SECOND EDITION

Contemporary
COMMUNICATION THEORY

Dominic A. Infante
Andrew S. Rancer
Theodore A. Avtgis
Erina L. MacGeorge

Kendall Hunt
p u b l i s h i n g   c o m p a n y

Book Team

Chairman and Chief Executive Officer   Mark C. Falb
President and Chief Operating Officer   Chad M. Chandlee
Vice President, Higher Education   David L. Tart
Director of Publishing Partnerships   Paul B. Carty
Senior Developmental Coordinator   Angela Willenbring
Vice President, Operations   Timothy J. Beitzel
Senior Permissions Editor   Caroline Kieler
Cover Designer   Jenifer Fensterman

Cover image © Shutterstock.com

www.kendallhunt.com
Send all inquiries to:
4050 Westmark Drive
Dubuque, IA 52004-1840
Copyright © 2017, 2010 by Kendall Hunt Publishing Company

ISBN 978-1-4652-8643-7

Printed in the United States of America

DOM INFANTE

Dominic A. Infante
1940–2014

His life as a Scholar, Teacher, Mentor,
Husband, Father, Grandfather,
and Friend illustrate his gravity
during his time on this earth

DEDICATION

Dedicated to our children

Laura and Jeffrey

Aimee

Aiden

Jesalyn and Carson

BRIEF CONTENTS

CONTENTS

PREFACE

This book is designed to introduce college students to theories in the field of communication. Theory courses are offered at many levels in the curriculum. If a course in communication theory is the only communication course a student takes, it is important that the material present a fairly broad picture of the current thinking in the discipline. The different approaches taken to understanding human communication, major theories within the structure of each approach, and representative research conducted to test the validity of theory building are all important areas to emphasize.

On the other hand, some students using this book will take multiple communication courses and become more than casual observers of communication. This type of student was also very much on our minds as we wrote. We attempted to reveal the importance of the field, the value of its teachings, and the richness of the discipline's thinking. We also tried to give equal treatment to the areas in which communication scholars specialize so that we do not influence the student to specialize in one area of the field instead of another.

FEATURES OF THE SECOND EDITION

There are several distinctive features of the Second Edition of this book that we would like to highlight. First, we emphasize the complementary, interdependent relationship of theory building and research in the communication discipline. We question how deeply a student understands a given communication theory if the student has no understanding of the research on which it was based, so each chapter has research examples that show students how theories are tested. In addition, we have incorporated the material on communication research methods formerly found in the Appendix directly into this edition as a separate chapter.

Second, this edition emphasizes the social scientific, or behavioral science, approach to the study of communication. A behavioral science approach emphasizes the orderly and highly rigorous accumulation of knowledge, and the corresponding development of theories that can be tested empirically. This is the type of research conducted extensively by the authors, who have devoted their careers to the social scientific approach to studying communication.

However, other approaches—often termed qualitative, or humanistic—are also noted and illustrated, especially where those approaches complement the social scientific perspective.

Third, this text emphasizes communication as human symbolic activity. As such we give greater emphasis to theories developed within the communication discipline. It will be evident to the reader that there is now no shortage of theory building in communication. However, where communication journals reflect sufficient interest in theories from outside the field (Petty and Cacioppo's Elaboration Likelihood Model, for example), we have used that criterion and included some of those highly influential theories from outside the discipline.

Fourth, our coverage of theory is broad, but selective. Books that attempt to survey an entire field are limited to a brief mention of many theories because of the vast amount of theory and research in each area. At the other extreme, if too few theories are covered, a sense of the scope of theorizing is lost. We chose an intermediate position in order to emphasize how contemporary scholars build on past theory and research. We hope this will be more intellectually satisfying than reading a "handbook" of statements about theories. In selecting this middle course, we have included a sufficient number of theories to present an overview of the different theory-building approaches in each area.

Fifth, this text presents both classic and relatively novel theories. A special attribute of the book is an emphasis on the trait approach to studying communication. In terms of sheer quantity of research, this approach is probably the major one taken by researchers during the past thirty-five years or so. A trait approach involves discovering what is characteristic of a person's communicative behavior—what regularities are consistent across situations. However, this Second Edition also includes expanded treatment of important "newer" areas of communication research and theory building. We now devote entire chapters to Relational, Computer Mediated, Health, and Cross-Cultural communication. These chapters illustrate how basic communication processes play out in a variety of different contexts, illustrating what we feel is one of the most important aspects of theory: theorists often build on previous work and extend existing approaches to new areas.

STRUCTURE OF THE TEXT

This book is divided into three parts. The first part provides an introduction and foundation. In these first three chapters, we conceptualize communication as a symbol-using activity, discuss the nature of theories, review the historical development of communication theory, and discuss methods of conducting communication research.

The second part of the book focuses on several major approaches to understanding human communication: communication traits, verbal behavior, nonverbal behavior, and persuasion. The third part of the book looks at communication theory building contextually. A good deal of the literature in the field pertains to the set of circumstances where communication takes place—the context. Eight chapters cover theory building in the interpersonal, relational, group, organizational, media, new media/computer-mediated, and cultural contexts.

As we wrote this book, we were reminded of the excitement scientists feel as they create theories and conduct research to test them. Theory building is an exploratory process designed to extend the frontiers of knowledge. We hope this text will convince the reader of the importance of building theory and will lead to shared enthusiasm for theory building in communication.

STUDENT-ORIENTED PEDAGOGY

Because we recognize the importance of assessing student learning, we have included the following features to facilitate students' understanding of the concepts.

Chapter Introduction—offers an overview of the material highlighted in the chapter

Running Glossary—provides a quick definition of key terms within the text

Figures and Tables—further illustrate theories visually

Chapter Summary—effectively reviews chapter elements presented

Key Terms—lists important concepts for each chapter

Glossary—includes all key terms found throughout the text

References—a comprehensive list documenting the extensive research cited

INSTRUCTIONAL ONLINE ENCHANCEMENTS

Look for the web icon in the page margins of the text to direct you to various interactive tools, accessed through the web code included in the textbook. The online materials are integrated chapter-by-chapter with the textbook to enrich students' learning.

STUDENT WEB CONTENT

Video interviews—showcase experts' explanations of theory

Review games—provide extensive concept review in game formats

Flash cards—offer an interactive version of the key terms

Exercises, research projects, activities—various tools encourage active learning and understanding of the material

INSTRUCTOR WEB CONTENT

Chapter outlines—highlight central ideas for each chapter and can serve as lecture notes

Comprehensive test bank—offers different question formats to better assess student knowledge

PowerPoint slides—illustrate important chapter concepts and can be made accessible to students

ACKNOWLEDGMENTS

We would like to thank the individuals at Kendall Hunt who were instrumental in conceiving of this project and whose guidance assisted us greatly in bringing it to fruition—Paul Carty and Angela Willenbring, along with the Kendall Hunt production team. We also appreciate the constructive comments of the colleagues who reviewed the content. They include:

Alicia Alexander
Southern Illinois University Edwardsville

Carolyn M. Anderson
University of Akron

Michael Irvin Arrington
University of Kentucky

Susan Avanzino
California State University Chico

Nathan Baxter
Gordon College

Monica Brasted
SUNY Brockport

Sakile Camara
California State University Northridge

David Carlone
The University of North Carolina at Greensboro

Debbie Chasteen
William Jewell College

Kathleen D. Clark
University of Akron

Leda Cooks
University of Massachusetts

Andrew Jared *Critchfield*
The George Washington University

Linda Czuba Brigance
SUNY Fredonia

John Dahlberg
Canisius College

Lucian F. Dinu
University of Louisiana at Lafayette

Norbert Elliot
New Jersey Institute of Technology

Celeste Farr
North Carolina State University

G.L. Forward
Point Loma Nazarene University

Merry E. George
Pikeville College

Jodi Hallsten
Illinois State University

Heidi Hamilton
Emporia State University

Mary Beth Holmes
Marywood University

Mark E. Huglen
University of Minnesota–Crookston

Laura Janusik
Rockhurst University

John Katsion
Multnomah University

William W. Kenner
University of Michigan Flint

Anastacia Kurylo
Marymount Manhattan College

Kara Laskowski
Shippensburg University

Susan Leggett
Westfield State College

Kristin Lindholm
Trinity International University

Hsin-I Liu
University of Incarnate Word

Tina McCorkindale
Cal Poly Pomona

Courtney Miller
Elmhurst College

Nancy Morris
Temple University

Anne Nicotera
George Mason University

Margaret Z. Ostrenko
Saint Leo University

Shara Toursh Pavlow
Florida Atlantic University

Barbara Penington
University of Wisconsin–Whitewater

Amber Peplow
Wright State University

Thomas E Ruggiero
University of Texas at El Paso

Brian Simmons
Cascade College

Sherry S. Strain
Keystone College

Yan Tian
University of Missouri–St. Louis

Beatriz Torres
Keene State College

Bill Wallace
Northeastern State University

John Warren
Southern Illinois University

Dennis L. Wignall
Dixie State College

MJ Woeste
University of Cincinnati

Edward Woods
Marshall University

ABOUT THE AUTHORS

Andrew S. Rancer (Ph.D., 1979, Kent State University) is Professor in the School of Communication at The University of Akron. He is the co-author of six books and numerous book chapters. His research has largely centered on argumentative and aggressive communication and has appeared in several national and regional journals including *Communication Education*, *Communication Monographs*, *Communication Quarterly*, and *Communication Research Reports*, among others. He is the recipient of several honors, including the Centennial Scholar, Distinguished Research Fellow, and Past President's Award from the Eastern Communication Association. In 2011, his teaching was recognized by the National Communication Association when he was the recipient of an Exemplary Teacher Award.

Theodore A. Avtgis (Ph.D., 1999, Kent State University) is Professor of Communication Studies and Director of the School of Communication at The University of Akron. He is also an Adjunct Associate Professor in the Department of Surgery at West Virginia University. Dr. Avtgis has authored over 70 peer-reviewed articles and book chapters on organizational communication, aggressive communication, risk and crisis communication, and health and medical communication. His work has appeared in journals such as *Management Communication Quarterly*, *Communication Education*, *Communication Research Reports*, *Communication Design Quarterly*, and the *Journal of Trauma and Acute Care Surgery* among others. He is co-author of over a dozen books and has served as Editor-in-Chief of Communication Research Reports. Among several awards, he was recognized as one of the twelve most prolific scholars in the field of communication studies (between 1996 and 2001), recognized as a member of the World Council on Hellenes Abroad, USA Region of American Academics, and received the Centennial Scholar, Research Fellow, Teaching Fellow, and Past President's Award from the Eastern Communication Association.

Erina MacGeorge (Ph.D., 1999, University of Illinois) is Associate Professor of Communication Arts and Sciences at Pennsylvania State University. Her research interests span interpersonal and health communication, with a focus on social support and social influence. With her students, she developed advice response theory, which explains advice outcomes for recipients as a function of message, advisor, situation, and recipient characteristics. Her work has been published in outlets that include *Communication Research*, *Journal of Health*

Communication, Human Communication Research, Communication Monographs, and the *Sage Handbook of Interpersonal Communication*. Recent studies examine advice between doctors and parents about childhood antibiotic use and breast cancer patients making surgical decisions with input from their social networks, as well as advice between college student friends coping with everyday problems. She is currently editing the *Oxford Handbook of Advice*, and is co-author of the textbook *Inter-Act* (14th ed.).

Part I

THEORY BUILDING IN COMMUNICATION

1. Introduction to Studying Communication

2. Perspectives on Communication Theory

3. Communication Research Methods

To introduce you to theory building in the field of communication, we will explore the following topics: What is the nature of communication? How do theories function? How has theory building in communication developed over time? What approaches have been used in building communication theories?

Chapter 1 describes communication as a transactional process: people interact and relate to each other by exchanging messages. There are many different definitions of communication, and each one explains communication from a different focus. One of the key differences between definitions is whether a message must be intentional to be considered communication. Another is whether we should use the term *communication* to describe all verbal and nonverbal expression. We believe definitions that claim all behavior is communicative obscure the significance of communication. After defining communication, we discuss several characteristics and points of controversy about communication.

Chapter 2 defines and explains theories. What is a theory? Are theories of communication different from other types of theories? Why do humans—both scientists and laypersons—invent theories? Theories are dynamic creations; they develop and change; they are seldom stagnant. Testing theories allows us to see how they can be changed to make them better. The testing process basically provides a theory with the opportunity to fail or to prove itself wrong. Evaluation of theories is an essential process. Without it, we would be unable to tell a good theory from a bad one. We will look at the criteria for a good communication theory and the criteria used in evaluating theories in general.

Chapter 3 introduces the methods used in communication research. Theory is built by conducting research which tests hypotheses and answers research questions. In this chapter we highlight the framework behind many of the theories which are discussed in the text. While there are numerous methods employed in communication research, we will largely focus on communication research methods which are employed in doing behavioral science research. The underlying foundation of this line of research involves controlled observation to understand individuals' communication behavior. Control is achieved by a good research design so that we have confidence in what is observed. Observation pertains to what is of interest and how it is observed; specifically, the concern is with measurement. Numerous ways of measuring aspects of human communication will be presented.

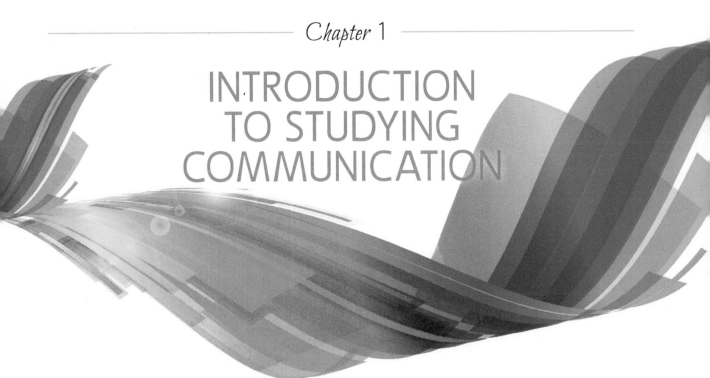

Chapter 1

INTRODUCTION TO STUDYING COMMUNICATION

As we shall see in this book, building useful communication theories is important for many reasons. Perhaps none is more significant than the idea that communication is vital to individuals, groups, and organizations in a democratic society.

What is unique about a free society? One distinguishing characteristic has been termed the "marketplace of ideas" (Cronkhite, 1976). People who have ideas are free to express them. If the ideas have merit, they will survive the competition with other ideas. This means freedom of speech is highly prized and protected from any possible erosion. It is assumed that people in the marketplace have the ability to select the best idea. Freedom of speech is crucial to ensure that there will be a wide variety of ideas available. This increases the probability that a very good idea will be present in the group of available ideas.

Communication is particularly prominent in *selecting* an idea from the marketplace of ideas. Aristotle believed that communication, especially persuasion, enabled people to discover what was good for society at a particular time and place. Public deliberation occurs when advocates and opponents for various ideas or proposals attempt to persuade people. If all proposals are not represented by competent advocates, the best proposal may not survive. The consequences of proposals must be clearly understood if the best decision is to be made. Advocates of an inferior proposal may deceive the audience by misrepresenting the superior proposal's advantages or potential disadvantages. If there were no competent spokespersons for the superior proposal, the audience might select the inferior proposal. People will do their best to make a good decision on an important matter. If awareness of the issues has been reduced by deception or incompetence, even the best ideas can go unnoticed. This is why effective communication is so important in our society. People will select the best candidate, approve worthy issues by referendum, or support good changes in the status quo—if the communication is of such quality that the significant issues are understood. This idea, of course, is not new. It was central in the thinking of both Aristotle and the writers of our Constitution. A major goal of the field of communication has been to prepare students to be effective participants in a democracy. The study of communication is more extensive in the educational system of the United States than in any other country in the world. This is no accident. It is difficult to find a country that has more freedom of expression than the United States. Our very existence depends on people making good decisions. As we have said, that is very unlikely without effective communication.

Despite the fact that our society is so advanced, we have not achieved complete equality of opportunity. Although there may be greater opportunity in the United States and the laws protect against discrimination, your sex, race, religion, or national origin may affect your achievements. However, communicative ability is an equalizer; our society rewards people who are effective communicators. For example, one of the most successful talk show hosts in the history of American broadcasting is Oprah Winfrey. Her success reaches well beyond television. Many suggest that her success is in part due to her excellence in public and interpersonal communication. Our society is not perfect, but that does not mean you cannot succeed. It is exciting to be part of the communication discipline; we commonly observe people "getting ahead" because of improvements made in their communication skills. As you study the material in the rest of this book, it is important to keep in mind the vital role of communication in our private and public lives. Because communication is so important, building the best possible communication theories and models is perhaps the most important activity scholars in our discipline can undertake.

When you take your first course in a discipline, you are sometimes completely unfamiliar with the subject matter. In your first chemistry course, for example, you probably had no knowledge about covalent and ionic bonding of elements. In other courses, you probably recognized some of the elements of what the discipline studies, but the knowledge was only superficial. For instance, if you took a course in meteorology, you would be acquainted with basic terms like weather, climate, or storms. The course would introduce you to new aspects of familiar phenomena. You might learn that a stationary high-pressure system in the Pacific Ocean west of the state of Oregon can direct the jet stream northward, creating a return flow of cold air to the northern states—resulting in unusually harsh weather.

Your first course in communication falls in the second category; you are already familiar with the subject matter. Because of personal interactions and what you have experienced through the mass media, there are few, if any, communication behaviors you have not encountered. As in our meteorology example, you probably expect to learn about the "whys" of the phenomena. For instance, why are some people more easily persuaded than others? Why are some people predisposed to communicate? How can you reduce your level of speech anxiety? What are the characteristics of a person who can talk effortlessly about any topic? How does the image people have of us influence how they react to our messages? How does your gender influence your verbal behavior? What nonverbal messages do we send to others?

We will begin to understand these and many other concepts as we examine *theory* in this book. A theory is a set of related statements designed to describe, explain, predict, and/or control reality. As we shall observe in the following chapters, there are several types of theories of communication, and all are useful in providing explanations. It is important to realize that theories are useful guides for behavior. They are not just abstract concepts; they provide a basis for practical application. For instance, a theory about communication in organizations might suggest that particular tasks require different communication skills. In practice, this theory would indicate that managers should be trained to communicate one way and that salespeople should be encouraged to communicate in other ways to make the organization more productive. This is representative of the control function of theory.

Theory A set of related statements designed to describe, explain, and/or predict reality

ISSUES IN UNDERSTANDING COMMUNICATION

BASIC COMPONENTS AND CONCEPTS

In this section, we will review some terms essential to your study of communication. As with our meteorology example, you have at least some familiarity with these concepts. Before we enter the complex area of defining communication, we will start with the somewhat easier, and less controversial, definitions of key elements in the process.

Source. A source designates the originator of a message. Some communication scholars have differentiated between the concepts of "source" and "sender." A sender is one who transmits messages but does not necessarily originate them. An example of a sender could be a radio announcer reading an ad for the program sponsors. A source could be a single person, a group of people, or even an institution.

Source Designates the originator of a message

Message. A message is the stimulus that the source transmits to the receiver. A message may be verbal, nonverbal, or both. Tone of voice, gestures, and facial expressions are all examples of nonverbal messages. Usually, both verbal and nonverbal messages are conveyed human communication transactions.

Message The stimulus that the source transmits to the receiver

Channel. A channel is the means by which the message is conveyed from source to receiver. Channels may be air waves, light waves, or even laser beams.

Channel The means by which the message is conveyed from source to receiver

Any of the five senses of human perception may serve as channels in the communication process. The number of channels being used by an individual can affect the accuracy of a given message. For example, in which case could a job applicant present more information about himself or herself—on a telephone or in a face-to-face interview? In the latter instance, the applicant would be using more sensory channels to convey his or her message, and the interviewer would be doing the same in receiving that message. Using more than one channel in conveying a message increases the *redundancy* (repetition) and, to a point, the accuracy of that message. Excessive redundancy, on the other hand, could be viewed by the receiver as insulting. When there is conflicting information presented over the verbal and nonverbal channels during a communication transaction, people may place a greater emphasis on the nonverbal cues. We will discuss this in greater detail in Chapter 6.

Receiver Decodes and interprets the message sent

Receiver. As the destination of a given message, the receiver decodes and interprets the message sent, whereas the source/sender encodes a message and transmits it. Encoding is defined as the process of taking an already conceived idea and getting it ready for transmission. Decoding, on the other hand, is the process of taking the stimuli that have been received and giving those stimuli meaning through individual interpretation and perception. In human communication transactions, the stimuli are signs and symbols, materials which stand for or represent something else. It is important to note that all individuals function as source and receiver. Because humans perform both the functions of encoding and decoding, they have been labeled "transceivers."

Noise Any stimulus that inhibits the receiver's accurate reception of a given message

Noise. Noise is any stimulus that inhibits the receiver's accurate reception of a given message. Noise is often classified as physical, psychological, or semantic. Examples of *physical noise* would be the thunder of a jet airplane overhead, car horns blowing, or the blaring of a stereo system next door. *Psychological noise* occurs when an individual is preoccupied and therefore misses or misinterprets the external message. As you are sitting and listening to a lecture in class, you may be thinking of what you are going to eat for dinner or about the quarrel you had this morning. If this activity prohibits the accurate reception of the professor's lecture, then psychological noise has occurred. *Semantic noise* occurs when individuals have different meanings for symbols and when those meanings are not mutually understood. For example, semantic noise occurs when you do not understand a particular word being used by another communicator or when the particular word or symbol used has many denotative or connotative meanings. When one of the authors moved to the Midwest from the East Coast and ordered "soda," he received an ice cream soda—not the carbonated beverage he thought he had ordered! Semantic noise occurred here. It is important to note that some element(s) of noise are always present in human communication transactions.

Feedback Allows a source to have a means of assessing how a message is being decoded

Feedback. Like all communication messages, feedback may be verbal, nonverbal, or both. Feedback is often called positive or negative. Positive feedback consists of responses perceived as rewarding by the speaker, such as applause or verbal/nonverbal agreement. Negative feedback consists of responses perceived as punishing or not rewarding. In interpersonal or public communication situations, frowns or whistles are examples of negative feedback. Even a complete lack of response on the part of the receiver could be perceived as negative feedback, because the source would have no cues by which to gauge the effects of the message. Thus, without feedback, a source would have no means of assessing how a message was being decoded, and subsequent inaccuracies might never be corrected. Because negative feedback implies that changes should be made, it is especially useful in helping us to send messages more effectively.

DEFINING COMMUNICATION

There have been numerous attempts to define communication. In fact, nearly every book on communication offers its own definition! No author seems satisfied with other authors' definitions, and the proliferation goes on and on. Why is this? You would think if we know what communication is, we should be able to agree on a definition. We reach this predicament because there is no *single* approach to the study of communication; there are many. Definitions differ on matters such as whether communication has occurred if a source did not intend to send a message, whether communication is a linear process (a source sending a message in a channel to a receiver who then reacts), or whether a transactional perspective is more accurate (emphasizing the relationships between people and how they constantly, mutually influence one another).

What this discussion means in terms of defining communication is that people disagree on definitions of communication because they disagree on the nature of communication. The many definitions raise a number of issues about the nature of communication. One important question is, "What makes human communication so powerful and distinctive?" If theorists can determine the answer, they can agree on what topics communication scholars should study.

The fact that we have no universally accepted definition of communication is not a debilitating problem. In fact, such a state of affairs is to be expected, given our current level of understanding. What is important is that we continue studying communication, learning as much as we can about this very significant set of human behaviors. The more we learn, the more precisely we will be able to define communication. At any time in our study we can stop and redefine. The definition would simply represent our present thinking. As we learn more, we surely would change our definition. As you read this text, you might try defining communication at the end of each chapter. The chances are you will feel a need to redefine communication as you progress. The more you learn, the more you will see the inadequacies in your earlier definitions.

Your authors have chosen to define communication as follows:

> *Communication occurs when humans manipulate symbols to stimulate meaning in other humans.*

Our definition emphasizes both sender and receiver. It also calls attention to the symbolic and intentional nature of communication. The next section presents some of the characteristics your authors believe communication exhibits: it is a social, symbolic process that occurs in a context. Some characteristics of communication are more controversial than others. After we present our position on the nature of communication, we will discuss three issues of controversy among scholars.

CHARACTERISTICS OF COMMUNICATION

1. Communication Is a Symbolic Process. Human symbolic activity is the very essence of communication and therefore should be the focus of the communication discipline. Cronkhite (1976) clarified this idea by differentiating three types of signs. A sign can be thought of as something that stands for another thing. A symptom is one type of sign. For instance, sneezing is a symptom of having an allergy. A symbol is a second type of sign. It is created to stand for something else. A symbol is arbitrary in that the creator is not limited in what can be used to represent something else. The idea is for the symbol to stimulate awareness of a particular thing when the symbol is used. Thus, for example, if you were an inventor who invented something, you would want to give it a unique name (i.e., a symbol) so that when the name is used, your invention would come to mind. A third type of sign is a ritual. This is a combination of being naturally produced, as in the case of a symptom, and being arbitrary or created, as would be a symbol. Many nonverbal behaviors are examples. For instance, grimacing in pain when we bump our elbow is a symptom. However, grimacing a certain way (e.g., with an accompanying laugh) because we are being observed and want to be seen as "tough" or impervious to pain is a ritual. Thus, a ritual involves *stylizing* a symptom so that it also becomes somewhat symbolic. It shows something natural, such as a sign of pain, but does it in a way that says something about the individual who exhibits the symptom.

Sign Something that stands for or represents another thing

Symptom One type of sign

Symbol A second type of sign created to stand for something else

Ritual A third type of sign that is a combination of being naturally produced and being arbitrary or created

> We agree with Cronkhite that symbolic activity represents what is and is not communication. Many academic disciplines study human symbols. However, the communication discipline is unique in that it gives primary attention to the human activity of using symbols.

2. Communication Involves Socially Shared Meaning. Our definition asserts that communication occurs when people use symbols to stimulate meaning in other people. This emphasizes that communication is a social process and involves more than simply perception of another person. Perception of another person at times might not involve communication, for instance, perceiving a person taking a nap in the library. If symbolic activity is not responsible for the perception, then communication did not occur. In the case of a nap, there may be no symbols or rituals involved. All the behavior may be symptoms. Perception is an important product of the communication process. But perception is produced by processes besides communication. These are studied by cognitive psychologists as individual processes. Communication is not an individual process, but a social one that involves symbolic activity of at least two people.

> Because we are from the same culture, we share meaning for symbols. That does not suggest that the meanings that you and a friend have for a given concept, such as "freedom of speech," are identical. What is suggested is that your meanings overlap so that you can discuss the concept with some common understanding. As a result of discussion, individuals might influence one another on what it means to have freedom of speech. Meanings are represented by symbols, and symbols can be used to change meanings in people. This emphasizes the idea that communication is a social process involving socially shared meaning.

3. Communication Occurs in a Context. A fundamental characteristic of communication is that it is highly contextual. To understand communication usually means taking into account the context in which it occurs. A communication context may be thought of as a particular type of communication situation. There is general agreement on the types of contexts. Most contemporary communication theory books present chapters on the various types. This text discusses how communication functions in several contexts including: interpersonal, relational, group, organizational, mediated, health, and intercultural.

Context A particular type of communication situation

> Interpersonal—communication between two people
>
> Group—communication between about three to fifteen people
>
> Organizational—communication within and between organizations
>
> Public—a speaker addressing an audience
>
> Mass & Mediated Communication—print, electronic, and socially mediated communication
>
> Intercultural—communication between people representing different cultures
>
> Family—communication in the family setting
>
> Health—communication between and among health-care providers and receivers
>
> Political—communication that involves persons governing our society

Communication tends to be influenced greatly by the context. For example, a negative assessment of a person's intelligence might be viewed as humorous in a family context but mean spirited in a small-group work setting, even though the very same words are used in both situations. Contexts vary on basic attributes, and that affects response to messages. For instance, because there is less immediate feedback in mass communication as compared to organizational communication, it could take longer for negative evaluations of a TV news anchor to lead to replacement than it would to replace a negatively evaluated work supervisor.

POINTS OF CONTROVERSY ABOUT COMMUNICATION

To understand the nature of communication and the characteristics that make it so complex and powerful, it is important for you to understand some key areas of disagreement among communication scholars. The following section will discuss three interesting questions currently disputed by communication theorists: Is communication intentional? Is communication **planned**? Is communication **transactional**?

Intentional Knowingly influencing the receiver of the message

COMMUNICATION AND INTENT

Has communication occurred if the source, the message sender, had no intention to influence the receiver of the message? Let us say Jan overhears Joe telling someone to take a particular course because Professor Smith is interesting. Jan then registers for that course. Should we say communication occurred between Jan and Joe? Certainly, meaning was stimulated in Jan's mind by the verbal behavior of Joe. Does communication always occur whenever meaning is stimulated? If Jan told Professor Smith that Joe mentioned how interesting the class was, and Smith then approached Joe and said, "Thanks for talking so favorably with Jan about my course," Joe would probably be very puzzled and would think, "I don't remember talking with Jan about the course." Suppose you read an article that discusses pupil dilation as an indication of favorable feelings (and you do not know there is controversy among researchers as to the meaning of pupil dilation). You then approach a potential romantic partner. As you are talking, you notice the person's pupils are dilating. Should you assume the other person sent you a message communicating attraction? Once again, meaning was stimulated, but was it stimulated intentionally? Clearly not in this case, because pupil dilation is an involuntary response. If intentionality is not required to designate behavior as communicative, then mere existence is all that is needed. Thus, if you were to observe a patient lying in a hospital bed in a deep coma, we would have to say you were "communicating" with the person.

Some people argue that if a message is sent, then communication occurs, regardless of the intended recipient. The central issue is whether there actually is a message. When the other person is unaware he or she is influencing you and you ask the person to repeat the "message," you would get only a confused look. If you read a message into another person's unintentional behavior, you act as both the message creator and the message consumer.

This issue illustrates a trend by some people to claim "everything is communication." Certainly communication is pervasive, but is it everywhere—all the time? That view dilutes the significance of communication. There is an old saying that if something is everything, it is nothing. Such exuberance in staking out territory is not necessary. If we consider communication to occur when humans manipulate symbols to stimulate meaning in other humans, the territory is vast enough to justify a field of study. This view of communication is neither too narrow nor too restrictive. It allows for the complexity of human interaction but avoids the task of accounting for unintentional behavior. Humans unknowingly stimulating meaning in other humans is interesting, yet it is not the same as humans knowingly doing so. An important point is that we are not claiming it is always possible to determine intentionality. At times, we cannot tell whether Sue sent a message to Anne or whether Anne both created and consumed a message about Sue. The issue is whether Sue sent a message. If Sue did so intentionally, communication occurred—regardless of Anne's reaction to the message.

Another reason for limiting communication to intentional behavior is to distinguish it from perception. **Perception** is a process through which individuals interpret sensory information. You might perceive that the walls of your classroom are painted "institutional green" or "institutional beige," but it would seem strange to say that you are communicating with the walls. Again, you might say that the painters communicated with you through the choice of color, but if you asked them to repeat their message, they would be puzzled if no message was intended. Instead, you observed and drew inferences from sensory data. Although perception is an essential part of the communication process because it enables us to receive and interpret messages sent by others, not all perception involves communication. Human communication requires at least two people who intend to send and to receive messages; communication is a social rather than an individual process.

Perception A process through which individuals interpret sensory information

Figure 1.1 illustrates our position. If the sender intends to communicate *and* the receiver recognizes the intention, *communication has occurred.* This situation is an example of what Brant Burleson (1992) terms a paradigm case, a case in which virtually everyone would agree that communication occurs. Burleson believes that face-to-face conversation is a paradigm case of communication behavior. Other situations are not so clear. What if you are walking down the street, notice a friend, and assume the friend is deliberately avoiding you? Suppose the friend did not see you. This event is attributed communication. Your friend did not intend to communicate with you, but you believed he or she intended to send a message about avoiding you. When a sender attempts to send a message, but the message is not received, this is an attempted communication. An example would be shouting to a friend who

	Sender intends to send a message	Sender does not intend to send a message
Receiver recognizes sender's intent	1. Communication occurs	2. Communication attributed
Receiver does not recognize sender's intent	3. Communication attempted	4. Perception, but not communication, occurs

Adapted from Burgoon & Ruffner (1978).

FIGURE 1.1 COMMUNICATION AND INTENTION

could not hear you because of traffic noise. No communication occurs in the fourth situation. If questioned, neither person would state that a message was sent or received. This situation might apply to behavior such as swatting at a fly that has settled on your book in class. Both you and another person in the room (the perceiver) are aware that you swatted at the fly, but neither inferred that a message was sent. This situation is an example of perception but not communication.

The axiom, "You cannot not communicate," was presented in the book, *Pragmatics of Human Communication* (Watzlawick, Beavin, & Jackson, 1967). For years after the publication of the book, this idea was embraced by many scholars in the communication field. Although the notion that everything is communication had a certain appeal, after a while other scholars began questioning whether everything about a person actually does represent a communicative message. This led to the issue of what exactly is a message, and what are the necessary conditions to declare that a message exists? The view emerged over time that symbolic activity was a necessary condition for communication to have occurred.

The controversy over what is and what is not communication was exemplified by the exchange between Motley (1990a, 1990b) and Andersen (1991). Motley postulated that for communication to have occurred, the behavior must have four features. It must be interactive, involve encoding, involve the exchange of symbols, and range in quality from high to low. Thus, when a person sneezes, it is not communication because it really does not have any of the four features (i.e., it does not meet any of the four necessary conditions for communication). This is because a sneeze is not a symbol but instead is a symptom of something such as an allergic reaction to tree pollen.

Andersen disagreed with Motley's position and asserted that types of symptomatic behavior constitute communication because attributes of a person such as body shape, body odor, and race are considered to have message value; they say something, they inform. Also, Andersen considers "informative communication" to have occurred if meaning is derived from observing things such as a person's height, gender, relaxation, or energy levels. In these instances, no intention to communicate may exist, yet receivers may believe there was intent and develop meaning accordingly. Andersen was particularly concerned that many symptomatic nonverbal behaviors occur along with symbols and are a part of the total meaning derived from a situation. He believed that excluding such symptoms would distort understanding of what happened in a situation. For instance, to ignore a person's coughing while explaining something would distort the fact that the person was trying to be helpful, even though he or she was sick.

Motley's postulates and ideas are consistent with our definition—*communication occurs when humans manipulate symbols to stimulate meaning in other humans.* This conceptualization provides active roles for the message source and the message receiver, covers both verbal and nonverbal symbolic behavior, considers the receiver's perceptions, and focuses on highly conscious symbolic behavior while also allowing for and recognizing behavior encoded at a very low level of awareness.

COMMUNICATION AS PLANNED BEHAVIOR

Communication plans offer answers to the issues raised in the previous section about intentionality, what constitutes a message, and when symbols are actually manipulated. Viewing communication as planned behavior, in essence, makes it clear that intentions are a necessary element of the communication process. The notion of communication plans defines when human behavior represents communication and when it does not.

INFANTE'S COMMUNICATION PLAN PERSPECTIVE

Dominic Infante was an early advocate and developer of the communication plan perspective. He developed a conceptualization of communication plans with the assumption that "people say what they plan to say." Thus, a communication plan is a set of behaviors that the person believes will accomplish a purpose. You might have a general plan to graduate from college, to get a good job, to raise a family, and to retire comfortably. Some plans are more specific: take the car to the garage the first thing tomorrow. This perspective assumes human communication behavior is *volitional*. The plans we form are controlled by our beliefs, attitudes, and values; plans are hierarchically arranged (Cronkhite, 1976). "I plan to major in journalism and work for a fashion magazine."

Communication plan
A set of behaviors that the person believes will accomplish a purpose

As Infante explained, there are two types of communication plans: verbal plans and nonverbal plans (Infante, 1980). A verbal plan is what you plan to say in a specific or general communication situation. A plan for a specific situation might be: "When Joan congratulates me on my award, I will tell her she helped me greatly." A plan for a general situation could be: "Whenever people congratulate me, I will act humble and thank them for whatever assistance they provided." Some verbal plans are formed well in advance of the utterance, whereas others are created and spoken immediately. For example, you may decide what to say when asked about your future profession years before you actually respond to an inquiry. However, you may form a plan to express your feelings about a particular presidential candidate only seconds before you speak. A verbal plan may resemble a topical outline where only the main ideas are specified. For instance, "Generally, I think education should be funded at the state level." Or a verbal plan may contain specific details and precise wording. For example, "The next time John loses his temper I will say, 'You're acting like a jerk again; I'm leaving.'"

Verbal plans vary in terms of how frequently they are used. Some are used only once or a few times. Others are used in recurring situations. For a large portion of our communication behavior, we recycle the same verbal plans. They work well, so we continue to use them. You can probably identify a large number of verbal plans you use habitually. When someone asks you what you think about college, do you have a standard reply? Once we determine a verbal plan, execute it, and decide it accomplishes the desired purpose, we reuse it in future situations with slight modification when necessary. We revise verbal plans from time to time. What we say in a given situation usually represents a verbal plan that has evolved over a period of time. For instance, you may have a verbal plan for telling another person you do not want to date him or her again. After using it, you decide, "Well, I could have said that better." So you revise your original plan, and the next time you are in a similar situation, you decline future engagements more tactfully.

Nonverbal plans sometimes precede or follow the execution of verbal plans, but usually they are formed along with our verbal plans. An example of a nonverbal plan preceding verbal behavior might be, "I'll get that person to come over and meet me by looking interested." Many nonverbal plans are formed along with verbal plans: "When I talk with my boss today, I'll display calm and confidence." As with verbal plans, nonverbal plans can be general or specific, formed well in advance or formed at the moment, used once or habitually, revised or unrevised.

In order to understand and predict communication behavior, it is necessary to understand and predict a person's communication plans. Research indicates that people learn to associate and/or anticipate consequences regarding their plans. How those consequences are perceived by the person permits a prediction of what the person will say. *Human communication represents the execution of the individual's most recently adopted communication plan (Infante, 1980).*

The idea of communication plans provides a way to address the issue of whether communication has occurred if one person is unaware that his or her behavior is stimulating a response in another person. Under the communication plans framework, we would say communication has occurred if we can trace the individual's behavior to a plan. If not, communication did not occur, even though meaning may have been stimulated in another person's mind. For instance, a student might purchase a sweatshirt with the school's logo to communicate her support for the school's athletic teams. Let us suppose that another student sees her (she is unaware of him) wearing the sweatshirt at a basketball game and says to himself, "She's a loyal fan!" According to the communication plan perspective, that would be an example of communication. When it is not possible to attribute behavior to a communication plan, we would say no communication has occurred. Meaning might have been perceived, but there was no communication. Of course, it is not always easy to determine whether a communication plan stimulated behavior. Plans, like other forms of knowledge, are usually discoverable. The only limitations are the ingenuity and resourcefulness of the researcher.

Messages molded and energized by communication plans are symbolic behaviors. This emphasizes the intentional versus the accidental nature of human communication. Messages are expressed with verbal and nonverbal symbols. Plans, of course, are also composed of symbols. However, the symbols in a plan are not necessarily the same ones that will appear in a message. Human judgment and volition transform plans into action. Plans can be modified and adapted to the given situation. For instance, suppose you have a plan for refusing to drink beer when it is offered to you. What you say might vary according to the situation. You could say it is "sinful" when talking with religious people or "unhealthy" when talking with physical fitness enthusiasts. The transformation process allows for revisions of a communication plan. This complex human ability presents a formidable obstacle for attempts to simulate human communication through the use of computers.

According to a communication plans framework, communication does not always entail a great deal of thinking by the people involved. If we do not have a plan for a situation, then substantial thinking is involved. However, much of our communication behavior is *habitual* in the sense that we prefer to place ourselves in familiar situations where we have communication plans that are very dependable—they always seem to work for us. Life would be difficult if we had to examine each situation thoroughly to determine what to say. Instead, we form plans that are as robust as possible and cover as many circumstances as feasible. It is easier to talk if we have reliable plans. Thus, people prefer familiar situations because they have already developed plans that have worked in the past. Having a dependable plan means the person may go on "automatic pilot" and not have to think much about the situation. According to this analysis, much human behavior is neither unique nor novel; it is repetitive and therefore predictable.

The concept of communication as planned behavior has been essential to the development of several theories of interpersonal communication, including the goals-plans-action theory (Dillard, 1990) and planning theory (Berger, 1997). Both are discussed in Chapter 8.

TRANSACTIONAL NATURE OF COMMUNICATION

The fact that communication is planned helps us recognize that communication is a transactional process. By that we mean communication involves people sending each other messages that reflect the motivations of the participants. People expect others to react to their messages; in turn they expect to respond to the messages of others. When we communicate, we attempt to affect our environment. We understand that others also communicate to exert such influence. We anticipate a "give and take" in communication—an interaction of human motivations. A simple linear process (a one-thing-leads-to-another description) does not adequately explain the communication situation. For instance, if we learn that Joel asked Rob for $1.50 for the candy machine, we don't have very much information. If Joel says, "I asked for a buck-fifty and got only a frown," the statement is more revealing because it describes a reaction to the request. In this case, Joel frowned because he just learned that his sister is dating Rob. Because Rob has a reputation for "breaking hearts," Joel is afraid his sister will be hurt. We could present more details, but the point should be clear. Communication is a process of mutual influence in which participants' motivations interact. Often, a linear description does not even identify the most important meaning in a communication situation. Not getting the money certainly was not the most significant meaning in this interaction. To identify a single message source, a single message receiver, and a single effect of a message may be accurate for a very limited period of time—at best. The

Transactional process Communication involves people sending each other messages that reflect the motivations of the participants

thinking of the people involved in a communication situation, their characteristic traits, the factors in the physical and social environments, and how all these things interact are necessary for a more complete understanding of communication in the particular situation.

The transactional nature of communication means each communication situation is unique, to a degree. A communication situation occurs with particular people, in particular physical and social circumstances, and during a particular period of time. Because what a person wants changes from one point in time to the next and, because the physical and especially the social environments are rarely if ever the same, we recognize that each of our communication experiences is at least somewhat unique. We are able to distinguish among communication situations, even though the people and places may be the same.

Even though communication scholars disagree on the points of definition discussed earlier, most would agree on the uses or functions of communication. The Roman orator Cicero believed the basic purposes of a speech were *to entertain, to inform,* and *to persuade.* In recent times, the purpose *to stimulate* has been added. The distinction made between persuading and stimulating is that persuading involves changing a listener from accepting to rejecting the speaker's proposal (or the reverse), whereas stimulating means moving a person who already approves, for example, to become even more intensely supportive. These purposes have been applied mainly to public speaking. Some contemporary theorists have explored other perspectives on the functions that communication fulfills for humans.

THE IMPORTANCE OF COMMUNICATION

CREATING COOPERATION

Because communication performs the functions discussed earlier, it plays a vital role in each of our lives. Humans are very interdependent. The arrangement of society is such that each of us depends on others to provide what we need. Communication is very important in enabling people to coordinate their efforts and to produce a variety of goods and services, which would be impossible if people were to work independently. Beyond this macroscopic view, there are many examples in our individual lives when we use communication to enlist the cooperation of others. We ask people for directions when we are lost. We want our friends to support us when we take a stand on a controversial issue. We suggest a division of work to our colleagues when we are assigned a time-consuming task. It is probably accurate to say that we do not live a day without asking for the cooperation of others and also cooperating with requests made by others.

Of course, some people get more cooperation than others. Communication skill is an obvious factor to explain this discrepancy. If people do not cooperate with us as much as we would like, it may be our communication behavior that is at fault. We have a need for control in our interpersonal relations (Schutz, 1958). If this need is not satisfied, we tend to feel powerless and view ourselves as relatively helpless—dependent on the whims of others. It is possible to desire too much control. When this happens, others view us as burdensome and prefer not to cooperate. We can ask too much of people. To be well adjusted interpersonally, we must learn what it is reasonable to ask of others and what we should reasonably give.

ACQUIRING INFORMATION

The second key role of communication is to help us acquire information. Information or knowledge is probably our greatest possession. Humans have always accumulated information; knowledge is power. At the international level, nations that have the most information also have the most economic power and prestige. Information is no less important at the microscopic level. For various reasons, we need a vast amount of information in our lives. We want facts about candidates to reach a decision when we go to the polls. Information about the weather affects our plans for the day. The principles of gardening are necessary to produce vegetables in our backyard. If we want to be bankers, we need a knowledge of finance. Other information satisfies our sense of curiosity with no apparent utility value. We read about the Bushmen of the Kalahari Desert because we are interested in extraordinary examples of survival. We listen to a lecture about black holes in space because we find the idea fascinating. We read a biography about a composer simply because we like his or her music. The cliché states that people thirst for knowledge: that the thirst is unquenchable seems to be a permanent condition of being human.

Communication plays a very important role in acquiring information. Other than in cases of direct experience with our physical environment, information without communication is rare. Here is an example of purely physical information, which you technically could acquire without communicating with other people. Let us say that you have just moved to another region of the United States and you wish to know where to catch a lot of fish. To do this independently, you would have to roam the countryside and search for lakes and streams. You would have to stay off highways because they contain signs, refrain from asking anyone about fishing waters, and reject consulting a map because all of these involve communication. Suppose you succeed in locating twelve lakes in a 15-mile radius from your new home without the benefit of communication. Would you have accomplished your goal of catching a lot of fish? Because not all bodies of water contain ample fish populations, your quest has only narrowed slightly.

Suppose you realize this and decide to communicate just once to find out which of the lakes contains the most fish. You ask a local expert; he names the best lake. Can you now proceed to accomplish your goal without further communication? Perhaps, but if the lake is large, you could spend the entire year there and not catch many fish. Even if you found the productive parts of the lake, there still is the matter of how to catch the fish. What bait, lures, and techniques work on this lake? You might catch a lot of fish without any human assistance. However, unless you are unusually lucky, it would take a very long time. Communication would not make the task easy, but it would make it simpler. Just find an experienced local fisherman and talk! Communication is vital in acquiring whatever information you need.

In this process of acquiring information, we have learned it is necessary to have a system of beliefs about the sources of information. According to Rokeach (1960), we have a set of beliefs about which sources are credible (believable) and which are not. Because we need information, we must know whether information is dependable. We have positive beliefs about highly credible sources and negative beliefs or disbeliefs about sources with low credibility. Consider the following piece of information: "Evidence indicates that fracking creates instability underground which may cause earthquakes." Whether you believe that information will depend heavily on the source. If it is announced on the CBS evening news, and if CBS is a credible source for you, you probably would see this as a very plausible possibility. However, if the source is a group you distrust, you probably would dismiss the idea as highly implausible and as further proof of the "conspiracy mentality" of extremists.

FORMING SELF-CONCEPT

The third area in which communication is useful is in forming our self-concepts. A commonly accepted principle of communication is that how we perceive ourselves greatly influences our communication behavior. If you believe you are worthwhile and a success, you say this in many ways and on many occasions. Your verbal messages reflect optimism and an unpretentious confidence in yourself. Nonverbally, your posture, gestures, tone of voice, and facial expression say you have positive beliefs about yourself.

People sometimes exude too much confidence. This communication behavior is also revealing. This type of individual may be uncertain about his or her self-worth and is attempting to convince others that he or she is productive and valuable. Such attempts at social influence may be termed *ego-defensive* communication behaviors. The person finds his or her unfavorable self-concept psychologically uncomfortable and seeks to remedy the condition by obtaining esteem from others. "My fears about myself must be wrong; how could I be a failure if people treat me like I am a success?" Of course, such self-deception is seldom sufficient to convince the individual of his or her worth, so the exaggerated communication behavior continues. This is not the only pattern of behavior that communicates an unfavorable self-concept. Other people say quite clearly in their verbal messages that they are pessimistic about their future or that they are helpless in their environments. Perhaps as a way of asking for help, people sometimes use facial expressions to say they are depressed, a message that is also communicated by their tone of voice and by posture and gestures.

Does communication influence who we think we are? That is, how does communication operate in the formation of our self-concepts? One theory claims our self-concept is a reflection of how we see ourselves in the responses of other people to us (Cooley, 1902). We communicate; others observe our communication behavior and react to it; we observe these reactions, and they become the basis for deciding who we are. Hence, the combination of our communication behavior and the communication behavior of others toward us controls our self-concepts. All of this is a very hopeful perspective about the idea of self-concept. It means we are partially responsible for the way we view ourselves because we stimulate the responses of others that result in our particular self-concept. There is hope because we can continue to communicate with people and obtain responses from them. People are discriminating. They respond differently according to the stimulus.

This is another way of saying you can change people's responses to you. You are partially responsible for and in control of your interpersonal world. This perspective says it is not valid for you to claim, "People do not show an interest in me or in what I am doing, so I must not be an interesting person." Instead, this orientation to self-concept would want you to conclude, "People do not show an interest in me because I do not encourage them to; I do not show an interest in them." The explanation for this would lie in your communication behavior. You probably do not ask many questions about others' interests when you talk. You give little if any positive verbal and nonverbal reinforcement to others when they show an interest in you. What could you do, according to this perspective? You could develop sincere interest in others—ask questions and show positive reactions to their responses to your questions. When people reciprocate by inquiring about your interests, you could show them that you are happy they asked. This should become an established pattern in your interpersonal relations, not something you try only once.

The point we are trying to make is that communication has been important in the formation of your self-concept, and communication can be used to change your self-concept. We can change our communication behavior, and that will cause people to react differently to us; the new responses toward us will cause us to perceive ourselves differently. There is considerable reason for adopting this "communication orientation" to self-concept. We are happier in life if we have a favorable self-concept. We are not happy if we believe others have not treated us fairly or have not given us what we deserve. We are happier when we believe in the communication process—that communicating to the best of our ability will produce results. They may not always be exactly what we wanted, but they will be satisfying nevertheless because of our active involvement in the process.

AS ENTERTAINMENT

The previous discussion of the importance of communication gives the impression that humans are serious, goal-oriented, information seekers proceeding through life in search of sober contentment. As we know, humans and other advanced animal species have a strong inclination toward entertainment. Once basic survival needs like safety and nourishment have been satisfied, it seems quite natural to occupy our time with less-serious matters. Sometimes this sequence of survival-then-entertainment is not followed exactly. Some college students, for example, have even been known to place entertainment before survival in college. Some of our students have said, if it were not for entertainment, they could not survive in college. The point is that entertainment is necessary.

Communication is vital for the entertainment side of the productive character orientation. True, some of our diversions seem to involve no communication. We might paint in a private place and never discuss our paintings with anyone. However, most entertainment involves communication. Movies, television, plays, books, and magazines are some obvious examples. It has been said that entertainment is the main purpose of the mass media. While that claim may be debated, there seems to be little doubt that mass media provide us with much of our entertainment.

We sometimes find entertainment in the way a person communicates. We often watch a particular television talk show not so much for the guests, but because we like listening to and watching the host. *The Tonight Show* host Jimmy Fallon's nonverbal behavior—the way he moves his eyes after a line and uses his voice to give additional meaning to words—adds to the entertainment value of the actual words. We like the way he says things and do not tire of his verbal and nonverbal mannerisms. The jokes told by comedians may not be as important as how they are told. Often leaders seem to be selected because of the way they express their ideas, even though the ideas may be rather commonplace.

Social conversations represent one of the most common forms of entertainment through communication. For many of us, this is our chief form of relaxation. We enjoy talking with people. Such conversations may have no serious purpose. We may not want to accomplish anything other than to enjoy ourselves. The topics may be trivial and the talk may be shallow because the purpose is pleasant diversion. Rational dialogue is also entertaining. Some of us find arguing a source of entertainment. We perceive an argument over a controversial issue as an exciting intellectual challenge—a verbal game of chess. The issue argued may not even be important to us; what matters is the activity.

We should emphasize further the importance of balancing work and rest. If all of our communication behavior is task oriented, we are conveying a less-than-desirable impression of ourselves. Most people feel uncomfortable with someone who is totally production oriented. People also find it difficult to rely on someone who takes the opposite extreme, a preoccupation with entertainment. The productive person is one who alternates between work and rest. Our more favorable impressions are probably formed of people who have such an orientation.

SUMMARY

Studying communication means acquiring a deeper understanding of familiar phenomena, such as the symbolic nature of communication. Communication is a transactional process that involves both content and relationship dimensions. We reviewed the reasons for a lack of agreement on a single definition of communication and then explained our position that communication involves humans manipulating symbols to stimulate meaning in other humans. We addressed the issue of intentionality by considering communication as planned verbal and nonverbal behavior.

Communication is influenced by the situation, the most familiar contexts being: interpersonal, small group, organizational, public, mass, intercultural, family, health, and political. We looked at the functions of communication from several perspectives: as purposes of public speeches (inform, entertain, stimulate, persuade). The importance of communication was discussed in terms of creating cooperation, acquiring information, forming self-concept, communication as entertainment, and in the evolution of ideas. As you explore the process of theory building in this text, we hope you develop an appreciation for the wealth of information communication researchers have painstakingly constructed about communication behaviors. We hope their work inspires you to reconceptualize behaviors you took for granted and to acquire a "communication mind-set" that enhances your own communication and provides new perspectives on the communication of others.

KEY TERMS

Channel	Noise	Symbol
Communication plans	Perception	Symptom
Context	Receiver	Theory
Feedback	Ritual	Transactional process
Intentionality	Sign	
Message	Source	

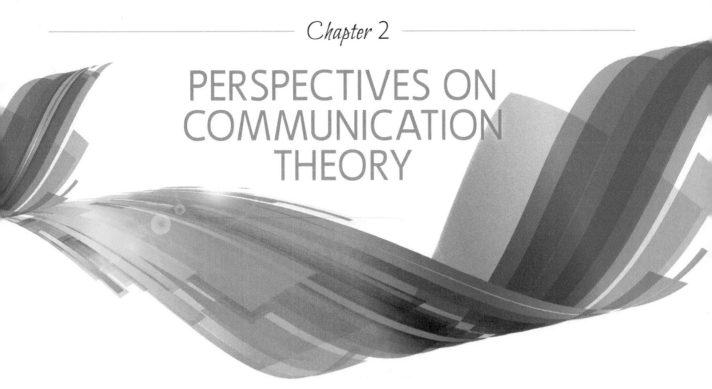

Chapter 2

PERSPECTIVES ON COMMUNICATION THEORY

Theory building is bound by the perspectives and biases of the people who develop the theories. A person can only make sense of an event based on their previous experience. This chapter will present elements that all theories have in common and focus on the criteria necessary for sound communication theory development.

Psychologist Kurt Lewin is attributed with the saying, "*There is nothing so practical as a good theory.*" This statement is echoed by Hoover (1992) in that "knowledge is socially powerful only if it is knowledge that can be put to use. Social knowledge, if it is to be useful, must be communicable, valid, and compelling" (p. 6). These arguments highlight the importance of systematic thought necessary for theory building in aiding our understanding of ourselves and our world.

As mentioned in the introduction of this book, the authors take a primarily social scientific approach to contemporary communication theory. Given this, we must answer the question, "What is scientific theory?" The scientific approach is based on principles developed in fields such as medicine, biology, chemistry, physics, and engineering. According to Hoover (1992), "Science is a mode of inquiry that is common to all human beings" (p. 5). Heider (1958) believed that human beings are naïve scientists who seek certainty in our environment. "The need to understand what is happening around us and to share experiences with others makes systematic thought and inquiry essential" (Hoover, 1992, p. 6). Karl Popper, who is believed to be the most influential philosopher of natural science in the twentieth century, did not believe that the aim of science is to simply establish correlations between observed events. Instead, he believed that the aim of science is to discover undiscovered worlds beyond the world of ordinary experience (Popper, 1996). In other words, to hear the unheard, see the unseen, speak the unspoken, and touch the untouched.

It is our innate curiosity to constantly discover new things about ourselves and our environment that has made science the hallmark of "truth" throughout the world. Given that science can be considered a living and breathing entity in that it is ever changing, Thomas Kuhn (1970) argued that "science is the constellation of facts, theories, and methods collected in current texts" (p. 1). The words *current texts* are important because what is contained in the latest texts in any given discipline is based on the most up-to-date research information. As such, theories contained throughout this book represent an up-to-date *constellation of communication theory.*

THE SCIENTIFIC METHOD

Social scientific method
Using the concept of systematic thought and the application of scientific principles

The concept of systematic thought and the application of scientific principles are the key to the social scientific method. All scientists, whether in the hard sciences or the social sciences, have to agree on a systematic way to investigate any given construct or concept. By agreeing on a particular method of inquiry, any doubt about the validity of a particular finding or study can be verified by conducting another study using the same systematic steps (Hoover, 1992). Replicating a study to assess any given theory building effort is crucial in science. Such a systematic method prompted Albert Einstein to remark, "Development of Western science is based on two great achievements: The invention of the formal logic system and the discovery of the possibility to find out causal relationships by systematic experiment" (MacKay, 1977, p. 51).

Hoover (1992) argued, "The scientific method seeks to test thoughts against observable evidence in a disciplined manner with each step in the process" (p. 33). Therefore, science can be considered reality testing where we take our theoretical assumptions about how a phenomenon works, and then seek to find objective and observable evidence that either confirms or refutes those assumptions. According to Hempel (1965), a scientific explanation for any given theory is one that could be thought of as a deductive argument. For example, a deductive argument may take the form of the following:

Major Premise: *All humans need oxygen to survive*

Minor Premise: *You are human*

Conclusion: *Therefore, you need oxygen to survive*

However, theories are actually built using not only deductive, but inductive and abductive processes.

THEORY BUILDING THROUGH DEDUCTIVE, INDUCTIVE, AND ABDUCTIVE APPROACHES

As communication scientists we can build theory through induction and deduction. In inductive theory building, we build theory from specific findings based on several research studies. We do this in order to try to develop a more general theory based on those specific findings. As such, in inductive theory-building, the research comes before or precedes the development of the theory.

We conduct a series of studies on a given topic or phenomenon in an effort to observe any factors or variables that might be related to that phenomenon, and then we try to develop a general theory based upon the results of those studies. Like inductive reasoning in argumentation, we reason from the specific (the research findings) to the general (the theory). For example, suppose we are trying to develop a theory which posits that an affirming managerial communicator style affects employee performance and employee satisfaction. Through a series of studies, we would study managerial communicator style, employee performance, and employee satisfaction. Once the findings of these many studies emerge, we try to propose a theory. In a purely inductive theory building effort, little to no prior theory is employed, and theory building activity has a strong experiential basis. As such, theory "emerges" from research findings, and without imposition of prior expectations.

In deductive theory-building (a.k.a., the hypothetico-deductive approach), we *begin* with a theory, then we design research which attempts to test the proposed theory. That is, we presume that a relationship exists between certain variables or factors ahead of time, then we deduce testable hypotheses and conduct the research. Using the same phenomenon as mentioned above, we might begin with a theory which that suggests "Managerial Communicator Style Influences Employee Work Performance and Employee Satisfaction." We would then derive hypotheses (e.g., "Managers who exhibit an affirming managerial communicator style (i.e., highly relaxed, friendly, and attentive) will engender increased employee work performance and employee satisfaction," and "Managers who exhibit a non-affirming communicator style (i.e., highly tense, unfriendly, and inattentive) will engender decreased employee work performance and satisfaction") and then test them. When enough research is conducted on this phenomenon, and, "If the data come out as predicted, support is inferred for the hypotheses and for the theory that led to the hypotheses" (Levine, 2011, p. 25).

Some scholars argue that deductive theory-building is seen as superior to inductive theory-building, "While purely inductive research is often considered low rent and the stuff for intellectual bottom feeders, the hypothetico-deductive (HD) approach in contrast, is often seen as the gold standard or the elite scientific ideal" (Levine, 2011, p. 30). As a consequence, Levine (2011) proposes that *abductive reasoning*, as applied to theory-building, may be a productive and valuable alternative. Levine (2011) conceptualizes abductive reasoning as a compromise between the inductive and deductive approaches to building theory, which "involves reasoning from the data to the best explanation of the data given the data" (p. 31). Thought of as a combination of induction and deduction, abduction is conceptualized as the process of forming well-thought-out explanations of phenomena, and then selecting for scientific examination the explanations which seem to fit the phenomena best. Abductive reasoning allows theorists to consider existing theory even as they consider the data and the explanations that are consistent with it. When using the abductive approach, you do not have to ignore prior theory as you would with a purely inductive approach. By employing abduction, researchers can better determine exactly the key or most important factors inherent in understanding a given phenomenon. Abduction further suggests that once theories have emerged, they should be compared with each other, and the one which offers the best explanation of the phenomenon under study should take precedence (Lipton, 2004). Levine's own work developing Truth Default Theory (described in Chapter 8) exemplifies the comparison of existing theory, data, and new theory.

Ontology What it is the theorist is examining and what is considered the exact nature of reality and the most basic measuring units of reality

The scientific approach to theory building makes certain assumptions about reality. Ontology concerns what it is the theorist is examining, what he or she considers to be the exact nature of reality as well as the most basic measuring units of reality. For the social scientific approach, it is assumed that reality exists beyond our human experience. For example, if you ask a scientist the classic question that students struggle with in any introductory philosophy course, "If a tree falls in the forest and no one is there to hear it, does it make a sound?" The scientist, given the ontological assumptions about reality, would probably respond, "Of course it does." Whether or not we are there to hear the tree fall does not affect the physical reality of the tree striking the ground and all the sights and sounds that go along with such a natural event. Another important assumption concerns how we come to know knowledge as well as how the theorist investigates the theory. This is known as epistemology. Scientists believe that true knowledge can only be discovered via the scientific method, by empirical observation and empirical evidence collected in an objective manner. The third set of assumptions concerns what constitutes findings that are valuable, important, and worthy for us to study as scientists, what values guide a theorist in building theory, and how theory contributes to the overall body of knowledge and practice. For the scientist, this concerns axiology, the discovery of worlds beyond the obvious, and how these worlds contribute to the overall quality of human experience. Given that one of the foundational assumptions of science is that of objectivity, can scientists truly be objective? Are they motivated by their preferences for doing research in a particular way, or, during the process of observing a phenomenon, does the researcher influence the phenomenon in any way? Although these questions are more ethical and aesthetic in nature, they are important for theorists to keep in mind when developing theories, as arguably we cannot escape our human condition even when we are engaged in the practice of science.

Epistemology how we come to know knowledge as well as how the theorist investigates the theory

Axiology The discovery of worlds beyond the obvious and how these worlds contribute to the overall quality of human experience

The scientific method is composed of five systematic steps that any study, to be considered valid, must move through in logical progression.

IDENTIFYING VARIABLES TO BE INVESTIGATED

The first step concerns identifying the communication phenomena that you want to observe and theorize about, and creating a useful way of conceptualizing, or creating an abstract description of that phenomena. For example, why do some people engage in more arguing with others? In their theoretical model of argumentativeness, Infante and Rancer (1982) conceptualized two competing motivations for arguing: a motivation to approach arguments with other people and a motivation to avoid arguments with other people. The two motivations comprise a person's general tendency to argue (see Chapter 4 for a complete discussion of trait argumentativeness). These motivations are stronger or weaker from person to person. Because they vary, theory can be constructed to explain why they vary; if they did not vary, there would be nothing to explain. Indeed, theoretical concepts are often referred to as variables, especially when referencing the idea of measuring those concepts. To provide empirical (i.e., information or data gathered by observation) evidence for their model, Infante and Rancer had to develop questions that actually assessed the approach and avoidance behaviors people used when faced with an argumentative situation. Examples of items to assess the motivation to approach arguments include: "Arguing over controversial issues improves my intelligence" and "I am energetic and enthusiastic when I argue." Motivation to avoid arguments is assessed through items such as "Once I finish an argument, I promise myself that I will not get into another" and "I prefer being with people who rarely disagree with me." These items are examples of how the argumentative motivation variables can be made observable through asking people questions about their behavior.

Variable Term referring to a theoretical concept emphasizing its variation and measurability

Empirical Information gathered by observation

DEVELOPMENT OF HYPOTHESES

The second step of the scientific method concerns the development of specific hypotheses that make predictions about possible relationships between variables. A hypothesis is generally considered an educated guess as to what the probable result will be when you measure your variables. According to Hoover (1992), "A hypothesis is a sentence of a particularly well-cultivated breed" (p. 27). In the Infante and Rancer (1982) example mentioned earlier, they hypothesized that, as a person's argumentativeness scores increase, so too would the person's desire to participate in debate (H1: Argumentativeness will be positively related to desire to participate in debate). What if these researchers were not sure of the direction of the relationship between the variables? What if there was no previous evidence suggesting that scores on the argumentativeness measure were linked to a desire to approach other people in argumentative communication? In this case, we would utilize a research question, or statements that do not predict relationships but inquire as to whether or not the variables are related (RQ1: Is there a relationship between argumentativeness and a desire to participate in debate?). Simply put, hypotheses predict associations in particular directions, whereas research questions inquire whether the variables are in any way related.

Hypothesis Tentative statement about the relationships between concepts of a theory; a statement of prediction about the relationships between variables

Research question Question guiding investigation; usually used when a hypothesis is not warranted

It is important to distinguish questions of science versus other types of propositions that people pose. People generally pose three types of questions, those of fact, value, and policy. Questions of fact concern whether something is or isn't, occurred or didn't occur, will or not will occur. Examples would include, "Does vitamin C decreases susceptibility to the influenza virus?" Factual questions are considered *scientific* in nature because they can be tested using the scientific method that assumes objectivity and is empirical in nature. Hypotheses are always formulated as questions of fact. Questions of value concern whether something is good or bad or favorable or unfavorable. Examples of value-based questions would include "Is abortion wrong?" or, "Is restricting

Questions of fact Concern whether something is or isn't, occurred or didn't occur, will or will not occur

Questions of value Concern whether something is good or bad or favorable or unfavorable

a woman's right to choose immoral?" According to Infante (1988), "People often differ considerably in what they believe is right or wrong, good or bad, valuable or worthless, desirable or undesirable when individuals apply their value standards . . . they come up with very different conceptions of whether the thing is favorable or not (p. 35). Values are idiosyncratic and specific to each person. Therefore, there is no way to form an assessment of value that is objective in nature and, as such, value assessments are not considered scientific in nature. Questions of policy concern whether or not something should or shouldn't be done. For example, "Should the government institute mandatory military service for all Americans under 35 years of age?" The fact that questions of policy are based on what people should or shouldn't do is considered a subjective question (as opposed to objective) and, as such, policy questions cannot be considered scientific in nature.

CONDUCT AN EMPIRICAL INVESTIGATION

The third step in the scientific method is conducting an empirical study. As stated earlier, the word *empirical* means to use observation in assessment of any given phenomena. According to Hoover (1992), "Science is the art of reality testing or taking ideas and confronting them with observable evidence drawn from the phenomena to which they relate" (p. 11). There are four methods through which theories can be empirically tested. These consist of experiments (measure the effects of the independent variable on the dependent variable), survey research (interviews or questionnaires), field research (observing something in its natural setting), and available data research (observing things from the past such as letters, artifacts, or e-mails). The method chosen is determined by the type of hypothesis that is derived in step 2 of the scientific method. Please refer to Chapter 3 for a detailed discussion of these different research methods.

COMPARE RESULTS TO THE ORIGINAL HYPOTHESIS

Once the data collection from your observation of the phenomena is complete, you must then evaluate the results to determine if the theoretically derived hypotheses are supported (either fully or partially) or rejected. If the hypothesis is rejected, we conclude that your theory (based on the results of your study) was not supported, and we must continue to accept the status quo. If, however, we find that our hypothesis is supported, then we accept our new finding as being supported, not proven (this will be discussed in more detail later in this chapter).

ASSESS THEORETICAL SIGNIFICANCE OF THE FINDINGS AND IDENTIFY THREATS TO VALIDITY

The final step in the scientific method is to assess the theoretical significance of the findings. When we use the word *significance,* we are referring to two different concepts. First, theoretical significance means the empirical findings either support or do not support the theory. Second, statistical significance reflects whether the results are due to chance. To say that a finding is statistically significant is not necessarily to say that it is theoretically significant and vice versa. Although the scientific method ensures a process that should lead to the development of quality theory development, it does not guarantee it.

WHAT MAKES A QUALITY COMMUNICATION THEORY?

Throughout this book you will be exposed to many theories that seek to describe, explain, predict, or control one or more particular aspects of communication. Some of these theories, as you will come to know, will have greater utility than others. A question that inevitably comes to a person's mind when considering any theory is, "How do I know if this theory is of any use?" If not for specific scientific guidelines, this question would be difficult to answer. However, theorists have compiled a list of criteria that serve to evaluate the worth of any given theory. These constituents of quality theory building include the need for theories to be testable, falsifiable, heuristic, parsimonious, logically consistent, and pleasing to the mind.

One of the major premises of the scientific method to theory building is the ability to test empirically the effectiveness of a theory to determine if it accounts adequately for the communication phenomena that it seeks to explain, predict, and/or control. Therefore, a theory must be empirically testable. A theory that cannot be tested can never be scrutinized to debate based on observation and, thus, is of very little utility to social scientists. By being able to test a theory based on agreed-upon steps (i.e., the scientific method) we can (a) draw conclusions about the utility and thoroughness of the theory, (b) determine whether the theory should be rejected or supported in its entirety, or (c) determine whether elements of the theory that are underdeveloped should be modified, and then, once modified, retest the new theory. The concept of testing should not be thought of as a one-time event. As society and technology change, constant testing should be conducted to account for such changes.

Testable Quality of a good theory; capable of being disproved or falsified

Replicable A study similar to an earlier study which determines if the results of the original study are similar when repeated

Not only should a quality communication theory be testable, but those tests should also conclusively reveal either support or lack of support for the theoretical assumptions under examination. Thus, the pursuit of falsification is one that the scientist should take extremely seriously because a theory that cannot be tested and objectively found to be supported or falsified is of no utility to science. The importance of theory falsification can also be seen in Popper's (1963, 1996) process of falsifying theory through systematic observation. Further, falsification should serve as the demarcation determining what is and what is not considered scientific theory in that only if the theory is falsifiable can it be considered scientific. Similarly, Hawkings (1996) believed that "any physical theory is always provisional, in the sense that it is only a hypothesis; you can never prove it. No matter how many times the results of experiments agree with some theory, you can never be sure that the next time the result will not contradict the theory. On the other hand, you can disprove a theory by finding even a single observation which disagrees with the predictions of the theory" (p. 15).

Falsification To find a theory to be false

For theory to be of any use, it should solve or explain some problem. The heuristic value of a theory lies within the theory's ability to solve problems or provide solutions that are the closest to the "best solution." One common business heuristic is known as K.I.S.S., which is an acronym for *keep it simple, stupid*. As these examples illustrate, heuristics are valuable for all types of theory-building efforts. In Chapter 7 we present Robert Cialdini's persuasive heuristics, which explain various reasons why people behave the way they do. Upon reading about the persuasive heuristics, you will get a better understanding as to the intuitive appeal they have in explaining behavior such as conformity and commitment.

Heuristic value A theory's ability to solve problems or provide solutions that are the closest to the "best solution"

Another attribute of theory is that it should be reduced to its simplest form possible or demonstrate parsimony. Perhaps one of the most popular examples of a parsimonious theory is Albert Einstein's *theory of relativity* (Stachel, 1989), which was reduced into two postulates. A postulate, also known as an axiom, is a proposition that is not proven or demonstrated, but simply considered true in nature.

Parsimony Reducing a theory to its simplest form possible

Postulate A proposition that is not proven or demonstrated, but simply considered true in nature

Axiom A proposition that is not proven or demonstrated, but simply considered true in nature

- **POSTULATE 1:** The laws of physics are identical for all observers in uniform motion relative to one another.
- **POSTULATE 2:** The speed of light in a vacuum is the same for all observers, regardless of their relative motion or of the motion of the source of the light.

Einstein also reduced, among other elements of his theory, the equivalent relationship of energy and mass into the mathematical formula: $E = mc^2$. As this example illustrates, great theories are not necessarily those that are composed of overly elaborate or ornate propositions but those that are expressed in the most concise and direct ways. Further, theories should contain as few assumptions as possible, yet be comprehensive enough to explain fully the phenomenon. For example, uncertainty reduction theory (URT) (Berger and Calabrese, 1975) assumes that when we first meet a person, people seek to reduce uncertainty. Therefore, this theory seeks to explain the process people go through when reducing uncertainty in initial interactions (see Chapter 8).

Another term used to represent the precision of theoretical explanation is known as Occam's razor and is named after the fourteenth-century English logician William of Ockham. He argued that "Entities must not be multiplied beyond necessity." The idea of simplicity comes from reductionist philosophy or the need to reduce units or concepts of a theory down to their simplest parts. This suggests that the fewer assumptions made in a theory, the better the theory.

Occam's razor Term used to represent the precision of theoretical explanation; stresses simplicity

The idea that theory should be **logically consistent** is based on the application of formal logic to theory building. Whether a theory is derived from inductive, deductive, or abductive reasoning, all theory building is based on principles that are consistent and related to one another. Consider the following objects and identify which of them do not belong: (a) suntan lotion, (b) towel, (c) swimsuit,

(d) sunglasses, and (e) hacksaw. It is not too difficult to determine that one of these items does not belong with the others, as a hacksaw has no logical reason to be included with the other elements of our "theory of going swimming." Given this, the propositions within a theory should serve to logically relate to one another, not contradict one another.

Another attribute of good theory building is the notion that any theory should have aesthetic value. That is, it should have intuitive appeal and be eloquently simple. Many theorists rely on diagrams or pictures when presenting complex ideas in an effort to pictorially represent theoretical models. The pictorial representation of this model simply "makes sense" to the everyday person. There is little cognitive work required to understand the assumptions of the model.

The constituents of communication theory discussed earlier represent both the desired and necessary characteristics that allow the field of communication studies to further its exploration of human interaction. Scholars that are engaged in theory building efforts will forward theories that may include all these characteristics or only a select few. As a general rule, when developing communication theory, a scholar should be aware of all the characteristics associated with good theory building and seek to make sure that their theory contains elements of each.

COMMUNICATION THEORY DEVELOPMENT

Theories are ever changing as a constant evolution must take place for any given theory to maintain the ability to describe, explain, predict, and control human events. Consider the annual drafting procedure of the National Football League (NFL). Each spring, the NFL evaluates the top college football athletes at an annual competition known as the NFL Combine. Each of the 32 professional football teams send representatives to evaluate the performance of each athlete. In the early days of the combine, athletes were assessed on speed, strength, and jumping ability. Therefore, the development of a theory as to what made a successful professional football player was somewhat simple (i.e., how strong, how fast, how tall). However, as professional football began to gain popularity and included lucrative product endorsement deals, increased celebrity, and other benefits, the NFL began to experience players who had exceptional speed, strength, and jumping ability, yet did not perform well at the professional level. When enough evidence indicating a theory's lack of explanatory or predictive power has amassed, the theorist should alter or discard the theory for one that better accounts for the phenomenon. In terms of our NFL Combine example, today's theories of what predicts successful performance at the professional level includes a host of physiological as well as psychological test factors that include dexterity, flexibility, intelligence, and psychological stability among others. Therefore, the theory of what makes a good NFL football player has had to evolve as the game, society, and the athletes have evolved. We cannot assume that once we explain and/or predict things effectively that explanation/prediction will forever be satisfactory. Recall the earlier discussion about statistical and theoretical significance. The vast majority of NFL theories concerning professional football prospects explain a very small percentage of success in the NFL; however, in this case, a theory that is correct one out of ten times would be considered a pretty good theory.

Extension Process in which a theory grows by adding knowledge and new concepts

Intention Process in which a theory grows by developing a deeper understanding of the original concepts and variables

How do theories grow and change? Theories can change through the process of extension or intention (Kaplan, 1964). The process of extension reflects the growing ability of a theory to describe, explain, and predict an ever-growing number of concepts and situations. For example, in Chapter 13 we discuss the social information processing theory (SIPT) of computer-mediated communication. According to Walther (2008), SIPT "explains how people get to know one another online, without nonverbal cues, and how they develop and manage relationships in the computer-mediated environment" (p. 391). This theory of mediated communication is believed to be a more comprehensive explanation of how people use technology than theories developed earlier because it accounts for newer technologies that were not in existence when earlier theories were developed. As new communication technologies emerge, theorists will probably try to apply SIPT to explain how people communicate via the new technology. Thus, SIPT will experience theoretical growth by extension. However, when theories grow by intention, they do not seek to further explain new concepts but instead seek a deeper understanding of the concepts that the theory already explains. An example of theoretical growth by intention is the development of information reception apprehension (IRA) (see Chapter 4). According to Wheeless, Preiss, and Gayle (1997), IRA is "a pattern of anxiety and antipathy that filters informational reception, perception, and processing, and/or adjustment (psychologically, verbally, physically) associated with complexity, abstractness, and flexibility" (p. 166). IRA was an extension of receiver apprehension, which sought to explain why some people become anxious when receiving communicative messages in general. However, IRA specifies the following types of factors that comprise the construct: listening apprehension, reading anxiety, and intellectual inflexibility. Therefore, the development of IRA was not necessarily intended to explain any new information as much as to provide a greater understanding of the different facets of anxiety associated with receiving information.

Regardless of the way that communication theories develop and evolve, all theory seeks to investigate the various phenomena and events that occur in nature. In the next section, we will cover the underlying functions and goals that are served/pursued by theory.

FUNDAMENTAL GOALS OF COMMUNICATION THEORY

There are particular goals that scholars pursue about any given event, and they use theory as a vehicle to achieve these goals. The four major goals of theory are to describe, explain, predict, and control. All these goals are central in determining the relative value of a theory.

The description goal of theory serves to focus the attention of scholars on particular parts of an event or phenomenon. For example, family communication scholars have long debated the definition of the word *family*. This debate has only become more complicated in light of reproductive technologies, same-sex unions, and other issues that confound the definition. However, once we are able to describe a particular phenomenon, scholars can then move to assess the efficacy with which a theory explains and predicts aspects of the thing being studied. Theories are designed to represent a phenomenon or event. The ability to describe the phenomena under investigation provides a blueprint with which the theory can be applied to other situations.

Description Focuses the attention of scholars on particular parts of an event or phenomenon

The importance of the descriptive function of theory can be illustrated in the parable of *the blind men and the elephant*. Once upon a time, a king summoned his servant and ordered him to gather up all the blind men in the village. The king presented the elephant to each man. To one man he presented the elephant's head, to another the ears, to another the tusks, to another the trunk, to another the foot, to another the back, to another the tail, and to the last man the tuft of the tail. He told each man that this was an elephant. The man who was presented the head described the elephant as a pot, the man presented with the ear described the elephant as a winnowing basket, the man presented with the tusk described it as a ploughshare, the man presented with the trunk believed the elephant was a plough, and so on and so forth. The men began to quarrel, shouting things such as, "Yes it is!" "No, it is not!" This quarrel continued until the men came to blows. The king, delighted to see this scene, shouted, "Just so are these preachers and scholars holding various views blind and unseeing . . . In their ignorance they are by nature quarrelsome, wrangling, and disputatious, each maintaining reality is thus and thus." This parable illustrates the need for a theory to describe in direct and clear terms exactly what it is the theory is addressing. By making sure everyone experiences the same concept of "what is an elephant," we can then have a description of an event that is understood by others.

The explanation goal of theory concerns understanding how a phenomenon or event occurs. To explain a communication phenomenon is vital to theory building in that to organize experience, which is one of the functions of theory explained earlier, we need to be able to explain how a communication process works. An example of a theory that does a particularly good job at satisfying the explanatory theoretical goal is the theory of groupthink (a.k.a., the groupthink hypothesis), discussed in Chapter 10. This theory is extremely effective in explaining a faulty decision-making process. However, although this theory

Explanation Understanding how a phenomenon or event occurs is very effective at explaining different types of interaction outcomes, it is considered a post-facto theory (that is, it is able to explain the past), as it has little predictive power in terms of the future. Therefore, theories that have been developed to explain a communication phenomenon may lack in the other goals of description and prediction.

Prediction The concept of knowing what events will occur in the future

The goal of prediction, the concept of knowing what events will occur in the future, is something that is vital to the survival of humankind as well as nature at large. Whether it is a tornado on the horizon, an oncoming recession of the economy, or an impending global war, our ability/need to predict events is a vital function that can be satisfied by theory. In his book *A Brief History of Time,* Stephen Hawking (1996) argued, "A theory is a good theory if it satisfies two requirements: It must accurately describe a large class of observations on the basis of a model which contains only a few arbitrary elements, and it must make definite predictions about the results of future observations" (p. 15).

The need to predict future events is a need that transcends science and is found in our everyday ways of thinking and explaining the world. For example, consider a time when you were walking home late at night on a dark street, and you saw a couple of people up ahead walking toward you. Most people would theorize (not scientifically but based on their own personal experience) that this situation has the potential to have adverse circumstances such as being robbed or physically assaulted. As such, you decided to cross the street, based on the prediction that this street-crossing behavior would result in reducing the probability of being in an altercation with the oncoming strangers.

For communication theorists, one of the most important aspects of a theory is the ability to predict communicative behavior. Many scholars develop models and theoretical frameworks designed to forecast a person's behavior in an expected way. For example, in Chapter 8 we present interaction adaptation theory (IAT). This theory is designed to predict how people will behave by accounting for, among other things, the communicator's requirements, expectancies, and desires. Several empirical investigations have supported the two propositions of IAT in terms of its ability to predict communication behavior. As will become evident in the later chapters of this book, some of the theories presented possess greater predictive powers than others. For many communication researchers, the degree of predictability of any theory is a direct translation of the overall quality of that theory.

Control The ability to alter elements in the present to achieve a specified outcome given certain situational factors in the future

The goal of control is made possible by our ability to predict, explain, and describe any given phenomenon or event. The explanation function of theory seeks to understand why events occur, whereas control concerns under what situations events will occur. When we use the term *control,* we are referring to the ability to alter elements in the present to achieve a specified outcome given certain situational factors in the future. For example, marketing and advertising professionals are aware of the theories of nonverbal communication and psychology regarding how humans react to color and the color spectrum. When advertising new products (whether they be on a Web page, magazine, or television commercial), marketers and advertisers will utilize the color red when they want the reader/viewer to attend to a message. Research indicates that the color red activates the human brain in different ways than other colors and that this activation has resulted in increased product sales. Knowing what we do about the influence of color on the human brain allows us to control the types of messages (in terms of color choice) that we want people to attend to.

The goals of theory discussed in this section transcend all disciplines. Whether we are developing theory based on biology, chemistry, physics, engineering, psychology, or communication, we all strive to satisfy these fundamental functions and goals.

HOW MANY THEORIES ARE ENOUGH?

This book presents dozens of theories across all contexts and aspects of human communication. There has long been a debate on the necessity of so many communication theories contrasted with other theorists who believe that we have too few. Berger (1991) presented a number of issues related to theory building in communication. First, was the lack of a theoretical paradigm, or touchstone theory. Instead, contemporary theory has its roots in many disciplines, including sociology, psychology, English, linguistics, and philosophy. Second, Berger believed that there is a scarcity of theory-building efforts throughout the entire field of communication studies. Berger argued that "we are hardly in danger of being buried under an avalanche of original communication theories" (p. 103). This critique was rebutted by Purcell (1992), who suggested that "there is a paucity of communication theories only if one assumes that theory construction began in the twentieth century" (p. 94), citing the contribution of pre-twentieth-century philosophers and scholars such as Descartes, Bacon, Blair, Campbell, and Whately. In sum, "the field of communication would be well served by communication theorists who attempt to bridge the broad span between interpersonal communication theory and classical rhetorical theory with covering communication theories" (Purcell, 1992, p. 97). The different perspectives of Berger and Purcell highlight the fundamental distinctions of what does/doesn't constitute contemporary communication theory.

Burleson (1992) offered yet another perspective on the number of communication theories. He rejected the question, "Why are there so few communication theories?" and rephrased the question to ask, "Why are there so few theories of human communication?" He argued that theorists have primarily been concerned with the content and uses that people put on communication rather than the development of a "philosophy of communication." A philosophy of communication should treat human communication holistically, providing a "characterization of the overall process of communication" (Burleson, 1992, p. 84). Such a philosophy should be general, leading to theories that transcend culture and context or are etic in nature (i.e., true to all people and cultures).

Still another unique perspective was offered by Craig (1993). He pointed out the paradox in communication theory building in that, even though there have been numerous and much more complex theories forwarded, "confusion, uncertainty, implicit dissention, and to a lesser degree, explicit controversy about the proper foci, forms, and functions of communication theory have markedly increased" (Craig, 1993, p. 26). In fact, Craig also reframed the original question of "Why are there so few communication theories?" to ask, "Why are there not so many communication theories?" He believes that although description, explanation, prediction, and control are fundamental goals of science, science should simultaneously advance moral and political objectives. In sum, he advocates that the field of communication studies be viewed as an integrative, practical discipline where all traditions (social science, critical, and interpretive methods) be used in any contemporary communication theory building.

SEVEN THEORETICAL TRADITIONS IN BUILDING COMMUNICATION THEORY

There are seven theoretical traditions in the constitutive model: the sociopsychological tradition, the cybernetic tradition, the rhetorical tradition, the phenomenological tradition, the sociocultural tradition, the critical tradition, and the semiotic tradition. These seven traditions and the interaction among them provide a comprehensive description of contemporary communication theory building (see Figure 2.1). That is, "each tradition is characterized by a unique definition of communication, conceptualization of communication problems, metadiscursive vocabulary (terms for talking about communication), and metadiscursive

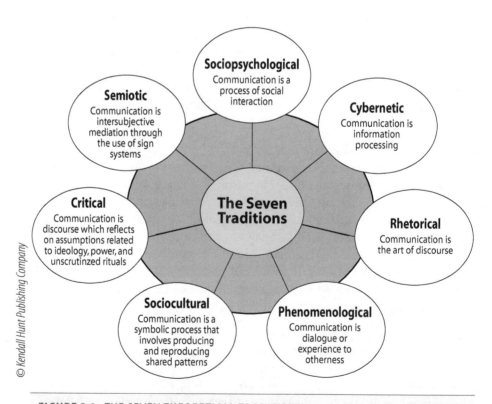

FIGURE 2.1 THE SEVEN THEORETICAL TRADITIONS

commonplaces (everyday assumptions about communication)" (Craig, 2006, p. 129). As the field of communication continues to develop, Craig (2007) believes that there may be more traditions developed as long as they: (a) comprise a unique and large body of evidence not found in other traditions, and (b) have a distinct perspective on communication problems, have a unique metadiscursive vocabulary, and have commonplace beliefs that are either embraced or rejected (Rancer & Avtgis, 2009). In this text, we focus primarily on theories which have been developed from the socio-psychological and socio-cultural traditions.

THE SOCIOPSYCHOLOGICAL TRADITION

The sociopsychological tradition is one of the newer traditions of communication theory building. Developed in the early 1900s, the sociopsychological tradition assumes that communication is a process of social interaction (Craig, 1999). The validation of theories from this perspective relies on the scientific method and the use of experimental designs in an effort to reveal cause-and-effect relationships along with control mechanisms to regulate these cause-and-effect relationships. Due to its reliance on the scientific method, some scholars refer to this as "communication science" (Berger & Chaffee, 1987).

Sociopsychological tradition Assumes that communication is a process of social interaction

Because this perspective focuses on the process of social interaction, theory building within this tradition has been contextual in nature (e.g., interpersonal, group, organizational, health) with further subdivision of each context (e.g., through within-organizational communication we may examine aggressive communication within the workplace). Even though the term *communication* existed in the early 1900s, it wasn't until the 1940s that psychologists overtly used communication as a focus in experimental research design (Hovland, 1948). Carl Hovland was the first person who advocated that all the social sciences (i.e., anthropology, psychology, political science, and sociology) utilize the scientific method to investigate communication. The sociopsychological tradition has been widely integrated into the field of communication studies and will continue to be one of the most prominent traditions for the foreseeable future. According to Craig (1999), this tradition views communication as "situations requiring manipulation of causes of behavior to achieve specified outcomes" (p. 133). The metadiscourses used in the sociopsychological tradition include vocabulary such as *attribute, behavior, cognition, effect, emotion, interaction, perception, personality,* and *variable* (Craig, 1999).

THE CYBERNETIC TRADITION

The cybernetic tradition treats communication theory building as information processing and concerns analyzing communication problems such as "noise; overload; a malfunction or 'bug' in a system" (Craig, 1999, p. 133). The vocabulary utilized in this metadiscourse includes *feedback, function, information, network, noise, receiver, redundancy, signal,* and *source* (Craig, 1999). This tradition was developed in the mid-twentieth century by researchers such as Claude Shannon and Warren Weaver (Heims, 1991).

Cybernetic tradition Treats communication theory building as information processing and concerns analyzing communication problems in a system

Theories that are developed in the cybernetic tradition focus on the flow of information and include noise, information overload, and incongruity between function and structure (Craig, 1999). Norbert Weiner (1948) originally coined the word *cybernetics* and was concerned with how humans and machines communicate. Weiner's principles were adapted to human relationships by Gregory Bateson (1972) as well as Paul Watzlawick, Janet Beavin, and Donald Jackson (1967). The systems perspective, which is widely used in communication studies, was developed from the cybernetic tradition. This tradition considers the larger context within which communication interactions occur.

THE RHETORICAL TRADITION

Rhetorical tradition
Conceptualizes communication as the art of discourse

The rhetorical tradition conceptualizes communication as the art of discourse (Craig & Muller, 2007). Theory building from this tradition looks at the direct relation to problems encountered within the sociohistorical context in which they occur. For example, consider Plato's critique of rhetoric as the art of deception, Aristotle's exploration of *logos,* and Burke's idea that all language is rhetorical (Craig & Muller, 2007). Craig (1999) believes that the rhetorical tradition "challenges the commonplaces that mere words are less important than actions, that true knowledge is more than just a matter of opinion, and that telling the plain truth is something other than strategic adaptation of a message to an audience" (p. 136). The rhetorical tradition approaches problems of communication as "social exigency requiring collective deliberation and judgment" (Craig, 1999, p. 133). Metadiscourse use in this tradition includes vocabulary such as *art, audience, commonplace, communicator, emotion, logic, method,* and *strategy* (Craig, 1999).

THE PHENOMENOLOGICAL TRADITION

Phenomenological tradition Views communication as dialogue or experience to otherness

The phenomenological tradition views communication as dialogue or experience to otherness (Craig & Muller, 2007). Craig (1999) argued that theorists operating from this perspective are concerned with "the necessity, and yet the inherent difficulty—even, arguably, the practical impossibility—of sustained, authentic communication between persons" (p. 139). Unlike some of the other traditions, the phenomenological tradition does not treat objectivity and subjectivity as mutually exclusive. Instead, both objectivity and subjectivity are believed to be necessary to understand the human experience. In terms of problems with communication, Craig (1999) believes that theorists treat problematic communication as "absence of, or failure to sustain, authentic human relationship" (p. 133). Metadiscourse common to this tradition includes vocabulary such as *dialogue, experience, genuineness, openness, other, self,* and *supportiveness* (Craig, 1999).

In terms of practical implications, phenomenological theorists assume that people experience events in very different ways and that we need to respect experiential differences as well as make good-faith efforts to seek common ground (Craig, 1999). Furthermore, there are practical applications in pursuing the goal of an ideal dialogue while simultaneously acknowledging problems associated with achieving the ideal dialogue.

THE SOCIOCULTURAL TRADITION

The sociocultural tradition reflects a "symbolic process that produces shared sociocultural patterns" (Craig, 1999, p. 144). Communication problems that are addressed by this tradition are problems of diversity and relativity as well as cultural change. Simply put, the sociocultural tradition views problematic communication as "conflict; alienation; misalignment; failure to coordinate" (Craig, 1999, p. 133). Metadiscourse common to this tradition contains vocabulary such as *co-construction, culture, identity, practice, ritual, rule, socialization, society,* and *structure* (Craig, 1999). It is believed that this tradition is the most diverse, as it includes theory building at the macro sociocultural level (e.g., functionalism and structuralism), at the micro sociocultural level (e.g., symbolic interactionism and ethnomethodology), or a combination of both (e.g., structuration). Edward Sapir and Benjamin Whorf are believed to be the pioneers of this tradition (Rancer & Avtgis, 2009). The theories contained in this tradition are diverse and include coordinated management of meaning (Pearce & Cronen, 1980), social action media theory (Schoening & Anderson, 1995), and more contemporary approaches to rhetorical theory (Ehninger, 1968). Further, in terms of practical use of this tradition, Craig (1999) believed.

> *Sociocultural theory is plausible from a lay point of view in part because it appeals rhetorically to the commonplace beliefs that individuals are products of their social environments; that groups develop particular norms, rituals, and worldviews; that social change can be difficult and disruptive; and that attempts to intervene actively in social processes often have unintended consequences. (p. 146)*

Sociocultural tradition
Addresses problems of diversity and relativity as well as cultural change

THE CRITICAL TRADITION

The critical tradition has its origins in Plato's development of the Socratic dialectic (Craig, 1999). Communication is conceptualized as a discursive reflection or discourse that freely reflects on assumptions that can be related to ideology, power, and unscrutinized rituals (Craig & Muller, 2007). The overarching goal of the critical tradition is to expose hidden elements that distort communication and to advocate for efforts to resist the use of power by these elements. Problems with communication are seen as "hegemonic ideology; systematically distorted speech situation[s]" (Craig, 1999, p. 133). Metadiscourse within this tradition includes vocabulary such as *consciousness-raising, dialectic, emancipation ideology, oppression,* and *resistance* (Craig, 1999). The contemporary critical tradition includes the writings of Karl Marx and Jürgen Habermas. More recently, current communication theories developed from this tradition involve political economy, critical cultural studies, feminist theory, postcolonial theory, and queer theory (Craig & Muller, 2007). Craig (1999) argued that the real-world application of the critical tradition lies in the commonplace belief of injustices and conflict that is ubiquitous in contemporary society. Further, this tradition serves to call into question the neutrality and objectivity assumed in science and technology.

Critical tradition Goal is to expose hidden elements that distort communication and to advocate efforts to resist the use of power by these elements

THE SEMIOTIC TRADITION

Semiotic tradition
conceptualizes communication
as intersubjective mediation
by signs

The final tradition is that of the semiotic tradition, and it can be traced back to the late seventeenth to early eighteenth-century writings of John Locke, who is considered the father of modern ideas of treating communication as transmission (Peters, 1989). This tradition conceptualizes communication as intersubjective mediation by signs, or "a process in which language and other sign systems come to have shared meanings and thereby serve as a medium for common understanding between individuals (subjects)" (Craig & Muller, 2007, p. 163). The semiotic tradition views communication problems as issues of transmission and representation that serve to reduce effective meaning exchange or misunderstandings or gaps between subjective viewpoints (Craig, 1999, p. 133). Metadiscourse common to this tradition includes vocabulary such as *code, icon, index, language, meaning, medium, misunderstanding, referent, sign,* and *symbol* (Craig, 1999).

According to Craig (1999), the future of organizing communication theory as an interrelated yet distinct tradition is based on the continued pursuit of new traditions that offer practical metadiscourse about practical problems associated with everyday interaction (Craig, 1999). As with any metatheoretical approach, new problems emerge as theory-building efforts continue in all traditions. Craig believes some of these problems include "the problem of strategy versus authenticity... , the problem of intentionality versus functionality... , the problem of proving the effectiveness of techniques... , the problem of instrumental reason as ideological distortion" (p. 130). With regard to the addition of new traditions in the future, Craig (1999) believes that a feminist tradition (if theorized as connectedness to others), an aesthetic tradition (if theorized as embodied performance), an economic tradition (if theorized as exchange), and a spiritual tradition (if theorized as communication on a mystical plane of existence) all hold interesting possibilities for the adaptation and addition to the constitutive metamodel of communication theory. The partitioning of communication theory into distinct traditions, yet also serving as a common ground by focusing theories on the task of explaining and rectifying everyday communication problems, serves as an innovative perspective that may reduce the splintering of approaches common to the communication discipline.

Theory-building efforts from scholars within the critical, cultural, and interpretive paradigms, as well as the postmodern tradition, have increased in recent years. Theorists and researchers from the social scientific tradition (such as the authors of this book) may find this trend of some concern because of the movement away from behavioral science. However, we readily acknowledge the contribution of these perspectives in increasing our understanding of human communication. According to Rancer and Avtgis (2009), "It is our contention that contemporary communication theory building efforts from all paradigmatic perspectives and theoretical traditions will simultaneously serve to fragment the discipline, yet unite it, based on the simple truth that we are all theorizing about the same phenomena—*communication.*"

SUMMARY

The material presented in this chapter is designed to expose you to the fundamental concepts, challenges, and procedures that every scholar must consider when engaged in theory-building efforts. Although some of these concepts may seem quite complex, whereas others appear quite simple, each concept is crucial to the integrity and foundation of quality theory-building efforts.

The scientific method and the steps that are associated with it provide a road map through which theories can be tested and modified. As evidenced in the chapter, theories that lack the ability to describe, explain, predict, and control are of little utility for scholars as well as researchers and practitioners. As society demands more problem-centered communication theories from the field of communication studies (i.e., theories that make a marked difference in the lives of people), adherence to the scientific method serves as a quality control process through which good theory can be rigorously developed and be applicable to the everyday communication problems that people face.

The final material in this chapter reflected Craig's constitutive metamodel that focuses on the utility that all traditions of communication theory building serve to alleviate everyday problems associated with or caused by problematic communication. This approach assumes that whatever the particular theory-building perspective, focusing on alleviating problems is a common thread that all communication theorists and theories can share.

KEY TERMS

Anticipatory function

Axiology

Axiom

Control

Critical tradition

Cybernetic tradition

Description

Empirical

Epistemology

Explanation

Extension

Falsification

Heuristic value

Hypothesis

Intention

Occam's razor

Ontology

Parsimony

Phenomenological tradition

Postulate

Prediction

Questions of fact

Questions of policy

Questions of value

Replicable

Research question

Rhetorical tradition

Semiotic tradition

Social scientific method

Sociocultural tradition

Socio-psychological tradition

Statistical significance

Testable

Theoretical significance

Variable

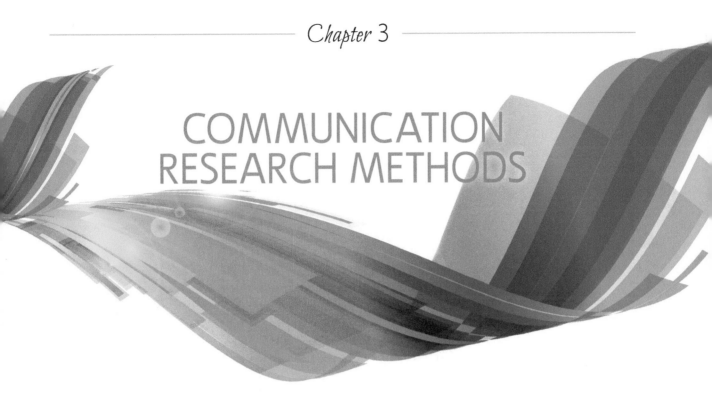

Chapter 3

COMMUNICATION RESEARCH METHODS

While it is normal practice to separate courses such as communication theory and research methods into two separate content areas, the two content areas are inextricably linked. That is, an understanding of research methods provides researchers a means of providing validation or falsification of theory. Research methods can be considered the theorist's "tool box" within which we derive evidence as to whether or not a theory is useful. We will introduce you to an overview of some methods used in communication research and theory testing. We cannot present all possible methods of research, as such an effort is well beyond the scope of this text. Instead, we would like to highlight the methodological framework behind many of the theories that are contained in this book. Thus, this chapter will provide a general overview of what is involved when conducting behavioral science research and theory testing.

Many methods are used to investigate the nature and origin of knowledge. In fact, one of the major areas of study in philosophy is dedicated to the origin of knowledge. This is known as **epistemology**. The vast majority of knowledge contained in this book was discovered through the practice of the behavioral science approach. The exclusion of other methods in the study of communication in no way reflects the superiority of one way of knowing over another. Instead, we have attempted to provide a solid foundation for perhaps the most popular method of investigation, the behavioral science approach. The underlying foundation of this line of research is that behavioral science research in communication involves controlled observation of humans in order to understand behavior. The two key words in this definition are *controlled* and *observation*. **Control** refers to carefully designed procedures which social scientists follow so they have confidence that what is being observed about humans and human communication is truly objective in nature and without personal bias. Such procedures are carefully modeled on the very same processes that physical sciences such as biology, geology, and physics, to name but a few, follow. Thus, good research design is an essential element of method that we examine further in this chapter. The second key word is **observation** and reflects the phenomenon of interest and how that phenomenon will be observed. More specifically, we are referring to measurement. Numerous ways to assess communication behavior will be presented later in this chapter.

THE SCIENTIFIC METHOD

Before we discuss specifics about research design and measurement, we need to explore some basic assumptions of scientific research. For example, let's say that you want to study the influence that trait verbal aggressiveness has on a person's preference for violent video game play (i.e., those having a rating of "M" for Mature). As described in Chapter 4 trait verbal aggressiveness is the predisposition to attack the self-concept of another person instead of or in addition to the positions they take on controversial subjects). Raymond Cattell (1966) developed guidelines for the scientific method that serve to hone our thinking and refine the specific questions that we are asking.

Induction leads to hypothesis

which leads to deduction

and finally to experimentation

Then, experiments lead to new induction

The induction phase involves an understanding of the research problem. For example, in our trait verbal aggressiveness/violent video game study, we can logically assume that a person who is high in trait verbal aggressiveness will have a greater tendency to prefer violent video games over non-violent video games when compared with people who are low in trait verbal aggressiveness. You may have also observed that some people curse and berate others who are also enjoying a particular type of gaming. Once your reasoning reaches this stage, you have entered the hypothesis stage.

The hypothesis stage consists of making predictions about what you believe will occur based on reviewing previous research. In this case, people high in trait verbal aggressiveness will prefer violent video games significantly more than people low in trait verbal aggressiveness. You have now entered the deduction phase. Your deduction is "The level of trait verbal aggressiveness will influence preference of video game genre."

Experimentation is the fourth phase. In this phase, from the deductive reasoning, you create an experimental design. It should be noted that experimentation can take multiple forms such as surveys, field research, traditional experiments, etc. The experiment will serve as a test of our hypothesis. Our design would lead us to separate high trait verbal aggressiveness from low trait verbal aggressiveness, as determined by, for example, the Infante and Wigley (1986) Verbal Aggressiveness Scale (the most reliable and valid scale assessing verbal aggressiveness). Once separated by level of verbal aggressiveness, our subjects will then be led to a lab that has a game system and an equal number of "G" rated non-violent games such as *Minecraft*, *Lego*, *Indiana Jones*, and *FIFA Soccer* as well as "M" rated violent games such as *Grand Theft Auto*, *Call of Duty*, and *Assassin's Creed*. The subjects will then be asked to choose a game that they would like to play and to begin playing that game. This design is known as a 2 × 2 factorial design. That is, you have two variables (trait verbal aggressiveness and preferred choice of games). Each of the variables is further divided into two categories (high versus low trait verbal aggressiveness and violent versus non-violent video games).

	Non-Violent Video Games	Violent Video Games
High Trait Verbal Aggressiveness		
Low Trait Verbal Aggressiveness		

FIGURE 3.1 ILLUSTRATES OUR 2 × 2 FACTORIAL DESIGN.

Let's suppose that you conducted this study. Once the results were obtained, does this mean that our study is concluded? According to our induction, hypothesis, deduction, experimentation model the answer is no. In fact, the findings obtained lead to new induction and the process starts over in a continuous cycle. In our study, let's say that, indeed, subjects who reported being high in trait verbal aggressiveness did choose violent video games significantly more often than did subjects who reported being low in trait verbal aggressiveness. With this finding, we begin to create other hypotheses that would illustrate other differences regarding aggressive communication traits. Perhaps even using different types of measurement for both video game choice and how we measure trait verbal aggressiveness would further extend our understanding of this relationship.

RESEARCH VARIABLES

In our previous example, "trait verbal aggressiveness" and "preference for video game genre" are both what researchers call concepts or constructs—or variables. The words concept, construct, and variable can be, and often are, used interchangeably. When discussing communication phenomena at the theoretical level, scientists generally use the terms concept or construct. Verbal aggressiveness and video game preference are both concepts/constructs—they are abstractions that encompass a range of actual behaviors and preferences. For example, verbal aggressiveness encompasses both Devin's tendency to swear at his little brother, and Alicia's habit of insulting her office mate, along with all the other specific behaviors that fit within the definition of trait verbal aggressiveness. On the other hand, when discussing how communication phenomena are studied and measured, scientists commonly use the term variable, a term that highlights the idea of variability. Both trait verbal aggressiveness and video game preferences vary, or differ, from person to person. If they didn't vary, it wouldn't be interesting to measure them, or to see how they relate to each other.

TYPES OF RESEARCH VARIABLES

According to Davis, Powell, and Lachlan (2013), there are several different types of variables. Dichotomous variables possess only two values (e.g., please indicate your political affiliation: Democrat or Republican). Continuous variables have more than two values (e.g., people can be separated into high, moderate, and low communication apprehension based on survey scores). In experimental research, independent and dependent variables are assumed to have a cause and effect relationship with each other. Independent variables can be considered the cause of something and their effects are determined by changes in the dependent variable or the results of the influence of the independent variable. Independent variables can be either manipulated (changed in some way) or not manipulated. For example, say we were studying the effect of humorous communication use in the classroom and the effect such messages have on student learning. Given that the independent variable in our study is humor use, we would manipulate humor in a way that in one condition or classroom, we would have the instructor use humor and in the other condition or classroom, we would have the instructor use no humor. Thus, by manipulating humor use (i.e., distinguishing between humorous and non-humorous conditions) we have effectively manipulated this independent variable.

Extraneous variables are variables that are uncontrolled or not part of the intended research but may have an impact on your study. In our humor and learning experiment, the time and day of the class are two extraneous variables. Students may be less receptive to humor on a Monday morning than they would be on a Friday afternoon. Confounding variables are a type of extraneous variable and serve to complicate relationships between the variables. For example, there are data that show that children who are breast fed perform academically better than children who were not breast fed. However, as a researcher and theorist, we must consider what else could affect this relationship. Mothers who choose to breast feed may have the choice of staying at home as opposed to having to work a full-time job. Where did these mothers in the study live? The suburbs or in the inner city? Does the time at home afford time for more nutritious meal preparation? What is the quality of education in those communities? These are just a few of the possible confounding

---

Dichotomous variables
Variable with two discrete values

Continuous variables
When there are meaningful degrees of a variable between the highest and lowest values

Independent variables
Variables that cause and/or predict dependent variables

Dependent variables
Presumed effect in cause-effect relationship with independent variables

---

Extraneous variables
Variables that are uncontrolled or not part of the intended research but may have an impact on your study

Confounding variables
A type of extraneous variable and serve to complicate relationships between the variables

variables that could complicate the relationship between breast feeding and school performance. Mediating variables are variables that come in between two variables and explain the relationship between them. For example, consider a study that showed people who receive graduate degrees enjoy greater salaries and more frequent promotion. However, this relationship, while true, depends on the major one chooses to pursue. In this case, the choice of major serves as a mediating variable. Moderating variables, on the other hand, are variables that moderate, or change, the influence of variable A on variable B. Consider the finding that a patient's communication competence has been linked to increased satisfaction with healthcare and a better patient experience with healthcare providers. However, the relationship between communication competence and satisfaction with health care is probably moderated by good health. Imagine two people, both of whom are highly competent communicators. However, one feels very healthy, while the other is very sick. The person who feels sick is going to have a harder time communicating effectively. This will weaken the relationship between his or her actual communication competence and satisfaction with health care. The person who feels very healthy is going to be able to exercise his or her communication skills to the fullest degree, which should strengthen the relationship between communication competence and satisfaction with health care. In this example, present health status is the moderating variable—it moderates, or changes, the relationship between communication competence and satisfaction with health care.

Mediating variables
Variables that come in between two variables and explain the relationship between them

Moderating variables
Variables that moderate, or change, the influence of variable A on variable B

TYPES OF RELATIONSHIPS

According to Davis et al. (2013), there are several types of relationships that can exist between variables. **Reversible relationships** reflect relationships that can go in either direction. More specifically, variable A influences B and it is equally true that variable B influences A. On the other hand, **irreversible-relationships** indicate that variable A has an influence on variable B but not the other way around. For example, excessive consumption of alcohol can have negative effects on the liver but liver function may not have an influence on excessive consumption of alcohol.

Deterministic relationships reflect relationships that assume that any changes in the dependent variable are directly due to the independent variable. Such relationships are also known as causal relationships. In order for this type of relationship to exist, there must be three conditions present. First, the independent variable must be related to the dependent variable. Second, the independent variable must occur before any effects are observed on the dependent variable. Finally, that the effect observed in the dependent variable can be attributed to any other variable factor than our independent variable. **Stochastic relationships** are not causal in nature but considered probable in nature. That is, causality can be assumed but such causality cannot be considered absolute. Most research in communication can be considered stochastic in nature.

Sequential relationships assume that variables must be in a particular order if the effect is to be observed. For example, in incidences of physical domestic violence, both verbally aggressive exchanges and shouting are usually present before the physical altercation occurs. However, in incidences of verbally aggressive exchanges, physical altercations and shouting need not necessarily be present. **Coextensive relationships** are believed to happen simultaneously or they co-occur. There is no set order assumed between or among variables.

Sufficient relationships assume that there is a certain level of one variable that needs to be present in order to bring about a change in the other variable. For example, most people experience some form of communication apprehension when they are about to give a public presentation. However, when the experience of communication apprehension reaches a certain level it can begin to affect the quality of the presentation. **Contingent relationships** are concerned with what other variables, beside the variable under investigation, must be present to bring about change in the other variable. For example, are the variables of making public anti-government statements, number of firearms owned, and visiting politically extreme websites contingent on the initiation of an investigation by the Department of Homeland Security? Finally, **necessary relationships** indicate that one variable must be present for the other variable to be influenced. For example, for natural gas to combust, there must be fire or an electric spark as well as certain levels of oxygen. **Substitutional relationships** assume that there are different variables that can affect a variable in similar ways. For example, HIV/AIDS is not only contracted by engaging in unprotected sexual behavior, it can also be contracted through the use of contaminated needles and other situations as well.

CONSTITUTIVE AND OPERATIONAL DEFINITIONS

Before any concept or theory can be investigated, we need to have a clear definition as to what constitutes any given communication phenomena. There are two types of definitions that are necessary for conducting sound social scientific research. Constitutive definitions define a concept by using other concepts. For example, we can define liking of a song as "a learned predisposition to evaluate a song in a consistently favorable or unfavorable manner." This constitutive definition contains the other concepts of learned predisposition, evaluation, and consistency. These three other concepts assist us in defining our new concept of liking a song. Utilizing other concepts is an indication that the given concept can be made theoretically meaningful (Kerlinger, 1986). Operational definitions define something in terms of the operations or procedures that were followed to experience the object of definition. Basically we are concerned with defining something based on observable characteristics. This is very important in terms of the ability to replicate any given study. Replication refers to the ability to replicate the procedures of a previously conducted study to investigate if similar findings will emerge if the study is conducted again. If similar operations and procedures are followed and similar results are obtained, it provides a validation of the concepts under investigation. Operational definitions provide a mechanism for this. There are two types of operational definitions: measured and experimental. **Measured operational definitions** provide essential information about how a variable was measured. For example, trait argumentativeness has traditionally been measured through

Constitutive definitions
Define a concept by using other concepts

Operational definitions
Define something in terms of the operations or procedures that were followed to experience the object of definition

the Infante and Rancer (1982) Argumentativeness Scale which is a 20-item scale, usually in a 5 to 7 Likert-type response format, which measures the two dimensions of argument avoidance and argument approach. An **experimental operational definition** outlines the procedures through which the findings were obtained. These can include how the data were gathered, what specific stimuli were used, etc.

HYPOTHESES AND RESEARCH QUESTIONS

Social scientists are in the business of asking questions or making statements, then employing well-disciplined methods to derive the best answer possible. Three hypotheses are important in scientific research. A research hypothesis is the prediction of the results of an experiment. That is, if the thinking that serves as the basis for a study is correct, then certain desired results should be observed. If the hypothesized results are observed, these results support what the researcher is thinking or quality of the theory being tested. Theories are tested by research hypotheses. For example, if we were studying employee satisfaction and its link to relational quality with their immediate supervisor, our research hypothesis may be "There will be a positive relationship between employee satisfaction and relational quality with their supervisor." In other words, as employee satisfaction increases, there is also an increase in relational quality. Research hypotheses are verbalizations of predicted outcomes. A statistical hypothesis is a statement of the research made in mathematical terms. For example, people who score two standard deviations above the mean on the trait argumentativeness will be termed high in trait argumentativeness and those scoring two standard deviations below the mean will be termed low in trait argumentativeness. By stating something in mathematical terms, we have a tangible referent for determining exactly what we are observing. One issue with the statistical hypothesis is that it cannot be directly tested due to both measurement and sampling error. That is, because we are not measuring every person in the population, we cannot be absolutely certain that our findings in our study will be reflective of the population (all people) when we go to generalize the results from our study. Finally, an experimental operational definition outlines the procedures followed in manipulating a variable. Thus, if other researchers want to study that independent variable, they would know how to replicate what the original researchers studied. When looking at a scholarly article, various types of definitions are generally found in the method/procedure portion of the article.

The final type of hypothesis is the null hypothesis. Because of the error that we just discussed, we need a standard for testing the statistical hypothesis. That is, are there real differences between these groups? Probability theory and inferential statistics provide a full explanation of such testing. In terms of this chapter, we will simplify the concept to say that the logic of testing the null hypothesis is to determine whether it is likely that the difference among the groups is due to error, not something that actually exists. For example, let's say we are measuring some variable (e.g., height, weight, or communication apprehension) for four groups of people. The four averages for each group will almost always differ. However, the issue is whether the differences are real or whether the

Research hypothesis
The prediction of the results of an experiment

Statistical hypothesis
A statement of the research made in mathematical terms

Experimental operational definition Outlines the procedures followed in manipulating a variable

Null hypothesis
Statement that relations observed in a study were due to chance

observed differences could be due to error. Error might be caused, for example, by using faulty measurement to measure height or simply by chance.

Research questions are questions that guide an investigation and are used when a hypothesis is not warranted or unable to be determined. There are many times when it is not possible to state a hypothesis because theory does not provide a basis for predicting what will happen. Further, there may be theory predicting one set of results and a second theory predicting a different outcome. For example, it can be hypothesized that men who regularly view sexist music videos reinforce the notion of male dominance and thus encourage males to "put-down" women. However, there is some other research indicating that women can be more derogatory about other women than men (e.g., Miller & McReynolds, 1973). Because of the uncertainty caused by the two conflicting explanations as to what determines derogation toward women, we cannot make a definitive statement about the relationship (i.e., a hypothesis) but instead pose a research question such as: "Do male and female viewers of sexist music videos differ in how they evaluate women after viewing such videos?"

RELIABILITY AND VALIDITY

Whenever researchers seek to measure any given variable or construct, they seek to do so in a consistent and meaningful manner. These concerns are issues of both reliability and validity. We will begin with a discussion of reliability and then introduce the concept of validity. Reliability reflects the ability to be consistent or obtain a high degree of agreement between items in a scale or between/among raters, among others. There are several different types of reliability that we will review here. **Test-retest reliability** reflects the degree to which we get the same result when we assess the same person at multiple times. For example, say we are developing a scale for communication apprehension (CA). Given that CA is considered a communication trait (i.e., consistent over time), we would expect that, if I assess a person's CA level and then assess it again in a week or so and then in a month or so, the results would be somewhat consistent. Thus, in this example, we have evidence of test-retest reliability. **Alternate forms reliability** reflects the degree to which the order of items on any given measure influence the way people respond (i.e., ordering effects). This is especially true when we have long surveys. For example, if a person is completing a survey that takes 15 minutes, the scales toward the end of the survey may be negatively influenced by the person being fatigued and not processing the questions as intended. To overcome this we would create different forms of the same scale to make sure that no one scale is adversely affected and that any possible errors due to fatigue or ordering effects are evenly distributed throughout each scale. **Spit-half reliability** reflects the degree to which parts of a measure relate to other parts of a measure. For example, let's say that we have a 50-item measure of relational satisfaction. To assess this type of reliability, we would randomly assign 25 of the items to one scale and the other 25 to another. We would then take these two split scales and administer them to our sample. We would expect that people who report high levels of relational satisfaction on one measure would also report similar levels of relational satisfaction on the other measure. Thus, such a result would provide evidence of split-half reliability. **Inter-item reliability** reflects the degree to which the total score of a scale relates to an individual item score. For example, let's say that we have a five-question scale concerning organ donation. However, one item asks about nutrition. We would expect that each of the four items that directly relates to organ donation should be more highly related to the overall scale score than the nutrition question. If a question has little relationship with the total scale, we would deem that item "bad" and discard it from our measure and our analysis. The final type of reliability is that of **inter-coder reliability**, which reflects the degree to which different people ascribe the same value to a particular item. For example, during the 2002 Winter Olympics in Salt Lake City, Utah, during the pairs' figure skating competition, the judge from France was caught cheating. How did the Olympic committee determine this? The scores that she assigned the skaters were considerably different from the scores the other judges assigned for the same performance. This lack of inter-coder reliability was evidence that the French judge was incompetent, which is highly unlikely, or complicit in a corrupt judging process.

In terms of validity, what we are concerned with is the degree to which we are measuring what we are intending to measure. Similar to reliability, there are different types of validity. **Face validity** concerns the degree to which the measure or processes "look" like they are measuring what they intend to measure. For example, let's say that you wanted to assess aggressive communication by developing a brand-new measure. To assess face validity, you may consult a leading aggressive communication scholar and ask them whether, in their professional opinion, the questions look like they are assessing aggressive communication. **Content validity** reflects the degree to which the measure looks like it is assessing all of the dimensions of the concept under study. Referring to our new aggressive communication measure, our dimensions may include types of attacks such as profanity or sarcasm, motivation for the attacks such as inflicting psychological pain or trying to soften the person's position on the issue, or other types of dimensions. It is rare that any given concept or construct contains only one dimension. Most measures in communication studies contain several dimensions, depending on what they are intended to measure. **Criterion validity** reflects the degree to which a particular measure is valid when compared to some outside criterion. Within the criterion validity, there two sub-types. The first, **predictive validity**, reflects the degree to which our measure accurately predicts some behavior in the future. Many of you are probably familiar with the SAT or ACT tests that many prospective students take to get admitted into college. These tests are developed to predict the probability that the student will be successful in college. However, as many of us know, these tests are suspect as some students who do well in these standardized tests flunk out of college whereas other students, who perform poorly on these tests, perform fine in college. Such findings raise concerns about the predictive validity of these tests. The second type of criterion validity is known as **concurrent validity** or the degree to which our new measure assesses a concept or construct similarly to more established measures assessing the same thing. For example, if we wanted to develop a new measure of communicator style, we would give our new measure of communicator style along with the Norton (1978) communicator style measure. If our new measure assesses

Validity The degree to which we are measuring what we are intending to measure

communicator style similar to that of the well-established Norton measure, we conclude that we have obtained evidence of concurrent validity for our new measure. The final type of validity is **construct validity** which reflects the degree to which your measure logically relates to other variables. Similar to criterion validity, construct validity also contains two dimensions of convergent validity and divergent validity. **Convergent validity** reflects the degree to which your measure is logically related to other concepts and constructs. Unlike concurrent validity where we are using similar measures to assess the same thing, convergent validity is looking at the extent to which our measure is logically related to other constructs. For example, if we develop a measure of health literacy, we would expect that our measure of health literacy will be positively related with measures of wellness. In other words, we can assume that people who are higher in health literacy would also be more likely to engage in wellness behaviors. These two concepts "converge" on each other. Regardless of the type of reliability or validity, the following concept will always be true:

RELIABILITY IS A NECESSARY CONDITION FOR VALIDITY

This truism simply states that if we are not measuring something consistently, we are not measuring anything at all. For example, say we step on a bathroom scale and it reads 150lbs. We then immediately step on the scale again and it reads 90lbs. We then immediately step on the scale and it reads 210lbs. Because the scale is failing to assess our body weight consistently, it is not measuring body weight.

LEVELS OF MEASUREMENT

Measurement can be thought of as a tool that a researcher uses to make abstract theory and ideas observable. Most of the research results discussed in this text were derived from questionnaires where people rated themselves or another person's behavior, messages, ideas, or aspects of a communication situation.

Measurement can be made at four different levels, also known as levels of measurement; they are the nominal, ordinal, interval, and ratio levels. As we present these four categories of measurement, they will be presented in an evolutionary manner beginning from the most basic units to the most advanced. The level of measurement directly impacts the types of statistical analyses that can be employed. At the most basic level is the nominal level of measurement and involves assigning an object of judgment into a category. For example, a common variable that is assessed in communication research is biological sex. A person can be assigned to either the male or female category. We could assign the value of "1" for males and "2" for females. However, the number we assign is meaningless as this type of data is meant to simply identify or categorize the object. Simply put, "2" is not greater or lesser than "1." This level of measurement serves as a way to put people or objects of study into particular categories.

Nominal level of measurement Level of measurement that results in assigning an object of judgment into a category

The ordinal level of measurement contains the characteristics of the nominal level of measurement but also has a logical rank order. For example, let's say we were judging five presentations and ranked them from one to five with one being the best and five being the worst. Such data would inform us as to which presentation is the best, second best, and so on. However, such data does not inform us as to the degree of difference, only that there is a difference. For example, there could be a tiny difference between the best presentation and the second best presentation, yet there could also be a huge drop in scoring between the second and third presentation. To put this in perspective, if you were to play a one-on-one basketball game with LeBron James, odds are that you would come in (i.e., rank) second. We cannot know how many points LeBron James won the game by. We only know that he ranked higher than you in terms of the results of the game.

Ordinal level of measurement Level of measurement where objects are rank ordered according to some standard

The interval level of measurement contains the properties of nominal and ordinal levels of measurement plus the intervals between data points that are equal, or approximately equal. For example, if we had a 10-point interval scale for measuring the quality of a presentation, quality would increase in equal amount from 1 to 2, 2 to 3, 3 to 4, and so forth. Thus, a presentation that received a rating of 8 would be considerably better than a presentation rated 4. An example of a scale measured at the interval level is the Infante and Rancer (1982) Argumentativeness Scale which can range from −25 to +40 which is a continuum or range from the tendency to avoid arguments (negative score) to the tendency to approach arguments (positive score).

Interval level of measurement Contains the properties of nominal and ordinal levels of measurement plus the intervals between data points that are equal, or approximately equal

The highest level of measurement is the ratio level of measurement. This level of measurement contains properties of nominal, ordinal, and interval levels of measurement plus an absolute zero point. Body weight would be considered a ratio level of measurement as a person who weighs 200 pounds is twice as heavy as a person who weighs 100 pounds and no one can have a negative body weight. We could not say the same for our presentation rating scale as we do not know where zero quality is for a presentation (it is somewhere below 1). Given this, we cannot say that a presentation rated 8 is twice as good as a presentation rated 4. However, if an absolute zero point is known, we can conclude that a presentation rated at "8" is twice as good as a presentation that was rated a "4."

Ratio level of measurement Level of measurement that contains properties of nominal, ordinal, and interval levels of measurement plus an absolute zero point

RATING SCALES

Measurement in communication research has utilized four primary methods for assessment: rating scales, behavioral observation, content analysis, and physiological measures.

Most communication research data has come from rating scales. There are three types of scales that have been employed almost exclusively: semantic differential, Likert scales, and simple linear scales. Semantic differential scales were developed by Osgood, Suci, and Tannenbaum (1957) in conjunction with their theory of meaning. They believed that the meaning of something can be located in "semantic space," which has three major dimensions: evaluation, potency, and activity. These dimensions are measured by scales

Semantic differential scales Rating scales that utilize a seven-point continuum bound by bipolar terms in order to locate an object in semantic space

Rate the song to which you just listened on the following set of six scales. For each pair of adjectives, a check in the space next to the word means "extremely," the second space from the word means "moderately," the third space means "slightly," and the middle space means "neutral." Remember, use only one check for each pair of words (six checks total on this page). Please make your checkmark on one of the blanks, not the spaces.

I personally feel the song was:

beautiful ____ : ____ : ____ : ____ : ____ : ____ : ____ ugly

awful ____ : ____ : ____ : ____ : ____ : ____ : ____ nice

unpleasant ____ : ____ : ____ : ____ : ____ : ____ : ____ pleasant

exciting ____ : ____ : ____ : ____ : ____ : ____ : ____ dull

interesting ____ : ____ : ____ : ____ : ____ : ____ : ____ boring

worthless ____ : ____ : ____ : ____ : ____ : ____ : ____ valuable

FIGURE 3.2 SEMANTIC DIFFERENTIAL SCALE.

composed of bi-polar adjectives which allows an object of judgment to be placed somewhere on the continuum between polar opposites. Figure 3.2 is an example of a semantic differential scale used to measure how much a song in a music video is liked. A rating of liking is considered a measure of attitude toward the object of judgment. Notice the instructions and also the scale format. The order of the bi-polar adjectives, in terms of whether the favorable or unfavorable adjective shall all appear on the left, is varied to discourage people from checking straight down a column without thinking about a given pair of adjectives. Having to determine the location of both the favorable and unfavorable ends of the continuum can result in the participant having to carefully consider the pair of adjectives.

Likert scales Rating scales that utilize a five or seven point agree-disagree format to rate value statements about an object

Likert scales were developed by Rensis Likert (1932) and are based on the idea of determining belief statements that are relevant to the object of judgment, assessing the extent to which a research participant accepts each statement, and then summing the person's acceptance across the total set of beliefs to derive a score for the person's attitude toward the object. Acceptance of a belief statement is usually measured by a five-point scale that spans from "strongly agree" to "strongly disagree." To discourage automatic response tendencies where some people tend to agree with statements that are positive and some people tend to disagree with items that are negatively worded, usually half the items are worded positively and half of the items are worded negatively to control for such tendencies. This pattern is illustrated in Figure 3.3: an example of a Likert-type scale for measuring attitude toward a song in a music video.

Behavioral observation Involves observing behavior, classifying it according to a framework, and determining the reliability of the classification

BEHAVIORAL OBSERVATION

In addition to studying what people verbally report on questionnaires, communication researchers sometimes use behavioral observation. The behavior

Several statements about the song to which you listened are presented. Indicate the extent to which you agree or disagree with each statement by placing a number in the space to the left of the statement. Use the following scale:

5 = strongly agree
4 = agree
3 = undecided
2 = disagree
1 = strongly disagree

_____ 1. That was one of the best songs I have heard in some time

_____ 2. I do not care if I ever hear that song again.

_____ 3. I would buy a recording of the song.

_____ 4. If that song comes on my car radio I would change the station.

_____ 5. I experienced very pleasant and favorable feelings while listening to the song.

_____ 6. The song fails to make a good impression.

FIGURE 3.3 A LIKERT SCALE.

might be studied "live" or recorded for analysis at a later time. The researcher usually does not rate or categorize the participant's behavior because the purpose of the study could cause the researcher to distort what is seen or be influenced in other ways. In other words, the researcher might find support for a hypothesis when there is no support. To overcome this, researchers will train research assistants, who are unaware as to the true reason for the study, to observe the participants and record behavior accordingly. This type of process controls for any possible bias introduced by the primary researcher(s).

CONTENT ANALYSIS

A limited amount of communication research has employed content analysis. In this very useful method of measurement, messages are examined for the occurrence of certain themes, types of language, organizational structures, types of evidence, and reasoning. The procedures are similar to those used for behavioral observation. Categories of things to look for in the message are formed ahead of time or after a preliminary reading of the messages if a given theory does not provide guidance for the categories. Coders are trained to use the coding system developed by the researcher(s). If there is not a sufficient amount of agreement among the coders (i.e., low reliability), the category system and instructions are revised until a sufficient level of agreement is reached. This may take several iterations to achieve. Content analysis can be used in a number of ways. For example, a single speech by a political leader could be analyzed for types of reasoning and emotional appeals that are used.

Content analysis Method of measurement for studying the content of messages, which utilizes a category system and check the reliability of categorizing message units

PHYSIOLOGICAL MEASURES

More recently, communication researchers have an increasing interest in **physiological measures** for explaining communication behavior. Some of these techniques include involuntary responses such as heart rate, blood pressure, skin conductivity (galvanic skin response), electroencephalograph, endocrinology (hormonal research), functional magnetic resonance imaging (fMRI; brain activation), and changes in pupil size. As Bostrom (1980) pointed out, there are a large number of causes of physiological change: alcohol, tobacco, caffeine, tranquilizers, various other drugs, controlled substances such as marijuana, and physical states such as fatigue, pain, hunger, and stress. Given this range of factors, it may be impossible to speak with someone who is not physiologically altered in some way. All of these factors can be classified into two categories: stimulants and depressants. For example, stimulants can result in greater persuasion whereas depressants can reduce persuasion effectiveness.

Communication researchers have active physiological research agendas in areas such as verbal aggressiveness (see, for example, Avtgis & Rancer, 2010; Beatty, McCroskey, & Floyd, 2009; Beatty & Pence 2010; Heisel, 2010), and affection (see, for example, Floyd, 2011) among others. Such investigations include techniques such as monitoring of cortisol levels, encephalography, heart rate, and galvanic skin response and fMRI among others.

SAMPLING

Seldom, if ever, does a researcher have access to study an entire population. Instead, part of any given population is examined with hopes that what we find in our sample is true and generalizable to the entire population. For example, if we are interested in the communication characteristics of parents that most influence the degree of perceived social support reported by their children, the population from which I would sample would be parents and their children from the United States. Because culture influences many different interpretations of family, it would be impossible to generalize this type of family communication research for all families throughout the world. Sampling is a method of studying part of a population in order to draw conclusions or make generalizations about the entire population. One of the main goals of sampling is to attempt to have the people you are sampling be as representative of the desired population as possible, which is otherwise known as **accuracy**. One way we do this is through the development of a **sampling frame** or the identification of the people/things that you identified as accessible for being selected for your study. Once that is identified, we need to determine what our **unit of analysis** will consist of. For example, the unit of analysis can be the individual person, romantic couples, schools, school districts, communities, or parts of a region, to name but a few. Let's now discuss some common sampling techniques used in communication research.

Sampling A method of studying part of a population in order to draw conclusions about the entire population

When we speak of sampling there are two basic types, random and nonrandom sampling. **Random sampling** simply assumes that everyone has an equal chance to be selected. For example, if you were to toss a quarter into the air and let it fall twenty times, we would expect that the result would be approximately 10 heads and 10 tails without too much variation (e.g., 18 heads 2 tails). The assumption here is that heads and tails have an equal probability of being selected. **Non-random sampling** simply states that not all people have an equal chance of being selected.

Random Sampling There are several different types of sampling techniques that communication researchers employ. The most basic is **simple random sampling** which gives everyone in the sampling frame an equal chance at being selected. However, sometimes not all categories are represented when using simple random sampling. How do we make sure that subcategories are all represented? **Stratified random sampling** allows the researcher to determine what categories need to be represented. Once that is determined, people from each of those categories are then randomly selected to ensure equal representation. For example, let's say that we are investigating social support and the link to socioeconomic status. We decide to create three economic groups: wealthy (above $150,000 annual income); middle class (between $35,000 and $149,000 annual income); and working poor (below $35,000). In order to ensure that each group is equally represented, once we determine wealthy, middle class, and working poor, we then go into each group and randomly select from each stratum. **Proportional stratified random sampling** reflects random sampling based on their proportion in the population. Let's say that we are interested in looking at binge drinking rates and incidents of verbal aggressiveness. We decide that three categories will be developed: heavy drinkers (5 or more drinks per day), moderate drinkers (2–4 drinks per day), light or non-drinkers (0–2 drinks per day). While we as researchers have determined the categories that comprise drinking behavior, we need to make sure that each group is representative proportionately. Let's say that heavy drinkers, based on our determination, represent 10% of the population, 80% are moderate drinkers, and 10% are light or non-drinkers. We will need to go into each group and make sure that we randomly select from each group so that we have a 10/80/10 representation. That is, for every 100 people, 10 will be heavy drinkers, 80 will be moderate drinkers, and 10 will be light or non-drinkers. The final type of random sampling, **cluster sampling**, is similar to stratified sampling except that the researchers do not determine the subgroups. Subgroups are determined by how they naturally occur. For example, a section of a city where someone lives or works is not determined by the researcher, so comparing people who live in New York City by comparing people in terms of the borough in which they live (i.e., Bronx, Brooklyn, Manhattan, Queens, Staten Island) and how they consume entertainment programming is a valid cluster sampling research design.

Non-Random Sampling is much more commonly used in communication research as it is not as expensive and time consuming as random sampling techniques can be. However, with that said, if everyone in our sampling-frame does not have an equal chance of being selected, any generalization based on the non-random sample can become suspect. Even with that concern, the social scientists, depending on what they are studying, deem the use of non-random sampling techniques as appropriate and accept the risks associated with their use. The first type is known as a **convenience sample** and consists of including people in your study who are easily accessible. For example, you may have been in a class where a graduate student or professor is working on a research project and you were asked to fill out a questionnaire. If you attend a larger university, you may have classes as large as 300 people. So in this case, in a matter of 15 minutes or so, the researcher can gather 300 responses. Such data gathering speed and ease to obtain make the convenience sample very popular among researchers. **Volunteer sampling** consists of people who want to help the researcher based on their own interest in the study. For example, people who have suffered a particular traumatic event may want to participate in a study investigating variables related to the traumatic event. Many retired football players from the National Football League have, upon their death, donated their brains for the study of traumatic brain injury and concussions. These players feel compelled to assist researchers to get a better understanding of the brain damage that can occur as a result of recurring head trauma. A **snowball sample** consists of having people go out and recruit other people they know or can access to participate in the study. Recall the example we described when discussing the convenience sample. Imagine if you had those same 300 students complete your questionnaire and then go out and get four friends to complete the survey. This would result in a total of 1200 responses. The final type of non-random sampling technique is **network sampling** and consists of using social and other types of networks to assess a desired sample. For example, using support groups for veterans for the purpose of studying their assimilation back into American society after being deployed in a forward area in Afghanistan. How could we go about this? Networking with the Veterans Administration (VA) to access a list of veterans who possess such characteristics to be included in our study may be a very effective technique for assessing your desired sample.

Sampling is a critical component for effective theory testing. The number of participants that any given study needs depends on many factors such as the level of accuracy we seek, the statistical tests we intend to use, and other factors. As have been evidenced thus far, theory and methods are inextricably linked.

EXPERIMENTS

The value of experimental research design is fairly obvious. When a variable is manipulated by other variables that are being controlled (i.e., held constant), the resulting effects can be viewed as being caused by the manipulated variable. Thus, we can have confidence in the fact that there is a causal relationship between the two variables. In fact, experimentation is the only methodology where inferences of **causality** can be determined. In other words, other methods allow us to observe relationships but not confidently infer that one variable is responsible for, or caused, the change in the other variable. Many people argue that whenever possible, research should utilize experimental design as it is considered the ideal scientific methodology when compared to other methodologies (Kerlinger, 1986). While the standard procedures associated with experiments are most desirable, the fact remains that in communication research, many of the questions that we seek to answer simply do not lend themselves to being answered via experimentation. For example, if we were assessing trait verbal aggressiveness, this is best assessed via the Infante and Wigley (1986) Verbal Aggressiveness Scale as opposed to conducting an experiment. Now we will review the various experimental designs available to researchers. Regardless of the type of design, any experiment must be concerned with both internal validity and external validity, the lack of which can threaten a study (Campbell, 1957; Campbell & Stanley, 1963). Internal validity is the degree to which the actual procedures are followed in a study; to ensure that it was not the procedures that were responsible for the results, we seek to verify that the variables of interest were responsible for the results. The four major threats to internal validity are **history** (i.e., previous experiences of your participants before the experiment that may influence their behavior), **maturation** (i.e., changes in your participants over time during the experiment and not do to manipulation), **testing** (i.e., participants respond differently as a result of becoming familiar with the measures being used in the study and not experimental manipulation), and **instrumentation** (i.e., when we use different measures to assess the same thing and the lack of consistency associated with this practice influences the results of the experiment). External validity, on the other hand, refers to the degree to which the findings of your study are generalizable to the larger population. That is, the degree to which the findings observed in our experiment are actually true in nature. Let's now review the various types of experimental designs.

Internal validity Check to determine whether something other than the independent variables such as history, maturation, measurement, or selection, could be responsible for results

External validity Concerned with the generalizability of a study; major threats are pretesting, experimental arrangements, sampling, and multiple treatment effects

EXPERIMENTAL DESIGN

Pre-experimental designs reflect experiments where there is no random assignment of participants, a lack of a pretest, or a lack of a control group (Campbell & Stanley, 1963). The specific types, moving from the most rudimentary to the more complex, include the **one-shot case study** (where "X" denotes the manipulation and "O" refers to observation of the results) (Davis et al., 2013). One major concern with using this type of design is that we cannot be sure where our participants stood regarding any given variable before the experiment and if it was in fact our manipulation that was truly responsible for the results. It is expressed as follows:

$$X \quad O$$

The next type of pre-experimental design is the **one group posttest design**. This type of design lacks random assignment, includes a pretest and posttest, but lacks a control group. While there is a pre and post assessment of participants we can make some comparisons. However, because we lack the control group, we cannot compare the results in those participants who received the manipulation to the results in people who did not receive the manipulation.

$$O_1 \quad X \quad O_2$$

The final type of pre-experimental design is the **static group comparison design**. This type of design lacks random assignment, has no pretest, but does have a control group. As can be seen, because we lack a pretest, we cannot be assured that any difference between the groups was truly due to the manipulation and not to their existing attitudes or experiences before we conducted the experiment.

$$X \quad O_1$$
$$O_2$$

The next class of experimental design is known as **quasi-experimental designs**; like pre-experimental designs, quasi-experimental designs lack random assignment, but they utilize pretests and posttests in unique ways (Campbell & Stanley, 1963). The first type of quasi-experimental design is the **time-series design**, which involves multiple pretests and posttests across time. By assessing participants at multiple times, we control for the threats to internal validity of maturation and history. However, given that we are lacking a control group, there are other threats in the use of this design (Davis et al., 2013). This design is expressed as follows:

$$O_1 \, O_2 \, O_3 \quad X \quad O_4 \, O_5 \, O_6$$

Another quasi-experimental design is the **nonequivalent control group design**. This design, while utilizing a control group so that the effect of the manipulated variable can be assessed, still lacks random assignment but does allow a more conclusive determination regarding the possibility of a cause and effect relationship (Davis et al., 2013). This design is expressed as follows:

$$O_1 \quad X \quad O_2$$
$$O_3 \qquad O_4$$

The final type of quasi-experimental design is the **multiple time-series design** which can be considered a combination of the previous two designs. That is, we are assessing participants at multiple times before and after manipulation and we now have a control group to which we can compare the effects. While still lacking random assignment, we can be more confident that the results of our experiment, due to multiple assessments at the pre and post manipulation phases, can draw conclusions about cause and effect relationships.

$$O_1 \, O_2 \, O_3 \quad X \quad O_4 \, O_5 \, O_6$$
$$O_7 \, O_8 \, O_9 \quad X \quad O_{10} \, O_{11} \, O_{12}$$

The final class of experimental designs is known as true experimental designs. These types of designs contain random assignment (which is denoted as "**R**") along with at least one experimental group and one control group (Campbell & Stanley, 1963). The most basic design is one that most everyone became aware of in grade school. That is, the **pretest posttest control group design** which includes random assignment, pretest, manipulation, control group, and a posttest. Most of the classic experiments that we read about in the social sciences have utilized this method (Davis et al., 2013).

$$R \quad O_1 \quad X \quad O_2$$
$$R \quad O_2 \qquad O_4$$

The **posttest-only control group design** controls for any effect that a pretest may have on the participants. For example, let's say that we are interested in investigating the impact of trait verbal aggressiveness on the predisposition toward the preference for playing violent video games. If we give a pretest assessing trait verbal aggressiveness, the participants may become sensitized by the pretest and change their responses. For example, if a participant answers several items that are worded in ways that are targeted toward hurting others, the wording may affect the way that participants behave in the experimental condition. Thus, they become sensitized to the pretest which may subsequently affect their behavior during the experiment. By not providing the pretest, we control for such an effect.

$$R \quad X \quad O_1$$
$$R \quad X \quad O_2$$

The final experimental design is by far the most elaborate in terms of controlling for threats to validity and is known as the **Solomon four group design**. Simply put, this experimental design controls for most if not all threats to internal validity. Given the power of such a design, one would have to ask; "why wouldn't researchers use the Solomon four design whenever conducting an experiment?" The simple answer to this question is time and money. The Solomon four design is extremely intricate and requires considerably more resources. For example, based on the limited resources, if you wanted to gauge the responses of 250 people, you would have to enlist 1,000 participants to populate each of the four conditions of the Solomon four design (Davis et al., 2013).

$$R \quad O_1 \quad X \quad O_2$$
$$R \quad O_3 \qquad O_4$$
$$R \qquad X \quad O_5$$
$$R \qquad \quad O_6$$

FACTORIAL DESIGN

A **factorial design** reflects the manipulation of additional independent variables beyond that of the usual experimental design. The number of manipulated variables in the field of communication studies typically varies from one to three independent variables simply based on manageability (i.e., resources, time, finances). For example, let's say that we are interested in a study using factorial design that includes looking at the effect of video game play (i.e., aggressive video games and nonaggressive video games), Gender (i.e., male, female), and verbally aggressive utterances during play (i.e., high, moderate, low). This factorial design would be notated as a $2 \times 2 \times 3$ factorial design which results in the researcher having to populate a combination of each condition or mathematically $2 \times 2 = 4$ and $4 \times 3 = 12$ groups. Each combination has to be populated by participants. That is, a study that has multiple participants meeting the criteria of being assigned to: violent video games, males, high in verbal aggressive utterances; violent video games, females, low in verbally aggressive utterances, etc.) One can see how difficult it would be to populate all of these cells with many participants. Therefore, researchers tend to limit the number of factors that they include in any one study to keep the project manageable.

FIELD RESEARCH

Field research is conducted in natural settings as contrasted to experiments which are generally conducted in some sort of laboratory. While experiments can be conducted in the field (see, for example, Rancer, Kosberg et al., 1997; Rancer, Avtgis et al. 1999), communication scholars rarely utilize such approaches. Organizational and health communication are two of the most common contexts utilizing field research. Researchers go into the subjects' natural setting (e.g., the workplace or hospital) as opposed to the subjects reporting to some sort of laboratory. Unlike experiments, there is usually no manipulation of variables, simply observing behavior in the natural setting. For example, in an effort to investigate the impact of electronic health records on the patient/provider relationship, we may shadow healthcare providers as they see their patients in an effort to assess this phenomenon.

SUMMARY

This chapter provided a general overview of research methods primarily from the social scientific perspective. A model of scientific research that involved induction, hypothesis, deduction, experiment, and feedback to the induction phase was discussed. Several concepts fundamental to behavioral research in communication were explained. The various types of variables were presented and discussed. The relationships that can exist among variables were also presented. We distinguished between constitutive and operational definitions and how they are used to guide research. The various types of scales available to social scientific researchers were presented. The four different levels of measurement (i.e., nominal, ordinal, interval, and ratio) were presented and their influence on the types of data they provide was discussed. Content analysis, in its various forms, was discussed along with the need for reliability between raters. Physiological measures provided insight into the latest types of technology that communication researchers are currently utilizing to explain a variety of communication phenomena. Various types of sampling techniques were discussed and the positive and negative issues associated with each sampling design were presented. Finally, we presented the various types of experimental designs and the implications that each design has on the research and the participants.

KEY TERMS

Independent variable	Reliability	Behavioral observation
Dependent variables	Validity	Sampling
Operational definition	Levels of measurement	Internal validity
Hypotheses	Semantic differential scales	External validity
Research questions	Likert scales	

THEORY BUILDING IN MAJOR APPROACHES TO COMMUNICATION

4. Trait Approaches

5. Verbal Behavior Approaches

6. Nonverbal Behavior Approaches

7. Persuasion Approaches

Part II introduces four major lines of communication research that have been investigated without being tied to a specific context: communication traits, verbal behavior, nonverbal behavior, and persuasion approaches. Ideas concerning persuasion, for instance, are assumed to apply in some form, regardless of the specific situation in which the persuasion occurs. Part III will discuss theory building in particular communication contexts.

Chapter 4 examines an extensively researched approach to communication. The concept of communication traits began with the study of persona[l] psychologists. We discuss four types of communication traits. A[pprehension] traits cover feelings of fear and anxiety about communicati[on]. [Presentation] traits comprise ways or styles of presenting verbal and [nonverbal.] Adaptation traits concern the different ways individ[uals adapt to] people with whom they communicate. Aggressio[n traits concern the tendency to] use force; these can be either constructive or destru[ctive.]

Chapter 5 focuses on verbal behavior theory and resear[ch, a popu]lar area of study for the past several decades. First we [discuss concepts] such as symbols, meaning, and perception. Next we exam[ine how] language communicates power and status. Then we revi[ew] behavior research in some detail: the theory of linguistic relativity, politeness theory and face management, communication accommodation, language expectancy theory, and information manipulation theory.

Nonverbal communication has emerged as one of the most popular areas of research in the communication field and has also generated a great deal of general public interest. Chapter 6 contrasts the effectiveness of verbal and nonverbal codes and discusses the influence of context, intentionality, emotional leakage, and the functions of nonverbal communication. We then examine nonverbal immediacy, cognitive valence theory, expectancy-violation theory, and interaction adaptation theory in detail because they have guided a good deal of nonverbal communication research and theory building.

Prior to the current line of research on communication traits, persuasion was probably the most popular research area. Chapter 7 conceptualizes persuasion as changing one's attitude or behavior as a consequence of a persuasive message or messages. We consider persuasion research on several variables: message variables and the source credibility approach to persuasion are discussed in some detail. Next we examine several theories of persuasion: cognitive dissonance, social judgment/ego-involvement, theory of reasoned action, theory of planned behavior, elaboration likelihood, compliance-gaining, and Cialdini's persuasive heuristics. We conclude with a brief look at preventing persuasion by focusing on inoculation theory and psychological reactance theory. We conclude this chapter by examining several personality traits and their influence on persuasion.

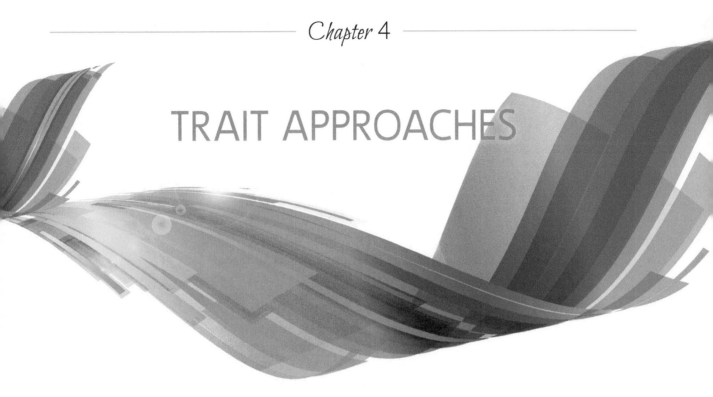

Chapter 4

TRAIT APPROACHES

What is a communication trait? The concept originated in personality theory. "Personality is an abstraction or hypothetical construction from or about behavior…a [personality] trait is a construction or abstraction to account for enduring behavioral consistencies and differences" (Mischel, 1968, pp. 4–5). Our interest is in communicative behavior—when individuals manipulate verbal and nonverbal symbols to stimulate meaning in others. The study of personality encompasses this and much more, for instance, traits such as compulsiveness, masochism, tolerance for ambiguity, richness of fantasy, and rigidity. Although these traits certainly might affect *how* we communicate, they do not constitute communicative behavior per se.

Communication traits are personality traits related specifically to human symbolic behavior. Communication traits thus represent a subset of the larger set of personality traits. An adaptation of Mischel's definition to make it more communication-oriented would be: *A communication trait is an abstraction constructed to account for enduring consistencies and differences in message-sending and message-receiving behaviors among individuals.*

Communication traits are hypothetical constructs. A hypothetical construct represents reality by structuring and giving meaning to experience. The traits we will examine in this chapter have an appeal because they appear to give meaning to certain communication behaviors and provide explanations that would not otherwise exist. It is important to note that a hypothetical construct in the social sciences is invented to represent and characterize something scientists cannot absolutely prove by observing it empirically with the five senses.

Communication trait
An abstraction constructed to account for enduring consistencies and differences in message-sending and message-receiving behaviors among individuals

For instance, the most prominent hypothetical construct in the history of the social sciences is probably *attitude*. An attitude is usually defined as a predisposition to respond favorably or unfavorably. This seems clear, for example, when we think of how favorable our feelings are toward a particular food. To say we have a favorable attitude toward that food makes sense. Remember, however, that "attitude" is a hypothetical construct, an invention to explain behavior. No one has actually ever seen an attitude. Likewise, we do not know that a given trait is "real." Researchers assume that if it is real, the data from a study will take a certain form. If it does, the researcher essentially says, "I'm right so far; the data don't contradict my assumptions. Now let's gather some different data to see if there is further proof." This process never really ends because somewhere along the line it will be possible to invent a different construct that explains the data better.

A major criticism of trait approaches is that they "beg the question." For instance, it is not very helpful to say some people argue a lot because they are high in trait argumentativeness. Using a label for one aspect of a trait as an explanation for behavior does not say much. However, the criticism is a "straw man" argument (describing and then refuting a position no one actually holds). Trait researchers do not use the label to explain the behavior. Instead, a theoretical framework is used. The label "high in argumentativeness" is a description of people who engage in arguments frequently. That label does not explain *why* they argue. The last section of this chapter will present a theoretical explanation that addresses competing motives and how people's perceptions interact with those motives to cause them to argue in a particular situation.

One of the reasons for interest in traits such as assertiveness, openness, friendliness, attentiveness, and aggressiveness is that it is easy to think of people whose personalities are defined mainly by one or another of these traits. Communication traits provide a basis for what to expect from others in various situations. It is useful to know in advance (at least to have an idea) how others will respond to us. Becoming more familiar with communication traits may provide an acceptable basis for predicting how others will respond in various communication situations.

CONTEXTS, TRAITS, AND STATES

Contextual view Behavior is consistent within contexts but varies across contexts

Distinctions are sometimes made between contextual, trait, and state behaviors. A contextual view of communication behavior contends that behavior is consistent within contexts but varies across contexts. Some examples of contexts would be family, school, and work. In this view, how one communicates on the job is not a good predictor of how one communicates at home. Communication competence is sometimes claimed to be contextual. For instance, being a competent communicator in public speaking situations does not mean one will be a competent interviewer or conversationalist. Similarly, a good interpersonal communicator may be a poor public speaker. The contextualist position is contrary to that of a trait theorist, who would expect someone who is very competent in one communication situation to be highly competent in all situations.

Trait behavior is assumed to be consistent across contexts and specific situations within particular contexts. That is, one's behavior regarding a trait is expected not to vary greatly from one situation to the next, nor from one point in time to the next. This does not mean that there should be no variability in trait behavior. Rather, types of behavior are usually predictable and reasonably consistent. Thus, a person who is assertive in one situation tends to be assertive in another. A person who is unassertive at age 13 tends to be unassertive at 23, 33, 43, and so forth. This does not mean that a given context or specific situation exerts no influence on behavior. Particular circumstances might, for instance, stimulate an unassertive person to speak up for his or her rights. In general, trait approaches maintain that there is a fairly high degree of consistency in trait behaviors across contexts, time, and situations. This idea has sparked a good deal of controversy, which we will review in the next section.

> **Trait behavior** Behavior is assumed to be consistent across contexts and specific situations within particular contexts

A state differs from trait and context in that state behavior varies from one situation to another within the same context. Trait communication apprehension predicts that a uniform level of fear will be associated with real or anticipated communication situations (McCroskey, 1970). State communication apprehension fluctuates with different circumstances. At times your fear might vary from your general trait behavior. You might normally be relatively free from fear about communicating (low in trait apprehension) but might experience a good deal of state apprehension in a specific situation. For example, a student who had usually been confident in the public speaking context trembled and was almost speechless when she had to recite a prayer in front of three thousand people at her graduation. She reported that if she had not written the prayer out beforehand, she would have been too afraid to think of a single word!

> **State behavior** Behavior that varies from one situation to another within the same context

Trait behavior, as we noted earlier, can be expected to vary somewhat across contexts and situations within those contexts. In fact, exhibiting precisely the same communication behavior regardless of the situation might indicate that a person is neurotic with obsessive-compulsive symptoms (Infante, 1987b). Trait theorists do not deny that the situation influences behavior. The question is how *much* does the behavior vary? Are situations basically different from one another, and do their varying characteristics force us to behave in ways that are unique to the given situation? Or, do we tend to place ourselves in contexts and specific situations that we view as functionally equivalent, thus enabling us to repeat familiar behaviors?

THE CROSS-SITUATIONAL CONSISTENCY FRAMEWORK

The issue of the stability of behavior across situations has been the subject of much debate in the field of psychology. The most recent controversy began with personality theorist Walter Mischel's (1968) analysis that a correlation of about. 30 seems to be the limit of the relationship of behavior in one situation to behavior in another situation. Thus, if we were to observe how *sociable* a group of people appeared to be in one situation by noting the number of smiles and then observed the same people in a different situation, the correlation would be rather low. A 1.00 correlation represents a perfect relationship; behavior in one situation could be predicted with perfect accuracy from behavior in another situation. In our example, if the rank order of the individuals in terms of the number of smiles were exactly the same in the first situation and the second, the correlation would be 1.00. Joe Smith smiled the most in both situations, Sally Jones was second in both, etc. A .30 correlation is low; it indicates considerable variability in smiling behavior from the first to the second situation. Joe Smith ranked first in smiling in Situation 1 but ranked tenth in Situation 2. Whereas a 1.00 correlation means perfect consistency, .30 means there is some but not much consistency between two sets of observations.

Situationist Approach to understanding communication that emphasizes the impact of situational variables

Those who support this idea have been termed situationists. In the social sciences, a situationist believes situations primarily determine behavior because situations are unique and present different demands on the individual. People experience these demands and try to adapt their behavior to the environment. Therefore, behavior is shaped by situations. Because situations are seldom the same, behavior is not consistent. Basically, this position maintains that personality is overwhelmed by the situation. For instance, a person may not be as sociable in one situation as compared to another because one situation is more task oriented and the participants simply do not have as much time or opportunity to act sociably.

Situationists also argue that stability in behavior across situations may be more in the mind of the observer than in the subject's actual behavior. That is, we may want to see consistency in the behavior of others because this reduces uncertainty in our lives. We want others to be predictable and dependable because it is easier to deal with reliable behavior than with unreliable behavior. Perhaps due to wishful thinking, we see people as cross-situationally consistent even if they are not; we distort the .30 relationship and make it closer to 1.00. Traits, according to this view, are more in the minds of perceivers than in the behavior of social actors.

Trait position Approach to communication that maintains there are broad predispositions that account for behavior

The trait position maintains that there are broad predispositions to behave in a particular manner. Trait theorists argue that a major reason why some research has failed to find consistent behavior across situations is that the studies were conducted in laboratory environments that placed people in unrealistic positions. Artificial situations cannot test the consistency or inconsistency of individuals in real life. According to the trait view, our personality traits predispose us to seek certain situations that allow us to "be ourselves," to behave characteristically, or to act in ways that reflect our uniqueness. If studies are not designed to permit people to select the situations in which they communicate, then the trait approach is not being fairly tested by researchers.

A trait approach to personality assumes that there are "ways of behaving" that we associate with the people in our lives. You have probably heard someone say, "That is just like her to do that," or "I knew he would do that." We tend to think of people in terms of a cluster of *central traits*. One person might be known for being assertive, dominant, and competitive, whereas another person might be shy, polite, and anxious. All traits are not equally important to everyone's personality. For a given trait, some people will show stronger patterns than others across situations, depending on how important the trait is in the makeup of that individual's personality. For example, the person described as shy, polite, and anxious might be consistently shy but might not show strong patterns regarding other traits.

According to trait theorists, another major reason why low cross-situational consistency has been noted is that too few behaviors have been observed in studies. A behavior such as smiling in one situation may not be related to smiling in another because situations can influence behavior to some extent. The idea of a trait is not that behavior in *two* situations should be consistent, but that there should be a pattern across *many* situations. A person who is very sociable (high in the sociability trait) might be friendly in one situation but not in another. However, in looking at the person's sociability behavior across a large number of situations, a distinct pattern should emerge. For example, behavior might be characterized as sociable in 35 out of 40 situations. A person who is not very sociable (low in the trait) might be sociable in Situation 1 and Situation 2, yet he or she may not be very sociable over time. Sociable behavior might occur in only 8 out of 40 situations.

The interactionist position emerged from the conflict between trait and situationist theorists. Interactionists maintain that behavior in a particular situation is a *joint* product of a person's traits and of variables in the situation. To ignore either of these influences on behavior results in less understanding of a person's actions. The interactionist position represents an attempt to integrate trait and situationist positions—to show they are compatible and not inherently antagonistic. According to an interactionist approach, trait and situational variables interact with one another to produce behavior. This means they influence one another and thereby create something that is unique— behavior that cannot be explained by the person's traits alone or by the situation alone. For instance, to predict whether a person will ask someone to turn down loud music, we must know not only whether the person has an assertive personality trait but also important characteristics of the situation. Is the loud music interfering with study for final exams? If the music is not blocking an important goal such as passing a difficult course, even an assertive person may say nothing. The interactionist position emphasizes the need to consider both trait and situational factors in predicting behavior.

Interactionist position
Assumes that behavior in a particular situation is a joint product of a person's traits and of variables in the situation

Three Positions on the Cross-situational Consistency Issue

SITUATIONIST:
Situation *primarily* determines behavior

TRAIT THEORIST:
Traits *primarily* determine behavior

INTERACTIONIST:
Traits and situation interact;
the interaction *primarily* determines behavior

Communication theories tend to be either trait or situationist in nature. It has been recommended that communication research should take an interactionist approach instead of the more fragmented approach of examining only traits or situations (Andersen, 1987; Infante, 1987a). Ignoring one factor leads to less than complete knowledge of communication. In the final section of this chapter we will examine a theory of argumentativeness that takes an interactionist approach.

The cross-situational consistency debate in psychology has been important for the field of communication because it has caused scholars to realize that there are trait and situationist approaches to communication. Unlike the field of psychology, trait and situationist researchers in communication have largely ignored one another. The situationist models of communication are inadequate because they cannot explain the many results found in trait research. Trait models are lacking because they cannot account for differences in behavior due to the situation. It seems obvious that combining the trait and situationist approaches would be desirable; taking an interactionist approach is a promising way for researchers to do so.

This debate in psychology has also been valuable because it has largely answered the question of how consistent behavior is across situations. Research indicates that behavior is consistent when enough relevant situations are considered. In addition to demonstrating cross-situational consistency, the research has suggested other areas for study. The focus on consistency has revealed that inconsistency occurs and also that scientists do not yet adequately understand why it occurs. Models need to be developed to account for differences in behavior. Is a given difference due entirely to occurrences within the situation? Why is someone very sociable at parties but very quiet when working as a librarian? Is there a trait that predicts whether sociable individuals will choose jobs in which sociable behavior is appropriate? Are unexpected, novel, and creative communicative behaviors even more revealing than regularities in communication?

We will examine four classes of communication traits in this chapter: apprehension, presentation, adaptation, and aggression.

APPREHENSION TRAITS

Communication Apprehension Due to the ambitious research program of James C. McCroskey and his associates, communication apprehension is probably the most thoroughly researched topic in the history of the communication discipline (for a good overview of the research see Richmond & McCroskey, 1985). Hundreds of studies have been conducted over the past four decades. As a result, an impressive body of knowledge exists today. In 1970 McCroskey defined communication apprehension as "a broadly based anxiety related to oral communication" (p. 270). This definition was expanded in later work to "an individual's level of fear or anxiety associated with either real or anticipated communication with another person or persons" (McCroskey, 1977, p. 78).

Communication apprehension A broadly based anxiety related to oral communication

There are four types of communication apprehension (CA). *Traitlike CA* is the relatively stable degree of anxiety a person experiences across communication contexts (public speaking, meetings, interpersonal, and group communication) and over time. Traitlike CA reflects a personality orientation and has been the major focus of study.

For some people, communication apprehension varies across contexts; this is termed *context-based CA*. For instance, some people are more fearful of speaking before a large crowd than of taking part in a group discussion. Other people have little fear of giving speeches but are uncomfortable talking with people on a one-to-one basis. Thus, it is meaningful to consider the context when studying CA.

Audience-based CA is fear experienced when communicating with certain types of people regardless of the time or context. The particular audience members trigger the fear reaction. A person who is apprehensive about communicating with parents, for instance, will experience CA when giving a speech if parents are in the audience even though the person has little fear of public speaking. The person experiences fear similar to that felt when talking with the parents interpersonally.

Situational CA is the degree of fear experienced in talking with people in a given situation. This is the apprehension created by variables unique to a particular situation. People who are high in CA are not always fearful, and low CAs sometimes do experience fear. What accounts for this inconsistency with one's trait? Variables in the given situation probably best explain such discrepancies. For instance, a person who is low in CA might become apprehensive if the person is told a great deal depends on a superior performance. Pressure can result in even very confident people "choking" in terms of performance.

There is basically only one internal effect of CA: The person feels psychologically uncomfortable. There are physical manifestations of this uncomfortable feeling, including "butterflies" in the stomach, shaking hands and knees, dry mouth, excessive perspiration, elevated heart rate, increased respiration rate, and increased blood pressure. What does it mean for someone to experience this internal effect on a regular basis? The research is striking in terms of how debilitating it is to be apprehensive about communication. For instance, people with high CA have less academic success, take jobs with lower communication requirements, are less satisfied with work, are not viewed as leaders, and are seen as less friendly and less attractive than people with low CA. Richmond and McCroskey (1985) concluded that the more talkative, low CA person "is perceived to be more competent in general, more communicatively competent, less anxious about communication, more composed and extroverted, more assertive and responsive, generally a leader and an opinion leader, more friendly and sociable, and more attractive" (p. 60).

There are several speculations about what causes CA. A *low self-esteem* explanation posits that people fear communication when they have an unfavorable concept of self and therefore anticipate that they will do poorly. A *parental reinforcement* model predicts that when children are positively reinforced for communicating, they communicate more and develop less CA. On the other hand, when children are negatively reinforced by being told not to disagree with adults or are inconsistently reinforced by being allowed to talk at the dinner table one day but not another, they learn to withdraw from communication and therefore become apprehensive about it because they have learned to expect punishment. An *inherited trait* explanation suggests that traits such as sociability are inherited. Persons who inherit a low sociability trait are especially susceptible to developing CA if their communicative behavior is not positively reinforced.

Three additional causes are linked to methods for reducing CA. *Excessive activation* refers to fear of communication as a result of a physiological over-reaction to an event—trembling, difficulty in swallowing, or temporary loss of memory. If the person is taught to control the overreactions, CA for all practical purposes is reduced. A method of therapy, *systematic desensitization,* is based on this assumption and appears to work very well. This involves learning to relax while thinking about various kinds of anxiety-producing communication events. *Inappropriate cognitive processing* posits that what high CA and low CA people experience physically is very similar, but, what they "think" they experience is very different. The physical sensation of "butterflies in the stomach" may be perceived by low CA individuals as a mild, normal, stimulating reaction to public speaking, whereas high CA people interpret it as a major loss of control. Thus, to change CA, one needs to change one's mind about communication. *Cognitive restructuring* is a therapy method employed for this. It involves identifying and changing irrational beliefs about self and also formulating new positive beliefs. The *inadequate communication skills* model of CA maintains people are apprehensive about communication because they know they are not very good at the activity. Fear is a normal and predictable response to a situation that one does not know how to deal with competently. The treatment approach for this is *communication skills training.* This is a very popular approach exemplified by speech and communication courses in educational institutions.

Beatty, McCroskey, and Heisel (1998) claimed that none of these speculations about what causes CA has been firmly established in research. They then offered an explanation based on the communibiological perspective. They believe CA has a biological origin because it is determined by "genetically inherited thresholds of neurobiological structures" (p. 198). That is, the extent to which certain parts of the brain are activated controls the extent to which a person experiences CA. The biology involves neurobiological brain mechanisms, which, when activated, stimulate certain cognitive and emotional activity and subsequent patterns of behavior.

The authors identified parts of the brain and the neurological circuits that connect them as constituting the behavioral inhibition system (BIS). People who are habitually anxious have overactive BISs, whereas less anxious persons have underactive BISs. According to Beatty, McCroskey, and Heisel, high CAs have overactive BISs and experience anxiety more often because they have a low tolerance for stimulation to their BIS. All communication situations produce at least a minimal degree of stimulation. That is a problem for high CAs because most communication situations provide what turns out to be the minimal degree of stimulation necessary in these persons to trigger their BIS and thus produce feelings of anxiety.

The authors also explain the brain biology of the behavioral activation system (BAS) and discuss why occasionally a low CA, for instance, will avoid making an oral presentation, whereas a high CA might not avoid the situation (even though you would probably expect it would be the high CA who would not speak because of his or her normally high level of anxiety). If the low CA is unprepared for the presentation, this could activate his or her BIS. However, a situation in which there is a large reward for a successful oral presentation might activate the BAS of the high CA but not trigger the BIS of the normally high CA individual. This example shows how and why traits do not always predict behavior.

The main point of their explanation is that the brain structures and circuitry involved in BIS and BAS are genetically determined, and the environment has very little to do with their biological development. Thus, this suggests that CA is based on one's genes and therefore is not susceptible to a great deal of change. If you are a high CA, undergoing treatment for CA can reduce your CA, but not a great deal (such as going from a very high CA to a very low CA). It is much more likely, the authors say, that with some effort the high CA will learn how to live with the anxiety by acquiring coping methods such as relaxation techniques and learning how to avoid uncomfortable anxiety-provoking communication situations. It should be noted that this explanation represents a major departure from the social learning model, which has been used almost exclusively in previous attempts to explain CA. For example, social learning suggests children develop CA after being discouraged from talking at the dinner table. We expect the communibiological perspective will stimulate some interesting controversy in future research and findings.

Receiver Apprehension   Lawrence Wheeless (1975) maintained that CA is a multi-faceted construct that includes dimensions pertaining to sending and receiving information in formal and informal contexts. The Personal Report of Communication Apprehension (PRCA) questionnaire developed by McCroskey (1970) focuses on fear of sending messages. A typical item on the scale is, "I look forward to expressing my opinion at meetings." If people are apprehensive about sending messages, it seems reasonable to speculate that they may also be anxious about receiving messages from others. According to Wheeless, receiver apprehension "is probably related more to fear of misinterpreting, inadequately processing, and/or not being able to adjust psychologically to messages sent by others" (p. 263). The Receiver Apprehension Test (RAT) was developed by Wheeless to measure this trait. His research suggests receiver and source apprehension appear to be two separate dimensions of CA. When dimensions are separate or independent, they are not related to one another.

Receiver apprehension
Fear of misinterpreting, inadequately processing, and/or not being able to adjust psychologically to messages sent by others

Thus, if you are high in source apprehension, you are not necessarily high in receiver apprehension.

For receiver apprehension, formal and informal communication contexts are not separate. This means the degree of receiver apprehension one feels in one context, such as a public speech, is similar to the degree experienced in other contexts, such as talking with a friend. Someone's level of receiver apprehension in one situation can be predicted from knowing about his or her receiver apprehension in another context. Wheeless's research suggests this is also true for source apprehension.

Wheeless's model of receiver apprehension is an example of theory building in communication because his conceptualization was influenced by work on communication apprehension. By building on earlier work, he expanded our understanding of the apprehension construct.

Informational Reception Apprehension Informational reception apprehension (IRA) is a relatively new trait that was developed from the trait of receiver apprehension (Wheeless, 1975). IRA is believed to be a secondary anxiety based on previous research on receiver apprehension (Wheeless, Preiss, & Gayle, 1997). IRA is defined as "a pattern of anxiety and antipathy that filters informational reception, perception, and processing, and/or adjustment (psychologically, verbally, physically) associated with complexity, abstractness, and flexibility" (Wheeless et al., 1997, p. 166).

The IRA construct is based on the idea that stimuli or message characteristics and cognitive processes interact with each other. Stimuli can vary in complexity, abstractness, and flexibility. Complexity reflects both the amount and details of the message, well as the cognitive capacity of the person receiving the information. Abstractness reflects how concrete the information is, as well as the capacity of the person receiving the message to think abstractly. Flexibility is "the demands of the external environment for openness, adaptability, change, etc., as well as the ability of a person to select, receive, and deal with such information" (Wheeless, Eddleman-Spears, Magness, & Preiss, 2005, p. 146).

Every person has a threshold for information processing that, when crossed, results in an impairment in a person's ability to properly process information. For example, consider the following two situations. In the first situation your professor enters the classroom and says, "Tomorrow we will have a quiz on this material, but we will not be grading the quiz." In the second situation your professor walks into the classroom and says, "Tomorrow we will have a quiz on this material, and the resulting grade will be your grade for the entire semester." As the environmental demands change (i.e., ungraded quiz versus an entire course grade), some students may have severe informational reception apprehension when studying or attending to the lecture due to the magnitude of the final course grade in the second example.

Informational reception apprehension A pattern of anxiety and antipathy that filters informational reception, perception, and processing, and/or adjustment (psychologically, verbally, physically) associated with complexity, abstractness, and flexibility

Informational reception apprehension is believed to contain the three dimensions of listening apprehension, reading anxiety, and intellectual inflexibility. Listening apprehension is the fear associated with either anticipated or real listening situations. Reading anxiety refers to the degree of anxiety a person experiences when reading information. Intellectual inflexibility reflects the degree to which people are unwilling to consider different points of view. In a study looking at IRA and argumentative and aggressive communication, Paul Schrodt and Lawrence Wheeless (2001) found that both listening apprehension and intellectual inflexibility were predictors of both argumentativeness and verbal aggressiveness. That is, people reporting high levels of IRA also reported higher levels of verbal aggressiveness and lower argumentativeness.

Within the classroom, Schrodt, Wheeless, and Ptacek (2000) found that informational reception apprehension has an influence on student motivation and achievement. More specifically, both listening apprehension and the intellectual inflexibility dimensions were correlated with lower motivation and achievement in the classroom. They concluded that researchers should consider informational reception apprehension to better explain student motivation and achievement beyond what has been explained by only communication apprehension. The development of the IRA trait has significantly expanded our understanding of apprehensive communication specific to receiving stimuli in the environment.

PRESENTATION TRAITS

Communicator Style Developed from a model by Robert Norton (1978, 1983), communicator style is concerned with how messages are communicated, not with the content of messages. According to Norton (1978) communicator style is "the way one verbally and paraverbally interacts to signal how literal meaning should be taken, interpreted, filtered, or understood" (p. 99). Style gives form to content and accumulates over time so that we develop a comprehensive, more global impression of a person's particular communicator style.

Communicator style may be viewed as an overall impression, a communicator image, composed of at least ten traits: impression leaving, contentious, open, dramatic, dominant, precise, relaxed, friendly, attentive, and animated. The degree to which an individual possesses each of these traits contributes to the person's image. With ten traits, there are numerous possible combinations. Each configuration creates a different overall impression. For instance, a person who is dominant, animated, and friendly is perceived as very different from another person who is also dominant and animated but unfriendly. The unfriendly trait might be so prominent that impressions of this person's other prominent traits might be perceived more negatively when compared with the same traits in someone else. The unfriendly trait might lead to the dominant and animated traits being viewed as manipulative and untrustworthy. How a person's traits combine, therefore, is crucial to the overall image that is created.

Listening apprehension The fear associated with either anticipated or real listening situations

Reading anxiety Refers to the degree of anxiety a person experiences when reading information

Intellectual inflexibility The degree to which people are unwilling to consider different points of view

Communicator style The way a person verbally and paraverbally interacts to signal how literal meaning should be taken, interpreted, filtered, or understood

Communicator image An overall impression of a communicator that is composed of at least ten traits

We will briefly review the meaning of each of the ten traits. Impression leaving is the attempt to create a lasting image in the minds of receivers. Communicators are aware of this goal when talking with others. Contentious is a disposition to challenge others when disagreements occur, to argue with others. Whereas arguing constructively is a very positive trait (to be discussed later), contentiousness appears to be a somewhat negative trait because it involves arguing too much, getting "carried away" by the emotion in a situation, being unwilling to end an argument gracefully, and pursuing it to "the bitter end." Open is a predisposition to reveal feelings, thoughts, and personal information. The open person takes pride in being honest and in not hiding things from others. Dramatic style involves telling jokes and stories to illustrate points, exaggerating for emphasis, and generally creating the impression of "acting" when talking with people. Dominant denotes coming on strong, speaking frequently, taking leadership roles, and wanting to control social situations. Precise includes insisting that people document what they are saying and that they give definitions. Generally, a person with this trait tries very hard to be accurate and thorough. Relaxed means not having nervous mannerisms in speech or bodily communication; pride is taken in appearing relaxed in stressful situations. Friendly involves praising, encouraging, and expressing liking for others. Attentive is the tendency to listen carefully to people, to be able to repeat back what others say, and to act so that people know you are listening. Animated is a trait that signifies extensive use of eyes, face, and gestures to express meaning.

Dominic Infante and William Gorden (1981) used the communicator style model to investigate communication between superiors and subordinates in organizations. They explored how similarities and differences in the communicator styles of an employee and a boss related to the employee's satisfaction. Are there certain traits on which subordinates like to be similar to their bosses? Are there other traits on which subordinates like to differ? The study found employees were most satisfied when dramatic and animated traits were similar, but relaxed, open, and attentive traits were different. If a boss is much more dramatic and animated, the subordinate may be uneasy and perhaps feel somewhat inferior because the boss exerts so much more energy than the subordinate.

Another study investigated the communicator style traits of fashion innovators and fashion laggards (Gorden, Infante, & Braun, 1986). A fashion innovator was conceived as one who adopts recent fashion changes, whereas a fashion laggard was one who adopts a fashion change after a long time, or one who never adopts it. The study found that fashion innovators, when compared to fashion laggards, were higher on impression-leaving, dramatic, friendly, and animated traits. These traits comprise what has been called the "energy expenditure" dimension of communicator style. This finding supported the hypothesis that people who communicate at a high energy level would also "dress for the part." That is, they would wear more dramatic, attention-getting, and current fashions.

Disclosiveness Self-disclosure, revealing intimate information about oneself, is a presentational trait that plays an important part in the development of close relationships. The general model is that trust is developed and strengthened when both persons self-disclose and show support for each other's disclosures. One person reveals something—a like, a fear, a secret goal. If the other person is supportive, this revelation encourages more and more intimate disclosures. The other person may feel a need to reciprocate the disclosure, so the individuals might take turns sharing. It may be impossible to develop a close personal relationship without self-disclosure. In fact, not to self-disclose is probably a way of telling another person that you do not want the relationship to progress to a more personal or intimate level. Wheeless (1975a) developed a scale to measure the tendency to self-disclose as a trait. According to Wheeless, disclosiveness represents "a person's predilection to disclose to other people in general—his or her generalized openness in encoding" (p. 144). Wheeless's model specifies that persons high in disclosiveness must also trust others. People who are not very trusting will be especially cautious about revealing feelings to others.

The Disclosiveness Scale measures the trait of self-disclosure in terms of five dimensions. The intent dimension involves the degree of awareness that one is revealing information about oneself. Having intent to self-disclose may mean that the individual views disclosure as a strategy in relating to other people. Amount pertains to the frequency of disclosure relative to other types of messages in interpersonal communication. Positiveness is a subscale that measures the extent to which the information revealed about the self is positive or negative. Depth refers to how superficial or intimate the information is. The honesty dimension involves the sincerity of disclosure.

ADAPTATION TRAITS

In contrast to the presentation traits just discussed, adaptation traits influence how we adapt to conversational partners. Five major categories of adaptation traits will be discussed in this section: communicative adaptability, rhetorical sensitivity, communication competence, interaction involvement, and cognitive flexibility.

Communicative Adaptability The communicative adaptability trait was originally developed as a way of integrating several dimensions of communication competence. Robert Duran (1992) defined communicative adaptability as "the ability to perceive socio-interpersonal relationships and adapt one's interaction goals and behaviors accordingly" (p. 320). The basic premise is that the greater the person's repertoire of social skills, the more likely they will be able to engage in successful communicative performance. Therefore, communicative adaptability is a component of social communication competence.

Communicative adaptability consists of six dimensions that are closely related to aspects of communication competence. These six dimensions are social composure, social confirmation, social experience, appropriate disclosure, articulation, and wit (Duran, 1992). Social composure is the degree to which

Disclosiveness Personality trait that reflects a person's predilection to disclose to other people in general

Social composure A dimension of communicative adaptability that reflects the degree to which a person is calm, cool, and collected in social situations

Intent A dimension of self-disclosure that involves the degree of awareness that one is revealing information about oneself

Amount A dimension of disclosiveness that pertains to the frequency of disclosure relative to other people

Positiveness A dimension of disclosiveness that measures the extent to which the information revealed about the self is positive or negative

Depth A dimension of disclosiveness that refers to how superficial or intimate the information is

Honesty A dimension of disclosiveness that involves the sincerity of disclosure

Communicative adaptability A trait that is the ability to perceive socio-interpersonal relationships and adapt interaction goals and interpersonal behaviors appropriately

Social composure
A dimension of communicative adaptability that reflects the degree to which a person is calm, cool, and collected in social situations

Social confirmation
A dimension of communicative adaptability that reflects the degree to which a person can affirm or maintain the other person's face or self-image while interacting

Social experience
A dimension of communicative adaptability that reflects the degree to which a person actually experiences, or is willing to experience, novel situations

Appropriate disclosure
A dimension of communicative adaptability that reflects the degree to which a person reveals personal information in the appropriate amount as dictated by any given situation

Articulation A dimension of communicative adaptability that reflects the degree to which a person is proficient or skilled in the expression of ideas

Wit A dimension of communicative adaptability that reflects the degree to which a person utilizes humor in appropriate situations to diffuse escalating aggressive communication exchanges

a person is calm, cool, and collected in social situations. Social confirmation is the degree to which a person can affirm or maintain the other person's face or self-image while interacting. Social experience is the degree to which a person actually experiences, or is willing to experience, novel situations. Appropriate disclosure is the degree to which a person reveals personal information in the appropriate amount as dictated by any given social situation. Articulation is the degree to which a person is proficient or skilled in the expression of ideas. This involves the mastery of the language, which includes appropriate syntax and semantic elements. The wit dimension reflects the degree to which a person utilizes humor in appropriate situations to diffuse escalating aggressive communication exchanges. Thus, sociocommunication competence is composed of psychological factors (i.e., social composure and social experience), sociological factors (i.e., appropriate disclosure and social confirmation), and communication factors (i.e., articulation and wit).

The Communicative Adaptability Scale (CAS) (Duran, 1983) was created to assess the six dimensions of sociocommunicative competence. Initial testing revealed that the CAS is related to both communication traits and psychological traits. More specifically, communicative adaptability was found to be a causal factor in satisfaction in roommate relationships (Duran & Zakahi, 1988) and is related to interpersonal assertiveness (Zakahi, 1985). In a study looking at the role of communicative adaptability and attractiveness, Robert Duran and Lynne Kelly (1985) found that the more adaptive a person was, the more cognitively complex they were (i.e., possessed the ability to develop multiple categories for describing abstract as well as concrete ideas). Further, adaptability was also linked to greater levels of interaction involvement (i.e., another communication competence-based construct that reflects the degree to which people are cognitively and behaviorally engaged in interpersonal interactions; Duran & Kelly, 1988).

Focusing on the psychological trait of locus of control, Theodore Avtgis and Scott Myers (1996) found that people with an internal locus of control orientation (i.e., people who see outcomes in their lives as being a function of their own purposeful action) reported greater adaptability than people with an external control orientation (i.e., people who see outcomes in their lives as being due to chance, fate, or other people). More specifically, internally oriented people are much more socially composed and have more social experience than externally oriented people. Recall that the cognitive flexibility trait suggests that a person needs to believe that they have the control to successfully execute the behavior. We can conclude from the Avtgis and Myers study that the belief in control over the behavior (i.e., self-efficacy) is also an important part of communicative adaptability.

In terms of measurement issues, the CAS is highly interrelated with the Norton (1978) communicator style questionnaire. These two traits, when combined, form three "super traits." That is, all six dimensions of the communicative adaptability trait and the eleven dimensions from the communicator style trait, when combined, form three larger dimensions of self-confidence, affect, and entertainment (Duran & Zakahi, 1984). More recently, the CAS can also be a valid measure when used by a third party (Hullman, 2007) to evaluate another person's communication adaptability (prior to Hullman, the CAS was used exclusively as a self-report measure).

In an effort to determine if a genetic basis for communicative adaptability exists, Michael Beatty, Lenora Marshall, and Jill Rudd (2001) administered the CAS to both identical twins (i.e., monozygotic twin pairs) and fraternal twins (i.e., dizygotic twin pairs). It is believed that monozygotic twin pairs are genetically identical, whereas dizygotic twins average about 50% identical. The overall findings of this research indicate that the CAS dimension of social composure is 88% heritable, wit is 90% heritable, and social confirmation is 36% heritable. These findings suggest several dimensions of communication adaptability may indeed have a genetic basis.

Communicative adaptability provides the field of communication studies with a generally stable trait that is conceptualized as a component of social competence. Although there is overlap with other competence-related and adaptive traits, communication adaptability is unique in that it encompasses cognitive, affective, and behavioral dimensions of competence.

Noble Self, Rhetorical Reflector, Rhetorical Sensitivity Persons who are noble selves (Hart, Carlson, & Eadie, 1980) believe in expressing exactly what they think or feel. To do otherwise, they believe, betrays their "real self." Thus, a noble self who dislikes something feels compelled to express that dislike, even though other people might not want to hear such a negative assessment, or even though the negative comments might create difficulties for the speaker. Noble selves do not value flexibility in adapting to different audiences. Noble selves view the idea of presenting a message one way to some people and another way to other people as misrepresenting their true beliefs. They believe a message should be created to suit oneself, not others. Thus, the noble self tends to have a script for a given topic and uses that script, with little change, in all situations in which the topic is discussed. For instance, if a noble self has a script of critical views on the president's domestic policy, he or she says essentially the same thing when talking to the president's supporters as when talking with critics. No attempt is made to appease the listener, to put the message in more "acceptable" terms.

> **Noble self** A person who believes in expressing exactly what they think or feel. Noble selves do not value flexibility in adapting to different audiences

The rhetorical reflector (Hart, Carlson, & Eadie, 1980) is at the other end of this spectrum. Rhetorical reflectors conceive of their "selves" not as fixed entities, but as social "characters" who take on whatever role is necessary for the particular situation. "Self" is a servant of the person and is highly changeable and adaptable. Rhetorical reflectors take pride in seeing the type of person needed in a situation and then becoming that person. They see flexibility as a most important trait. They emphasize "telling people what they want to hear," expressing a position on an issue in terms of the attitudes, values, hopes, fears, and desires of the receiver. The rhetorical reflector believes in being the kind of person others want him or her to be. This does not mean being dishonest. For rhetorical reflectors honesty is not the issue. Their concern is with the *requirements* of the situation. What type of person are people looking for, and what do they want to hear? As you would expect, the scripts of the rhetorical reflector are not as fixed as those of the noble self. Rhetorical reflectors probably

> **Rhetorical reflector** People who have the tendency to conceive their "selves" not as fixed entities, but as social "characters" who take on whatever role is necessary for the particular situation

have very general scripts for controversial issues and situations, which they adapt to the given situation.

Rhetorical sensitivity (Hart, Carlson, & Eadie, 1980) is intermediate with respect to the noble self and rhetorical reflector extremes. The rhetorically sensitive person believes there is no single self but a complex network of selves, such as father, husband, accountant, church member, golfer. Rhetorically sensitive persons do not adopt the constantly changing character of the rhetorical reflector, but neither do they agree with noble selves that individuals have only one immutable self. Rhetorical sensitives are flexible, but they neither sacrifice their values to please others nor ignore the needs of other people when communicating with them. Rhetorical sensitivity avoids the rigidity of the noble self and the chameleon character of the rhetorical reflector. Whereas the rhetorical reflector sees messages as a means to please others, the rhetorical sensitive is more concerned with the function of messages in creating understanding. Thus, messages on a topic vary from audience to audience in terms of what it takes to make an idea clear and meaningful to people. The rhetorical sensitivity trait involves an appreciation for the idea that communicating ideas and feelings to people need not be either rigid or overly accommodating.

SELF-MONITORING OF EXPRESSIVE BEHAVIOR

Developed by social psychologist Mark Snyder (1974, 1987), self-monitoring of expressive behavior refers to the way people use verbal and nonverbal communication to control the way they present themselves to others in social situations and in interpersonal encounters such as at parties, job interviews, professional meetings, at school, and in other contexts (Snyder, 1980). It is considered a trait which comes under the umbrella term of "impression management," or the way in which people control the impressions of self that they present to others.

In order to understand the trait of self-monitoring, it is best to distinguish between two categories of people who consistently differ in the manner in which they control their verbal and nonverbal behavior during self-presentation. Snyder (1974, 1980, 1987) refers to these two categories of individuals as those who are high versus those who are low in self-monitoring. Individuals high in self-monitoring control the images of self that they project to others. That is, high self-monitors are more likely to tailor their verbal and nonverbal behavior, and even to some extent their attitudes, to fit who they are communicating with. That is why high self-monitors have been called "polished actors" in that they can skillfully adopt the verbal and nonverbal mannerisms of those they are communicating with. For example, high self-monitors have been observed adopting a reserved, withdrawn, and introverted style of communication with one group of people, and then when the situation calls for it, just as convincingly portray a gregarious, outgoing, and extroverted personality. Synder argues that certain professions tend to attract individuals higher in self-monitoring, among them, professional actors, trial lawyers, salespeople, and politicians. Indeed, Snyder (1980) points to onetime New York City mayor, Fiorello LaGuardia (whom LaGuardia Airport in NYC is named for) as being particularly adept in his ability to employ verbal and nonverbal communication to match the particular group of constituents he was addressing. It is said that he was so skillful at this type of symbolic expression that when watching silent films of LaGuardia's campaign speeches, you can easily and accurately guess which group of constituents he was addressing!

On the other hand, individuals classified as low self-monitors tend to communicate and behave in a very consistent manner, regardless of whom they are communicating or interacting with. That is, they possess a great deal of cross-situational consistency in their communication behavior and in the expression of their attitudes and beliefs. In other words, low self-monitors tend to "tell it like it is" regarding the expressions of attitudes and behavior.

The Self-Monitoring Scale (Snyder, 1974) is used to classify individuals as either high or low in this trait. Items on the scale which tend to be endorsed by high self-monitors include: "I would probably make a good actor," "In different situations and with different people, I often act like very different persons," and "I'm not always the person I appear to be." Items on the scale which tend to be endorsed by low self-monitors include: "I have trouble changing my behavior to suit different people and different situations," "I can only argue for ideas which I already believe," and "At parties and social gatherings, I do not attempt to do or say things that others will like" (Snyder, 1987, pp. 16–17).

While those high in self-monitoring may be quite skillful in altering their communication behavior and attitudes to fit the particular group or individual they are communicating with, they do not do so for deceptive or manipulative purposes (Snyder, 1980, p. 36). As such, self-monitoring of expressive behavior is not correlated with Machiavellianism. According to Snyder (1980), high self-monitors are "eager to use their self-monitoring abilities to promote smooth social interactions" (p. 36). However, high self-monitors were able to more accurately correctly identify when others engage in deception (Brandt, Miller, & Hocking, 1980). In addition, those individuals high in self-monitoring are also more conversationally sensitive (Daly, Vangelisti, & Daughton, 1987), are more likely to emerge as leaders in small groups (Zaccaro, Foti, & Kenny, 1991), are more likely to be promoted (Kilduff & Day, 1994), and are better able to accomplish negotiation goals (Jordan & Roloff, 1997).

This is not to suggest, however, that it is always preferable to be high in self-monitoring. Indeed, and especially in more contemporary thought, the notion of presenting your "true self" to others (i.e., being low in self-monitoring), regardless of who you are talking with or what you are talking about, is often viewed favorably by many as being honest, trustworthy, and having character. In addition, low self-monitors are more likely to present their "true" selves in online dating sites (Hall, Park, Song, & Cody, 2010), and may also develop deeper and more trusting relationships (Gangestad & Snyder, 2000). Finally, as Snyder (1980) suggests, those individuals who are high in self-monitoring may ultimately "be unable to communicate their private feelings" (p. 40). This last finding may help explain the finding that high self-monitoring can result in lower levels of relational quality. That is, self-reported self-monitoring was related to lower levels of intimate communication, relational satisfaction, and commitment in a romantic relationship (Wright, Holloway, & Roloff, 2007).

AGGRESSION TRAITS

Although not typical of the majority of our communicative behaviors, the final type of traits to be discussed is very important. A communicative behavior "may be considered aggressive if it applies force physically and symbolically in order, minimally, to dominate and perhaps damage or, maximally, to defeat and perhaps destroy the locus of attack. The locus of attack in interpersonal communication can be a person's body, material possessions, self-concept, positions on topics of communication, or behavior" (Infante, 1987b, p. 158). Thus, communication is aggressive when a person tries to "force" another person to believe something or to behave in a particular way. To force someone means to put such pressure on them that they do not really have much of a choice. According to this model of aggressive communication, force can be constructive or destructive in interpersonal relations. Aggression is constructive if it facilitates interpersonal communication satisfaction and enhances a relationship. Examples of physical aggression that can do this are sports, games, and playfulness such as mock assaults. Examples employing symbolic aggression might be defending one's rights without infringing on the rights of other people, as in persuading someone to cooperate on a new venture. On the other hand, aggressive communication is destructive when it produces dissatisfaction and reduces the quality of a relationship. Destructive types of physical aggression include violence against persons (for example, spouse beating) and violence directed at objects (for example, crushing someone's favorite hat). Examples of destructive symbolic aggression include insulting a person, swearing at someone, and expressing bitter resentment.

Infante's model of aggressive communication maintains that symbolic aggression is energized by a set of four personality traits. The idea is that the aggressive dimension of our personalities is not composed of a single trait but rather a complex combination of competing predispositions. Two of these traits are constructive, and two are destructive. The generally constructive traits are assertiveness and argumentativeness, whereas the usually destructive traits are hostility and verbal aggressiveness.

A recent book by Andrew Rancer and Theodore Avtgis (2014) presents a comprehensive review of aggressive forms of communication. In addition to reviewing the research on the various types of aggressive communication, which we are about to discuss here, the authors explained how aggressive communication is measured and how it functions in family, interpersonal, organizational, instructional, intercultural, mass media, and persuasion contexts. Rancer and Avtgis also gave attention to how a better understanding of aggressive communication and training in communication skills can result in desirable societal outcomes such as less-destructive physical aggression.

Assertiveness Assertiveness is a person's general tendency to be interpersonally dominant, ascendant, and forceful. Alberti and Emmons (1974), who were influential in popularizing assertiveness training, said assertiveness involves people acting in their own best interests, defending their rights without undue anxiety, expressing honest feelings comfortably, and exercising their rights without denying others' rights.

Lorr and More (1980) developed a questionnaire for measuring assertiveness and discovered four major dimensions. Directiveness involves leadership: taking charge in group situations and seeking positions where one can influence others. Social assertiveness occurs when the individual is able to start conversations with strangers, feels comfortable around a wide variety of people, and is generally able to initiate desired relationships. Defense of rights and interests is a dimension of assertiveness that pertains, for example, to a person's willingness to return a defective purchase, to tell others when they are creating a disturbance, or to confront people who are taking advantage of others. Independence involves maintaining personal convictions, even when in the minority and receiving pressure from the majority to conform.

Lorr and More's research suggests there are low to moderate relationships among the four dimensions. Thus, if you are very directive, for instance, you are not necessarily likely to be very socially assertive. With four dimensions a variety of combinations are possible, so that many people tend to be assertive in some ways but not in other ways. At the extremes, some people are assertive in all four ways, whereas others are not assertive at all.

Assertiveness training has been popular for a number of years. Its purpose is to teach people who are low in assertiveness how to behave assertively. The focus of this training has been primarily on the defense of rights and interests dimension, with some degree of attention paid to social assertiveness. A variety of assertiveness training programs have emerged. Some are designed for a particular group of people such as assertiveness training for women. Others constitute a form of psychotherapy. The programs vary greatly in length. An assertiveness "workshop" for nurses, for instance, might last an evening or weekend, whereas an assertiveness program in psychotherapy can be quite lengthy.

Assertiveness is conceived as a generally constructive aggressive trait. It is aggressive because it involves using verbal and nonverbal symbols to create a force that dominates in such ways as taking control of a group activity, getting what one deserves, or stopping violations of one's rights. Of course, dominance could be destructive if such actions are used to hurt other people, as in making a person seem foolish when you insist on your rights. If that happens, the trait of hostility, rather than assertiveness, is involved. Hostility will be discussed later in this chapter.

Argumentativeness This is a subset of assertiveness because all arguing is assertive, but not all assertive behavior involves arguing. Argumentativeness is a person's tendency to present and defend positions on controversial issues while attempting to refute the positions others take. Argumentativeness includes

Directiveness A dimension of assertiveness that involves leadership: taking charge in group situations and seeking positions where one can influence others

Social assertiveness A dimension of assertiveness that reflects an individual being able to start conversations with strangers, feeling comfortable around a wide variety of people, and generally being able to initiate desired relationships

Defense of rights and interests A willingness to confront others to protect rights and interests

Independence A dimension of assertiveness that involves maintaining personal convictions even when in the minority and receiving pressure from the majority to conform

Argumentativeness A person's tendency to present and defend positions on controversial issues while attempting to refute the positions others take

two competing motives: the tendency to approach arguments and the tendency to avoid arguments. The person's argumentativeness trait is the difference between the approach and avoidance tendencies. The more the desire to approach exceeds the desire to avoid arguments, the more argumentative the individual tends to be.

Infante and Rancer's (1982) Argumentativeness Scale is a questionnaire that measures these tendencies. A person who is highly argumentative has strong approach and weak avoidance tendencies, whereas a person low in argumentativeness is low on approach and high on avoidance. There are at least two types of moderate argumentatives. A moderately argumentative person with **conflicting feelings** is high on both approach and avoidance. This person would like to argue often, but strong feelings of anxiety about arguing hold him or her back. This type of moderately argumentative person tends to argue only when the probability of success is high, such as arguing with someone who has little knowledge of the controversial issue. A moderately argumentative person termed **apathetic** is low on both approach and avoidance. This individual does not like arguing controversial issues, but does not really dislike the activity either. This type of moderately argumentative person argues mainly when the incentive for success is high—when there is something of importance to be gained by arguing.

Conflicted feelings Experienced by a moderate argumentative person who is high in both approach and avoidance

Apathetic feelings Experienced by a moderately argumentative person who is low on both approach and avoidance

Infante and Rancer's model of argumentativeness is an interactional model of personality because it suggests that a person's motivation to argue in a given situation is a function of both the person's argumentativeness trait and the influence of situational variables. The situation is represented in their model by the individual's perceptions of the probability and importance of success and failure in arguing. These perceptions of the situation interact with traits to produce one's motivation to argue in a given situation. This model can explain why a person who is high in trait argumentativeness does not always argue, or why a person who is low in the trait does argue at times. The model predicts that, in a given situation, high argumentatives will not argue if they perceive that failure is likely and important and that success is unlikely and unimportant. Further, there are situations in which persons low in argumentativeness do argue. This does not happen often. When it does, it is because these individuals perceive that arguing in the situation is likely to produce an important outcome and there is low likelihood that bad consequences will occur.

A good deal of research suggests that arguing produces valuable outcomes (Infante, 1987b; Infante & Rancer, 1996; Johnson & Johnson, 1979; Rancer & Avtgis, 2014). For instance, arguing has been shown to produce more learning by stimulating curiosity about the topics argued. Arguing is also related to greater social perspective-taking ability because arguing with others requires understanding their vantage points and engaging in less egocentric thinking and more mature reasoning. Arguing has been associated with enhanced credibility; when people argued more, they were viewed as more believable. Other research has found highly argumentative individuals to be more skilled and competent communicators, less easily provoked to use verbal aggression, leading to greater marital satisfaction and less marital violence. Argumentativeness has been linked with leadership and favorable assessments of supervisors by subordinates. Because arguing constructively can lead to so many positive outcomes, this basic skill should be taught to children early in their schooling. The inability to argue effectively is an unnecessary handicap because it is not difficult to learn how to argue well.

Hostility Hostile people are often angry. Hostility, in terms of communication, has been defined as symbolic expression of irritability, negativism, resentment, and suspicion. Irritability is communicated by having a very quick temper in response to the slightest provocation, being generally moody and grouchy, showing little patience, being exasperated when there is a delay or something goes wrong, and being rude and inconsiderate of others' feelings. Negativism is expressed by refusing to cooperate, expressing unwarranted pessimism about the outcome of something when other people are very hopeful, and voicing antagonism concerning authority, rules, and social conventions. Resentment is a dimension of hostility that involves expressing jealousy and hatred, brooding about real or imagined mistreatment so that feelings of anger develop, and indicating that others do not really deserve success. Suspicion is communicated by expressing an unjustified distrust of people, expecting that others do not have goodwill, believing that others are planning to harm you, and treating people as if their characters are flawed.

Hostile persons might vary along these four dimensions. For instance, one hostile person might be high on resentment but low on the other three components. Another person might be high on suspicion and negativism and moderate on the other two dimensions. A person high on all four aspects would be particularly hostile.

As explained in the previous section for argumentativeness, an individual's perceptions of a situation can modify the behavior normally predicted by the person's trait. For example, a person who is very high on the negativism dimension of hostility might express no antagonism toward an authority figure in a particular situation and might cooperate readily. In the same situation, another person who is low in negativism might curse the authority figure and refuse to cooperate. In the first case the hostile urges toward the authority might be suppressed because the person has a stronger need, such as wanting a promotion. In the second case, the usually mild individual might behave in a hostile manner because of a belief that he or she was betrayed by the person in the position of authority.

One analysis of the hostile personality is particularly illuminating (Berkowitz, 1962). The hostile person is not one who is chronically angry; rather, the person has learned to behave aggressively, a trait that remains latent until aroused by frustration. Frustration stimulates anger. In time, merely thinking about a frustrating event can produce the anger. The frustration is sometimes generalized in the person's mind, so that even very ambiguous situations or events are seen as frustrating. For instance, a person who sees his or her father as frustrating might come to view all men that way. Hostile responses are learned. They can be influenced, for example, by the disciplinary method one experiences as a child. To a degree, a child learns from parents whether

Irritability A dimension of hostility that is reflected in a quick temper in response to the slightest provocation, being generally moody and grouchy, showing little patience, being exasperated when there is a delay or something goes wrong, and being rude and inconsiderate of others' feelings

Negativism A dimension of hostility that is expressed by refusing to cooperate, expressing unwarranted pessimism about the outcome of something when other people are very hopeful, and voicing antagonism concerning authority, rules, and social conventions

Resentment A dimension of hostility that involves expressing jealousy and hatred, brooding about real or imagined mistreatment so that feelings of anger develop, and indicating that others do not really deserve success

Suspicion A dimension of hostility that is reflective of expressing an unjustified distrust of people, expecting that others do not have goodwill, believing that others are planning to harm you, and treating people as if their characters are flawed

or not to behave aggressively. If a child is physically punished for not behaving in a particular way, and if the child then behaves as the parent desires, the lesson learned is, "Hitting someone must be a good way to influence people; it certainly worked on me!" Nonpunitive methods such as rewards for desired behavior can help children restrain hostile words and actions.

Encouraging people to talk about frustrations or to vent anger is not an effective way to limit aggression (Berkowitz, 1962). In fact, just the opposite happens. Talking about the hostile urge rekindles the anger. Because anger is the necessary prerequisite, aggression becomes more likely. Encouraging someone to talk about a frustration only facilitates the learning of the hostile response. This idea challenges the practice, sometimes popular in interpersonal communication courses, of encouraging students to "open up," to express their true feelings concerning their relations with others. Instead, the framework suggests that individuals should be taught nonhostile, rational methods for dealing with frustrating situations and should avoid mentally rehearsing hostile responses. Thus, if a husband and wife have bitter verbal fights over money, they could be taught methods of argumentation so that they can debate rather than fight about finances.

Verbal Aggressiveness As in the case of argumentativeness, which is a subset of assertiveness, verbal aggressiveness is a subset of hostility. That is, hostility is the more global trait of which verbal aggressiveness is a facet. As a subset of hostility, all verbal aggression is hostile. Verbal aggressiveness is defined as the trait of attacking the self-concepts of people instead of, or in addition to, their positions on issues (Infante & Wigley, 1986). Whereas a physically aggressive person tries to inflict bodily pain, a verbally aggressive person attempts to create mental pain. A verbally aggressive person tries to hurt others by making them feel badly about themselves. In a sense, a "verbal punch" is thrown at a person's self-concept.

Verbal aggressiveness
Attacking the self-concepts of people instead of, or in addition to, their positions on issues

There are many types of verbally aggressive messages. All are forms of insults: character attacks, competence attacks, personal background attacks, physical appearance attacks, curses, teasing, ridicule, profanity, threats, and nonverbal emblems. You probably recognize most of these and may have been the victim of some. The last on the list, nonverbal emblems, may seem to contradict the idea of "verbal" aggression. However, a nonverbal emblem is functionally equivalent to a word. Thus, to roll your eyes when someone says something can be a rather severe attack on the person's competence. An exaggerated look of disbelief would also be an insulting nonverbal emblem.

Verbal aggression produces a number of effects in interpersonal communication. The most fundamental effect is self-concept damage. A person can recover from many types of physical aggression such as being punched in the nose. Recovery from some forms of verbal aggression never occurs. The effects can last for a lifetime, for example, telling a child he has a "pig's nose."

Verbal aggression has both lasting and temporary effects on interpersonal communication. Hurt feelings, anger, irritation, and embarrassment may cause relationships to deteriorate. If those feeling subside, it may be possible to repair the damage. However, verbal aggression sometimes results in termination of the relationship. A very serious effect of verbal aggression, from a personal and a social perspective, is that verbal aggression can lead to physical violence. A good deal of research suggests murder, for example, is commonly preceded by verbal aggression in the form of threats, character attacks, or ridicule. Some research indicates that when there is verbal aggression in a marriage, physical assault is more likely. Verbal aggression also has negative effects in work situations. Verbally aggressive bosses are particularly disliked, and less success, lower motivation, and less credibility are also associated with verbal aggression on the job.

Four causes of verbal aggression have been posited (Infante, Trebing, Shepherd, & Seeds, 1984). Transference is a psychopathological basis for verbal aggression. People use verbally aggressive messages to attack persons who remind them of an unresolved conflict. For instance, childhood memories of humiliation by someone older might cause a person to project the undesirable characteristics of that particular older individual onto all persons "older." This transference from the unresolved conflict leads the person to feel justified and to derive pleasure when saying something verbally aggressive to any older person. Disdain is marked by the desire to communicate dislike for a person through verbally aggressive messages. Social learning serves as a cause for verbal aggression if people have been rewarded for such behavior in the past. For example, people laugh when one person "puts down" another person. We also learn things vicariously by observing someone "modeling" the behavior—seeing a "hero" on TV use verbal aggression. Verbal aggression sometimes results from an argumentative skill deficiency. If people do not know how to argue skillfully, they resort to attacking self-concepts because they are unable to attack positions on topics. This "misdirected" attack is less likely to occur when one is skilled at arguing positions.

It is difficult to say how much of the verbal aggression in society is due to each of the four causes. However, the first two causes are probably responsible for a rather small portion. That is, psychopathologies are not pervasive in the population, and we structure our lives so that we talk as little as possible with others we dislike. Social learning and argumentative skill deficiencies are probably responsible for more of the verbal aggression in society. If this is the case, there is hope that the destructiveness of verbal aggression can be reduced substantially. Education can be a solution. People, especially children, can be taught how to argue constructively and thus reduce the inclination to use verbal aggression. Children can also be taught constructive methods for dealing with verbal aggression when it does occur.

Michael Beatty and James McCroskey (1997) also have speculated on the causes of verbal aggressiveness. As they did for communication apprehension, they conceptualized verbal aggressiveness as an expression of inborn neurobiological structures. That is, verbal aggressiveness is a temperament that is inherited. Just because there is a genetic basis for the trait, however, does not mean simply that verbal aggressiveness is passed down from one generation to the next. For example, traits can skip generations. Thus, you

Transference Cause of verbal aggression that involves using verbal aggression against people who remind one of unresolved sources of conflict and pain

Disdain Cause of verbal aggression that involves the desire to communicate dislike for a person through verbally aggressive messages

Social learning Cause of verbal aggression brought about by direct reinforcement of verbally aggressive behavior or by modeling the behavior after an esteemed person

Argumentative skill deficiency Cause of verbal aggression due to an inability to argue skillfully; attack and defend needs are not satisfied

may inherit the verbal aggressiveness of one of your great-grandfathers. Moreover, because the genes of both of your parents are involved, there can be some rather complex genetic interactions. Like the color of your eyes, the influence of both parents can sometimes be found in personality traits such as verbal aggressiveness.

Beatty and McCroskey posit three neurological circuits that are the biological basis for verbal aggressiveness. In addition to the behavioral inhibition system and the behavioral activation system explained earlier in this chapter for communication apprehension, the authors specified the fight-or-flight system. This system involves response to a threat—either fleeing or staying and facing it aggressively. For each of the three systems Beatty and McCroskey identify the regions of the brain involved, the particular brain activity, and the chemical reactions. In doing this they have in essence identified the biology of aggression in general and verbal aggression specifically.

If Beatty and McCroskey are correct, then their efforts represent a major step toward understanding why people are verbally aggressive. What needs to be resolved, however, is just how immutable the trait is. If a person is verbally aggressive, is there any hope of getting him or her to use fewer self-concept attacking messages? Interestingly, there is some research evidence that verbal aggressiveness can be lowered using educational activities (Colbert, 1993; Sanders, Wiseman, & Gass, 1994). If some change in aggressive communication is possible, quite a few educational activities have been suggested for this purpose (Infante, 1995).

Finally, we will examine two rather recently developed communication traits that pertain to aggressiveness. These provide additional ways to view conflict in human interaction.

Taking conflict personally
A communication trait that reflects the degree to which we have a negative emotional reaction to participating in a conflict

Direct personalization
A dimension of taking conflict personally reflecting the hurt a person experiences during a conflict episode

Persecution feelings
A dimension of taking conflict personally that reflects the perception that other people are just seeking to pick a fight with you and purposely seek to engage in conflict

Taking Conflict Personally The communication trait of taking conflict personally (TCP) was developed by Dale Hample and Judith Dallinger (1995). This trait reflects "a negative emotional reaction to participating in a conflict" (p. 297). This negative emotional reaction constitutes low verbal aggressiveness. People who are high in this trait (i.e., take conflict personally) believe that conflicts are "antagonist, punishing interactions" in which the central goal of conflict communication is to purposely hurt the other person (Hample, 1999). TCP can take the form of either aggressive or avoidant behavior and is believed to bring about similar reactions from others with whom we are communicating.

The TCP trait is believed to comprise six dimensions: direct personalization, persecution feelings, stress reaction, positive relational effects, negative relational effects, and like/dislike valence. Direct personalization reflects the hurt a person experiences during the conflict episode. Persecution feelings reflects the perception that other people are just seeking to pick a fight with you and purposely seek to engage in conflict. It is believed that people who have feelings of persecution see conflict as a combative experience where there is a clear winner and a clear loser. Stress reaction is the level of physiological response one has when in a conflict episode (e.g., upset stomach, headache).

Positive relational effects reflects the extent to which people feel conflict communication can be positive for both social and task relationships. Negative relational effects is the extent to which people feel that conflict communication can have negative outcomes for both social and task relationships. The final dimension of the TCP trait is that of like/dislike valence and is defined as the degree to which people enjoy engaging in conflict. Hample and Dallinger (1995) believe that the like/dislike valence is very similar to the argumentativeness trait discussed earlier in this chapter but point out that argumentativeness is a person's intended behavior, whereas like/dislike valence reflects an emotional reaction.

The TCP trait is believed to be a product of both the situation and a person's predisposition to behave. Hample (1999) believes "TCP is a stable personality trait…permitting, among others, the simple generalization that some people are more predisposed toward personalization than others" (p. 173). People differ in their predisposition to be tolerant, trusting, self-interested, self-confident, generous in their attributions, and generally more or less easily hurt when involved in a conflict episode (Avtgis & Rancer, 2003).

Research findings using TCP revealed that people who are high in TCP (i.e., see conflict as punishing) tend to have a high motivation to avoid arguments, whereas people who think that conflict is productive reported a high motivation to approach arguments (Hample & Dallinger, 1995). Further, adult children with an internal conflict locus of control (i.e., see conflict outcomes with their parents as being under their control) reported less direct personalization, less persecution feelings, less stress reaction, less negative relational effects, and more positive relational effects than adult children with an external conflict locus of control (i.e., see conflict outcomes with their parents as being out of their control) (Avtgis, 2002).

In a study comparing the United States, New Zealand, and Australia, Theodore Avtgis and Andrew Rancer (2003) found that Americans reported significantly less feelings of persecution, less direct personalization, yet greater stress reaction than either New Zealanders or Australians. The findings indicate that, overall, Americans have less tendency to interpret conflict behavior as a personal attack. Why, then, would Americans be higher in stress reaction? According to Avtgis and Rancer (2003), an "epidemic of incompetent communication permeates within the United States as well as between Americans and other cultures. Perhaps the lack of communication skills can be attributed to the arousal of stressful feelings in Americans when faced with conflict" (p. 115).

Taking conflict personally has also been associated with rumination, or the consistent and repetitive thinking about negative experiences with others (Miller & Roloff, 2014). The researchers thought that individuals may differ in their ability to "put behind them," or reach closure after receiving hurtful messages such as insults and teasing. One of the factors that they felt contributed to decreasing this rumination tendency and achieving closure after a hurtful and negative experience with others is the predisposition of taking conflict personally. Two hypotheses were offered. The first hypothesis predicted that

Stress reaction A dimension of taking conflict personally that reflects the level of physiological response one has when in a conflict episode

Positive relational effects A dimension of taking conflict personally that reflects the extent to which people feel conflict communication can be positive for both social and task relationships

Negative relational effects A dimension of taking conflict personally that reflects the extent to which people feel that conflict communication can have negative outcomes for both social and task relationships

Like/dislike valence A dimension of taking conflict personally that reflects the degree to which people enjoy engaging in conflict

TCP would be positively related to one's desire to avoid interaction with the offender, and the second hypothesis predicted that TCP would be positively related to seeking revenge toward the offender. To test these predictions, Miller and Roloff (2014) asked participants to "recall an instance when someone made a comment that hurt their feelings" and record that comment. They were also asked questions about how much repetitive thinking (i.e., rumination) they engaged in about that incident, how much hurt they felt, their desire to avoid the offender, and the degree to which they wanted to seek revenge toward the offender. Participants' level of TCP was also measured.

The results of the study supported both hypotheses, as TCP was found to be positively related to both avoidance and revenge motivation toward the offender. As such, Miller and Roloff (2014) suggest that "Those who take conflict personally may have a much more difficult time achieving closure during a hurtful episode and therefore engage in rumination while attempting to accomplish closure" (p. 207). Those high in TCP (in particular in the direct personalization dimension of the trait) have a desire to avoid the person who hurt them, and to seek revenge both during and after the hurtful interaction.

Along with argumentativeness and verbal aggressiveness, the taking conflict personally trait will continue to prove to be a valuable tool in the explanation of conflict behavior. If society becomes ever increasingly hostile and segmented, looking at communication traits such as TCP will become important for theorists, researchers, and practitioners alike.

Tolerance for Disagreement Tolerance for disagreement (TFD) is a communication trait that is defined as "the amount of disagreement an individual can tolerate before he or she perceives the existence of conflict in a relationship (Richmond, McCroskey, & McCroskey, 2005, p. 178). TFD was originally developed by James McCroskey and Lawrence Wheeless (1976) and later expanded (Knutson, McCroskey, Knutson, & Hurt, 1979). Most research on conflict relies on a unidimensional continuum that ranges from good conflict to bad conflict. McCroskey and Wheeless distinguished between disagreement, which is a difference of opinion on issues, and conflict, which involves competition, suspicion, distrust, hostility, and self-perpetuation.

Although TFD was originally conceptualized as something that is a product of the interaction and is relationship specific, Knutson et al. (1979) argued that due to each individual's interpretation of what is considered disagreement and conflict, these interpretations are more cross-contextual and thus should be considered traitlike. More specifically, they argued that "the existence of an individual difference variable, which they labeled tolerance for disagreement (TFD), which they employed to explain why some people will perceive the presence of conflict much sooner than others will" (Teven, McCroskey, & Richmond, 1998, p. 210). The distinction between disagreement and conflict is very similar to the distinction between argument and verbal aggression, respectively (McCroskey, 2006). That is, argument (as well as trait argumentativeness) is considered constructive, whereas verbal aggression (as well as trait verbal aggressiveness) is considered destructive. All disagreement is considered constructive, and all conflict is considered destructive to the relationship.

Tolerance for disagreement A communication trait that reflects the amount of disagreement a person can tolerate before he or she perceives the existence of a conflict in a relationship

Disagreement Part of the tolerance for disagreement communication trait that reflects the difference of opinion on issues

Conflict Part of the tolerance for disagreement communication trait that reflects competition, suspicion, distrust, dislike, hostility, and self-perpetuation

The TFD trait is also influenced by situational factors such as a low degree of affinity (i.e., liking) between the people that is present in a disagreement on an issue. These situational triggers are similar to those situational triggers identified for verbally aggressive behavior (Wigley, 2006). Given that TFD is a joint function of the trait and situational cues, TFD is conceptualized from the interactionist trait perspective (Magnusson & Endler, 1977).

People who are high in TFD are relatively resistant to engaging in conflict, whereas people low in TFD are much more likely to engage in conflict across a wide range of relationships, regardless of the issue at hand. These differences are based on a person's threshold at which disagreement transforms into conflict. This consistency in the tendency to engage in either disagreement or conflict is rooted in the larger supertraits of assertiveness, which contains disagreement and hostility, which involves conflict.

Virginia Richmond and James McCroskey (1979) investigated the extent to which employee satisfaction was related to the employee's and supervisor's level of TFD. The findings indicated that employee satisfaction (which involves satisfaction with supervisor, work, and pay) were influenced more by the supervisor's TFD than the employee's TFD. Therefore, the greater supervisor tolerance for disagreement, the more satisfied the employee. Further evidence reveals that TFD is also related to cognitive flexibility and communication flexibility (Martin, Anderson, & Thweatt, 1998) in that "the flexible communicator appeared to be willing to argue and disagree with others. These individuals tend to approach arguments and do not avoid confrontations where there may be a difference of opinions" (Teven, McCroskey, & Richmond, 1998, p. 212).

SUMMARY

This chapter explored trait approaches that have been taken to understand human communication. The approach has its origin in the study of personality from the field of psychology. Distinctions were made between trait, contextual, and state behaviors. The trait approach was contrasted with situationist and interactionist positions. The cross-situational consistency of behavior framework was reviewed because of its relevance to understanding traits. Four classes of communication traits were discussed: apprehension, presentation, adaptation, and aggression. In the apprehension traits category, we examined communication apprehension and receiver apprehension along with informational reception apprehension. The presentation traits presented were communicator style and disclosiveness. The category of adaptation traits included communication adaptability, rhetorical sensitivity, noble self, rhetorical reflector, and self-monitoring of expressive behavior. The last class of communication traits explored consisted of aggression traits: assertiveness, argumentativeness, hostility, and verbal aggressiveness, along with taking conflict personally and tolerance for disagreement.

KEY TERMS

Animated

Apathetic

Appropriate disclosure

Argumentative skill deficiency

Argumentativeness

Articulation

Attentive

Communication apprehension

Communication trait

Communicative adaptability

Communicator image

Communicator style

Conflict

Conflicted feelings

Contentious

Contextual view

Directiveness

Disagreement

Disclosiveness

Disdain

Dominant

Dramatic

Friendly

Honesty

Impression leaving

Informational reception apprehension

Intellectual inflexibility

Intent

Interactionist position

Irritability

Listening apprehension

Negative relational effects

Negativism

Noble self

Open

Persecution feelings

Positive relational effect

Positiveness

Precise

Receiver apprehension

Relaxed

Resentment

Rhetorical reflector

Rhetorical sensitivity

Situationist

Social assertiveness

Social composure

Social confirmation

Social experience

Social learning

State behavior

Stress reaction

Suspicion

Taking conflict personally

Tolerance for disagreement

Trait behavior

Trait position

Transference

Verbal aggressiveness

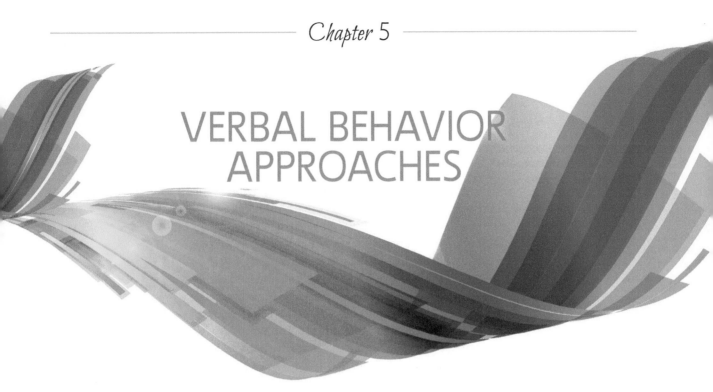

Chapter 5

VERBAL BEHAVIOR APPROACHES

Human beings are the only creatures on earth that can talk themselves into trouble. Perhaps you told someone that they were "interesting," only to discover that rumors had spread across campus about your new intimate relationship! You might have made what you thought was a witty remark in class and suddenly found yourself in disfavor with the professor because of your "wisecrack." If you promised your mother that you would vacuum the house "soon," she might have been upset because you did not do it that *morning*.

If these examples sound familiar, you are aware of the difficulties that can arise when people communicate. Some students assume that the formal study of human communication will be an "easy" subject to master, remarking, "After all, I've been communicating since I was born and talking since I was twelve months old." The problem is when we've been doing something for so long, we repeat our behaviors automatically. We are often not particularly aware of what is actually happening. For example, we may not like being perceived as being unsure of ourselves, and we might not know that certain language choices (such as using verbal qualifiers) are contributing to this impression. Understanding our language choices can enable us to change.

SIGNS, SYMBOLS, AND SIGNALS

Some of the difficulty in understanding and practicing effective communication can be traced to the core symbol system of verbal communication.

Language can be thought of as a collection of signs, symbols, codes, and rules used to construct and convey messages. These elements form the medium through which we communicate our ideas, desires, and feelings.

As we discussed in Chapter 1, the concepts *sign, symbol,* and *signal* are related and often confused with each other. Signs stand for or represent something else. The object or concept the sign represents is called a referent. There are two types of signs: natural signs are called signals; artificial or conventional signs are called symbols. **Signals** stand in a direct one-to-one relationship with what they represent. They are not ambiguous or arbitrary but are linked with specific responses. Cronkhite (1986) defined a signal as, "That type of sign that stands for its significate by virtue of a natural relationship, usually by some relationship of causality, contingency, or resemblance" (p. 232). Signals technically cannot be arranged because they occur naturally; they are discovered, not created. This definition of signal differs significantly from common usage of the term "traffic signal." In order to avoid confusion, Cronkhite has substituted the word symptom for signal. A "symptom is a sign that bears a natural relationship to that for which it stands" (p. 232). For example, thunder, lightning, and dark clouds are symptoms of an approaching rainstorm. Calloused hands are symptoms of physical labor. High temperature, sneezing, and congestion are symptoms of a head cold or flu.

Signs also exist as conventional, human-made, artificial phenomena called *symbols.* Artificially created or conventional symbols provide meaning when a particular society has agreed on what they will look like and what they will represent. Increase in foreign travel has necessitated the creation of international traffic signs. These signs are now found on major freeways and highways across the world. For example, a sign with a hand facing you, palm exposed, means stop. The meaning of that sign is becoming universally accepted.

One important characteristic of symbols is that they are *arbitrary* and *ambiguous;* they do **not** have a direct relationship with their referents. The word *elephant,* for example, does not possess any of the physical characteristics of a large animal. Unlike a physical sign or signal, a symbol can have many referents. A picture of an elephant in a children's book is another possible referent for the word-symbol *elephant.* The picture of the elephant is also a nonverbal symbol of the animal. Just like the word, the picture stands for, or represents, something other than itself.

A third category of sign behaviors, which are neither totally arbitrary nor symptomatic, are rituals. The fidgeting and foot-shuffling that occur just before the end of a class are examples of rituals (Cronkhite, 1986).

The communication discipline has focused largely on the study of human *symbolic activity.* Although research has been conducted into forms of nonsymbolic behavior and some communication scholars still argue that "all behavior is communication" (see Chapter 1), other scholars, including Cronkhite (1986), have suggested that the focus of our field needs to be more narrowly and realistically defined. They argue that primary attention should be focused on

---

Signs Something that stands for another thing

Symbols Type of sign that is created to stand for something else

Symptom Type of sign that bears a natural relation to an object

---

Ritual Type of sign that is a combination of being naturally produced, as in the case of a symptom, and being arbitrary or created, as would be a symbol

the effects of symbol systems and those who use them. The study of language and verbal behavior is inherently connected to the study of human symbolic activity.

LANGUAGE AND MEANING

The symbols used to create language are arbitrary and ambiguous. Yet communication is a process of exchanging mutually understood symbols to stimulate meaning in another (Steinfatt, 1977). Indeed, human language exists to allow us to share meanings. If symbols themselves do not contain meaning, how then is meaning created out of symbols? Meaning is accomplished when human beings *interpret* symbols. Meaning is a human creation: "Words don't mean; people mean." That is, the meaning of symbols is supplied by people and their culture. Symbols themselves carry no innate meaning; they may mean one thing to one person and something different to someone else. For example, the word-symbol *rock* can mean a hard substance found in quarries, a type of contemporary music, or a valuable stone set in a ring.

An eleven-year-old boy noticed that his mother was unusually quiet and did not appear to be "herself." When he asked his mother what was wrong, she replied that she was feeling depressed and did not know why. The son suggested that his mother see a psychiatrist to find out what was wrong. Before he could finish his sentence, he noticed that both of his parents became quite angry. They admonished him for being rude and impolite to his mother and punished him by sending him to his room! The boy honestly did not understand why he was being punished or why his parents had reacted so strongly. The parents soon forgot the incident, but it continued to haunt the boy. Several years later, while studying language and communication at college, he finally understood what had happened. To the mother and father, the word *psychiatrist* meant "doctor who treats crazy people." To the son, *psychiatrist* meant "counselor, advisor, and mental health professional who helps people understand their problems." The two generations had very different meanings for the symbol *psychiatrist*.

We learn meanings from our past experiences, from the mass media, and from interactions with friends, family, and authority figures. Even though the meaning of a given symbol can appear quite similar, no two people have the *exact* same meaning for the symbol. If people do not share the same meaning for symbols, how is communication possible? To answer this, we must distinguish between two types of meaning, denotative and connotative.

Denotative refers to the "actual" or "agreed-upon" meaning or meanings of a word. Denotative meaning is frequently referred to as the literal or "dictionary" meaning of a word. Connotative meaning refers to subjective associations—the personal and emotional attachments that people associate with a word or symbol. Connotative meaning contains all the judgments and evaluations that individuals have for a word or symbol. The word *college,* for example, has both denotative and connotative meaning. Its denotative meaning is, "An institution

Denotative meaning
The objective, descriptive, or agreed-upon meaning of a word. A dictionary definition

Connotative meaning
Subjective associations, personal, or emotional attachments people associate with symbols

of higher learning furnishing courses of instruction usually leading to a bachelor's degree." Its connotative meaning can differ considerably. One connotative meaning might be, "A place to party for four or more years." Another connotative meaning for college is, "An institution that will prepare me to get a job." Yet another connotative meaning could be, "The place where I became an adult and learned responsibility." Communication could not occur if people did not operate with some denotative meanings. Dictionaries are created to provide us with the "correct" or "accepted" definitions of words. We still run into difficulty, however, when the dictionary provides us with multiple definitions of symbols. For example, there are twelve different definitions of "college" in a large dictionary.

LANGUAGE AND PERCEPTION

Language influences our thoughts and our actions. Culture strongly influences the way a linguistic system develops and is transmitted. All languages have their own unique organization patterns. Language, as a set of signs, symbols and signals, has a grammar associated with it. Communication becomes possible when individuals share a system of order or grammar. Linguists and semanticists Benjamin Lee Whorf (1956) and Edward Sapir (1958) suggested that the language system we learn from our culture has a profound influence on how we interpret the world: "Language shapes perceptions of reality."

THEORY OF LINGUISTIC RELATIVITY

Theory of linguistic relativity Assumes that all higher level of thought depends on language and the structure of the language we use influences the way we understand our environment

The theory of linguistic relativity (also referred to as the Sapir-Whorf hypothesis) contains two fundamental principles: (1) all higher levels of thought depend on language; and (2) the structure of the language we use influences the way we understand our environment (Chase, 1956). The theory of linguistic relativity has never been tested through scientific experiments. Little if any research has explored the relationship between linguistic structure and actual behavior. Cronkhite (1976) stated that the theory "would be impossible to 'prove' even if it were true" (p. 271). We have no way of interpreting reality without thinking thoughts expressed in some language. Suppose we met a being from outer space who could perceive but had no means to communicate. Without language we could not share this creature's understanding of the world.

One study, although it was not a controlled experiment, did lend support to the theory of linguistic relativity. This study indicated that people with differences in words for colors perceive colors differently. The researchers discovered that differences in the ability to recognize and recall colors is associated with the availability of names for those colors (Brown & Lenneberg, 1954). More recent research appears to support the finding that linguistic differences affect thoughts and perceptions, including the categorization of color (Nisbett & Norenzayan, 2002; Roberson, Davies, & Davidoff, 2000). Researchers studied members of the Berinmo culture in Papua, New Guinea, and contrasted their perceptions of color with British participants. With both sets of participants, the experimenters pointed to color chips and asked participants in their respective native language to "Tell me what it is called." Each participant was also asked to give their best example of all the names they had given. It was discovered that the Berinmo have five basic color terms: white (including all pale colors); black; red; the color range of yellow/orange/brown; and a range of colors constituting green/yellow-green/blue, and purple, which correspond to words in their language system. The British participants had a significantly larger color categorization system based on the English language. This finding suggests that the possession of color terms in a language affects the way colors are perceived and organized into categories, the greater the number of words for color, the greater the color differentiation. The researchers concluded that color categories are formed primarily by language and that the results "in a substantial way…present evidence in favor of linguistic relativity" (p. 394).

Because languages develop in part in response to environmental conditions, a language is likely to have many words for classifying phenomena important to its physical and cultural environment. For example, the Eskimo language has many different words for snow. Eskimos are more likely to notice and think about differences in snowfalls than are native speakers of English, who have only a single term for snow. English leads us to "lump" all types of snow together and to ignore differences that the Eskimo notices (Cronkhite, 1976).

Much of the data that Whorf reported compares standard American English vocabulary to the language structure of Hopi, a Native American language. The Hopi and standard American English linguistic systems have very different rules for the discussion of time. Time in the Hopi system is a psychological time rather than a quantitative measure. Standard English makes a distinction between nouns and verbs. Objects or things are separated from action. Hopi language emphasizes differences in duration. Ellis (1992) clarified this distinction between the two linguistic systems. He stated that in the Hopi language, "the day or the year 'moves along' or 'gets later' but it cannot be broken into units" (p. 27).

The Sapir-Whorf hypothesis is important because it suggests that there is a connection between one's language and one's behavior. If language shapes perception and perception shapes behavior, then language can strongly influence one's actual behavior. Standard American English contains a great many polarized words—pairs of opposites. Think of the bipolar adjectives thick and thin, smart and stupid, tall and short, ugly and beautiful. Now try to think of a word that will fit exactly in the middle between those bipolar adjectives. The English language provides us with a ready store of opposites but does not provide us with many "moderate" words. We have difficulty finding them and using them (DeVito, 2001).

How does this linguistic situation influence our behavior? Let us suppose that your friend shows you a new outfit he or she has just purchased and asks your opinion of it. Suppose your attitude is somewhere right in the middle between love and hate. You don't want to say, "It's okay," as that answer sounds somewhat vague. What other alternatives quickly come to mind? "Nice" and "fair" do not accurately reflect your feelings. Thus, you are almost "forced" to say that you "love" or "hate" it. The constraints imposed on you by the linguistic system influence what you say. Indeed, you may then come to like the outfit more or less (another pair of opposites!) based on the word you chose.

LANGUAGE AND POWER

Power, control, and status are at the core of many social relationships (Giles & Wiemann, 1987). More powerful speakers can exercise greater control over a communication interaction and even the entire relationship. Can you recall a situation where language made you feel powerless or low in status? Perhaps you remember a time when you felt inadequate because of your conversational partner's vocabulary level. Some individuals, for example, report feeling "left out," "ignorant," and "passive" when they communicate with their physicians. Doctors who lack effective communication skills often appear to "talk down" to their patients. They do this by using professional jargon and by interrupting when patients ask questions.

COMMUNICATING POWER AND STATUS

People commonly use several forms of verbal behavior that communicate powerful or powerless positions. These forms of language can influence how much power people believe that you have, and also your level of status in society.

Verbal Intensifiers Verbal intensifiers include adverbs such as *so, such,* and *quite* and expressions such as "It was *really* nice." By increasing the intensity of the emotion being conveyed, intensifiers actually can reduce the strength of an utterance. Instead of saying, "The concert was delightful," including a verbal intensifier would modify the utterance to "The concert was really delightful." The extra adverb swings the audience's focus to the emotions of the speaker and away from the message, thus creating a more powerless position.

Verbal Qualifiers Verbal qualifiers also reduce the strength and impact of an utterance. Examples frequently cited are "you know," "possibly," "perhaps," "I guess," and "in my opinion." Instead of saying, "A communication degree will prepare me well for many careers," a lower-status or less powerful speaker might add a verbal qualifier to the statement: "In my opinion, a communication degree will prepare me well for many careers." The new statement sounds as if the speaker doubts that hearers will agree.

Tag Questions In this form of verbal behavior, the speaker adds ("tags on") a question to the end of a statement. Tag questions often weaken the assertions of the speaker. Note, for example, the difference in the strength of the following statements: "Usher is a great singer," and "Usher is a great singer, isn't he?" The second speaker appears to be insecure and seeking reassurance. Some scholars argue that tag questions are used to draw a response from reluctant communicators (Pearson, 1995). However, tag questions appear to weaken the verbal behavior of the speaker by making assertions appear less certain.

Lengthening of Requests The power and status of a speaker is often related to lengthening of requests. For example, if you want someone to open the window, you may say, "Open the window." If you want to appear more polite you might add, "Please open the window." People who add additional words to their requests are making "compound requests." Lengthening a request softens it and suggests that the speaker is less powerful, less assertive, and of lower status. For example, some speakers may add the additional phrase, "If it is not too much trouble" to the sentence. Although lengthening a request appears to signal politeness, it also makes the speaker appear to be more tentative, hesitant, and weak.

The interaction of context and linguistic indicators of power poses interesting questions for communication theorists to investigate (Bradac, 1988). For example, is it sometimes possible to increase power by hedging or being indefinite in language? Will high-power persons such as corporate presidents be able to enhance their power if they use low-power forms of verbal behavior? How will people respond to a woman C.E.O. who uses "feminine speech?"

SEX, GENDER, AND POWER: DIFFERENCES IN VERBAL BEHAVIOR

Over the last two decades, scholars have studied sex differences in verbal behavior (Bate & Bowker, 1997). Much of the early research indicated that females tend to use more verbal intensifiers, qualifiers, tag questions, and lengthening of requests than males (Lakoff, 1975). Because of this, "female speech" was often characterized as less powerful and less assertive than "male speech."

During the last thirty years, society has become more sensitive to verbal displays of power. The feminist, senior citizen, LGBTQ, African-American, physically challenged, and Hispanic/Latino movements have also had a significant impact on the language choices we make (Bate & Bowker, 1997). The women's movement, in particular, has done much to alter the verbal behavior of males and females. It has sensitized us to expressions of power and status in speech. As a consequence of this heightened sensitivity, changes have occurred in people's language. We now avoid using the masculine pronoun to stand for both males and females, and we avoid sex-stereotyped job titles such as *policeman* in favor of the gender-neutral *police officer.* Like *Mr.,* the title *Ms.* does not require a speaker or writer to know someone's marital status to address her politely.

Anthony Mulac, James Bradac, and Pamela Gibbons (2001) tested their gender-as-culture hypothesis in three different studies. They found that although men and women speak the same language, they do so differently because they learn to use language in very different cultures. Much of this learning takes place in groups of same-sex peers between the ages of 5 and 15. Learning how to carry on friendly conversations in two very different social contexts results in males and females developing different language preferences. These learned differences can produce communication breakdowns when members of one sex try to use their language behaviors in talking with members of the other sex. For instance, males may not be as skilled as females in using language to identify particular emotional states. This limits understanding in the interaction. A woman might conclude, "I just don't know what he is referring to." If men and women disagree on the interpretation of a given communicative behavior due to their different language models, the interaction will be affected. Thus, a man might see a woman's tag question as a sign of uncertainty and less self-confidence while she views the tag question as a method for involving the other person in an observation. Because men and women learned to use language differently, cross-gender interactions can be affected by differences in verbal behavior.

LANGUAGE INTENSITY AND OPINIONATION

Language Intensity One of the verbal behavior variables most frequently studied during the last forty years is the intensity of a speaker's language in a persuasive message. Language intensity is "the quality of language which indicates the degree to which the speaker's attitude toward a concept deviates from neutrality" (Bowers, 1964, p. 345). Speakers who use intense language exhibit more emotion and utilize stronger expressions, opinionated language, vivid adjectives, and more metaphors than speakers using less-intense language. For example, during a period of strained relations, President Ronald Reagan made a public speech calling the former Soviet Union an "evil empire." This term is clearly stronger and more intense than if the president had referred to the Soviet government as a "difficult power."

Language intensity is related to a communicator's use of metaphors, modifiers, and obscure words. One study tested whether sex and death metaphors used in the conclusions of speeches would have greater persuasive impact than less-intense, more literal conclusions (Bowers & Osborn, 1966). The statement, "Too long, we ourselves have stood by and permitted the ruination of our western economies by those who have proclaimed the doctrine of protective tariff" was used to test a literal conclusion. In the metaphorical conclusion, the word "rape" was substituted for "ruination." Speeches with metaphorical conclusions were more persuasive than speeches with literal conclusions. This finding contrasts with a previous study (Bowers, 1963) in which highly intense language produced less attitude change than low-intensity language. However, metaphors were not used in the earlier study.

Carl Carmichael and Gary Cronkhite (1965) reasoned that the frustration level of a receiver interacts with the language intensity of the speaker to affect persuasion. They speculated that a very intense persuasive message would be less effective when listeners were frustrated. Because frustrated people are already aroused, they should reject an intense message because it would push their level of arousal into an "uncomfortable zone." Carmµichael and Cronkhite tested this relationship and found that frustrated listeners reacted less favorably to a highly intense message. Language intensity, however, made no difference to listeners who were not frustrated.

Thirteen generalizations about the relationship between intense language and persuasion were isolated after an extensive review of over twenty studies (Bradac, Bowers, & Courtright, 1979). Language intensity interacted with several variables to influence attitude change. Receivers hearing intense language will be more likely to change their attitudes when: (a) they view the speaker as highly credible; (b) the speaker is male; (c) the speaker advocates a proposal the receivers already support; and (d) the receivers are low in arousal and stress. These findings are useful to political and organizational communicators. For example, a sales manager wishing to increase quotas for the coming quarter and speaking to a staff that has just experienced record sales should use highly intense language to motivate them. Following the same line of reasoning, a political advisor confidently urged former President George H. Bush to use intense metaphors when speaking to the Veterans of Foreign Wars about a constitutional amendment to outlaw burning the American flag.

Opinionated Language A form of highly intense language, opinionated language, has received much attention from communication theorists and researchers (see Chapter 6). When speakers use opinionated language, they indicate both their attitudes toward the topic and their attitudes toward those who agree or disagree with them. For example, a speaker might proclaim, "Only a fool would oppose the construction of nuclear power plants across the country," or, "Any intelligent person recognizes the danger in building nuclear power plants." The first statement is considered an "opinionated-rejection" statement. This type of statement reflects an unfavorable attitude toward people who disagree with the speaker. The second statement is considered an "opinionated-acceptance" statement. This type of statement expresses a favorable attitude toward people who agree with the speaker about the topic.

Researchers have conducted several studies on the effects of opinionated language. One study examined the effects of opinionated language in persuading open- and closed-minded listeners (Miller & Lobe, 1967). For one audience, two opinionated-acceptance and two opinionated-rejection statements were inserted in a message that advocated outlawing the sale of cigarettes (a proposal with which the audience disagreed). For the other group, no opinionated statements were inserted. The messages were otherwise identical and were attributed to the same highly credible source. Opinionated language was more persuasive than nonopinionated language if the source was highly credible. Opinionated language strengthens the intensity of the bond between the message *source* and the message *proposal*. When a highly credible source uses opinionated language, receivers think the speaker feels very strongly about an issue. Receivers are likely to change their attitudes to agree with the speaker. Using opinionated language also helps speakers emphasize the rewards listeners can expect if they accept the speaker's recommendations. Another study found that a highly trustworthy male speaker was more persuasive when he used opinionated language, but an untrustworthy speaker was more persuasive when he used nonopinionated language (Miller & Baseheart, 1969).

Other researchers have investigated the relationship between opinionated language and intensity of initial attitude toward a topic (Mehrley & McCroskey, 1970). A message containing opinionated language may be more or less persuasive depending on listeners' *initial* attitudes toward the topic. When listeners initially hold strongly negative or positive attitudes toward a topic, messages containing nonopinionated language enhance persuasion. However, when listeners hold relatively neutral attitudes, opinionated language results in greater persuasion. These findings can be explained by dissonance theory (see Chapter 6). The more a speaker pressures receivers to change their attitudes, the less their attitudes will change. When listeners are initially neutral, nonopinionated language statements are not strong enough to change attitudes, and opinionated language can be more effective. When listeners hold intense attitudes toward proposals, the opposite is true. Opinionated language statements are considered too strong, so that speakers who use opinionated language with intense listeners may find less attitude change and lower credibility ratings. No simple generalizations can be made about the effects of opinionated language; rather, outcomes depend on the interaction among a number of source, message, and receiver variables.

Forewarnings Messages that warn the audience by mentioning the type of arguments an opposing speaker will present

Several years later, other researchers examined opinionated language used in a particular type of message. Forewarnings are messages that warn the audience by mentioning the type of arguments an opposing speaker will present. For example, parents often warn their children not to accept candy or rides from strangers. Politicians often warn voters about upcoming attacks by their opponents. In studies of forewarnings and opinionated language, participants read an excerpt from a "symposium TV program," then indicated their reactions to the program. On the first page of the booklet containing the synopsis, participants read a message from either an authoritative (professor) or less-authoritative (freshman student) source. These sources used either opinionated or non-opinionated language to warn the reader about another authoritative (a second professor) or less-authoritative (a second student) speaker. Examples of opinionated statements included: "Any intelligent person will come to this same conclusion after considering the matter," and, "Only the most uneducated individual will accept the arguments that he is going to present..." For less-authoritative speakers, using a nonopinionated warning yielded greater persuasion. However, the use of opinionated language by an authoritative warner was effective in reducing the impact of a persuasive message. Thus, opinionated language appears to be one way to motivate listeners to resist persuasion (Infante, 1973).

A follow-up study tested whether opinionated language strengthened the attitudes of those later exposed to a message with which they disagreed. Each participant received both a "pro" and a "con" speech. Two groups received the "pro" speech before the "con" speech, and two groups received the "pro" speech after the "con" speech. One group received six opinionated rejection statements in the "pro" speech, and one group received six non-opinionated statements in the "pro" speech. Participants read the speeches, then evaluated the proposal and the character and authoritativeness of the two speakers. The "pro" speaker was viewed as less authoritative and less moral when he used opinionated language. With a favorable audience, using non-opinionated language seems to make the audience resistant to prior or subsequent persuasive efforts (Infante, 1975b).

Studying opinionated language has helped theorists develop "guidelines" for persuaders. Salespeople, advertisers, politicians, and public relations practitioners can use these findings to make their messages more successful.

THEORETICAL APPROACHES TO VERBAL BEHAVIOR

COMMUNICATION ACCOMMODATION THEORY

Derived from social psychological principles, communication accommodation theory (CAT) examines underlying motivations and consequences of shifts in verbal behavior (Giles & Wiemann, 1987). Similarity-attraction is a principal contributor to CAT, the idea being that we are attracted more to people who are similar to us. Two premises are central to communication accommodation theory: (1) During communication, people try to accommodate or adjust their style of speech to one another. (2) They do this to gain approval, to increase communication efficiency, and to maintain positive social identity with the person to whom they are talking. A core assumption of CAT is that our *perceptions* of another's speech determine how we will evaluate and behave toward that person. Two speech strategies, convergence and divergence, are central to this theory. In both speech convergence and divergence, the movement toward or away from the speech style of the other is motivated by an assumption about the other's speech style (Giles, Mulac, Bradac, & Johnson, 1987). Using convergence, individuals adapt to each other by slowing down or speeding up speech rate, lengthening or shortening pauses and utterances, and using certain forms of politeness, tag questions, and verbal intensifiers in their speech. Basically, when individuals try to converge their speech with the speech of another person, they try to match such things as the person's speech rate, volume, pitch patterns, tone quality, vocal energy, phrasing, pronunciation, and enunciation. Divergence refers to the way speakers accentuate vocal and linguistic differences to underscore social differences between speakers. In some situations, communicators often deliberately wish to maintain a social distance between themselves and others. Speech divergence is likely to occur when individuals believe that others are members of undesirable groups, hold distasteful attitudes, or display unsavory appearances (Street & Giles, 1982).

Communication accommodation theory A language theory of how we have our language converge or diverge with the language of others

Convergence A dimension of communication accommodation theory that is a strategy where individuals alter their speech to adapt to each other

Divergence A dimension of communication accommodation theory that reflects accentuating vocal and linguistic differences to underscore social differences between speakers

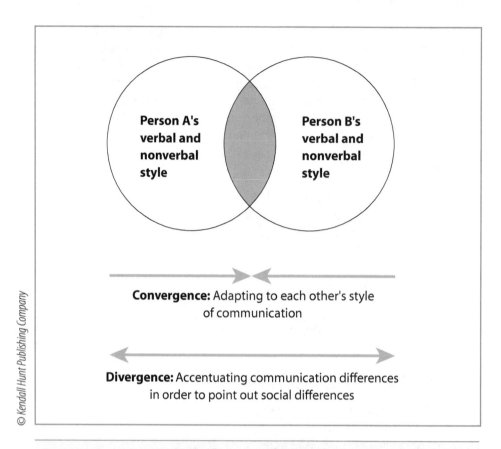

FIGURE 5.1 COMMUNICATION ACCOMMODATION THEORY.

For instance, if Person A wants to diverge in speech from Person B, A might pronounce a word correctly that was mispronounced by B (see Figure 5.1).

Use of Convergent Strategies Researchers have explored situations in which people use convergent and divergent forms of speech. In the area of gender and communication, Virginia Wheeless (1984) found that individuals classified according to gender orientation (masculine, feminine, androgynous, undifferentiated) rather than biological sex differed in their language use. Feminine and undifferentiated individuals were more accommodating than masculine and androgynous individuals. This finding is consistent with research that shows that "feminine language" is viewed as more considerate, cooperative, helpful, submissive, and accommodating (Stewart, Stewart, Cooper, & Friedley, 1996).

Stereotypes or expectations of others' abilities often influence the speech convergence process. For example, some nurses use "baby talk" to the institutionalized elderly, regardless of the individual's actual capabilities. Blind persons report that people who communicate with them often shout or exhibit other exaggerated behaviors completely unrelated to their ability to see. Attempting to adjust one's style to others in circumstances with which one has no experience can lead to "overconvergence." This conveys a sense of being talked down to and detracts from effective and satisfying communication.

Speech convergence suggests that people find approval from others satisfying. The greater the need for social approval, the greater the tendency for speech convergence. Power also plays a part in the degree to which convergence will be exhibited. Powerless individuals tend to adopt the verbal and vocal styles of those with power. This finding helps to explain some of the sex differences in verbal behavior. Females may use speech convergence in organizational communication contexts to "say the right thing" and to "fit in" with male organizational superiors. Communication theorists interested in gender and communication have identified the "double-bind" women face in organizations when they are asked to "speak like a man, but act like a lady."

In several instances, communication accommodation may be a scripted behavior. Individuals may "automatically" use a convergence script to make their speech appear more similar to another's (Giles et al., 1987). We may have a speech convergence verbal plan (see Chapter 1) ready to use when we need it.

Use of Divergent Strategies Groups with strong ethnic pride often use speech *divergence* or speech *maintenance* to underscore their identity and distinctiveness (Giles et al., 1987). In Chapter 4, we discussed the communication trait *rhetorical sensitivity. Noble selves* would be more likely to use speech divergence as a way of maintaining their identity than would rhetorical sensitives or rhetorical reflectors.

Occasionally, speech divergence is used as a power marker or to control the behavior of others. We may adopt a more formal, jargon-laden speech style when we wish to highlight educational differences. One professor uses speech divergence as a way to remind students gently and humorously that she has the power to determine when class will end. When students shuffle their feet and rearrange their books toward the end of a class period, the professor has been heard to say, "I see that you are engaging in significant leave-taking behaviors!" Giles and his colleagues report that we sometimes slow down our speech rate when we are talking with people who speak rapidly to slow them down. Parent–child interaction is another context in which speech divergence is frequently exhibited. As a child, you may have known you were "in trouble" when your parent called for you by using your first, middle, and surnames. This divergence was an attempt to increase the perceived (or real) status differences between parent and child.

Communication accommodation theory has also been used to investigate nonverbal communication. David Buller and Judee Burgoon (1986) found that changes in overall tone of voice and rate of speech (vocalics) altered listeners' interpretations of a speaker's level of intimacy and psychological closeness. Buller and James Aune (1988) tested the prediction that when a speaker seeks compliance with a request for help, the similarity of the speaker's speech rate to the listener's speech rate (a vocalic cue) improves compliance. It was thought that the similarity of speaker speech rate to listener speech rate would make the speaker appear more socially attractive. The study found that listeners who were better at decoding and interpreting vocalics (meaning stimulated by how we say something rather than what we say) were more likely to match the speech rate of the speaker and to comply with requests for help from a speaker with a fast rate than listeners who were poorer decoders. This finding suggests that perceived similarity in speech rate influences perceptions of a relationship and compliance with requests for help.

Although communication accommodation theory has generated considerable research, Howard Giles and his colleagues suggested that more questions need to be answered. For example, how do one's communication accommodation behaviors change during the course of a lifetime, and what is the relationship between communication accommodation and empathy? Communication scholars will explore these issues and continue to refine the theory.

LANGUAGE EXPECTANCY THEORY

Language expectancy theory A message-based theory of persuasion that focuses on how cultural expectation of language use affects both the change and reinforcement of attitudes and beliefs

Language expectancy theory (LET) was developed by Michael Burgoon in 1995 and is based on an accumulation of research on how people are persuaded. Because language behavior is at the core of this theory, we have chosen to include it in this chapter. LET focuses on language and how language affects both the change and reinforcement of attitudes and beliefs. It is considered a message-based theory of persuasion in that it seeks to explain why some linguistic forms of persuasive messages are more effective than others (Burgoon, 1995; Burgoon, Denning, & Roberts, 2002).

The concept of language expectation was adapted from the work of Brooks (1970), who believed that our stereotypes (later called expectancies) about what a source has to say, as well as the way they are expected to say it, influence the attitudes and beliefs of the receiver. For example, consider a person who has conservative views about financial investing and is about to hear a presentation from two different speakers. Both speakers share the same attitudes about investing (being fiscally conservative). One speaker is a male with a heavy Brooklyn, New York, accent and an animated presentation style, whereas the other speaker is a mid-western female with a more "standard American" accent and reserved presentation style. Based on our expectations concerning how we "think they should speak" and on their use of language, who will be more effective? Who will be less effective? LET is not concerned about each person's individual expectations (e.g., "This woman looks like my ex-girlfriend who was irresponsible with money, so therefore, this woman presenter has no credibility") as much as the expectations set forth by society and our culture at large (e.g., What language expectations do we have about financial advisors? Male financial advisors? Female financial advisors?).

The idea that the strategic linguistic choices made by persuaders can significantly predict success (Burgoon, Jones, & Stewart, 1975) served as the impetus for the development of language expectancy theory. LET assumes that language is a rule-governed system and that people, through socialization of their home culture, come to expect and prefer particular message and language strategies over others. That is, when people engage in persuasion, they need to consider how the audience was culturally programmed to determine what is considered competent and appropriate persuasive communication as well as what is considered inappropriate and ineffective language use (Burgoon et al., 2002). Further, these culturally/socially developed expectations affect persuasibility based on whether the language conforms (i.e., is consistent with) or does not conform (i.e., is inconsistent with) to our expectancies. When we violate linguistic norms (either positively or negatively), these violations have effects on the perceived appropriateness and effectiveness of the persuasive message. Language expectancies are impacted by three factors: the communicator, the relationship between the interactants, and the context in which the interaction takes place.

The formation of linguistic expectations can encompass entire social categories such as sex or ethnicity, and as such, these categories serve to define what is considered appropriate communication behavior. For example, people who are male have greater linguistic freedom (Burgoon et al., 2002). Having greater linguistic freedom is called having a wide bandwidth and results in a greater variety of persuasive linguistic strategies that will be seen as appropriate or falling within an expected range (Burgoon et al., 2002). Other social groups may be constrained to a smaller bandwidth regarding what is considered "appropriate linguistic strategies." These linguistic strategies can include variations in language intensity (e.g., fear appeals, opinionated language, language intensity, and aggressive compliance-gaining strategies). Simply put, people with greater bandwidth are allowed to "get away with" utilizing more linguistic variation than others. An example of this would be an ex-convict addressing a group of at-risk youth about the benefits of staying in school. This speaker would be afforded a much greater bandwidth (e.g., be allowed to use profanity, intimidation, sympathy, support) than would a pastor addressing the same group. Societal expectations concerning a pastor's linguistic strategies are much more constricted when compared to those of an ex-convict.

Bandwidth variations have also been identified in the study of language use and gender. According to Burgoon et al. (2002), rigid norms have developed concerning what is and what is not acceptable use of language by men and women. The research suggests that males are allowed more linguistic variability. For example, men are afforded the cultural expectation that use of intense language can still be persuasive. On the other hand, women using intense language were not seen as persuasive because the use of intense language was perceived as a violation of expectations of what constitutes appropriate and effective persuasive messages for use by females.

Source credibility (i.e., people who are perceived as being trustworthy and having expertise) has also been interpreted using LET. People with high credibility are afforded greater bandwidth than people with low credibility (Hamilton, Hunter, & Burgoon, 1990). When we believe that a person has a degree of expertise or is highly trustworthy, we tend to afford them more latitude in the types of language they use when trying to influence us.

LET reflects how cultural and societal expectations about language use and how violations of norms, gender, and trustworthiness affect the persuasive process.

Wide bandwidth A term from language expectancy theory that reflects when people have a greater variety of persuasive linguistic strategies that will be seen as appropriate or within an expected range

Smaller bandwidth A term from language expectancy theory that reflects when people have a smaller variety of persuasive linguistic strategies that will be seen as appropriate or within an expected range

Language intensity Quality of speaker's language about objects or concepts that indicates a difference in attitude from neutral

Opinionated language Highly intense language that indicates a speaker's attitude toward topics and attitude toward others

However, LET also allows for the explanation of the contradictory research regarding the persuasiveness of fear appeals. More specifically, some research indicates that fear appeals are effective (e.g., getting a person to stop smoking by telling them they will die of lung cancer should they continue to smoke), whereas other research indicates that the use of fear appeals is not persuasive (see Chapter 7). When interpreted through the expectations of the culture at large, expectancies about fear-arousing appeals as well as other intense language types is dependent on the audience. For example, Burgoon (1989, 1990) reported that when a person is perceived as having low credibility, the use of fear-arousing messages results in negative expectancy violation. On the other hand, males' use of fear appeals and other intense language was perceived as being more persuasive. This illustrates the different bandwidths that are created by cultural influence concerning language expectancy.

This research is further confounded by the particular state of mind of the receiver or audience. When the receiver is highly aroused (e.g., angry, anxious, uncertain), then fear and intense language results in negative expectancy violation. When the receiver is calm or not aroused, fear and intense language results in positive expectancy violation. In other words, intense language use is more persuasive when it is delivered to an audience that is relatively calm. On the other hand, when the audience is uncertain or anxious, a smaller bandwidth is acceptable, and intense language results in negative expectancy violation.

LET was also applied to the research on the effects of preexposure to persuasive language. When a person is preexposed to persuasive language, it results in the creation of expectations. In turn, when the actual persuasive encounter occurs, the receiver has already developed an expectation that serves as a benchmark from which to compare the persuasive attempt (Burgoon, Cohen, Miller, & Montgomery, 1978; Miller & Burgoon, 1979). For example, parents often talk to their children about the types of language strategies that other people will use to get them to try illegal drugs or engage in underage drinking (e.g., "It is cool!" "Everyone is doing it!" "Don't you want to be part of the group?" "Only losers don't drink!"). This defines these language expectations for the child before they actually encounter the situation. When the child experiences the actual situation, the degree of persuasibility will be determined by whether there is no violation, positive violation, or a negative violation of language expectations. Given that the creation of language expectations is a factor in the degree to which a person is persuaded, the question then becomes: "Is it better to create highly intense language expectancies or low-intensity language expectancies?" There is no benefit or pitfall to the creation of high- or low-intensity language expectations, but if there is a high-intensity language expectancy and the persuader uses low-intensity language, then they are seen as more persuasive. On the other hand, if we are expecting low-intensity language and encounter a persuader using high-intensity language, then there is minimal persuasive effect.

Seventeen propositions guide LET. Propositions 1–3 suggest that people develop expectations about language which influence whether a persuasive message will be accepted or rejected. If the language in a persuasive message violates expectations positively, this facilitates persuasion, resulting in potential attitude and/or behavioral change. If the language in a message violates expectations negatively, either no persuasion will occur, or changes opposite to those advocated by the persuader may result. Propositions 4–5 deal with the factors of sender credibility and freedom to select different and varied language strategies (i.e., having a wide bandwidth). It is suggested that individuals low in perceived credibility are more persuasive if they use low aggression or more prosocial compliance-gaining strategies. Conversely, individuals high in credibility have a wider bandwidth, that is, they enjoy more freedom to select varied language strategies and compliance-gaining strategies. Propositions 7–9 deal primarily with gender, fear, and language intensity. Males are more persuasive when using highly intense appeals, while females are more persuasive using low-intensity and less aggressive appeals. Propositions 10–12 suggest that individuals experiencing cognitive stress use lower intensity messages, and if they use high intensity language, the cognitive stress experienced can result in negative attitude and/or behavioral change. Propositions 13–14 suggest that forewarning receivers about future attacks can create maximum resistance to persuasion. Propositions 15–17 suggest that low-intensity attack messages are generally more effective than highly intensive messages in overcoming resistance to persuasion, and that the first message in a series of messages can affect the acceptance of subsequent messages. That is, when expectations are positively violated in the first message, the second message will likely be persuasive, and when expectations are negatively violated in the first message, the subsequent message will not be persuasive.

Although the studies supporting LET have relied primarily on experiments using college students in American universities, every culture has expectations about what constitutes the appropriate use of language and what constitutes competent communication. Therefore, language expectations transcend all cultures, but the definition of what constitutes appropriate language use is specific to each culture. In the end, LET is based on human expectations, which are believed to be important factors in many theories of human communication (Burgoon & Burgoon, 2001).

POLITENESS THEORY AND FACE MANAGEMENT

When individuals engage in competent communication, their messages come across to others as effectively as possible, even when the given communication event may be marked by potential embarrassment, criticism, complaining, disagreement, and stress. Not only does the message sender want to come across effectively, but he or she also wants to inflict as little embarrassment and discomfort on the receiver as well.

One theory has emerged which speaks to how individuals employ "politeness" in their verbal behavior to "grease the gears of social interaction" (McGlone & Giles, 2011, p. 211). This theory, labeled politeness theory, focuses on how we use language strategically to come across as competent, civil, and having regard for those who are the recipients of our messages. The theory also explores the use of communication strategies which can both create and maintain social harmony. When we are in an interaction with others, there are occasions when we refrain from saying exactly what we mean to say in the most direct way possible. Why do we do this? Why do we avoid saying exactly what we mean to select others? What are some factors which emerge during an interaction which cause us to engage in this type of circumvention behavior? Politeness theory, developed by Brown and Levinson (1978, 1987), seeks to address these and other questions such as "What is the best and most direct way to secure what we want or need while still coming across as politely as possible to our receivers?," and, "On the occasions when we do employ language which is more strident, how are those messages received?" and, "How can we craft and deliver messages which would allow both the sender and receiver of these messages to 'save' or 'maintain face' during these episodes?"

"Face" is defined by Brown and Levinson (1987) as "the public self-image that every member wants to claim for himself [or herself]" (p. 61). As such, all of us have a preferred "self-image" that we want others to perceive in us; it is the identity that we want to present to others when engaged in communication. However, under politeness theory, face does not refer to what we think about ourselves, often called our self-image or self-esteem. Rather, in this theory, face is referred to as "what kind of image is revealed in your own and others' actions" (Goldsmith, 2007, p. 220). As such, face is considered how our language behavior conveys who we are trying to be. Every time we use language in order to secure an action or seek compliance from another person we are enacting our public face.

Politeness theory conceptualizes "face" as the desire to exhibit one's self-identity to others, to be seen appropriately by others, and the understanding that your conversational partner has their own face needs as well. The theory suggests that there are two kinds of face: positive face and negative face. *Positive face* is our wish to have the person or persons we are interacting with approve the self-identity we exhibit during the interaction, in essence, to validate our self-identity. It is also conceptualized as a person's desire to have select others like and admire them (Dainton & Zelley, 2015). *Negative face* is conceptualized as our desire that others will not disrespect the identity we envision for ourselves. It is also seen as the ability to communicate without restrictions imposed on us by others. As Goldsmith (2007) suggests, "Although there are exceptions, the unspoken agreement to honor one another's face is a basic operating principle in most of our everyday interactions" (p. 222).

Three major assumptions underlie politeness theory: (1) Individuals in interaction, to the extent that it is possible, desire to maintain face. (2) As communicators, we make choices and decisions regarding the selection and delivery of messages in order to maintain face. These choices are tied into our relational and task goals. (3) Despite our best efforts to communicate in a manner which upholds the face of our receiver, there are occasions in which our choice of messages and message strategies will threaten someone's face, and their message choices are similarly occasionally likely to threaten our face needs (Dainton & Zelley, 2015, pp. 77–78).

Our desire to "honor face" is often cited as a major reason why we do not always say what we want to say to someone else in a direct and efficient way. Goldsmith (2007, 2008, 2009) suggests that several actions exhibited during conversations can potentially be seen as threatening to our own or another person's face. What are some of these "face-threatening communication behaviors? Goldsmith suggests that warnings, orders, requests, and even giving advice can threaten negative face. Questioning someone else's actions, disagreeing, interrupting, criticism, and complaints can also threaten another person's positive face.

What can be done verbally or linguistically to save another person's face, or make a face-threatening action seem less threatening? Applying politeness theory, Goldsmith (2007, 2008, 2009) delineates a five-part system for identifying and categorizing forms of politeness that people use to manage threats to face. (1) *Bald-on-record strategies*—deliver the face-threatening actions bluntly and directly, defined as bald-on-record. Goldsmith provides an example to illustrate each of the five types of face-threatening actions. Let us say you are thirsty and in need of a drink. Using bald-on-record strategies, you might say to your conversational partner, "Get me a glass of water." This request is made without any adaptation to face, and with little else to the message. (2) *Positive face redress*—this strategy involves stating the face-threatening action (e.g., when making a request directly, ask for what you want, or when providing a criticism, say exactly what you think is wrong), but use the language of solidarity, association, or similarity to make a connection between you and your partner. You can do this by using in-group language, joking, showing understanding, using terms of endearment, promising something, or pointing out commonalities between both parties. Using the same request for a drink example as above, you might say to your partner, "Honey, some water?" which, according to Goldsmith, uses the language of solidarity. (3) *Negative face redress*—This strategy suggests that the face-threatening action is stated in a way that minimizes disrespect, appears more deferential by "toning down" its forcefulness so as not to offend the target. Some verbal behaviors employed in this strategy are asking questions or using hedges, giving options to the hearer, apologizing and being deferential to the other, and addressing the receiver by title and last name. Again, using the drink request, you might say, "Could I trouble you for a little drink, please?" When using negative face redress, the speaker attempts to appear more subordinate to the target. (4) *Off-record strategies*—When employing this strategy, the speaker employs hints or ambiguous language to deliver the face-threatening action so that the request (i.e., the threat) is hidden between the lines. Again, employing the request for a drink, the speaker could say "I sure am parched!" When employing off-record strategies, the speaker can deny that the request was face threatening (e.g., "I wasn't asking for water; I was just saying I was parched"). (5) *Avoidance or refraining*—The final option is simply not to engage in a face-threatening action. Goldsmith suggests that silence or not engaging in the action or verbal behavior is a potential way of handling a situation in which a face-threatening action might be committed. However, not discussing an issue of importance to avoid a threat to face may result in less favorable relational outcomes than using one of the other strategies.

On a continuum from most polite to least polite, strategies that are more polite demonstrate greater regard for "face." As such, avoidance, or not engaging in the face-threatening action, would be the most polite. Off-record strategies would be the next most polite, followed by negative redress, then positive redress. Bald-on-record would be considered the least polite face-threatening action (Goldsmith, 2007, 2008, 2009).

According to politeness theory, several factors influence the degree of politeness both source and receiver will employ during a communication encounter. In particular, prestige, power, and risk are three factors which can influence the use of politeness strategies (Dainton & Zelley, 2015). For example, if your interaction partner has more *prestige* than you (e.g., someone with a higher status and/or a person who is well-known), the face-threatening actions you engage in may be more polite. If your interaction partner has *power* over you (e.g., your boss, your parent) you may engage in more polite face-threatening verbal behavior. Finally, if your message is likely to be seen as dangerous or hurtful to another person (e.g., you are going to break off a relationship with another, or you going to turn someone down if they ask you out on a date) then your face-threatening message will likely be more polite.

An interesting test of politeness theory was conducted to explore politeness strategies adult children imagined they would use to initiate a conversation with their aging parent about the need for eldercare (Pitts, Fowler, Fisher, & Smith, 2014). The researchers sought to explore how adult children might honor their parent's positive and negative face needs in imagined conversation openers about later life care, and how those imagined conversational openers might also threaten their parent's positive and negative face needs.

Participants were asked to think about, and then write out exactly what they would say to raise the topic of elder care needs with a parent. Most of the participants constructed openers imagining that they were addressing their mothers. Overall, a majority of the messages (80%) were coded as honoring or threatening parents' positive and/or negative face. Very few (6%) included just bald-on-record statements. Messages *honoring parents' negative face* were the most frequent, and included five themes which focused on the child's desire to give their parent independence and control of the conversation: (e.g., "Let's discuss the things that are most important to you and talk about situations you'd want to avoid," "I was wondering if you would like to talk about…," "When would you like for us to put your wishes into effect?," "I know how much you value your independence"). Messages *honoring parents' positive face* also emerged, and included six themes that centered on supporting parents' fellowship and competence face (e.g., "Dad, you know that I love you, and I am concerned about your health," "We care about you and your well-being and we wanted to talk about how we can help take better care of you," "I would like to take care of you while I can, like you took care of me when I was young").

Messages that threatened parents' negative and positive face also emerged. Messages which *threatened parents' negative face* included "It's time you come and live with me," "I'm going to call and set up a doctor's appointment for you," "When the time comes that you can no longer take care of yourselves," and "Someday you won't be able to live alone." *Threats to positive face* also emerged, although much less frequently. Some examples included, "As you are aging, we all need to figure out how you would like to be cared for," "I am concerned about your plans," and "We are worried about being able to take care of you properly."

In summary, many of the tenets of politeness theory emerged from the narratives constructed by adult children in this study. As such, politeness theory can be effectively utilized to help individuals understand the outcomes of conversational interactions, as well as to help prepare people to deliver more effective messages prior to sensitive conversational events.

INFORMATION MANIPULATION THEORY

Information manipulation theory (IMT) was developed by Steven McCornack (1992; 2008) in order to help explain how individuals create messages which contain both honest and deceptive information. Rather than suggesting that messages exchanged between individuals are either completely "truthful" or completely "dishonest," McCornack argues that most interpersonal communication exchanged between people falls somewhere between these two extremes. While most communication involves largely the presentation of honest information, a great deal of information exchanged between conversational partners often contains information which has been altered, edited, and even distorted. This results in the dissemination of a great deal of less than honest information. As such, IMT is "a theory designed to explain how people deceive and how people are deceived" (McCornack, 2008, p. 216).

IMT suggests that people create messages by manipulating the information that they share so that the resultant messages are both somewhat honest and somewhat deceptive. Deception occurs through the inclusion of certain information and omission of other information, ambiguity in how the information is presented, falsification of certain parts of a message, and the use of evasive strategies.

IMT is based on a set of maxims articulated by Grice (1989) called the cooperative principle. Grice believed that during an interaction, communicators try to cooperate with each other to achieve a common purpose in order to move toward a common communication direction when they exchange messages with each other. In order to do this, communicators utilize four maxims: quantity, quality, relation, and manner. *Quantity* refers to the amount of information that is expected in the messages exchanged between communicators. We expect that in a conversation with another person we will share as much relevant detail as possible; information should not be left out. The maxim of *quality* refers to the expectation that your messages are truthful and correct. That is, messages should not be false or lack evidence. The maxim of *relation* (*relevance*) refers to the expectation that people will present information relevant to the subject matter or the conversation going on at the time. The final maxim, *manner*, refers to how things are said rather than what is said. There is an expectation that conversational messages should not be ambiguous or obscure, that they should be presented in a parsimonious and well-ordered way.

Information manipulation theory suggests that when there is a violation of any or all of these maxims, information has been manipulated, hence, deception has occurred. As such, individuals can "produce one of five messages in any situation: a message that discloses all of the relevant information for the situation (a fully cooperative message), or messages involving manipulations of quantity, quality, relation, or manner" (McCornack, 2008, p. 220).

McCormack (1992, 2008) uses a case study to illustrate each of these five message and information manipulation choices. This case study presents the following hypothetical situation for you to consider:

> *Imagine you have been dating "Terry" for nearly three years, and that you feel very close and intimate toward him or her. Because Terry goes to a different school upstate, the two of you have agreed to date other people. Nevertheless, you feel jealous and possessive toward Terry. You see Terry only occasionally, but you call each other every Sunday and talk for an hour. Unbeknownst to you, on Friday one of Terry's friends invites Terry to go to a party on Saturday, but it's a date party. Terry presumes you cannot visit for the weekend, so Terry asks someone from communication class, someone attractive. The two of them go to the party and end up having a great time together. Throughout Saturday, however, you call Terry but get no response. Worried, you drive upstate on Sunday. Arriving at Terry's doorstep, you tell Terry, "I decided to drive down for the day and surprise you. I tried calling you all day, but kept getting your voice mail. What were you doing last night? (McCornack, 2008, p. 220).*

Given this situation, what message options does IMT suggest can be employed? The first option is that Terry can be *fully cooperative*, honest, and totally disclose all of the information about the situation, e.g., "I went to a party with someone I am interested in, I didn't think you could make it down. Sorry to have worried you. Perhaps we need to talk about our agreement to date others." McCornack (1992, 2008) suggests that few people in this situation employ this type of message strategy, instead, they opt for some manipulation of the information. A second option would be to engage in a *quantity* violation, that is, produce a message with somewhat less information than would be required for this situation (e.g., "I went to a party and had a lot of fun, sorry to have worried you"). This message can be seen as deceptive since it left out critical information which would alter your perception of Terry's behavior. A third option would be to engage in a *quality* violation, that is, present false information (e.g., "I was feeling ill, so I turned off my cell phone and went to bed"). This option clearly results in deception. A fourth option would be to engage in a *relation* violation. Again, this would involve presenting information which is irrelevant to the situation (e.g., "Why didn't you tell me you were coming? Isn't it a bit extreme to drive all the way up here just to check up on me?"). A fifth option would be to engage in a *manner* violation, that is, presenting messages which are irrelevant, ambiguous, and vague (e.g., "I was really busy with stuff and turned my phone off").

McCornack argues while we might want to believe otherwise, "most of the messages we present to others in daily communication involve some form of information control or 'manipulation'" (2008, p. 222). As such, some form of "information manipulation" (i.e., deception) is evident in the majority of interpersonal encounters. The tenets of IMT have been used in a variety of contexts to help explain the way individuals control, "spin," and manipulate information in conversational interaction.

SUMMARY

Many theories of communication account for the verbal behavior of individuals. Language is at the core of verbal behavior, and human beings are distinct in their ability to use language-incorporating signs, symbols, and signals. Language helps shape our perceptions and influences our behavior. We presented five theoretical approaches to verbal behavior. The theory of linguistic relativity (a.k.a., the Sapir-Whorf hypothesis) argues that all higher level thought depends on language, and the structure of the language we use influences the way we understand our environment. Communication accommodation theory suggests that people accommodate or adjust their style of speech to gain approval, maintain social identity, and make communication more effective. Speakers use convergence to adapt to another's speech style and divergence to maintain social distance between themselves and others. Language expectancy theory focuses on how language affects both the change and reinforcement of attitudes and beliefs. The theory assumes that language is a rule-governed system and that people, through socialization of their "home" culture, come to expect and prefer certain message and language strategies over others. Politeness theory focuses on how we use language strategically to come across as competent and civil communicators who have regard for those people receiving our messages. It suggests how both senders and receivers of messages craft and deliver messages which allow both communicators to "save" or "maintain" face during interaction. Finally, information manipulation theory helps explain how people create messages to be either truthful during an interaction, or how individuals might manipulate the information contained in a message in order to engage in some deception.

KEY TERMS

Communication accommodation theory

Connotative meaning

Convergence

Denotative meaning

Divergence

Forewarnings

Language expectancy theory (LET)

Language intensity

Manner

Opinionated language

RitualSigns

Smaller bandwidth

Symbols

Symptom

Theory of linguistic relativity

Wide bandwidth

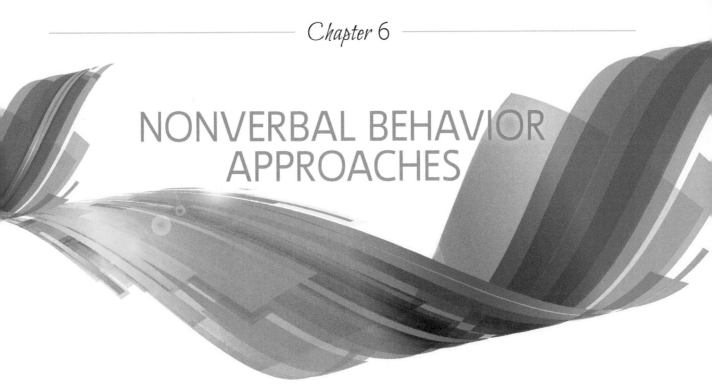

Chapter 6

NONVERBAL BEHAVIOR APPROACHES

Communication often involves more than a verbal message. We typically send and receive several messages simultaneously. Messages sent without using words are called "nonverbal" messages. For instance, a person's verbal message concerning a new shirt you are wearing might be, "I really like your new shirt." If the person accompanied the verbal message with nonverbal behavior such as erratic eye contact, a downward twist of the lower lip, words spoken in a slightly higher than average pitch, shoulders turning away from you, eyes blinking, and feet shuffling, you might decide that the verbal message was inconsistent with the nonverbal cues. Which would you tend to believe? Probably you would conclude the person really does not like your new shirt and is simply trying not to offend you.

Our example suggests that nonverbal communication is important because it is highly believable. Understanding what people mean is central to how effective we are socially; determining what people mean is not always easy. Verbal statements are affected by a number of factors, including the desire not to offend, social pressure to agree when others are present, the desire to make a commitment when time and resources may not be available, worries about other issues that divert attention, and deceptive comments just to avoid questions asked. For example, individuals believe one thing but say they believe something else, claim to pay attention but are actually thinking about their next vacation, and say they will behave one way while intending to do just the opposite. The better we can "read" people, the more we know what to expect and can plan accordingly. Understanding nonverbal communication is a very valuable social tool.

There is widespread interest in nonverbal communication by both the general public and those in the communication field. The book *Body Language* (Fast, 1970) continues to enjoy popularity even after 46 years, and several dubious conclusions it contains about nonverbal communication. In the communication discipline, nonverbal behavior is one of the major lines of research.

Nonverbal behavior is thought to be at least as important as verbal behavior in understanding communication. Some researchers have argued that nonverbal behaviors typically stimulate much more meaning than the meaning created by the words used in a communication situation (Mehrabian, 1981). The nonverbal code may be viewed as a language, one that we begin learning just as early in life as we do the verbal code.

The popularity of nonverbal communication makes it necessary to emphasize that it is not a "cure-all" for social problems; studying nonverbal communication does not guarantee social effectiveness. Popular books sometimes characterize nonverbal codes as "secret weapons," requiring only that you learn the secrets to conquer any task. However, nonverbal communication is only one dimension of communication competence. Competence with the verbal code, constructing effective arguments, and good delivery are also very important.

AFFECTIVE-COGNITIVE DIMENSIONS OF COMMUNICATION

The potency of verbal and nonverbal communication varies according to what is being communicated. Understanding the **affective** and **cognitive dimensions** of communication will clarify the variation. The affective dimension includes the communication of emotion (such as anger, love, fear, or happiness), attitude (how much something is liked or disliked, for example), and predispositions (such as anxiousness, confidence, or depression). These feelings can be communicated by the verbal code, but the task is difficult. For instance, when you try to tell a friend how much you love another person, you may feel that you have not really been understood. Some ideas are difficult to put into words but can be expressed very clearly nonverbally. Simply observing how a person looks at you communicates a good deal about the degree of affection, for instance. Nonverbal behavior is particularly effective in communicating affect.

The verbal code, on the other hand, is more effective when the goal is to communicate thoughts or cognitions. The cognitive component of communication refers to beliefs about what is and/or is not related to the object of communication. You can have beliefs about attributes, characteristics, and consequences of an object. For instance you might believe that a candidate for the presidency is honest, sincere, friendly, and an expert in domestic issues, but a novice in foreign affairs. Beliefs have to do with how things are related. This might also be thought of as "an idea" or "thinking." Typically, abstract processes such as spatial reasoning are necessary to comprehend a belief. These processes are very difficult to express nonverbally. The verbal code seems to have been designed especially for communicating the cognitive aspects of our internal processes. In our example, expressing beliefs about a candidate's relationship to domestic issues and foreign affairs could be done verbally without much difficulty. However, to do this nonverbally would be a nearly hopeless task. Expressing affect for the candidate through the nonverbal code could be accomplished very easily. A negative opinion about the candidate could be expressed with a look of disapproval; positive feelings could be expressed with smiles, head nodding, or clapping.

THE CONTEXTUAL NATURE OF NONVERBAL COMMUNICATION

The idea that the meaning of a message depends on its context is important in understanding nonverbal communication. A context involves situations and variables in the situations that make it different from other contexts. These differences occur along the lines of who, what, how, why, where, and when. The characteristics of the context influence the meaning of a message. Take a symbol such as a handshake. In a situation where you are introduced to someone, the handshake might indicate "I'm very glad to meet you," whereas the very same behavior in greeting an old friend could mean "I'm so glad to see you again." A handshake with rivals before a contest can mean, "May the better person win"; after closing a business deal, "It was a pleasure to do business with you"; after a bitter quarrel, "Let's put this fight behind us." The behavior is essentially the same in all these examples. However, the meaning is considerably different. The reason is quite simple; we have learned that a given symbol (or set of symbols) means one thing in one situation but something different in another. Thus, the meaning of a message is influenced by context. We should note the context in which a message is presented when we decide on its meaning.

Despite the fact that the contextual nature of communication is discernible, some of the popular books on nonverbal communication overlook this concept. Instead, they suggest that certain nonverbal behaviors mean only one thing and ignore the other possible meanings that could be created by changes in the situation. For instance, a possible interpretation of a woman talking to a man with her arms folded in front of her is that she is signaling unavailability; he is "closed out." What if this behavior occurs in a chilly room or even in a warm room by a woman who has just come in from the cold? In such cases, the nonverbal arm behavior might say nothing about the woman's desire for a relationship. It is misleading to treat a set of nonverbal behaviors as a formula for social knowledge. In certain circumstances it might be true that "a woman is interested in you if she moves her shoulders back, is slightly flushed, and tilts her head to one side a bit." These behaviors might indicate interest in an intimate setting. If you are walking across campus to your next class, they might signal that she had a good workout at the gym, is stretching her deltoids, and is reacting to the muscle stimulation.

NONVERBAL BEHAVIOR AND INTENTIONALITY

In Chapter 1 we explained that all human behavior is not communicative behavior. *Communication occurs when humans manipulate symbols to stimulate meaning in other humans.* Symbols are only one of several things that can stimulate meaning. Non-symbolic behavior can stimulate a response; however, intention is not involved. A woman may fold her arms for many reasons. If sending a message about unavailability is not one of her reasons, then communication about approachability does not occur when she folds her arms. Of course, others might "read meaning into" her behavior. She cannot stop people from thinking. Meaning can be stimulated by both symbolic and nonsymbolic elements. If a woman's arm folding is nonsymbolic regarding accessibility, imagine her confusion if a man said, "Why did you just send me a message that said you are unavailable?" Her response, in the terminology of this book might be, "I cannot stop you from seeing meaning in nonmessage behavior. If you do, do not act as though I am communicating with you. Realize that you are creating meaning for yourself that may have no relation to my ideas and feelings."

Perhaps one of the reasons the area of nonverbal communication has become so popular is that nonverbal behavior provides clues to detecting attitudes, traits, and deception. There are many examples. Pupil dilation shows interest. Frequent head nodding indicates a feeling of lower status. Deception is signified by less forward body lean. Nervousness is evidenced by fewer gestures. Such behaviors seem to reveal information that people themselves usually would not volunteer. As such, these nonverbal behaviors appear to be a valuable means for understanding people. Despite this appeal, the behaviors in question usually do not constitute communication because intentional manipulation of symbols to send messages is not apparent. Instead, the behaviors are more like symptoms as defined by Cronkhite (1986). For example, a drooping posture may be a symptom of sadness or depression.

Emotional leakage
A term used to describe when a person's feelings "leak out" through one or more nonverbal channels

Similarly, emotional leakage is a consequence of the perception of symptoms. Emotional leakage is the term used to describe when a person's true feelings "leak out" through one or more nonverbal channels. Unknowingly, or at a very low level of awareness, individuals reveal their true emotions because of their nonverbal behavior. If you are bored with a conversation but pretend you are interested, emotional leakage might occur if your laughter were less relaxed and you used fewer vocal expressions and head nods. The idea that a person's boredom would leak out and foil the person's attempt to create a particular impression is intriguing. However, the "leaky" behaviors are not symbolic; most likely they are symptoms. As our conception of communication makes clear, all meaning does not result from communication. Although highly pro-vocative, "emotional leakage" is not a communication behavior because it does not involve a deliberate message on the part of the sender. Instead, one-way meaning is formed in the mind of the observer based on naturally occurring symptoms or behaviors that cannot easily be controlled.

NONVERBAL COMMUNICATION ABILITIES

People vary widely in how well they encode and decode written and spoken messages. Because individuals range from very high to very low in verbal language abilities, we would expect to find differences in nonverbal communication as well. Research suggests that the ability to encode and decode nonverbal behavior may be an attribute of certain personality traits. People who are extroverted are more skilled at portraying emotions through vocal and facial codes. Introverts are less able to communicate emotions nonverbally, if for no other reason than they have not had as much practice due to their tendency to withdraw from people.

Self-monitoring of expressive behavior (see Chapter 4) is another trait that appears related to nonverbal encoding ability (Snyder, 1974). High self-monitors are very aware of the impression they make on others. They are able to assess their behavior and reactions to it and make adjustments in their performance accordingly; high self-monitors are very adaptive. High self-monitors are also skilled at communicating emotions nonverbally when compared to low self-monitors. Having the motivation to monitor one's behavior with respect to the reactions of others appears necessary for the development of the ability to encode nonverbal messages skillfully.

Self-monitoring of expressive behavior
A trait that involves monitoring one's nonverbal behavior and adapting it to situations in order to achieve communication goals

Greater encoding skill by high self-monitors has been investigated in terms of deceptive communication (Miller, de Turk, & Kalbfleisch, 1983). Research participants were asked to tell the truth or to lie about the feelings that they had while viewing pleasant or unpleasant slides. Both high and low self-monitors took part in the experiment. Participants either spoke immediately or were given twenty minutes to rehearse what they would say. Observers viewed videotapes of the participants' messages and judged whether the individual was telling the truth or not. When rehearsal was permitted, high self-monitors were more effective in deceiving observers. The more time they had to practice their behavior, the more successful they were. Low self-monitors who had not rehearsed displayed more pauses and had a higher rate of nonfluencies such as "um." This experiment confirmed the hypothesis that high self-monitors would be more effective in deceiving others.

There may be a sex difference in the ability to communicate emotions facially and vocally (Zaidel & Mehrabian, 1969). Females seem to be more skilled than males. One explanation for this is that culture has taught females to be more expressive and to reveal emotions. Males, on the other hand, have been conditioned to be more stoic and to inhibit expression of feelings. Because males engage less in emotionally expressive behavior, they are less skilled at encoding it. Nonverbal decoding ability is also related to sex. Psychologist Robert Rosenthal and his associates (1979) developed the PONS (Profile of Nonverbal Sensitivity) test to measure ability to decode nonverbal messages. One of the most consistent results in research using this test is that females tend to score higher in comparison to males. The finding that females are higher in both nonverbal encoding and decoding abilities further illustrates the point that the two abilities are related. That is, if you are high on one, you tend to be high on the other; if you are unskilled regarding one, you tend to be unskilled regarding the other.

Although females generally score higher on the PONS test, there are some males who score equally well. These tend to be males who are in very communication-oriented professions that require sensitivity to the needs of others. Teachers, clinical psychologists, and actors are examples. This finding further supports the social-influence explanation given earlier for male-female differences in nonverbal behavior.

High scorers on the PONS test differ from low scorers in several ways in addition to gender. Low scorers tend to be younger. Just as with verbal language, nonverbal ability seems to improve with age. High scorers tend to function better socially, to have closer same-sex relationships, and to predict future events with greater accuracy.

In developing the PONS, Rosenthal experimented with the amount of time a scene was shown to people. He found when exposure was reduced from five seconds to 1/24 of a second, some people were still able to identify the emotion portrayed. These individuals who appeared to be especially sensitive to the nonverbal code reported that they had less satisfactory relationships with other people. Perhaps it is possible to see "too much" in the behavior of others, and this creates dissatisfaction with people. That is, extreme accuracy in decoding may make one more aware of the "common deceptions" that are a regular component of social interaction. Common deceptions refer to "white lies," behaving one way but preferring something else, or concealing the truth because of a desire to protect someone's feelings.

FUNCTIONS OF NONVERBAL COMMUNICATION

Functional approaches have been used extensively to examine a number of areas in communication such as credibility, persuasion, and mass media. Viewing nonverbal communication in terms of the functions that it fulfills for the individual is similarly valuable. We will briefly examine six important functions.

SENDING UNCOMFORTABLE MESSAGES

Some messages are much easier to present nonverbally. Overt delivery of a verbal message could result in embarrassment, hurt feelings, discomfort, anxiety, and anger. One example of such a message involves initiating or preventing interaction. For instance, at a party Jamie might realize that Sean across the room wants to approach and talk. If Jamie does not want to meet Sean, a possible verbal message would be, "Don't bother coming here to talk with me; I don't want to get to know you." Of course, that is a difficult message to present in a social situation. An "easy way" to deliver the idea would be preferable. Nonverbal codes such as eye and facial behavior and the directness of body orientation can send the message without as much embarrassment. In fact, even in a crowded room, probably only Sean would be aware of Jamie's message of discouragement.

Once interaction has been initiated, another difficult message is to inform someone that you wish to terminate the interaction. Imagine that Sean in our previous example ignored the nonverbal message and approached Jamie anyway. The verbal message: "Why did you come across the room to talk with me? Couldn't you see I'm not interested? Please leave" would be a very difficult message to deliver. Nonverbally, the task would be easier. Jamie could avoid eye contact, turn so as not to face Sean directly, and talk in short phrases with little expression (sound bored).

These examples illustrate that negative messages are communicated with efficiency by the nonverbal code. However, some types of positive messages also are easier to say nonverbally. One example is communicating love. Some people find it difficult to say "I love you" and instead rely on eye behavior, **touch**, and **close proximity**. Another example is communicating favorable internal states such as feeling very good about oneself. Nonverbally, this can be done by sounding confident (vocally), reflecting this feeling in facial behavior, and walking with a confident gait.

Eye behavior Nonverbal behavior that communicates attitude, interest, dominance, or submission

FORMING IMPRESSIONS

Nonverbal communication is especially useful in the process of forming first impressions. Initial interaction and the early stages of a relationship are influenced a good deal by the first impressions that people form of each other. Communication between people is viewed as ranging from impersonal to interpersonal (Miller, 1978). At the *impersonal* end of the continuum, people use sociological variables such as age, sex, and race to form an impression that guides what to say and how to say it. When communication is impersonal, you rely on assumptions about what people are like to guide your communicative behavior. We typically place a good deal of importance on first impressions because we do not want to say something that the other will view as foolish. We are strongly motivated to reduce uncertainty about the other so that we can predict with confidence how to and how not to communicate. (You will read more about this process in the discussion of uncertainty reduction theory in Chapter 8).

When communication is *interpersonal,* the impression of the other that guides interaction is based mainly on *psychological* data. In comparison to sociological data, psychological is more personal. The major types of psychological data are values (very strong, wide-ranging beliefs that guide behavior), attitudes (like or dislike for things), and personality (traits that define the person). Thus, when communication is interpersonal, it is less stereotypic and is individualized according to the psychological characteristics of the people involved.

The nonverbal messages we send contribute substantially to the first impression others form of us. This impression then guides how people talk with us in the early stage of interaction. Many of these messages pertain to physical appearance—fashion, grooming, body type, and attractiveness. For instance, the first impression that you make might be: a male, late teens, highly fashion conscious, very neat and clean looking, a "physical fitness" type who values being attractive. These cues would provide a basis for others to guess how to communicate with you. For instance, clothes or physical fitness would be "excellent bets" for successful topics of communication.

Nonverbal cues provide data relevant to your psychological characteristics. If the cues are clear, communication moves from the impersonal to interpersonal levels more readily. The cues just discussed, fashion consciousness and physical fitness, are a few examples. Other cues derive from nonverbal codes such as the way we use our voices. For instance, a person might sound very self-confident or move very confidently. Another individual's movements might suggest nervousness or apprehension. If the nonverbal cues are not clear, then there is the tendency for communication to remain at the impersonal level. For instance, if the messages from your eyes, face, and body movements make it unclear whether you are a very cautious or a carefree person, a person talking with you will exercise discretion, selecting only "safe" topics such as the weather, one's major, or hometown.

MAKING RELATIONSHIPS CLEAR

In addition to content, communication has a **relationship** dimension (Watzlawick, Beavin, & Jackson, 1967). Content refers to the topic of the message. For instance, a parent might say, "Did you have a nice time at the party last night?" The content is clear. It has to do with how favorable your experience was with the party. The relationship dimension refers to the interpersonal relationship between the individuals, and this influences how the message will be handled. For instance, you might respond, "Oh, I had a great time!" If a friend had asked the same question, you might have said: "I was having a great time...until I reached the point where I had too much to drink!" The relationships we have with people exert a powerful force on our communicative behavior.

Nonverbal communication functions to establish and clarify the relationship dimension of communication. It does this very well because at times the relationship message would be offensive if spoken verbally. For example, "I am your boss even though you do not like it." Communicating such a message without words serves to "soften" the message, making a destructive outcome of the situation less likely. If the relationship is not clarified, the danger of a misunderstanding increases. For instance, in the early stages of a new job you might be uncertain as to whether you must comply with what a certain person tells you to do. This uncertainty could result in your responding to the person with indifference when the other person's expectation was for you to be compliant. This would be a costly mistake if the person was your superior and not a peer.

There are many types of relationships that are important in communication. Some of these are parent–child, superior–subordinate, spouse–spouse, partner–partner, friends, and siblings. Others are based on competition, cooperation, liking, love, or disdain. Nonverbally, we tell one another what we believe the nature of our relationship to be. If there is correspondence between the parties, the relationship dimension of communication can recede to the background. For instance, if you want to be dominant in a relationship, you might communicate that by steady eye contact, holding the floor most of the time, interrupting and touching the other person more. If the other person accepts this relationship definition, there is no problem. Nonverbally, this acceptance might be communicated by eyes cast downward while looking "up" to you, frequent head nods, and passive smiles. On the other hand, if the nonverbal messages that people send one another about the nature of their relationship are not congruent, then the definition of the relationship becomes an issue and usually predominates until resolved. When a relationship issue emerges, it becomes more likely that the attempt to define the relationship will shift from the nonverbal to the verbal code. That is, it is easier, less disruptive, and less offensive if we tell one another nonverbally of the nature of our relationship. If this fails to produce an agreeable outcome, then more overt communication is necessary; there is a need to talk about the relationship.

Regarding our earlier example, suppose you are new on a job and respond with indifference to someone who says you should stop what you are doing for a while and work at a different task. Suppose further that this person's eye contact was not steady and the tone of voice was unsure—two behaviors that do not indicate a superior relationship. Because the command is incongruent with the nonverbal cues, it probably would be necessary to clarify the relationship verbally. This could be done by having your supervisor explain to you whom else in the organization you must obey.

REGULATING INTERACTION

Regulating our interaction with others is a fourth major function of nonverbal communication. Imagine the following: two people recognize one another in a college library. They begin to talk in a pleasant tone with occasional laughter. They take turns talking with little silence between utterances. After about 15 minutes the conversation ends, and they return to separate places in the library. Imagine further that both individuals derived considerable satisfaction from the interaction. This is an example of successful communication.

Although such episodes are extremely common, we could also view them with amazement—an example of complex human activity made to look easy. A major reason why communication events such as this go smoothly is they are carefully and skillfully regulated. The central regulating mechanism appears to be nonverbal communication. As a regulator, nonverbal behavior operates in terms of *initiating interaction, clarifying relationships, directing turn-taking, guiding emotional expression,* and *leave-taking.*

Greeting behaviors that suggest a desire to interact are largely nonverbal. In our example, each person could send such messages by raising eyebrows while widening the eyes, raising the chin with a smile, and perhaps waving the hand in greeting. When the individuals approached one another and positioned themselves about three feet apart, the conversation could begin.

During the conversation, several nonverbal behaviors regulate the interaction. We discussed the function of clarifying relationships in the previous section. Directing turn-taking involves communicating when you want the floor and when you are or are not willing to relinquish the floor. When we want the floor (our turn to speak), a number of nonverbal messages may be used: throat clearing, vocal sounds such as "uh, uh," opening the mouth as if beginning to speak, raising eyebrows, and opening eyes wide. Willingness to give up the floor is indicated by pausing, looking to the other as if searching for a response, nodding approval to begin, or gesturing toward the person to begin. Wanting to hold the floor when someone desires to talk is expressed by increasing volume somewhat, employing an aggressive tone in the voice, breaking eye contact, and adopting a determined facial expression.

Guiding emotional expression involves the tone of the conversation. Nonverbally we say whether the tone should be happy, sad, angry, hurried, or serious. As we explained earlier, nonverbal communication is especially effective at expressing the affective or emotional dimension of communication.

Regulating leave-taking is accomplished nonverbally in many ways (Knapp, Hart, Friedrich, & Shulman, 1973). Messages that indicate a desire to end the conversation include breaking eye contact and glancing around the area, looking at a watch, shuffling feet, and leaning in the direction of the exit. The actual leave-taking will either be positive or negative, depending on the desire for future communication. Some positive nonverbal messages are a handshake, a smile, and a wave. Negative messages include an abrupt ending, turning and leaving with no goodbye, an angry goodbye, and a gesture of disgust on exiting.

INFLUENCING PEOPLE

Nonverbal communication appears to be very important in the process of persuasion. Certainly the verbal message matters. However, there is increased awareness that people are influenced by nonverbal messages as well. Whether the verbal message is accepted seems to depend on how well the persuader communicates nonverbally. The adage, "It's not what you say but how you say it," is an overstatement, but "What you say cannot overrule how you say it" is accurate.

There are several types of nonverbal messages that can enhance a source's persuasiveness. Some involve physical appearance that appeals to the receiver, such as dress and grooming. Others include body movement or eye and facial behavior—creating a dynamic image, a sincere look, or appearing sociable. Vocal behavior, meaning the way the voice is used, is also important. This entails sounding dynamic and interesting. These nonverbal messages all contribute to the individual's *image* or total impression. In political communication especially, there is increased use of terms such as image building, image management, and image rebuilding or repairing. The use of these terms acknowledges the principle that one's nonverbal messages are not independent of the verbal message. Perhaps this causes you to think that the influence process, whether it occurs in the political, business, or personal arena, is extremely superficial because appearances matter so much. However, there is a very good reason for this. People pay close attention to persuaders' nonverbal behavior as a basis for deciding whether to *trust* the person. Trust is a necessary condition for persuasion in almost all cases.

A person's nonverbal behavior provides a major source of data in deciding on a person's character. Eye behavior is usually emphasized as a criterion for deciding whether to trust someone. Voice is also a focus. What qualities do we look for when deciding trust? The answer is rather well established in terms of research. We are more attracted to people and trust them when they are similar to us (Infante, 1978). Similarity tends to breed attraction, and the more our nonverbal behavior says to a person, "As you can see, I am a lot like you," the more the person probably will trust you. This is true mainly because they know what to expect from a similar other. They assume the person is guided by similar values.

This analysis has identified an approach to nonverbal communication in persuasion that has been termed nonverbal response matching (Infante, 1988) and may be considered an aspect of communication accommodation theory, which was discussed in Chapter 5. The idea is for the persuader to match the receiver's nonverbal behavior so that a bond of trust develops because the receiver perceives similarity between self and the persuader. For instance, if the receiver talks fast with short, quick gestures, the persuader would adopt this style to identify with the receiver. This is not mimicry, which is a form of insult. Instead, it is a message that says, "I understand how you are, and I like being that way myself." This behavior confirms the saying, "Imitation is the sincerest form of flattery." Studies that compared successful salespersons to mediocre ones revealed that the successful sellers used response matching, whereas the unsuccessful ones did not (Moine, 1982). Clearly, our nonverbal behavior provides important input in our decision about whether to trust others.

Nonverbal response matching Matching another's nonverbal behavior in order to create perceived similarity, which leads to trust

REINFORCING AND MODIFYING VERBAL MESSAGES

Finally, one of the most basic functions of nonverbal communication is to affect the verbal message. The verbal and nonverbal messages are often produced together. As such, there is not one message but several, comprising a set of messages. The idea of a set emphasizes that things go together, influence one another, and the whole is more than simply a sum of the parts. Thus, a given configuration of nonverbal messages along with certain words will communicate one thing, whereas the very same words with a different set of nonverbal messages will communicate something else. Nonverbal communication may reinforce or modify the verbal message.

Nonverbal communication reinforces verbal messages in a variety of ways. Imagine gestures that would accompany the phrases in parentheses in the following sentence. Gestures are used to illustrate size ("the fish was this big"), position ("I was here; the fish jumped there"), effort ("I struggled to keep the rod tip high while he pulled really hard"), movement ("I reached into the water quickly and picked up the fish by the lower jaw"). Facial, eye, and vocal behavior are especially effective in emphasizing the emotional content of a message. For instance, if you are talking about hunger in America, your nonverbal messages should reflect concern and reinforce the seriousness of this social problem. While you discuss the issue, your face, eyes, and voice could express sympathy and gravity. If proposing a solution such as a guaranteed job program, your face, eyes, and voice could communicate hope, enthusiasm, and confidence.

At times, nonverbal messages are used to modify verbal messages. This is especially likely when we do not want our words to be taken literally. There are at least four ways this happens. One is when it is socially desirable to say one thing, but we want to express our displeasure with the contents of the verbal message. For example, imagine working for a company that invested much of its resources in a new but very unsuccessful product. In talking with coworkers your verbal message might be, "Oh, yes, our...is a wonderful innovation." Nonverbally, with eyes, face, and tone of voice, you might say that the product is not so wonderful and actually not much of an innovation either. Mock verbal aggression is a second means of altering literal meaning; it includes playfulness commonly termed "kidding" or "teasing." However, one must be careful to avoid miscalculation. Receiving a birthday present wrapped in paper that reads, "Happy birthday to a sweet old buzzard" may or may not be taken as a joke! Third, nonverbal messages are used to modify the verbal message in requests. Terry asks Dale for something, and Dale really would like to say "no" but uses a nonverbal message that says, "OK, I will if you *really* want me to." The verbal "yes" is expressed with little enthusiasm, looking away, and breathing out while drooping the shoulders (as if burdened by a great load).

NONVERBAL EXPECTANCY VIOLATIONS THEORY

Nonverbal expectancy violations theory Theory that explains a wide range of communication outcomes associated with violations of expectations about nonverbal communication behavior

Judee Burgoon (1978, 1983, 1985) and Steven Jones (Burgoon & Jones, 1976) originally designed nonverbal expectancy violations theory (NEVT) to explain the consequences of changes in distance and personal space during interpersonal communication interactions. NEVT was one of the first theories of nonverbal communication developed by communication scholars. NEVT has been continually revised and expanded; today the theory is used to explain a wide range of communication outcomes associated with violations of expectations about nonverbal communication behavior.

According to NEVT, several factors interact to influence how we react to a violation of the type of nonverbal behavior we expect to encounter in a particular situation (Burgoon & Hale, 1988). NEVT first considers our **expectancies**. Through social norms we form "expectations" about how others should behave nonverbally (and verbally) when we are interacting with them. If another person's behavior deviates from what we typically expect, then an expectancy violation has occurred. Anything "out of the ordinary" causes us to take special notice of that behavior. For example, we would notice (and probably be very uncomfortable) if a stranger asking for directions stood very close to us. Similarly, we would notice if our significant other stood very far away from us at a party. A violation of our nonverbal expectations is unsettling; it can cause emotional *arousal*.

We learn expectations from a number of sources (Floyd, Ramirez, & Burgoon, 1999). First, the culture in which we live shapes our expectations about different types of communication behavior, including nonverbal communication. As we will describe in our discussion of nonverbal immediacy behaviors, contact cultures have more eye contact, more frequent touch, and much smaller zones of personal distance than noncontact cultures. The context in which the interaction takes place also affects expectations of others' behavior. A great deal of eye contact from an attractive other may be seen as inviting if the context of the interaction is in a social club, whereas the same nonverbal behavior may be seen as threatening if that behavior is exhibited in a sparsely populated subway car late at night. Depending on the context, "a caress may convey sympathy, comfort, dominance, affection, attraction, or lust" (Burgoon, Coker, & Coker, 1986, p. 497). The meaning depends on the situation and the relationship between the individuals. Our personal experiences also affect expectancies. Repeated interactions condition us to expect certain behaviors. If our usually cheerful roommate suddenly stops smiling when we enter the room, we encounter a distinctly different situation than we expected. NEVT suggests that expectancies "include judgments of what behaviors are possible, feasible, appropriate, and typical for a particular setting, purpose, and set of participants" (Burgoon & Hale, 1988, p. 60).

Our *interpretation and evaluation* of behavior is another important element of the theory. NEVT assumes that nonverbal behaviors are meaningful and that we have attitudes about expected nonverbal behaviors. We approve of some and dislike others. **Valence** is the term used to describe the evaluation of the behavior. Certain behaviors are clearly negatively valenced, such as being subjected to a rude or insulting gesture (e.g., someone "flips you the bird" or rolls their eyes at you). Other behaviors are positively valenced (e.g., someone signals "v" for victory after a touchdown or "thumbs up" for your new sweater). Some behaviors are ambiguous. For example, imagine that you are at a party and a stranger to whom you are introduced unexpectedly touches your arm. Because you just met that person, that behavior could be confusing.

You might interpret the behavior as affection, an invitation to become friends, or as a signal of dominance. NEVT argues that if the given behavior is more positive than what was expected, a positive violation of expectations results. Conversely, if the given behavior is more negative than what was expected, a negative violation of expectations results. In ambiguous situations, the following element tips the balance.

Communicator reward valence is the third element that influences our reactions. The nature of the relationship between the communicators influences how they (especially the receiver) feel about the violation of expectations. If we "like" the source of the violation (or if the violator is a person of high status, high in credibility, or physically attractive), we may appreciate the unique treatment, and the violation behavior may be seen positively. However, if we "dislike" the source, or if the person engaging in the violation behavior is seen as low in credibility, gives you negative feedback, is seen as unattractive, we are less willing to tolerate nonverbal behavior that does not conform to social norms; we view the violation negatively.

NEVT posits that it is not just a matter of the nonverbal behavior violations and the reactions to them. Instead, NEVT argues that who is doing the violations matters greatly and must be accounted for to determine whether a violation will be seen as positive or negative. Unlike other nonverbal interaction models such as discrepancy arousal theory (see LePoire & Burgoon, 1994), NEVT predicts that even an "extreme violation of an expectancy" might be viewed positively if it was committed by a highly rewarding communicator (Burgoon & Hale, 1988, p. 63). That is, if a person you have just met at a club puts their arm around you, and you view this person as highly attractive (both socially and physically), high in credibility, and high in status, you may valence this violation behavior positively. Thus, NEVT suggests that it is not just a matter of the nonverbal behavior violations and the reactions to them. Instead, who is doing the violation matters greatly, and must be accounted for in order to determine whether the violation will be seen as positive or negative.

Nonverbal expectancy violations theory has generated much interest and research. We will mention a few studies based on this theory. Burgoon and Jerold Hale (1988) conducted an experiment in which individuals participated in discussions with friends and with strangers who either increased, reduced, or acted normally regarding immediacy behaviors (especially prox-

Proxemics How people use space to communicate

emics, body orientation, forward lean, eye contact, and open posture). They found that low-immediacy behaviors (i.e., negative violations of expectations such as less eye contact than normal or indirect body/shoulder lean) resulted in lower credibility ratings than high or normal levels of immediacy in both the friends and the stranger conditions. Being less immediate than expected was perceived as communicating detachment, lower intimacy, dissimilarity, and higher dominance. However, being more immediate than normal (e.g., standing closer, leaning forward) was viewed as expressing more intimacy, similarity, and involvement.

Burgoon and Joseph Walther (1990) examined a variety of touch behaviors, proxemics, and postures to determine which are expected or unexpected in interpersonal communication and how expectations are influenced by the source's status, attractiveness, and gender. Some findings were that a handshake is most expected, whereas an arm around the shoulder is least expected. Erect posture is most expected, and tense posture is least expected.

Several studies have examined the role of expectancy violations in different kinds of interpersonal relationships. For example, NEVT was used to study sexual expectations and sexual involvement in initial dating encounters. Previous research suggested that males enter female-initiated first dates with heightened sexual expectations (Mongeau, Hale, Johnson, & Hillis, 1993), and that less sexual intimacy is reported in female-initiated as compared to male-initiated first dates (Mongeau & Johnson, 1995).

Using an experimental design, Paul Mongeau and Colleen Carey (1996) varied the directness in initiating a date. Male and female participants read a scenario in which a female asks a male out on a date to a movie (*female asks*), a female indicates interest in seeing a movie followed immediately by the male asking her on the date (*female hints*), or the male asks the female on the date without the preceding hint (*male asks*). The gender of the target varied; half the participants evaluated the male target and the other half the female target. The extent to which the target took an active role in making the date, measures of dating and sexual expectations, and the target's general level of sexual activity were measured. Mongeau and Carey report that the results of this study were consistent as predicted by expectancy violations theory: "males enter female-initiated first dates with inflated sexual expectations. As a consequence, that less sex occurs on female-initiated first dates is certainly consistent with a negative violation of the males' expectancies" (p. 206).

Kory Floyd and Michael Voloudakis (1999) used NEVT to explore the communication of affection in adult platonic friendships. Their study involved 40 mixed-sex dyads. The first encounter consisted of conversation between the participants. For the second encounter, the researchers asked some participants (confederates) to increase or to decrease their "affectionate involvement" with the naive subject. The researchers hypothesized that unexpected increases in affection would be considered positive expectancy violations, whereas unexpected decreases would be considered negative expectancy violations. The research supported their hypotheses. In addition, naive participants in the low-affection condition saw the confederates as less immediate, less similar to themselves, less composed, and less equal to themselves. Again, these findings support NEVT's prediction that negative expectancy violations can produce negative outcomes.

One study manipulated the reward value of the communicator and the valence and extremity of the violation behavior to explore their effects on student-professor interactions (Lannutti, Laliker, & Hale, 2001). A scenario was created involving a student-professor conversation. An experimental study manipulated the location of a professor's touch (no touch, touch on arm, or touch on thigh), reward value for the professor (e.g., low—"one you dislike and disdain," or high—"one you like and admire"), and sex of the participant (male or female). The sex of the professor was also adjusted so that it was always the opposite sex of the participant. Evaluation of the professor, desire to interact with the professor, and perceptions of sexual harassment were measured.

Nonverbal expectancy violations theory was "partially supported" in this study in that female participants' evaluations of the professor became more negative as the intimacy of touch increased, regardless of the reward value of the professor. The more unexpected the touch, the less favorable the professor and the interaction were evaluated by the female participants (Lannutti, Laliker, & Hale, 2001).

Nonverbal expectancy violations theory continues to generate research; modifications and revisions of the theory are still emerging. NEVT makes us more aware of the influence of our nonverbal behavior (i.e., distance, touch, eye contact, smiling). It suggests that if we engage in nonverbal communication behavior that violates expectations, it might be wise to contemplate our "reward value." Unless our "reward value" is sufficiently high to offset a violation of expectations, it might be wise to rethink our behavior.

INTERACTION ADAPTATION THEORY

Interaction adaptation theory A theory of how we alter our behavior in response to the behavior of another person

Interaction adaptation theory (IAT) was conceptualized to explain behavior that is "mindful, intentional, and symbolic" (Burgoon, LaPoire, & Rosenthal, 1995, p. 11). IAT assumes that adaptation is a systematic pattern of behavior that is in direct response to the interactive pattern of another communicator (Burgoon et al., 1995). Therefore, there are no random adaptations when people interact with each other. This suggests that all adaptation is considered intentional. IAT also assumes that our relationships with each other are based on both verbal and nonverbal messages that are adapted to the behavior of the interaction partner. Adaptation reflects the degree to which we alter our behavior in response to the behavior of another person. Further, adaptation during interaction serves as a signal to the interactants and observers of the interaction as to the nature or basis of the relationship between the two communicators (White, 2008). That is, the way people engage in adaptive behavior during an interaction relays important relational information that can include the type of relationship, degree of positive/negative affect between the interactants, as well as power and status differences.

The two adaptation patterns that people utilize when in an interaction reflect patterns that either **reciprocate** or **compensate**. Adaptation that "reciprocates" reflects matching behavior or reciprocating the behavior of the other person. This is similar to the communication accommodation theory concept of converging our speech patterns to the other person to show liking and affiliation (see Chapter 5). Convergence means we adapt our interaction patterns to match those of the other person. Matching, within the IAT framework, refers to both verbal and nonverbal behavior and is not restricted to just verbal or paraverbal behavior as it is in communication accommodation theory. To illustrate how IAT accommodations function, consider a scenario where a close friend is very upset and discloses to you that their mother is gravely ill. When communicating with this friend, you will probably use matching adaptation reflecting behavior that is somber, empathetic, and caring.

Adaptation that "compensates" reflects the "balancing out" of the other's behavior and seeks to represent the "whole spectrum" of the interaction. An example of this would be a friend who is very excited and calls us to say that they are putting their entire life savings into the buying and selling of real estate based on an investment product that they had purchased from an infomercial they just viewed on television. In this case, our interaction pattern may be one of a cautious, reserved, and skeptical tone, thus not matching the euphoric, excited, and determined patterns of our friend. This concept of compensation is also reflective of the yin and yang concept found in Chinese philosophy. The yin and yang concept reflects the intertwining of opposing forces. In the current example, your behavior is cautious, reserved, and skeptical and is exhibited to compensate for your friend's overly euphoric, excited, and determined behavior.

Although adaptation is considered nonrandom (i.e., intentional), IAT treats interaction adaptation as a primal survival need. That is, we choose our adaptation in a way that satisfies survival needs and seeks to establish important links to other people, thus ensuring or significantly increasing our survival (i.e., strength in numbers). There is more to adaptation than the simple idea that we engage in reciprocating or compensating patterns or we do not. The theory also speaks to the amount to which we engage in adaptation. The degree of adaptation is influenced by both the role we play in society (i.e., societal norms) and idiosyncratic personal preferences. For example, a person who is a mortician will probably have a much more restricted degree of adaptation than a professional athlete due to the fact that societal norms for a mortician's behavior are far more conservative than they are for the professional athlete.

IAT assumes that several main factors (both socially and personally derived) influence a person's needs, wants, and expectations of other people when engaged in interaction. More specifically, when we first encounter someone in conversation, we bring with us a host of **requirements**, **expectations**, and **desires** with regard to the person and the specific interaction conversation. These three components of the theory were originally conceptualized as being hierarchically organized so that "requirements" influence "expectations," which in turn influence "desires." The theory maintains conversational requirements are a person's basic psychological/physiological needs related to approach-avoidance behavior (a.k.a. the fight-or-flight biological activation of the brain). These requirements are believed to be primarily unconscious and are said to influence our conversational expectations. The expectations are formed by societal norms of appropriateness as well as the degree of knowledge that we have developed from past interactions with that specific person.

These expectations, in turn, influence our desires, which are "highly personalized and reflect things such as one's personality and other individual differences" (White, 2008, p. 193). This hierarchical approach was later refuted by the research findings of Floyd and Burgoon (1999). However, the three components, although not hierarchically organized, are believed to be highly interdependent and the requirements, expectations, and desires can be weighted differently based on the specific interaction. In other words, in one interaction, expectations may play more of a role than desires or conversational requirements, whereas in another interaction, another factor may be weighted more heavily. For example, a person may have a great need to avoid a particular person (i.e., conversational requirement) that is so strong that this need for avoidance supersedes our expectations (i.e., what is socially appropriate behavior in that situation) and our desires (i.e., individual interests).

The three components—requirements, expectations, desires—combine to form a unique collection of individualized communication information known as a person's **interaction position**. According to Burgoon et al. (1995), an interaction position represents "a net assessment of what is needed, anticipated, and preferred as the dyadic interaction pattern in a situation" (p. 266). By understanding a person's interaction position, people have better predictability about how one interprets a communication situation and the likely communicative behaviors that they will enact.

Interpersonal adaptation theory offers two basic predictions about a person's response to behavior and is based on the dynamic relationship between the interaction position and the actual behavior that is enacted (Burgoon & Ebesu Hubbard, 2005).

- **P1:** When the interaction position is more positively valenced than the actual behavior, the interpersonal pattern is divergence, compensation, or maintenance.
- **P2:** When the actual behavior is more positively valenced than the interaction position, the anticipated interpersonal pattern is convergence, matching, or reciprocity.

In terms of how this would work in explaining communication, consider the example of a supervisor who is about to conduct a meeting with a subordinate concerning the quarterly performance review of the subordinate. The supervisor has, throughout their career, engaged in many conversations with subordinates concerning both positive and negative aspects of their performance. According to IAT, any given conversation is influenced by the supervisor's psychological and/or physiological needs at any given time. These may take the form of the need to mentor, need for affiliation, or need to control. This would constitute the supervisor's conversational "requirements." Second, the supervisor has an "expectation" about how employees generally respond to negative evaluations and even more specific expectations about how a particular employee will respond to such information (e.g., anger, sorrow, remorse, embarrassment). Finally, the supervisor has a "desire" for employees to be open, involved, and eager to make needed changes to improve performance. These three components constitute the supervisor's "interaction position."

Imagine that a subordinate who has had a history of poor performance and a generally negative attitude is about to come into the supervisor's office for the performance evaluation meeting. Based on the supervisor's interaction position described earlier, the supervisor would expect a hostile and generally emotionally charged interaction. Therefore, the supervisor would prepare herself to console the subordinate and try to give some comforting words. However, imagine further that when the subordinate arrives for the review, he is proactive in strategies to improve his performance and optimistic about his future contribution to the department and the organization as a whole. Interaction adaptation theory predicts that the supervisor will have an interaction style of convergence, matching, and reciprocity due to the fact that the subordinate was more positively valenced than the supervisor's interaction position. Thus, P2 is what would be predicted for such a communication situation.

According to White (2008), important research directions in the application of interaction adaptation theory include romantic and intimate relationships and the particular communicative exchanges that occur within these relationships (e.g., problematic interactions). For example, when studying deception in interpersonal interactions, White and Burgoon (2001) found support for IAT in that the interaction position of both deceivers and truth-tellers influenced their initial behavior. That is, both deceivers and truth-tellers were affected by the behavior of the interaction partner.

STRENGTHS AND WEAKNESSES OF IAT

One of the many strengths of IAT is that it conceptualizes expectancies as being formed by personal and biological factors as well as the degree to which these factors are further influenced by actual communicative behavior. IAT can be considered a cousin of expectancy violations theory discussed earlier in this chapter as it accounts not only for the expectations of the communicators but also integrates actual communicative behavior in the prediction of interaction behavior. The primary weakness of IAT lies in the fact that it is a relatively new theory with modest empirical support. However, the evidence that does exist lends support for the assumptions of IAT and holds exciting implications for interpersonal scholars.

NONVERBAL IMMEDIACY

Imagine the following scenario. You have been waiting at the doctor's office for about half an hour and have finally been called into the examination room. Your level of anxiety is already high, as you wonder if your lower abdominal pain and discomfort is serious. After waiting another ten minutes in the examination room, you hear a knock on the door and the doctor enters. The doctor looks at you very briefly and then turns away. He takes a seat at the other end of the examination room. He appears somewhat tense as he asks you to identify the nature of your medical concern. During his questioning, he speaks with a dull and monotonous voice, does not smile very much if at all, uses very few gestures, and avoids eye contact throughout the interview. He asks you to sit on the examination table but fails to mention what will happen next. As the medical interview progresses, you become more worried and concerned than you were before the doctor came in.

Perhaps you can relate to the scenario outlined. Many patients describe such experiences during initial interaction with their physician. Patients often describe such interactions as being uncomfortable at best and frightening at worst, even if their medical condition was easily diagnosed and treated. Quite often patients delay return visits to the doctor or seek alternative health-care options rather than subject themselves to a repeat of this scenario. The anxiety and frustration can happen in communication encounters in other contexts as well, from close interpersonal interactions (such as a first date) to relatively impersonal communication interactions (such as communication with a sales-person in an automobile dealership).

The degree of closeness between individuals is an important factor influencing the ease of communication. Researchers have identified and labeled a set of nonverbal behaviors that influence the degree of perceived closeness. **Immediacy behaviors** is the term used to describe a set of messages (both verbal and nonverbal) that signal feelings of warmth, closeness, and involvement with another person (Andersen, 1999, p. 187). Immediacy behaviors can result in positive or negative interpersonal communication outcomes, depending on how they are manifested (Richmond & McCroskey, 2000b).

Immediacy behaviors
Messages that signal feelings of warmth, closeness, and involvement with another person

Although originally conceived by the psychologist Albert Mehrabian (1971), research and theory-building efforts in identifying and understanding the impact of nonverbal immediacy has come largely from communication scholars such as Peter Andersen, Janis Andersen, Virginia Richmond, and James McCroskey among others. Peter Andersen (1985, 1999) suggested the following four functions of immediacy behaviors:

- Immediacy behaviors signal to others that we are *available* for communication and make others feel included in the interaction.
- Immediacy behaviors signal *involvement*—that we are interested in those with whom we are communicating. It makes receiver(s) feel that we are closer to them. Immediacy behaviors that signal involvement can be something as benign as a wave or as intimate as a kiss or prolonged eye contact.
- Immediacy behaviors *stimulate our senses* both psychologically and physiologically. Andersen argued that blood pressure, heart rate, and brain activity are increased when we receive immediacy cues from another person.
- Immediacy behaviors communicate *closeness and warmth.* In positive relationships immediacy behaviors (such as looking another person in the eye or smiling) bring people closer. Lack of nonverbal immediacy can do just the opposite.

What are nonverbal immediacy behaviors? A cluster of several nonverbal behaviors constitute what we now call "nonverbal immediacy behaviors." These include tactile (touch) behaviors, proxemic (personal space), oculesic displays including eye contact, kinesic (body motion and movement) behaviors including facial expressions, smiling behavior, head nods, and body position, and paralinguistics or vocalics (i.e., how a person says something, not what they say).

One especially powerful set of immediacy cues is associated with eye behavior, specifically *eye contact* and *gaze*. When someone locks eyes with you, they offer an invitation to engage in communication and to interact. Gaze functions as a primary immediacy cue in a number of contexts including relational and instructional communication.

Proxemics, the use of personal space, is the most frequently studied nonverbal immediacy cue; closer proxemic distances convey greater feelings of immediacy. Recall in our earlier example that the physician sat at the far end of the room, conveying a sense of avoidance rather than immediacy. Other proxemically oriented immediacy behaviors include interacting on the same physical plane (the same level) as your receiver and leaning forward when communicating with another.

Personal space Zones of space that surround us: intimate, casual-personal, socioconsultative, public

Touch has also been identified as a powerful nonverbal immediacy cue, especially in intimate relationships. Perceptions of touch, however, are modified by the nature of the interpersonal relationship (the level of intimacy), the culture a person comes from (some cultures use more touch than others), personal norms concerning touch, and the context in which the individuals are communicating (on the job or in a romantic setting, for example).

Kinesics, body motion and movements, comprise a fourth set of immediacy behaviors. Kinesic behaviors that communicate immediacy include facial expressions such as smiling, head nods (signaling agreement), gestures that show approval, open body positions (e.g., arms open, head up, legs not crossed), and speaking with someone while facing them directly (as opposed to turning away from them).

Paralinguistics (vocalics—not what we say, but *how* we use our voice to express feelings) is a fifth set of immediacy cues. Vocal synchrony (adjusting your paralinguistic style to fit or match the person with whom you are communicating) is another type of vocalic immediacy cue. Perhaps you can recall an instance when you spoke more softly to match the tones of the person with whom you were talking. One of the authors recalls that his father occasionally took on the accent of the person he was talking to in an effort to promote immediacy and to achieve vocal convergence (see our discussion of communication accommodation theory in Chapter 5). When discussing this cluster of nonverbal immediacy behaviors, it is important to point out that individuals do not receive these behaviors in a fragmented fashion.

What causes a person to communicate using this cluster of immediacy behaviors? Peter Andersen (1999, 1998, 1985) suggested several antecedents that either promote or dampen the exhibition of immediacy behaviors. A powerful antecedent (cause) of exhibiting nonverbal immediacy (or not) is a person's *culture*. Certain cultures have been called "contact cultures," and people from these cultures tend to use more nonverbal immediacy behaviors when they communicate. That is, they may use more gestures, touch each other more, and stand closer together. A second cause of immediacy behavior is the *valence of the interpersonal relationship*, which refers to whether the relationship is seen as positive or negative. We tend to exhibit of a lot of immediacy behaviors (e.g., closer distance, greater use of gestures, greater eye contact) with someone whom we like. A third cause of immediacy behavior is the *perception of the stage of the relationship;* as relationships develop, more immediacy cues are exhibited. *Individual differences and traits* constitute another cause of immediacy behaviors. Factors such as biological sex, orientation to touch, and communication and personality traits can influence the exhibition of nonverbal immediacy behaviors. *The nature of the situation* or environment can influence expressions of immediacy. Touching someone in public may be perceived as situationally inappropriate; however, the same type of touch might be seen as appropriate if you were in more private surroundings. Finally, the *temporary state* of the individual can influence the exhibition of immediacy behaviors. Feeling physically ill, in a "bad mood," or "stressed out" can dampen one's exhibition of nonverbal immediacy cues.

What are the consequences of engaging in nonverbal immediacy cues? A great deal of communication research during the last several decades supports the potency of employing nonverbal immediacy in a variety of contexts. One of the contexts in which the exhibition of nonverbal immediacy has a significant impact is instructional communication. In one of the first studies to introduce the immediacy construct in the communication discipline, Janis Andersen (1979) found that teacher immediacy favorably influenced students' attitudes toward the teacher and the course. Highly immediate teachers increased student liking for both high school and college courses (Flax, Kearney, McCroskey, & Richmond, 1986). Teachers highly skilled in immediacy behaviors were perceived as higher in competence, trustworthiness, and caring (Thweatt & McCroskey, 1998). The influence of teacher immediacy does not appear to be bound by culture. Increases in teacher immediacy resulted in increased learning across four cultures including mainland American (U.S.), Australian, Finnish, and Puerto Rican (McCroskey, Sallinen, Fayer, Richmond, & Barraclough, 1996). Thus, when students perceive that their instructor employs nonverbal immediacy they have more positive feelings for the instructor, more positive feelings for the course, and report more cognitive learning ((Witt, Wheeless, & Allen, 2004).

Research in the health-care context has also pointed to the advantages of nonverbal immediacy behaviors. Patients' perceptions of their physicians' nonverbal immediacy behaviors influence their reported satisfaction with those physicians (Conlee, Olvera, & Vagim, 1993). In addition, physicians who were perceived as immediate had patients who reported lower levels of fear (Richmond, Smith, Heisel, & McCroskey, 2001). Doctor–patient relationships might yield very different outcomes if the physician used more nonverbal immediacy behaviors. Parents' perceptions of their pediatrician's nonverbal immediacy, in relationship to their communication satisfaction with the physician, feelings, emotions, and acceptance of their doctor's advice and recommendations was studied (LaBelle, Odenweller, & Myers, 2015). The results revealed that parents who saw their pediatrician as nonverbally immediate, as well as clear and receptive to them, reported greater communication satisfaction (i.e., greater positivity toward the doctor in fulfilling their needs) and affective learning with that doctor. These results suggest the importance of a physician employing nonverbal immediacy behaviors, appearing relaxed and approachable, and recognizing parents' input during an office visit. In such situations, parents will leave the visit to the doctor more satisfied and more likely to follow the doctor's recommendations (LaBelle, et al., 2015, p. 66).

Nonverbal immediacy also operates in the organizational context, especially in superior–subordinate communication. Immediacy stimulates a reciprocity of immediacy; subordinates report more satisfaction with supervisors who exhibit nonverbal immediacy and engage in more immediacy behaviors themselves (Richmond & McCroskey, 2000a). Supervisors who use immediacy cues make subordinates feel more valued, respected, and relationally attractive (Koermer, Goldstein, & Fortson, 1993).

Marital relationships also appear to be influenced by immediacy cues. Research has found that "individuals who engage in nonverbal immediacy behaviors tend to be more inclined to be liked by their marital partners than are those who are not nonverbally immediate" (Hinkle, 1999, p. 87). In addition, use of immediacy behaviors and liking for your spouse appear to persist throughout the duration of a marriage (Hinkle, 1999).

COGNITIVE VALENCE THEORY: AN EXTENSION OF NONVERBAL IMMEDIACY

Working from an interactionist approach to studying communication and relationships, Peter Andersen (1999) considered the question, "When one person increases intimacy or immediacy, how can you explain the response of their partner?" (p. 454). Cognitive valence theory (CVT) maintains that when a person in an interaction perceives an increase in immediacy behaviors "cognitive schemata" are activated. Cognitive schemata are expectations about the consequences of behaving in a certain way that allow people to interpret, explain, and act upon information (Andersen, 1998, p. 47).

Cognitive valence theory A perceived increase in immediacy behaviors from one person in a relationship activates expectations

An important component in CVT is *arousal*. Arousal is "the degree to which a person is stimulated or activated" (Andersen, 1999, p. 161). When arousal is increased, there is a tendency to engage in more nonverbal immediacy behaviors, which builds even greater levels of arousal. Levels of arousal that are too low produce virtually no change in the relationship. However, too much arousal can lead to negative relational outcomes. CVT suggests that moderate levels of arousal (found in most interactions) are most likely to activate cognitive schemata.

CVT suggests that relationships usually develop when individuals communicate using immediacy; that is, one person sends messages using immediacy cues, and the other person reciprocates. Interactions such as these are called "positively valenced." Sometimes, however, immediacy behaviors exhibited by one person are not seen favorably by another; they are instead "negatively valenced." CVT also addresses the question, "What happens when efforts to increase relational closeness by using nonverbal immediacy are rejected?" If the cognitive schemata are positively valenced, the theory states positive relationship outcomes will result; if cognitive schemata are negatively valenced, negative relationship outcomes are more likely.

According to CVT, six cognitive schemata (similar to the factors that influence immediacy discussed earlier) form the basis of whether the relationship will become positively or negatively changed as a result of an increase in immediacy and intimacy (Andersen, 1999).

1. **Cultural Appropriateness.** Cultures vary in the degree to which they use immediacy behaviors. As we have mentioned, some cultures use touch more than others. Noncontact cultures (Japan, for instance) prefer little touch; contact cultures (such as Greece) prefer greater amounts of touch. When communicating with a person from Japan, using a great deal of touch would be culturally inappropriate and thus negatively valenced.

2. **Personal Predispositions.** Personality and communication traits (such as dogmatism, self-esteem, communication apprehension, and interaction involvement), as well as personal predispositions such as touch-avoidance, influence reactions to increases in immediacy behaviors. For example, an increase in eye contact might be seen as positive for an extrovert, while the same behavior may be negatively valenced for the person high in communication apprehension.

3. **Interpersonal Valence.** According to Andersen (1999), "interpersonal valence is the evaluation of another person's qualities, not one's relationship with that person" (p. 232). CVT suggests that an increase in immediacy by someone who has qualities we admire (for example, credibility or physical attractiveness) will be positively valenced, whereas the same behavior will be negatively valenced if it comes from someone whose qualities we evaluate less positively.

4. **Relational Appropriateness.** These schemata deal with expectancies about where one individual thinks a relationship should be heading, the "relational trajectory." According to CVT, nonverbal immediacy behaviors that correspond to the anticipation of greater relationship intimacy should be seen positively. According to Andersen (1999), "the key to relational success is to anticipate your partner's desired relational trajectory and to behave accordingly" (pp. 232–233). If your relational partner has expressed a desire for the relationship to become more intimate, then engaging in immediacy behaviors should result in positive outcomes. If you engage in more touch, greater eye gaze, and less proxemic distance, your partner will likely judge those immediacy behaviors positively because they fall along his or her perceived relational trajectory (i.e., the desire for increased intimacy). On the other hand, immediacy behaviors that do not correspond to another person's anticipated relational trajectory will likely be seen negatively.

5. **Situational Appropriateness.** Immediacy behaviors that are inappropriate to the situation or context are likely to be negatively valenced. For example, behavior that would be acceptable in a romantic restaurant could be considered inappropriate in a college classroom.

6. **Psychological or Physical State.** These schemata "represent intrapersonal, internal dispositions (Andersen, 1999, p. 235) and refer to our moods, our temporal physical conditions (e.g., having a bad cold or flu), and temporal emotional and psychological states such as feeling happy or sad, tired, or excited. Getting a costly traffic ticket, receiving an unexpected grade of "A" on a course paper, receiving a compliment on your appearance from a valued other, or having a fight with your roommate can influence how you will react to immediacy and intimacy behaviors. CVT suggests that, in general, positive psychological or physical states are related to positive reactions to immediacy and intimacy behaviors, whereas negative psychological or physical states are related to negative reactions to immediacy and intimacy behaviors.

If the immediacy behaviors exhibited by person A match person B's six cognitive schemata, those immediacy behaviors will be positively valenced and positive relationship outcomes will ensue. Relationships develop based on a number of factors, including the degree of preferred closeness. CVT suggests that for relationships to become closer and more satisfying, one must match the relationship partner's cultural, personal, interpersonal, situational, state, and relational schemata (Andersen, 1998, 1999).

SUMMARY

Nonverbal behavior functions best in communicating affect; it is highly believable. The meaning of nonverbal behaviors depends on the communication context. Similarly, our expectations of appropriate nonverbal behaviors depend on the situation and the relationship between individuals. The authors believe symbolic activity is a necessary condition for nonverbal behavior to be considered communicative. Without an intention to convey a message, the behavior is usually a symptom. We use nonverbal communication to perform a number of important functions: to express messages that are uncomfortable to present verbally, to form impressions, to clarify and establish the nature of the relationship between the people who are communicating, to regulate the interaction between people, to persuade people by conveying a basis for trust, and to reinforce and modify verbal messages. Research on nonverbal immediacy and expectancy violations helps us understand the effects of various nonverbal behaviors. Our responses to violations of expectations are determined by our expectancies, our interpretation and evaluation of the behavior, the valence of the violation (positive or negative), and the reward level of the person with whom we are communicating. These ideas were explored in the theories covered: expectancy violations theory, interaction adaptation theory, nonverbal immediacy, and cognitive valence theory.

KEY TERMS

Cognitive valence theory

Emotional leakage

Eye behavior

Immediacy behaviors

Interaction adaptation theory

Nonverbal expectancy violations theory

Nonverbal response matching

Personal space

Proxemics

Self-monitoring of expressive behavior

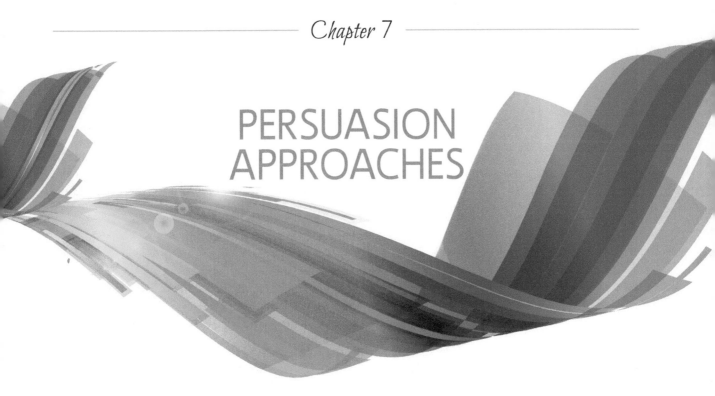

Chapter 7

PERSUASION APPROACHES

CONCEPTUALIZING PERSUASION

At its most basic level, **persuasion** *may be thought of as an attitude and/or behavioral change that results from a message designed to alter beliefs about a proposal.* A proposal is a recommended course of action. For instance, "We should give a piece of land in our state back to Native Americans," or, on a more personal level, "Let's go to the movies tonight." Attitude is defined as how favorably we evaluate something. This is represented by feelings such as good versus bad, right versus wrong, nice versus awful, valuable versus worthless. An example of an attitude toward a proposal might be, "I feel giving that piece of land to the Native Americans is good and the right thing to do." A belief is a perception of how two or more things are related. In terms of persuasion, beliefs are perceptions of the consequences of a proposal. For instance, "If we return the land to the Native Americans, a number of farmers will have to be relocated."

If a persuader wants to influence a specific behavior, he or she must use messages to create a favorable attitude. If we want to influence someone to sign a petition, we need to address the individual's attitude toward the object of the petition. If the petition proposes returning a tract of land to Native Americans, persuasion involves presenting a message that will help the person form beliefs in support of giving land to a Native American tribe; for example, "A previous wrong would be corrected." If beliefs about the proposal are positive, the attitude toward the proposal will be favorable. Of course, if beliefs are negative, the

Attitude How favorably we evaluate something

Belief A perception of how two or more things are related

attitude will be unfavorable. A mixture of positive and negative beliefs results in a moderately favorable or unfavorable attitude, depending on the proportion of positive to negative beliefs.

By persuading a person to favor a proposal, a persuader provides justification for the receiver to choose to behave in a particular manner. In order to have persuasion and not some other type of *social influence,* the receiver must feel free, not constrained, to choose. Thus, **perceived choice** is a distinguishing characteristic of persuasion. Persuasion uses symbols to modify an attitude to achieve a particular behavior. Attitude represents a predisposition to behave in a certain way. In persuasion the source is willing to let success depend on attitudinal influence.

In other types of social influence, the source is unwilling to allow behavior to be controlled by attitudes. Instead, the source applies force or pressure as a substitute for the motivation provided by attitudes. Coercion involves the use of physical aggression and verbal aggression (for example, threats, insults, ridicule, and profanity) as substitutes for attitudinal influence. If coercion is used, no choice is perceived: "The person is holding a gun to my head, so I must sign the petition."

Coercion Source applies force or pressure as a substitute for the motivation provided by attitudes

Placing persuasion within the framework **Belief Change → Attitude Change → Behavior Change** helps to verify whether *persuasion* or some other type of social influence took place. Isolating behavior change alone is not evidence of persuasion. For example, we might encourage a friend who dislikes fishing to go on a fishing trip by saying, "This trip is a chance to renew our friendship" (an example of compliance). If the person enjoys the experience (forms positive beliefs about fishing), the attitude toward fishing becomes more favorable. However, there was no persuasion in this situation because it was not a message from one person that caused the other to change an attitude. The fishing trip was not a message because it was not an intentional exchange of symbols. Catching a large fish on the trip was not symbolic activity; fish do not manipulate symbols to stimulate a feeling of exhilaration. Instead, engaging in the behavior produced an internal change in attitude. A message is required for persuasion to take place; no message about fishing was presented before the behavior. A person can be induced through coercion or compliance to behave in a certain manner that can lead to attitude change. However, the steps involved in coercion or compliance are often the reverse of the belief-to-attitude-to-behavior model and are not examples of persuasion.

SELF-AWARENESS AND PERSUASION

In studying persuasion, one can form the impression that the persuader is constantly thinking: analyzing the receiver, situation, and topic; composing the message a split second before delivering it; continually monitoring feedback from the receiver; and adjusting the message, along with delivery, to the feedback. The idea of the persuader as so completely alert and actively controlling the shape, content, and sound of the message is rarely the case (for a review see Roloff, 1980).

Individuals seem to follow a cognitive course of "least resistance" in communication, which leads them to rely on previously prepared communication plans. A plan is a meaningful sequence of events a person expects in a situation as either an observer or a participant. You may recall we discussed this concept in Chapter 1. A person may have found that a certain message was effective in a given situation. In a similar situation, the person simply recalls the message and repeats it, modifying perhaps a word or two. Persuaders often essentially rely on communication plans, reading from a previously prepared script. This requires very little effort and allows the source to communicate on "automatic pilot."

The idea that receivers are not very attentive, that their minds wander away from the message, is an ancient one. Add to it the recent notion of a source similarly preoccupied, and we have a model of persuasion where the source and receiver are physically present in the situation but mentally "in-and-out." This may be more the rule than the exception. One reason why this may be the case is that our personalities predispose us to prefer certain situations. Given a choice, we approach some situations and avoid others. Thus, we usually find ourselves in familiar situations. Because we are seldom in an unusual situation, we are seldom without a plan. That is, having been in certain types of situations virtually guarantees that we possess a plan that has enjoyed at least some previous success. Among other things, this suggests that we do not do much composing of original messages. We usually can recall a communication plan that is appropriate. If not, we revise one that is close to what is needed.

APPROACHES TO UNDERSTANDING PERSUASION

In this chapter we will focus on several approaches and theories that have stimulated the most persuasion research in the field of communication. Then we will turn to theories explaining how to resist persuasion.

LOOKING AT THE SOURCE, MESSAGE, CHANNEL, AND RECEIVER: THE VARIABLE-ANALYTIC APPROACH

A good deal of persuasion research, especially research from 1940 through 1969, explored specific variables in the persuasion process because they seemed to be important—not because they were part of a particular persuasion theory. Experiments targeted numerous variables relating to the source, message, channel, and receiver in persuasion. Much of the early research tried to determine how sources who are more and less believable (source credibility) influence attitude change and what factors influence source credibility (Andersen & Clevenger, 1963). Later in this chapter, we will examine three approaches to the study of source credibility.

There is a large body of research on the message in persuasion (for summaries, see Burgoon & Bettinghaus, 1980; Cronkhite, 1969). At least three categories seem relevant: message structure, message appeals, and language. The message structure research investigated such variables as whether the strongest argument in a message should be placed first (anticlimactic arrangement), last (climactic), or in the middle of the message (pyramidal) (Gulley & Berlo, 1956); whether two-sided messages are more persuasive than one-sided messages (Hovland, 1957); whether the opposition's argument should be refuted before or after presenting one's own case (Thistlethwaite, Kamenetsky, & Schmidt, 1956); and whether the speaker or receiver should draw conclusions from arguments in the speech (Tubbs, 1968). Message appeals explored were the use of fear or anxiety appeals, evidence, reward appeals (McCroskey & Wright, 1971), humor (Gruner, 1965, 1970), logic (Scott & Hurt, 1978), emotion (Ruechelle, 1958), and self-esteem (Spillman, 1979). Language variables included language intensity, use of qualifiers for arguments (Feezel, 1974), rhetorical questions (Zillman, 1972), opinionated language (Infante, 1975b), and obscenity (Bostrom, Baseheart, & Rossiter, 1973). We will examine some of the research in a later section of this chapter.

The channel in persuasion has received a limited amount of research. A major focus has been on comparing live, tape-recorded, and written messages for differences in persuasiveness (Knower, 1935; Wilkie, 1934).

The receiver in persuasion has been studied in a variety of ways: sex (Scheidel, 1963), ego involvement (Sereno & Bodaken, 1972), and attitude intensity. Probably the major way the receiver has been studied is in terms of personality. Some of the traits investigated have been persuasibility (Hovland & Janis, 1959), authoritarianism (Adorno, Frenkel-Brunswik, Levinson, & Sanford, 1950), dogmatism (Rokeach, 1960), self-esteem (Infante, 1976), richness of fantasy (Infante, 1975c), and tolerance of ambiguity (Infante, 1975a). Some of this research will be discussed in the next section.

These are just a sample of the persuasion variables that have been investigated. Despite the vast amount of research, some conclusions remain tentative and subject to qualifications. For instance, a message that tries to frighten the receiver will vary in its persuasiveness, depending on how important the topic is, how believable the source is, and how specific the solutions presented are. Thus, a high fear message can be more persuasive than a low fear message when the source is highly believable and the solution for the problem is very specific, but only if the topic is important to the receiver.

RESEARCH ON MESSAGE VARIABLES

Throughout the last four decades, communication theorists have identified several message variables that appear to influence our reaction to persuasive messages (Sussman, 1973). Two will be examined here: fear appeals and evidence.

FearAppeals The study of fear-arousing message content has its roots in antiquity. Aristotle discussed the use of fear and other emotions in the *Rhetoric*. Aristotle suggested that speakers must understand the emotional predispositions of their audience and then use that knowledge as one of the "available means of persuasion." Modern research considers fear appeals to be arguments that take the following form:

1. You (the listener) are vulnerable to a threat.
2. If you are vulnerable, then you should take action to reduce your vulnerability.
3. If you are to reduce your vulnerability, then you must accept the recommendations contained in this message.
4. Therefore, you should accept the recommendations contained in this message. (Boster & Mongeau, 1984, p. 371)

A typical fear appeal might be a variation on the following:

1. Smoking has been found to increase the chances for disease and death.
2. Because you do not want disease or death, you must do something to prevent them.
3. An effective way to prevent these outcomes is to stop smoking.
4. Therefore, you must stop smoking.

During an average evening, we may witness several fear-arousing messages in television commercials. From smoke detectors to life insurance, to the latest pharmaceutical drugs, advertisers make frequent use of the fear appeal to influence consumers.

The contemporary study of fear in persuasion can be traced to the work of Irving Janis and Seymour Feshbach (1953). In their seminal study, high school students were randomly assigned to one of two experimental groups who heard messages on dental hygiene. For one group, a *moderate fear* appeal was used; for the other, a *high fear* appeal was created. A third group of students was also tested. They served as a *control group* and were exposed to an entirely different message on the structure and operation of the human eye. The high fear appeal urged dental care and recommended vigorous and proper brushing of the teeth; pictures of rotting gums and decaying teeth accompanied the message. In the moderate fear appeal, these pictures were omitted. Janis and Feshbach discovered that the moderate fear appeal was more effective than the high fear appeal in changing students' attitudes toward proper brushing and dental care.

These findings led to several decades of experimental research testing the relationship between the level of fear in a message and attitude change. Some studies discovered the opposite outcome: attitude change was more likely when a high fear appeal was used (Beck & Davis, 1978; see Miller, 1963, for a summary and analysis of the early research). Because experimenters sometimes arrived at different results when they studied fear appeals, scientists tried to reconcile these contradictions.

Six explanations of fear appeal effects have been offered (Boster & Mongeau, 1984). The **drive explanation** suggests that the fear aroused by a persuasive message creates a state of drive, which receivers find unpleasant. Individuals experiencing this state of drive are motivated to reduce it by changing their attitudes and/or behaviors. According to the drive explanation, the greater the amount of fear in a message, the greater the attitude change in the direction recommended by the message.

The **resistance explanation** finds that as perceived fear in a message decreases, individuals' attitudes and/or behaviors will move closer to those recommended in the message. The rationale is that receivers will pay attention to messages low in threatening content; they will resist more threatening messages. Low fear appeals are less threatening than high fear appeals. Thus, messages containing low fear appeals are more likely to be heard than messages containing high fear appeals.

According to the **curvilinear hypothesis**, when receivers are either very fearful or very unafraid, little attitude or behavior change results. High levels of fear are so strong that individuals block them out; low levels are too weak to produce the desired effect. Messages containing *moderate* amounts of fear-arousing content are most effective in producing attitudinal and/or behavior change.

The **parallel processing explanation** suggests that fear-arousing messages activate fear control and danger control processes in listeners. *Fear control* is a coping process by which receivers strive to reduce the fear created by the message. *Danger control* refers to a problem-solving process in which listeners search for information on how to deal with the threat presented. These two processes interact to influence message acceptance. According to the parallel response explanation, when a fear-arousing message primarily activates the *danger control* process, a *high* fear appeal will most influence attitudes and/or behaviors. When a fear-arousing message primarily activates the *fear control* process, a *low* fear appeal is most influential.

The **protection motivation explanation** states that a receiver's attitude toward the topic is a result of the amount of "protection motivation" produced by the message. Protection motivation refers to receivers' drives to avoid or protect themselves from a threat. As protection motivation increases, conformity to attitudes and/or behaviors recommended in the message also increases. Thus, the greater the fear in a message: (a) the more likely a threat will occur; and (b) the greater the ability to deal with the threat by following the recommendations provided in the message; thus (c) the greater the attitude and/or behavioral change in the direction of the message.

The sixth explanation is labeled the **threat control explanation**. Reactions to fear appeals depend on logical, not emotional, factors. A fear-arousing message stimulates *response efficacy* and *personal efficacy* processes in listeners. Response efficacy refers to the receiver's perception of how effective the recommended attitudes or actions will be in reducing or eliminating the threat. Personal efficacy refers to whether or not the receiver is capable of taking the actions recommended by the message. These two responses combine to produce threat control. Threat control is a person's perceived probability of success in controlling the threat. This explanation suggests that, as threat control increases, listeners will adopt attitudes more closely corresponding to the recommendations of the message. As fear increases in a message, so too should the amount of attitude and/or behavioral change in the listener.

Boster and Mongeau concluded that all six explanations were less than adequate in explaining the results of experiments studying fear-arousing messages and persuasion. A more comprehensive approach to understanding how fear appeals work was offered by Kim Witte (1992, 1994) which combines components of the drive, parallel processing, and protection motivation explanations. We will now describe this model.

WITTE'S EXTENDED PARALLEL PROCESS MODEL: AN EXTENSION OF PREVIOUS RESEARCH ON FEAR AROUSAL AND PERSUASION

Witte realized that the influence of fear-arousing messages on persuasion was more complicated than first realized, even after the significant theoretical contributions of Boster and Mongeau with their six explanations of fear appeal effects. Witte reasoned that other factors impact the relationship between fear appeals and attitude and behavior change. To that end, he developed the **extended parallel process model** (EPPM) (Witte, 1992). This model identifies conditions in which fear appeals are effective, but also when they may not work.

In order to resolve the inconsistencies observed in previous research, Witte suggests that some factors need to be reconsidered, and others added, in order to better predict whether the use of fear-arousing messages will create or stimulate behavioral change. In particular, the EPPM combines the drive, parallel processing, and protection motivation explanations described earlier into a new model labeled the extended parallel process model.

The EPPM adds factors identified as threat, danger control, fear control, perceived efficacy, perceived response efficacy, and perceived self-efficacy to develop a new model in order to more effectively predict the effects of fear inducing messages. One of the key elements in the model is labeled *threat* which is defined as a "danger or harm that exists in the environment whether we know it or not" (Witte, Cameron, McKeon, & Berkowitz, 1996, p. 320).

In its most basic explanation, EPPM suggests that fear appeals will cause individuals to take action, but only if the fear arousing message convinces the receiver that they are susceptible to the given threat. *Perceived efficacy* is the belief that there is a definite course of action which the individual can take to avoid the threat. The type of response to the fear appeal depends upon their degree of perceived self-efficacy to avert the threat. Self-efficacy is the belief that the message receiver is able to engage in, or perform, the recommendations offered in the message to avert the threat (Wong & Capella, 2009).

The first scenario suggests that the message receiver believes that the threat to them is low, insignificant, or irrelevant. As a consequence, they will likely not experience fear, and thus will not respond to the fear appeal. If, however, the individual perceives that a threat does exist, they will likely experience fear. It is then that they will either engage in danger control or fear control, depending upon their level of perceived efficacy (Witte & Allen, 2000).

If an individual perceives a high threat, and perceived self-efficacy is high, then they will likely engage in *danger control* which focuses on the solutions to the threat which tends to reduce the fear. They will begin to think about the recommendations offered in the message, and will likely adopt at least a few of them to control the danger.

If, however, individuals challenge the recommendations offered in the message, and do not experience perceived efficacy, that is, they do not believe that there is a clear course of action they can take to avoid the threat, then they will likely engage in *fear control* which focuses on the problem, not the solution. And, as Gass and Seiter (2014) suggest, people who engage in fear control often engage in "denial, avoidance, or panic" (p. 288). An example of fear control regarding a message designed to persuade an individual to use sunscreen might include denial (e.g., "I'm not at risk for getting skin cancer, it won't happen to me"), avoidance (e.g., "This is just too scary, I'm simply not going to think about it"), or even reactance (e.g., "They're just trying to manipulate me, I'm going to ignore them") (Witte & Allen, 2000, p. 594).

Additionally, another set of factors must also be considered when employing fear arousing messages. According to EPPM, both perceived response efficacy and perceived self-efficacy need to be stimulated. *Perceived response efficacy* refers to how much the receiver believes in the recommendations of the message, while *perceived self-efficacy* refers to whether the receiver believes that she or he has the ability to engage in the recommended course of action.

For a fear appeal to be successful, the fear arousing message needs to be crafted in such a way that the receiver feels vulnerable to the given threat, and the fear appeal message needs to stimulate danger, rather than fear, control. This is the essential recommendation of EPPM as messages which prompt danger control usually lead receivers to take positive actions to remove the threat. In sum, using high threat and high efficacy persuasive messages are most effective, while low threat and low efficacy messages are the least effective in producing behavioral change (Witte & Allen, 2000). Thus, Gass and Seiter recommend that when using fear appeals in persuasion, "a persuader must provide workable, practical remedies, thereby triggering danger control and constructive responses" (2014, p. 288).

A study by Wong and Capella (2009) employed the tenets of EPPM in order to examine antismoking threat and efficacy appeals on intentions to stop smoking cigarettes. Recognizing that a limitation to fear appeal studies was the reliance on primarily text-based messages, the researchers sought to explore whether video-based television health-oriented PSA's (i.e., public service announcements/advertisements) would be effective in motivating behavioral change especially regarding smoking cessation.

Two television ads were used. The first presented the harms done by smoking to the brain by showing blood clots in a smoker's brain, and further suggesting that smoking leads to strokes, cancer, and blindness. This ad invoked the "fear of disease and/or death." The second ad invoked "fear of social rejection" by showing how smoking is unattractive and attracts social disapproval. A high and low threat message was created for each ad.

In addition to the threats contained in both ads, the ads also manipulated the efficacy appeals which provided solutions to the threat to help smokers quit. One ad was a commercial for a nicotine lozenge as a substitute for smoking, while the other ad discussed how "Chuck" used a smoker's helpline to deal with cigarette cravings after quitting which recommended activities such as taking a walk, eating an apple, or taking a nap (Wong & Capella, 2009). Adult smokers were the participants in the study who were assigned to watch either the high threat or low threat ad, followed by either an ad for the use of the nicotine lozenge, an ad recommending the use of the smokers "quit-line," or no ad at all. After viewing the respective ads, participants responded to scales measuring their intentions to quit smoking, intentions to seek help to quit, the effectiveness of the ad, and how much threat they perceived in the ad.

The results suggested that intentions to quit smoking were highest for those "who felt at risk because of their smoking and felt confident that calling the quit-line or using the nicotine lozenge would make quitting easier" (*Communication Currents, NCA*, Vol. *4*, Issue *1*, February 2009, *http://www.natcom. org/CommCurrentsArticle.aspx?id=910*). For smokers not ready to quit, "it was important for them to both feel at risk because of their smoking and confident in the solution promoted to help them quit successfully" (*Communication Currents, NCA*, Vol. *4*, Issue *1*, February 2009, *http://www.natcom.org/Comm CurrentsArticle.aspx?id=910)*. These findings underscore the necessity of creating messages which present both the threats and risks of smoking, and the strategies for quitting, both components of EPPM.

Evidence in Messages When we hear the term *evidence,* images of attorneys arguing cases come to mind. Television shows such as *Law and Order* depict the powerful effects of good evidence. Clearly evidence is a critical component in any trial. Evidence is also an important verbal behavior variable in less-formal communication contexts. When we become the target of a persuasive effort, we usually challenge our adversary to *prove* the case to us. When a new drug claims to prevent baldness, all but the most desperate or trusting of souls require some type of evidence before they spend huge sums of money on it.

Communication theorists beginning with Aristotle have focused on evidence as a determining influence on individual belief systems. Evidence consists of "factual statements originating from a source other than the speaker, objects not created by the speaker, and opinions of persons other than the speaker that are offered in support of the speaker's claims" (McCroskey, 1969, p. 170). A slightly different definition is "any statement of fact, statement of value, or definition offered by a speaker or writer which is intended to support a proposition" (Florence, 1975, p. 151). Contemporary communication courses, especially argumentation and public speaking, stress the relationship between evidence and persuasion. However, the findings of almost two decades of communication research do not appear to support a direct, positive association between evidence and persuasion. It has not been conclusively shown, for instance, that an audience will be more easily persuaded if more evidence is presented.

After reviewing over twenty studies on the influence of evidence in persuasion, James McCroskey concluded that several variables interact with evidence to produce changes in attitudes or increases in perceived speaker credibility: *evidence and source credibility, evidence and delivery effectiveness,* and *prior familiarity of evidence.*

There is a relationship between the use of evidence and the credibility or believability of the speaker. If a speaker is already perceived to be very credible, including "good" evidence will do little to change attitudes or enhance speaker credibility. However, speakers who are perceived as low to moderate in credibility may increase their credibility by employing evidence. This increase in perceived credibility may in turn increase attitude change.

In several studies on evidence and message topic, McCroskey believed that other factors were influencing the evidence—attitude change relationship. By interviewing participants after the experiments, he discovered that the quality of the delivery made a difference. To investigate the relationship further, he conducted several studies using live, audiotaped, and videotaped versions of a well-delivered and a poorly delivered presentation. The amount and type of evidence were the same for each version in each medium. From these studies, he found that: (a) including good evidence influences attitude change very little if the message is delivered poorly; and (b) including good evidence can influence attitude change and speaker credibility immediately after the speech if the message is well-delivered, the speaker initially has only low-to-moderate credibility, and the audience has little prior knowledge of the evidence. Because the results were consistent for all versions, he concluded that the medium of presentation has little effect on the use of evidence in persuasion.

McCroskey also believed that prior familiarity with evidence should be considered when assessing the evidence—persuasion relationship. Post-experimental interviews led him to conclude that "old" evidence does little to influence listeners. "Old" evidence has already been heard and processed cognitively. If any dissonance had been created by the message, it was already resolved or defense mechanisms were created to prevent a recurrence. These assumptions are consistent with explanations derived from information theories and cognitive dissonance theory (discussed later in this chapter). For evidence to affect listeners' attitude change or perceptions of the source immediately, McCroskey found that the evidence must be "new" to the listener. Including evidence has little, if any, impact on receivers if they are already familiar with it. McCroskey concluded that although considerable information has been uncovered about the influence of evidence in persuasion, communication theorists should continue their research efforts.

One researcher examined the theoretical foundations of previous research and reformulated the existing theories concerning evidence and persuasion (Florence, 1975). According to these findings, evidence influences persuasion only if the proposal, idea, or policy it supports is *desirable* to the audience. Both the credibility of a source of evidence and the evidence itself influence the desirability of a proposal. More recently, Dale Hample (1977, 1979, 1981) developed a theory of argument in which evidence plays a major role. In this theory, the relative power of evidence was measured. Hample argued that the power of evidence is one of the best predictors of attitude change. Because evidence is a key verbal message variable in the communication process, researchers will no doubt continue to examine its influence in persuasion.

SOURCE CREDIBILITY AND PERSUASION

A great deal of research has been based on the idea that source credibility is important in explaining persuasion (for early summaries and analyses see Andersen & Clevenger, 1963). Generally, the research has failed to establish that source credibility is a necessary condition for persuasion. That is, some studies find that credible sources persuade more people, whereas other studies find no relationship between attitude change and source credibility. Such inconsistency seems strange, especially because the idea that credibility affects persuasion seems self-evident, hardly worth investigating. There are two major models of source credibility in the communication field: factor and functional.

The Factor Model The factor model of credibility has been dominant for the past 2,500 years. Aristotle promoted *ethos,* the Greek term for credibility, as one of the three major ways speakers persuade audiences. The others are *logos* (the words, ideas, and arguments in the speech) and *pathos* (arousing the audience's emotions and feelings). Aristotle believed there are three aspects of credibility: a source's competence or expertise, character, and goodwill toward the audience. Eventually, these three dimensions were viewed as factors of credibility. A factor is a cluster of perceptions—for example, perceptions of a source's intelligence, authoritativeness, and ability to inform—contributing to the source's perceived expertise.

Factor model of credibility Aspects of credibility are a source's expertise, character, and goodwill

According to the factor model, source credibility is represented by how favorably the receiver judges the source on each of the factors of credibility. Thus, credibility exists in the mind of the receiver; it is not an actual characteristic of the source like eye color or hair color. If a source has an I.Q. of 160, is a published author on the subject of her speech, and presents an enormous amount of information on that topic, that does not mean that the audience will necessarily view her as an expert. One person may consider the source an expert on the topic, but another person may not. Credibility is strictly in the eye of the beholder.

Over the last thirty-five years, factor approach research has found that the expertise dimension appears to function independently from the character dimension. Thus, sources viewed as experts are not necessarily also thought to have good character. Some may be seen that way whereas others may not; one factor does not depend on the other. In the case of character and goodwill, however, the factors are not distinct. They work together. If we believe sources have our best interests in mind, we also perceive them as having good character. If we think they are trying to deceive us, we rate their character poorly.

A number of other variables may affect credibility: energy (dynamism), sociability, power, impact, mental balance, cultivation, and charisma. If credibility is a list of factors, critics wonder about the length of the list. Does a longer list imply a better understanding of credibility? This raises the issue of whether a "laundry list" of factors really tells us anything. Does each new factor increase understanding or cause confusion? Another criticism of the factor approach is that the model does not specify whether a receiver uses all the factors in assessing a source's credibility. A plausible expectation is that in some persuasion situations some factors matter more than other factors; some receivers will find certain factors more relevant than will other receivers. Thus, the characteristics used to judge the source's credibility can change with different sources, situations, and audiences. These and other criticisms of the factor model have led to the development of two additional models of credibility.

Functional model of credibility Credibility is determined by the extent to which a source fulfills the receiver's needs

The Functional Model The functional model of credibility views credibility as the degree to which a source satisfies the receiver's needs. Three simultaneous processes occur in a persuasive situation. First, the receiver becomes aware of the source's characteristics. Some, like height and voice quality, are observable; others, like education and social status, must be inferred. Second, the receiver determines criteria for judging the source in the situation. That is, the receiver becomes aware of the functions that the source could serve for the receiver (for example, to provide recent information, to entertain). Third, the receiver compares the characteristics with the functional criteria. An audience at a banquet might judge the extent to which a speaker has both informed and entertained them. The more needs that are fulfilled by the source, the more credible the source is. For example, the more the audience enjoyed the speech, the more credible they consider the speaker (Cronkhite & Liska, 1980).

Another group of researchers developed a method for measuring credibility according to the functional approach and then compared the functional model to the factor model to determine which explains persuasion best. The two models performed equally well in explaining differences, so the test was inconclusive. However, because the factors did not explain persuasion better than a general measure of credibility, the functional model was judged to be promising (Infante, Parker, Clarke, Wilson, & Nathu, 1983).

COGNITIVE DISSONANCE THEORY

Social psychologist Leon Festinger's cognitive dissonance theory (1957) is the most thoroughly researched of a family of cognitive consistency theories and therefore the one we shall discuss in this chapter (for a review of other consistency theories, see Kiesler, Collins, & Miller, 1969). Consistency theories of persuasion are based on the idea that inconsistency is psychologically uncomfortable. Inconsistency results when we believe A should have a certain relationship to B but it does not, or when A has an unexpected, undesirable relationship with something. For instance, inconsistency would be felt if we see that a program to reduce poverty in our city is not reducing hunger among children as we had expected. Instead, the program is reducing hope and aspirations among disadvantaged people.

Cognitive dissonance theory assumes that two beliefs are related either in a state of consonance or dissonance. A state of **consonance** is characterized by consistency: "I like my sorority, and my good friend likes my sorority." **Dissonance** is marked by inconsistency: "I like my sorority, but my good friend does not like it." The idea is that it would "bother" us (we would feel dissonance) if our friend did not also value what we value, and we would be motivated to get rid of the uncomfortable feeling. A central tenet of the theory is: The more the mental discomfort (dissonance), the more we are motivated to change something to make things comfortable.

Cognitive dissonance theory Assumes that two beliefs are related either in a state of consonance or dissonance

The theory identifies a number of factors that influence the amount of dissonance experienced (See Figure 7.1). Perhaps the most important one is whether the person's self-concept is involved in the dissonant relationship. If one belief is, "I just said that I liked a task that I really hate" ("I lied"), and a second belief is, "I am an honest person," the dissonance involves self-concept—our mental picture of the kind of person we are. What will be done to reduce dissonance? Research suggests individuals tend to change so that their attitude toward the task is more favorable, "I actually do like that task." This change in attitude permits consistency with the belief, "I am an honest person." We try to protect our self-concepts by rationalizing our actions and decisions so we do not "look bad" to ourselves. Changing the second belief to "I am dishonest" would also have restored consistency: "I lied" and "I am dishonest." However, we seldom reduce dissonance by changing a favorable belief about ourselves.

This principle can be used to explain the results of a classic study by Aronson and Mills (1959). To join a very dull discussion group, individuals were required either to recite a list of sexual terms (mild initiation) or to recite a list of "obscene" words (severe initiation). The research participants were then asked how much they liked the group. Did the severe or the mild initiation lead to greater liking for the group? In line with the theory's prediction, persons given the severe initiation liked the group more. Why? Because they experienced more dissonance. Their beliefs could be characterized as: "I am efficient," so "I just put forth a great effort, and I got something worthwhile." To conclude that the group was worthless would force the belief about self to be: "I am inefficient" because "I just put forth a great effort for little reward." Individuals who experienced the mild initiation did not distort their feelings about the group. "I am efficient," and "I got little benefit from the discussion, but I did not put much into it, so I have not lost."

Dissonance can be reduced in many ways besides changing beliefs, as in the preceding example. Attitude change toward a speaker's proposal and attitude change toward the speaker are two basic methods of resolving dissonance. Attitude change toward the speaker might involve criticizing the source of the information: "I won't listen to the American Cancer Society public service announcement warning about the health risks of smoking because the American Cancer Society is biased against cigarette smoking." Other methods of reducing dissonance are not as obvious. Selective exposure involves seeking information that supports your opinion but avoiding information that is unfavorable toward your opinion. The listener can also misinterpret the speaker's position so that the speaker seems to agree with the listener. One could also consider the dissonant elements unimportant so that the dissonance does not really matter. "The new car I just bought has little pickup, but I really don't need power and speed in a car anyway." Another alternative is to add consonant elements to "drown out" the dissonance. "Besides, my new car has great lines, a beautiful interior, an excellent stereo, and perfect handling."

Selective exposure Exposing oneself only to agreeable messages; avoiding situations, such as public speeches by a political opponent, requiring us to listen to those with whom we disagree

A basic idea about persuasion from dissonance theory is that to persuade people, you must cause them to experience dissonance, then offer your proposal as a way to get rid of the dissonance. A persuader might try to make receivers feel dissonance about energy policies in the United States and then present a proposal for developing alternative and renewable energy sources such as hydrogen fuel cells or solar energy to free the United States from dependence on foreign oil. When a speaker arouses dissonance, the receiver will try to reduce it, using one of the methods just listed. However, dissonance can also be reduced by adopting or agreeing with the speaker's proposal. Although there is no guarantee that the audience will reduce dissonance by changing their minds, the speaker does have a chance to achieve persuasion.

According to the theory, if no dissonance is aroused, there will be no persuasion. People do not change an attitude unless they feel they need to change it. Feeling dissonance provides the motivation to change. The theory predicts that to persuade someone, you must first "upset" the person (make them feel dissonance) concerning the topic of your proposal. If you fail to persuade the audience, perhaps the dissonance they felt was not great enough to motivate action.

SOCIAL JUDGMENT/EGO-INVOLVEMENT THEORY

This approach to persuasion is distinctly different from cognitive consistency theories of persuasion. Ego-involvement or social judgment theory (Sherif, Sherif, & Nebergall, 1965) predicts successful persuasion by a message depending on how the message is related to the person's current beliefs. Research in physiological psychology indicates that if a person is given an "anchor" in

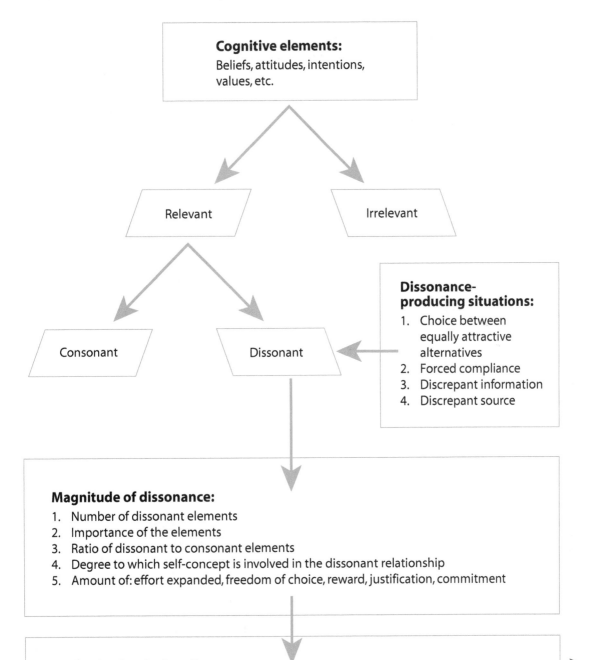

Cognitive elements:
Beliefs, attitudes, intentions, values, etc.

Relevant

Irrelevant

Consonant

Dissonant

Dissonance-producing situations:
1. Choice between equally attractive alternatives
2. Forced compliance
3. Discrepant information
4. Discrepant source

Magnitude of dissonance:
1. Number of dissonant elements
2. Importance of the elements
3. Ratio of dissonant to consonant elements
4. Degree to which self-concept is involved in the dissonant relationship
5. Amount of: effort expanded, freedom of choice, reward, justification, commitment

Methods of reducing dissonance:
1. Selective exposure
2. Change attitude
3. Change behavior
4. Derogate the source
5. Reject the message
6. Distort the source's position
7. Change the importance of the dissonant elements
8. Add consonant elements to change the dissonant-consonant ratio

FIGURE 7.1 COGNITIVE DISSONANCE.

making judgments, objects close to the anchor are seen as more similar to the anchor than they really are (they are assimilated). Objects far from the anchor are perceived as even more dissimilar than they really are (they are contrasted). If you were handed a bar and told it weighs 10 pounds, you would probably judge too low when asked to guess what a 12-pound bar weighs. You probably would judge the 12-pound bar as just about the same as the 10-pound anchor; you would assimilate it. Next, if asked to guess the weight of a 40-pound bar, you probably would judge it heavier than it really is. It would seem more distant from the anchor; the contrast effect would occur.

Ego-involvement
Characterized by a wide latitude of rejection and narrow latitudes of acceptance and noncommitment

Assimilation The degree to which a person accepts the influence of the new culture or environment

What does this have to do with persuasion? Ego-involvement or **social judgment theory** indicates that assimilation and contrast effects also occur in persuasion. Assimilation constitutes persuasion; a **contrast effect** represents a failure to persuade. In the case of persuasion, the receiver's position on the topic of the persuasive message serves as the **anchor**. If a speaker slightly opposes gun control and you moderately oppose it, you tend to interpret the speaker's position as basically the same as yours. On the other hand, the more you favor gun control and the more the speaker opposes it, the greater the likelihood that you will view the speaker's position as more extreme than it really is (that is, a contrast effect). Basically, we accept assimilated messages but reject contrasted messages.

Although interesting, the assimilation—contrast notion leaves several questions unanswered. Under what conditions are messages assimilated or contrasted? Why do two individuals with the same position on an issue react differently to the same message about the issue, one person assimilating the message while the other person contrasts it? The concepts of latitude of acceptance, rejection, and noncommitment are needed to answer these questions.

Latitude of acceptance
Consists of all statements the person finds acceptable. This can include the favorite position or the anchor

Latitude of rejection
Consists of all of the positions on an issue the person rejects

Latitude of noncommitment
Consists of all of the positions a person neither accepts nor rejects

The latitude of acceptance consists of all statements the person finds acceptable, including the favorite position, the anchor. Figure 7.2 illustrates the latitudes of acceptance for two individuals on an issue with 11 positions. Notice that Chris and Pat have the same most acceptable position (A) or anchor belief: "Final exams should be optional for graduating seniors." Chris rejects Statement 6 and Statement 7, while Pat agrees with them. The latitude of rejection (r) consists of all of the positions on the issue the person rejects (finds objectionable). Pat and Chris have latitudes of rejection that vary in width. Pat rejects only Statement 1, the position that final exams should be required of all students, whereas Chris rejects statements 1–7. The latitude of noncommitment (nc) consists of all positions the person neither accepts nor rejects. The person is noncommittal or neutral on these issues. Chris is neutral about Statement 8; Pat is neutral about statements 2–5.

The latitudes of acceptance, rejection, and noncommitment determine whether a given person will assimilate or contrast a message. Messages falling in the latitudes of acceptance or noncommitment will be judged closer to the favorite position (anchor belief) than they really are (assimilated). Messages falling in the latitude of rejection will be judged farther away (contrasted). According

		Chris									
Topic Positions	1	2	3	4	5	6	7	8	9	10	11
	r	r	r	r	r	r	r	nc	a	A	a

		Pat									
Topic Positions	1	2	3	4	5	6	7	8	9	10	11
	r	nc	nc	nc	nc	a	a	a	a	A	a

A = most acceptable position
a = other acceptable positions

r = positions which are rejected
nc = positions on that the person is neutral

POSITION STATEMENTS

11. Final exams should be optional for all students.
10. Final exams should be optional for graduating seniors.
9. Final exams should be optional in elective courses.
8. Final exams should be optional for students with an A average.
7. Final exams should be optional for students with an A or B average.
6. Final exams should be optional for students with an A, B, or C average.
5. Final exams should be optional for students with a passing average.
4. Final exams should be optional at the professor's discretion.
3. Final exams should be required only of freshmen.
2. Final exams should be required only of freshmen and sophomores.
1. Final exams should be required of all students.

FIGURE 7.2 EGO-INVOLVEMENT OR SOCIAL JUDGMENT THEORY.

to ego-involvement theory, a basic principle of persuasion is that to change a person's most acceptable position on a topic, the message must fall within the person's latitude of acceptance. A persuader can also attempt to widen the latitude of acceptance by advocating a position in the person's latitude of non-commitment. If successful, the persuader will widen the receiver's latitude of acceptance, thus creating a larger "target" for a second persuasion attempt.

The latitudes also indicate whether the person is ego-involved. According to the theory, high ego-involvement is characterized by a narrow latitude of acceptance (the person's own favorite position is about the only position accepted), a wide latitude of rejection (almost everything other than one's own position is rejected), and a narrow latitude of non-commitment (nearly all positions are either accepted or rejected; the person is neutral about very few positions). Low ego-involvement is the opposite. The latitude of acceptance is wide (people are able to accept several other positions on the issue besides their anchor position), the latitude of non-commitment is wide (there are many positions on the topic that the person is neutral about), and the latitude of rejection is narrow (there is not much left to reject if one accepts most positions and does not care about most of the remaining ones).

Chris is highly ego-involved, and Pat is not ego-involved with final exam regulations. According to the theory, even though they both hold the same most acceptable position (Statement 10), they would react differently to a message that advocated Statement 6. Chris would contrast the message because it falls in the latitude of rejection; it would be "heard" as a more extreme message than it actually is. On the other hand, Pat would assimilate the message, perceive it closer to the anchor (Statement 10) than it really is because it is one of the acceptable positions. Thus, Pat would be persuaded by the message; Chris would not.

This theory permits us to conceptualize how persuasion can be achieved with a highly ego-involved individual. In our example, to persuade Chris to change from Statement 10 to Statement 2 would take many messages. One message would not be enough—it would be contrasted. Persuasion would require many messages over a long period of time, each gradually expanding the latitude of acceptance and slowly moving the favorite position (anchor belief). This probably is a realistic view of persuasion. It is very difficult to persuade someone who is very ego-involved in a topic. The theory represents this idea clearly. When a person is highly ego-involved, a "one-shot" attempt to persuade the individual is surely doomed to failure. A "persuasive campaign" composed of many messages over a period of time is a more realistic way to try to change someone who is ego-involved.

THE THEORY OF REASONED ACTION

Theory of reasoned action A theory of persuasion that is based on attitudes, belief strength, and the evaluation of the meaning of the belief

The theory of reasoned action by Martin Fishbein and Icek Ajzen has been used a good deal by communication researchers (e.g., see research by Edwards, 1998; Stewart & Roach, 1998; Park, 1998). It is also a good example of theory building. The theory was introduced in the 1960s and enhanced through the next several decades (for instance, see Ajzen, 1985; Ajzen & Fishbein, 1980; Fishbein & Ajzen, 1975).

The theory of reasoned action began with Fishbein's theory of attitude toward an object (an object could be a person, a physical thing, an idea, a social program, etc.); he conceptualized attitude as a sum of the beliefs that we have learned to associate with the object. Suppose we consider your attitude toward physical fitness. You might have learned to associate seven beliefs with physical fitness. The extent to which each belief contributes to your attitude depends on (a) belief strength and (b) evaluation of the meaning of the belief. You might have a belief that it is extremely likely (belief strength) that a physical fitness lifestyle results in a very favorable (evaluation) consequence, an attractive body shape. This belief would favorably affect your attitude toward physical fitness; you have a strong belief that the object produces something good. A second belief might be that you think it is slightly unlikely (belief strength) that you will get frequent colds if you are in good physical condition. This belief also is positive because it asserts that you will be less likely to experience something bad, but because it is not a very strong belief, it will have less impact on your attitude. If your remaining five beliefs followed the pattern of these two examples, you would have a moderately favorable attitude toward physical fitness. That is, if we add the degree of favorable feelings in your seven beliefs, the total would be much closer to the favorable end than to the unfavorable end of the attitude object continuum.

In the 1960s, psychology and sociology researchers found that attitude theories such as this one were poor predictors of a given behavior. For example, we could design a study to measure your attitude toward physical fitness. If your attitude was very favorable and we gave you a coupon for a free workout at a local gym, the prediction would be that you would use the coupon. Typically, that prediction would not be very accurate. In fact, flipping a coin might be just as accurate in predicting behavior as measuring attitude.

Fishbein, who was later joined by Ajzen, expanded the theory to deal with this problem of why attitude toward an object does not accurately predict a specific behavior relevant to the object. Fishbein declared that attitude does predict behavior, but not in the way that previous researchers had assumed that it should. The problem was the measure of behavior. A single act, observed once, was what most studies used as the criterion. This was a mistake because there is no theoretical reason why attitude toward an object should be closely related to a single behavior, unless there is only one behavior that is relevant to the object, which is seldom the case. Typically, many behaviors are relevant to an attitude object. When that is the case, attitude toward the object should be related to the total set of behaviors. Thus, one act, observed once, does not measure the entire set of relevant behaviors. The correct behavioral measure was what Fishbein called the multiple-act, repeated observations criterion. This means all the relevant behaviors should be counted; ideally, they should be observed more than once over a period of time.

Multiple-act A behavioral prediction in research based on a set of relevant behaviors ideally observed more than once over a period of time

In terms of our example, then, your attitude toward physical fitness probably would not predict whether you will show up at the gym. We would be a bit more accurate if we could observe you showing up next week, the week after, and the next week, and so on (this would be a single-act, repeated measures criterion). An even better predictor would be observations of all other relevant behaviors, observed more than once. Two possibilities would be observing you eating a healthy diet each day for a month, or noting that you watched physical fitness shows on TV for a month. If we designated ten behaviors and observed them for a month, the total number of occurrences of the ten would constitute a multiple-act, repeated observations criterion. Research by Fishbein and others found an improved behavioral measure such as this is strongly related to attitude toward the object.

What this means in terms of persuasion, then, is if you succeeded in persuading someone who had an unfavorable attitude toward physical fitness to have a favorable attitude (probably by arguing successfully that several good things would likely follow), you should expect the total pattern of the person's fitness-related behaviors to change. However, any single behavior might not change. For instance, the person might go to the gym often, watch exercise shows on TV, attend fitness lectures, etc., but continue eating high-fat fast food. We might wonder at this point whether it is possible to target a single behavior not only for prediction but also for change in persuasion situations.

The theory of reasoned action was developed to deal specifically with the problem of predicting a single behavior, even if it is observed only once. Fishbein and Ajzen built on their earlier research. A core idea of the theory of reasoned action is that behavior is intentional; very little behavior is accidental. When people engage in a given behavior, it is because they formed intentions to do so, and they had reasons for their decisions to actualize their intentions. Thus, much of our behavior can be characterized as "reasoned action."

Attitude toward the specific act is one of two major components of a behavioral intention. The second is what has been called the *normative component*. Keep in mind that the Fishbein and Ajzen model works backward from a specific behavior. That is, a specific behavior is predicted or controlled by an intention to behave; that intention is predicted and controlled by two factors, attitude toward the act and the normative component. Each of these two components is controlled by particular factors.

Attitude toward the specific act is controlled by the beliefs that the person has about the consequences of performing the act. As with Fishbein's earlier theory of attitude toward an object, two aspects of each belief are important: belief strength and evaluation. Continuing with our gym visit example, suppose you have five moderately strong beliefs about five somewhat desirable consequences of accepting the offer for a free workout at a gym: the gym has superior equipment; it is easy to get to the gym because of its location; membership rates could be cheaper after a trial visit; a gym membership would increase motivation to exercise; you could meet interesting people there. At this point it might be tempting to predict that you probably will go to the gym. The five beliefs are reasons for action or inaction. In this case the reasons tilt somewhat toward action. However, there is more to the theory. The second determinant of an intention is the normative component, and we need to consider it before making a prediction about behavior.

The normative component is composed of our beliefs about what valued others expect us to do regarding the behavior. Each belief is weighted by our motivation to comply with the wishes of other people. In terms of our example, suppose one normative belief is that your good friend would not want you to join that gym, because he is planning on having a gym in the basement of his home and wants you to work out there so the two of you can motivate one another. Perhaps another normative belief is that your significant other does not like the manager of the gym and therefore is less than enthusiastic about the prospect of you being a member there. Suppose further that you have fairly strong motivation to comply with these normative expectations.

On the basis of these two components, attitude toward the act and the normative component, can we now offer a prediction of whether or not you will go to the gym for the trial workout? Often information about these two components is enough to make an accurate prediction. However, in a case like this where you are being pulled one way by one component and another way by the second component, more information is needed. The *subjective weights* of each component help evaluate conflicting influences. For some behaviors we feel that we can do whatever we feel like doing (i.e., we let our attitude toward the act guide us and feel no constraint from other people). For other behaviors we decide what we do must be compatible with the preferences of valued others (i.e., we look to the normative component for guidance).

In our example, suppose on a 1–10 scale your weight for attitude toward the act is 3 and your weight for the normative component is 8. In view of this data the theory would predict that you will not go to the gym for the trial workout. Suppose that the theory is accurate (as it has been most of the time), and you do not go to the gym. However, what would have happened if we had made a prediction based only on the first attitude that we considered, attitude toward physical fitness? Because the attitude in the example was moderately favorable, the prediction would have been that you would go to the gym. The prediction would have been wrong. If the prediction had been based only on attitude toward the act, once again it would have been wrong. An accurate prediction was achieved only when both components were considered and weighted. The theory became more accurate as it developed—an excellent illustration of the advantages of theory building. The theory of reasoned action has been a popular one in communication research because of its accuracy.

In addition to prediction strengths, the theory provides implications for persuasion. For example, if you want to influence a person to perform a specific behavior, do not devote much time to trying to change attitude toward the object. Instead, try to determine what the person's current attitude is toward that act and also the normative component. Importantly, how is each component weighted? Such analysis directs your focus for the persuasive attempt. The fundamental persuasion tactics would involve arguing the consequences of performing the act. For a favorable attitude toward the behavior you would claim good consequences would be likely and bad consequences would be unlikely. For an unfavorable attitude, the opposite would be argued (i.e., that good things would not happen, but bad things would occur). Influencing the normative component involves maintaining that persons valued by the individual either expect certain behaviors or do not want certain things to happen. Sometimes it could be necessary to convince people that they should have high motivation to fulfill the expectations of valued others. In other circumstances persuading people to perform a given behavior necessitates moving them to ignore the wishes of others and to act mainly on the basis of self-interest. This tactic could be especially difficult to accomplish because it is not unusual in persuasion situations for need for approval to be a major factor.

THE THEORY OF PLANNED BEHAVIOR

As explained in the previous section, the core of Fishbein and Ajzen's theory of reasoned action is the notion of the behavioral intention; a person's intention of performing a given behavior is the best predictor of whether or not the person will actually perform the behavior. It may have occurred to you, however, that several factors can work against this behavioral intention → behavior sequence. Think about some examples where you, to use a cliché, "had the best intentions" to perform a behavior (e.g., taking your sibling to the mall to go shopping next Saturday morning) but certain personal limitations (e.g., you were too tired and overslept) and/or external obstacles (e.g., you didn't have a car available to you that day) prevented you from actually performing that behavior. The successful performance of a behavior also depends on one's ability to control factors that either allow or prevent performance of that behavior (Ajzen, 1988).

To resolve some of the difficulties in predicting behavior precisely, Ajzen (1985, 1988, 1991) proposed the theory of planned behavior (TPB), an extension of the theory of reasoned action (TORA). TPB is also based on the premise that the best predictor of an actual behavior is a person's behavioral intention. However, unlike its predecessor theory, TPB suggests that there are three, rather than two, factors associated with a person's behavioral intention (see Figure 7.3).

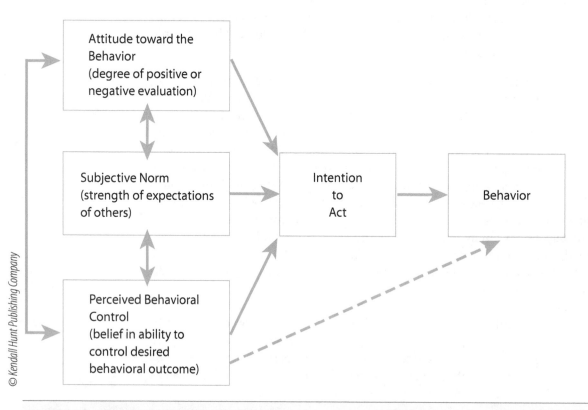

FIGURE 7.3 THEORY OF PLANNED BEHAVIOR.

In TPB, the first two factors associated with a behavioral intention are the same as in TORA: (1) attitude toward the specific act (or behavior), and (2) the normative component, our beliefs about what valued others expect us to do regarding the behavior in question. Ajzen (1985, 1988, 1991) added a third factor, perceived behavioral control, to TPB. Perceived behavioral control refers to "the degree to which a person believes they can control the behavior in question" (Roberto, Meyer, & Boster, 2001, p. 316)—how easy or difficult the person believes it will be to perform a given behavior.

TPB suggests that, in general, more favorable attitudes toward the specific act (or behavior), more favorable subjective norms (normative component), and greater perceived behavioral control (the ease of performing the behavior in question) strengthen the intention to perform the behavior. According to TPB, perceived behavioral control is directly related to behavioral intentions and to actual behavior.

Ajzen (2001) suggests that perceived behavioral control influences a person's confidence that they are capable of performing the behavior in question. Perceived behavioral control is, in essence, a combination of two dimensions, self-efficacy (ease or difficulty in performing the behavior or likelihood that the person can actually do it) and controllability (people's beliefs that they have control over the behavior, that the performance of the behavior is—or is not—up to them).

Returning to the physical fitness lifestyle example, let's say you want to predict whether a person will walk on a treadmill in a physical fitness center for at least 30 minutes each day in the next month (Ajzen, 2001). To assess the self-efficacy dimension of perceived behavioral control, you might ask the person to respond to an item such as, "For me to walk on a treadmill for at least 30 minutes each day in the forthcoming month would be" [impossible—possible]. To assess the controllability dimension of perceived control, you could ask, "How much control do you believe you have over walking on a treadmill for at least 30 minutes each day in the forthcoming month" [no control—complete control].

Thus, if you want to assess more accurately whether a person will actually perform a given behavior, you will need to measure perceived control, along with an assessment of the person's *behavioral intention*, "I plan to walk on a treadmill for at least 30 minutes each day in the forthcoming month" [strongly disagree—strongly agree], their *attitude toward the behavior*, "I believe walking on a treadmill for at least 30 minutes each day in the next month is [harmful—beneficial, worthless—valuable], and their subjective norm, "Most people who are important to me think that [I should—I should not] walk on a treadmill for at least 30 minutes each day in the next month" (Ajzen, 2001, pp. 4–7).

When put to the test, TPB has been able to predict a number of health-related behaviors such as weight loss (Schifter & Ajzen, 1985), adolescent use of alcohol (Marcoux & Schope, 1997), and adolescent abstinence from sex and/or use of condoms during sexual relations (Basen-Engquist & Parcel, 1992).

Perceived behavioral control The degree to which a person believes that they control any given behavior

Self-efficacy The degree of ease or difficulty in performing the behavior or likelihood that a person can actually perform a behavior

Controllability People's belief that they have control over the behavior, that the performance of the behavior is or is not up to them

Perceived control The degree to which people believe that they have control over a situation or behavior

Subjective norm The pressure a person feels to conform to the will of others to perform or not perform a behavior

Communication researchers have recently adopted TPB to predict actual behavior. For example, Roberto, Meyer, and Boster (2001) used TPB to predict adolescent decisions about fighting. In their study, several hundred seventh-grade boys and girls were questioned about their participation in physical fights "where two or more people hit, punch, slap, push, or kick each other in anger" (p. 317). They completed a survey instrument that measured their actual behavior (e.g., "During the last month how many times did you get into a fight?"), their behavioral intentions (e.g., "How many times do you think you will get into a fight in the next month?"), the perceptions of subjective norms (e.g., "Do most of the kids you know think you should get into fights?"), their attitudes toward fighting (e.g., very cool—very uncool), and their *perceived behavioral control* (e.g., "How easy or hard is it for you to stay out of fights?," and "When someone tries to start a fight with you, how easy or hard is it for you to avoid the fight?").

The results supported several of the assumptions of TPB in that attitudes toward fighting and perceived behavioral control were both related to an individual's behavioral intentions. That is, those adolescents who felt they were more "in control" of their fighting behaviors and who expressed unfavorable attitudes toward fighting were less likely to get into fights. Both behavioral intentions and perceived behavioral control emerged as predictors of actual behavior (Roberto et al., 2001).

TPB has also been used to predict smokers' interests in participating in a smoking-cessation program (Babrow, Black, & Tiffany, 1990). TPB suggests that measuring a person's attitudes toward participating in a particular smoking-cessation program would allow better prediction of participation in the program than attitudes toward smoking in general or attitudes toward quitting smoking in general. Intentions to participate (behavioral intentions), attitude toward participation, beliefs about the consequences of participating, perceptions of the subjective norm, and perceived behavioral control were measured ("how frequently would the following factors: flexibility of program hours, participation with other friends, convenience of location, etc. affect your ability to participate in this particular smoking-cessation program?" [never—constantly]). Babrow et al.'s (1990) findings generally supported TPB. Beliefs about the consequences of participating in the program were related to attitude toward participation. Most important, attitude, subjective norm, and perceived behavioral control beliefs were strongly related to individuals' intentions to participate in the smoking cessation program.

The development of TPB in response to an earlier theory, TORA, allows us to see how theories are built by extension, where new theories emerge from expansion of existing theories. By adding new information, factors, and knowledge to existing theories, we can better explain, predict, and thus, control behavior.

Elaboration likelihood model A model of persuasion that assumes persuasion results primarily from characteristics of the persuasive message or from characteristics of the situation

ELABORATION LIKELIHOOD MODEL

Petty and Cacioppo (1986) developed the elaboration likelihood model (ELM). They recognized that persuasion results primarily from characteristics of the persuasive message or from characteristics of the persuasion situation. ELM analyzes the likelihood that receivers will cognitively elaborate—engage in issue-related thinking—on the information presented in a persuasive message.

At times persuasion occurs because the receiver of a message considers the content of the persuasive message carefully and has favorable thoughts about the content. The favorable thinking about the message content causes a favorable attitude to form toward the object of the message. This represents one type of persuasion—the central route to persuasion, characterized by a good deal of persuasive, issue-related thinking. At other times persuasion occurs because the receiver is guided not by his or her assessment of the message but because the receiver decides to follow a principle or a decision-rule derived from the persuasion situation. The rule might be: "When everyone else goes along with the speaker's recommendation, I should too unless I have a very good reason to deviate from the group." This is an example of persuasion through a peripheral route.

According to Petty and Cacioppo, when persuasion takes a peripheral route, there is little or no elaboration of message content; that is, there is a lack of issue-related thinking. When a decision on a persuasive message is not based on the message itself, the receiver looks to other things to guide the decision, as in the preceding example. The persuasive situation provides many principles for evaluating a message if one does not want to engage in a critical assessment of the message content. We sometimes base message acceptance on the trustworthiness of the source, the expertise of the source, or even the physical attractiveness of the source. Also, a decision-rule can be based on rewards or punishments. "I will accept the source's position if I can realize a financial gain from it or if I can avoid a punishment such as higher taxes." Sometimes we are guided by our relationship with the persuader, as in "I need to return a favor."

The ELM is based on the idea that people realize their attitudes are important because attitudes guide decisions and other behaviors. This importance motivates people to form attitudes that are useful in their lives. Although attitudes can result from a number of things, persuasion is a primary source. When a persuasive message attempts to influence an attitude the receiver realizes is significant to his or her life, the likelihood increases that the receiver will cognitively elaborate on the content of the message. This process takes a good deal of effort, so it is avoided whenever possible. That is, people generally prefer not to have to work hard mentally and will follow the "easy way" whenever possible. This probably is due not so much to people being lazy as to the reality of our cognitive limits. Our physical limits are pretty obvious. For instance, we cannot run a marathon as a sprint. The central route to persuasion is probably more like a "mental sprint." You can do it only for a limited period of time.

A peripheral route to persuasion is "easy" because not much thinking is necessary. All one has to do is realize an appropriate guiding principle and make a decision on the persuasive message based on the principle. "The source is a real expert so I can trust what she is saying." Little, if any, elaboration takes place when a simple principle, like this example, is used to guide assessment of a persuasive message.

Central route The favorable thinking about the message content causes a favorable attitude to form toward the object of the message

Peripheral route When there is little or no elaboration of a message, situational cues persuade people instead of the message

It is important to note that persuasion, or lack of it, can take place with either route. What matters is the *cognitive product* of the process. When one takes the central route, thinking about the content of the message might result in unfavorable assessments of the source's arguments. This negative reaction would inhibit persuasion. Similarly, persuasion could fail to occur through a peripheral route when a receiver utilizes the negative side of a principle. "The source has no real credentials to speak on this topic, so I would not even consider changing my opinion."

Because elaboration or issue-related thinking is central to this theory, a good deal of research has explored the factors that influence how much we elaborate when we receive a persuasive message. Basically, two types of factors have been identified: (a) factors that influence our *motivation* to elaborate, and (b) factors that influence our *ability* to elaborate.

Motivation to elaborate has been investigated in terms of the receiver's involvement in the persuasive issue; the more the person is personally involved in the topic, the more likely he or she will elaborate on the message. Also, motivation to elaborate is increased when several sources present arguments on the topic. The variety of arguments presents a sense of conflict, and conflict tends to attract attention. The research also has discovered that some people are more likely than others to elaborate. Specifically, people who have a strong need for cognition (they enjoy thinking a lot) are more likely to elaborate on the content of a message.

Need for cognition
A stable individual difference in people's tendency to engage in and enjoy effortful cognitive activity

The need for cognition trait is defined as "a stable individual difference in people's tendency to engage in and enjoy effortful cognitive activity" (Cacioppo, Petty, Feinstein, & Jarvis, 1996, p. 198). Cognitive activity refers to the degree of critical thinking a person engages in. People range from being high to being low in need for cognition. Individuals high in need for cognition enjoy thinking about abstract issues and often engage in contemplative thought, whereas people low in need for cognition tend to rely more on simple social cues that provide a shortcut to effortful thought. These cues can be things such as attractiveness and source credibility, as illustrated in the elaboration likelihood model of persuasion. That is, people who are high in need for cognition have a tendency to process information through the central route, whereas people low in need for cognition have a tendency to process information through the peripheral route.

Although it may appear that people high in need for cognition are somehow smarter than people low in need for cognition, this is not the case. Of course people high in need for cognition have to have a degree of critical thinking capacity. Sanders, Gass, Wiseman, and Bruschke (1992) compared Asian Americans, Hispanic Americans, and European Americans in need for cognition, argumentativeness, and verbal aggressiveness. The results of this study reveal that need for cognition was positively related to argumentativeness and negatively related to verbal aggressiveness. Further, Asian Americans reported being lower in need for cognition than both Hispanic Americans and European

Americans. A similar link between need for cognition and argumentativeness was also observed by Mongeau (1989).

It is important to note that need for cognition is a motivational trait, not a behavior skill-related trait. Similar to the competing motivational tendencies that comprise the trait of argumentativeness, need for cognition simply suggests that we either enjoy abstract thinking or we do not. Need for cognition is an important motivational factor in the elaboration likelihood model of persuasion. The need for cognition is a very important trait for researchers and theorists interested in a source-based factor that influences how people are persuaded.

The ability to elaborate is also influenced by several factors. Distractions are a key element. If people are distracted during the presentation of a message, they are less likely to elaborate on the content. They are more likely to take a peripheral route. For instance, distracting a friend by dining in a good restaurant while trying to persuade him or her makes it less likely that your friend will exert the cognitive effort to elaborate on the message (attention to the food subtracts from the attention available for message elaboration). In this example, it is again more likely that a peripheral route to persuasion will be taken. "Coming from so generous a friend, the message is probably valid." Knowledge of the topic also is a factor that influences ability to elaborate. Knowing little about the topic makes elaboration very difficult, and peripheral routes are welcomed when we find ourselves in such a circumstance. Similarly, the comprehensibility of a message influences elaboration. A very vague message or one that relies heavily on very difficult material reduces the ability to elaborate. However, this might not reduce persuasion if, instead of elaborating on the message content, the receiver relies on a principle such as "the speaker is such an expert that the message position surely is correct." Diverting receivers to a particular peripheral route at times could be a successful strategy of persuasion.

It should be noted that the two routes to persuasion are not mutually exclusive. Probably only one route is taken under circumstances of extremely high or extremely low elaboration. Thus, when elaboration of the message content is very extensive, no consideration might be given to a peripheral route. On the other hand, when there is no elaboration of the message, a peripheral route is taken exclusively. Between those extremes, however, probably both characteristics of the message and characteristics of the persuasion situation matter. For instance, after receiving a persuasive message, a person might say: "After thinking extensively about what was said, I must conclude that I am persuaded a bit, but not as much as I would have been if the speaker had been motivated less by self-interest." Research by James Stiff (1986) suggests people are influenced in persuasion not only by cues associated with the central route but also by cues pertaining to peripheral routes. Stiff demonstrated that, when they want to, people can "stretch" their capacity for processing information and process both message and situation information. Therefore, it is overly simplistic to view persuasion in an "either/or" (as in either a central or a peripheral route) sense. Allowing for both provides a richer explanation of persuasion.

We can avoid being overly simplistic also by saying that characteristics of sources (such as expertise or attractiveness) do not always pertain to peripheral routes. For instance, an actor's beautiful tan could be considered part of the persuasive message when trying to sell suntan lotion; the tan would constitute data (an example) for the claim that having a tan enhances physical attractiveness. In other circumstances, such as the actor talking about aiding the homeless, the tan would function as a component of attractiveness that, for some receivers, might be a peripheral route to persuasion.

O'Keefe's (1990) assessment of the ELM being most promising as a theoretical development is probably quite accurate. The theory is generating a good deal of research and is attracting the attention of a sizeable body of researchers. Although cognitive dissonance theory was the dominant theory of persuasion in earlier periods of persuasion research, the ELM might very well play a similar role in the future.

COMPLIANCE-GAINING

A good deal of social influence research in the communication discipline focuses on **compliance-gaining**. Compliance-gaining and persuasion are two different types of social influence as persuasion often involves attitude change, while a main emphasis of compliance-gaining is on the various strategies that people use to influence another person to behave in a particular manner (Dillard, 1990; Wheeless, Barraclough, & Stewart, 1983).

Compliance-gaining is important because we often do not desire attitude change; instead, we want to have someone perform a desired behavior or do something for us. That is, compliance-gaining interactions can have important and practical outcomes. People seek compliance for a number of reasons and from a number of different individuals. We may seek the compliance of a friend when we ask them not to drink and drive, or when we ask them if we can borrow some money. We may seek compliance from our roommate when we ask them to turn down their music so that we may study for an exam. We may seek compliance when we ask one of our professors or supervisors to write a letter of recommendation for us when we apply to graduate school or a new job. In addition, we often seek compliance from strangers, such as when we ask, "Can you hold my place in line while I use the restroom?" Solicitors from organizations regularly phone us asking for donations to their respective charities.

Although persuasion and compliance-gaining share many similarities, there are several differences between them. Persuasion tends to focus on public or mass communication contexts, while the focus of compliance-gaining efforts tend to occur in more interpersonal contexts when we are interacting with family members, friends, and colleagues at school and at work. Scholarly efforts designed to understand persuasion have focused primarily on message processing and messages effects, while research on compliance has focused more on message production and the choices people make in selecting the strategies to use to get someone to do something for them.

While differences between these two forms of influence do exist, they do inform and often help guide each other. Steven Wilson, a contemporary communication scholar who has focused numerous research studies on compliance-gaining has suggested that, "Although the traditional persuasion and compliance-gaining literatures differ in focus, they inform each other. Questions about message effects and message choices are complementary. Even if we know how parents can persuade their children to study or how dentists can convince patients to floss their teeth (message effects), we also need to understand why parents and dentists do not always use the most effective persuasive strategies (message choices)" (Wilson, 2002, p. 7).

Compliance often involves more subtle forms of psychological pressure: "I (and/ or others) will like you if you comply"; or "I (and/or others) will dislike you if you do not comply." There are many compliance-gaining strategies for each of these two forms. An example of the first is, "I will do something for you if you do this for me." "Our friends will be disappointed if you do not do this," illustrates the second. Instead of allowing the receiver's attitude toward the proposal to control the receiver's behavior, the source in a compliance situation implies that the desired behavior will make the receiver more socially accepted. An individual's attitude usually remains unchanged in compliance situations.

Compliance Social influence attempts designed to influence another person to behave in a particular manner

An early line of compliance-gaining research had its beginning in the field of sociology, where Gerald Marwell and David Schmitt (1967) derived sixteen different compliance-gaining strategies, which were later introduced to the communication field (Miller, Boster, Roloff, & Seibold, 1977). Figure 7.4 presents a definition of each strategy with an example from the Marwell and Schmitt typology. Generally, research was conducted by presenting a hypothetical situation (for example, your roommate is playing the stereo too loudly). The set of compliance-gaining strategies was then presented, and participants were asked to rate the likelihood that they would use each strategy in the hypothetical situation. Another method was to ask participants to write what they would say in such a situation. Researchers then analyzed the written content to determine preferred strategies.

Prior to the 1980s compliance-gaining research was largely atheoretical, that is, research on compliance was not informed by theory. Since the 1980s, communication and persuasion scholars have attempted to study and understand compliance-gaining message strategies, choices, and selections utilizing several theoretical frameworks. As such, more recent developments in understanding why individuals seek and resist compliance have employed several theories which have been, or will be, discussed in this text, such as politeness theory (Chapter 5), and the goals-plans-action theory of persuasion (Chapter 8). Over the past several decades, scholars such as Steven Wilson have grounded compliance-gaining research in theoretical frameworks which highlight directives, face, goals, and obstacles in order to explain how compliance-gaining efforts function. The assumption made is that people understand situations in terms of influence goals, and they attempt to develop and use messages which help them achieve their goals.

The situation analyzed here involved a father attempting to persuade his son, Dick, to study.

1. **Promise**
   If you comply, you will be rewarded.
   Offer to increase Dick's allowance if he increases his studying.

2. **Threat**
   If you do not comply, you will be punished.
   Threaten to forbid Dick the use of the car if he does not increase his studying.

3. **Expertise (Positive)**
   If you comply, you will be rewarded because of "the nature of things."
   Point out to Dick that if he gets good grades he will be able to get into a good college and get a good job.

4. **Expertise (Negative)**
   If you do not comply, you will be punished because of "the nature of things."
   Point out to Dick that if he does not get good grades he will not be able to get into a good college or get a good job.

5. **Liking**
   Actor is friendly and helpful to get target in "good frame of mind" so that he will comply with request.
   Try to be as friendly and pleasant as possible to get Dick in the right "frame of mind" before asking him to study.

6. **Pre-Giving**
   Actor rewards target before requesting compliance.
   Raise Dick's allowance and tell him you now expect him to study.

7. **Aversive Stimulation**
   Actor continuously punishes target, making cessation contingent on compliance.
   Forbid Dick the use of the car and tell him he will not be allowed to drive until he studies more.

8. **Debt**
   Compliance is owed because of past favors.
   Point out that you have sacrificed and saved to pay for Dick's education and that he owes it to you to get good enough grades to get into a good college.

9. **Moral Appeal**
   You are immoral if you do not comply.
   Tell Dick that it is morally wrong for anyone not to achieve good grades and that he should study more.

10. **Self-Feeling (Positive)**
    You will feel better about yourself if you comply.
    Tell Dick he will feel proud if he studies more.

11. **Self-Feeling (Negative)**
    You will feel worse about yourself if you do not comply.
    Tell Dick he will feel ashamed of himself if he gets bad grades.

12. **Altercasting (Positive)**
    A person with "good" qualities would comply.
    Tell Dick that since he is mature and intelligent, he naturally will want to study more and get good grades.

13. **Altercasting (Negative)**
    Only a person with "bad" qualities would not comply.
    Tell Dick that only someone very childish does not study.

14. **Altruism**
    Your compliance is very badly needed, so do it as a favor.
    Tell Dick that you fervently want him to get into a good college and that you wish he would study more as a personal favor to you.

15. **Esteem (Positive)**
    People you value will think better of you if you comply.
    Tell Dick that the whole family will be very proud of him if he gets good grades.

16. **Esteem (Negative)**
    People you value will think worse of you if you do not comply.
    Tell Dick that the whole family will be very disappointed in him if he gets poor grades.

From Marwell & Schmitt, Dimensions of Compliance-gaining Behavior, 1967, pp.357–58.

FIGURE 7.4 COMPLIANCE-GAINING STRATEGIES: FAMILY SITUATION EXAMPLES.

Employing the concepts of directives, face, goals, and obstacles, Wilson (2002, 2010) has expounded on how compliance-gaining functions in interaction episodes. *Directives* are speech acts used to get a target to do something (i.e., perform an action) that they might otherwise not do, or at least object to. This concept suggests that the compliance-gaining request is attempting to overcome resistance on the part of the target. An example shared by Wilson (2002) involved asking his then-9-year-old stepdaughter to make her bed. In attempting to enact this compliance-gaining request, the requestor recognizes that the target likely will object to the request because the target may feel there is no need for the action (i.e., making the bed), lacks the willingness to comply (i.e., she does not want to make her bed), denies the legitimacy of the request (i.e., the requestor has no right to make the request), lacks the ability (i.e., she is too busy to make the bed), or that the requestor has no right to make the request (i.e., she can keep her room any way she wants to). Directives are employed when the requestor suggests that the "rules" for compliance are in effect, and that the target should follow those "rules."

Face involves the identity that a person tries to project during interactions with others (see Chapter 5 on Verbal Behavior, and Chapter 15 on Cultural Contexts for a more comprehensive treatment of "face"). The concepts of positive and negative face are integral to a discussion of face and facework in compliance. Positive face involves the desire to have one's actions approved and accepted by important others, while negative face involves not having one's actions restricted. Certain compliance-gaining requests are seen as face-threatening in that they restrict the autonomy of the target. As such, directives can be seen as face-threatening. Wilson (2002, 2010) argues that compliance-gaining requests are perceived as more face-threatening when the target has more power (e.g., asking for help from the boss vs. a co-worker), when the relationship between requestor and target is more distant (e.g., an acquaintance vs. friend), and when the compliance-gaining request is large vs. small (asking to borrow $100.00 vs. $1.00).

Goals are conceptualized as "future states of affairs that an individual is committed to achieving or maintaining" (Dillard, 2008, p. 66). During compliance-gaining efforts, the requestor's goal is to change or modify the target's behavior. It is suggested that compliance-gaining requests should be viewed more as the attainment of goals versus the seeking of compliance. Indeed, typologies of influence goals, or lists of reasons why people seek compliance (e.g., for help, advice, permission, change, relational change) have been developed (Wilson, 2002). Understanding which goal a requestor has helps to determine which compliance-gaining strategy would be most effective to employ.

Obstacles refer to the cluster of reasons why the target may refuse to cooperate with the compliance-gaining request. Wilson (2002, pp. 201–202) suggests that if the target of our compliance-gaining request is reluctant or hesitant, or even outright refuses to comply, the target will reveal reasons for noncompliance. It is suggested that those individuals who are requesting a compliance-gaining attempt anticipate potential obstacles as they formulate their message plans. If obstacles to the request are offered, then the requestor needs to determine whether they want to persist or continue with the request, and if so, whether they should address the obstacles which the target revealed.

One way of obtaining a better understanding of obstacles is through attribution theory. Attributions are judgments about the causes of events, or speculations as to why someone did, or did not, do something to, or for, you (e.g., "Why did my partner get so angry when I informed her/him that I could not drive her/him to the airport next Tuesday?"). Wilson, Cruz, Marshall, and Rao (1993) used an "attribution analysis" to predict how long requestors would persist with a compliance-gaining request after encountering resistance from a target, and how directly would the requestor address the "obstacles" to noncompliance (p. 352).

Weiner's (1979, 1985, 1986) attributional analysis was used as the theoretical framework for their study. This framework suggests that judgments about the causes of interpersonal events vary along three dimensions: (1) *locus*, whether the cause for the event is due to the actor (internal) or some other situational factor (external); (2) *stability*, whether the cause is unstable (fluctuates over time) or stable (constant over time); and (3) *controllability*, whether the cause is under the target's (or others') control (controllable) or beyond the actor (or others') control (i.e., is uncontrollable). The researchers predicted that requestors would persist with a compliance-gaining request when the target stated reasons for noncompliance that were unstable, internal, and controllable by the target. Conversely, requestors would be less likely to persist when their obstacles were stable, external, and uncontrollable by the target. This was due to the speculation that such obstacles have little chance of being overcome, hence, compliance would much less likely (Wilson, et al., 1993). In addition, the researchers speculated that requestors would use more "anti-social" compliance-gaining strategies when a target reveals noncompliance due to internal/controllable reasons rather than external/uncontrollable reasons.

Rather than simply employing "hypothetical situations," this study had participants actually engage in a "real" compliance-gaining effort. Participants were given a list of 20 "students" (actually, confederates in the study) who had "signed up" to earn extra credit for completing a study being conducted by a professor. The real participants were told to call these students to remind them about the time and place of their own study. If any of the 20 students changed their minds about participating, the real participants were asked to try to persuade them to honor their promise about completing the study. The researchers manipulated compliance. Of the 20 phone calls, 10 were answered by confederates who said that they would show up, one phone call went to a wrong number, and one call was never answered. The other eight calls were answered by confederates who said no, they would not show up and they offered different reasons for noncompliance which varied on the three dimensions of locus, stability, and controllability.

Nine compliance-gaining strategies, organized into four categories, were used: (1) *direct requests*—message sources simply requested that the target fulfill their obligation to participate in the study (e.g., "We were hoping you could make it"); (2) *resource-oriented strategies*—message sources either warned the targets about the negative consequences of not complying, emphasized the advantages of complying, or downplayed the disadvantages of complying (e.g., "You will get no extra credit points if you don't show up, and neither will your partner"; "You can always use the extra points"; "It should only take about an hour of your time"); (3) *obstacles to compliance*—message sources tried to clarify the reason the target was not complying, suggested methods of overcoming the obstacle, or denied that whatever excuse that was given could be easily overcome (e.g., "Do you have a conflict?"); and (4) *normative strategies*—message sources emphasized that the target was obligated to comply, or appealed to guilt or unselfish concerns to encourage compliance (e.g., "Well, can I just remind you that you signed up"; "You are also inconveniencing the other person that you have signed up with").

The results of the study suggested that message sources persisted most when they encountered reasons for noncompliance that were internal and controllable by targets, but this effect occurred primarily with unstable cases. With targets who disclosed unstable reasons for noncompliance (refusing to honor their commitment), participants persisted longer, challenged the obstacles offered by the target more, used guilt more, and saw their targets as more sincere if their reasons for noncompliance were internal/controllable" rather than "external/controllable." The authors suggest that these findings underscore the benefits of employing "attributional analysis" as a framework for understanding noncompliance to compliance-gaining requests.

CIALDINI'S PERSUASIVE HEURISTICS

Robert Cialdini (1988) developed six principles of compliance-gaining based on his experience in a variety of occupations, including advertising, public relations, and fundraising. He defines compliance as "action that is taken only because it has been requested" (Cialdini, 1987, p. 165). He noted that there are consistencies across all occupations in terms of getting people to comply with a request, which he labeled "persuasive heuristics." The six heuristics consist of reciprocity, commitment and consistency, social proof, liking, authority, and scarcity.

The reciprocity principle assumes that when someone gives you something, you should give them something in return. The sense of owing someone something is believed to be a powerful compliance-gaining strategy. People are constantly being given things in an effort to enhance compliance. Whether it is free food samples in a supermarket, free mailing labels from a charity, or free Avon products, the feeling of obligation is powerful and transcends cultures. In a study of charitable solicitations, Cialdini and Ascani (1976) used the reciprocity principle to increase blood donation. A request was made for people to join a long-term blood donor program. When this initial request was rejected, the researchers then made a second smaller request of a one-time blood donation. This smaller request resulted in a 50% compliance rate as opposed to a 32% compliance rate for simply asking for the one-time donation. This compliance technique is also known as the door in the face technique.

Reciprocity heuristic
A compliance-gaining strategy that assumes that when someone gives you something, you should give them something in return

Commitment and consistency heuristic
A compliance-gaining strategy that assumes that when people take a stand on an issue, there is internal pressure to be consistent with what they committed to

Social proof heuristic
A compliance-gaining strategy that assumes that we determine what is correct by finding out what other people think is correct

Liking heuristic
A compliance-gaining strategy that assumes that we comply with requests because we like the person

Authority heuristic
A compliance-gaining strategy that assumes that people should be more willing to follow the suggestions of an individual who is a legitimate authority

Scarcity heuristic
A compliance-gaining strategy that assumes that people want to try to secure those opportunities that are scarce

Door in the face technique
A compliance-gaining strategy that utilizes a large request followed by a smaller request. People are more likely to agree to the smaller request after rejecting the larger request

The commitment and consistency principle assumes that when people take a stand on an issue, there is internal pressure to be consistent with what they committed to. For example, it is common practice in the toy industry to purposely understock the more popular toys around the holiday season. Parents promise their children the most popular toys for the holidays. When the parent goes to the toy store and finds that the promised toy is out of stock, other toys are purchased to make up for the promised toy. Conveniently, after the holidays there is an ample amount of the most popular toys. The parent, more often than not, will return to get the promised toy, thus increasing the toy stores' overall sales.

The social proof principle states that "we determine what is correct by finding out what other people think is correct" (Cialdini, 1988, p. 110). This is especially powerful when we are uncertain about what is correct behavior. To determine what is correct behavior, we look around us to see how other people are behaving. This serves as a guide as to what is correct. Consider your favorite television comedy. The producers will purposely include "laugh tracks" to cue the viewer when to laugh. It is common practice in churches to "salt" the collection plate (i.e., put a one or five dollar bill in the plate before it is passed to the parishioners). Doing this sets a standard amount for the donation. This also works in bars, where the bartender will "salt" the tip jar to indicate the standard rate of tipping.

The liking principle assumes that we comply with requests because we like the person. The police use this principle when interrogating suspects. If you have ever seen an episode of *CSI* or *Law and Order*, you most certainly are familiar with the "good cop/bad cop" interrogation technique. The principle behind this technique is that one interrogator will threaten and be aggressive to the suspect, and the other will be more understanding and calm. When the aggressive interrogator leaves the room, the suspect will have a greater tendency to give information to interrogator that he or she "likes" more. It is a common practice in sales to build a relationship with your clients and then work toward the sale. It is well documented that **homophily**, or similarities of attitudes and backgrounds, increases liking (Byrne, 1971; Stotland & Patchen, 1961). In a study of peace marchers, Suedfeld, Bochner, and Matas (1971) found that people were more likely to sign a petition if the person requesting the signature was similarly dressed.

The authority heuristic holds that "one should be more willing to follow the suggestions of an individual who is a legitimate authority" (Cialdini, 1987, p. 175). Our culture is filled with authority figures that tell us what to think, who to vote for, and what to buy. One study revealed that people were three and a half times more likely to follow a jaywalker into traffic when he wore a suit as opposed to just a shirt and pants (Lefkowitz, Blake, & Mouton, 1955). The authority heuristic, similar to that of social proof, is particularly effective in times of uncertainty. When we are uncertain, we look to authority figures to help us determine what is appropriate.

The final persuasive heuristic is scarcity. Ciladini (1987) defined this principle as "one should want to try to secure those opportunities that are scarce" (p. 177). The fact that something is offered for a limited time or in limited quantity makes the item that much more valuable. This concept is illustrated in television infomercials. It is a common tactic for vendors to put a counter in the corner of the television screen informing the viewer of how many units are left. This strategy gives the viewer the perception that once they are sold out of the product, there will be no more available.

The persuasive heuristics developed by Robert Cialdini continue to represent one of the most comprehensive efforts in explaining the complex process of compliance-gaining. Recall in the elaboration likelihood model (ELM) of persuasion that people process messages either through the central route (critical thinking) or the peripheral route (cues in the environment). The persuasive heuristics presented here would be processed through the peripheral route of the ELM.

PREVENTING AND/OR RESISTING PERSUASION

We turn now to theories that explain how to prevent persuasion. In emphasizing how to persuade people, it is easy to forget that the reverse is often our goal. It is not unusual for us to want another person to resist being influenced by a third party. We might want a wavering Democrat to resist appeals to vote Republican. In a sense, we try to "persuade" a person not to be persuaded. There have been five approaches in persuasion research to the problem of how to prevent persuasion.

The *behavioral commitment* approach advises public statements about positions. If you know that someone supports your proposal, you would want him or her to express that opinion publicly. When other people learn someone holds a given position, it is more difficult for that person to change the position. Because the position has been associated with the individual, "losing face" might result from changing what was previously declared.

The *anchoring approach* is based on the idea that someone will be less likely to change a position if the position is anchored or "tied" to things that are significant for that person. With this approach you would try to convince an individual who valued others (friends, family, etc.) to agree with a position by pointing out that other people and/or reference groups (religious, political groups, etc.) also agree. You might add that important values (freedom, for instance) are upheld by the position. Changing an opinion would involve disagreeing with family and friends, would violate group norms, and would undermine values.

A third approach is creating *resistant cognitive states*. People are more difficult to persuade when they are in certain frames of mind. The major research finding in this area is that when persons experience an increase in self-esteem, they are particularly resistant to persuasion because people who feel high self-esteem believe they are valuable; they are confident and therefore less likely to say they were wrong in holding a position that a persuader tries to change. It is relatively easy to raise or lower self-esteem in a research laboratory. The main technique for raising self-esteem is to lead individuals to believe they have succeeded at an important task. Conversely, believing they have failed lowers self-esteem. Because a person with low self-esteem is particularly easy to persuade, an ethical issue arises. Is it acceptable to try to persuade someone who has just experienced failure? The person may be especially vulnerable at that time, and attempting persuasion may be taking advantage of him or her (Infante, 1976).

Training in critical methods is an approach that has met with mixed results. The idea appears sound. Train people to think critically when listening to a speech, to recognize fallacies in reasoning, and to detect propaganda techniques; they will then not be so easily persuaded. In one study, students were trained in methods for critically evaluating speeches. Later they listened to a tape-recorded speech. Women in the study were persuaded less than the control group of women who had not been taught the evaluation methods. However, male participants were persuaded more than the control group of untrained men. American culture may have influenced men to be more dogmatic in their positions than women; therefore, men may pay less attention to opposing positions in the message. The training might have neutralized this cultural effect and made men more sensitive to the content of the message (Infante & Grimmett, 1971), thus yielding the variable results.

INOCULATION THEORY

Inoculation theory
Approach to preventing persuasion based on the biological analogy of preventing disease

Inoculation theory from social psychology is the fifth approach (McGuire, 1964). This theory assumes that preventing persuasion is like preventing a disease. To keep a dangerous virus from causing a disease, the body can be inoculated with a weakened form of the disease-producing virus. The body's immune system will then create antibodies to destroy that type of virus. If the actual virus does invade the body at a later date, the defense will be in place and will prevent the disease. To prevent persuasion, according to this biological analogy, the person's cognitive system needs to be inoculated so a defense is in place when a strong persuasive message "invades the mind." How does *cognitive inoculation* work? The counterpart of the weakened virus would be weak arguments in support of an opponent's position. In theory, when an audience hears the weak arguments, they think of refutations for them. These refutations, like antibodies against a disease, form the foundation for attacking stronger arguments heard later. Thus, preventing persuasion from this approach involves "strengthening" the mind's defense systems so it will be able to destroy strong, attacking arguments.

PSYCHOLOGICAL REACTANCE THEORY

Have you ever experienced a situation when someone "took something away from you," or restricted your ability to choose? As a consequence of this, you wanted that "something" even more than you did before? An example of this resonates with many parents with the suggestion, "Tell your teenage daughter that you disapprove of her new boyfriend and she'll like him even more" (Gass & Seiter, 2014, p. 65). During a persuasive effort, if people feel that their choice-making ability is threatened, your persuasive effort may indeed backfire. This is sometimes referred to as the "boomerang effect" and is an essential component of the **psychological reactance theory of persuasion** (PRT) developed by Brehm (1966).

When individuals react negatively to a perceived loss of control, to threats, or a loss of freedom it stimulates psychological reactance. Psychological reactance theory deals with our resistance to persuasion and social influence. Any restriction or persuasive message that eliminates our freedom to choose will likely stimulate a reactance response in us. This is referred to as *state reactance*. Brehm and Brehm (1981) define reactance as a "motivational state that is hypothesized to occur when a freedom is eliminated or threatened with elimination" (p. 37). Reactance creates a desire to restore our attitudinal and/ or behavioral freedom (Shen & Dillard, 2005).

Four components form the basis of PRT: freedom, threat to freedom, reactance, and restoration of freedom (Quick, Shen, & Dillard, 2013). *Freedom* represents our perceptions about the way we can behave, the choices we have available to us. It includes our actions, emotions, and attitudes. *Threats* are anything that we believe restricts our freedom. Psychological *reactance* is a motivational state we experience when we believe that our freedom of choice has been restricted, eliminated, or even threatened with elimination, for example a parent telling his or her college student, "I forbid you to major in communication!"

Restoration of freedom suggests that when individuals believe that their freedom has been restricted or eliminated, they are motivated to restore it. Quick et al. (2013) suggest a number of behaviors are available which can serve to help us restore our freedom. The most direct form of restoration is actually engaging in the forbidden act or behavior. Thus, after your parent restricts your choice of a college major, you formally declare the major which was just forbidden! Freedoms can also be restored indirectly by: (1) becoming more favorable to the threatened choice, (2) derogating the source of the threat, (3) denying the existence of the threat, and (4) choosing a different freedom to feel more in control (Quick, et al., 2013, p. 168).

Using the example mentioned above about the parents' restriction on the child's choice of major in college, let us assume that Meghan experiences psychological reactance after being told that she cannot major in communication in college. What are some actions that Meghan can employ which will restore her feelings of freedom? First, she can act in direct opposition to her parent's mandate, that is, she can choose communication as her major in college. She can express an even greater desire or favorability of majoring in communication in college (indirect), she can think much less highly of her mother and decide not to abide by her mother's wishes (indirect), she can believe that her mother really has no say in her choice of college major (indirect) and should "butt out" of this issue, or she can choose to major in social psychology and minor in communication (indirect). In each case, however, Meghan is responding to the threat to or elimination of her freedom, and thus is engaging in psychological reactance.

Reactance restoration can be measured by employing the RRS (the Reactance Restoration Scale (Quick & Stephenson, 2007). When using this scale, individuals are presented with a set of three statements in which they are asked to respond to a set of semantic differential-type scales (motivated—unmotivated, determined—not determined, encouraged—not encouraged, inspired—not inspired) based upon a particular persuasive message. Participants use the three semantic differential-type scales to indicate their intended behavior. For example, this scale was given to participants after they read a persuasive message which advocated sunscreen usage when directly exposed to the sun. An example of one of the statements on the scale is: "*Right now, I (am) _____ to use sunscreen the next time I am exposed to direct sunlight for an extended period of time (greater than 15 minutes).*"

Psychological reactance has also been conceptualized as an "individual difference," or a trait (see Chapter 4 for a review of communication and personality traits). That is, individuals can vary in the amount of self-determination and need for autonomy. Individuals who self-report that they are high in trait reactance have a strong need for autonomy and independence, and tend to resist authority (Quick, Scott, & Ledbetter, 2011).

A Psychological Reactance Scale (Hong & Faedda, 1996) was developed to measure this individual difference, called trait reactance. The scale consists of four factors: (1) *emotional response toward restricted choice* (e.g., "I become frustrated when I am unable to make free and independent decisions"); (2) *reactance to compliance* (e.g., "When something is prohibited, I usually think, 'That's exactly what I am going to do'"); (3) *resisting influence from others* (e.g., "When someone forces me to do something, I feel like doing the opposite"); and, (4) *reactance to advice and recommendations* (e.g., "Advice and recommendations usually induce me to do just the opposite").

In a study in the context of health communication, Quick et al. (2011) investigated, among other concerns, whether trait reactance would be positively related with a perceived threat to a freedom (organ donation). In this study, participants read messages which advocated organ donation. One of the messages advocating organ donation was deemed freedom threatening (e.g., "Stop the denial! Given the need for organ donors, a reasonable person would consent to be an organ donor. Becoming an organ donor is something you simply have to do"). The other message did not threaten the freedom to donate (e.g., "You are the only one that can decide if becoming an organ donor is right for you").

Participants were assessed on their level of trait and state reactance, their attitudes toward organ donation, their intentions to donate, and their level of perceived threat to their freedom which the message contained. The results of the study revealed that trait reactance significantly predicted a threat to their freedom. That is, those individuals who were self-identified as high in trait reactance felt that the message severely restricted their freedom, and their attitudes and intentions to donate were less favorable. This led the researchers to suggest "the importance of avoiding overtly persuasive communication when promoting organ donation to trait-reactant individuals" (Quick et al., 2011, p. 674).

Psychological reactance theory represents a powerful and evolving theory of persuasion which helps explain why some individuals are more likely than others to resist persuasion. Its tenets can be profitably applied to numerous communication contexts including interpersonal, organizational, group, media, health, and intercultural communication.

PERSONALITY TRAITS AND PERSUASION

In Chapter 4 we presented several communication and personality traits which impact on communication behavior. Many communication studies have explored how personality influences communication, especially in persuasion situations. As we conclude this chapter, we will present several personality traits which primarily impact on persuasive communication.

Persuasibility Research reported in the book *Personality and Persuasibility* (Hovland & Janis, 1959) suggests that a personality trait predicts how much a person is influenced by persuasion attempts—regardless of the topic, source, or situation. This idea appears to be valid. Some people seem easy to persuade. They rarely resist pressure to move in one direction or another. This willingness to change can be viewed as persuasibility. Also, other individuals seem consistently difficult to persuade. They rarely budge on any issue. In essence, they seem resistant to persuasion.

> **Persuasibility** Personality trait indicating willingness to be persuaded

The idea of a persuasibility trait appears to be an uncomplicated way to explain susceptibility to social influence. However, conceptually the matter is not so clear. Is there such a trait, or are there other personality traits sometimes related to persuasion that create the illusion of a general persuasibility trait? In that regard, the traits that follow have been found to be related to persuasion. The amount of persuasibility indicated by each trait, when viewed as a whole, could create the impression that there is a more global persuasibility trait.

Self-Esteem Self-esteem refers to how favorably the individual evaluates himself or herself and is a trait related to persuasion. When individuals have low self-esteem, they lack self-confidence in general, and they have little faith that their positions on controversial issues are valid. They tend to be high in persuasibility. When told by a speaker that their positions should be changed, they tend to believe the speaker: "The speaker must know what is right on this, for I certainly do not know." High self-esteem, on the other hand, is thought to be related to low persuasibility. When people feel very good about themselves, they are also confident about their positions on controversial issues because opinions are a part of one's identity. Satisfaction with oneself usually discourages change. Therefore, individuals with high self-esteem tend to resist persuasion.

> **Self-esteem** How favorably the individual evaluates himself or herself is related to persuasion

Dogmatism Rokeach (1960) conceptualized dogmatism in terms of individuals' willingness to consider belief systems (what one associates with an object or issue) other than the ones they hold. Open-minded individuals are willing to consider other sets of beliefs, even if they feel very strongly about an issue. Dogmatic or closed-minded persons are unwilling to do so. They have a firm set of beliefs for an issue, and they do not want to be bothered by other belief systems.

> **Dogmatism** The individual's willingness to consider other belief systems

Dogmatic people find it very difficult to separate a source from the source's message. Thus, if dogmatic people like a source, they tend to accept the source's message; if they dislike a speaker, rarely will the speaker's message persuade them. The open-minded person, however, has less trouble reacting differently to source and message—for example, "I can't stand the speaker, but he makes a good point." When the source is viewed as credible, dogmatism is associated with persuasion. This is especially true when the persuasion topic is not very important to the individual. Dogmatic people tend to be rather easy to persuade when given a credible source and a less important topic. This also suggests that open-minded persons are not necessarily easy to persuade. When the source is credible and the topic rather unimportant, open-minded people are more difficult to persuade than dogmatic individuals.

Machiavellianism An orientation in which people believe that manipulating others is a basic strategy of social influence

Machiavellianism The trait of Machiavellianism refers to an orientation in which people believe that manipulating others is a basic strategy of social influence. Individuals who are high in Machiavellianism think it is ethical to tell people only what they want to hear, to use the receivers' doubts, fears, and insecurities to motivate action, and even to distort facts so they become more acceptable. Generally these people are willing to use whatever strategy works in persuasion; they are very pragmatic. High Machiavellians tend to act rather detached and to be less emotional than other people. They believe the end justifies the means. Persons with a high level of this trait have a strong need to influence others. They like leadership positions, and they are usually the dominant parties in their relations with other people.

Low Machiavellians, on the other hand, are very non-manipulative in dealing with people. They want to avoid pressuring others, to allow others maximum freedom to decide for themselves. Low Machiavellians tend to have little need to dominate and influence others. They tend to be more emotional than high Machiavellians when discussing a controversial issue.

Need for social approval A person's need for approval from others influences how they react to persuasive messages that imply approval-disapproval

Opinionated acceptance Language that expresses a favorable attitude toward people who agree with the speaker

Opinionated rejection Language that expresses an unfavorable attitude toward people who disagree with the speaker

Need for Social Approval People vary in their need for social approval and the extent to which they fear social disapproval. According to this idea, a source who offers social approval or threatens social disapproval when the receiver has a strong need for approval ought to be very persuasive. Various forms of opinionated language specified by Rokeach (1960) provide a way to test this relationship. Opinionated acceptance language expresses a favorable attitude toward those people who agree with the speaker—for example, "Intelligent and responsible people will agree that my proposal is needed." Opinionated rejection language states a negative attitude toward those who disagree with the speaker's position—for example, "Only a bigoted fool would oppose this plan." Opinionated acceptance language represents social approval, whereas opinionated rejection constitutes social disapproval. Baseheart (1971) found support for the idea that opinionated language leads to more persuasion when people have a strong need for social approval. In such a circumstance, opinionated rejection was as successful as opinionated acceptance in stimulating persuasion. Having a strong need for social approval probably heightens a person's sensitivity to language that suggests the speaker is evaluating the receiver in some way.

SUMMARY

Persuasion is an integral topic for communication study because the skill of the persuader in using verbal and nonverbal symbols affects the interaction. In this chapter, we defined persuasion as attitude change toward a source's proposal. Persuasion differs from coercion because audience members can choose to agree or disagree. In this framework, belief change leads to attitude change, which can then produce behavior change. Adapting to the audience and the situation makes persuasion more effective.

As we said at the beginning of this chapter, persuasion research has changed greatly in recent years. We think it is important for persuasion research to continue with the enthusiasm it has enjoyed in the past. Current researchers are especially interested in how people influence one another in interpersonal relationships. The advertising and public relations professions provide another important persuasive context for the application of communication theory.

Research that enhances our understanding of the persuasion process is inherently valuable. Of course, there are other ways of influencing another person's behavior. Two particularly distasteful methods are physical aggression and coercion. Persuasion is infinitely more desirable than these alternatives because the process of persuasion respects the dignity of others and their right to choose among alternatives based on their beliefs. Persuasion offers hope for people to resolve differences in a satisfying and constructive manner.

KEY TERMS

Assimilation

Attitude

Authority heuristic

Behavioral intention

Belief

Central route

Coercion

Cognitive dissonance theory

Commitment and consistency heuristic

Compliance

Controllability

Dogmatism

Ego-involvement

Elaboration likelihood model (ELM)

Factor model of credibility

Functional model of credibility

Inoculation theory

Latitude of acceptance

Latitude of noncommitment

Latitude of rejection

Liking heuristic

Machiavellianism

Multiple-act

Need for cognition

Need for social approval

Opinionated acceptance

Opinionated rejection

Perceived behavioral control

Perceived control

Peripheral route

Persuasibility

Reciprocity heuristic

Scarcity heuristic

Selective exposure

Self-efficacy

Self-esteem

Social proof heuristic

Subjective norm

THEORY BUILDING IN COMMUNICATION CONTEXTS

The idea that communication is highly contextual is widely accepted. A message that has one meaning in one context can take on a much different meaning in another context. Chapter 8 discusses theory building in interpersonal communication contexts. This has been one of the most active research areas in the field. We discuss the interpersonal communication motives model, goals-plans-action theory, planning theory, constructivist theory, relational framing theory, truth default theory, and uncertainty reduction theory. These theories address questions that include why people communicate, how they produce messages, why messages get interpreted in different ways, and why some people are more effective communicators than others.

Chapter 9 explains theory building in Relational Contexts. The chapter begins with a discussion of similarity and attraction, which provides key historical backdrop to the development of theorizing about communication and relationships, including predicted outcome value theory, the relationship interaction stages model, the relationship maintenance model, relational dialectics theory, the relational turbulence model, and communication privacy management theory. The chapter concludes with a discussion of family communication patterns theory, an influential theory of communication in family relationship contexts.

Chapter 10 introduces you to the different types of groups and the various roles that people play in those groups. We also introduce the different types of group leadership, unique forms of conflict types, and conformity issues specific to group communication. We then present some of the major theories within the group communication context.

Organizational communication is examined in Chapter 11. The evolution of organizational communication theory is traced through three major approaches in the field of management and communication. We present the theories developed from an interdisciplinary perspective and those specific to the discipline of communication such as the theory of independent mindedness. We then introduce you to theories and approaches to leadership and motivation as well as how workers are socialized to organizations. We conclude the chapter with a discussion of ethics within the workplace.

Chapter 12 identifies basic questions explored by mass media researchers. After reviewing early theory-building efforts in mass communication, we discuss the functions of mass media. Next, we present agenda-setting theory, which addresses the powerful influence of the media. The theory of parasocial interaction, uses and gratifications, cultivation theory, spiral of silence, and media dependency theory probe the effects of the media on users.

Recently, theories have emerged which attempt to explain the communication in computer-mediated contexts, including cell phones, tablets, desktop and laptop computers, and other technologies. Chapter 13 presents three sets of computer-mediated communication (CMC) theories. "Cues-filtered-out" theories include social presence theory, the lack-of-social-context-cues hypothesis, and the social identity model of deindividuation effects. Channel selection theories include media richness theory, channel expansion theory, and media synchronicity theory. Adaptation theories include social information processing theory, the efficiency framework, and the hyperpersonal model.

In Chapter 14 we introduce the evolution of health communication, the functions of communication, and various personality characteristics that influence patient-provider interaction. We then introduce a variety of health communication theories that include uncertainty management, diffusion of innovation, and the transtheoretical model.

We conclude our treatment of theory building in communication in Chapter 15 by discussing contemporary and influential efforts to understand how culture influences communication and its outcomes. The four theories discussed in this chapter are Hofstede's dimensions of national culture, face negotiation theory, anxiety/uncertainty management theory, and cross-cultural adaptation theory.

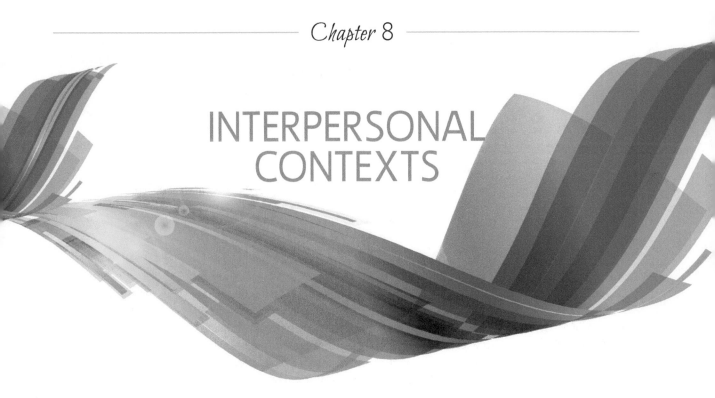

Chapter 8

INTERPERSONAL CONTEXTS

During the late 1950s and early 1960s, few communication scholars engaged in research and theory building about interpersonal relationships. Research in interpersonal interaction was conducted primarily by sociologists, social psychologists, and anthropologists. When the study of dyadic (one-on-one) communication began in earnest, researchers investigated how communication could be used to develop and improve interpersonal relationships with friends, lovers, and spouses. The first textbooks in interpersonal communication appeared in the early 1970s (Giffin & Patton, 1971; Keltner, 1970; McCroskey, Larson, & Knapp, 1971). Later in the decade, the communication discipline experienced a surge in researching and theorizing about interpersonal communication (Delia, 1987)

Interpersonal communication has been a focus for so many scholars, and defined in so many ways (Burleson, 2010), that it can be challenging to determine what "counts" as a theory of interpersonal communication. However, one useful distinction is between theories that focus on message production and interpretation processes that occur in most, if not all, types of dyadic interactions and relationships (even between strangers), and theories that focus primarily on processes specific to the development, maintenance, and termination of personal relationships. We address the first type of theory in this chapter, and the second in Chapter 9, Relational Contexts.

This chapter will introduce you to seven theories of interpersonal communication: the interpersonal communication motives model, goals-plans-action theory, planning theory, constructivist theory, relational framing theory, truth default theory, and uncertainty reduction theory. These theories address questions that include why people communicate interpersonally, how they produce messages, why messages get interpreted in different ways, why some people are more effective communicators than others, why it is difficult to tell when someone is lying, and what happens when strangers meet. Although these are only a few of the useful theories of message production and interpretation created by communication scholars, they are a good starting point for students, and will offer you considerable insight into everyday experiences interacting with others.

THE INTERPERSONAL COMMUNICATION MOTIVES MODEL

Theory of interpersonal communication motives A theory that identifies the motives people have for interpersonal communication

The interpersonal communication motives model (ICM) was developed by Rebecca Rubin, Elizabeth Perse, and Carole Barbato to describe important differences in why people communicate interpersonally (Barbato & Perse, 1992; Rubin, Perse, & Barbato, 1988; Graham, Barbato, & Perse, 1993). Their work drew on two existing theories: interpersonal needs theory (Schutz, 1958), and the uses and gratifications theory of mass media (Lazarsfeld & Stanton, 1944, see Chapter 12). Consistent with uses and gratifications theory, ICM assumes that communication behavior is "purposeful and goal-directed," and "that people are mindful of their communication choices" (Graham, Barbato, & Perse, 1993, p. 173). Thus, the purpose of ICM is to identify key reasons, or motives, explaining *why* people engage in interpersonal communication. As defined by the theory, a motive is an internal state of readiness to act to achieve a goal.

Motive An internal state of readiness to act to achieve a goal

The initial work to develop ICM examined how motives for communicating were associated with communication apprehension and satisfaction (Rubin, Perse, Barbato, 1988). This work identified six motives for engaging in interpersonal communication, and developed the Interpersonal Communication Motives Scale to measure these motives (see Figure 8.1). It also showed that low communication apprehension was associated with the pleasure, affection, and control motives, whereas high communication apprehension was associated with the inclusion motive, and that communication satisfaction was most strongly associated with the pleasure, affection, and relaxation motives.

1. **Affection**—interpersonal communication used to express concern, caring, and appreciation for others
2. **Control**—interpersonal communication used to gain compliance from others, to get others to do what you want them to do
3. **Escape**—interpersonal communication used to avoid engaging in other activities and to "fill the time"
4. **Inclusion**—interpersonal communication used to share feelings, avoid loneliness, be with others (i.e., companionship)
5. **Pleasure**—interpersonal communication used for social benefits, for fun, stimulation, and entertainment
6. **Relaxation**—interpersonal communication used to help relax and unwind

From: Rubin, R. B., Perse, E. M., & Barbato, C. A. (1988). Conceptualization and measurement of interpersonal communication motives. *Human Communication Research, 14*, 602–28. Copyright 1988 by Wiley–Blackwell. Reprinted by permission.

INSTRUCTIONS: Here are several reasons people give for why they talk to other people. For each statement, provide a number that best expresses your own reasons for talking to others. Use the following scale:

Put a "5" if the reason is exactly like your own reason.
Put a "4" if the reason is a lot like your own reason.
Put a "3" if the reason is somewhat like your own reason.
Put a "2" if the reason is not much like your own reason
Put a "1" if the reason is not at all like your own reason.

"I talk to people . . ."

_____ 1. Because it's fun.
_____ 2. To help others.
_____ 3. Because I need someone to talk to or be with.
_____ 4. To put off something I should be doing.
_____ 5. Because it relaxes me.
_____ 6. Because it's a pleasant rest.
_____ 7. Because I want someone to do something for me.
_____ 8. Because it's exciting.
_____ 9. To let others know I care about their feelings.
_____ 10. Because I just need to talk about my problems sometimes.
_____ 11. To get away from what I am doing.
_____ 12. Because it allows me to unwind.
_____ 13. To thank them.
_____ 14. Because it makes me feel less lonely.
_____ 15. Because I have nothing better to do.
_____ 16. To get something I don't have.
_____ 17. To have a good time.
_____ 18. To tell others what to do.

Scoring: Total your scores for each subscore below. The range for each subscore is 3–15.

Your score:

Pleasure:	(Items 1, 8, 17)
Affection:	(Items 2, 9, 13)
Inclusion:	(Items 3, 10, 14)
Escape:	(Items 4, 11, 15)
Relaxation:	(Items 5, 12, 6)
Control:	(Items 7, 18, 16)

FIGURE 8.1 THE INTERPERSONAL COMMUNICATION MOTIVES SCALE.

Since the initial research, ICM has stimulated a large number of studies that situate motives within a constellation of predictors and outcomes. Some of this work examines personality and demographic factors that are associated with interpersonal motives (Barbato & Perse, 1992; Rubin, Fernandez-Collado, & Hernandez-Sampieri, 1992). For example, one early study (Rubin & Rubin, 1992) examined the relationship between locus of control and interpersonal motives. This study found that individuals with an *external* locus-of-control orientation (those who believe that chance and powerful others control their lives) seem to be motivated by the inclusion motive to communicate with others. People with an *internal* locus-of-control orientation (those who feel that they exert control over their environment and lives) tend to be motivated to communicate by the control motive.

Another set of studies examined interpersonal communication motives in various relationships and contexts. The results suggest that we tend to communicate with family members, spouses and lovers, and close friends for affection, pleasure, and inclusion. For example, parents report communicating with their children primarily for affection and pleasure motives, and secondarily for relaxation and inclusion (Barbato, Graham, & Perse, 2003). Similarly, inclusion, affection, and pleasure accounted for a great deal of communication between fathers and young adult children (Martin & Anderson, 1995). Another study found that escape, control, inclusion, and pleasure motives accounted for much communication between mothers and adult children (Anderson & Martin, 1995a). In the organizational context, employees are most satisfied with co-worker relationships when their interpersonal communication motives involve affection (and not escape), and with their supervisor relationships when their interpersonal communication motives involve pleasure and inclusion.

Finally, a body of research has been devoted to examining relationships between interpersonal motives and communication behavior. One study showed that affection, control, and inclusion are significant motives for resolving conflict between romantic partners (Myers, Zhong, & Mitchell, 1995). Another study explored differences in interpersonal communication motives between "competent communicators" and those who are less competent. In this study, competent communicators were defined as people who are both assertive (dominant, competitive, aggressive) *and* responsive (gentle, friendly, empathic). Competent communicators seem to communicate more for affection and pleasure, whereas less competent individuals seem to communicate more for control and escape (Anderson & Martin, 1995b). In the context of small-group communication, the interpersonal motives of escape, control, inclusion, pleasure, and affection influence members' satisfaction with a group (Anderson & Martin, 1995c).

ICM helps to explain how demographic and personality characteristics affect communication behavior, the "profile" of communication in different relationships, and why some communicators may be more effective than others. As research connected with this theory proceeds, scholars are recognizing a need for attention to the scope and validity of the ICM scale. Although items from the original scale continue to be used, many researchers add items to measure additional motives, depending on their research interests (e.g., Myers, Zhong,

& Mitchell, 1995). These adaptations raise important questions about which motives are consistent across individuals, relationships, and contexts. Further, as statistical techniques for analyzing scales continue to improve, scholars have questioned whether there are actually six distinct motives being measured by the ICM, or whether some of them should be divided or combined (Frisby & Martin, 2010). In all, ICM scholars need to address the issue of which motives matter, and how best to assess them. Despite this concern, ICM research continues to grow. A recent set of studies examines communication motives in sibling relationships, which are historically understudied compared to other kinds of familial relationships (Rocca, Martin, & Dunleavy, 2010).

GOALS-PLANS-ACTION THEORY AND PLANNING THEORY

Like interpersonal motives theory, goals-plans-action theory (GPA; Dillard, 1990) and planning theory (Berger, 1997) both emphasize communicators' choices about how they communicate. However, whereas IMT examines broad motives for communicating with others, these two theories focus on more specific goals and plans that guide message production during interaction. GPA was initially designed as a theory of interpersonal influence (Dillard, 1990), and still retains a principal focus on situations in which one person tries to affect what another person thinks or does. Yet GPA increasingly functions as a general theory of message production. Because planning theory (Berger, 1997) focuses primarily on the relationship between plans and messages (action), it provides detail about the effects of planning that is missing from the broader GPA model. Both theories are consistent with the communication plan perspective (Infante, 1980) described in Chapter 1.

Goals-plans-action theory A theory that explains message production as resulting from goals and the plans made to achieve them

Planning theory A theory that describes message effectiveness as a consequence of plan characteristics, especially plan complexity

GPA THEORY

GPA theorist James Dillard describes goals as "future states of affairs that an individual is committed to achieving or maintaining" (Dillard, 2015, p. 65). Although this definition might encompass goals that people can pursue alone, the focus of GPA is really on interaction goals: the types of goals we pursue by talking with others, such as influence or support. Frequently, if not typically, people pursue multiple goals in interaction. GPA theory distinguishes between primary goals and secondary goals. Primary goals are the motivators for interaction: they stimulate thoughts and behaviors necessary for message construction. In essence, primary goals "have to do with the specific purpose of talk" (Meyer, 2004, p. 168). Dillard and colleagues have described six common types of primary influence goals (Dillard, Anderson, & Knobloch, 2002): *gaining assistance* ("Can you help me move my furniture?"), *giving advice* ("I think you should see a doctor about that cough."), *sharing activity* ("Let's go see that concert this weekend!"), *change orientation* which is to change another person's position or stance on an issue ("You should really think about Bernie Sanders!"), *change relationship* ("I think we need to get engaged."), *obtain*

Goals Future states of affairs that an individual is committed to achieving or maintaining

Pimary goals Principal reasons for interaction, determining subsequent plans and actions

permission ("Can I go to the party even if you cannot be there?"), and *enforce rights and obligations* ("You said you would help me with my statistics homework since I cleaned the apartment."). Other scholars have described primary goals relevant to support (MacGeorge, 2001) and conflict (Samp & Solomon, 1999) interactions. In addition to motivating behavior, primary goals also affect how we perceive and interpret behavior. For example, if your primary goal is changing a friendship to a romantic relationship, you will probably pay more attention to certain kinds of nonverbal behavior (e.g., proximity, touch) and attach different meaning to that behavior than if your primary goal were getting your friend to stop borrowing your tennis racket without permission.

Secondary goals Concerns that arise when pursuing a primary goal

In the pursuit of a primary goal, other concerns often emerge. Secondary goals are concerns that arise because of the desire to pursue a primary goal. Dillard has described five categories of secondary goals (Dillard, Segrin, & Hardin, 1989). *Identity goals* are focused on upholding personal standards and ethics, and may "push" people away from unethical or distasteful behavior such as lying to get something they want. *Conversation management goals* are focused on managing impressions and protecting face (see theories in Chapters 5 and 15). *Relational resource goals* are about maintaining the relationship. These goals motivate communicators to consider "relational costs" when pursuing their primary goals (e.g., "I am considering asking my partner to sleep in a different room because s/he snores; how will that request impact our level of intimacy?"). *Personal resource goals* are about preserving one's own resources (e.g., time, energy, material goods). They help determine aspects of message construction (e.g., "I cut the conversation short because I realized I was wasting my time," Dillard, 2008, p. 69). Finally, *affect management goals* are the concerns message producers have for creating, sustaining, or preventing emotional responses. For example, when asking someone to go out with you, you may be dealing with anxiety, or trying to avoid being embarrassed.

For any given primary goal and interaction, different secondary goals become more or less relevant. If your roommate continually forgets his agreed-upon job of taking out the garbage, you might have the primary goal of enforcing that obligation, and the secondary goals of making sure that you don't have to take on the job (a personal resource goal) and keeping a cordial relationship (a relational resource goal). Secondary goals vary in their compatibility with primary goals and with each other, with less compatible goals creating challenges for interaction. In the roommate example, there is a tension between getting the trash taken out, not doing it yourself, and maintaining the relationship.

GPA theory has stimulated considerable theorizing and research. To illustrate, one study tested the theory in the context of students' decisions to discuss disappointing grades with their instructors (Henningsen, Valde, Russell, & Russell, 2011). Based on GPA theory, the researchers predicted that students who were more concerned about primary and secondary goals would do more planning for interacting with the instructor, which in turn, would lead to a decision to engage in (or not) an attempt to influence the instructor to reconsider or change the grade. In the study, participants were asked to think of a class in which they had received a disappointing grade. Although they had received this grade, they had not as yet spoken with the faculty member who gave them that grade. Participants who fulfilled these criteria completed a survey that contained measures of concern for primary and secondary goals relevant to this situation, amount of planning, and decision to engage the instructor. For example, the *influence primary goal* was measured with items such as, "It is very important that I convince the faculty member to reconsider my grade. *Conversation management secondary goals* included items such as, "In the conversation with the faculty member, I will avoid saying things that are socially inappropriate." *Relational resource secondary goals* were measured with items such as, "During the conversation about the disappointing grade, I am not willing to hurt our faculty-student relationship to get what I want." In addition, *amount of planning* was measured with items such as, "I have planned out how to discuss my disappointing grade with my faculty member," and the *decision to engage* (action) was measured with items such as, "I have decided that I want to discuss my disappointing grade with the faculty member" (Henningsen et al., 2011). The results of the study generally supported GPA theory. Several goals (the influence primary goal, the conversation management secondary goal, and the relational resource goal) were found to stimulate planning, the amount of planning led to the decision to engage in the influence attempt with the instructor, and the decision to engage actually predicted whether or not the student actually discussed the grade with the faculty member (e.g., "I directly discussed the grade with my faculty member" (Henningsen, et al., 2011, p. 186).

PLANNING THEORY

Both GPA and planning theory (PT) describe goals as determining the plans that people make and utilize for interaction, but PT offers a more detailed analysis of plan characteristics and their effects on communicative action. Theorist Charles Berger describes plans as "cognitive representations of action sequences that enable people to achieve goals" (2015, p. 90). PT contends that whenever individuals are engaged in communication with each other, plans are being developed or recalled, and used. Planning, or the process of developing plans, can take multiple forms: communicators can recall a verbal or nonverbal plan that they have already used in a similar situation (sometimes referred to as a "canned plan"), they can observe the plans enacted by credible others or role models, they can enact a plan developed by another person, or they can create a plan by imagining the interaction (Berger, 1997). Sometimes, extensive planning takes place prior to the interaction. For example, when you were younger your parents may have left you home alone for the evening. While running around the house playing with your sibling or friend, you broke an expensive item of furniture. In the effort to reduce punishment, you may have spent much of the remaining evening devising a plan for communicating with your parents on their return home! However, planning is often extemporaneous ("on the spot"), as you start with a pre-existing plan and rapidly modify it to adapt to the interaction as it proceeds. For example, when you realize your boss knows you were posting party photos on Facebook when you were home "sick," you may have to quickly plan a way of explaining your behavior.

Plans Cognitive representations of actions to be taken to achieve goals

Planning Processes involved in developing plans

PT describes plans as hierarchically organized, with more abstract plan elements organizing more concrete elements. For example, a plan for obtaining food at a restaurant might include two major elements of placing the order and paying for the food. The element of placing the order might include sub-elements such as greeting the restaurant employee, stating what you want, and answering questions if asked. Similarly, the paying for the food plan might be broken down into sub-elements that include handing over cash or swiping a credit card, checking that all items are present, and thanking the employee. (GPA makes a less precise distinction between strategy-level plans, or general approaches, and tactic-level plans, which specify step-by-step behaviors.) Plans vary in how specific or detailed they are, and how many contingencies (if X happens, then do Y) they include.

Plan complexity
The specificity of a plan, including its level of detail and number of contingencies

Planning theory refers to variation in detail and contingency as plan complexity, and contends that greater plan complexity usually results in more effective communication. In a test of this contention, Berger and Bell (1988) asked individuals to respond to a series of questions regarding a potential dating request. Participants were asked to assume that they met an attractive other at a party and decided that they would like to date this person. They were asked to respond to the following questions: "How would you go about asking the person for a date?" "What would you say to the person?" "What would you do to achieve your objective, that is, what steps would you go through to get the date?" Each response to those questions was evaluated by a panel of male and female judges on the effectiveness of the plan (effective–ineffective), plan complexity (as measured by plan length or the number of specific actions mentioned), plan breadth (i.e., actions to be taken if the plan failed), and plan contingencies (a ratio of plan length and plan breadth). Results indicated that plans judged to be more effective contained more actions, had greater breadth, and contained more anticipated contingencies (i.e., future actions to use in case the request for the date was rejected).

However, PT also acknowledges that beyond a certain point, plan complexity can be detrimental. When plans fail, research indicates that communicators whose plans are extremely complex are slower to respond, impairing their fluency and credibility (Berger, 1997). In addition, complex plans do not guarantee effectiveness, because communicators must possess the appropriate "performance skills" to be able to enact the plan. Thus, no matter how effective the plan may appear "on paper," if a communicator cannot deliver the plan with competent verbal and nonverbal behavior, the plan may not be successful. Individuals whose jobs require a great deal of competence in developing message plans (e.g., script- and screenwriters, public relations practitioners, news writers, etc.) often rely on communicatively competent and dynamic others such as actors, news anchors, and politicians to carry out their communication plans (Berger, 2015, p. 97). Further, some individuals with competent performance skills may not be competent message plan creators.

The **hierarchy principle** of PT explains how people respond to failed communication plans. According to this principle, when we realize that a communication plan hasn't worked, our first changes are usually to the simplest, most concrete elements of our plans. Imagine that you state your fast-food order, but the employee just stares at you. What do you do? In all likelihood, you'll repeat your order, perhaps more loudly and emphatically. If that doesn't work, you might then begin to alter your plan more substantially, to include elements like "finding a responsive employee," but initial changes are typically to the simplest elements of the plan. Because simple plan changes often work (most restaurant employees are going to respond when the order is repeated), this tendency saves effort. But it can also backfire, especially when goals are more complex than ordering food, and when initial plans are too simple or abstract. If your plan to borrow your friend's car is simply "Ask for the car" and the request is denied, asking again or adding "please" probably won't change the response. On the spot, it will be difficult to devise a more sophisticated plan that includes "acknowledge imposition," "offer compensation," and "convey gratitude" (and your friend will be especially aware those new elements are included specifically for persuasive impact).

FROM GOALS AND PLANS TO ACTION

Neither PT nor GPA theory specifies all the many message features that might be affected by goals and plans. (Indeed, these may be infinite.) However, GPA describes *influence* messages as varying on four dimensions that are likely to be affected by message producers' plans and in turn affect how message targets respond. These dimensions are explicitness (the transparency or "obviousness" of the goals), dominance (how much power or status the influence message asserts), argument (whether the message includes reasons for the desired action), and control over outcomes (whether the message includes promises or threats that the message producer can carry out) (Dillard, 2015).

GPA and PT have exerted considerable influence on interpersonal communication scholarship, such that most scholars currently describe message production as a process of goal pursuit and plan enactment. However, these theories also have limitations. Both are restricted to explaining intentional behavior. Research to test the theories depends on participants' capacity to report their own goals and plans, which may alter in the process of being reported (Dillard, 1997). GPA remains somewhat tied to its original roots as a theory of influence. Most PT research has focused rather narrowly on plan complexity. Both theories have informed substantial bodies of research, but will continue to benefit from greater testing and elaboration. Such work is proceeding. For example, Palomares has developed a theory of how people detect others' goals (Palomares, 2008). Caughlin has presented a "multiple goals theory," which echoes the GPA's emphasis on the multiplicity of goals and their potential to conflict and create challenges for message producers, but also adds a new focus on the persistence of certain goals within relationships over time (for example, always trying to get your parents to relax, or your best friend to feel better; Caughlin, 2010).

CONSTRUCTIVIST THEORY

Constructivist theory, also called constructivism, was developed and introduced to the communication discipline by Jessie Delia during the mid 1970s. Multiple communication scholars, most notably James Applegate, Brant Burleson, Ruth Anne Clark, Barbara O'Keefe, Daniel O'Keefe, and Wendy Samter, have contributed to the testing, extension, and application of this theory (Burleson & Caplan, 1998).

Constructivist theory has historical connections with social constructionist theories that emphasize human beings as active interpreters and agents in their social worlds, rejecting the notion that people passively follow "laws" of human behavior (Gubrium & Holstein, 2008). Thus, reality is socially constructed and individually interpreted and is not fully separable from the perceiver. However, constructivist theory also asserts that individual interpretation has certain regular properties across people, so like most of the theories in this textbook it is better understood as a scientific or post-positivist theory than an interpretive one.

At the heart of constructivist theory is the idea of personal constructs. Personal constructs are assumed to take the form of bi-polar dimensions (e.g., rich–poor, kind–cruel, arrogant–humble, stingy–generous). Some personal constructs are very concrete, such as those dealing with the physical attributes of others (e.g., tall–short), whereas others are more abstract and deal with the personality and behavior (e.g., friendly–unfriendly). Personal constructs are "the basic cognitive structures through which persons interpret, anticipate, evaluate, and understand aspects of the world" (Burleson & Caplan, 1998, p. 236). In other words, our constructs affect how we make sense of people and events, and consequently influence all aspects of our interactions with others (Nicotera, 1995).

People differ in the specific constructs they possess and rely on. For example, one person might rely heavily on the spiritual–secular construct (or religious–nonreligious) construct, placing everyone they meet somewhere on this dimension, and choosing how to interact on the basis of this (and other constructs they possess). Another person might make little use of the spiritual–secular construct for thinking about people, but instead rely on a different construct such as poor–wealthy. Constructivist theory assumes this kind of variation in the content of constructs; indeed it suggests that no one's constructs are exactly the same (e.g., my religious–nonreligious construct does not have to be exactly the same as yours). However, constructivist theory has focused less on the specific constructs people use, and more on the *quantity* of constructs they use.

Early research testing constructivist theory showed that people vary in the number of constructs they have, and that having a larger construct system typically means also having a more abstract and organized system (Burleson,

2007). In other words, people who have more constructs typically also have more constructs that focus on things like personality and behavior rather than physical characteristics, and they also use multiple constructs simultaneously (for example, being able to describe how someone is wealthy and religious and progressive and anxious and inflexible). Individuals who have more constructs, and whose constructs are more abstract and better organized, are said to be higher in cognitive complexity.

Cognitive complexity is measured using an instrument called the Role Category Questionnaire (RCQ; Crockett, 1965). When using this measure, participants are asked to provide written descriptions of two peers whom they know quite well, usually one they like and one they dislike. Participants are instructed to describe each peer in as much detail as possible and to focus on the peer's traits, personality characteristics, habits, beliefs, mannerisms, and the way they treat others. The written impressions generated by the Role Category Questionnaire are scored for the number of different interpersonal constructs they contain. The resulting score is seen as a measure of construct quantity and, hence, a measure of cognitive complexity.

To illustrate differences in cognitive complexity, Burleson (2007) provides the following examples of how two individuals might describe their romantic partners. One person might offer something like, "My partner, Chris, is a generally happy person, who has a great smile. Chris works hard in school, is concerned about physical appearance, and is really good-looking. Chris is a caring and good friend. Chris likes to be the center of attention, but also has a good sense of humor. I think Chris's jokes are really funny. Chris treats people with respect. We are a lot alike in many ways." Another person might offer something like, "My partner, Jamie, is self-confident, outgoing, friendly, and curious about the world in general. Jamie is open-minded and is always willing to learn new things. Jamie is open to constructive criticism and new ways of thinking. Jamie sometimes gets frustrated and shows some temper, but channels that negative energy into a positive form of expression. Jamie has a caring and supportive nature. Overall, Jamie is an independent and compassionate individual." Each of these written impressions contains the same number of words, but the second description includes more constructs focused on personality and behavior rather than appearance. In other words, it is more abstract. It is also better organized: it does a better job of showing how the different characteristics are connected. The second writer would earn a higher score on the RCQ.

Research on cognitive complexity and communication supports two general conclusions. First, cognitive complexity tends to increase with age until late adolescence or early adulthood (essentially, the college years), after which it remains largely stable in adulthood (Burleson & Caplan, 1998). Second, being higher in cognitive complexity is associated with more effective communication strategies in many domains, including informing, persuading, and disciplining (Burleson, 2007). For example, Clark and Delia (1977) tested whether the use of persuasive strategies associated with higher levels of perspective-taking ability increased with age. Children in grades 2 through 9 were given the RCQ and also presented with three scenarios in which they needed to

Cognitive complexity
The extent to which a person's construct system is differentiated, abstract, and well-organized

persuade someone to act on their behalf, such as getting a stranger to take care of a lost puppy. They were then recorded speaking what they would say in each situation. Children's messages were coded as "0" if they failed to offer any support, "1" if they demonstrated a need for the request (e.g., "The puppy looks skinny"), "2" if they dealt with counterarguments either in the statement or request (e.g., "I'll bring you food to feed the dog if you'll keep it"), and "3" if they supplied an advantage to the other, or attempted to adapt to the interests and values of the other (e.g., "This dog would be a good watchdog. A dog makes a good companion," or "If I were you and I lived alone, I'd like a good watchdog like this one"). The results indicated that older children were more cognitively complex and consequently used more higher-order strategies (2s and 3s) and fewer lower-order strategies (0s and 1s) than did younger children.

Constructivist theory was extraordinarily influential for the discipline of communication, especially in the 1970s and 1980s, when it contributed to a maturing social science of communication. Like most theories, however, constructivism has received its share of criticism. Many of these criticisms have been leveled at the reducing of complex processes of individual interpretation to measurement of cognitive complexity with the RCQ (Gastil, 1995). The inadequacy of constructs as a depiction of cognitive processes seems especially on-target as models of cognitive psychology develop over time. However, constructivist theory continues to be recognized as an influence on current theory and research. In particular, the extensive work on comforting behavior by Brant Burleson and colleagues (see Burleson, 2003), has been integral to the development of a thriving domain of communication research focused on supportive communication (including comforting or emotional support, advice, esteem-building, etc., see MacGeorge, Feng, and Burleson, 2011). Overall, this work shows that people who are higher in cognitive complexity tend to use comforting strategies that validate, rather than reject, how distressed targets feel (e.g., "I get why you feel that way…" vs. "This is no big deal, move on"). These validating, or "person-centered" comforting strategies, are consistently evaluated more positively than the rejecting ones, and actually reduce emotional distress more effectively (Jones & Wirtz, 2006; for a review, see MacGeorge, Feng & Burleson, 2011).

RELATIONAL FRAMING THEORY

Relational framing theory A theory that explains cognitive structures through which we interpret communication behavior and its effects

Have you ever watched two people interact, and concluded that one of them was "calling the shots"? Or decided that your dating partner "wasn't all that into you"? Relational framing theory (RFT), developed by James Dillard, Denise Solomon, and Jennifer Samp, explains that these conclusions are influenced by the **frames**, or cognitive structures, through which we interpret communication behavior (Dillard, Solomon, & Samp, 1996). You can think of frames as mental eyeglasses through which you "see" interaction.

Foundational to RFT is the assumption that all communication conveys not just content (the literal or conventional meaning of words), but also implicit claims about the relationship between the communicating parties. These two types of meaning are sometimes called content and relational messages (Watzlawick, Beavin, & Jackson, 1967). Some relational messages are rather obvious. For example, if you see someone with an angry expression shouting obscenities at another person, you're probably not going to conclude that the two really like each other. But other relational messages can be much more ambiguous. What does a smirk and a "Shut up!" really say about the relationship between the speaker and message target? RFT helps to explain why the "same" behavior might be understood differently by different people, or in different situations (McLaren & Solomon, 2015).

According to RFT, at any point in an interaction, people perceive and interpret communication behavior through one of two frames. The dominance-submissiveness frame focuses attention on status, power, and control. When we "read" interaction through this frame, we pay attention to behaviors that signal dominance or submissiveness, and we tend to interpret ambiguous behavior as informative about these characteristics. Overall, when this frame is active, or guiding interpretation at that moment, people focus on who is "one-up" or "one-down" in the relationship. So, with this frame active, you would have a tendency to perceive a smirk and "Shut up!" as one person's effort to control another, even if that wasn't the speaker's intention.

Dominance-submissiveness In relational framing theory, a cognitive frame that focuses attention on status, power, and control

The affiliation-disaffiliation frame is about regard, liking, or admiration. When we perceive interactions through this frame, we attend to behaviors that signal affiliation or disaffiliation, and ambiguous behavior is interpreted as indicative of these attributes. When we view interactions through this frame, we focus on how well the interacting parties get along. If this is the frame activated when you see the smirk and "Shut up!" you would perceive the behavior as conveying something about how much the two people like each other. (Notice that this could be either liking or disliking; other behaviors might help you make that judgment.)

Affiliation-disaffiliation In relational framing theory, a cognitive frame that focuses attention on regard, liking, or admiration

RFT makes a differential salience hypothesis, claiming that only one of the two frames is likely to be in use at any given time, because competition between the two frames makes interpretation challenging (Dillard, Solomon, & Samp, 1996). However, the theory allows for the possibility of relatively rapid switching between frames, so that communicators could move back and forth between frames in the course of a single interaction (McLaren & Solomon, 2015). RFT also acknowledges that interactions vary in involvement or intensity—the degree to which interacting parties are coordinated, engaged, and immediate with each other. According to the general intensifier hypothesis, perceptions of involvement polarize judgments within the other two frames. In other words, as people exhibit more involvement in the interaction, we will tend to perceive greater disparities in dominance if that frame is active, and stronger affiliation or disaffiliation if that frame is active. Imagine that the smirk is very exaggerated and the "Shut up!" quite loud and emphatic. If your dominance frame is active, you will probably see the speaker as more dominant (and the target as more submissive) than if the smirk was subtle and the "Shut up!" spoken quietly. Similarly, if you have two positive interactions with acquaintances, and view both through the affiliation-disaffiliation frame, you are likely to perceive the acquaintance who was more animated as liking you more than the less animated one.

Differential salience hypothesis In relational framing theory, the claim that only one cognitive frame will be in use at any given time

Involvement In relational framing theory, the degree to which interacting parties are coordinated, engaged, and immediate with each other

General intensifier hypothesis In relational framing theory, the claim that perceptions of involvement polarize judgments within the other two frames (dominance-submissiveness, affiliation-disaffiliation)

RFT contends that the relational frame activated at any given time is influenced by multiple factors (Solomon, 2006), including social and cultural norms, individual predispositions, relationship history, the function of the interaction, and the content of specific messages. Thus you are probably more likely to view interaction through the dominance-submission than the affiliation-disaffiliation frame when in your boss's office than when in your friend's living room (a social norm), if prior supervisors have been authoritarian rather than egalitarian (relationship history), or if you expect a performance review (function of interaction). On the other hand, having an anxious personality (individual predisposition) may provoke you to view the interaction with your boss through the affiliation-disaffiliation frame, as could messages like "It's such a pleasure to work with you."

A series of studies (reviewed in McLaren & Solomon, 2015) have examined how frames become activated as a consequence of specific variables representing each of these factors. For example, a recent pair of studies (McLaren, Dillard, Tusing, & Solomon, 2014) examined the perceived relevance of the two frames when requests to engage in a shared activity were made directly or obliquely and delivered in the context of cooperative or competitive relationships. Student participants read hypothetical scenarios describing Pat, a neighbor in their dorm, as either cooperative (friendly, warm, and complimentary) or competitive (critical, bossy), and requesting that the participant join a ping-pong game either directly ("We're playing ping-pong and need a fourth. Come on.") or obliquely (highly indirectly: "We're playing ping-pong in the den. Sound good?"; McLaren et al., 2014, p. 524). Participants then rated the relevance of the dominance-submissiveness frame (on items such as dominance/submission and controlling/yielding) and affiliation-disaffiliation frame (on items such as liking/disliking and attraction/aversion). The dominance-submission frame was rated as more relevant to understanding the direct request than the oblique request, and to understanding the competitive relationship than the cooperative one. Contrary to prediction, the affiliation-disaffiliation frame was not rated more relevant to understanding the oblique request (versus the direct one), but this frame was rated more relevant to understanding the cooperative relationship. A second study with somewhat different scenarios and messages produced similar results. As the authors explain, the pair of studies supports RFT's claims about message features and relationship history affecting the relevance of frames, though they do this more consistently for the dominance-submission frame than for the affiliation-disaffiliation frame. The authors suggest the possibility of an affiliation bias that makes this frame relevant to many social interactions, regardless of variation in message or relationship qualities.

A major part of RFT's value comes from its potential to explain why ambiguous messages can sometimes be interpreted very differently, so that one person experiences insult or hurt where none was intended (Solomon, 2006). Compared to other theories of interpersonal communication presented in this chapter, RFT has also been more lightly and intermittently tested. Some research studies have failed to support the differential salience hypothesis, suggesting either that people are able to apply multiple frames simultaneously, or, alternatively, that existing methods are not well-designed to track rapid changes in the use of frames (MacLaren & Solomon, 2015). As new scholars apply this theory, its accuracy and value will become more evident.

TRUTH DEFAULT THEORY

Whereas relational framing theory describes interpretive processes relevant to virtually any interaction, truth default theory (TDT) is a theory of how people assess each other's credibility and detect deception, developed by Timothy Levine and colleagues (Levine, 2014). Deception can be defined as intentionally, knowingly, and/or purposely misleading another person (Levine, 2014). Although some older studies suggested that deception is common practice in everyday life, with the average person telling as many as two lies per day (DePaulo, Kashy, Kirkendol, Wyer, & Epstein, 1996), more recent research indicates that such averages are inflated by a small number of highly prolific liars, and that most people tell the truth most of the time (Serota & Levine, 2014). Accordingly, TDT is based on the contention that most people are honest most of the time, that we enter most interactions correctly assuming that others will communicate honestly (truth default), and that this assumption is functional for human interaction. In this respect, TDT is distinct from older theories of deception and deception detection that regarded deception as far more prevalent and truth bias as dysfunctional for communicators (e.g., interpersonal deception theory, see Burgoon & Buller, 2015).

Truth default theory
A theory of credibility assessment and deception detection in interpersonal communication based on the idea that people typically presume others to be honest (truth default)

Truth default
The presumption of honesty that usually underlies interaction

TDT is a relatively complex theory, recently articulated as a series of 14 propositions (Levine, 2015). The following summary paraphrases these propositions.

1. Most people communicate honestly most of the time. Deception occurs, but is infrequent, and must be infrequent to avoid detection.

2. Most lies are told by a few people ("prolific liars").

3. People believe most of what is said by others, so most messages are presumed to be honest (truth default). The truth default makes communication efficient.

4. Because most people communicate honestly, the truth bias and truth default usually lead to correct judgments of honesty, but also make people vulnerable to occasional deception.

5. Deception is usually purposeful, selected as a tactic when honesty is believed ineffective or counterproductive for the communicator's goals.

6. People understand that deception is purposeful, and evaluate others' motives when making judgments of honesty or deception.

7. People continue to believe that others are honest unless a trigger event provokes suspicion. Trigger events include realizing there is a motive for deception, observing behaviors associated with dishonesty, messages that are incoherent, lack of correspondence (mismatch) between message content and known reality, and warnings from others about potential dishonesty.

8. When trigger events are sufficiently strong, people become suspicious, temporarily abandon the truth default, and scrutinize messages, comparing them against available knowledge.

9. Based on available information, messages may be judged deceptive or honest.

10. Trigger events and deception judgments may occur well after the deception has occurred.

11. Deception is not usually detected by observing the sender's nonverbal behavior, or demeanor. The likelihood of detecting a lie based on demeanor is only slightly better than chance.

12. Deception is usually detected by comparing the message to pre-existing knowledge or external evidence, or because the deceiver confesses.

13. Effective questioning can help to reveal information that leads to deception detection, but poor questioning will reduce accuracy at detecting deception.

14. Expertise at detecting deception is largely based on skill at eliciting useful information (e.g., questioning), not observing demeanor.

Although presentation of the theory is recent, Levine began testing some of its propositions in the 1990s. There is now research support for each of the propositions, and many are supported by multiple studies. For example, Proposition #11 is supported by a large number of studies conducted by a wide range of scholars in communication, psychology and allied disciplines. Despite the widespread belief that liars can be identified by their demeanor (nonverbal behavior), laboratory studies show little consistency in the demeanor of liars (Levine et al., 2011), and people's average ability to detect lies from demeanor hovers around 50% (i.e., is no better than chance) (Bond & DePaulo, 2006).

As a test of Propositions #10–12, Park, Levine, and colleagues conducted a study they titled "How People Really Detect Lies" (Park, Levine, McCornack, Morrison, & Ferrara, 2002). In this study, undergraduates were asked to recall a recent situation in which they discovered someone had lied to them, and to report when and how they found out. Participant descriptions of their discovery methods were examined; most could be classified ("coded") into one or more of the following categories: third party information, physical information, solicited direct confession, unsolicited direct confession, at-the-time verbal or nonverbal behavior, and inconsistencies with prior knowledge. The most commonly reported discovery methods were third party information (52% of participants), physical evidence (30%), and solicited confessions (18%). Frequently two of these discovery methods were combined. Detecting lies through at-the-time behavior (i.e., demeanor while lying) was reported by only 11% of participants, and usually in combination with a method that did not depend on demeanor. In addition, most lies (85%) were not detected until after the interaction in which deception occurred, with 60% detected at least a day later, and 40% detected more than a week later.

Although there is already a great deal of support for TDT's propositions, it continues to be tested and extended by active researchers, and is likely to grow and change beyond its recent presentation. For example, one critic has suggested the theory could do a better job of explaining why people lie, extending it more fully into the realm of message production (Van Swol, 2014). This goal might be achieved through greater integration with information manipulation theory (see Chapter 5) and its successor, information manipulation theory II (McCornack et al., 2014). However, for the present, TDT appears to provide a current, accurate account of interpersonal deception and its detection.

UNCERTAINTY REDUCTION THEORY

Developed by Charles Berger, **uncertainty reduction theory** (URT; Berger, 1979; Berger & Calabrese, 1975) explains interpersonal communication during the *beginning* of an interaction. Because initial interactions can lead to relationships, URT provides a bridge between this chapter, focused on basic interpersonal processes, and Chapter 9, which examines communication in relational contexts. The core assumption of this theory is that when strangers meet, they seek to *reduce uncertainty* about each other. Reducing uncertainty makes others' behavior more predictable, and enables us to choose appropriate behaviors for ourselves. URT was initially presented as a series of axioms (universal truths that do not require proof) and theorems (propositions assumed to be true) that describe relationships between uncertainty and interaction behavior. These axioms and theorems are presented in detail elsewhere (Berger, 1979; Berger & Calabrese, 1975); here, we summarize key ideas.

THREE STAGES OF INITIAL INTERACTIONS

URT contends that there are three stages in initial interaction, characterized by different behaviors. During the entry phase of relationship development, we observe physical appearance and surroundings to determine things like sex, age, and economic or social status. We then supplement this information with additional biographic and demographic information obtained through interaction. Behavior in this entry phase is controlled by communication rules and norms. For example, it is considered improper to ask strangers for intimate details about their lives. When communicators begin to share attitudes, beliefs, values, and more personal data, the personal phase begins (Berger & Calabrese, 1975). During this phase, the communicators feel less constrained by rules and norms and tend to communicate more freely with each other. The third phase of initial interaction is the exit phase. During this phase, the communicators decide on future interaction plans. They may discuss or negotiate ways to allow the relationship to grow and continue. However, any particular conversation may be terminated at the end of the entry phase.

Entry phase Dimension of uncertainty reduction theory that reflects the initial phase of relationships where physical appearance, sex, age, socio-economic status, and other biographic and demographic information is most important

Personal phase A dimension of uncertainty reduction theory that reflects communicating attitudes, beliefs, values, and more personal data

Exit phase Dimension of uncertainty reduction theory that assumes that during this phase, the communicators decide on future interaction plans

UNCERTAINTY REDUCTION AXIOMS

The axioms of URT describe seven foundational assumptions ("taken-for-granted truths") about seven important factors in any dyadic exchange: verbal communication, nonverbal expressiveness, information-seeking behavior, intimacy, reciprocity, similarity, and liking. For example, the first axiom of the theory can be phrased "if uncertainty levels are high, the amount of verbal communication between strangers will decrease." The more we learn about someone, the less uncertain we are, and the amount of verbal communication increases.

Two other factors that reduce uncertainty between communicators are information-seeking behavior and the degree of similarity individuals perceive in each other. When strangers first meet and interact, the amount of information they seek from each other is quite high. As a relationship progresses, the amount of overt information-seeking behavior decreases. The degree of perceived similarity (in background, attitudes, and appearance) among communicators reduces uncertainty. Individuals use cues about similarity and dissimilarity (especially background and attitude cues) to help them understand why other people communicate as they do. For example, if I am talking with Dana, who comes from a large city similar to mine, then I would have some basis to explain why Dana uses an assertive or aggressive communication style. Similarity in background (real or imagined) may help us explain and predict attitudes and beliefs. Indeed, Berger (1979) found that perceived background similarity led to predictions of attitude similarity.

If communicators are very uncertain, URT suggests they will exchange information and will self-disclose at about the same rate. High levels of uncertainty will produce high and about equal rates of information exchange between communicators. Under conditions of high uncertainty, such as when strangers meet, an imbalance in the exchange of information may create tension. One person may be accused of dominating the conversation, and the relationship may be terminated.

Nonverbal expressions of interest and attention increase as uncertainty decreases. Communicators may exhibit more direct eye contact, touch more, and sit closer to each other. As uncertainty decreases further, intimate messages may be exchanged. Self-disclosing statements reveal more intimate information and may rapidly move the relationship from the entry phase. The final result of less uncertainty is that communicators will like each other more because they feel they know and understand each other better.

UNCERTAINTY REDUCTION THEOREMS

Charles Berger and Richard Calabrese also developed twenty-one theorems about how the seven factors in the axioms are related and interact to reduce uncertainty. Six of the theorems suggest that when the *amount of communication* between strangers in initial interaction increases, nonverbal expressions of interest (such as direct eye contact, head nods, pleasantness of voice), intimate communication content, liking, and similarity also increase. More communication lessens the need for immediate and equal exchanges of information.

Five other theorems deal with nonverbal cues associated with affiliation or liking (factors of nonverbal expressiveness). These theorems suggest the greater the *nonverbal expressiveness*, the more intimate content, perceived similarity, and liking there will be. Nonverbal expressiveness also reduces the need for information-seeking behavior and for equal, immediate exchanges of communication.

Four theorems are related to the *intimacy level of communication content*. As communication content becomes more personal, perceived similarity and liking between communicators increase. In addition, as self-disclosing messages become more intimate, the tendency to seek information and the need for immediate and equal exchanges of information also decrease.

Three theorems address the concept of *information seeking*. One suggests that strangers use less information-seeking communication as they begin to like each other more. As a relationship develops, there is less need to ask questions and "interrogate" people; they are more willing to volunteer information about themselves.

Two theorems deal with *reciprocity*, or *rates of information exchange*. As two individuals perceive greater similarity and are more attracted to each other, they feel less need to exchange information with equal frequency. However, the theory also suggests that when uncertainty is high, communicators tend to echo behaviors; as one person increases information seeking, so does the other.

The final theorem suggests that the greater the real and perceived similarity between communicators in a developing relationship, the more likely attraction or liking will exist. During the last thirty years, social psychological and communication researchers have conducted much research into the relationship between similarity and liking. For uncertainty reduction theory (URT), the key to this relationship is our need to reduce uncertainty. Berger and Calabrese suggested that the concept of uncertainty reduction explains many of the research findings concerning the similarity-attraction relationship.

MOTIVES TO REDUCE UNCERTAINTY

The motivation to reduce uncertainty varies from one interaction to another. One type of motive is incentive. Typically, we want to know more about people who control rewards or who can satisfy our needs. The more we learn, the better our strategies to obtain the rewards. For example, we may develop relationships with fraternity or sorority members so that our new friends can help us earn an invitation to join their group. When they can help us, these people possess *high incentive value*. We monitor their behavior, as well as our own communication with them, more closely. For example, we may look at how they respond to praise. If we discover that they enjoy being complimented and are more gracious and giving after being praised, we may then compliment them frequently to speed the relationship development.

A second motive that stimulates information seeking is the unpredictable behavior of others. When a communication behavior deviates from our expectations, we monitor the communication of others more closely to get additional

Incentive In uncertainty reduction theory, the motive to reduce uncertainty about people who control rewards or who can satisfy our needs

Unpredictable behavior In uncertainty reduction theory, the motive to reduce uncertainty about people whose behavior deviates from our expectations

information. We often respond less favorably to the unusual or unpredictable behavior of others than to behavior consistent with our expectations. Berger (1979) found that if a stranger in an initial interaction gave more compliments, he or she was rated as friendlier. However, he or she was also judged more dishonest and less sincere. Interactants probably imputed *ulterior motives* to the stranger to explain the increase in compliments. Thus, when a person's communication follows conventional norms and rules, we may pay less attention to it. However, when a person's communication deviates from conventions, rules, and norms, we pay closer attention to that behavior (increase our monitoring) to generate more reliable information about the person.

Likelihood of future interaction In uncertainty reduction theory, the motive to reduce uncertainty about people whom we anticipate meeting again

A third and final motive for acquiring information about others is the likelihood of future interaction. Generally, desire for future contact causes people to pay closer attention to their own and others' communication. Expecting future interaction strongly influences our evaluation of another's behavior. People who believe that they will be communicating with another person in the future may change their communication behavior to be viewed more favorably. People generally do not disclose intimate information to strangers. However, spontaneous and intimate self-disclosure to strangers does occur in some situations. The "stranger-on-the-plane" situation is one context in which we suspend normal communication rules because we never expect to meet the other person again. You may recall a long airplane ride during which your seatmate revealed intimate personal details after meeting you only a few hours earlier. An out-of-town pub or bar is another context in which we may ignore the rules we typically follow for self-disclosure (Berger, 1979).

STRATEGIES TO REDUCE UNCERTAINTY

Passive strategy An uncertainty reduction strategy that involves watching someone without being observed

Active strategy An uncertainty reduction strategy that requires effort to discover information, but there is still no direct contact between the two parties

Interactive strategy An uncertainty reduction strategy that consists of obtaining information directly through asking questions (interrogation) and offering personal information about yourself

There are three general strategies to reduce uncertainty about others. Passive strategies involve watching someone without being observed. You may have engaged in a passive strategy to reduce uncertainty about someone to whom you were attracted. You may have unobtrusively observed this person talking with other students in class, in the cafeteria, or in the dormitory. Note that while you were gaining information, no *direct* communication occurred between you. We often observe others in informal social situations where norms and rules are frequently relaxed and more revealing information may emerge (Berger, 1979). Active strategies of uncertainty reduction require more effort to discover information, but there is still no direct contact between the two parties. An active strategy may include finding out about another person by asking third parties for information. You may have discovered someone's "availability" for a relationship by asking friends whether the person was involved with someone. Interactive strategies include obtaining information *directly* through asking questions (interrogation) and offering personal information about yourself (self-disclosure). The self-disclosure strategy relies on the fact that self-disclosure by one person stimulates self-disclosure in another. If I reveal something important about myself to others, they feel "obliged" to reveal something equally important about themselves to me. A party is a good place to observe people using interactive strategies.

TESTING AND EXTENDING UNCERTAINTY REDUCTION THEORY

In the years since the initial presentation of URT, many communication scholars have examined its assumptions through quantitative and empirical research (for a review, see Berger, 2011). Some of this work has focused on uncertainty reduction in the initial development of romantic relationships. Well before the development of Facebook or other social media, Parks and Adelman (1983) argued that networks of friends and family members help to reduce uncertainty about romantic partners by providing "third-party" information. For example, observing your partner's interactions with family members may tell you a great deal. The mere act of meeting a partner's larger social network or family may also reduce uncertainty. Indeed, failing to introduce a partner to one's friends and family may make the partner uncertain and provoke such questions as, "If I'm so important to you, how come I've never met your friends?" (p. 58). Using interviews and questionnaires, Parks and Adelman found that people who received support for their romantic involvement from family and friends expressed less uncertainty about their relationships and were less likely to terminate the relationship than people who received less support. More recently, researchers have examined the use of uncertainty reduction strategies by people engaged in online dating (Gibbs, Ellison, & Lai, 2011), using surveys conducted with current users of online dating sites (e.g., eHarmony, Match.com, Yahoo! Personals). This study showed that online daters who had more uncertainty about personal safety, misrepresentation (deceptive behavior by others), or recognition (having their dating profile identified), used more uncertainty reduction strategies, including strategies that were passive (e.g., comparing the photo with the written profile), active (e.g., saving e-mails or chats to check for consistency), interactive (e.g., asking questions in phone conversations), and extractive (e.g., online searches to uncover and verify personal information).

The value of URT has been demonstrated, in part, by its capacity to motivate the development of theories that go beyond the context of initial interactions (Berger, 2011). Some of these theories are discussed in later chapters, including theories of uncertainty in ongoing relationships (relational turbulence model; Knobloch & Solomon, 2002; see Chapter 9), uncertainty in interactions about health issues (uncertainty management theory; Brashers, 2001; see Chapter 14), and uncertainty in intercultural communication (anxiety/uncertainty management theory; Gudykunst, 1995; see Chapter 15). URT has also influenced the development of a competitor theory, predicted outcome value theory (Sunnafrank, 1986). As explained in Chapter 9, this theory explains initial interaction somewhat differently than URT.

SUMMARY

This chapter explored several theories of message production and reception in interpersonal communication. These theories included the interpersonal communication motives model, goals-plans-action theory, constructivist theory, relational framing theory, truth default theory, and uncertainty reduction theory.

KEY TERMS

Active strategies

Affiliation-disaffiliation

Cognitive complexity

Constructivism

Differential salience hypothesis

Dominance-submissiveness

Entry phase

Exit phase

General intensifier hypothesis

Goals

Goals-plans-action theory

Hierarchy principle

Incentive

Interactive strategies

Involvement

Likelihood of future interaction

Motive

Passive strategies

Personal constructs

Personal phase

Plan complexity

Planning theory

Planning

Plans

Primary goals

Relational framing theory

Secondary goals

Theory of interpersonal communication motives

Truth default theory

Truth default

Unpredictable behavior

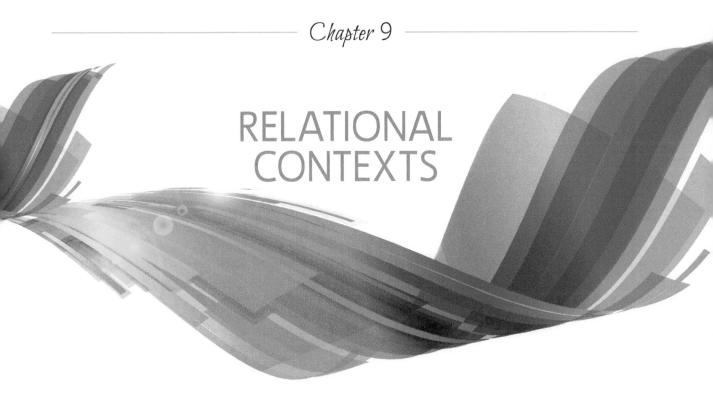

Chapter 9

RELATIONAL CONTEXTS

A great deal of interpersonal communication occurs in personal relationships, including romantic relationships, friendships, and families. Correspondingly, there has been considerable scholarly interest in developing theories to explain how communication contributes to relationship development and mainte-nance (Solomon & Vangelisti, 2014), and how relational partners can use com-munication to accomplish goals and manage issues effectively (e.g., Vangelisti, 2011; Caughlin, Koerner, Schrodt, & Fitzpatrick, 2011). The theories covered in this chapter represent a subset of the many that are relevant to communication in relational contexts. Some of the selections presented here emphasize roman-tic relationships, but most also have relevance to friendships and families. In addition, the chapter discusses families as a unique context for communica-tion, and describes one theory that is specific to family interaction. The chapter begins with a discussion of similarity and attraction, which provides key his-torical backdrop to the development of theorizing about communication and relationships, especially theories of romantic relationship development.

SIMILARITY AND INTERPERSONAL ATTRACTION

Attraction is key to explaining the development of voluntary relation-ships, or relationships that we choose for ourselves. For most of us, romantic

Voluntary relation-ships Relationships we choose for ourselves relationships and friendships begin with attraction to the other person. Being hired for a job or invited to join a volunteer organization may also be influenced by attraction. Psychologist Donn Byrne launched the study of interpersonal attraction, and devoted much of his career to studying why we like some people and dislike others. Byrne (1971) believed that most of interpersonal attraction was explained by the principle of reinforcement: we like and are attracted to those people who reward us, and dislike individuals who punish us. Rewards and punishments take a wide variety of forms. For example, you might find another person rewarding because they are beautiful, funny, or kind to you, or find someone punishing because they have strong body odor, a sour disposition, or try to make you look bad.

Principle of reinforcement The idea that we like and are attracted to those people who reward us

Building on the principle of reinforcement, Byrne argued that attitude similarity is particularly rewarding and therefore a reliable indicator of whether people will like each other (see Figure 9.1). Knowing that another person sees the world much as you do is comforting (Byrne, Griffitt, & Stefaniak, 1967) and makes interacting with them more predictable. The attitude similarity need not be real. Communicators frequently infer the attitudes of others (e.g., based on appearance and behavior), especially if they have not known them long enough to have heard them express many opinions. Thus, perceived similarity—the degree to which we *believe* another person is similar—is often sufficient to attract us to others. This idea prompted extensive research examining the influence of perceived similarity on interpersonal attraction.

Attitude similarity The degree to which people's attitudes are consistent with each other

Perceived similarity The degree to which we believe another's attitudes are similar to ours

In much of his research on attraction and attitude similarity (for a review, see Byrne, 1997), Byrne employed the "bogus stranger" technique. In this method, participants completed an attitude questionnaire (scale). They were then given another scale supposedly completed by a stranger; the researcher actually chose the answers on "the stranger's" questionnaire. The researcher divided people into two groups to create two experimental conditions: the "similar"

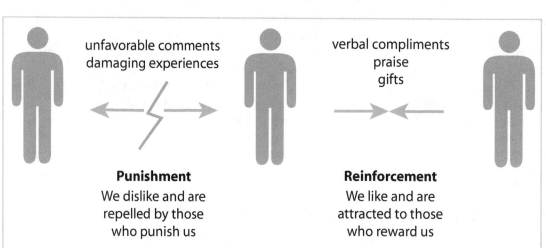

unfavorable comments
damaging experiences

verbal compliments
praise
gifts

Punishment
We dislike and are repelled by those who punish us

Reinforcement
We like and are attracted to those who reward us

© Kendall Hunt Publishing Company

FIGURE 9.1 BYRNE'S REINFORCEMENT THEORY.

and "dissimilar" attitude conditions. In the "similar" condition, the stranger's scale almost duplicated the responses of the research participant. In the "dissimilar" condition, the questionnaire had almost opposite responses from those of the participant. Studies of this type consistently showed that participants were attracted to the "stranger" who responded with similar attitudes.

As communication scholars began to join psychologists in their study of attitude similarity and attraction, they discovered relationships between attitude similarity, attraction, and communication. We are more likely to be persuaded by communicators if we believe they are similar to us (Berscheid, 1966). Similar individuals communicate more with each other (Rogers & Bhowmik, 1970). Communication scholars also examined different types of similarity. McCroskey, Richmond, and Daly (1975) offered four dimensions of similarity: attitude similarity, value similarity (morality), background similarity, and appearance similarity. They developed a questionnaire to measure perceived similarity between communicators and tested it with high school, college, and adult participants. Consistent with Byrne's original contention, attitude similarity was the most important factor in perceived similarity.

However, communication scholars also began to develop critiques of Byrne's work, and that of other social psychologists. A basic concern was that Byrne's experimental methods were too contrived and artificial to model how people are actually attracted to each other. We rarely read questionnaires completed by those we have just met and might be considering as friends! Consequently, critics questioned whether the findings could be generalized to authentic attraction situations (Eiser, 1980; Gergen, 1980). Beyond this concern, communication scholars wanted theory and research to address the *communication* of attitudes, beliefs, and values between individuals (Duck, 1985), and more generally how similarity affects attraction when people have the opportunity to interact.

Michael Sunnafrank and his associates began by studying the similarity-attraction relationship when people have a chance to interact with each other, and ended up not only critiquing the idea that similarity creates attraction, but also creating a competitor to uncertainty reduction theory (Chapter 8). Sunnafrank and colleagues' early research (Sunnafrank & Miller, 1981; Sunnafrank, 1985) examined how perceived similarity and interaction predicted attraction. In one study (Sunnafrank & Miller, 1981), participants were told that they would be working on a project with a stranger who had attitudes either like or unlike their own. Half the participants engaged in a five-minute interaction with their partner; the other half did not. The participants then completed a questionnaire that measured how much they were attracted to their partner. Participants from the half that did not interact preferred the "similar" stranger. Those who did communicate were more attracted to a stranger unlike themselves. Participants who met dissimilar strangers but had no opportunity to communicate with them were the least attracted of the four groups. Sunnafrank (1985) extended this research by studying what happens when strangers are prompted to discuss their similar and dissimilar attitudes. He found that both ordinary getting-acquainted conversations *and* getting-acquainted conversations that were followed by attitude discussions made people more attracted to dissimilar strangers, but not to similar strangers. If you already believed that a stranger shared your attitudes, your expectations were merely confirmed and did not increase your attraction to the stranger. However, if you believed that you would meet someone very different from you, conversation often reduced the threat posed by the different attitudes, allowing attraction to occur. On the basis of these studies, Sunnafrank challenged the idea that attitude similarity *causes* interpersonal attraction, arguing that ordinary getting-acquainted conversations quickly override any effect of attitude similarity on attraction (Sunnafrank, 1992). He also proceeded to challenge uncertainty reduction theory, contending that predicted outcome value predicts the effect uncertainty will have (Sunnafrank, 1990).

PREDICTED OUTCOME VALUE THEORY

Predicted outcome value theory Theory that explains behavior in initial interactions and subsequent relationship development as a consequence of predicted rewards and costs of the relationship

Rewards Anything that we see as a benefit from a relationship

Costs Anything that we see as a punishment or detriment from a relationship

Predicted outcome value A prediction about whether a relationship is likely to be rewarding (positive) or costly (negative)

Uncertainty reduction theory (see Chapter 8) treats uncertainty as the primary motivator for behavior in initial interaction (Berger & Calabrese, 1975). However, according to Michael Sunnafrank's **predicted outcome value theory** (POVT; Sunnafrank, 1986, 1990), people in initial interactions are primarily motivated by something else: the desire to maximize their own relationship outcomes. In other words, they want to increase relationship *rewards* and decrease relationship *costs* for themselves. When people are first meeting, they have had no real experience with each other, so they aren't able to assess the actual rewards or costs that a relationship would bring. Instead, based on whatever information is available, they predict whether the relationship is likely to be rewarding (positive) or costly (negative)—this is the **predicted outcome value**. Predicted outcome values are used to determine whether to pursue a relationship, which in turn affects how interaction proceeds.

POVT modifies all seven axioms of URT so that predicted outcome value (rather than uncertainty) is the primary influence on how people communicate in initial interactions. According to POVT, a positive outcome value motivates the kinds of behavior described by URT: greater quantity and intimacy of interaction (i.e., talking more and about more personal topics), more nonverbal expressions of liking, and the use of more information-seeking tactics (questions, self-disclosures, and nonverbal encouragers). In other words, the more positive you predict the relationship will be, the more you will tend to communicate in ways that convey an interest in developing the relationship, whereas predicting that the relationship will be negative for you leads to communicating in ways that cut off the opportunity for relationship development (e.g., restricting the flow of information, ending the interaction more quickly).

There is convincing research support for POVT. In one study (Sunnafrank & Ramirez, 2004), students in the same class were paired randomly on the first day of class, had a brief interaction, and then predicted how positive they thought a future relationship with each other would be (i.e., predicted outcome value).

Uncertainty about each other was also assessed. In the ninth week of the semester, students were asked again about the relationship with that same classmate. Predicted outcome values reported on the first day predicted the closeness of the relationship in the ninth week, with the more negative of the two POV's exerting the stronger effect. (In other words, relationships tended to become only as close as the POV of the less-interested person.) With predicted outcome accounted for, uncertainty had little impact on behavior during the interaction, or on the development of the relationship.

Relative to URT, POVT has had less influence on scholars in interpersonal and relational communication. URT was formally articulated earlier than POVT, and its propositions have received greater testing. In addition, Berger (URT theorist) has asserted that predicting outcomes is just an uncertainty-reducing activity, and thus he contends that POVT is an expansion of URT rather than a competing alternative (1986). As noted in Chapter 8, scholars have also found the concept of uncertainty useful for theories that extend beyond initial interactions and the development of personal relationships; predicted outcome value has not proven to have the same value for stimulating theoretical growth. Nonetheless, POVT provides a well-reasoned and supported theory of early relationship development, and one that continues to be tested and expanded. For example, Ramirez, Sunnafrank, & Goei (2010) provide evidence that POVT can be extended to explain how ongoing relationships fare when relational partners encounter unexpected events.

RELATIONSHIP INTERACTION STAGES MODEL

Many theories of relational communication address the association between communication in relationships and their development or deterioration. Although most theories focus on specific processes or elements, some have attempted to encompass the entire spectrum of relationship development and decline. The most influential of such models is Mark Knapp's (1978) relationship interaction stages model (RISM). This model was designed to explain how communication in romantic relationships evolves as the relationships change over time.

Relationship interaction stages model A model that describes change in communication as relationships change over time

As indicated in Figure 9.2, Knapp (1978) presented his model using a dual "staircase" metaphor. All relationships are represented as having characteristics of ascending (i.e., coming together), descending (i.e., coming apart), and stabilizing (i.e., periods of balance and consistency). Based on social exchange theory, Knapp asserted that movement up and down the staircase was based on the ratio of rewards received from the relationship to the costs received from the relationship. In other words, "relational rewards and costs result in decisions about where the relationship will go and how fast it will get there" (Avtgis, West, & Anderson, 1998, p. 281). The model also assumes that movement is relatively systematic and sequential, though it is possible to skip "stairs" or move rapidly from one to another.

Initiation stage A stage of the relationship interaction stages model that reflects the first interactions of relational partners

Experimenting stage A stage in the relationship interaction stages model that reflects relational partners focusing on finding similarities between them

Intensifying stage A stage in the relationship interaction stages model that reflects relational partners seeking to find similarities in terms of morals and values

Integrating stage A stage in the relationship interaction stages model that reflects when relational partners begin to talk about the future together and share a sense of being committed

Bonding stage A stage in the relationship interaction stages model that reflects a strong emotional and psychological link between relational partners

Differentiation stage A stage in the relationship interaction stages model that reflects highlighting how different you are from your relational partner

Circumscribing stage A stage in the relationship interaction stages model that reflects relational partners focusing communication on everyday matters in order to avoid conflict

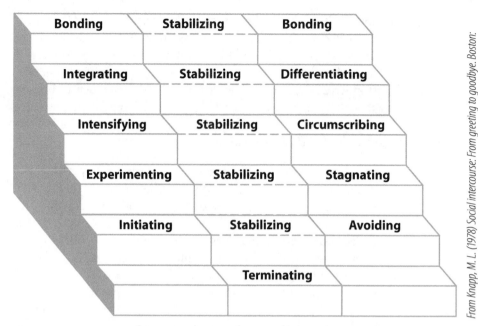

FIGURE 9.2 RELATIONSHIP INTERACTION STAGES MODEL.

There are ten stages in RISM, five of which describe how relational partners "come together," and five stages which describe how relational partners "come apart." The stages of coming together consist of the initiation stage, the experimenting stage, the intensifying stage, the integrating stage, and the bonding stage. The stages of coming apart consist of the differentiation stage, the circumscribing stage, the stagnation stage, the avoiding stage, and the terminating stage. The definitions of each stage are shown below:

Avtgis et al. (1998) conducted an inductive study (see Chapter 2 for the distinction between induction and deduction), which sought a more precise identification of cognitions, feelings, and behaviors associated with each relationship stage. The results of the study indicated that in the initiation stage, people talk about relaxing things and commonalities, feel nervous and cautious, smile, and use flirting nonverbal behaviors. In the experimenting stage people talk about past relationships and try to create a good impression, feel connected and comfortable, call on the telephone, and freely violate each other's personal space. In the intensifying stage people probe about the partner's morals and values, feel loving and happy, display affectionate behaviors, and buy gifts. In the integrating stage people share intimate feelings and talk about the future, feel unhappy when apart and feel one with their partner, go on vacations together, and meet each other's family. In the bonding stage people pledge love for the other person and make arrangements about the future, feel a sense of unity and overwhelming joy, have joint possessions, and make sacrifices.

In the stages of coming apart, the differentiation stage is characterized by people arguing and talking about incompatibility, feeling lonely and inadequate, and attempting to make compromises. In the circumscribing stage people talk about simple everyday matters, feel frustrated and distant, and pursue different activities. In the stagnation stage people give short answers to questions, feel unwanted and bored, and stop physical contact. In the avoiding stage people only discuss general matters and avoid talking about the relationship, feel nervous and helpless, and spend a lot of time away from each other. In the terminating stage, people talk about discussing where the relationship failed, feel unhappy but relieved, and spend time dividing up belongings.

Despite its enduring popularity, RISM has never been precise enough to function as a basis for highly specific prediction, and is better understood as a general framework for organizing diverse communication behaviors in relationships, paired with a social exchange account for why relationships change. However, a handful of empirical studies have been conducted to assess and improve the model. One study suggests that the model extends, with some adaptation, to nonromantic relationships such as those between coworkers (Welch & Rubin, 2002). A recent study (Fox, Warber, & Makstaller, 2013) found that college students' use of Facebook had changed how they communicated in several stages. For example, "creeping" (reviewing another person's Facebook site without posting) functioned as a partial replacement for superficial interaction in the initiating and experimenting stages. In addition, becoming "Facebook official (FBO)" was an important marker of relationship stability in the integrating stage. As this study illustrates, the continued value of the model for relational communication scholars and students probably depends on whether the stages continue to represent common patterns of communication in relationship development and deterioration in the face of societal and technological change.

RELATIONSHIP MAINTENANCE MODEL

The relationship maintenance model (RMM) describes "actions and activities used to sustain desired relational definitions" (Canary & Stafford, 1994, p. 5) and connects the use of those behaviors to relationship characteristics and outcomes. In large measure, RMM is focused on describing the different behaviors people use strategically to keep intimate relationships satisfying, but theorists also recognize that relationship maintenance can be unintentional or nonstrategic, and can be used to *reduce* intimacy or satisfaction. The original research (Canary & Stafford, 1992) identified five maintenance behaviors, which Stafford (2011) expanded to seven in conjunction with research providing evidence that these seven can be measured as distinct: positivity, understanding, assurances, self-disclosure, relationship talk, sharing tasks, and involvement with social networks.

The use of most relationship maintenance strategies is positively associated with relationship commitment, satisfaction, liking, love, and control mutuality (agreement on the decision-making structure in the relationship), while being negatively associated with loneliness (Canary & Stafford, 1992; Dainton, Stafford, & Canary, 1994; Henson, Dybvig-Pawelko, & Canary, 2004). The

Stagnation stage A stage in the relationship interaction stages model that reflects the boredom experienced in a relationship

Avoiding stage A stage in the relationship interaction stages model that reflects the physical or communication avoidance of a relational partner

Terminating stage A stage in the relationship interaction stages model that reflects the ending of a relationship

Relationship maintenance model A model of actions and activities that sustain desired relational definitions

Understanding A type of relationship maintenance behavior that encompasses understanding, cooperation, and patience with the relationship partner

Positivity A type of relationship maintenance behavior that involves being optimistic and cheerful with the relationship partner

use of maintenance strategies also appears very similar across same-sex and opposite-sex marriage (Haas & Stafford, 2005).

The relationship maintenance model itself is largely descriptive, focused on identifying types of relational maintenance behavior rather than offering explanations for their use or outcomes. However, over time, research has connected relational maintenance to relationship outcomes in increasingly sophisticated ways, typically through merging the RMM with other concepts and theories. One study (Ramirez, 2008) examined how both married partners' relational maintenance strategies influence several aspects of their commitment to the relationship: personal commitment (I "want to" remain in the relationship), moral commitment (I "should" remain in the relationship), and structural commitment (I "have to" remain in the relationship). All three types of commitment were affected by maintenance behaviors, but personal and moral commitment were more strongly affected than structural commitment. Personal commitment to the relationship was especially strongly predicted by one's own assurance and positivity, and by partners' assurances, positivity, and openness (a combination of self-disclosure and relationship talk). Other studies examine relationship maintenance strategies and social media, engaging with theory to explain how people use different strategies via different media to maintain their relationships (Ledbetter, 2009; Ledbetter & Kuznkeoff, 2012). Thus, RMM exhibits continued value for explaining behavior in relationships.

RELATIONAL DIALECTICS THEORY

At some point in a relationship, you may have realized that you wanted two opposing things—at the same time. For example, you may have wanted to be very involved in the life of your romantic partner, but also to be an independent person, making your own plans and decisions. You may have wanted your relationship to be tightly connected to family and friends, and yet wanted to be "your own couple," not controlled by the needs and preferences of others. According to Leslie Baxter's relational dialectics theory (RDT; Baxter, 1990; Baxter & Erbert, 1999), relational dialectics are opposing forces or tensions that affect relationships and can never be fully eliminated, only understood and managed. Relational dialectics can be internal dialectics, internal to the dyadic (two-person) relationship, or external dialectics, resulting from the embedding of the dyadic relationship within a larger social network (friends, family, and others).

According to RDT, one dialectic in relationships is the dialectic of expression, or tension around how much should be disclosed or kept private. When this dialectic is internal (focused on the dyadic relationship), it is called openness-closedness. *Openness* is the desire to share intimate ideas and feelings with your relationship partner. *Closedness* is the desire to maintain your individual privacy from your partner. Between relationships and their social networks, the dialectic of expression is called the revelation-concealment dialectic. *Revelation* refers to sharing information from the relationship to the social network, whereas *concealment* refers to keeping information private, within

Assurances A type of relationship maintenance behavior that involves messages about the desire to continue the relationship

Self-disclosure A type of relationship maintenance behavior that involves sharing thoughts and feelings that are not specifically about the relationship

Relationship talk A type of relationship maintenance behavior that involves discussing the nature of the relationship and what is desired for it

Sharing tasks A type of relationship maintenance behavior that involves performing responsibilities, such as household chores

Involvement with social networks A type of relationship maintenance behavior that involves interacting with friends and relatives

Relational dialectics theory A theory that describes opposing forces or tensions (relational dialectics) that affect relationships

Relational dialectics A set of opposing forces or tensions that individuals experience as a consequence of being in a dyadic relationship

Internal dialectics In relational dialectics theory, a set of opposing forces or tensions that are internal to the dyadic relationship

the relationship. During pregnancy, couples may become especially aware of this dialectic as they decide what to tell and what to keep to themselves.

According to RDT, a second dialectic is the dialectic of integration, or tension between being involved versus being separate. The internal version of this dialectic is called connection-autonomy. *Connection* is the desire to link your actions and decisions with those of your relationship partner. *Autonomy* is the desire to act and make decisions independent of your relationship partner. For example, in relationships with co-workers, this dialectic may take the form of wanting to be cooperative and helpful, yet assertive and able to look out for yourself. The external version of the dialectic of integration is called inclusion-seclusion. *Inclusion* is the desire relationship partners have to spend time as a dyad with family and friends, whereas *seclusion* is the desire to spend time together but apart from everyone else.

The third dialectic in RDT is called the dialectic of certainty, which is tension around being stable and routine, versus being changeable and surprising. As an internal dialectic, this is called novelty-predictability. *Novelty* is the desire for originality, freshness, and uniqueness in your partner's behavior or in your relationship. *Predictability* is the desire for consistency, reliability, and dependability. At the same time that we want a romantic partner to be "the person I've always known," RDT contends that we also him or her to be "the new kid on the block." As an external dialectic, the dialectic of certainty is called conventionality-uniqueness. *Conventionality* refers to wanting your relationship to be like those of your friends and family, whereas *uniqueness* refers to wanting a relationship that is distinct from those in your social network.

RDT asserts that it is normal for people in relationships to experience relational dialectics. At any given time, one or both people in a relationship may be aware of these tensions, or concerned about them. At such times, they may be explicitly discussed. At other times, dialectics will go largely unnoticed, though the theory contends that they are a force within relationships whether recognized or not. Early research associated with RDT identified a number of strategies that people use to manage the relational dialectics they experience (Baxter, 1990). *Selection* is the strategy of exclusive focus on one pole of a dialectic. For example, someone might manage the openness-closedness dialectic by attempting to be completely open about absolutely everything with his or her spouse. *Cyclic alternation* is a strategy of addressing each side of a dialectic in turn, over time. Relational partners who are geographically separated might choose to be completely independent when they are apart, but spend all their time together when they are able to be in the same place. *Topical segmentation* involves choosing certain areas in which to satisfy one side of a dialectical tension while choosing other areas to satisfy the opposite side. For instance, with your grandmother you may choose to be open about certain topics or aspects of life, such as school and work, but remain closed about your sex life and your political activism. *Neutralization* is a strategy of compromise: addressing each pole in the dialectic to a limited extent. For example, a couple might work at being sufficiently like others in their social network to avoid standing out, but different enough to retain the feeling that they "play by their own rules."

External dialectics
In relational dialectics theory, a set of opposing forces or tensions that result from the embedding of the dyadic relationship in a larger social network

Dialectic of expression
In relational dialectics theory, a tension around how much should be disclosed or kept private

Openness-closedness
From relational dialectics theory, an internal dialectic between the desire to share intimate ideas and feelings with one's relational partner and the desire to maintain individual privacy

Revelation-concealment
From relational dialectics theory, an external dialectic between the desire to share information from the relationship to the social network and the desire to keep information private, within the relationship

Dialectic of integration
In relational dialectics theory, a tension around being involved versus being separate

Connection-autonomy
From relational dialectics theory, an internal dialectic between the desire to link your activities with those of your relational partner and the desire to act independently

Inclusion-seclusion From relational dialectics theory, an external dialectic between the desire to spend time as a dyad with family and friends versus the desire to spend time with the relational partner apart from everyone else

Finally, *reframing* is a strategy of deemphasizing dialectical contradiction, looking at the poles differently so that they no longer seem quite so contradictory. For instance, maybe you are uncomfortable because you perceive that you are more spontaneous (novel) and your partner is more planned (predictable). You might choose to reevaluate your partner as more spontaneous than other people you know, or notice that your partner's predictability creates the structure in which you are able to be spontaneous. These cognitive strategies do not eliminate the dialectic, but can make it less problematic or even positive.

During the early development of RDT, theorizing and research remained compatible with the scientific paradigm emphasized in this text, insofar as there were efforts to verify that people experience dialectics in their relationships and employ dialectic management strategies, and to connect dialectics and management with relationship outcomes (Baxter, 1990). For example, Pawlowski (1998) asked a small sample of young married couples to identify turning points in their relationships (significant events or changes) and choose three that represented early, recent, and mid-relationship turning points. She then asked them to describe each turning point, with interview questions designed to elicit details about thoughts, feelings, events, issues, and involvement from others. Transcripts of these interviews were read by trained coders, who marked statements that indicated experience of one of the six dialectic tensions (three internal, three external). The couples also completed scales measuring how important they thought each tension was at each turning point. The results showed that connection-autonomy was most frequently experienced by these couples, and revealment-concealment the least. The experience of these tensions varied by turning point; for example, connection-autonomy was more frequently reported at the first turning point than the second or third. Across turning points, the openness-closedness, autonomy-connection, and inclusion-seclusion dialectics were rated more important than the other three.

However, since the late 1990s, research connected with RDT has been almost exclusively qualitative and interpretive, avoiding efforts to generalize or predict in favor of "rendering a rich evocative understanding of the meaning-making process, privileging the words and perspectives of the participants" (Baxter & Braithwaite, 2008, p. 350). Baxter & Braithwaite (2008) describe the quantification of dialectics as lacking depth of insight into the dynamics of specific situations, and Baxter & Norwood (2015) recently contended that "the post-positive paradigm is generally an ill fit for RDT" (p. 280). Indeed, recent research has concentrated on detailed description of dialectic tensions in various relationships and populations (e.g., first-generation college students and their families; Lowery-Hart & Pacheco, 2011), and Baxter has moved toward an explicitly non-scientific, critical version of the theory (labeled RDT 2.0; Baxter, 2011; Baxter & Norwood, 2015) that is outside the scope of the present text. Consequently, despite considerable influence on multiple generations of relationship researchers and students, the future of RDT as a scientific theory of relational communication will depend on the interests and efforts of future scholars. Scholars Robert Duran and Lynne Kelly have published a scale assessing experience of the connection-autonomy dialectic (Duran, Kelly, & Rotaru, 2011); this is a positive step in sustaining scientific research to test and improve RDT.

RELATIONAL TURBULENCE MODEL

Denise Solomon and Leanne Knobloch developed the relational turbulence model (RTM) to explain why many romantic relationships go through periods of "drama" or **turbulence**, during which the relationship is experienced as unstable, chaotic, disorderly, and even dysfunctional (Solomon & Knobloch, 2001; Solomon & Knobloch, 2004). Some of the theory's ideas connect with uncertainty reduction theory (Berger & Calabrese, 1975, see Chapter 8) and relational dialectics theory (Baxter, 1990; see above), but the theory has evolved well beyond these roots.

Relational turbulence model A model that explains why relationships experience periods in which they are experienced as unstable

RTM starts with the observation that certain life events or circumstances tend to provoke relationship change, or periods of transition. The life events or circumstances that necessitate relational change vary from couple to couple, but certain kinds of transition periods are common across couples (e.g., moving in together). Solomon and Knobloch initially developed the theory with a focus on the transition from casual dating to a committed relationship (Solomon & Knobloch, 2001), but subsequently extended it to encompass transitions more generally, including those centered on significant challenges (breast cancer, infertility, military deployment; Knobloch, 2015, Solomon, Weber, & Steuber, 2010). Relationships often become turbulent during such transitions. RDT explains this as resulting from changes in relational uncertainty and partner interference.

Transition In the relational turbulence model, refers to a life event or circumstance that tends to provoke relationship change

Relational uncertainty is defined as "the degree of confidence individuals have in their perceptions of involvement within a relationship," including how I feel about our relationship (self-uncertainty), how my partner feels about our relationship (partner uncertainty), and the status of the relationship (relationship uncertainty; Solomon, Weber, & Steuber, 2010, pg. 119). High relational uncertainty is being very uncertain about your own feelings, your partner's feelings, and the status of the relationship, whereas low relational uncertainty is being very certain about all of those things. Partner interference occurs when a relational partner exerts influence that disrupts life routines. As relationships develop, partners become interdependent, which means that they allow each other to influence their activities. For example, as relationships between college students develop, people who once ate, studied, worked out, and partied independently, begin to do all of those things together, or interdependently. In married and cohabiting couples, many life activities become highly interdependent, such that even small changes in one partner's life naturally affect the other. Partner interference arises when a partner feels that the other partner's influence is *disruptive* of their normal routines. Imagine that your boyfriend or girlfriend joins an Ultimate Frisbee group that meets Wednesday nights. If you've been accustomed to eating and watching TV together, and changing this plan is negative for you, that's partner interference. If however, this frees you to have friends over to watch a TV show your partner hates, RTM describes that as *partner facilitation*, not interference.

Relational uncertainty The degree of confidence individuals have in their perceptions of involvement in a relationship

Partner interference Influence of a relational partner that disrupts life routines

According to RTM, relational transitions often generate both relational uncertainty and partner interference. Imagine moving to a new town so your husband or wife can move up the career ladder more easily, requiring that you also change jobs and leave friends and family behind. If your spouse throws him or herself into the new job, is rarely home, and is often tired or stressed, you might reasonably develop concerns about your importance to your spouse and the future of your relationship (relational uncertainty). Your spouse's single-minded focus on work may also force you into taking on more of the domestic tasks, which intrudes on your own job search, fitness routine, and efforts to develop a social life in your new community (partner interference). Under the influence of relational uncertainty and interference, research shows that relational partners become more reactive. In part, reactivity is emotional and cognitive. Partners experience more anger, sadness, fear, and jealousy, perceive irritating and hurtful events as more threatening to the relationship, and generally perceive their relationships as more tumultuous (for reviews of this research, see Knobloch, 2015; Solomon, Weber, & Steuber, 2010). Reactivity is also present in how partners produce messages directed at each other, and in how they interpret each other's messages.

Reactive In the relational turbulence model, refers to excessive emotional and cognitive response to a partner's behavior

In one study testing RTM, Theiss and Knobloch (2013) surveyed 220 military personnel who had recently returned home from deployment. These participants completed measures of relational uncertainty and partner interference, open and aggressive communication (reported for themselves and their partners), and perceived affiliation and dominance in their partners' behavior. Consistent with RTM, increased relational uncertainty and partner interference were associated with less openness and more aggressiveness in communication by and from the partner. Further, partners who were seen as using less open and more aggressive communication were viewed as less affiliative and more dominant (see Relational Framing Theory, Chapter 8). This is one of several dozen studies conducted over the past 15 years to test RTM. As this research has accumulated, the authors have made revisions where appropriate. For example, RTM was originally envisioned as explaining the transition from casual to committed in romantic relationships, and included the claim that relational uncertainty and partner interference peak at this transition (i.e., at moderate levels of relational intimacy). However, variation in the findings from different studies have made this claim problematic (Solomon, Weber, & Steuber, 2010), and the theoretical focus has shifted toward understanding the consequences of turbulence in the context of any transition, not just changes in relationship definition and intimacy.

COMMUNICATION PRIVACY MANAGEMENT THEORY

Communication privacy management theory
A theory that explains how people reveal private information as well as how people conceal private information

Communication privacy management theory (CPM) was developed by Sandra Petronio to understand "the behaviors, decisions, and changes salient in managing private information" (Petronio, 2013). According to Petronio and Durham (2008), "CPM views 'disclosure' as the process of revealing information, yet always in relationship to concealing private information" (p. 310). Like relational dialectics theory (discussed above), CPMT describes an on-going dialectical tension, or opposition, between revealing and concealing private information. For example, when we start to date another person, we are usually careful about what and how we disclose to the other person. We need to disclose private information in order to develop intimacy. Yet simultaneously we need to control information that we believe is exclusively ours and not appropriate for sharing in the developing relationship. In RDT, this tension is called openness-closedness; in CPMT, it is named the public-private dialectic.

CPM was first presented as a formal theory in 2002, and has undergone development since that time. Recently, Petronio and colleagues have begun describing the theory as having three principles, or elements (Child, Petronio, Agyeman-Budu, & Westermann, 2011; Petronio, 2013). The first principle of CPM is the principle of privacy ownership, which states that people believe that their private information belongs to them, just as they own other possessions such as cars and houses. Relatedly, when people share private information they do not relinquish ownership but instead allow others to become co-owners.

The second principle of CPM is the principle of privacy control, which asserts that people believe they have the right to control what others know about them, and to make decisions about the disclosure of their private information to others. For individuals, privacy control is accomplished with the assistance of privacy rules, or personal guidelines that specify when and how to disclose private information. In part, privacy rules are acquired through social learning. Children learn what to share and keep secret from parents' and older siblings' overt and covert messages. For example, you may have been told "Don't tell anyone outside of our immediate family how much money we make" or realized that no one ever talked about what a certain uncle did for a living. The acquisition of privacy rules is not limited to childhood. Newcomers to any group or organization learn what is considered private in that new group. For example, if you belong to a fraternity or sorority, you were probably taught not to share the initiation process, secret handshake, and other rituals. And some companies require signed non-disclosure agreements of new employees. Privacy rules are also affected by our experiences. If you disclose something private to someone and that person turns around and tells someone else, chances are that you will not disclose anything private to that person again. Thus, this event will alter your privacy rules for that person, and may also affect your privacy rules for others. Although privacy rules are individual, CPMT contends that that they are affected by culture, gender, motivations, contexts, and the ratio of risk to benefit. Some cultures encourage more openness than others, and traditionally, women disclose somewhat more than men. People vary in their motivations for revelation and concealment, and often feel more comfortable disclosing in some contexts or relationships than others. Finally, privacy rules typically reference the benefits and pitfalls of revealing private information.

Individual privacy rules guide personal sharing of private information, but when private information is shared, making others into co-owners, these rules

Public-private dialectic The ongoing tension, or opposition, between revealing and concealing private information

Principle of privacy ownership The belief people have that their private information belongs to them

Co-owners People with whom an original owner shares private information

Principle of privacy control People's belief in the right to control what others know about them, and to make decisions about the disclosure of their private information to others

Privacy rules Personal guidelines that specify when and how to disclose private information; influenced by culture, gender, motivation, context, and risk-benefit ratio

are no longer sufficient. CPMT uses the term privacy boundary to describe distinctions between people who have ownership or co-ownership of private information, and people who lack that access. If you have a secret that no one else knows, there is a privacy boundary separating you from everyone else. However, many privacy boundaries are shared. If, as a child, you and your brother stole candy from your neighborhood grocery story but neither of you have ever told anyone, you and your brother have a *shared* privacy boundary distinguishing you as owners of the information from everyone else. Shared boundaries can be dyadic (two people) group, family, organizational, or even societal (Petronio & Durham, 2008).

CPMT describes original owners and co-owners as utilizing different types of coordinated rules to manage privacy boundaries. Coordinated linkage rules control who else is allowed to know. For example, if a friend tells you that she has an eating disorder and you agree not to share that information with anyone, the two of you have constructed a boundary around yourselves and the information. Coordinated ownership rules affect whether co-owners are allowed to share the information independent of the original owner. If you announce your engagement to your best friend, you may still want to be the one who shares the information with other friends and family. Finally, coordinated permeability rules determine how much information is shared. Your co-worker may be willing for others to know that he has a prison record, but not want the details of his crime and sentence shared with others the way he shared them with you.

The third principle of CPM is the principle of privacy turbulence. This principle contends that when owners and co-owners do not sufficiently coordinate privacy boundaries, such that unauthorized others obtain access to private information, turbulence occurs in the form of privacy violations and other unwanted consequences. In some cases, privacy turbulence arises without intentional violation of a coordinated rule. For example, you may reveal to your best friend that you are unhappy in your marriage. Your best friend may know that this information is to be kept strictly between you, yet neither of you realize that your friend's spouse has overheard you from another room. If your friend's spouse tells your spouse, privacy turbulence will result, even though your friend broke no coordinated rules.

Like relational dialectic theory, CPMT is an interpretive rather than post-positivistic or scientific theory; it provides a framework for describing the disclosure and concealment of private information but largely omits predictive claims about relationships between its constructs. Correspondingly, much of the research associated with CPMT has been descriptive, focused on using the theoretical constructs to explicate the experience and management of privacy dilemmas in various contexts. For example, in one recent study (Toller & McBride, 2013), researchers interviewed parents to examine their motivations for talking or not talking about the death of a family member with their young children. Qualitative analysis of these interviews revealed two parental motivations for revelation (showing that death is a part of life, and modeling grief); parents also described being "selectively honest" and using religion as a reference point. However, recently, CPMT has also been used in conjunction with other theories and quantitative methods in studies that appear to be developing a more predictive theory. For example, one study based on CPMT and uses and gratifications theory (of media use, see Chapter 12) reported that bloggers' motives for deleting previously posted material were predicted by their level of disinhibition, privacy rule orientations, amount of time blogging, and privacy management practices (Child, Haridakis, & Petronio, 2012). This kind of theoretical adaptation is likely to expand the theory's appeal and utility for scholars.

FAMILY COMMUNICATION PATTERNS THEORY

UNDERSTANDING FAMILIES

As defined by Kathleen Galvin and Bernard Brommel (2000), families are "networks of people who share their lives over long periods of time; who are bound by ties of marriage, blood or commitment, legal or otherwise, who consider themselves as family, and who share future expectations of connected relationship" (p. 3). This definition encompasses numerous interpersonal associations and diverse interaction patterns. Indeed, conceptualizations of family range from the nuclear family (parents and children) to kinships of various sorts, which can include friends and even pets (Trost, 1990). The previous four theories described in this chapter—relationship maintenance, relational turbulence, relational dialectics, communication privacy management—are all relevant to this range of both traditional and less traditional family relationships.

However, some theories, such as the one described in this section, have been developed specifically to explain communication in nuclear families. Such theories recognize that nuclear families have certain unique characteristics that shape the process and outcomes of communication in those contexts (Yerby, Buerkel-Rothfuss, & Bochner, 1990). Nuclear families are characterized by nonvoluntary relationships, at least for children. Although you can choose your friends, you do not choose to be born into a specific family. The history, sets of relationships, and network of relatives are already established when we are born. Additionally, nuclear families exhibit longevity of influence: the influence of one's family, whether functional or dysfunctional, often endures for a lifetime. Typically, families are also characterized by high levels of intimacy and commitment—beyond those that are usual for friendships or romantic relationships in their earlier stages. Family members often spend a great deal of their time together and see each other in a wide range of circumstances. Relatedly, their commitment to remaining connected is usually strong, and may even be taken for granted. Correspondingly, families are usually the strongest influence on the development of self-concept. Families are probably our most potent sources of information and influence that shape how we see ourselves. Finally, families are systems of relationships, exhibiting nonsummativity and interdependence. Nonsummativity means that the family is

Nonvoluntary A characteristic of many family relationships; we do not choose to be born to a specific family

Longevity of influence A characteristic of families; the influence of one's family endures for a lifetime

Commitment and intimacy A characteristic of families; typically, families experience a stronger sense of inseparability and interconnection than in other relationships

Development of self-concept A characteristic of families; our self-concepts are strongly influenced by interactions with family members

Nonsummativity and interdependence A characteristic of families; families are more complex than their set of members, and each member influences all others

more complex than the individuals that are its members, and interdependence means that all members of the family influence other members. Suppose that one spouse in a dual-career family is suddenly unemployed. Understanding the influence of this change on the family cannot be fully understood by focusing solely on the now-unemployed spouse. This change will permeate all parts of the family system. Possible functional consequences might be: greater frequency and quality of interaction between family members, more time for the children to spend with the unemployed parent, and potential realignment of family roles and responsibilities. One dysfunctional consequence could be the highlighting of status differences within the family. One member is now the "breadwinner" in the family. With decreased family income, greater conflict between the family members regarding individual and family spending may also result.

PATTERNS OF COMMUNICATION IN FAMILIES

Family communication patterns theory A theory that differentiates types of families based on their routine ways of communicating with each other, and connects such patterns with outcomes for family members, especially children

Family communication patterns theory (FCPT) (Koerner & Fitzpatrick, 2002, 2006) differentiates types of families based on their routine ways of communicating with each other, and connects such patterns with outcomes for family members, especially children. Historically, the theory's roots go back to the 1970s, when media scholars began theorizing about how families responded to messages in the media (McLeod & Chaffee, 1972, 1973). Family communication scholars extended the theory and developed improved ways of measuring key constructs in the 1990s and 2000s (Ritchie & Fitzpatrick, 1990; Ritchie, 1991). Recently, the theory has enjoyed something of a renaissance, and in 2014 was featured in a special issue of the *Journal of Family Communication*.

Co-orientation Two or more people attending to the same social or physical "object"

The theory starts with the assumption that families tend to communicate in stable, predictable ways. These patterns are described as resulting from co-orientation, which occurs when two or more people attend to the same social or physical "object." In families, co-orientation occurs on a very frequent basis, as family members collectively encounter many of the same circumstances and events both in their family environments and in the community (e.g., living in the same place, going to the same schools and stores, seeing the same television programs). As families co-orient to shared experiences, they become aware of each other's attitudes, beliefs, preferences, etc., and have the opportunity to respond to the similarities and differences they observe. For example, imagine young children playing at a park under their parents' supervision encountering other children engaged in "play fighting" with water guns or Nerf swords. Some parents are opposed to their children playing with such items, or even with other children engaged in play fighting of any kind, whereas other parents are indifferent to, or positive toward, this type of play. Children, too, vary in how much they find this type of play appealing. In this situation, as parents and children co-orient to toy weapons and the activity of play fighting, both will learn something about how the other responds to it, parents have the opportunity to influence their children's attitudes and behaviors, and in some cases, children may influence their parents in return.

FCPT describes two dimensions of family communication that characterize how families co-orient to multiple issues and events over time. One of these dimensions is called **conformity orientation**, and refers to the "the degree to which family communication stresses a climate of homogeneity of beliefs, values, and attitudes (Koerner & Schrodt, 2014, p. 6). The other is called **conversation orientation**, defined as "the degree to which families create a communication environment in which family members are encouraged to participate in unrestrained interaction about a wide range of topics" (Koerner & Schrodt, 2014, p. 5).

"Crossing" conformity orientation with conversation orientation generates a typology of four family types, illustrated in Figure 9.3 below. **Protective families** exhibit high conformity orientation and low conversation orientation. Communication in these families emphasizes parental authority and child obedience. Children's opinions rarely matter in decision-making, which can be detrimental for the development of decision-making skills. Conflict is rare, and unlikely to be productive. In such a family, children might be forbidden to play with toy weapons with little or no explanation; alternatively it might be understood (without saying) that it was OK. **Consensual families** show high conformity orientation combined with high conversation orientation. Communication in these families is characterized by the desire to preserve the family hierarchy while also having open interaction. Problem-solving is valued, but volatile conflict is seen as inappropriate, and children tend to adopt parents' values and beliefs. The parents in this type of family might explain why they do not want their children playing with toy weapons—or conversely, discuss the fun they had as a child in neighborhood mock battles, or praise the child's "combat skills" as "just like your uncle in the Army." **Laissez-faire families** display low conformity orientation and low conversation orientation.

Conformity orientation
The extent to which family communication emphasizes homogeneity of beliefs, values, and attitudes

Conversation orientation
The degree to which families encourage unrestrained interaction about a wide range of topics

Protective families
Families high in conformity orientation and low in conversation orientation

Consensual families
Families high in conformity orientation and high in conversation orientation

Laissez-faire families
Families low in conformity orientation and low in conversation orientation

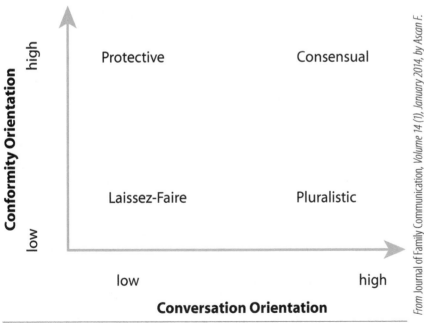

From Journal of Family Communication, Volume 14 (1), January 2014, by Ascan F. Koerner and Paul Schrodt. Copyright © 2014 Routledge. Reprinted by permission of Taylor & Francis, Ltd. http://www.tandfonline.com

FIGURE 9.3 FAMILY COMMUNICATION PATTERNS THEORY FOUR FAMILY TYPES.

Because interaction between family members is minimized, family members make their own decisions and rarely engage in influence or conflict. Children in such families may be especially susceptible to peer influence as they attempt to develop their own views and behaviors. In this type of family, lack of involvement with each other and unconcern about differences between them would probably keep toy weapons and aggressive play from being discussed at all. Finally, pluralistic families combine low conformity orientation and high conversation orientation. Communication is open and unconstrained, and opinions are judged on their merits rather than who expressed them. Such families do not avoid conflict, but work at finding positive resolution. Consequently, if the parents disagreed with each other, or with the children, about toy weapons and play fighting, they would discuss and perhaps argue about their different points of view, while seeking any necessary compromises (e.g., allowing a child to save up allowance for a Nerf sword rather than the parents purchasing it).

Pluralistic families
Families low in conformity orientation and high in conversation orientation

Early discussions of FCPT tended to describe the different family types in relatively neutral terms, deemphasizing differences in value or advantage to the children (Koerner & Fitzpatrick, 2002). However, considerable research has accumulated to suggest that children benefit from a higher conversational orientation and a lower conformity orientation. A meta-analysis of 56 studies (Schrodt, Witt, & Messersmith, 2008) demonstrated the effects of family communication patterns, and especially conversation orientation, on a range of psychological, social, behavioral, and information processing outcomes. For example, within families higher in conversation orientation and lower in conformity orientation, children experience more positive interaction, affection, self-disclosure, understanding, and relational satisfaction. They also tend to have better conflict resolution skills, and are mentally and physically healthier than children from lower conversational and higher conformity orientations. One study (Schrodt & Carr, 2012) examined the association between family communication patterns as reported by young adults (with their families of origin) and the trait of verbal aggressiveness. Communication behavior is verbally aggressive if it attacks a person's self-concept to inflict psychological pain, including attacks on character or competence, harsh teasing, insults, and ridicule (see Chapter 4). The trait of verbal aggressiveness (VA) is the tendency to engage in this type of behavior, which is generally destructive to personal and professional relationships. In Schrodt and Carr's study, 474 university students completed the Family Communication Patterns Scale to assess conversation and conformity orientations in their families, and an abbreviated version of the Verbal Aggressiveness Scale to assess the tendency to engage in verbally aggressive behavior. Analyses of this data showed that students from families with lower conversation orientation or higher conformity orientation were somewhat more verbally aggressive. Correspondingly, students from protective families were the most verbally aggressive, whereas students from pluralistic families were the least. As the authors argue, "to the extent that parents co-create a family environment that encourages expressiveness and reduces overt conformity to parental viewpoints based on parental authority, such an environment may help mitigate the activation and use of verbally aggressive behavior in adolescence and young adulthood."

Recent critique of FCPT identifies several issues for family communication scholars to address in subsequent work (Koerner & Schrodt, 2014). One of these is "better explication of the causal mechanisms linking family communication to outcomes" (Koerner & Schrodt, p. 12), or why family communication patterns have the effects that have been observed. For example, does higher conversation orientation have positive effects for children because discussion and deliberation builds more sophisticated ways of thinking about and communicating with others (see Constructivist Theory in Chapter 8)? Or do positive effects for high conversation orientation stem from children developing self-esteem and confidence when adults are interested in their ideas and opinions? Koerner and Schrodt (2014) suggest both are possible, but need to be tested. In support of this testing, they also advocate further improvement of the Family Communication Patterns Scale, with a focus on questions that measure conformity orientation. As they note, some conformity tactics have never been well represented (e.g., inducing guilt or shame), and societal norms have shifted since the 1990s, to the extent that typical parental means of encouraging conformity may be less dictatorial than they once were. Extending the theory and improving measurement of its key constructs will ensure its continued relevance to explaining family communication well into the future.

SUMMARY

This chapter presented several theories of interpersonal communication in relational contexts. These theories included predicted outcome value theory, the relationship interaction stages model, relaionship maintenance model, relational dialectics theory, relational turbulence model, communication privacy management theory, and family communication patterns theory.

KEY TERMS

Assurances

Attitude similarity

Avoiding stage

Bonding stage

Circumscribing stage

Commitment and intimacy

Communication privacy management theory

Conformity orientation

Connection-autonomy

Consensual

Conventionality-uniqueness

Conversation orientation

Coordinated linkage rules

Coordinated ownership rules

Coordinated permeability rules

Co-orientation

Co-owners

Costs

Development of self-concept

Dialectic of certainty

Dialectic of expression

Dialectic of integration

Differentiation stage

Experimenting stage

External dialectics

Family communication patterns theory

Inclusion-seclusion

Initiation stage

Intensifying stage

Internal dialectics

Involvement with social networks

Laissez-faire

Longevity of influence

Nonsummativity and interdependence

Nonvoluntary relationships

Novelty-predictability

Openness-closedness

Partner interference

Perceived similarity

Pluralistic

Positivity

Predicted outcome value

Predicted outcome value theory

Principle of privacy control

Principle of privacy ownership

Principle of privacy turbulence

Principle of reinforcement

Privacy boundary

Privacy rules

Protective

Public-private dialectic

Reactivity

Relational dialectics

Relational dialectics theory

Relational turbulence model

Relational uncertainty

Relationship interaction stages model

Relationship maintenance model

Relationship talk

Revelation-concealment

Rewards

Self-disclosure

Sharing tasks

Stagnation stage

Termination stage

Transition

Understanding

Voluntary relationships

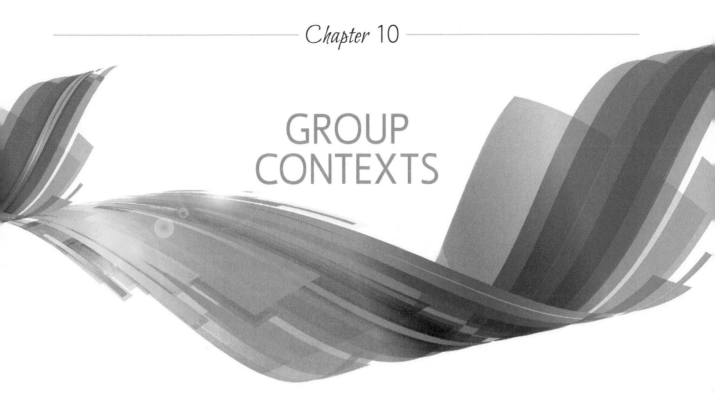

Chapter 10

GROUP CONTEXTS

Important aspects of relationships (affection, trust, and attraction, for example) differ when they occur between two individuals as opposed to when they occur in a small group. The feeling of trusting an other person is not the same feeling as trusting a group of people. Differences in communication between two individuals and the communication among several people necessitate identifying interpersonal and small group communication as two distinct contexts. After clarifying certain aspects of groups, we will discuss several concepts that set communication in groups apart from communication in other contexts. Then we will examine some recent and significant developments in the field of communication studies in terms of building group communication theories.

NATURE OF GROUPS

GROUP SIZE

Small-group communication refers to communication in gatherings that vary in size from three to about fifteen people. A group is considered small if members are able to switch roles from receiver to source with relative ease (DeVito, 2012). When groups are composed of fifteen people or more, it becomes difficult to switch from receiver to source. In such a situation, the order of speaking is often assigned, and more formal rules of parliamentary procedure may be followed such as the use of Robert's Rules.

Small-group communication
Communication in gatherings that vary in size from three to about fifteen persons

The size of a small group influences the likelihood that everyone will get along with one another. A group of four people involves six dyadic relationships, whereas a group of twelve has sixty-six. The greater the number of possible relationships, the more potential for individual dyads within the group to be incompatible. Group size affects satisfaction. The larger the group, the greater the probability that some members will not be able to talk as much as they would like. Size can also impair group performance, as implied in the adage "too many chefs spoil the broth." There may be an optimal number of people for solving a given problem; additional people may cause confusion and impede, rather than help, group progress.

TYPES OF GROUPS

When you think of "groups," what comes to mind? You can probably identify quite a few reasons for people to gather together. A group's *purpose* provides perhaps the clearest way of distinguishing one type of group from another.

Task-oriented groups are those that have a specific task to accomplish. Task groups can be further divided into problem-solving, decision-making, and idea-generating groups. A **problem-solving group** attempts to discover a solution to a problem by analyzing it thoroughly. **Decision-making groups** are also concerned with problem solving. However, they have the added function of actually deciding which solution will be implemented, when and how it will be put into effect, how progress will be monitored, how changes in the solution will be handled, and how the program involving the solution will be evaluated. The **idea-generation group** is a third kind of task group. The purpose of idea-generation groups is to discover a variety of solutions, approaches, perspectives, or consequences for a topic. The idea-generation group is often called a "brainstorming" group.

A second type of group is the **therapy group**. The purpose of therapy groups is to help the individual solve personal problems. These groups are conducted by professionals such as clinical psychologists. There are many different kinds of therapy groups. Some of the most common are encounter groups, T-groups, and sensitivity groups, all of which hope to promote personal growth. Some therapy groups include support for losing weight, alcohol or drug addiction, and chronic physical disease among many others. The communication discipline has conducted little research and has had little experience with therapy groups because few communication scholars are trained therapists.

Consciousness-raising groups exist to increase members' awareness of shared characteristics or concerns. These commonalities can be characteristics such as gender, nationality, or religion; a value such as respect for animal rights; an experience such as serving in the military; an ability such as intercollegiate athletics; or a profession. The purpose of consciousness-raising groups is to have members realize more vividly who they are, to be proud of what makes them unique, and to have members change their behavior so it is more in line with this new consciousness. For instance, a consciousness-raising group might help members realize how widespread domestic violence is in our society.

Learning groups constitute a fourth type of group. The purpose is for individuals and the group to acquire more information and understanding of a topic. This type of group is sometimes used in educational settings such as high schools and colleges. There are some advantages to group versus individual efforts in learning. For example, group members can divide the work; each member adds his or her unique perspective to enrich what the group learns; members gain insight from discussing information that may not have been gained in the absence of such discussion; and motivation to continue learning can be enhanced.

Therapy, learning, and consciousness-raising groups have been studied generally by the fields of psychology, sociology, education, and counseling. As mentioned earlier, group communication theory and research in the communication field has focused primarily on problem-solving and decision-making groups. We will now examine several important elements in such groups.

GROUP ROLES

Certain communicative behaviors in groups (such as using humor to get members to relax) are intended to accomplish certain goals such as releasing group tension. Someone enacting those behaviors can be described as playing or taking a given role. In 1948 Benne and Sheats provided an analysis of roles that has remained influential over the years. They said there are three main categories of roles that can be enacted by group members. *Group task roles* pertain to group discussions aimed at selecting, defining, and solving problems. The specific task roles identified by Benne and Sheats are

1. **Initiator–Contributor**—proposes new ideas, changes, procedures.
2. **Information Seeker**—asks questions about information and others' suggestions.
3. **Opinion Seeker**—asks questions about the values guiding the group.
4. **Information Giver**—presents evidence relevant to the group problem.
5. **Opinion Giver**—states his or her position on issues.
6. **Elaborator**—clarifies what is being considered, extends the analysis of an issue.
7. **Coordinator**—gets people to function together, puts information together.
8. **Orienter**—keeps group focused on goals, points out departures from goals.
9. **Evaluator–Critic**—argues the evidence and reasoning pertaining to issues.
10. **Energizer**—motivates group toward a quality decision.
11. **Procedural Technician**—performs routine tasks, busywork.
12. **Recorder**—writes group proceedings so a record exists.

These roles are often performed by more than one person in a group. One person might perform several of the twelve task roles during the course of a discussion. In fact, a single incident of communication might involve several roles. For example, a member offers an opinion, follows that with a question, and then tries to energize the group so it will not lack the necessary motivation to accomplish the task.

The second category of roles is termed *group building and maintenance*. These roles are concerned with the socioemotional climate in the group. That is, the feelings that group members have for one another. Such roles are very important in terms of the group achieving its task goals. These roles are

1. **Encourager**—provides positive feedback to members, shows warmth.
2. **Harmonizer**—reduces tension between members and mediates conflict.
3. **Compromiser**—attempts to have each party in a conflict gain something.
4. **Gatekeeper**—promotes open channels of communication and participation by everyone.
5. **Standard Setter**—suggests and uses standards to evaluate the group.
6. **Group Commentator**—describes the processes operating in the group to change or reinforce the group climate.
7. **Follower**—conforms to group ideas, acts as a good listener.

These seven roles and the first twelve roles are all concerned with the group achieving its purpose. Thus, each of these nineteen roles of task completion and socioemotional support are very group centered. However, not all behavior in a group conforms to this selfless behavior. Sometimes a person tries to satisfy individual needs, which may be totally irrelevant or even counterproductive to the group's task. These behaviors are termed *individual roles*.

1. **Aggressor**—attacks self-concepts of others to assert dominance.
2. **Blocker**—is hostile by being negative and opposing things unreasonably.
3. **Recognition-Seeker**—offends members by calling too much attention to self.
4. **Self-Confessor**—works personal problems into the discussion in hope of gaining insight.
5. **Playboy**—indicates a desire to be somewhere else, preferably having fun.
6. **Dominator**—interrupts, manipulates, and tries to control others.
7. **Help-Seeker**—wants sympathy, acts insecure, confused, and helpless.
8. **Special Interest Pleader**—argues for a "pet" idea, often based on prejudice.

GROUP LEADERSHIP

It is not difficult to imagine how chaotic our institutions, corporations, organizations, clubs, and political parties would be if they had little leadership. Without leadership, the groups would never have formed in the first place. The many fields studying leadership have produced an enormous body of literature about group leadership or ineffectiveness. In his classic analysis of leadership, Ralph Stogdill (1974; Stogdill & Bass, 1981; see also Bass & Stogdill, 1990) identified forty major topics and examined over 3,000 books and articles. He found that most topics were organized around seven main categories: leadership theory, leader personality and behavior, leadership stability and change, leadership emergence, leadership and social power, leader–follower interactions, and leadership and group performance.

The communication field has taken four approaches to leadership: trait, functional, style, and situational. The **trait approach to leadership** is based on the idea that leaders have traits that distinguish them from followers. You will recall from Chapter 4 that a trait is a characteristic of an individual that is generally consistent from one situation to the next. Trait research suggests leaders are more likely than followers to be high on traits such as self-esteem, extroversion, open-mindedness, aggression, achievement motivation, analytical thought, sociability, and argumentativeness.

The **functional approach to leadership** focuses on the leadership behaviors needed by a group to accomplish its goals (Barnlund & Haiman, 1960), not on the individual as in the trait approach. The leadership behaviors that are essential to the success of a group do not have to be performed by a single person. Instead, leadership can be enacted by any number of group members. Two types of leadership behaviors are task and group maintenance. One person in a problem-solving group might provide leadership for the task, another person for group maintenance, while a third person might provide some help in both areas. Task leadership behaviors include initiating ideas and procedures, coordinating members' contributions, summarizing to let the group know its progress, and elaborating on ideas. Group maintenance behaviors involve releasing tension that builds to an unproductive level, regulating the amount of talk by each member, improving group morale, and mediating group conflict (Beebe & Masterson, 2003).

John Cragan and David Wright (1999) provided a useful analysis of the leadership behaviors needed in a problem-solving or decision-making small group. Leadership communication behaviors in the *task area* are contributing ideas, seeking ideas, evaluating ideas, asking others to evaluate ideas, and fostering understanding of ideas. The leadership behaviors in the *procedural area* are setting goals for the group, preparing an agenda or outline for the group to follow, clarifying ideas, summarizing at various points in the discussion, and verbalizing when the group is in complete agreement on something. There also are several leadership communication behaviors in the *interpersonal relations area*: regulating participation so no one feels "left out," creating a positive emotional climate, promoting group self-analysis, resolving conflict in the discussion, and instigating conflict to stimulate a more thorough examination of issues.

The **style approach** has identified three major types of leadership: authoritarian, democratic, and laissez-faire (White & Lippett, 1968). Each style represents a unique set of leadership behaviors. In contrast to individual traits or functions any group members can perform, the emphasis is on different ways of leading.

The **authoritarian style** involves the leader being very directive in terms of the group goals and procedures, the division of work, and deciding the outcome of conflict. Group members do not feel free to argue with this type of leader on these matters. Research suggests that groups can be quite productive with an authoritarian leader; however, members' satisfaction with their experience in the group tends to be lower than with other leadership styles. The authoritarian style is said to be most appropriate in situations that are highly stressful or dangerous (e.g., emergencies) or highly competitive (e.g., athletic contest). The belief is that argument in such situations can be counterproductive; what works best is a strong, competent central figure who guides the group forcefully down an efficient and productive path.

In contrast, the **democratic style** views all issues (including goals, procedures, and work assignments) as matters to be discussed by the group. The actual decision on the issues can be made in one of three ways. A *majority decision* is produced when members vote. The agreed-upon percentage (e.g., 51 percent, 67 percent) of votes must be obtained for an idea to pass. *Consensus* occurs when the group tries to find a resolution to the given issue that everyone in the group can support. This can be difficult to achieve. If such a solution can be found, it will enjoy significant group support. A *participative decision* involves members contributing ideas and the leader then being guided by the expressed preferences in making the decision. On a more macro level, of course, this is a central feature of our representative form of government. The democratic style of leadership tends to produce the most member satisfaction, even if the group is not as productive as those operating under another leadership style.

The **laissez-faire style** of leadership involves a minimum of involvement by the leader in group activity. Basically, the leader provides as much information as needed, and then the group members are left to make decisions as a group, to act as individuals, or as subgroups. This lack of direction from a leader can be counterproductive, especially in groups with low motivation for a task. However, this style can work very well with people who are highly motivated, experienced self-starters who work well together. The leader says in essence, "You don't need me to tell you what to do."

GROUP CONFLICT

The term *conflict* has negative connotations for some people. Certainly, there are types of conflict that are destructive. However, not all forms of conflict are necessarily bad. In fact, certain kinds of conflict are essential to the success of a problem-solving or decision-making group. The theory of groupthink discussed later in this chapter illustrates rather vividly what happens when there is too little conflict in important decision-making groups.

Conflict exists in a small group when proponents of differing positions on an issue are motivated to defend their positions. Overt disagreement in a group is another way to think of conflict. According to B. Aubrey Fisher (1970), problem-solving and decision-making groups typically go through four stages: orientation to the task, conflict over what the group should do, the emergence of a group position, and group reinforcement of the decision. The conflict stage is especially important in determining how the group will progress and the resulting quality of the decisions.

The influence of conflict on the group product was clearly illustrated in research by Charlan Nemeth (1986). She discovered that conflict in a small, problem-solving group improved the quality of the group's process in making decisions. The conflict she studied took the form of an argumentative minority that opposed the majority opinion. Nemeth found that having a vocal minority view did not necessarily persuade the majority away from their initial position. Instead, an argumentative minority tended to stimulate the majority toward a more careful, thoughtful, and thorough decision. This illustrates an important function of conflict in small groups. The conflict does not have to result in the proponents of one position "converting" the believers of another position. Instead, conflict can lead to a more carefully considered decision. More specifically, one that looks at a number of advantages and disadvantages before reaching a conclusion.

Conflict in small groups can be viewed in terms of argument. That is, the interaction in problem-solving groups can be analyzed according to the issues over which there was disagreement, the positions taken and defended by the various group members, the attempts to refute the positions, and whether these aspects of argument help explain the group outcome, especially the quality of the group decision. An argumentative approach to studying small group communication holds considerable promise. Randy Hirokawa's functional theory (discussed later in this chapter) reveals that certain kinds of communication in small groups, including argument, distinguish effective from ineffective problem-solving groups.

GROUP CONFORMITY

Conformity is sometimes a product of group communication. Conformity can be defined as: *"A change in behavior or belief toward a group as a result of real or imagined group pressure"* (Kiesler & Kiesler, 1969, p. 2). Conformity is a type of group influence, a change in the individual brought about by pressure (real or imagined) for the person to behave in a manner advocated by the group. For example, some students in a study group might say, "Let's take a break and finish this job tomorrow." One member might dissent and say he or she wants to continue and to finish the job today. After all the other members of the group express dissatisfaction with continuing, the lone dissenter says, "Well, OK, let's call it quits for now." The person was not able to resist the pressure to conform to the wishes of other members. This experience is generally a universal one. All of us at times decide to conform to what the group wants to do rather than to resist, especially when resisting may have negative relational consequences that outweigh the benefits of continuing to resist the group's will.

One type of conformity is *public compliance;* the individual behaves in the way desired by the group only when being observed by group members, because the person does not really believe in the behavior. This type of conformity recognizes that our behavior is not always consistent with our beliefs and attitudes. Sometimes we believe one way but behave in another manner because of group pressure. *Private acceptance* is a second kind of conformity. Here the person behaves as suggested by the group because the group produces a change in the person's beliefs and attitudes. Thus, the person is not "pretending" when behaving in a particular manner but actually believes the group's position (Kiesler & Kiesler, 1969).

In our study group example, one of the members in the majority might say to the lone dissenter, "You are suggesting that we make this a marathon session. However, I recently read some research that showed the quality of performance for a group with a task such as ours falls off sharply right about where we are now in the number of nonstop hours worked." Our lone dissenter might then say, "I didn't realize that, but it certainly is plausible given other things that I've read about achievement. OK, let's finish tomorrow." Conformity in this instance is different because it is based not only on group pressure but also on an internal change in the dissenter.

There also is the possibility that one does not have to change a behavior to conform. A group can essentially reinforce the individual's ideas by pressuring him or her to remain a certain way, to continue a certain behavior and not to change. For example, binge drinking on college campuses across the nation is a growing epidemic. The group pressure to binge drink or encourage the practice might keep the person from making more healthy decisions. In this case, the group influenced the person by strengthening or reinforcing previous beliefs (e.g., people who binge drink have more fun at a party) and patterns of behavior (e.g., choosing to go to places where people are binge drinking). This reinforcement can be viewed as a type of conformity.

There are several reasons for our compliance with group pressure. Being a member of a given group partially satisfies our *need to belong,* to be included. Thus, if the group threatens to exclude us because we do not want to go along, our feelings of belonging are endangered. The group is also influential because it serves a valuable *reference function* by informing members on what is and what is not acceptable behavior. The group provides a basis for comparison so that individuals can evaluate their behavior. "I must be dressing OK; everyone in the group dresses just like me." *Group attractiveness* is a third reason for being influenced by group pressure. Generally, the more attractive a group is to us, the more we are likely to be influenced by it. If we are attracted to a group, we have strong feelings of liking, and it is difficult to go against those feelings unless the issue is very important. Moreover, because we usually evaluate a group as attractive because its members express liking for us, we find it difficult to resist pressure from the group because we fear members will stop liking us. This is a powerful incentive to yield to group pressure because we have a need for affection and generally dislike losing the respect of others. Such a loss could threaten our need to belong (the first reason). Finally, *group maintenance* sometimes is a reason for conforming. We realize that the group needs to put on a united front. If one member behaves differently, it will weaken the image of the group. Thus, we may conform for the good of the group.

FUNCTIONAL THEORY OF GROUP DECISION QUALITY

Randy Hirokawa's functional theory involves the communication characteristics of group interaction that lead to quality decisions. Stating such principles in probability terms constitutes a law: if a group does A, B, and C, it is highly likely that they will make a quality decision.

One study analyzed videotaped discussions of various groups who were judged to have reached an effective or an ineffective decision (Hirokawa & Pace, 1983). Four communication characteristics distinguished effective from ineffective groups. The first was that effective groups rigorously evaluated the validity of opinions and assumptions made by the individuals in the group. Ineffective groups, however, glossed over the evaluation procedure and accepted opinions and assumptions as facts without critical analysis. A second difference in communication pertained to how groups evaluated alternatives. Effective groups analyzed possible solutions thoroughly with very critical attention paid to consequences such as what would happen if the solution were adopted. Ineffective groups were superficial and uncritical. Usually they simply said a given solution did or did not meet the criteria for a good solution; they did not argue why. Third, effective groups based their decisions on reasonable premises (assumptions) whereas ineffective groups based their decisions on inaccurate, highly questionable premises. No member of the ineffective groups made an effort to correct these mistakes. The fourth communication characteristic was the quality of leadership. In effective groups, the leaders encouraged *constructive argumentation* by introducing issues, challenging other positions, and identifying fallacies in reasoning. The leaders of ineffective groups exerted a negative effect on the quality of the group's decision by influencing the group to accept faulty ideas, introducing ridiculous ideas, or leading the group on a tangent.

Interestingly, this study also identified communication characteristics that did *not* distinguish effective from ineffective groups: participating equally, trying to identify important information, attempting to generate a number of possible solutions to a problem, and using a set of criteria in evaluating the various possible solutions. These characteristics were found in both effective and ineffective groups.

Hirokawa's functional theory maintains that a group needs to fulfill four critical functions to reach an effective, high-quality decision:

1. Achieving a thorough understanding of the problem that requires a decision
2. Discovering a range of realistic and acceptable possible solutions
3. Identifying the criteria for an effective, high-quality solution
4. Assessing the positive and negative consequences of possible solutions to select the solution with the most desirable consequences

Hirokawa (1985) conducted a study that examined the communication behavior of groups and found that the more the four functions were satisfied, the higher the quality of the group's decision. Statistical analysis revealed that understanding the problem and recognizing the possible negative consequences of each potential solution best differentiated the groups that reached effective decisions from those which were ineffective. In a later study Hirokawa (1988) found the amount of time spent talking about the four functions did not predict decision quality. Instead, it was the quality of talk that mattered.

Hirokawa and Scheerhorn (1986) identified factors that contribute to a group making a faulty decision. Their basic idea is "that group members influence the quality of a group's decision by facilitating or inhibiting the occurrence of errors (for example, faulty interpretations and conclusions) during various stages of the decision-making process" (p. 63). The five factors are:

1. Inadequate assessment of the problem (failing to recognize signs of the problem, its full extent, seriousness; not identifying the causes of the problem)

2. Inappropriate goals and objectives for dealing with the problem (not identifying objectives that will correct the problem; selecting unnecessary objectives that burden the group)

3. Improper assessment of consequences (ignoring or underestimating the positive and/or negative consequences of a possible solution; overestimating the positive and/or negative consequences)

4. Establishment of an inadequate information base (flawed information, group rejecting valid information, group collecting too little or too much information)

5. Invalid reasoning from the information base (making mistakes in reasoning; using only the information that supports a preferred but flawed choice)

These five sources of faulty decisions result from the communication of the group members. A group member facilitates the errors through social influence by convincing members to accept an invalid inference. Group members can also prevent these five factors from contributing to a bad decision. This too is accomplished through communication, as when a member corrects a fallacious conclusion by another group member.

Dennis Gouran and Randy Hirokawa (1986) termed this kind of corrective communicative behavior **counteractive influence**. It counteracts by neutralizing or negating faulty communication. In doing so, the group is then able to make progress toward an effective decision. This type of influence is very important in getting a group back on track. Both effective and ineffective groups make mistakes. However, a characteristic of effective groups is that counteractive influence is prevalent, and uncorrected mistakes are rare in comparison to ineffective groups. Counteractive influence is another illustration of the positive role of argument in group decision making.

Hirokawa's theory, and the one by Janis discussed next, represent the laws perspective for theory building. The emphasis is on discovering conditions that lead to certain outcomes; this probabilistic reasoning takes an "if this, then that" form. There is a direct interest in what happens to groups and the antecedent conditions that lead to an outcome, such as decision quality. Hirokawa's theory represents an important step in understanding the communicative conditions that need to exist for a group to reach a quality decision. Future research will build on that foundation and further our understanding of the type of communication necessary for effective decision making in groups.

THEORY OF GROUPTHINK

Social psychologist Irving Janis's (1982) theory of groupthink is also concerned with the quality of decisions reached in groups. However, whereas functional theory centered on explaining superior group decisions, the theory of groupthink is about group failures or decisions that in hindsight seem incredibly poor, ill advised, and generally incompetent. The basic problem Janis tried to solve is how a group of persons, who individually are quite competent, can make a collective decision that is utterly incompetent. The theory was based on historical analyses of national fiascoes such as the Bay of Pigs invasion, inactivated defenses at Pearl Harbor, escalation of the Vietnam War, and the decision to launch the space shuttle *Challenger*. The theory of groupthink was offered as an explanation of such failures.

Groupthink is a communication process that sometimes develops when members of a group begin thinking similarly, greatly reducing the probability that the group will reach an effective decision. To explain groupthink, we will first say what it is *not*. Groupthink is not critical thinking, where decisions are based on thorough discussions of the problem and the possible good and bad consequences of potential solutions. Groupthink is not an attitude that says, "I am going to present this objection to what the group favors even if it means some people will be a little upset with me for not going along."

The definition by negation, then, suggests several features of groupthink. When groupthink develops, there is a high level of cohesiveness among members and a great deal of reluctance to deviate from the group position. Cohesiveness is the feeling of "oneness" in a group, being "close-knit," bound to one another, and united, as members of a team. Cohesiveness is normally a desirable condition in groups. It is undesirable when members place such a priority on solidarity that they do not analyze problems thoroughly and reach decisions without adequately considering the consequences of proposed solutions. As a result, groups reach consensus on a course of action prematurely. This can cause a group of superior individuals to make a very inferior decision and to select the wrong solution. The communication in a group that is operating under groupthink lacks argumentation and has little rigorous clash of positions on issues. Figure 10.1 presents a summary of the theory of groupthink.

Cohesiveness The feeling of "oneness" in a group, being "close-knit," bound to one another, and united as members of a team

Facilitating Conditions	Symptoms of Groupthink	Defective Decision Making	
Cohesive group	Overestimation of power and importance a. illusion of invulnerability b. belief in the inherent morality of the group	Inadequate analysis of problem Limited range of solutions No rigorous assessment of consequences of preferred solution Failure to reconsider initially rejected solutions	Successful Solution Unlikely
Group structure a. too isolated b. biased leadership c. lack of procedure	Closed-mindedness a. collective rationalizations b. stereotypes of out-groups	Inadequate research Biased processing	
Environment a. external pressure b. lack of alternatives c. low self-esteem	Great pressure toward consensus a. self-censorship b. illusion of unanimity c. direct pressure on dissenters d. self-appointed mindguards	Lack of contingency plans	

Adapted from Janis (1982), p. 244.

FIGURE 10.1 THE THEORY OF GROUPTHINK.

According to the theory, groupthink is more likely when three conditions are present in decision-making groups. The first is a necessary condition but not a sufficient one. For groupthink to develop, *the group must be cohesive* with a strong desire for the group to remain that way. However, just because a decision-making group is cohesive is not sufficient for groupthink to develop. At least two other conditions are necessary: group structure that promotes groupthink and an environment where groupthink flourishes.

The *structure of a decision-making group* can lead to groupthink. For example, if a group is isolated from information and from other persons in a larger organization, the structure can preclude exposure to differing opinions. A biased leader, one who clearly establishes very early the solution he or she prefers, creates a group structure conducive to groupthink. Group members may not advance other possible solutions and may be reluctant to question critically the leader's preferred solution. Another structural factor occurs when the group does not have established procedures for making decisions. Having a set of rigorous procedures (such as bringing in outside experts before the final decision is reached) can reduce the chance of a disastrous decision. Without a tradition of rigorous decision-making procedures, a group can more easily succumb to pressure toward uniformity and thus agree to a very flawed course of action.

The *nature of the situation* represents another facilitating condition for groupthink. Stress nurtures groupthink, especially when the group feels pressure from outside sources to solve a particular problem. A group can make a very bad decision because they feel pressure to present a united front and not to "rock the boat." If the group fails to consider and evaluate a number of solutions, perhaps because they do not have sufficient resources or time, they may agree to one solution without considering other possibilities. If a group feels low in esteem because of recent failures, they will also be more susceptible to pressure toward consensus.

Three major symptoms indicate the groupthink syndrome. First, the *group tends to overestimate its power and importance*—believing strongly that "right" is on its side and that opposing forces are "evil." This creates a false sense of confidence that entices groups to take greater risks than they otherwise would. A second symptom is that the *group becomes very closed-minded*. In selecting a risky course of action, they discount clear warnings and avoid considering information that refutes their choice. The third symptom of groupthink is *great pressure in the group to reach consensus*. Individuals minimize the importance of their doubts to preserve unanimity. Pressure is exerted against any group member who expresses a strong argument against the group's positions. When these symptoms occur, the process of groupthink is probably operating.

Groupthink impairs decision making, greatly increasing the probability of a flawed decision. There are several major defects with decisions affected by groupthink. First, the pressure of cohesiveness results in faulty analysis. The problem is not understood thoroughly; thus, its causes are not well known. Because a solution should deal with a problem's cause, this defect is indeed serious. There are also other deficiencies. Other possible solutions are ignored or dismissed because there is an early preference for a particular solution. The consequences of the preferred solution are not examined rigorously. This is perhaps the most fatal flaw in the process. Also, there is not enough reanalysis of solutions that were initially rejected. When groupthink operates, there is typically a lack of research and thus a shortage of necessary information. Because there is an early preference for a particular solution, information is processed in a biased fashion. A final defect is that groups tend not to make contingency plans when they fall into the trap of groupthink because of the unjustified confidence they have in their solution. For example, if a decision was made by a company to save labor costs by moving its manufacturing plant to a developing country, a necessary contingency plan would deal with possible political instability in that country.

Although groupthink can be a serious problem in decision-making groups, Janis pointed out that several strategies can avoid groupthink. All the procedures are designed to prevent a group from reaching premature consensus and to keep feelings of cohesiveness from turning into group pressure for uniformity.

- The leader of a decision-making group should encourage group members to voice doubts, concerns, or objections.
- The leader should be impartial in presenting the task to the group by using unbiased language and being careful not to show a preference for a particular solution.

- The organization or larger group should set up more than one group with different leaders to work on the same problem.
- The decision-making group should at times divide into two or more sub-groups that work separately and then meet together to debate differences.
- Each member should get the reactions of someone outside the group and report concerns back to the group.
- Trusted members of the organization who are not members of the actual decision-making group should be brought into some meetings to challenge the positions of the group.
- To stimulate debate, one member of the group should be assigned the role of devil's advocate when solutions are being evaluated.
- When the decision involves rivals, such as a competing organization, scenarios of the rival's possible reactions should be created. Emphasis should be placed on the potential risks of the various solutions.
- Once preliminary agreement is reached on a solution, a "last chance" meeting should be held for members to present lingering doubts and to rethink the issue before making the final decision.

Although the theory of groupthink has been used mainly to study historical accounts of bad decisions, one study demonstrated that groupthink can be examined in a laboratory setting (Courtright, 1978). The results supported the theory of groupthink. This support is important for a laws theory. Remember that a basic goal of laws theories is to identify the antecedent conditions that lead to the prediction.

MULTIPLE SEQUENCE MODEL OF GROUP DECISIONS

Unitary sequence model
Model of group decision making that identifies stages that groups go through as they move toward a decision

There have been two distinctive approaches to how groups reach decisions in discussions concerned with problem solving. The unitary sequence model suggests groups pass through certain stages as they move toward a decision. For instance, a problem-solving group first determines the nature of the problem to be solved, the standards that a solution should meet, which of the available solutions best meet the standards, and how the solution selected should be implemented and evaluated. According to Marshall Scott Poole (1981) the unitary sequence model represents a logical ideal of how groups should move toward a decision.

One study looked at forty-seven group decisions to determine the paths taken in reaching decisions (Poole & Roth, 1989). Only eleven of the forty-seven decisions followed the unitary sequence. Fourteen of the decisions followed a solution-oriented path because almost none of the communication pertained to the problem. Twenty-two of the decisions involved complex paths in which the group followed from two to seven problem-solution cycles.

Research such as this suggests a second approach to how groups reach decisions. The **multiple sequence model** (Poole 1981, 1983a, 1983b) contends groups can have different patterns of sequences because they can take various paths to a decision, depending on the contingencies in the situation. This model uses a systems perspective; the emphasis is on patterns of interaction and situational contingencies. The multiple sequence model identifies three separate tracks of group communication activity: *task, relational,* and *topical.* The three **activity tracks**, in a given decision-making group, develop simultaneously but usually at uneven rates. The development of the tracks is influenced by breakpoints that tend to interrupt the development of the activity tracks. There are three kinds of **breakpoints**: *pacers, delays,* and *disruptions.*

The **task activity track** includes the processes in which the group engages to accomplish its task. Some of these are deciding how to proceed, gathering information, analyzing the problem, establishing standards for solutions, and selecting a solution. Imagine a group responsible for drafting football players for a National Football League (NFL) team. They begin meeting well before the NFL collegiate player draft in April. Their task is to decide which eligible collegiate players they should draft to strengthen their team. One of the tasks the director of player personnel would introduce early is a problem analysis. Specifically, what positions were weakest this past season? Where is the need for new talent greatest? If it is decided that the need is most apparent at defensive tackle, another task process would be to establish the standards for a solution. For instance, what should the player's time be in the 40-yard dash? What height and weight are ideal, does he have to be a proven pass-rusher, etc.? The process of selecting a solution would involve strategies such as: in the first round of the player draft, if our first choice for defensive tackle has been selected, we will go to our second; if the second has also been selected, we will switch to our first, second, and third choices for free safety (our second greatest need).

The **relational activity track** involves the activities that emphasize the relationships among the group members that pertain to how the group works together. These include how ideas are introduced and criticized, how conflict is managed, and how roles are defined and reinforced. In our pro football example, the director of player personnel might specify how scouts will work together to evaluate players. At meetings where prospective players are evaluated, one person in the group might be asked to give an overview of a player's strengths and weaknesses, and then the other members are invited to argue for or against drafting the player. When traveling to evaluate players, hotel room assignments might be made so that good friends room together.

The **topical activity track** is made up of the content of the issues and arguments of concern to the group at various times in the discussion. The distinction between the first two tracks and the topical track is process versus content. The first two tracks concern the paths the group follows in discussing content. An example of the topical process track in our pro football example might be: player A has the size and speed that we are looking for but he only had three quarterback sacks last season; player B managed fifteen sacks, but he is not quite big enough for us. This topic could be considered while a group is selecting a solution (task track) or while managing a conflict (relational track).

Breakpoints influence how decisions develop. There are three types of breakpoints. **Pacers**, or normal breakpoints, determine how a discussion moves along. A topic shift is the most common breakpoint influencing pacing. Other normal or expected breakpoints are adjournments, planning periods, or getting away to reflect on topics. **Delays** occur when the group cycles back to rework an issue. The group might go back through the very same analysis several times to solve a problem. For instance, an argument might be repeated several times. This may be a difficult period for the group, but it can also stimulate great creativity if the group rises to meet the challenge. **Disruptions** are a type of breakpoint that occurs in at least two different forms. The first is a major disagreement. When this happens, all three activity tracks could be disrupted. Even after the disagreement is settled, it may take the group a while to get back on track. For example, relational difficulties might be created by conflict that hinders task and topical activities. In our example, two scouts who dislike each other (a relational difficulty) may argue about a particular player, slowing down the decision-making procedure (a task activity). Further, they might distort the player's strengths and weaknesses (topic track), which makes it difficult for the group to get back to a productive discussion. A second type of disruption occurs when a process adopted by the group fails. This could occur when the work is divided among group members, but one assignment turns out to be many times more difficult than the others. Another example is a group selecting the wrong criteria for a solution. In our pro football example, this could involve emphasizing the size of a player when, instead, the number of quarterback sacks should have been the major consideration.

The activity tracks and the breakpoints in Poole's model identify what goes on when a group meets to solve a problem. The objective of all the activities is to accumulate what is needed to complete the task. What is needed to solve a problem might be thought of as *prerequisites* for decision making. Sometimes a group will begin a problem-solving discussion with some of the prerequisites already satisfied. For a decision-making group, the prerequisites include recognition of the need to make a good decision, analysis of the problem to be solved, determining the criteria for a good solution, discovering the possible solutions, adapting the solutions to the needs of the group, selecting a solution, and planning to implement and also to evaluate the solution.

Groups can vary greatly on how ready they are to satisfy each of these prerequisites for a decision. If a group has completed most of the prerequisites, the path to a decision could be relatively simple. On the other hand, if a group has satisfied none of the prerequisites, the path to a decision could be very complex; there could be several problem-solution cycles.

The decisions resulting from a given path or cycle are governed by several contingencies. Poole's model emphasizes two. The first is the nature of the task.

Two dimensions are important. *Difficulty* refers to the amount of effort necessary to complete the task. *Coordination requirements* pertain to the degree that members must integrate their actions and work together. The likelihood of a group accomplishing its task is influenced by these factors. That is, the likelihood of task accomplishment is lower when task difficulty and coordination requirements are higher.

A second contingency of decision development is *group history*. What happened earlier in a group creates expectations about what will happen in the future. Such expectations influence current progress toward an effective decision. Poole (1983b) identified three aspects of a group's history that affect how decisions develop. One aspect pertains to how *involved* members are in the group. Low levels of involvement indicate an individualistic, competitive climate. Higher levels of involvement indicate that members are more dependent on one another. This is typified by a more cooperative climate of decision making. A second factor of a group's history relates to their beliefs about *leadership*. Who the leader is, whether leadership changes over time, and the functions of the leader are relevant concerns. The third factor involves *procedural norms*. A group develops rules, procedures, and roles for guiding its work.

Poole's multiple sequence model of group decisions has emerged as an elaborate and sophisticated explanation of communication and group decision making. The idea that there are three interlocking tracks of activity involved in group decision making is a powerful concept, especially when combined with the concepts of breakpoints and prerequisites.

SUMMARY

This chapter examined communication in the small-group context or discussions involving three to approximately fifteen members. The problem-solving group is the one studied most by communication scholars. The kinds of roles that people take in groups are task roles, group building roles, maintenance roles, and individual roles. Leadership behaviors needed in problem-solving groups include task behaviors, procedural behaviors, and interpersonal relationship behaviors. Conflict in group communication can be either constructive or destructive. Argumentation is essential for constructive conflict. Conformity is a frequent outcome of group communication. Two types of conformity are public compliance and private acceptance. Group pressure creates conformity because of the need to belong, the reference function of groups, the influence of group attractiveness, and the desire for group maintenance.

Three theories of group communication were discussed in some detail. Hirokawa's functional theory of group decision quality attempts to explain effective and ineffective group decisions according to the communication that takes place in the group. The theory posits critical functions groups need to fulfill to reach a quality decision. Janis's theory of groupthink also addresses decision quality. The theory identifies the conditions that encourage groupthink, its symptoms, and its consequences; it also suggests methods for controlling groupthink. Poole's multiple sequence model of group decisions explores the paths groups take in reaching decisions. Activity tracks are identified along with breakpoints and discussed in terms of how they develop in problem-solving discussions.

KEY TERMS

Conflict	Group size	Trait approach to leadership
Conformity	Roles	
Counteractive influence	Small-group communication	

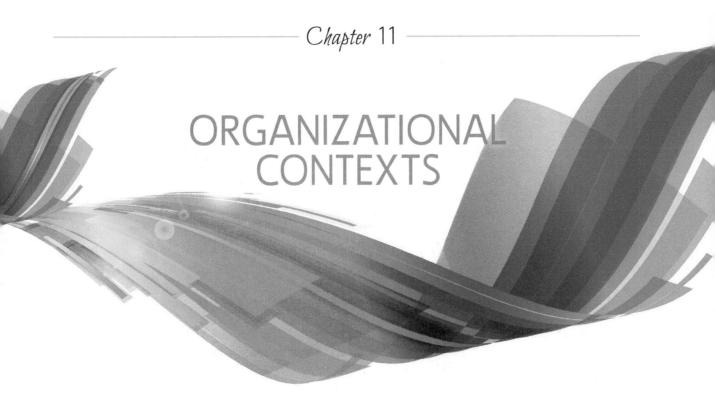

Chapter 11

ORGANIZATIONAL CONTEXTS

Communication theory within the organization requires that any useful scientific-based theory have bottom-line effects for both organization members as well as organization productivity. Recall in Chapter 2 that the predictive function of theory is paramount for social scientific theory. To that end, many organization theories have been developed, discredited, and/or ignored because they either lack predictive power (e.g., critical cultural theories) or are simply bad/flawed theories (see the human relations approach presented later in this chapter). In contemporary organizations, we live in a world in which organizations sometimes operate in unethical and immoral ways in efforts to maximize profits for the few, from the labor of many. Whether it be Volkswagen's willfully lying to customers about pollution control or the Toshiba Corporation overstating earnings by nearly 2 billion dollars, communication and communication theory serve as the matrix through which organizations operate. Given this, some organizations utilize theory for prosocial and noble causes, whereas others use theory for the systematic manipulation of the markets with which they serve.

This chapter will present some of the most popular theories that have guided organizations and organizational researchers since the early twentieth century. As will be evidenced in this chapter, communication, although not explicitly termed in early organizational theory building, serves as the main factor for organization productivity and worker satisfaction.

CLASSICAL MANAGEMENT PERSPECTIVES

The first theories addressing how organizations function primarily focused on how to get workers to be efficient producers. With the development of the Industrial Revolution, people moved from the agricultural and rural areas throughout the United States and into industrialized centers. To organize human beings, managers had to become more effective communicators in an effort to coordinate work shifts, give job instruction, and make sure the organization ran as smoothly as possible. It should be noted that these early efforts at organizing workers were fraught with worker exploitation and manipulation. The lack of concern for worker needs permeates early organizational theories, which are known as the classical management perspective.

Classical management perspective A management perspective that seeks to maximize productivity and has little concern for the worker

SCIENTIFIC MANAGEMENT THEORY

Scientific management theory A management perspective that assumes any worker can be productive if given a scientifically efficient task

The scientific management theory was developed by Frederick Taylor in 1911. He tested his management approach at the Bethlehem Steel Mill in Cleveland, Ohio. In observing workers in the steel mill, Taylor concluded that workers intentionally work below their full capacity. This intentional underachieving behavior is known as soldiering. Soldiering is believed to occur because (a) workers believe that increased productivity will result in a reduction in the number of workers needed to perform a specific task, (b) a wage system does not compensate more productive workers and actually encourages lower productivity from employees, and (c) most worker training has been conducted through unstandardized on-the-job training, which leads to inefficient job performance.

The scientific management approach has three basic assumptions. First, any worker can perform at a high level if given a task that is scientifically efficient. A task is considered scientifically efficient when all elements of the task are analyzed, scrutinized, and made optimally efficient. Consider the task of shovel coal into a furnace necessary for the production of steel. To be made scientifically efficient, we would need to consider the distance between the pile of coal and the furnace, the size and type of shovel, and the technique used to pick up, carry, and deposit the coal into the furnace. Once all these elements are analyzed and made optimal, the result is the scientifically efficient way to shovel coal. This process is known as a time-motion study. Second, workers are motivated by money and will only perform if paid. This principle "cheapens" human beings in that workers see no other value in high levels of performance other than a means of achieving money. This is what is known as the dangling carrot approach to performance. Unfortunately, millions of people get up every morning and go to jobs simply because they pay well, not because they are proud of what they do. Once the job stops paying well, the worker simply finds another well-paying job. Scientific management is not concerned with how you feel as much as how you perform. The third assumption holds that any tasks assigned to workers should be simple and unambiguous. The types of message exchange associated with scientific management theory consist of upward communication (i.e., messages that flow from workers to supervisors) and downward communication (i.e., messages that are handed down from management to workers).

The overall principles of scientific management are logical and relatively simple to institute. However, this perspective tends to treat workers like cogs in a wheel or parts of a machine. In today's society, scientific management is still used in many industries. For example, the fast-food industry utilizes scientific management theory. All employees are trained in performing simple tasks in the same way. Because the training of new employees is so standardized, or scientifically efficient, the high employment turnover rates associated with the fast-food industry do not adversely affect the earnings of these restaurant chains.

BUREAUCRACY MANAGEMENT THEORY

Max Weber (1947) developed a management theory that emphasized tight structure and control over employees. His bureaucratic management theory makes a distinction between power and authority. Power is the ability to force people to do what you want, regardless of their willingness to do so, whereas authority is the ability to get people to voluntarily obey orders. Perhaps the most notable contribution of this theory was the rational-legal authority system. The term *rational* refers to designing the organization to achieve certain goals with maximum efficiency, and the term *legal* refers to the use of authority through rules and regulations set forth by the organization.

Bureaucratic management A management perspective that advocates a tight structure with many levels in the hierarchy as well as control over employees

A main assumption of the bureaucratic structure is that it is believed to be the optimal means for organizing people. This structure has many levels set in a hierarchy. Each hierarchical level regulates the level beneath it. There is also a strong emphasis on depersonalization, which refers to a clear separation between personal matters and business matters. It is assumed that this large hierarchical structure and tight organizational rules and regulations allows for control and coordination of worker behavior. One of the drawbacks of this approach is that there is little personal accountability for the quality of production. This lack of accountability has been linked to the emphasis on the depersonalization of the worker from the organization (see Jablin & Putnam, 2001).

EFFECTIVE MANAGEMENT THEORY

The effective management theory forwarded by Henri Fayol (1949) assumes that management action should be composed of planning for the future, organizing, commanding, coordinating, and controlling. Fayol is best known for his military-like principles of management, which are highlighted in Table 11.1. As you can see from the table, many of Fayol's tenets involve communication and are relationally based. Although Fayol's tenets do indicate some concern for the worker, his approach to management is considered a classic management theory because it overwhelmingly is designed for maximizing organization function and productivity.

Effective management theory A theory that assumes management action should be composed of planning for the future, organizing, commanding, coordinating, and controlling

TABLE 11.1 FAYOL'S FOURTEEN FUNDAMENTAL TENETS TO EFFECTIVE MANAGEMENT

TENETS	DESCRIPTION
Division of Work	Workers who are trained in one task become experts and, thus, most productive.
Authority	The ability to issue orders as well as use power in an appropriate way.
Discipline	Employees will only follow orders to the degree to which management provides effective leadership.
Unity of Command	Employees should only have one manager, thus keeping information clear and consistent.
Unity of Direction	Employees who do similar tasks should all be given the same plan of action.
Subordination of Individual Interest to General Interest	Management must put the needs of the organization above those of any single employee.
Remuneration	Compensation is an important motivating tool.
Centralization or Decentralization	Whichever management chooses to do should be based on current personnel as well as the current health of the organization.
Scalar Chair	Clear hierarchy of information is necessary, and lateral communication is encouraged.
Order	Order is needed at both the production level as well as the personnel level.
Equity	There must be a degree of respect for employees as well as equal justice throughout the organization.
Stability of Tenure	Keeping quality management is crucial, given the cost and time involved in training new management.
Initiative	Employees at all levels of the organization should be allowed to be innovative.
Esprit de Corps	Management is responsible for maintaining high morale levels for all employees.

By far, the most significant contribution of this approach lies in the scalar chain concept of information transfer. The scalar chain is the clear hierarchical information exchange between different levels of the organization. Similar to the communication structure used in the U.S. Armed Services, Fayol believed that there should be clear lines of both upward and downward communication. Further, organizational members at the same level should be able to share information with one another as long as the organization is aware of this exchange. This lateral exchange of information is known as a gangplank, or Fayol's bridge (see Figure 11.1). Reflecting back on the U.S. Armed Services analogy and the scalar principle, the military uses the term GI when referring to a soldier. GI is an acronym for *government issue,* indicating that the soldier is the property of the military (as are tanks, jeeps, and boots). As this indicates, there is concern for the soldier, but in the end, it is about the optimal function of a military force.

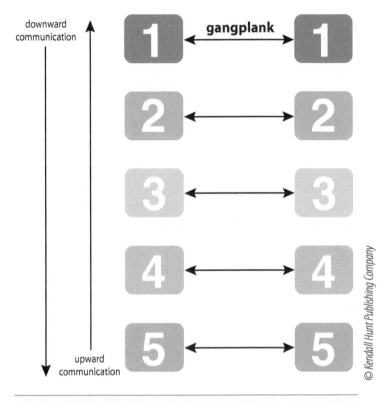

downward communication

gangplank

upward communication

© Kendall Hunt Publishing Company

FIGURE 11.1 FAYOL'S BRIDGE.

The classic management approaches, which advocated productivity over concern for the worker, were a reflection of early industrialization, where organizations had a large uneducated workforce that was easily exploited. In the next section, we see the repercussions of this type of worker treatment.

HUMAN RELATIONS MANAGEMENT PERSPECTIVES

Unlike the classical management approaches that focus on maximizing productivity with little regard for the worker, the human relations perspective emerged as a direct result of the poor treatment of workers. The researchers most noted for their pioneering work in this area are Elton Mayo, Fritz Roethlisberger, and William Dickson. These researchers served as consultants for what has become known as the Hawthorne studies. Between the years of 1927 and 1932, a series of experiments were conducted to determine the effects of illumination on productivity at the Western Electric Company's Hawthorne Plant located in Chicago, Illinois.

The employees at this plant assembled induction coils needed for telephone systems produced by Western Electric. Because assembling induction coils was considered a "specialized" job, a new management team was assembled

Human relations perspective A management approach that advocates that management should satisfy the interpersonal and emotional needs of workers

Organizational Contexts 255

to oversee production. The workers were assigned to either the experimental group, consisting of workers who assembled the coils in varied lighting conditions, or a control group, consisting of workers who assembled the coils under normal lighting conditions. Other manipulations during the experiment included additional work breaks, performance-based compensation, and altering lunch and work schedules.

The initial results indicated that there was an increase in productivity. Mayo and his colleagues concluded that the reason for the increased productivity was not the lighting conditions, but the attention given to the workers by the experimenters and the management team. Further, it was also concluded that the strong interpersonal relationships that developed among coworkers made for a cohesive and supportive work group, resulting in increased productivity.

Mayo strongly believed that the workers' need for supportive and high-quality relationships within the workplace was a result of a breakdown in society (Roethlisberger & Dickson, 1949). As a result of industrialization, people who moved away from family and friends to find employment developed unfulfilled relational needs that must be fulfilled by the organization. In this light, Mayo (1933) argued that one of the major functions of management was to foster spontaneous cooperation, which refers to the fostering of teamwork and quality relationships. With regard to conflict, the human relations management perspective strongly advocates that competition and conflict be avoided at all costs, as it has a negative effect on spontaneous cooperation.

These conclusions from the Hawthorne studies marked a paradigmatic change in management approaches from the classic management assumption of maximizing efficiency and productivity to the focus on quality interpersonal relationships and satisfying the psychological needs of the worker.

In more recent years, researchers have reinterpreted the findings of the Hawthorne studies and offer alternative conclusions to those of Mayo, Roethlisberger, and Dickson. Augustine Brannigan and William Zwerman (2001) argued that the major findings of the study came about when one particular group, known as the mica splitting test group, were moved into isolation from the other groups in the experiment, resulting in a 15% increase in productivity. The increased productivity of the mica splitting test group led to the experimental effect known as the Hawthorne effect. The Hawthorne effect is defined as a threat to the internal validity of the experiment where a change in experimental conditions (e.g., moving the mica splitting test group into isolation) brings about a change in the behavior of the participants that the experiment was originally intended to identify.

In a study using the original data from the Hawthorne studies, it was found that managerial discipline, financial incentives, the economic hardship of the Great Depression, and increased rest periods significantly predicted worker productivity. Although Mayo concluded that quality interpersonal relationships were responsible for increased productivity, it appears that Mayo, Roethlisberger, and Dickson ignored other factors that influenced performance and only focused on the human relationships in an effort to forward the human relations ideology (Franke & Kaul, 1978). In summary, the human relations approach to management resulted in lower productivity because it was based on faulty information and faulty interpretation of the data obtained from the Hawthorne studies. However, as a result of the human relations approach, management theorists began to consider the psychological well-being of the worker, which brought about needed change in working conditions and theorizing about communicating in the organization.

HUMAN RESOURCE MANAGEMENT PERSPECTIVE

The most contemporary approach to management is the human resource management perspective. The underlying assumption of this approach is that the employee is viewed as a valuable asset of the organization who needs to be developed to meet the needs of both the employee and the organization. Unlike the previous two approaches to management, theorists from this perspective have developed several theories that are used in contemporary organizations.

Human resource management perspective A management approach that assumes employees are a valuable asset who should be developed for the benefit of both the organization as well as the worker

SYSTEM 4 MANAGEMENT THEORY

The system 4 management theory of Rensis Likert (1961, 1967) contains management styles that range from low concern for workers to high concern for workers. **System 1** is the exploitive-authoritative type management, which regularly uses threats and fear to motivate workers. Decision making within this management style is conducted at the top levels of the organization then handed down to workers. Downward communication is most valued in these organizations. The content of the communication is primarily task focused. Upward communication is discouraged and kept to a minimum, as this discouragement serves to keep supervisors and subordinates psychologically distant from one another.

The second system is known as **system 2**, or benevolent-authoritative type management, which uses punishment similar to that of system 1, but also incorporates some level of reward. However, system 2 still devalues employee input and only considers management input in decision making. Although communication is generally downward, the amount of upward communication is greater than that found in system 1 and consists of only messages that are deemed important by management.

The third system is **system 3**, or consultative type management, which uses both reward and punishment along with considering some employee input. Although employee input is considered, major decisions are still made at the higher levels of the organization, whereas smaller decisions (i.e., those that have relatively little impact on the organization) are left to lower-level employees to solve. Both downward and upward communication are utilized. System 3 contains some relational messages, with the majority of messages being those that serve the benefit of the organization.

The most employee-centered system is **system 4**, or participative type management, and reflects management's valuing and encouraging input from subordinates. There is a strong psychological connection between the superior and subordinate, with quality communication flowing in both upward and downward directions. It is believed that system 4 management results in high productivity and quality interpersonal relationships at all levels of the organization. This also results in employees who are more committed to the organization.

X,Y MANAGEMENT THEORY

X, Y management theory A
theory of management that
contains bi-polar assumptions
about employee behavior

The approach to management developed by Douglas McGregor (1960, 1966) focused on the manager's assumptions about the work ethic of employees. The X, Y management theory represents bi-polar assumptions about employee behavior. Theory X assumes three basic assumptions about employees. First, employees are lazy, have a tendency to do the minimum, and actively seek to avoid work. Second, because of this dislike for work, management must use threats, coercion, control, and direction as motivational tools to achieve organizational goals. Third, employees have little ambition and strive for a world free of uncertainty. This need for certainty is why employees desire to be controlled (Pugh & Hickson, 1997).

On the other hand, Theory Y contains six basic assumptions about workers. First, within every worker there is an internal motivation to be productive and excel. Second, managerial control is only one of many devices that can be used to increase productivity. Third, the pursuit of satisfaction and maximized potential is the most valued reward for employees. Fourth, employees can not only be taught to accept responsibility, but also can be taught to actively seek opportunities for responsibility. Fifth, employees are much more capable of contributing to creative problem solving than they are given credit for. Sixth, the employees' full potential as an attribute of the organization is sorely underutilized by the organization (Pugh & Hickson, 1997). As McGregor's theory indicates, Theory X assumes a much more classic management approach when contrasted to Theory Y. These dichotomous approaches are developed from a manager's past employment experiences as well as the manager's assumptions about human nature.

THEORY Z OF MANAGEMENT

One of the first management approaches focusing on culture and management was William Ouchi's (1981) Theory Z approach to management. In the late 1970s and 1980s, due to the incredible growth and success experienced by Japanese organizations within the United States and in international markets, it became common practice for theorists to compare and contrast American organizations (type A organizations) with Japanese organizations (type J organizations). Type A organizations encourage individual decision making, performance appraisals based on short-term behavior, and specialized career paths. In contrast, type J organizations encourage collective decision making, long-term performance appraisals, and nonspecialized career paths. Table 11.2 indicates differences between type A and type J organizations.

There was a prevailing assumption that due to the success of Japanese management techniques, simply importing these techniques into American organizations would result in similar success. However, most of these attempts at integrating management approaches failed to be effective when applied outside the culture of origin. That is, the Japanese management models were interwoven with Japanese culture, not that of the United States.

Ouchi (1981) believed that the most effective management theory should be based on the specific culture within which it is going to be applied. A major assumption of Theory Z is that workers are actively involved in the process and success of the organization. Further, this active involvement represents the key to optimal productivity. The theory is grounded in four components consisting of: (a) trust between superior and subordinate in that all interactions between workers and management are conducted in an open and honest fashion; (b) management should have implicit personal knowledge of each employee and use this knowledge to match people who are compatible with one another; this compatibility should be based on personality and job specialty to

TABLE 11.2 OUCHI'S COMPARISON OF TYPE A VERSUS TYPE J ORGANIZATIONS

TYPE A ORGANIZATION (AMERICAN)	TYPE J ORGANIZATION (JAPANESE)
Employment is short term.	Employment is long term and often for a lifetime.
Evaluation and promotion occur frequently and at a rapid rate.	Evaluation and promotion are slow and usually are within the same organization.
Specialized career paths that may lead them to switch employment to competing organizations.	Nonspecialized career paths that are malleable to the needs of the organization.
Explicit control mechanisms that leave no ambiguity as to what rules and regulations the organization wants followed by employees.	Implicit control mechanisms that reflect the more subtle organizational/societal expectations of worker performance and productivity.
Individual decision making is encouraged, whereas innovation and creativity are seen as individual pursuits that are the primary influence in decision making.	Collective decision making is encouraged, and individuality is discouraged while group rule and group harmony are primary influences in decision-making behavior.
Individual responsibility as a cultural assumption reflects accountability for oneself and not coworkers. Employees are rewarded and punished based on individual performance.	Collective responsibility as a cultural assumption reflects that everyone has a stake in the whole organization, and a failure or success at any one level or by any one employee is a failure or success for the entire organization.
Segmented concern as cultural assumptions dictate localized problems and localized solutions without regard to implications on the greater good or the organization as a whole.	Holistic concern as cultural assumptions dictate the subordination of local concerns if those concerns are harmful to the whole. Individual sacrifices are expected if the organization as a whole will prosper.

Adapted from Ouchi, W. G. Theory Z: How American business can meet the Japanese challenge. Reading, MA: Addison-Wesley.

maximize efficiency; (c) productivity is based on a certain standard of performance that is expected of all employees at all levels of the organization; and (d) a level of intimacy that reflects the belief in caring, support, and selflessness through quality relationships among all members of the organization.

Unlike McGregor's theory, which focused on employees' work ethic, Theory Z is focused on the attitudes and individual responsibilities of each employee. Ouchi (1981) believed that collective beliefs and attitudes of employees should be based on mutual respect for each other as well as for the organization. The type J cultural assumption of lifetime employment speaks to the concept of collective beliefs and attitudes. Approximately 20% of the Japanese workforce is under lifetime employment in government and large corporations (Kato, 2001). Theory Z holds that workers are loyal to their employer, are not looking to leave the organization at the first sight of an opportunity for advancement at another company, and will typically wait 5, 10, or even 20 years for a promotion, which generally occurs within the same organization. The Theory Z approach advocates that organizations spend a large amount of time and money in the development of interpersonal skills of every employee within the organization. Given the organization's stress on competent employee communication, processes such as decision making and information exchange are greatly improved.

MODEL I AND MODEL II THEORY

Chris Argyris (1965) believed that the personal and professional growth of a person is directly related to, and affected by, their work situation. Previous management approaches (i.e., classical management) were so focused on bottom-line productivity/profit goals that they became communicatively incompetent with regard to growing employees and utilizing employee creativity and potential. This myopic focus results in employees developing a preventative or reactive posture as opposed to a proactive posture. This development of a preventative or reactive posture is known as defensive routines (Argyris, 1985). Simply put, workers are so resistant to change, even when change can enhance their careers, that they develop a "work to not get fired" perspective, as opposed to a "work toward excellence perspective." When workers internalize this "work to not get fired" philosophy, it results in a form of learned helplessness (Seligman, 1992). An example of this can be seen in an employee who shows initiative on the job, yet continually receives negative feedback for this initiative. The employee will eventually cease to show initiative. This learned helplessness is not self-induced, but induced by the organization in that most organizations tell employees to be focused on long-term personal and organizational goals, yet proceed to evaluate employees in short-term cycles (e.g., quarterly job performance reviews).

Chris Argyris and Donald Schon (1978) argued that workers are constantly caught in a paradoxical situation. For example, employees are constantly being encouraged to "think outside the box." But to do so requires breaking existing organizational rules. Any deviation from organizational rules and norms, more often than not, results in reprimand, demotion, or termination. This paradox is perpetuated in two different theories employed by management. The first is known as espoused theory and concerns what the manager tells an employee about the manager's behaviors, ethics, and management philosophy. The second is known as theory in use and reflects the actual behaviors, ethics, and management philosophy enacted by the manager. For example, a manager may tell the employees that he or she is employee centered, values feedback, and has an open door policy (i.e., espoused theory). However, when this manager is approached by an employee, the manager dismisses the feedback as trivial, seems impatient, and is nonverbally confrontational toward the employee (i.e., theory in use; Argyris & Schon, 1978).

Model I and model II approaches to management are believed to bring about distinctively different outcomes for employees and the organization. Model I assumes four types of managerial behavior. First, the manager sets unilateral goals that are then pursued by employees. Second, the manager is self-reliant to the point where the manager seeks to maximize success and minimize failure. Third, the manager rarely, if ever, expresses negative affect or behavior in public and keeps opinions and attitudes private. Fourth, the manager treats all issues objectively and rationally to the point where any emotional expression will be minimized if not absent. These behaviors are believed to bring about single-loop learning in workers. Argyris (1985) argued that this type of learning is self-oppressive. Single-loop learning is the understanding of *how* a process is conducted, not *why* the process is conducted. For example, in the fast-food industry there is a large amount of single-loop learning. Employee training is so scripted and standardized that employees are taught how to assemble a particular hamburger, reset the fryer, make coffee, and so forth. What these employees are not shown is why the tasks are performed in a particular order and how the appropriate execution of these tasks results in the employee contributing to the overall success of the organization.

Model I approach
Management approach that assumes unilateral goals, self-reliance, failure to disclose negative opinions, and reliance on objectivity and logic

Model II approach
Management approach that assumes pro-action, consultative decision making, solution implementation, and the ability to adapt should the solution need adjustment

The model II approach to management allows for organizational learning and growth. Model II managers routinely engage in the following three behaviors: (a) the manager takes action on information they see as valid, regardless of who the information comes from or whether it is based on logic or emotion; (b) the manager consults all the people who are both relevant to and competent to make decisions; the manager then acts on that decision; and (c) the manager is committed to the decision and is active in the implementation yet flexible enough to adjust the course of action if needed. By utilizing these behaviors, managers are open to feedback and trusting of others. This results in double-loop learning, also known as generative learning. Generative learning reflects learning the process, understanding the rationale for the process, and knowing how this process contributes to the function of the entire organization. This model of management allows for employee feedback and employee identification with the task, the manager, and the organization.

In an effort to train managers to utilize model II behaviors, Argyris (1993) conducted a 5-year study of managers, which resulted in the development of a seminar directed at improving model II communication and management skills. It is believed that this type of training aids in overcoming the defensiveness and mistrust that results from model I management behaviors. This training approach to model II management indicates that effective management behaviors can be learned and that these skills can be acquired and utilized by any manager.

MANAGERIAL GRID THEORY

Instead of conceptualizing concern for task and concern for a worker as a single continuum, Robert Blake and Jane Mouton (1964, 1978) proposed the managerial grid theory. The grid contains two continua compring concern for worker and concern for task that result in a managerial style profile. Managers are assessed on a scale from 1 (very low) to 9 (very high) on the degree to which they have concern for their workers and an identical scale assessing concern for the task.

Managerial grid theory
A theory that contains two continua resulting in five managerial profiles ranging in concern for task and concern for relationship

The impoverished manager is a person who scores low in concern for worker and low in concern for task (i.e., scoring at or near 1 on both scales). Impoverished managers are ineffective, are costly to the organization, and have less tenure in management positions (see Figure 11.2).

The country club manager is a person who scores high in concern for worker and low in concern for task (i.e., at or near 9 on concern for worker and at or near 1 on concern for task). Country club managers are valued by subordinates due to a high level of communication and relational competency that fosters positive affect (feelings) from subordinates. Given that this type of manager is reflective of human relations, the country club manager is not valued by upper-level management because of the lack of focus on the task (see Figure 11.3).

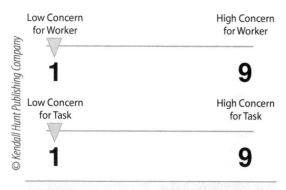

FIGURE 11.2 IMPOVERISHED MANAGER.

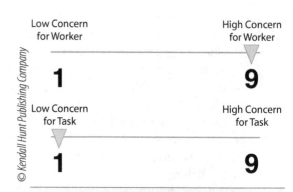

FIGURE 11.3 COUNTRY CLUB MANAGER.

The task manager is a person who scores low in concern for worker and high in concern for task (i.e., scoring at or near 1 on concern for worker and at or near 9 on concern for task). The task manager is not well liked by subordinates but is highly valued by the organization because of the bottom-line productivity that is associated with a high focus on task. This style of management is most representative of the scientific management approach (see Figure 11.4).

The moderate manager is a person who scores moderate in both concern for worker and task (i.e., scoring at or near 5 on both scales). This management style results in average success with regard to productivity and average levels of relational quality with subordinates. More people report using a moderate management style than any other style because people tend to score in the middle of both scales, with fewer people scoring on the extremes of the measures (e.g., country club and task managers; see Figure 11.5).

The team manager is considered the optimal management style because the manager has a high concern for worker and a high concern for task (i.e., scoring at or near 9 on concern worker and on concern for task). The team manager enjoys both high levels of productivity and quality interpersonal relationships with workers (Blake & Mouton, 1982). Dean Tjosvold (1984) found that employees reported working hardest when the manager was high in both concern for worker and task (i.e., team manager). Further, people reported working the least for managers who were high in concern for worker and low in concern for task (i.e., country club manager). The team manager style is most reflective of the human resource approach (see Figure 11.6). The value of the Blake and Mouton (1964, 1978) managerial grid can be found in the way different combinations of management styles can be derived from treating concern for task and concern for the worker as two separate independent dimensions that range from low to high concern.

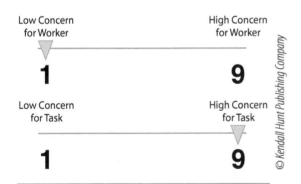

FIGURE 11.4 TASK MANAGER.

FIGURE 11.5 MODERATE MANAGER.

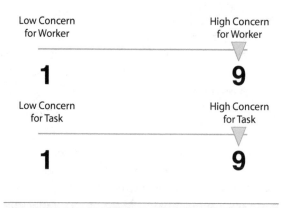

Low Concern for Worker		High Concern for Worker
1		**9**
Low Concern for Task		High Concern for Task
1		**9**

FIGURE 11.6 TEAM MANAGER.

THEORY OF INDEPENDENT MINDEDNESS

Theory of independent mindedness A communication based organizational theory that advocates cultural congruity between the organization and the larger culture within which it operates

The theory of independent mindedness (TIM) (Infante, 1987a, 1987b) is a uniquely communication-based theory as opposed to being economic, business, or psychologically based. The TIM seeks congruity or similarity between the culture created within the specific organization (i.e., microculture) with that of the larger culture (i.e., macroculture) within which it operates (see Figure 11.7). The cultural coordination advocated by the TIM also serves as the foundation of Ouchi's (1981) Theory Z. American culture values freedom of expression and individual rights. Both of these values are made explicit in the Constitution of the United States. The TIM assumes that these values should be reflected and fostered within the organization.

As a corporatist theory, the TIM is believed to bring about employee motivation, satisfaction, and productivity. Employees should be active in decision-making processes, and those processes should include the robust exchange of ideas and perspectives. However, unlike most Eastern management approaches that advocate the downplaying of power and status, the TIM, conceptualized from a Western perspective, advocates that power and status differences should not be downplayed, but acknowledged and emphasized as they are in the larger American culture (Avtgis & Rancer, 2007).

This theory is a radical departure from classical management-based theories that emphasize the use of unilateral control and power (Ewing, 1982; Infante & Gorden, 1987). In fact, the TIM assumes that power and control are fluid ideas that move both downward from superior to subordinate as well as upward from subordinate to supervisor. In an effort to exert control and power in an appropriate fashion, competent communication skills must be developed. More specifically, three communication traits are believed to influence the degree of independent mindedness in an organization: argumentativeness (Infante & Rancer, 1982), verbal aggressiveness (Infante & Wigley, 1986), and communicator style (Norton, 1978).

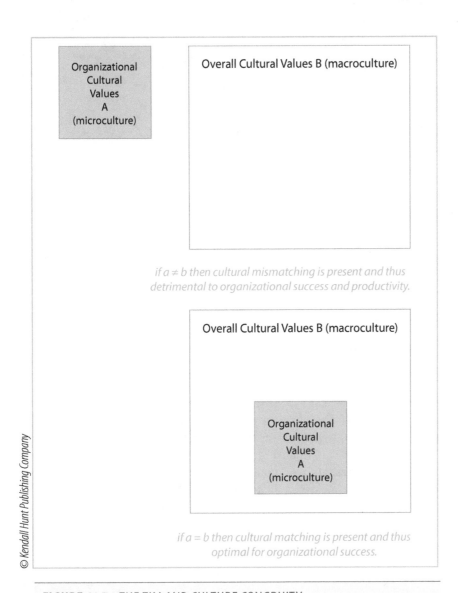

FIGURE 11.7. THE TIM AND CULTURE CONGRUITY.

As discussed in Chapter 5, trait argumentativeness is believed to be a constructive trait that has been found to bring about many organizational benefits, such as the appropriate expression of organizational dissent (Kassing & Avtgis, 1999), greater job satisfaction (Infante & Gorden, 1985), and solution-oriented conflict resolution strategies (Martin, Anderson, & Sirimangkala, 1997). Trait verbal aggressiveness is a destructive trait that has been found to be linked to employee inattentiveness and unfriendliness, lower levels of job satisfaction (Infante & Gorden, 1989), and the use of ineffective and inappropriate organizational dissent strategies (Kassing & Avtgis, 1999). The trait of communicator style represents the ten distinct styles of communication, including dominant style, dramatic style, contentious style, impression leaving style, animated style, relaxed style, open style, attentive style, precise style, and friendly style. Of these ten dimensions, certain combinations of these styles create either

TABLE 11.3 COMMUNICATION TRAIT PROFILES OF THE THEORY OF INDEPENDENT MINDEDNESS

PROFILE	TRAIT LEVEL	OUTCOME
ONE	High Argumentativeness	High Employee Commitment
	Low Verbal Aggressiveness	High Employee Satisfaction
	Affirming Communicator Style	High Employee Productivity
TWO	High Argumentativeness	Moderate Employee Commitment
	Low Verbal Aggressiveness	Moderate Employee Satisfaction
	Nonaffirming Communicator Style	Moderate Employee Productivity
THREE	Low Argumentativeness	Lower Employee Commitment
	Low Verbal Aggressiveness	Lower Employee Satisfaction
	Affirming Communicator Style	Lower Employee Productivity
FOUR	Low Argumentativeness	Lowest Employee Commitment
	High Verbal Aggressiveness	Lowest Employee Satisfaction
	Nonaffirming Communicator Style	Lowest Employee Productivity

an affirming communicator style (i.e., communicating in a way that validates another person's self-concept) or a nonaffirming style (i.e., communicating in a way that negates or threatens another person's self-concept). Combining the ten communicator style dimensions along with argumentativeness and verbal aggressiveness represents particular trait profiles that range from complete independent mindedness (i.e., Profile 1) to the absence of independent mindedness (i.e., Profile 4). Table 11.3 indicates the various profiles.

THEORIES OF ORGANIZATIONAL LEADERSHIP

A common assumption in our culture is that everyone should "shoot for the stars" and strive to achieve great things. Leaders have always been part of history and folklore. Consider great leaders such as Robert E. Lee, Margaret Thatcher, Franklin Delano Roosevelt, Martin Luther King, and General George C. Patton. Most people ascribed great personality characteristics and sense of mission to their pursuits. This section will review several theories of leadership that seek to explain how and why people are either put into, or emerge into, positions of leadership.

TRAIT APPROACH TO LEADERSHIP

The trait approach to leadership assumes that people possess the characteristics to be effective leaders based on predispositions or traits that are either biologically derived or developed through the environment. The study of leaders and leadership is not a recent development. For centuries people have studied the qualities of effective leaders in an effort to determine what traits and behavior make an effective leader. These efforts have been called the great man theories of leadership. In one of the first major social scientific approaches to trait leadership, Ralph Stogdill (1948, 1974) believed that any leadership research should take the perspective that leadership qualities are part of a person's personality, and therefore, personality traits should always be accounted for.

Trait approach to leadership Assumes that leaders have traits that distinguish them from followers

Several traits have been associated with leadership. First, leaders possess the trait of narcissism, which is the belief that they, as opposed to someone else, are qualified to lead. This trait assumes a higher level of self-confidence and self-love than those levels found in followers. Second, the trait of charisma reflects the leader's ability to display a high degree of communication competence, the ability to inspire subordinates, as well as have the subordinates buy into the leader's vision (Conger, Kanungo, & Associates, 1988). The term communication competence refers to the ability to be effective (i.e., achieve a desired goal) and appropriate (i.e., achieve goals in a way that respects other people and is deemed socially appropriate). The study of organizational leadership can be seen in the work of Max Weber (1947), who distinguished between charisma based on behavior (i.e., pure charisma) and charisma based on the position of power the person holds within the organization (i.e., routinized charisma). Charisma is a trait that has been possessed by effective leaders such as John F. Kennedy, Oprah Winfrey, David Koresh, and Charles Manson. As this list illustrates, charisma can be used to lead people to perform either constructive or destructive behaviors.

How people interpret events has also been found to distinguish effective leaders from ineffective leaders. The trait of locus of control is a trait that concerns how people attribute causes to outcomes in life (Rotter, 1966). Carl Anderson and Craig Schneier (1978) found that people who exhibit an *internal locus of control* (i.e., see outcomes as being a function of their own behavior) were more likely to be leaders than people who exhibited an *external locus of control* (i.e., see outcomes as being a function of luck, chance, fate, other people). Internally oriented people also reported having greater amounts of previous leadership experience (Hiers & Heckel, 1977) and emerge as group leaders more frequently than people who reported being externally oriented (Lord, Philips, & Rush, 1980).

Perhaps the most well known trait that affects so many behaviors is that of biological sex. Much debate and research has centered on whether men or women make more effective leaders. Sex and gender are considered biological and psychological traits, respectively. Research indicates that men and women do, in fact, have different approaches to leadership and that each approach includes both effective and ineffective behaviors. Rosabeth Moss Kanter (1977) found that women in organizations tend to be more nurturing and socially sensitive whereas men tend to be more assertive and use more overt power. Recent research indicates that the most effective leaders are those who display a more gender neutral or androgynous style that comprises both masculine and feminine behaviors (Hackman & Johnson, 2000). Although trait leadership studies have declined in recent years, the predispositions and traits (whether physical or psychological) that effective leaders possess have provided important insight into what makes some people more effective leaders than others.

SITUATIONAL APPROACH TO LEADERSHIP

Situational leadership approach Assumes that there is no such thing as a born leader as much as people acting as leaders depending on the specific situation

The situational leadership approach assumes that there is no such thing as a born leader as much as people acting as leaders, depending on the specific situation. Consider the following list of people and whether they would be considered leaders without the particular situations in which they were involved: Rosa Parks (without segregation), Abraham Lincoln (without the Civil War), Winston Churchill (without the Battle of Britain), Martin Luther King, Jr. (without the civil rights struggles of the 1960s), Rudy Giuliani (without the terrorist attacks on the World Trade Center), and Mother Teresa (without Third World oppression). The situational leadership theory of Paul Hersey and Kenneth Blanchard (1977) assumes that any leadership style should be based on both the employees' *psychological maturity* (i.e., degree of self-efficacy and willingness to accept responsibility) and *job maturity* (i.e., degree of skills and knowledge of the task). As employees' maturity increases, the most appropriate leadership style would be more relationally focused than task focused. More specifically, a hierarchy of maturity levels requires a degree of both task and relational leadership styles.

At the most basic maturity level, a leader would use the tell style, which is high task focus and low relationship focus. The tell style is advocated because employees have low self-efficacy and are unmotivated. Therefore, the leader must simply instruct or train employees in skills to accomplish the task. Second on the continuum would be the sell style, and it assumes that employees have some maturity and are resistant to being told what to do, yet are not fully motivated to show initiative. Therefore, the leader should be high in both task and employee focus. This type of leadership style includes explaining decisions and advising employees in an effort to motivate them for task accomplishment. At the third level is the participative style. This style assumes that employees have high levels of job maturity and low levels of psychological maturity. Therefore, a low task focus and high relational focused style is required, as employees are capable of performing the task but are unwilling or resistant to perform the task. The final approach is the delegating style and reflects high levels of employee psychological and job maturity. With these types of employees, a low task focus and a low employee focus is required. In this case, employees are capable of performing the task and are motivated to do so. Therefore, the leader should simply allow employees to perform (Hersey, 1984).

EXCHANGE APPROACHES TO LEADERSHIP

The exchange approaches to leadership focus on the quality of the relationship between leaders and their followers. The quality of the relationship is believed to be the determining factor for effective leadership. Leader-member exchange theory (LMX) is one such theory that focuses on the quality of relational linkages between both the leader and followers (a.k.a. members). It is assumed that relational linkages are the main influence on effective leadership (Dansereau, Cashman, & Graen, 1973). How the leader and followers negotiate their specific roles directly affects how the leader and followers will interpret work and the work experience. LMX theory assumes that leaders behave differently with different individual members of the organization based on the nature of the dyadic relationship. The nature of the linkage can be either high or low in quality. High-quality linkages between the follower and leader are termed *in-group relationships,* whereas low-quality linkages are termed *out-group relationships* (Dansereau, Graen, & Haga, 1975). The development of high-quality linkages is the key to effective leadership. Research findings indicate that subordinates with high-quality linkages report more rapid promotion and were more team oriented than out-group members (Erdogan, Liden, & Kraimer, 2006; Scandura, Graen, & Novak, 1986).

> **Exchange approaches to leadership** A leadership approach that assumes the quality of the relationship is believed to be the determining factor for effective leadership

Another exchange approach to leadership is that of transformational leadership theory. Given that American culture is one that values equal rights, justice, competition, and commitment, transformational leadership is focused on the empowerment of individual workers and aiding the organization in adapting to change in both internal and external environments. Among all the leadership theories discussed thus far, transformational leadership is believed to be the most paradigmatic, as it is based on a worldview rather than just another approach to explaining leadership behavior. The three basic premises are (a) the leader is an agent of change, (b) the leader emphasizes the self-actualization of subordinates, and (c) leaders pursue the goals of the organization as well as satisfying the higher-level needs of the followers. Noel Tichy and Mary Anne Devanna (1986) highlighted the seven characteristics that separate transformational leaders from other types of leaders. Table 11.4 describes these characteristics.

Another variation in situational leadership-based theories is that of Fred Fiedler's (1972) contingency theory. This theory assumes that the degree of success of any leader is contingent on the situational demands as to whether the leader should have a task or employee focus and the amount of influence and control the leader has over the situation. When situations are extreme in nature (i.e., there is a possibility of a high degree of success or a high degree of failure), it is best to adopt a task-focused approach. If the situation is moderate in gravity (i.e., there is a possibility of moderate success or moderate failure), it is best to adopt an employee-focused approach. Contingency leadership theory assumes that you cannot change the internal qualities of the leader and that we should find situations (i.e., task focused or employee focused) that match the leader's specific style as well as situations that offer a degree of control and influence over subordinates. For example, in professional sports you will find

TABLE 11.4 CHARACTERISTICS OF TRANSFORMATIONAL LEADERS

TRANSFORMATIONAL CHARACTERISTICS	THOUGHTS, FEELINGS, AND BEHAVIORS
Is identified as a change agent	Understands that the only thing that remains stable in organizations is instability. Welcomes the challenge of being innovating and changing as the environment demands.
Shows courage	Will risk being ridiculed for the success of the organization and followers.
Has a clear vision	Has the ability to constantly envision the future and possibilities that accompany change and innovation.
Is driven by values	Demonstrates impeccable moral fiber and integrates this moral code into the day-to-day function of the organization and organizational members.
Never stops learning new information	Is a lifelong learner who is always interested in better ways of doing things. Rarely satisfied with the status quo and always looking for the next innovation.
Welcomes uncertainty and ambiguity	Thrives on chaos and welcomes complex challenges. Uncertainty and ambiguity are motivating and represent an opportunity for growth.
Believes in workers	Has an undying commitment to bettering organizational members through opportunities for learning and growth.

coaches who have accomplished incredible things in terms of turning around a losing franchise or getting the most from a particular player. However, when this same coach goes to a different team with a different culture and different players (i.e., the situation changes), they may only experience average success.

WORKER MOTIVATIONAL THEORIES

Many researchers have hypothesized why some people are more motivated to work than others. We all know people who, when given a task, will put all their effort into making sure the job is completed to the best of their ability. On the other hand, we also know people who, when given a task, will put out only enough effort to meet the minimum standards. The difference between these two kinds of people can be explained by analyzing the factors that motivate them. This section presents some of the most popular theories of motivation that researchers use to explain human behavior in the organization.

HIERARCHY OF NEEDS THEORY

Abraham Maslow (1943) proposed a theory of motivation that was based on the attempt to fulfill human needs. This hierarchical approach to motivation holds that primary needs have to be satisfied before a person can pursue higher-level needs. The lower or more primary needs concern those that sustain physiological survival. These are reflected in the need for air, water, food, and so on. Once the physiological needs are met, we then are motivated to satisfy our safety needs. Safety needs reflect a life free of turmoil, relative stability, and a preference for predictability. After meeting the safety needs, we are then motivated to satisfy our love needs, which are reflected in the pursuit of affection and belonging. Once the love needs are met, people are then motivated to satisfy their esteem needs, which are reflected in pursuing recognition, appreciation, and respect from other people. This leads to the highest level of needs and satisfaction known as self-actualization. To be self-actualized is to achieve the pinnacle of human potential and achievement. Figure 11.8 reflects the Maslow hierarchy of needs.

MOTIVATOR HYGIENE THEORY

This theory of motivation was developed by Fredrick Herzberg (1968) and is based on the degree of satisfaction and dissatisfaction that workers experience in the workplace. Motivator hygiene theory is a departure from the more traditional theories of motivation that work on a single continuum ranging from satisfied to dissatisfied. Instead, Herzberg proposed a two-continua model in which the first continuum reflects a range from being satisfied to not being satisfied, whereas the second continuum reflects a range from being dissatisfied to not being dissatisfied. Figure 11.9 illustrates these continua. The rationale for creating two continua is based in the logic positing the opposite of something is not something different. This is best illustrated when verdicts are handed down in our legal system. When a person is found not to have committed a crime of which they were accused, they

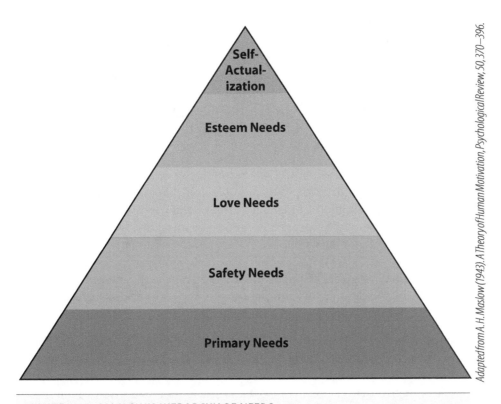

Adapted from A. H. Maslow (1943). A Theory of Human Motivation, Psychological Review, 50, 370–396.

FIGURE 11.8 MASLOW'S HIERARCHY OF NEEDS.

are found to be not guilty, as opposed to innocent. The absence of something (e.g., guilt) cannot be something else (e.g., innocent). Instead, it is not guilty. Simply put, the opposite of apple is not apple, as opposed to orange.

Similar to Maslow's lower-level needs (i.e., physiological and safety needs), the factors related to job dissatisfaction concern the person's need to avoid being deprived of physical and social rewards. Herzberg (1968) illustrated the pursuit of these needs using an analogy of the biblical characters Adam and Abraham. The Adam personality concept reflects behavior that occurred after Adam was sent out of the Garden of Eden. That is, he was faced with the need to satisfy the primal needs of food, security, and safety. The motivation to satisfy these needs become Adam's sole focus. This is similar to the hedonic philosophy of life, or the idea that life is about the pursuit of pleasure and happiness for the individual.

The factors associated with being satisfied in a job are similar to Maslow's concept of self-actualization and reflect the need to achieve the maximum of human potential and perfection (Pugh & Hickson, 1997). This type of motivation is reflected in the biblical character Abraham and is known as the Abraham personality. According to the Bible, God summoned Abraham because he believed that Abraham was capable of accomplishments that were far beyond primal needs. The pursuit of self-realization and great achievement for an entire people was his primary focus, as opposed to just Abraham's own immediate needs. The Abraham personality is reflective of the eudaimonic philosophy of life in that people seek deeper meaning in life and move beyond the simple pursuit of pleasure and happiness.

Although both the Adam and Abraham type personalities seek to be satisfied at work, they seek satisfaction in different places. The Adam personality seeks to avoid pain or, in this case, avoid being dissatisfied. This motivational force results in seeking out things within the immediate environment to avoid pain. These can be things such as pay, good coworker relationships, and working environment. Therefore, this person is motivated to avoid being dissatisfied as opposed to being motivated to be satisfied. The Abraham personality seeks achievement, recognition, and opportunity for growth.

Herzberg (1968) termed the things that make us dissatisfied hygiene factors (e.g., pay, working conditions). Using a biological analogy, poor hygiene can lead to disease, but good hygiene does not necessarily stop disease. In other words, just providing a worker with good pay and good working conditions does not mean that they will be motivated. On the other hand, the things that make us satisfied are known as motivator factors or growth factors and concern the need for great accomplishment, human growth, and self-realization. The lack of motivator factors will not cause a worker to be dissatisfied (assuming good hygiene is present) but will cause a worker to not be satisfied.

To test this theory, Herzberg (1982) assessed over 1,600 employees and found that 81% of motivator factors reflected human growth and development, whereas 69% of hygiene factors contributed to dissatisfaction. The overall principle of motivator-hygiene theory is that workers should be given all the appropriate tools to perform well. Although providing these tools will not motivate

FIGURE 11.9 HERZBERG'S MOTIVATOR-HYGIENE CONTINUA.

someone, it will simply keep them from becoming dissatisfied. Further, this theory encompasses the complexity of human nature and the innate need for human growth. Figure 11.9 illustrates this concept.

ACQUIRED NEEDS THEORY

The influence of culture on the individual is the underlying assumption of the acquired needs theory of motivation. This theory assumes that people are motivated to work to acquire the things that the culture at large deems important (McClelland, 1962). All the needs that are dictated by the culture can be broken down into three main or overarching needs that, according to Western culture, are pursued by people through work.

Acquired needs theory
Theory of motivation that holds that people are motivated to behave in order to acquire things that the culture at large deems important

The first is the need for achievement. People who are high in this need are motivated to acquire positions of responsibility and strive to achieve moderate goals. The reason people pursue moderate goals is that goals that are seen as too easy will be reached by everyone and thus are not viewed as a significant success. On the other hand, goals that are seen as too difficult will be reached by very few and thus can be viewed as a failure. Research indicates that workers who are high in the need for achievement are also open, are sensitive, and report higher levels of job satisfaction (Mitchell, 1984). The second need is the need for power. People who are high in this need are motivated to aspire to greatness and positions of respect (Kotter, 1988). This motivation also includes the pursuit of control, influence, and being responsible for other people. Although it may seem that people who pursue the need for power have selfish intent, people who are high in the motivation for power use this power to help others around them (McClelland, 1975). The final need is the need for affiliation, and it reflects the need to develop and enjoy quality relationships with others, avoid conflict, and be less dogmatic and assertive in an effort to maintain these relationships. Overall, acquired needs theory highlights the different motivating factors that people possess and utilizes these factors to explain why people are motivated to perform certain jobs at certain productivity levels. For example, a productive social worker who makes an annual salary of $22,000 per year is motivated by different needs than a productive stockbroker who makes $220,000 per year.

Theories of worker motivation seek to predict, explain, and understand the things that motivate people to work as well as how to tap into these motivating factors to achieve maximum employee performance. Motivation will continue to be an intriguing part of productive organizational function. Beyond the theories reviewed here, there are many different perspectives concerning how or why workers are motivated. Most, however, differentiate the more primal needs (i.e., physiological needs) from those higher-level needs (i.e., psychological needs). Regardless of how you view motivation, the fact remains that people are complex beings that have a wide range of needs that they strive to satisfy. Communication and relationship building and maintaining play central roles in these theories of worker motivation. The ability to satisfy workers' physiological, psychological, and interpersonal needs, by most accounts, results in motivated, committed, and long-term employees.

ORGANIZATIONAL SOCIALIZATION

MODEL OF ORGANIZATIONAL ASSIMILATION

Organizational assimilation is defined as "the process by which individuals become integrated into the culture of an organization" (Jablin, 2001, p. 755). Frederic Jablin's model proposes that people move through three distinct stages of assimilation. These stages consist of anticipatory socialization, organizational entry and assimilation, and disengagement and exit.

The anticipatory socialization stage reflects how people develop expectations about work. These expectations begin to develop at a very young age through sources such as our parents and the media. Listening to our parents discuss their jobs is our first exposure to what we should expect from our work life. Our educational system is another powerful influence on the creation of our organizational expectations as it exposes children to hierarchical order and information about specific vocations. How to communicate in the workplace is another important facet of anticipatory socialization. We learn appropriate behaviors from watching television shows based on certain occupations (e.g., *CSI, Grey's Anatomy, The Office*). Some of these communication skills that we develop include emotional control, conflict management, and role taking. People engage in information gathering in developing expectations about work. Information can be gathered from organizational newsletters, websites, current employees, and other people with knowledge of the organization. According to Katherine Miller and Frederic Jablin (1991), newcomers utilize surveillance (observation of past behaviors), testing limits (breaking of organizational rules and norms, and then observing the reaction of others), indirect questions (hinting at a topic without directly asking about the topic), third party (soliciting information from coworkers when the newcomer should really be asking the supervisor), disguising conversations (disguising information seeking within everyday conversation), and observing (information seeking by observing the behavior of others).

The second stage in the assimilation model is the organizational entry and assimilation stage. According to Jablin (2001), assimilation "is generally considered to be composed of two dynamic interrelated processes: (1) planned as well as unintentional efforts by the organization to socialize employees, and (2) the attempts of organizational members to individualize or change their roles and work environments to better satisfy their values, attitudes, and needs" (p. 755). People entering the organization are called *newcomers* and are given more latitude with regard to making mistakes. This latitude is based on the fact that the newcomer has to adapt to a new environment, new procedures, new policies, and new relationships.

The final stage of organizational assimilation is the organizational disengagement/exit stage. When people decide to leave the organization, they begin a slow withdrawal process that includes deidentifying with the organization and other organizational members. For example, a person found a new job and gave a four-week notice to their supervisor. During that four-week period, the employee will slowly decrease communication with others as well as increase relational distance. Organizational exit can take the form of being terminated, transferring to another department within the same organization, retiring, or quitting.

ORGANIZATIONAL INFORMATION PROCESSING

INFORMATION SYSTEMS THEORY

Karl Weick (1979) proposed a theory of how people make sense of information in an environment. The main goal of the information systems theory is to explain how information and sense-making is a perceptual process that varies from person to person. This general systems-based theory seeks to identify how ambiguity and equivocal information lead people to different realities. Thus, the organization should seek to ensure a "most single" reality that is shared by all members of the organization. Simply put, organizations should seek to reduce uncertainty or equivocation (i.e., requisite variety).

Information systems theory An information processing theory that seeks to explain how information and sense-making is a perceptual process that varies from person to person

Weick (1995) argued that organizations operate or exist within an environment that is both physical and informational. People within the organization are in a constant state of *organizing*. Weick believes that we should use verbs such as *managing* and *organizing* as opposed to nouns such as management and organization. The use of verbs is advocated to reflect the fluidity of the sense-making process as opposed to using nouns that reflect stationary or fixed entities. People create their environment through enactment, which is the action of making sense. Any one person will attribute different realities to information. Given that people have different perceptual schemas and selective perception, people create different information environments. When there is a low equivocal environment, people use assembly rules, which are standard processes that aid people in standard routines for making sense of information. Sense-making does not only involve interpreting information but also includes generating what was interpreted. As Weick argued, "People know what they think when they see what they say" (Weick, 1979, p. 175). For example, your college or university has a student handbook, which explicitly provides all students standardized procedures for everything from academic standards of conduct to applying for graduation. These standards help increase the probability that each student will enact in a similar way. On the other hand, when there is high equivocation, people engage in communication cycles. Communication cycles are sense-making actions where people create and react to ideas. For example, a professor assigns her students an assignment with only the following instructions: "I want you to develop a term paper on the Civil War. The length of the paper should be long enough to be complete." The information provided by the professor is full of uncertainty and equivocal information. In this case, the students will probably engage in communication cycles to make sense of the equivocal directions. Weick (1979) believes that both assembly rules and communication cycles are utilized most during the selection stage of organizing. "The selection process selects meanings and interpretation directly and it selects individuals, departments, groups, or goals indirectly" (Weick, 1979, p. 175). On the other hand, when sense-making is effective, people are sharing the same information environment, and people should use the retention stage of organizing as the organization should save both the assembly rules and the communication cycles as a rubric for future sense-making processes. The retention stage of organizing involves deciding whether or not assembly rules and communication cycles should be retained or discarded in future sense-making. It is argued that the more information that is retained from past information processing, the more difficult it will be to process more complex information in the future. However, some retention of past sense-making is valuable. Simply put, Weick believes we should "treat memory as a pest." The variety of rules that an organization has developed and engages is known as organizational intelligence (Kreps, 1979) (see Figure 11.10). Information systems theory serves as a rubric from which shared sense-making can be accomplished in the process of organizing.

Adapted from Karl Weick. (1973). The Social Psychology of Organizing. Reading, MA: Addison-Wesley.

FIGURE 11.10 STRUCTURE OF THE ORGANIZING PROCESS.

ORGANIZATIONAL ETHICAL PERSPECTIVES AND THEORIES

Throughout the history of industrialized society, employees have taken unfair advantage of workers, customers, and competitors. What does it mean to be ethical? What is right? Appropriate? Good? The answers to these questions are difficult to derive due to their subjective nature. This section will introduce you to several ethical traditions that seek to explain the various ways that people interpret ethical behavior.

The foundational ethical perspective assumes that ethics and ethical behavior are absolute and universal across all people and cultures. A standard code of ethics is to be adhered to by all people. Foundational ethics can be found in classic religious documents such as the Bible, Torah, or Koran. Many professions also have universal codes of ethics. Some of these codes are legally binding, and some are used to serve as general guidelines for behavior. For example, Table 11.5 reflects the modern version of the Hippocratic Oath (Lasagna, 1964) that is recited by newly appointed medical doctors entering the field of medicine and the oath of enlistment that is required of all new recruits enlisting in the U.S. Armed Services.

The situational ethical perspective assumes that people make ethical decisions based on the situation and not a universal truth. Situation-based ethics holds that ethical standards change based on the specific circumstances in which the behavior occurs. For example, consider the following question: "Is stealing wrong?" To answer this question from the situational ethics perspective would be, "It depends on the circumstances." Another term used to describe ethics in this tradition would be *contingency ethics*. Recall when Hurricane Katrina ravaged the city of New Orleans. The media made a distinction between people who were stealing diapers, food, and clothing from those who were stealing jewelry and electronics. The former were referred to as foragers (and thus behaving ethically), and the latter were referred to as looters (and thus behaving unethically).

The deontological ethical perspective is also known as virtue ethics. Deontological ethics extend back to Aristotle and his writings on Nichomachean ethics. This perspective is based on the intentions of the person. If a person's intent is based on sound and ethical reasoning, then the resulting behavior is seen as ethical. For example, if a pharmaceutical company markets a drug that will increase the quality of life for millions of people, but the development and testing of the drug resulted in the deaths of dozens of animals and human test subjects, the intention to help millions of people would make any resulting loss of life be seen as unavoidable, resulting in the pharmaceutical company's pursuits being seen as ethical.

The utilitarian ethical perspective is considered the opposite of the deontological perspective in that ethical behavior is based on outcomes, not intentions. This perspective can be associated with philosophers such as Jeremy Bentham, John Stuart Mill, and Henry Sidgwick and makes a distinction between a person's moral commitments (e.g., a person's personal sense of duty) and the actual

TABLE 11.5 THE MODERN HIPPOCRATIC OATH AND THE OATH OF ENLISTMENT

MODERN HIPPOCRATIC OATH

I swear to fulfill, to the best of my ability and judgment, this covenant. I will respect the hard won scientific gains of those physicians in whose steps I walk, and gladly share such knowledge as is mine with those who are to follow.

I will apply, for the benefit of the sick, all measures that are required, avoiding those twin traps of over-treatment and therapeutic nihilism.

I will remember that there is art to medicine as well as science, and that warmth, sympathy, and understanding may outweigh the surgeon's knife or the chemist's drug.

I will not be ashamed to say "I know not," nor will I fail to call in my colleagues when the skills of another are needed for a patient's recovery.

I will respect the privacy of my patients, for their problems are not disclosed to me that the world may know. Most especially must I tread with care in matters of life and death. But it may also be within my power to take a life. This awesome responsibility must be faced with great humbleness and awareness of my own frailty. Above all, I must not play as God.

I will remember that I do not treat a fever chart, cancerous growth, but a sick human being, whose illness may affect the person's family and economic stability. My responsibility includes those related problems, if I am to care adequately for the sick.

I will prevent disease whenever I can, for prevention is preferable to cure.

I will remember that I remain a member of society, with special obligations to all my fellow human beings, those sound of mind and body as well as the infirm.

If I do not violate this oath, may I enjoy life and art, respected while I live and remembered with affection thereafter. May I always act so as to preserve the finest traditions of my calling and may I long experience the joy of healing those who seek my help.

OATH OF ENLISTMENT

I, (name), do solemnly swear (or affirm) that I will support and defend the Constitution of the United States against all enemies, foreign and domestic; that I will bear true faith and allegiance to the same; and that I will obey the orders of the President of the United States and the orders of the officers appointed over me, according to regulations and the Uniform Code of Military Justice. So help me God.

behavior of the person. The assumption is that a person's moral commitments and behaviors should be in a dialogue. That is, both the intention and the behavior are considered when deciding if a specific action is ethical. Although considered together, intent and behavior may not necessarily be related to each other (i.e., the behavior may or may not be reflective of a person's moral commitments). The underlying assumption of utilitarianism should be aimed at increasing utility or happiness. That is, the best ethical decision is the one that guarantees the most happiness. If the overall result is positive, then the action is ethical.

The rights/justice-based ethical perspective assumes ethical behavior is derived from natural law. An ethical person or organization is one in which a certain level of dignity, justice, and fairness is afforded to all people. An example of rights/justice-based ethics can be seen in Wal-mart's decision to provide a variety of generic prescription medications for three dollars each. This decision resulted in making medications affordable to a much wider segment of the population. The two general types of rights/justice are distributive justice and procedural justice. Distributive justice reflects normative or societal definitions of what is just or right with regard to the allocation of goods within an organization. Procedural justice reflects decision making and implementing those decisions based on fair and sound principles.

The relationship-based ethical perspective assumes that ethical behavior is a creation of, and maintained through, communication. All relationships within the organization as well as between organizations and their various external publics are based on quality and honest communication. Honest communication involves spontaneous interaction that is void of ulterior motives. Another assumption of the relational ethical perspective is that dialogue is the foundation for which all relationships are developed, maintained, or terminated. Any person communicating should be mindful of the effect that dialogue (i.e., communication) has on the other person and that dialogue should be focused on the development of the other person. Richard Johannesen (1996) argued that the relationship-based ethical perspective "allows free expression, seeks understanding, and avoids value judgments that stifle. One shows desire and capacity to listen without anticipating, interfering, competing, refuting, or warping meanings into preconceived interpretations" (p. 68).

The final ethical perspective is known as stakeholder theory. The term *stakeholder* refers to parties whose interests are directly affected by business activity. Stakeholder theory emerged as a reaction to the writings of Milton Friedman (1970) in his article entitled, "The Social Responsibility of Business Is to Increase Its Profits." Friedman believed that the social world is organized into separate zones of activity. Simply put, people are trained in different disciplines in different ways. For example, a businessperson is trained differently from a doctor, who is trained differently from a philosopher. Each of these professions, as well as many others, have different ways of looking at the world and thus interpreting what is and what is not ethical. This separation of spheres is also true to political, economic, and social activity, and social activity should not be commingled with the others.

> **Stakeholder theory**
> A theory that assumes the sole responsibility of an organization is to those people who own the instruments of production

Friedman (1970) argued that the sole responsibility of the organization is to those people who own the instruments of production (i.e., stakeholders). Therefore, according to stakeholder theory, the organization and its members are behaving ethically if they generate profits for the stakeholders. Ethical behavior, within the corporate world, is solely based on maximizing shareholder profit within the limits of the law. For example, when people argue that "big oil" companies are posting enormous quarterly profits and should be investigated, people are basing their ethical judgment from the right/justices-based perspective, as opposed to stakeholder theory, which argues that if profits are not as high as they could be within the limits of the law, then the organization and organizational members are not behaving ethically.

Stakeholder theory was developed over thirty-five years ago. Since then, the concept of stakeholder has been expanded to include members of the board of directors, managers, and production workers, as well as shareholders. Outside the organization, stakeholders include customers, suppliers, competitors, local committees, and government regulating bodies. In the end, stakeholders fall into the five categories of shareholders, customers, employees, suppliers, and communication.

PRACTICES OF ETHICAL ORGANIZATIONS

Steve May (2006) believed that for an organization to be considered ethical, it should follow six practices. First, alignment refers to the ethical practice that matches the organization's formal practices (e.g., performance appraisal policies, employee pay and benefits) with the informal practices of the organization (e.g., norms, rituals) that serve the needs of the organizational members. Alignment requires effort on the part of both the organization and organizational members. Second is the practice of dialogic communication, which refers to having open channels of communication that constitute the cornerstone of teamwork. Dialogic communication should be decentralized and lack a hierarchical structure. Regardless of a person's position or status, all employees are encouraged to interact. Third is the practice of participation, which reflects the value of feedback and the recognition of contributions from members. Transparent structure is the fourth practice and reflects that every practice that the organization and its members engage in should be up front and open (i.e., aboveboard) to both internal and external members (e.g., customers, community). This transparency should be in all organizational practices, including hiring policies and employee appraisals. The fifth practice is that of accountability and reflects exceeding the minimal standards set by the industry in which the organization operates as well as governmental standards. Courage is the sixth practice and concerns the degree to which the organization values employee dissent, listening to dissent, admitting when the organization is wrong, and promises to rectify any injustice. These six practices are the hallmarks of ethical organizations.

SUMMARY

This chapter began with the development of management theories that have evolved over the nineteenth and twentieth centuries. These efforts included scientific management, human relations, and human resource perspectives. In all these perspectives, the importance of communication, whether it be controlled (i.e., scientific management) or encouraged (i.e., human relations and human resource), is central to explaining human production. We then discussed leadership theories that highlight the various perspectives on how effective leadership is conceptualized and implemented. These varying perspectives include leadership that is believed to be a feature of personality (e.g., trait approaches), a feature of the circumstances (e.g., situational leadership), or a function of the relationship between the leader and the members (e.g., leader–member exchange). The theories of worker motivation discussed included the need for becoming self-actualized (e.g., hierarchy of needs theory), the need for recognition (e.g., motivator-hygiene theory), and the need to satisfy various inner needs (e.g., acquired needs theory). All these theories hold that there is indeed a drive within workers that moves them in varying degrees to accomplish organizational goals. The model of assimilation presented in the chapter maps how a person becomes a member of the organization. As discussed, this process begins in childhood and follows us through retirement. Each of us has a different experience in the organization, and that is why so much effort is expended in the creation of a socialization process that provides a similar experience for all new employees. This sense-making function was also highlighted in information systems theory that utilizes assembly rules and communication cycles in an effort to organize information. Finally, we presented various theories of ethics and how these theories affect how we view something as right or wrong. These perspectives ranged from ethical behavior as being universal to all people (i.e., foundational ethics) to those that are dependent on the situation (i.e., situational ethical perspectives).

KEY TERMS

Acquired needs theory

Bureaucratic management theory

Classical management perspective

Effective management theory

Exchange approaches to leadership

Human relations perspective

Human resource management perspective

Information systems theory

Managerial grid theory

Model I approach

Model II approach

Scientific management theory

Situational leadership approach

Stakeholder theory

Theory of independent mindedness (TIM)

Trait approach to leadership

X, Y management theory

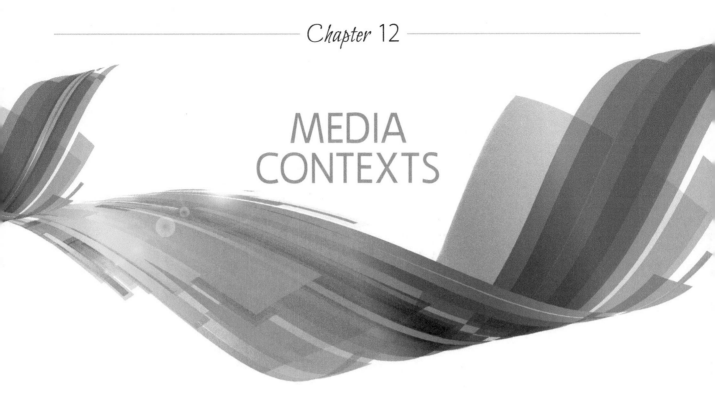

Chapter 12

MEDIA
CONTEXTS

Contemporary society maintains a reciprocal, interdependent relationship with the mass media. Society influences the media and is itself influenced by mass or mediated communication. Rarely a day goes by without some mention of how the media and mass communication affect our lives. Through mass media, people learn almost immediately about major happenings across town or across the globe. As readers and viewers, we are eyewitnesses to global events both joyous and tragic. At the same time, newspaper, radio, and Internet reports scream headlines such as, "Studies link teen suicides with TV, social media, and movies," and "Kids, TV Don't Mix." The **reflective-projective theory of mass communication** asserts that the mass media acts like a mirror for society. The media reflect society's attitudes and values as they simultaneously project idealized visions of a society. Individuals interpret these reflections, seeing both their own images and alternative realities. Interpretations are affected by the intellectual, emotional, and sensory responsiveness of each individual. Lee Loevinger (1979) argued that nations or communities are not necessarily formed by maps or geographical boundaries. Rather, nations or communities are formed by common images and visions, along with common interests, ideas, and culture.

Reflective-projective theory of mass communication A theory that asserts that the mass media act like a mirror for society

Definitions and conceptualizations of mass media and mass communication have changed considerably over the last several decades. At one time, not too long ago, mass media was defined primarily as radio, television, newspapers, and magazines. Today, the term *media* is likely to conjure terms such as streaming and on-demand video such as *Netflix*, *cable* and *satellite television*, *satellite radio,* and *interactive media,* also referred to as computer-mediated communication (CMC; see Chapter 13). Indeed, "the idea of 'new media' captures both the development of unique forms of digital media, and the remaking of more traditional media forms to adopt and adapt to the new media technologies" (Flew, 2002, p. 11). That is, new media combines computing and information technology, communications networks, and digitized media and information content. There are a few fundamental differences between what has been termed "new media" and traditional media. The new mediated technologies allow the user to communicate in a two-way fashion with others. In the past, after reading a story in a print newspaper, you had an opportunity to write a letter to the editor and send that via conventional (or snail) mail. Today, after reading the same story on a web-based version of the news source, you can send immediate feedback to the source via e-mail, Twitter, Facebook, and other forms of social media. This immediacy factor represents another major difference. Putting a print newspaper or magazine together takes an enormous amount of time. Adding a story to a news Internet site, complete with video, reduces that time frame considerably.

One consequence of these innovations and of the changing nature of media use has been the development of new theories of mass media. These theories attempt to explain how individuals respond to media, to predict how rapidly a society will adopt these innovations, and to determine what effect mass communication has on individuals, society, other forms of human communication, and culture. Current research looks at the role of society, culture, and the individual in the *production* of mediated content. The distinction between mass communication and interpersonal communication has stimulated a considerable amount of investigation by communication researchers. Some theories address how mass communication and interpersonal communication *jointly* influence an individual's decision-making processes. Other theories attempt to offer a synthesis of interpersonal and mass communication, which has been labeled *mediated interpersonal communication* (Gumpert & Cathcart, 1986). Three broad questions have stimulated much of the research and theory building in mass communication:

1. What is the impact of a society on its mass media?
2. How does mass communication function?
3. What effect does exposure to mass communication have on people?

The bulk of mass media theory and research has concentrated on the third question. Many theorists have investigated how mass media messages affect people's perceptions and behaviors. Examples of these more traditional media theories will be detailed in this chapter. Chapter 13 will detail the development of theories focusing on "new media." Some of the theories in this chapter explore audience involvement in mass communication. Other theories try to explain how mediated messages shape our perceptions of reality. Yet another body of research examines how communication rules are used to guide audience members' collective interaction with mass media.

EARLY THEORY-BUILDING EFFORTS IN MASS COMMUNICATION

During World War I, the new mass media were used to help activate the population. The mass media presented messages designed to stimulate support for the war effort. The newly developed media effectively promoted the beliefs of the warring nations. Mass communication became an important tool used by individuals engaged in large-scale persuasive efforts. The term *propaganda* first emerged during this time. After World War I, U.S. society witnessed an increasing growth in diversity; the society became less homogeneous. Individuals were no longer so closely dependent on one another. The term "mass society" was created by sociologists to describe not merely a large number of people in a given culture but the *relationship* between the individuals and the social order around them (DeFleur & Ball-Rokeach, 1982).

THE "MAGIC BULLET" THEORY

Sometimes referred to as the "hypodermic needle theory," the magic bullet theory was one of the first developed to explain the influence of the new forms of communication on society. The bullet theory and the many variations of it were derived from the stimulus-response perspective of several early mass communication theorists and researchers (e.g., Lasswell, 1927). This view asserts that any powerful stimulus such as a mass media message can provoke a uniform response from a given organism, such as an audience. Recall that the mass media at this time were thought to exert powerful, direct influence over the audience. The magic bullet or hypodermic needle theory suggested that the mass media could influence a very large group of people *directly* and *uniformly* by "shooting" or "injecting" them with appropriate messages designed to trigger a desired response.

Magic bullet theory
A theory of mass communication that suggests media influences people directly and uniformly

The popularity of these early stimulus-response theories of mass communication was consistent with that of the existing psychological and sociological theories of mass society. In addition, "evidence" of the power of the media existed in its ability to mobilize support for the country's war effort. The newly emerging mass media did have a profound effect on the audience, but several intervening factors also exerted considerable influence on audiences during that time. After years of additional research, mass communication theorists concluded that the early stimulus-response theories lacked explanatory and predictive power. They developed alternative theories that address both the power of the media to influence attitudes and behavior and also the influence of different message sources and different audience reactions. Examples of these alternative theories will be presented later in this chapter.

THE TWO-STEP FLOW THEORY

Several researchers had designed a study to examine how individuals from different social groups select and use mass communication messages to influence votes (see Lazarsfeld, Berelson, & Gaudet, 1944). The researchers expected to find empirical support for the direct influence of media messages on voting intentions. They were surprised to discover, however, that *informal, personal contacts* were mentioned far more frequently than exposure to radio or newspaper as sources of influence on voting behavior. When questioned further, several participants revealed that they had received their information about the campaign *first* from *others* (who had received information directly from the mass media).

Two-step flow Theory that asserts information from media is processed first by opinion leaders who then pass it along via interpersonal channels

Opinion leader A component of the two-step flow theory that reflects a person who pays close attention to the mass media then exerts their influence on others concerning the messages received from the media

Armed with this data, Elihu Katz and Paul Lazarsfeld (1955) developed the two-step flow theory of mass communication. This theory asserts that information from the media moves in two distinct stages. First, individuals who pay close attention (are frequent "attenders") to the mass media and its messages receive the information. These individuals, called opinion leaders, are generally well-informed people who pass information along to others through informal, interpersonal communication. Opinion leaders also pass on their own interpretations in addition to the actual media content. The term "personal influence" was coined to refer to the process intervening between the media's direct message and the audience's ultimate reaction to that message. Over the last fifty years, a substantial amount of research has contributed to our knowledge about opinion leadership.

Several characteristics of opinion leaders have been identified. Opinion leaders are quite influential in getting people to change their attitudes and behaviors and are quite similar to those they influence. Think of an individual whom you consult before making a major purchase. Perhaps you have a friend who knows a great deal about cars. You may hear a number of messages on television about the favorable qualities of the Ford Fusion and the Toyota Camry. The mass media have clearly provided you with information about each car, but do you rely solely on this information to decide which car to buy? If you are like most people, probably not. You may check *Consumer Reports* to determine what it says about those two cars. Will this information be enough to persuade you to prefer one car to the other? Possibly, but chances are you will also seek out the advice of someone you consider an opinion leader on the topic of automobiles.

The two-step flow theory has improved our understanding of how the mass media influence decision making. The theory refined our ability to predict the influence of media messages on audience behavior, and it helped explain why certain media campaigns may have failed to alter audience attitudes and behavior. Despite this contribution, the two-step flow theory has also received its share of criticism. First, some major news stories seem to be spread directly by the media with only modest intervention by personal contact. Acts of terrorism or natural disasters are often heard first from the media, then discussed interpersonally. Second, definitions of opinion leadership are often vague. Werner Severin and James Tankard (2001) suggested that some opinion leaders are self-nominated and are not reported to be opinion leaders by their supposed followers. Another difficulty is that opinion leaders have been found to be both active and passive. The two-step flow theory argues that opinion leaders are primarily active media seekers, whereas their followers are primarily passive information "sponges." This distinction between media behavior of leaders and followers does not necessarily hold true. Finally, although Katz and Lazarsfeld argued the need for a *two-step* model, the process of media dissemination and audience behavior can involve more steps. Thus, the two-step flow theory gave way to the concept of multistep flow, often used to describe the *diffusion of innovations*.

DIFFUSION THEORY

Diffusion theory examines how new ideas spread among groups of people. The two-step flow theory of mass communication was primarily concerned with the exchange of information between the media and others. Diffusion research goes one step further. It centers on the conditions that increase or decrease the likelihood that a new idea, product, or practice will be adopted by members of a given culture. Diffusion research has focused on five elements: (1) *the characteristics of an innovation* that may influence its adoption; (2) *the decision-making process* that occurs when individuals consider adopting a new idea, product, or practice; (3) the *characteristics of individuals* that make them likely to adopt an innovation; (4) the *consequences* for individuals and society of adopting an innovation; and (5) *communication channels* used in the adoption process (see Rogers, 1995).

Diffusion theory
The study of how new ideas spread among groups of people

Communication channels include both the mass media and interpersonal contacts. The multistep flow and diffusion theories expand the number and type of intermediaries between the media and the audience's decision making. In multistep diffusion research, opinion leaders still exert influence on audience behavior via their personal contact, but additional intermediaries called change agents and gatekeepers are also included in the process of diffusion. Change agents are those professionals who encourage opinion leaders to adopt or reject an innovation. Gatekeepers are individuals who control the flow of information to a given group of people. Whereas opinion leaders are usually quite similar to their followers, change agents are usually more educated and of higher status than either the opinion leaders or their followers. A change agent might be a representative from a national cable television company who tries to persuade local opinion leaders in a community (town officials, for example) to offer cable television or a computer company representative who convinces local school officials to introduce a particular computer into the school system. This representative is probably more knowledgeable about the computer system than the opinion leaders (school officials). However, the task of influencing the school board to budget money still rests with the local opinion leaders. Recall that opinion leaders are similar to those they represent. Previous research suggests that similarity or homophily enhances attraction, liking, and influence. A gatekeeper might be the editor of a local news show or newspaper. This person decides what stories will be printed or broadcast. Gatekeepers represent yet another intermediate step in the flow of information between the media and

Change agents
Professionals who encourage opinion leaders to adopt or reject an innovation

Gatekeepers People who control the flow of information to a given group of people

audience. Thus, a number of intermediaries and channels are involved in the process of information dissemination and influence.

Early theory-building efforts in mass communication relied heavily on psychological and sociological theories. The field of mass communication has since produced theory that can "stand on its own." Several contemporary theories developed by communication scholars will be presented next. The first theory, the functional approach, was based on the early research and continues to be refined today.

THE FUNCTIONAL APPROACH TO MASS COMMUNICATION THEORY

The mass media and mass communication serve many functions for our society. Clearly, one of the main attractions is escapism and entertainment value. We go to the movies, watch our favorite television comedies, game and reality shows, or dramatic programs, and attend to social media for entertainment value. Another major use of the media is to provide information. Driving to school or work, we turn on the radio and catch the latest news, weather, and sports scores. We may listen to our favorite talk program to hear what others think about relations between the United States and China. Harold Lasswell (1948) articulated three functions of mass communication: *surveillance, correlation,* and *cultural transmission.* Charles Wright (1960) added a fourth function, *entertainment.* In 1984, Denis McQuail added a fifth function: *mobilization.*

Surveillance A dimension of the functional theory of mass communication that is the information and news providing function of mass communication

Surveillance refers to the information and news-providing function of mass communication. When we turn on the radio to obtain the latest weather, traffic, or stock market reports, we are using the media primarily for its surveillance function. When the stock market dropped 508 points on October 19, 1987, millions of Americans turned on their radio and television sets to obtain information about the plunge. In every major office in the country that day, workers were "glued" to their radios to discover how much their companies' stocks had fallen. Individuals who did not own stock read in-depth reports in local newspapers concerning the potential influence of the stock market crash on the national and global economies.

Correlation A dimension of the functional theory of mass communication that concerns how the mass media select, interpret, and criticize the information they present to the public

The second function, correlation, deals with how the mass media select, interpret, and criticize the information they present to the public. The editorials on radio and television and the persuasive campaigns waged using the media are primary examples of the correlation function. "USA for Africa," "Live Aid," "Farm Aid," and "Hands Across America" were campaigns whose origins and major fundraising drives were stimulated by and developed in connection with the media. The outpouring of funds to help the starving people of Ethiopia was largely stimulated by the poignant images that came into our homes via television. Many political critics suggest that the media, and not the American people, select our political leaders. They point to the tremendous media coverage and scrutiny given to the private lives of politicians and media celebrities as an example of the correlation function of the media. Along with criticism and selection of events, the correlation function of the media also *confers status* on selected individuals. The mass media choose to highlight a number of individuals who then become "legitimized" to audiences.

The third function, cultural transmission, refers to the media's ability to communicate norms, rules, and values of a society. These values may be transmitted from one generation to another or from the society to its newcomers. Cultural transmission is a teaching function of the media, which brings many social role models into the home. Those role models frequently engage in behaviors considered appropriate in a given society (prosocial behaviors). Johnston and Ettema (1986) cited shows such as *Mister Rogers' Neighborhood, Sesame Street*, and the *ABC Afterschool Special* as examples of children's programs that attempt to teach or to promote such prosocial behaviors as being polite, dealing with anger or fear, handling new situations, coping with death, persisting at tasks, caring, and cooperating. Primetime television shows such as *The Middle, The Goldbergs*, and *Black-ish* have been mentioned as programs that promote values such family harmony and a solid work ethic. As the number of television hours watched increases, regional and subcultural differences appear to be decreasing. The media's powerful cultural transmission of "common" messages has caused us to speak, think, and dress more alike. These common or unifying messages may have further "homogenized" U.S. culture by dictating the "proper" way to act.

Cultural transmission A dimension of the functional theory of mass communication that concerns the media's ability to communicate norms, rules, and values of a society

The fourth function of mass communication, entertainment, may be the most potent one. Mass communication helps fill our leisure time by presenting messages filled with comedy, drama, tragedy, play, and performance. The entertainment function of mass communication offers an escape from daily problems and concerns. The media introduce us to aspects of culture, art, music, and dance that otherwise might not be available to us. The mass media can stimulate excitement in viewers (as with sporting events) or calm us (as with classical music broadcasts). Mass communication as entertainment provides relief from boredom, stimulates our emotions, fills our leisure time, keeps us company, and exposes us to images, experiences, and events that we could not attend in person. Numerous critics, however, assert that the media and its messages lower expectations and reduce fine art to pop art.

Entertainment A dimension of the functional theory of mass communication that reflects how mass communication helps fill our leisure time by presenting messages filled with comedy, tragedy, play, and performance

McQuail's fifth function of mass communication, mobilization, refers to the ability of the media to promote national interests (as we saw in the discussion about World War I), especially during times of national crisis. Although this mobilization function may be especially important in developing nations and societies, it can occur anywhere. We may have seen evidence of it in the United States during the days after the assassination of President John F. Kennedy and during the coverage of the terrorist attacks of 9/11. The media's central function was not only to inform us but also to counsel us, strengthen us, and pull us together.

Mobilization A dimension of the functional theory of mass communication that reflects the ability of the media to promote national interests

AGENDA-SETTING THEORY AND MASS COMMUNICATION

Agenda setting A theory that holds that intense media attention increases the importance of certain topics, issues, and individuals

Agenda setting describes a very powerful influence of the media—the ability to tell us what issues are important. For example, if the media choose to highlight declining wages and lower standards of living for the current generation of adults, then concern over the economy becomes an important issue, regardless of the level of importance we placed on it before the media attention. Books addressing the issue start to sell across the country. Suddenly, people are concerned about loss of leisure time compared to previous generations. Entertainers joke about children in their thirties moving home to live with their parents.

Agenda setting has been the subject of attention from media analysts and critics for years. As far back as 1922, the newspaper columnist Walter Lippmann was concerned that the media had the power to present images to the public. Because firsthand experiences are limited, we depend on the media to describe important events we have not personally witnessed. The media provide information about "the world outside"; we use that information to form "pictures in our heads" (Lippmann, 1922). Political scientist Bernard Cohen (1963) warned that "the press may not be successful much of the time in telling people what to think, but it is stunningly successful in telling its readers what to think about." Prior to the early 1970s, the prevailing beliefs of mass communication research were that the media had only limited effects. Most research assumed the following sequence: the media generate awareness of issues through presentation of information; that information provides a basis for attitude change; the change in attitude includes behavior change. Most research looked for attitude and behavior change and found very limited influence. A study by Max McCombs and Donald Shaw (1972) in Chapel Hill, North Carolina, changed the emphasis of research efforts and stimulated a flurry of empirical investigations into the agenda-setting function of the mass media.

McCombs and Shaw focused on awareness and information. Investigating the agenda-setting function of the mass media in the 1968 presidential campaign, they attempted to assess the relationship between what voters in one community *said* were important issues and the *actual* content of media messages used during the campaign. They first analyzed the content presented by four local papers, the *New York Times,* two national newsmagazines, and two national network television broadcasts. They ranked importance by looking at the prominence given a story (lead, front-page, headline, editorial, etc.) and the length. The researchers then interviewed 100 undecided voters (the assumption being that voters committed to a candidate would be less susceptible to media influence). McCombs and Shaw concluded that the mass media exerted a significant influence on what voters considered to be the major issues of the campaign. In addition to pioneering an entire line of research, McCombs and Shaw provided an excellent example of the thinking on which this textbook is premised. They believe that effective scientific research builds on previous studies. As a result, their study of the next presidential election (Shaw & McCombs, 1977) extended the scope of the original study, the objectives, and the research strategies. The study took place in Charlotte, North Carolina, and extended the analysis over time using a panel design. One of the interesting objectives added to this study was the investigation of what types of voters would be more likely to depend on the media. The researchers looked at two factors—the relevance of information to an individual and the degree of uncertainty—in determining need for orientation.

Need for orientation is a psychological trait which suggests that people have an underlying need to understand their environment. We experience an uncomfortable feeling until we explore and understand key features of a given environment. For example, when we visit a new city we may initially feel discomfort until we figure out the "lay of the land." According to McCombs (2002) we may also experience this need for orientation when we are faced with voting decisions and must make candidate and issue choices based on limited information.

As a trait, individuals vary in need for orientation. Some people experience high need for orientation in all situations they encounter. Others have little or no need for orientation. Need for orientation contains two dimensions: relevance and uncertainty. Relevance deals with how applicable or inapplicable a given topic is for you. If a topic is irrelevant to you, your need for orientation would be low. Thus, if the topic is irrelevant, people would pay very little attention to news media reports, and would demonstrate "weak agenda-setting" effects (McCombs, 2002). Uncertainty ranges from high to low; if a person has all of the information that he or she needs or desires about a topic or situation, their uncertainty about that topic/situation would be low. For those for whom topic relevance is high, and uncertainty about the topic or situation is also high, their need for orientation would be high. As such, this type of person would likely be a strong and robust news consumer, and strong agenda-setting effects would be identified by this person. Thus, voters with a high need for orientation would be more likely to be influenced by the media in determining the importance of issues when issues were relevant and uncertainty was high. While the original focus of agenda-setting research had been largely on politics, later researchers have extended investigations of agenda setting to the areas of business, sports, entertainment, education, the economy, advertising, the environment, and medicine and other health issues.

In addition, research on agenda setting now recognizes the importance of the Internet, cable news, talk radio, and new media, especially social media. This new body of research is labeled "online agenda-setting research," and examines the influence of sources of news and information such as political campaign blogs, campaign websites, online political advertisements, cable TV news sites (e.g., CNN), news websites (e.g., CNN.com, Google News, Yahoo News), online bulletin boards, and the many social media sites such as Facebook, Twitter, Instagram, Tumblr, Pinterest, Google+, personal blogs, and other social media sites (Tran, 2014).

The difference between traditional media (e.g., print newspapers, terrestrial radio, network broadcast television) and the "new media" (a discussion of new media will be presented in Chapter 13) in agenda setting has been examined in

Need for orientation
Part of the agenda-setting theory of mass communication concerning the relevance of information to an individual and the degree of uncertainty

several studies. One study examined whether readers of the print versus online versions of the *New York Times* would have different perceptions about the importance of certain political issues (Tran, 2014). Since online news affords the reader greater control in what to focus on, the results of the study found that individuals who primarily use online news developed different perceptions about what were considered "important problems" than those who primarily used print newspapers (Althaus & Tewksbury, 2002).

One goal of political campaign efforts is to increase the importance of a candidate's "issue agenda" and to secure media coverage for a candidate (Kiousis, Mitrook, Wu, & Seltzer, 2006). Today, Internet-based tools such as candidate blogs, campaign websites, and online political advertisements augment the use of traditional media in order to attain this goal. Research has discovered there is a symbiotic relationship between traditional broadcast television news and candidate blogs in the development of agenda-setting effects (Sweetser, Golan, & Wanta, 2008). Candidates are engaging in agenda setting on their own via social media, candidate bulletin boards, and YouTube videos. In addition, the speed and personalization of social media and online communication have altered agenda-setting. People's reactions to Internet and social media based information make agenda-setting more rapid, constant, and instantaneous. With new methods of gathering data for agenda-setting research, such as the number of mentions people and topics receive online and in social media (i.e., to determine what is "trending"), new ways of setting the agenda have emerged.

In addition, "entertainment news" programs such as *The Daily Show* have recently been added to the list of media which exert an agenda-setting influence. It has been suggested that these entertainment news programs make the news more accessible and palatable to viewers which makes consumption of the messages contained in these program more persuasive. One study investigated whether the presentation style of news influenced individuals' perceptions on agenda setting (Kowalewski, 2014). News content was presented either as a traditional news program or as an entertainment news program. Results of the study showed that people did not react differently to the information presented regardless of the format in which the information was presented (hard news or entertainment news). One conclusion reached by the study was that "In other words, the findings here indicate that entertainment programs could set the public's agenda" (Kowalewski, 2014, p. 149). It is clear, however, that agenda-setting theory continues to be relevant in a new-media world.

MASS COMMUNICATION AND PARASOCIAL INTERACTION

Parasocial interaction
A relationship that exists between television viewers and remote media communicators

The influence of mass communication and the media extends into the domain of relationship development. The concept of parasocial interaction has received considerable attention from both mass communication and interpersonal communication theorists. The concept was introduced sixty years ago by Horton and Wohl (1956) to describe a new type of "relationship" that exists between television viewers and remote media communicators. In a parasocial relationship, members of the audience view performers or the characters they portray as belonging to the audience's peer group. Media performers with whom audiences develop parasocial relationships include entertainers, talk show hosts, journalists, sport personalities, and a number of other national and local media personalities.

We often develop a sense of involvement with media performers. We follow their careers just as we follow the careers of actual friends and colleagues. We may look forward to reading Internet, newspaper, magazine, and social media accounts of their lives. We may even go to great lengths to try to meet them in person. One of your authors, for example, is a fan of "talk radio" programs. For years, he listened to former national talk radio host Bruce Williams give advice to listeners on a variety of topics. When visiting other cities, the author would scan the dial to locate the nationally syndicated program. This gave the feeling of having the performer "travel with him" and made it seem that he had a "friend," even in the most distant city. When Bruce Williams scheduled a local appearance at a very large ballroom; the author immediately purchased tickets. Convinced that he would be among only a small audience on a wintry evening, the author arrived only fifteen minutes before the event was to begin. He was amazed to discover a capacity crowd, with only a few seats left in the very back of the ballroom! Clearly, he had underestimated the number of people who had also developed a *parasocial relationship* with this particular radio celebrity.

In parasocial interaction, viewers believe that they know and understand the media personality in the same way that they know and understand their "real" friends (Perse & Rubin, 1989). The parasocial relationship is based on the belief that the media performer is similar to other people in their circle of friends (Rubin, Perse, & Powell, 1985). For most audience members, these parasocial interactions augment their actual face-to-face relationships.

In another study, researchers hypothesized that viewers would regard their favorite media performer as "closer" to them than actual "acquaintances" but more distant than "friends." Because most of our interpersonal relationships can be classified as "acquaintanceships," this hypothesis projected that we place our favorite media personality as "closer" to us than many people with whom we interact. Results showed that television personalities hold an intermediate position in "closeness" between friends and acquaintances. Koenig and Lessan (1985) suggested that the term *quasi-friend* may be most appropriate in describing the relationship between viewer and television personality.

Levy (1979) reported that news viewers occasionally reply to a newscaster's opening greeting with a greeting of their own. Almost 70 percent of network news viewers said they noticed when their anchorperson was on vacation, and 25 percent of viewers indicated that the anchorperson's absence "upset" them (p. 72). Levy also portrayed parasocial interactions as an alternative to face-to-face relationships for some people who have few or weak social ties with other people. A report by the American Psychological Association's Task Force on Television and Society reported that the elderly watch television more than any other age group. For this group in particular, as well as for other isolated individuals, television viewing becomes a parasocial activity that helps create the illusion of living in a world surrounded by people. Parasocial relationships with media personalities often fill the "gaps" caused by the death of a spouse or by children leaving home. Alan Rubin and Rebecca Rubin (1985) argued that "it is possible and beneficial to see media in certain contexts as being functional alternatives to interpersonal communication" (p. 38).

THE INFLUENCE OF INTERPERSONAL COMMUNICATION THEORY ON PARASOCIAL RELATIONSHIPS

In Chapter 8 we discussed the major assumptions of uncertainty reduction theory, which suggests that individuals seek to reduce uncertainty about those with whom they wish to develop relationships. We communicate more to reduce the uncertainty we feel about how to behave. We are more comfortable when we have more information. Rubin and McHugh (1987) applied these principles to understand parasocial interaction relationships. They examined whether increased television exposure leads to increased liking and whether parasocial interaction results from both exposure and attraction. The researchers found that television exposure was not influential in either parasocial interaction or attraction to a media personality. This finding contrasts with the assumptions of uncertainty reduction theory. They did discover, however, that parasocial relationships develop only when we are attracted to the media persona.

A study by Turner (1993) attempted to unite another theory of interpersonal communication with the research on parasocial interaction. Interpersonal attraction and attitude similarity argues that similarity (in attitudes, background, value/morality, appearance) between individuals leads to interpersonal attraction or "liking." Turner found that attitude similarity emerged as the factor most closely related to parasocial interaction. Background and appearance similarity were also related to parasocial interaction, but the relationship was not as strong. Turner contributed additional insight into what leads to the development of a parasocial interaction and reinforced the mutual influence of interpersonal communication theory and media research.

MEASURING PARASOCIAL INTERACTION

Rubin, Perse, and Powell (1985) developed a reliable and valid questionnaire to measure relationship importance and affinity with media personalities. The Parasocial Interaction (PSI) Scale is a 20-item measure designed to assess an individual's feelings of friendship, involvement, and personal concern for a television newscaster and news team. By modifying the target (from newscaster to another type of persona), you can obtain a measure of parasocial interaction with any media personality.

The PSI (see Figure 12.1) includes such items as: "When I'm watching the newscast, I feel as if I am part of their group"; "My favorite newscaster keeps me company when the news is on television"; and "I think my favorite newscaster is like an old friend." Individuals respond to each of the 20 items by choosing one of five response options ranging from "strongly agree" (5) to "strongly disagree" (1). The PSI addresses the concepts of empathy, perceived similarity, and physical attraction. The researchers suggested that a fondness for television news would make a viewer feel more attracted and similar to the newscaster, thus contributing to the likelihood of a parasocial interaction.

The PSI was used in a study (Auter, 1992) conducted to determine if parasocial interaction can be increased by certain camera techniques and behavior by

---

_____ 1. The news program shows me what the newscasters are like.

_____ 2. When the newscasters joke around with one another it makes the news easier to watch.

_____ 3. When my favorite newscaster shows me how he or she feels about the news, it helps me make up my own mind about the news story.

_____ 4. I feel sorry for my favorite newscaster when he or she makes a mistake.

_____ 5. When I'm watching the newscast, I feel as if I am part of the group.

_____ 6. I like to compare my ideas with what my favorite newscaster says.

_____ 7. The newscasters make me feel comfortable, as if I am with friends.

_____ 8. I see my favorite newscaster as a natural, down-to-earth person.

_____ 9. I like hearing the voice of my favorite newscaster in my home.

_____ 10. My favorite newscaster keeps me company when the news is on TV.

_____ 11. I look forward to watching my favorite newscaster on tonight's news.

_____ 12. If my favorite newscaster appeared on another TV program, I would watch that program.

_____ 13. When my favorite newscaster reports a story, he or she seems to understand the kinds of things I want to know.

_____ 14. I sometimes make remarks to my favorite newscaster during the newscast.

_____ 15. If there were a story about my favorite newscaster in a newspaper or magazine, I would read it.

_____ 16. I miss seeing my favorite newscaster when he or she is on vacation.

_____ 17. I would like to meet my favorite newscaster in person.

_____ 18. I think my favorite newscaster is like an old friend.

_____ 19. I find my favorite newscaster to be attractive.

_____ 20. I am not as satisfied when I get my news from a newscaster other than my favorite newscaster.

From Rubin, A. M., Perse, E. M., & Powell, R. A. (1985). Loneliness, parasocial interaction, and local television news viewing. Human Communication Research, 12, 155–180. Copyright 1985 by Wiley-Blackwell. Reprinted with permission.

FIGURE 12.1 PARASOCIAL INTERACTION SCALE.

mediated personalities "in order to help 'blur' the line between audience and characters" (p. 174). To conduct the study, Auter used a 1950s episode from the *George Burns and Gracie Allen Show*. This show was unique at the time because George Burns frequently stepped out of character to address the audience, thus "breaking the fourth wall." This same technique is used by the actor Kevin Spacey when he addresses the viewers in his character of Congressman, turned President, Francis Underwood in the Netflix show *House of Cards*. Two versions of the program were created, one in which George Burns addressed the audience in asides and one in which those segments were edited out to create a "standard" situation comedy. Students were randomly divided into two groups and shown one version of the show. After watching the tape, the students completed a version of the PSI scale. The results of the study found that parasocial interaction scores were higher for those students who saw the "out of character" version of the program. In addition, the highest parasocial interaction scores came from those who saw that version and those who chose George Burns as their favorite character. The results suggest that not only does the PSI Scale measure what it says it does but that the development of parasocial interaction is "affected by message attributes and audiences' predisposition to interact with television characters" (p. 180).

Parasocial interaction is an important concept in assessing the relationship between the media and audience members. It offers many avenues for future research. A recent study distinguished between a parasocial relationship, parasocial interaction, and a new construct labeled a parasocial breakup (Hu, 2015). While the concept of a parasocial interaction (PSI) and parasocial relationship (PSR) have been used interchangeably, it is argued that there are differences between the two concepts. *Parasocial interaction* examines the effects of a target's verbal and nonverbal communication on the viewers' "cognitive, affective, and behavioral responses during viewing" (Hu, 2015, p. 2). PSR conceptualizes a *parasocial relationship* similar to an interpersonal relationship. Hu (2015) suggests that this distinction between the two concepts can be illustrated by examining items coming from scales designed to measure PSI and PSR. He suggests that an item representing PSR might be "I miss seeing my favorite TV personality when his or her program is not on," while an item measuring PSI might be, "I sometimes make remarks to my favorite TV personality during their programs" (Hu, 2015, p. 2). To further differentiate between the two concepts, Hu suggests that when audience members are engaged in parasocial interaction with a target personality, "the interaction stays within the viewing episode" and viewers perpetuate the interaction by imitating the target's verbal and nonverbal communication, or even attempting to contact the target (2015, p. 2). This is contrasted with the concept of a parasocial relationship which is conceptualized as a more enduring and long-term concept which continues even after the television is turned off, just as an interpersonal relationship continues after both parties leave the interaction (Hu, 2015). Hu argues that PSI may ultimately lead to PSR.

A new concept has been introduced in this theory, labeled a parasocial breakup (PSB). PSB is "defined as people's negative emotional reactions to termination of PSR with their liked personae" (Hu, 2015, p. 3). The most frequent cause of a parasocial breakup is when a show ends, when a given TV performer (i.e., a favorite news anchor or weather caster leaves for another market), or when a character is taken off the air, possibly due to when something happens to the actor or actress who plays the given character.

USES AND GRATIFICATIONS THEORY

As director of the Office of Radio Research at Columbia University, Paul Lazarsfeld published the first work on uses and gratifications (Lazarsfeld & Stanton, 1944). One of his former students, Herta Herzog, worked extensively on a program of research on daytime radio serials. She investigated the characteristics of women who listened to serials, the uses they made of the information they listened to, and the gratifications they received from their choice of programming (Lowery & De Fleur, 1995). The perspective that resulted from this early research presented a direct challenge to the powerful effects conceptualization of the magic bullet theory.

The next major study from this perspective was by Schramm, Lyle, and Parker (1961). They conducted eleven studies from 1958 through 1960 on how children used television. The emphasis was on the choices of programming children made to satisfy their needs and interests. After these pioneering efforts, numerous studies have mined this vein of research. Uses and gratifications theory attempts to explain the *uses* and *functions* of the media for individuals, groups, and society in general.

Earlier we looked at the five functions of mass communication in terms of the *content* of mass media. The emphasis on content implies a passive audience absorbing what is offered. Uses and gratifications research changed the emphasis to audience members as active participants selecting particular forms of media.

Uses and gratifications theory A theory of mass communication that attempts to explain the uses and functions of the media for individuals, groups, and society in general

OBJECTIVES OF USES AND GRATIFICATIONS THEORY

Communication theorists had three objectives in developing uses and gratifications research. First, they hoped to explain *how* individuals use mass communication to gratify their needs. They attempted to answer the question: *What* do people do with the media (A. Rubin, 1985)? A second objective was to discover the *underlying motives* for individuals' media use. *Why* does one person rush home (or stay up late at night) to watch the local news on television while another person prefers reading the newspaper during breakfast or after dinner, while another prefers to get news only from the Internet? Why do some people only watch HBO movies? These are some questions that uses and gratifications theorists attempt to answer in their research. A third objective of this line of theory building was to identify the positive and negative *consequences* of individual media use. Relationships between the individual and the mass media, media content, the social system, alternative channels of communication (such as friends), and the consequences of media choice are all avenues of inquiry for systems researchers.

EXAMPLES OF USES AND GRATIFICATIONS RESEARCH

At the core of uses and gratifications theory lies the assumption that audience members actively seek out the mass media to satisfy individual needs. For example, Rubin (1979) uncovered six reasons why children and adolescents use television: learning, passing time, companionship, to forget or escape, excitement or arousal, and relaxation. Television viewing for passing time, for arousal, and for relaxation emerged as the most important uses of television for this age group. Rubin also designed a questionnaire called the Television Viewing Motives Instrument to discover reasons why people watch television. Complete the survey in Figure 12.2 to get a sense of your primary motives for watching TV.

Rubin (1983) designed another study to explore adult viewers' motivations, behaviors, attitudes, and patterns of interaction. The study looked at whether TV user motivations could predict behavioral and attitudinal consequences of television use. Five primary television viewing motivations were examined: pass time/habit, information, entertainment, companionship, and escape. The strongest viewing motivation relationships were found between pass time/habit and both companionship and escape viewing. The two categories of viewers identified in this study were predecessors to the *ritualized* and *instrumental* users of television discussed next. The first group of viewers used television to pass time and out of habit. The second group used television to seek information or as a learning tool.

Ritualized use Using television viewing primarily as a diversion

Instrumental use Using television viewing primarily for information acquisition

Rubin (1984) identified two types of television viewers. The first type (habitual) consists of people who watch television for ritualized use. This type has a high regard for television in general, is a frequent user, and uses television primarily as a diversion. The second type (nonhabitual) consists of people who attend to television for instrumental use. This type exhibits a natural liking for a particular television program or programs and uses media content primarily for information. This person is more selective and goal oriented when watching television and does not necessarily feel that television is important. Rubin argued that ritualized television use represents a more important viewing experience for the audience member, whereas instrumental television use represents a more involving experience for the viewer.

In a study of Swedish television users, Levy and Windahl (1984) identified three types of audience activity. The first, called *preactivity,* is practiced by individuals who deliberately seek certain media to gratify intellectual needs. For example, some viewers deliberately select newscasts to be informed about current events. The second type, *duractivity,* deals with the degree of psychological attentiveness or involvement audience members exhibit during a

INSTRUCTIONS: Here are some reasons that other people gave us for watching TV. Please tell us how each reason is like your own reason for watching television. (Put one check in the correct column for each reason.)

I watch television . . .	A Lot	A Little	Not Much	Not At All
1. Because it relaxes me	_____	_____	_____	_____
2. So I won't be alone	_____	_____	_____	_____
3. So I can learn about things happening in the world	_____	_____	_____	_____
4. Because it's a habit	_____	_____	_____	_____
5. When I have nothing better to do	_____	_____	_____	_____
6. Because it helps me learn things about myself	_____	_____	_____	_____
7. Because it's thrilling	_____	_____	_____	_____
8. So I can forget about school and homework	_____	_____	_____	_____
9. Because it calms me down when I'm angry	_____	_____	_____	_____
10. When there's no one to talk to	_____	_____	_____	_____
11. So I can learn how to do things I haven't done before	_____	_____	_____	_____
12. Because I just like to watch	_____	_____	_____	_____
13. Because it passes the time away	_____	_____	_____	_____
14. So I could learn about what could happen to me	_____	_____	_____	_____
15. Because it excites me	_____	_____	_____	_____
16. So I can get away from the rest of the family	_____	_____	_____	_____
17. Because it's a pleasant rest	_____	_____	_____	_____
18. Because it makes me feel less lonely	_____	_____	_____	_____
19. Because it teaches me things I don't learn in school	_____	_____	_____	_____
20. Because I just enjoy watching	_____	_____	_____	_____
21. Because it gives me something to do	_____	_____	_____	_____
22. Because it shows how other people deal with the same problems I have	_____	_____	_____	_____
23. Because it stirs me up	_____	_____	_____	_____
24. So I can get away from what I'm doing	_____	_____	_____	_____

SCORING INSTRUCTIONS FOR TELEVISION VIEWING MOTIVES INSTRUMENT:

Give a numerical value for each statement in each column. Use the following scale:

A Lot = 4
A Little = 3
Not Much = 2
Not At All = 1

Add your score for each of the following viewing motive factors:

Viewing Motive	Statement Numbers	Mean Score
Relaxation	1, 9, 17	2.41
Companionship	2, 10, 18	1.68
Habit	4, 12, 20	1.97
Pass Time	5, 13, 21	2.13
Learning About Things	3, 11, 19	1.84
Learning About Myself	6, 14, 22	1.84
Arousal	7, 15, 23	1.67
Forget/Escape	8, 16, 24	1.67

After you have added up the scores for each factor, divide that score by 3 to obtain a mean or average score for each television viewing motive factor. Compare your average score on each dimension with the norms obtained from a nonrandom sample of 464 adults (Rubin, 1983).

FIGURE 12.2 TELEVISION VIEWING MOTIVES INSTRUMENT.

television viewing experience. The focus is on how individuals interpret and decipher mediated messages. The comprehension, organization, and structuring of media messages leads to certain intellectual and emotional gratifications for viewers. For example, trying to figure out the plot or ending of a dramatic program on television is one example of the duractivity use of the media. The third type of audience activity, *postactivity,* deals with audience behavior and message use after exposure to mediated messages. People involved in postactivity attend to a mediated message because they feel the information may have some personal or interpersonal value. Individuals who actively seek out television news to provide content for interpersonal communication such as "small talk" exhibit postactivity audience behavior.

Another assumption of uses and gratifications theory is that audiences use the media to fulfill expectations. For example, you may watch science fiction movies such as *Star Wars* and television programs such as *Extant* or *Helix* to fantasize about the future.

A third assumption of uses and gratifications theory is that audience members are aware of and can state their motives for using mass communication. In Levy and Windahl's study, participants were able to describe how particular media gratified certain needs. The researchers found that the primary motivation for watching TV news was to gain information about the world, rather than for diversion. Studies that investigate how individuals use the media for gratification primarily employ *self-report measures*, questionnaires that ask participants about their motives for using the mass media. The television viewing motives instrument is one such questionnaire.

One study addressed several social and psychological factors associated with patterns of audience media use. Donohew, Palmgreen, and Rayburn (1987) tested a random sample of subscribers to cable television. Through telephone and mailed questionnaires, they collected demographic (age, sex, income, education, marital status) and lifestyle information. Participants also provided information on their social, political, economic, cultural, and communication-related behaviors. The researchers asked questions about the need for stimulation, gratifications sought from cable TV, satisfaction with cable TV offerings, number of hours of cable TV viewing per day, and number of newspapers and magazines subscribed to by the respondents. Four lifestyle types emerged. Type I was labeled the disengaged homemaker. This individual was primarily female, middle-aged, lower in education and income, and used the media for companionship and to pass the time rather than for information or arousal. According to Rubin's classifications, the disengaged homemaker appears to represent the *ritualized* media user. The second type of individual, the outgoing activist, was also frequently female, somewhat younger, well-educated, had a good income, and was less likely to be married. Outgoing activists were highest in need for stimulation among the four types. They enjoyed staying informed and were primarily print media users. They did not watch a great amount of television and were least gratified by cable TV. Donohew, Palmgreen, and Rayburn speculated that type II's active lifestyle leaves them little time for television viewing. The third type of individual was labeled the restrained activist. These individuals were older and had the highest educational levels. More than half were female, and they were likely to be married and to have relatively high incomes. They had low need for sensation but high need for intellectual stimulation. They exhibited strong informational needs and viewed themselves as opinion leaders. They were heavy users of both print media and television, especially for informational purposes. Their media use patterns follow those of Rubin's *instrumental* user. The final type of user identified was called the working class climber. This person was primarily male, lower in education and income, and middle-aged; most were married. Working class climbers were ambitious and self-confident. They did not engage in an activist lifestyle and ranked low in need for intellectual stimulation. They were highest among the four types on television exposure and satisfaction with cable TV. They were quite low on print media usage. According to Rubin's taxonomy, they would be classified more as ritualized than as instrumental media users. The results of this study helped clarify our understanding of the many lifestyle variables that influence mass media use.

Disengaged homemaker
A lifestyle type indicating primarily female, middle-aged, lower in education and income, and use the media for companionship and to pass time

Outgoing activist
A lifestyle type primarily consisting of female, younger, well educated, with a high need for stimulation, good income, and less likely to marry

Restrained activist
A lifestyle type primarily male and female who are older, highly educated, opinion leaders likely to marry, and have high incomes

Working class climber
A lifestyle type primarily consisting of males, lower in education and income, middle-aged, and married

CULTIVATION THEORY

Cultivation theory of mass communication This theory asserts that television influences our view of reality

Enculturation A type of cultural adaptation reflecting when we learn to speak, listen, read, interpret, and understand verbal and nonverbal messages in such a fashion that the messages will be recognized and responded to by the individuals with whom we communicate

The cultivation theory of mass communication effects was developed by George Gerbner and his associates at the Annenberg School for Communication at the University of Pennsylvania. The theory has been tested by numerous empirical studies. Cultivation theory asserts that television influences our view of reality. Cultivation theory (Gerbner, Gross, Morgan, & Signorielli, 1980, 1986) asserts that television is primarily responsible for our perceptions of day-to-day norms and reality. Establishing a culture's norms and values was once the role of formal religion and other social initiations. Previously the family, schools, and churches communicated standardized roles and behaviors, serving the function of enculturation. Television often serves that function, as one of the major cultural transmitters for today's society (Gerbner & Gross, 1976a, 1976b). "Living" in the world of television cultivates a particular view of reality. Some argue that television provides an experience that is more alive, more real, and more vivid than anything we can expect to experience in real life!

THE INTERACTION OF MEDIA AND REALITY

One of the authors read an article in a local newspaper that illustrates the tendency to confuse a real event with images absorbed from television. A reporter had stopped his car at the intersection of a rural road and a larger highway. He noticed a car speeding on the highway at approximately 100 miles per hour. As the car reached the point where the reporter was stopped, it suddenly tried to make a left turn without slowing down. It clipped a light pole and flipped over on its back, wheels still spinning. No one else was in sight. The reporter described staring forward, not believing what he had just seen. He recalled his mind saying to him very clearly, "What you are seeing isn't real, You are just watching a movie." For almost ten seconds he just sat there, waiting to see what would happen next. Of course, nothing happened, and he realized that it was up to him to help. He fell prey to two fears as he approached the car—one artificial (induced by previous television images) and one very real (which contradicted other images received). Television portrayals of overturned cars invariably end with fires and explosions. With televised accidents, no "real man" thinks twice about rushing to a scene where someone may be dead or horribly mutilated. The reporter was very afraid on both counts. Television is so pervasive that the line between illusion and reality is blurred. We sometimes mistake a real event for a televised one; we probably make the opposite mistake more frequently. This phenomenon provided the basis of the research into cultivation theory.

HEAVY VERSUS LIGHT TELEVISION VIEWERS

George Gerbner's participation in two national studies provided the foundation for cultivation theory. He contributed a content analysis of television programming to the National Commission on the Causes and Prevention of Violence in 1967 and 1968 and for the Surgeon General's Scientific Advisory

Committee on Television and Social Behavior in 1972. Gerbner and his colleagues tracked the incidents of violence portrayed during a randomly selected week of fall primetime programming plus children's weekend programming. They compiled the percentage of programs marked by violence, the number of violent acts, and the number of characters involved in those acts. They found violent acts portrayed in 80% of primetime programming; children's shows were the most violent of all. Older people, children, women, and minorities were the most frequent victims—despite the fact that three-quarters of characters portrayed on television were white middle-class males.

Building on this work, the researchers surveyed viewers to determine the number of hours spent watching television daily, the programs selected and why, attitudes about the probability of being a victim of crime, perceptions about the number of law enforcement officials, and general attitudes about trusting other people. Gerbner and his associates classified people as heavy viewers (four or more hours daily) and light viewers (two hours daily or less).

Cultivation theory predicted that heavy viewers would perceive the world as more dangerous because of repeated exposure to violent television portrayals. Persistent images of danger and violence color views of reality and create the perception of a mean world. Heavy viewers overestimated their chances of being involved in a violent crime. They also overestimated the number of law enforcement workers in society.

Individuals frequently confuse media-constructed reality with actual reality. Gerbner and Gross (1976b) reported that in the first five years of its broadcast life, the television show *Marcus Welby, M.D.* (a fictional doctor portrayed by the late actor Robert Young, which aired from1969 to 1976), received over a quarter of a million letters from viewers. Most of the letters contained requests for medical advice! Television is highly effective in the cultivation process because many of us never personally experience some aspects of reality but the pervasive presence of television—constantly available for relatively little expense—provides a steady stream of mediated reality. We may have limited opportunities to observe the internal workings of a real police station, hospital operating room, or municipal courtroom. Thus, the media images become our standards for reality. Have you noticed that the New Year's Eve parties we actually attend *never* seem quite as exciting as the New Year's Eve parties we see on television?

The theory predicted uniform effects for all heavy viewers—regardless of factors such as gender, education, socioeconomic group, or media preferences (for example, reading newspapers versus viewing televised newscasts). As the primary source of socialization, television's messages provide a symbolic environment that transcends demographic differences. The only factor that seemed to have an independent effect on perceptions was age. Respondents under thirty consistently reported that their responses were more influenced by television than those of people over thirty (Gerbner & Gross, 1976b). Because people thirty and under have been "weaned" on television, the influence of media messages may be especially potent.

REFINEMENT OF CULTIVATION THEORY

In response to criticisms that cultivation theory ignored the contributions of other variables (see next section), Gerbner and his associates introduced the factors of mainstreaming and resonance (Gerbner, Gross, Morgan, & Signorielli, 1980). Mainstreaming refers to the power of television to present uniform images. Commercial sponsors want to appeal to the broadest possible range of consumers, so television presents mainstream images. Differences are edited out to present a blended, homogenous image acceptable to a majority of viewers. Differences in perceptions of reality due to demographic and social factors are diminished or negated by the images projected on television. Ritualistic patterns reinforce sameness and uniformity. Resonance describes the intensified effect on the audience when what people see on television is what they have experienced in life. This double dose of the televised message amplifies the cultivation effect.

Despite the large data set supporting the theory, the cultivation effect has encountered several challenges. Certain personality characteristics related to the selection of television programs were not controlled in the earlier studies (Hughes, 1980). It has also been suggested that television may actually cultivate realistic and functional perceptions of the world. Hirsch (1980) found that if other variables are controlled simultaneously, very little effect remains that can be attributed to television. In his review of the original data, he found that even people who did not watch television perceived the world as violent and dangerous.

Potter (1986) concluded that the cultivation effect may be more complex than is currently stated; the amount of exposure to television may be less important than the attitudes and perceptions of individuals exposed. The interactions of audiences, television, and society are complex and cannot be reduced to simple cause and effect. Cultivation theory links heavy television viewing with a distrustful view of a violent world. The final criticism questions the meaning of that link. The research has demonstrated a correlation between certain behaviors and certain attitudes, but has it proven the direction of influence? Do people who are distrustful watch more television because they have few friends? Cause and effect have not been established. There is no doubt that the controversy surrounding the media's influence on our perceptions and behavior will continue to rage. We can expect more research from scholars of mass media in this area. New findings will refine and advance our efforts to theorize about the effects associated with the mass media.

THE SPIRAL OF SILENCE THEORY

The spiral of silence theory was developed by Elisabeth Noelle-Neumann, a German researcher, in 1974. The theory has implications in three areas: (1) mass media and communication, (2) the individual and interpersonal communication, and (3) public opinion (Salmon & Glynn, 1996). It is considered one of the "most highly developed and one of the most researched theories in the field of public opinion" (McDonald, Glynn, Kim, & Ostman, 2001, p. 139).

The theory has generated a considerable amount of research, as well as controversy, since its debut. It offers, however, many insights for both practitioners and scholars interested in media bias, media effects, individual perception, and collective conformity (Donsbach, Tsfati, & Salmon, 2014).

Contemplating the question: "Are you more or less willing to express your beliefs on an issue depending on whether you think those beliefs are widely shared by those individuals around you?" guides us to an appreciation of the theory. Noelle-Neumann's spiral of silence theory argues that individuals who think that their opinions and beliefs are not widely shared by others (in a given reference group, or in society in general) will feel pressure to express another opinion (the majority opinion) or will choose to remain silent.

According to the theory, people assess whether their opinions match those of the majority from several cues in their environment (Glynn, Hayes, & Shanahan, 1997). The media are important sources for these cues. The mass media often "serve as the representation of the dominant views in society" (Perse, 2001, p. 110) and help shape public opinion. People depend on the media as a primary source of information about social norms, customs, acceptable styles of dress and fashion, and even what to think.

Spiral of silence theory suggests that people have a fear of social isolation; that is, they do not want to be seen as different from the majority. Adolescents are especially sensitive to "fitting in" with the majority regarding the clothes they wear and the expressions they use to communicate. Noelle-Neumann believes that most people also strive to avoid social isolation by refusing to express beliefs and opinions that they feel do not enjoy majority support. To express a belief that is either "old-fashioned" or "socially unacceptable" is more than most people are willing to do (Salmon & Moh, 1992). Indeed, isolating yourself from others by expressing your true belief, when it goes against the majority view, is seen as a far worse outcome than remaining silent (Glynn, Hayes, & Shanahan, 1997). As a consequence, the theory asserts "that an individual withholds his or her opinion when confronted with a dissonant climate of opinion" (Donsbach, et al., 2014, p. 7). Noelle-Neumann suggested that this "spiral of silence" leads one viewpoint or one position to dominate public opinion, while others (perceived minority viewpoints) often disappear from public awareness because the people who hold less accepted views or positions remain silent. However, if people find that their opinions are widely shared by the majority or are gaining acceptance, they will be more likely to express their positions.

Some people do not succumb to the spiral of silence. Labeled "hardcores," these people do not feel the same constraints of social pressure or fear the social isolation attached to expressing minority viewpoints. Hardcores have an unusually high amount of interest in the issue; their positions remain relatively unchanged (McDonald, Glynn, Kim, & Ostman, 2001). Hardcores represent only about 15 percent of the population (Salmon & Moh, 1992).

The issue of cigarette smoking in public offers an excellent example of the effects of majority opinion on verbal (and nonverbal) behavior. For many years nonsmokers were apprehensive about speaking out against smoking in public, and the nonsmoker almost certainly did not approach smokers and request that they put out their cigarettes. In the last three decades, however, this situation appears to have changed dramatically. The nonsmoker now represents the majority opinion—that smoking has no place in public contexts (Salmon & Glynn, 1996). The reticence about criticizing smoking behavior disappeared when public opinion changed.

How did this change occur? How did the former "minority view" become the current "majority view"? The spiral of silence theory suggests that the changing messages projected by the mass media contributed greatly to the change of public opinion. According to the theory, individuals scan the environment for information about which opinions are gaining support and which are losing (Gonzenbach, King, & Jablonski, 1999). Clearly, over the last two decades the media's predominant message has been one of "antismoking." The removal of ads for cigarettes on broadcast television, the increased frequency of "public service" spots describing the dangers of smoking, and the reports in the media that fewer Americans are smoking today compared to three decades ago have helped create change. Today, the smoker is caught in the "spiral of silence" regarding expressing opinions about smoking in public. This reversal of positions is a prime illustration of a tenet of the theory: willingness to speak out changes the climate of opinion so that the dominant opinion becomes stronger. In turn, the dominant view as presented in the media yields a greater likelihood that individuals will speak up (Gonzenbach et al., 1999).

People who hold the less-dominant position will become increasingly reluctant to express their position. Their silence erodes the less-supported position even more. When the media report that adherents to a given position are frequently criticized or even physically attacked (Gonzenbach et al., 1999), they reduce the probability that individuals will voice the unfavored position. For example, when the antifur message of groups such as P.E.T.A. (People for the Ethical Treatment of Animals) received more attention from the media, including reports of individuals wearing natural fur being physically attacked, individuals who had previously expressed support of natural fur clothing grew more silent.

Communication studies have examined the role of the spiral of silence theory regarding a number of different issues and from several methodological perspectives to help refine and extend the theory. One study tested the spiral of silence theory that judgments about majority opinion are made through direct observation and, in particular, from television. The researchers measured both the exposure to media by individuals in the national sample and their perceptions of what position was most supported on the issue of whether gay people should be allowed to serve in the U.S. military. The study found that respondents with higher levels of media exposure believed that more of the public agreed with them, whereas those with low levels of media exposure perceived lack of support for their position on that issue (Gonzenbach et al., 1999, p. 290).

Spiral of silence theory was also used to test public opinion on another controversial issue: whether the United States should declare English as the official language (Lin & Salwen, 1997). The study hypothesized that an individual's willingness to speak out about this issue would be related to his or her perception of national and local public opinion. Participants in two diverse cities (Miami, FL, and Carbondale, IL) were randomly surveyed by telephone. They were asked whether they were "willing" or "unwilling" to express their opinion about this issue in public with another person who held a different opinion about the issue of making English the official language of the United States. The findings generally supported the assumptions of the spiral of silence theory. Respondents in both cities indicated greater willingness to discuss the issue in public when the media coverage of this issue was seen as generally positive or supportive (Lin & Salwen, 1997). As the national and local media coverage of this issue became more positive, younger and better-educated respondents indicated even more willingness to express their opinion on this issue (Lin & Salwen, 1997).

Some researchers have explored how the realism of the setting for the expression of public opinion might affect an individual's willingness to speak out (Scheufele, Shanahan, & Lee, 2001). Would people in a more realistic setting be less willing to present their position than those who were asked to speak out in a hypothetical situation? College students responded to questions concerning their levels of media use, their knowledge about genetically altered foods, and their attitudes toward that topic. Half of the respondents were asked if they would be willing to discuss their opinion about the topic at a hypothetical "social gathering." The other half were told that there would be a second part of the study in which they could express their opinions about genetically altered food in greater detail with other students in a focus-group interview context. The study supported a major tenet of the spiral of silence theory: fear of isolation was negatively related to people's willingness to express an opinion on genetically altered food. The data also suggested that the situation influences willingness to speak out on an issue. Respondents who were told that they would be presenting their opinions in a focus group interview context were less willing to present their opinions than those in the hypothetical "social gathering" context.

MEDIA DEPENDENCY THEORY

Media dependency theory was developed by Sandra Ball-Rokeach and Melvin DeFleur (1976).

Media dependency theory argues that the more dependent an individual is on the media for having his or her needs fulfilled, the more important the media will be to that person. Although some communication scholars consider media dependency theory to be an offshoot of the uses and gratifications theory of mass media, there are some differences. A major issue in uses and gratifications theory is, "*Where* do I go to gratify my needs?" whereas media dependency theory focuses on the issue, "*Why* do I go to *this* medium to fulfill *this* goal?" (Ball-Rokeach, Power, Guthrie, & Waring, 1990). Dependency theory suggests that media use is primarily influenced by societal relationships, whereas uses and gratifications theory places greater emphasis on individual

Media dependency theory A theory of mass communication that assumes that the more dependent an individual is on the media for having his or her needs filled, the more important the media will be to the person

media selection. Uses and gratifications theory focuses more on a person's active participation with mass media, whereas dependency theory tends to focus more on the social context in which media activity occurs.

Dependency theory emphasizes the *relationship between society and the media*. There are a number of mutual dependencies. The media rely on government for legislation to protect media assets and for access to political information. The political systems of a society rely on the media to reinforce political values and norms, to help mobilize citizens to vote, and to inspire active involvement in political campaigns. Society depends on the media for the creation of information, advertising, and technology that it uses (Rubin & Windahl, 1986). The commercial broadcasting system of the United States, for example, is built on dependency between the media, advertisers, and audiences. Television programs are produced to attract large audiences so that advertisers can sell their products and services to those audiences. The media then depend on this advertising revenue to stay in business. Each system depends on the other.

The *relationship between the media and the audience* is crucial as well, for it influences how people use mass media. Audiences may depend on the media for information, for escape, and for "information" on what is considered appropriate or normative behavior. Television programs that emphasize pro-social messages such as honesty and morality are designed to teach acceptable behavior in our society.

The *relationship between society and the audience* examines how society influences the audience and vice versa. Society depends on audiences because individuals who comprise a society are seen as potential voters, potential consumers, and as members of different social and cultural groups who contribute in numerous ways to the development of a society and its culture.

The theory's authors define dependency as a relationship in which the attainment of goals by one party is contingent on the resources of another party. People develop dependency relationships with the mass media as a way of attaining their goals of understanding, orientation, and play (Grant, Guthrie, & Ball-Rokeach, 1991). According to the theory, people develop expectations that the media can help them satisfy their needs. Thus, people develop "dependency relations" with the media (or a particular medium) that they believe will be most helpful in attaining a particular goal (Loges & Ball-Rokeach, 1993).

The theory identifies dependency relations on media information sources. Ball-Rokeach and DeFleur suggested that individuals depend on media for information in situations ranging from the need to identify the best buys at the supermarket to more general informational needs such as how to maintain a sense of "connection" with the world outside your neighborhood. The theory suggests that an individual's reliance on mass media develops when the person's informational needs on certain issues cannot be met by direct experience.

Media dependency is also linked to media *influence*. That is, the more important the media are to an individual, the more influence the media exert on that individual. Our society relies heavily on the mass media for information, entertainment, and the communication of societal norms and values. In our society, information is considered a prized commodity; we regard information as power. Today, most people use their personal computers to access information sources on the Internet. The theory recognizes, however, that dependency on the media varies greatly from one individual to another, from one group to another, and even from one culture to another.

A number of key assumptions about the media, the audience, and audience dependency have been identified: (a) If the media influence society it is because the media meet the audience's needs and wants, not because the media exert any "control" over individuals. (b) The uses people have for media in large part determine how much the media will influence them. For example, the more the audience depends on information from the media, the greater the likelihood the media will influence the audience's attitudes, beliefs, and even behavior. (c) Because of the increasing complexity of modern society, we depend a great deal on the media to help us make sense of our world, to help us make decisions that allow us to cope better with life. The theory suggests further that we come to understand and even experience our world largely through the media. What a person learns about the world beyond their direct experience is influenced by the media. Our understanding of international politics, the global economy, and music, for example, are in part shaped by the content offered by the media (Baukus, 1996). (d) Individuals who have greater needs for information, escape, or fantasy will be more influenced by the media and have greater media dependency.

Ball-Rokeach and DeFleur suggested that media dependency ranges on a continuum from individuals who are totally dependent on the media to satisfy their needs to individuals who satisfy their needs independently from the media. (Remember that Shaw and McCombs addressed a similar concept with their *need for orientation*.) In addition, each individual displays variations within each category of media dependence. For example, you may depend heavily on news and newsmagazine shows for information yet have very little interest in escape and fantasy programs such as soap operas or situation comedies. Others may depend totally on the media for business news—monitoring sources such as CNN Business News, and CNBC, but ignoring the Weather Channel.

Most individuals are media dependent when conditions demand quick and accurate information. If you live in a climate that is prone to many tornadoes or hurricanes during the summer months or blizzards during the winter months, you may need an almost constant source of information about the weather. Your dependency on the media for weather-related information may even have stimulated you to purchase a "weather radio," which broadcasts bulletins and information from the local office of the National Weather Service. During times of weather-related crises, individuals become very dependent on the media.

Constant attention to and dependence on the media also emerged during the explosion of the space shuttle *Challenger* in 1986, the stock market crash of 1987, the war in the Persian Gulf in 1991, the bombing of the federal building in Oklahoma City in 1995, and protests and disturbances in several American cities in 2014 and 2015 in response to what some have argued was excessive use of force by police. Other crises, both local and national, also cause individuals to become more dependent on the media. For example, in the days following an airplane crash individuals tend to become more media dependent on the medium they believe will best satisfy their informational needs. For some this may mean attending to national newspapers and their companion websites, such as *USA Today* and usatoday.com, which will devote additional coverage to this type of story. For others, this may mean monitoring *CNN* or cnn.com throughout the day. Still others may turn to one of the many news-related websites or social media apps to learn more details as they become available. Given the complex interactions of the individual, the media, and society, the social context often dictates the level of dependency. In times of conflict and uncertainty, the need for information increases, and dependency on the media also rises. During relatively calm periods of stability the audience relies less heavily on the media for guidance.

Media dependency is related to the complexity of the society in which a person lives. In a society as complex as ours, the media provide a number of essential functions: they provide information useful for the elections that are the centerpiece of democracy, they serve as whistle-blowers if the government oversteps its authority, they announce important economic or technological developments, they provide a window to the rest of the world, and they are a primary source of entertainment. The more functions served by the media, the more important they become.

Depending on the type of information goal a person has, he or she may choose one particular medium over another. Different media require different degrees of effort in satisfying one's informational goal. Preferences for particular media (for example, television, newspapers, Internet, radio, social media), differ according to information needs, the sources of media available, and the effort expended by the information seeker. For example, an individual may prefer to get information from television due to its immediacy, but because that medium may not be available in an office or an automobile, they must use radio instead. Some individuals choose newspapers over television because newspapers are perceived to cover stories in greater depth than television.

Media dependency theory asserts that the media have powerful effects on individuals and society. Several studies have investigated the assumptions of media dependency theory. One study investigated the union of media dependency theory and the theory of parasocial interaction discussed earlier. Grant, Guthrie, and Ball-Rokeach (1991) wondered if the development of parasocial interaction with a television personality increases the intensity of one's dependency on that medium or the reverse. Did an intense media dependency relationship stimulate the development of a parasocial interaction? They used the medium of television shopping (such as QVC and the Home Shopping Network) to investigate this relationship. One of the most important findings was that individuals who developed strong media dependency relationships with television shopping tended to develop parasocial relationships with television shopping personalities.

In addition, they found that purchasing a product from a television shopping channel reinforced media dependency on that channel because it gave viewers a greater sense of connection to the show. The researchers also suggested that people tune in to television shopping not only to purchase products but to satisfy their entertainment goals and to learn about new products. The more the viewers had these goals, the more they watched, and the more parasocial interactions they developed with television shopping hosts.

Alan Rubin and Sven Windahl (1986) proposed a combination of uses and gratifications theory and media dependency theory. They offered a "uses and dependency model," which incorporates elements of both theories. The uses and dependency model recognizes that the audience is somewhat active in their media-related behavior, and that individuals seek media that will fulfill personal needs. The model also represents the society-media-audience interaction and the mutual influences working to create interests and to influence the selection of particular media to satisfy goals. Needs are not always the sole product of the social and psychological characteristics of individuals; they are influenced by culture and society. This union of two theories also bridges the gap between the limited effects model of uses and gratifications and the powerful effects posited by dependency theory.

One test of the uses and dependency model found that "television dependents" contrasted with "newspaper dependents" (Baukus, 1996). Television dependents tend to see media coverage of conflict as "entertainment." This may account for why heavy television users may have been more likely to watch a great deal of coverage of the trial of O.J. Simpson or watch cable channels such as truTV and the Science Channel. The study also found that television dependents believed the media are a source of information that helps us better understand the impact of social conflict on a community, country, or culture. Highly involved television-dependent groups differed from the other groups in their information belief. People who are highly involved *and* television dependent seem to want information as quickly as possible, and the ability of television to cover an event instantly with accompanying video is very important to this type of individual. Another study observed that dependency needs for understanding oneself and society were related to newspaper readership. Individuals who had greater need for understanding how society and its institutions function were more dependent on the newspaper than those without that need (Loges & Ball-Rokeach, 1993). Thus, media dependency theory helps us understand the relationships between the media and society, dependency relations with particular media, and the choice of particular media to satisfy information goals.

SUMMARY

Mass communication and other forms of mediated communication exert a profound influence on the world. Mass communication is said to serve five functions for a society: surveillance, correlation, cultural transmission, entertainment, and mobilization. The mass media also serves an agenda-setting function as they influence our attitudes and perceptions of events by selectively focusing attention on certain issues. The media influence extends into the domain of relationship development. Parasocial interaction theory suggests that we often develop a sense of personal involvement and a type of "relationship" with media performers such as news and weather forecasters, talk show hosts, and other media celebrities and personalities. Uses and gratifications theory explains the underlying motives for individual use of mass communication. A core assumption of this theory is that an audience is an active group that seeks out and uses certain media to satisfy their needs. Cultivation theory suggests that television is largely responsible for the development of perceptions of day-to-day norms and reality. The theory argues that cumulative exposure to television's ritualistic patterns of images manipulates how we see ourselves, others, and society in general. Spiral of silence theory argues that because people are reluctant to express beliefs contrary to widely accepted opinions and because the media are often the source for conveying accepted opinions, the media contribute to a spiral of silence in which minority views are suppressed, which creates a climate that reinforces majority views. Media dependency theory is derived from the systems approach and examines the multiple interactions of audience, media, and society in determining why a medium is selected, for what goal, and the dependencies created by the intricate relationships.

KEY TERMS

Agenda setting

Change agents

Correlation

Cultivation theory of mass communication

Cultural transmission

Diffusion theory

Duractivity

Enculturation

Entertainment

Gatekeepers

Instrumental use

Magic bullet theory

Mainstreaming

Media dependency theory

Mobilization

Need for orientation

Opinion leaders

Parasocial interaction

Postactivity

Preactivity

Reflective-projective theory of mass communication

Resonance

Ritualized use

Spiral of silence theory

Surveillance

Two-step flow theory

Uses and gratifications theory

Chapter 13

COMPUTER-MEDIATED COMMUNICATION CONTEXTS

Xun Zhu, David L. Brinker & Erina L. MacGeorge

What was the first thing you did when you woke up this morning? Did you reach for your phone to check your notifications—for texts, instant messages, e-mails, or other digital forms of communication? Today, for most people in developed countries like the United States, and especially for Millennials, communicating via a computer is a taken-for-granted aspect of life, whether that "computer" is a phone, tablet, laptop, desktop, or some other device. According to a Pew Research Center report, 84% of Americans use the Internet (Perrin & Duggan, 2015) and one-fifth report going online "almost constantly" (Perrin, 2015). The number of applications available for communicating with others via these technologies has increased dramatically, and they continue to be developed, even as older applications decline in popularity, or become used for specific purposes or by specific populations. For example, MySpace was developed before Facebook, but is now principally used by musicians and their followers (Knopper, 2013). In addition, although e-mail continues to be broadly used, younger generations rely more heavily on text and instant messaging, and a recent survey (Mander, 2015) found that among 16- to 24-year-olds, Facebook usage was declining. The world of technology changes so rapidly that there could well be a new and popular way of communicating via computer developed between the time this book is written and the time you are reading it. As you read this chapter, it is useful to keep in mind that this presents an extra challenge for theorizing about computer-mediated communication (CMC): to some extent, the phenomena being theorized about are constantly changing.

CMC is an intriguing phenomenon for communication scholars. There are now a sizeable number who identify their specialty as computer-mediated communication, or CMC; not surprisingly, this has become a particularly attractive specialty in the last decade, with the rise of social media like Facebook. The *Journal of Computer-Mediated Communication* is a Web-based, peer-reviewed scholarly journal whose entire focus is on social science research on computer-mediated communication. The drive to study CMC is partly due to its pervasiveness and dynamism (constant change), but also because it presents interesting theoretical challenges. In particular, CMC theorists must continuously wrestle with the question of whether CMC is better understood as being fundamentally different from, or just a variation on, face-to-face (FTF) communication.

Theorists have identified qualities that can be used to describe how different forms of CMC are different from each other, and from FTF communication. Four important qualities are hypertextuality, multimedia, synchronicity, and interactivity (Newhagen & Rafaeli, 1996; Walther, Gay, & Hancock, 2005). Hypertextuality is the extent to which CMC includes interlinking of information. When you read a traditional, printed book, the author is not able to directly connect you with other sources of information; the best he or she can do is reference other work that you have to leave the book in order to access. However, when you read a book using reading applications such as Kindle or Google Reader, you are often able to click on links that take you directly to definitions, encyclopedia entries, other works by the same author, etc. Multimedia references the extent to which computer-mediated communication includes not only text, but visual images and sound, including the range of human nonverbal behavior. Whereas early texting was largely limited to letters, numbers, and punctuation, we can now "text" emojis, voice messages, photos, and videos. Thus, current texting is far more of a multimedia experience than it was recently. Interactivity can be defined as the extent to which message sender and receiver are interchangeable roles, each exerting influence on the other (Walther, Gay, & Hancock, 2005). Face-to-face conversation is generally highly interactive: what each of you say is interpreted by and responded to by the other party. Historically, mass media were largely not interactive, because most people weren't able to respond directly to the broadcasters or political figures who produced the messages that were conveyed. Today there are innumerable variations on the level of interactivity in computer-mediated contexts. Skype or Google Hangouts permit a level of interactivity similar to face-to-face interaction, and television shows often have websites where viewers can post reactions that may make their way back to message producers. Synchronicity refers to the immediacy of responding between interacting parties. "Snail-mail" is relatively nonsynchronous because you have to wait for the other person to write back and for the postal service to deliver the letters. E-mail and text allow for a range of synchrony (from very delayed to near-immediate responsiveness), and face-to-face interaction requires immediate response—even nonresponsive will usually be

Hypertextuality
A quality of CMC, referencing the extent to which it includes interlinking of information

Multimedia A quality of CMC, referencing the extent to which it includes not only text, but visual images and sound, including the range of human nonverbal behavior

Interactivity A quality of CMC, referencing the extent to which message sender and receiver are interchangeable roles and exert influence on each other

Synchronicity
A quality of CMC, referencing the immediacy of response between interacting parties

interpreted as meaningful. These qualities, and especially the latter three, are part of the complexity that theories of CMC are required to encompass.

This chapter presents three sets of CMC theories. The first, cues-filtered-out theories, focus on the limitations of CMC as compared against FTF communication. The second, channel selection theories, focus on the selection of media to minimize limitations and improve communication outcomes. The third set of theories, adaptation theories, emphasize human capacity to adapt to the limitations of CMC, and even to benefit from those limitations.

CUES-FILTERED-OUT
THEORIES OF CMC

In face-to-face interactions, we form our impressions about others partly based on nonverbal cues. We observe whether they are young or old, how attractive they are, and how politely they behave. In interactions via CMC, however, the nonverbal cues may not be always available, especially when the channel is asynchronous (e.g., an e-mail, an online discussion board). We exchange opinions about a local restaurant on Yelp without seeing how other users behave. A group of theories have been formed to explain how people develop perceptions of and relationships with others when nonverbal cues are limited or completely absent. This group of theories, referred to as **cues-filtered-out** theories (Culnan & Markus, 1987), shares the assumption that CMC precludes the fulfillment of communication functions served by the nonverbal cues. If no other communication cues that perform similar functions are available, the development of interpersonal perceptions and relationships online is deterred (Walther & Parks, 2002). In this section, we discuss three theories in the cues-filtered-out family: social presence theory, lack of social context cues theory, and the social identity model of deindividuation effects. These theories were intuitively appealing and were foundational for early research on CMC. But, as we will discuss later, theories in the cues-filtered-out family have been heavily criticized due to their assumptions about mediated communication and contradictory findings in research studies testing the theories. As a consequence, these theories no longer serve as the basis for much research, but are important for understanding both CMC and the development of more sophisticated theory.

SOCIAL PRESENCE THEORY

Social presence theory, developed by John Short, Ederyn Williams, and Bruce Christie (Short, Williams, & Christie, 1976), explains why some communication media facilitate interpersonal communication while others do not. According to Short et al. (1976), communication media have two critical attributes:

Social presence theory
A theory that explains the effects of a communication medium on the way people communicate

Bandwidth The capacity of a medium to transmit nonverbal communication cues

Social presence The degree to which a communicator is aware of the presence of his or her interactional partner

bandwidth and social presence. Bandwidth refers to the quantity of nonverbal communication cues a medium can transmit. Communication media vary in their bandwidth. When we video chat with friends via FaceTime or Skype, we can have eye contact, observe facial expression, posture, body language, and dress, and listen to vocal cues, in addition to receiving verbal messages. In contrast, the range of nonverbal cues that can be transmitted is more limited if we talk over the phone or post comments on an online discussion board. Bandwidth is connected with the second attribute of media: social presence, or the degree to which a communicator is aware of the presence of his or her interactional partner. Social presence describes the extent to which a medium can make people feel that their interactional partner is *being there as a real person* (Gunawardena, 1995). In a state of social presence, communicators think about characteristics and internal feelings of their interactional partners, and attend to each other's uniqueness (Short et al., 1976).

Social presence theory argues that the bandwidth of a medium and the degree of social presence determine how people experience their mediated interactions. In particular, the more bandwidth a medium affords, the greater the degree of social presence created by the medium. For example, some multiplayer role-playing games were designed to create a high level of social presence among users by affording the transmission of both verbal and nonverbal cues. In game tasks, players can video chat with other users to coordinate individual actions, see avatars of their own and others' heroes, and be immersed in a game world that mimics reality. When you play the games with more social presence, it is not uncommon to feel that other users are there together with you, no matter how geographically distant you are from each other. In contrast, the sense of separation may not be reduced as much when you play a game where only text-based communication is supported. Communication via a medium with high bandwidth and high social presence is judged as warm, sociable, and involved, while communication via low bandwidth and social presence is seen as aloof, insensitive, and impersonal (Lowenthal, 2009; Short et al., 1976; Walther & Carr, 2010).

Although the ideas of social presence theory are intuitive and appealing, they have received serious critique from communication researchers (Walther & Carr, 2010). A major challenge targets the core concept of social presence. Walther (1992) questioned whether social presence was an objective characteristic of a communication medium, or users' subjective perceptions of the medium. Although early statements of the theory define social presence as a quality of the medium itself (Short et al., 1976), researchers typically measure it as a perception of the media user. This leaves unclear whether communication differences are caused by features of the media or individual variations in perceptions of media (Walther, 1992). Researchers who rely on the theory have attempted to clarify the concept of social presence, but "nearly everyone who writes about social presence continues to define it just a little differently," making it difficult to draw conclusions about its nature and effects (Lowenthal, 2009, p. 130).

LACK OF SOCIAL CONTEXT CUES

Another framework in the cues-filtered-out family is the lack of social context cues hypothesis (Siegel, Dubrovsky, Kiesler, & McGuire, 1986; Sproull & Kiesler, 1986). It was developed to explain the effects of reduced social context cues on communicative behavior (Sproull & Kiesler, 1986). Communication does not occur in a vacuum. Instead, people communicate in a context filled up with cues that define the nature of the social situation and the relationships between communicators (Spoull & Kiesler, 1986; Walther, 1992). These cues are referred as social context cues, and include the physical and social environment where communication occurs, communicators' position in a social hierarchy, and their nonverbal behaviors (Sproull & Kiesler, 1986). According to the theory, social context cues put constraints on communicative behavior, and convey expectations about what behaviors are socially appropriate. People in interactions perceive and interpret social context cues, and decide what information is communicated, how it is conveyed, and with whom the information is exchanged. For example, in an organization where most people are casually dressed and managers share office space with their teams, new employees may interpret these cues as signs of open-mindedness and equality. To meet the expectations conveyed by the social context cues, newcomers may address managers by their first names and converse with coworkers about personal topics. Social context cues can be either static or dynamic. Static cues emanate from people's appearance and artifacts (e.g., a spacious office, job title), while dynamic cues include people's nonverbal behaviors that change over the course of an interaction (Sproull & Kiesler, 1986).

According to the theory, "all communication technologies attenuate to at least some degree the social context cues available in face-to-face communication" (Kiesler and Sproull, 1992, p. 103). In other words, when we communicate via technology of any kind, some cues are muted or removed, and this is especially true for text-based media. When e-mailing, we lack many dynamic cues. We do not know if our recipients nod with approval, frown with displeasure, or squint with disappointment. Static cues are also minimized. We may not know what our recipients look like, how old they are, or what their race is. Information on status and affiliation is also lost unless e-mail signatures are used (Sproull & Kiesler, 1986). Even though new technologies allow for synchronicity and greater interactivity, the quantity of social context cues is still less than that transmitted via face-to-face communication (Kiesler and Sproull, 1992). For example, nonverbal cues such as brief facial expressions may be lost when video quality is low or the Internet connection is slow. When we have a job interview via FaceTime, we may not be able to tell if the interviewer's office is on the top floor. As a result, mediated technologies filter out the cues (e.g., office location) we often use to imply a person's status in the hierarchy of an organization.

Sproull and Kiesler (1986) argued that when social context cues are strong, people's communicative behaviors tend to be other-focused and controlled, and reflect the status differentiation between message senders and receivers. In contrast, the reduction or absence of social context cues was argued to

Lack of social context cues hypothesis A theory that explains how reduced social context cues affect communication behavior

Social context cues Cues that define the nature of social situations and the relationships between communicators

result in more extreme, more impulsive, and less socially regulated behavior (e.g., the use of swearing, insults, and hostile language, referred to as flaming; Walther, 1992). Moor, Heuvelman and Verleur (2010) examined the frequency of flaming on YouTube. About 65% of YouTube users they surveyed reported seeing flaming often when reading comments on videos. One video blogger who posted over 700 videos on YouTube said that "no video is exempt of being flamed" (p. 1541).

Like social presence theory, the idea that lack of social context cues produces unregulated communication behavior has intuitive appeal. However, research challenging the accuracy of this idea appeared not long after Sproull and Kiesler first proposed it. In both natural settings and lab experiments, researchers noticed that CMC users exhibit both pro-social (e.g., polite comments) and anti-social behaviors (e.g., flaming) when the social context cues were absent (Lea, O'Shea, & Spears, 1992). Although the theory predicts the uninhibited behavior, its premise that normative, regulated behavior will not occur when social context cues are weak or missing has not been supported (Walther, 2010). These concerns are addressed in more detail by the next theory.

THE SOCIAL IDENTITY MODEL OF DEINDIVIDUATION EFFECTS

Social identity model of deindividuation effects A theory that explains how people develop perceptions of others and regulate their own behavior based on identification with social groups to which they belong

The social identity model of deindividuation effects (SIDE model; Spears & Lea, 1992; Reicher, Spears, & Postmes, 1995) explains how people develop perceptions of others and regulate their own behavior based on identification with social groups to which they belong. The SIDE model begins with the observation that CMC users do not always exhibit unregulated communication behavior when nonverbal cues are absent. For example, Lea and his colleagues (1992) reviewed studies on uninhibited behavior in CMC and noticed that uninhibited remarks such as swearing and rude expressions accounted for less than 5% of all messages exchanged via CMC. Instead, CMC users behaved in a more normative and more socially regulated manner than previous theories such as lack of social context cues would predict (Spears & Postmes, 2015). The SIDE model takes this inconsistency as the basis for developing a new theory (Postmes, 2010).

Visual anonymity Occurs when CMC users exchange messages without seeing people to whom they are communicating

Deindividuation Temporary loss of one's own uniqueness or individuality

According to the SIDE model, there are two factors that drive CMC users' perceptions of others and online behavior: visual anonymity and the salience of a social identity (Spears & Lea, 1992; Reicher et al., 1995; Walther & Carr, 2010). Visual anonymity occurs when CMC users exchange messages without seeing people with whom they are communicating (Walter & Carr, 2010). The SIDE model contends that a lack of visual cues creates two cognitive states: depersonalization and deindividuation. Deindividuation refers to a temporary loss of one's own uniqueness or individuality. When CMC users cannot see their interactional partners, SIDE argues that they are not able to form impressions based on the individual, unique, or idiosyncratic characteristics of others. Instead, they become highly sensitive to cues indicating group membership. They may pay attention to whether other users are from the same cities, ethnic groups, or have the same gender. As a consequence, people in a state of deindividuation tend not to focus on individual differences between themselves and others, but instead identify with commonalities they share with their own social group(s). In addition to deindividuation, visual anonymity also leads to **depersonalization**, which refers to the inability to tell that other people are uniquely different from one another. As a result, people tend to treat other people as interchangeable members rather than distinguishable individuals. "So, whereas deindividuation implies *a loss of self in the group*, depersonalization refers to *the emergence of group in the self*" (Spears & Postmes, 2015, p. 27). Deindividuation and depersonalization can be seen in many online groups (Postmes, 2010). For example, users of TripAdvisor, an online travel website, rarely know each other individually or meet in person. But they share experiences, opinions, and advice to help other users to plan their travel. Deindividuation occurs when users appear to be bonded by a strong sense of community without much attention to how unique they themselves are. Users may also feel depersonalized when they see other travelers as a group who have common interests in travelling as opposed to a collection of individuals who want to seek information for their unique travel needs.

Depersonalization
The inability to tell that other people are uniquely different from one another

All individuals belong to a variety of social groups, ranging from large-scale social categories such as race, nationality, and gender to small-scale groups such as runners or yoga enthusiasts. Which social groups do CMC users orient to when they are visually anonymous to each other? According to the SIDE model, the social group a person references in relating to other CMC users depends on the **salience of a social identity**, or the extent to which the feelings of belonging to a group are present and important (Lea & Spears, 1992; Walther, 2011). Identity salience can be activated by noticing common characteristics of a group of people. For example, regional identity may become salient when people notice that other CMC users are from the same state (e.g., via IP addresses). Identity salience can also arise from attacks on groups to which one feels a sense of belonging (Walther, 2010). In an online discussion forum, one's identity of being a student from a certain university may be activated if others post a critique of that institution.

Salience of a social identity The extent to which feelings of belonging to a social group are present and important

The SIDE model was initially applied to explain social influence in online groups (Spears & Postmes, 2015). Specifically, the model contends that the attitudes and behaviors of CMC users are more influenced by their online groups when they experience strong deindividuation, depersonalization, and identity salience than when these factors are less strong (Walther, 2010). A number of studies have shown that the social groups with which CMC users identify exert greater influence on their attitudes toward controversial topics, compliance with group norms, and the use of language when they are in a state of deindividuation and depersonalization (Spears & Postmes, 2015; Walther, 2010). Recent development has extended the SIDE model to account for other interpersonal phenomena (Walther, 2011). For example, the model predicts that deindividuation and depersonalization lead to a person's liking of a group as whole, regardless of his or her liking of a specific member of the group (Walther, 2010). In other words, although visual anonymity deters impression formation about individuals, CMC users can still form perceptions of a group of people based on their shared membership.

Nonetheless, the SIDE model also has its critics and limitations. One challenge is the rise of new media technologies (Walther, 2011). Instagram, for example, allows users to post photos, videos, or interactive diagrams. The new technologies make communication online visually identifiable, "the conditions for which SIDE predicts no systematic effects" (Walther, 2011, p. 453). Scholars have also observed research findings that are not well explained by SIDE. For example, Walther and Carr (2010) noticed that social influence within online groups almost disappeared when the behavior of a single group member did not align with group norms, even when visual anonymity and identity salience were strong. The SIDE model used to be one of the most dominant theories of CMC. However, scholars will have to contend with these challenges as research and theorizing progress (Walther, 2011).

CHANNEL SELECTION THEORIES

Theories in the cues-filtered-out family focused on potential negative effects of limited cues. Theories of channel selection also address how missing cues affect communication via CMC, but shift focus to the selection of appropriate media to minimize such limitations. Three related theories—media richness theory, channel expansion theory, and media synchronicity theory—all incorporate the idea that certain media can carry more information to better facilitate understanding, while other media carry less information but are more efficient.

MEDIA RICHNESS THEORY

Media richness theory
A theory that characterizes communication media as "richer" or "leaner" to summarize how well they facilitate mutual understanding, and contends that selecting the right channel for particular tasks is key to maximizing the efficacy of these communications

Equivocal
Open to multiple interpretations

Media richness theory (MRT) characterizes communication media as "richer" or "leaner" to summarize how well they facilitate mutual understanding, and contends that selecting the right channel for particular tasks is key to maximizing the efficacy of these communications. The theory was developed by organizational communication scholars Richard Daft and Robert Lengel, who observed that managers have to use communication to turn complex organizational information and motivations into clear goals, strategies, and tasks for their employees (Daft & Lengel, 1984, p. 191). MRT claims that managers (and people, in general) can optimize the flow of information by attending to features of communication media that make them more or less appropriate to particular situations or tasks. The theory starts with the observation that communication may be more or less equivocal—or open to multiple interpretations. For example, a manager might say "this is our top priority," but one employee might interpret "priority" to mean something to be done quickly, while another might interpret it as a thing to be done carefully, and the manager might actually mean that the job is not that important at all, but has to be represented that way when clients might be listening! The theory also notes that communication may vary in uncertainty, which refers to the possibility that information may actually be missing.

In MRT, media richness refers to features of a medium that give it the capacity to resolve equivocality and uncertainty. The theory describes four factors that determine the richness of a medium: how many nonverbal cues it can convey, how immediately speakers receive feedback (synchrony), how natural (versus technical or formal) the language is, and how personal or individualized the communication can be. FTF communication is usually considered the richest possible medium. An ordinary telephone call is less rich than FTF communication because it has fewer cues (no facial expressions), but is still relatively rich because it is synchronous, natural, and directed at a particular person. A memo to all staff in a particular division is much less rich, because nonverbal cues are lacking, there is no mechanism for feedback, language is typically more formal than natural, and the communication is directed at the entire staff, not a particular individual. Online, these same features differentiate "lean" typed text interactions (e.g., text messaging) from richer media such as video conferencing.

Media richness
Features of a medium that give it the capacity to resolve equivocality and uncertainty

How does richness relate to task in CMC contexts? Imagine you need to work with a colleague who is in another city. You might prefer to organize a meeting time by e-mail, but to conduct the meeting by video chat. The MRT explanation for these choices is that the leaner medium, e-mail, is more appropriate to the scheduling task because that task has less potential for equivocality or uncertainty than the work to be done in the meeting itself.

Although MRT was first proposed to explain media selection in work organizations, researchers have gone on to examine it in other contexts. For example, Sheer (2011) studied how students' perceptions of media richness influenced which online communication features they utilize for particular communication tasks. She asked students to rate different features of a social media platform (e.g., instant messaging, webcam chat, personal profile pages), asking them to evaluate how rich the features were and how well they facilitated self-presentation. She found that richer features, which enable message personalization and convey a bigger variety of cues, were perceived as more appropriate for self-presentation. Specifically, students chose richer media for talking about more personal topics (e.g., relationships) and less rich media for straightforward communication tasks (e.g., finding out about homework assignments).

MRT offers an intuitive general framework for understanding how channel selection might be optimized based on task. However, despite some research findings consistent with the theory (such as those of the Sheer study described above), the body of research directly testing the theory's predictions indicates that people do not seem to choose media that match the equivocality or uncertainty of their communication tasks (Dennis, 2009; Dennis, Fuller, & Valachich, 2008). This serious shortcoming of MRT has led directly to the articulation of two theories that address this problem in different ways: channel expansion theory (CET) and media synchronicity theory (MST).

CHANNEL EXPANSION THEORY

Do you know people who post very personal information on Facebook, or who use text messaging for important conversations? Media richness theory doesn't provide a good explanation for this kind of behavior, because the equivocality and uncertainty of the communication is not well matched to the media being selected. As an alternative, the channel expansion theory proposed by John Carlson and Robert Zmud (1999) argues that expertise and past experience with a channel (i.e., medium) determines our perceptions of media richness, and this in turn determines our likelihood of utilizing that channel. In CET media richness is the perceived ability to understand and be understood using a particular channel—it is a perception of the media user and not an inherent trait of the channel.

Channel expansion theory A theory that defines media richness as a perception of the user and argues that it is influenced by channel, topic, organizational context, and communication partners

The theory posits four kinds of influential experiences that influence richness perceptions: channel, topic, organizational context, and communication partners. Experience using a particular channel increases a person's comfort with the particular ways of expressing oneself that it allows. Familiarity with a topic and the context increase a person's confidence that his or her symbolic choices will be decoded as intended. Experience with a particular partner enables a person to both be confident in the words and terms he or she chooses, and enables a person to know how their channel choice will be perceived.

Researchers testing CET have found support for the idea that richness is a matter of personal perception, and that channel, topic, organizational context, and communication partners are empirically related to perceived channel appropriateness. For example, Scott D'Urso and Stephen Rains (2008) hypothesized that people would perceive FTF, telephone, e-mail, and instant message channels as more or less rich based on their experience, and statistically controlled for the influence of structural differences (e.g., synchronicity) and peers' use of these media. They found that perceptions of a channel as personal were related to topic and partner familiarity, and experience with the channel drove perceptions of how many cues the media conveyed. This study suggests that people who post highly personal information on Facebook or use text messaging for important conversations do so because they actually perceive those media as richer than other people do.

Media synchronicity theory A theory that divides communication into two kinds of tasks: conveying information and converging on meaning. The theory claims that information is better conveyed asynchronously, while shared meaning is more effectively reached synchronously

MEDIA SYNCHRONICITY THEORY

Like CET, media synchronicity theory provides an alternative reformulation of MRT, but does this by reconceptualizing communication tasks. Rather than describing tasks as varying in equivocality and uncertainty, theorists Alan Dennis and Joseph Valacich (1999) argued that tasks varied in the desirability of synchronous communication. According to this theory, conveyance communication tasks involve disseminating information, and such tasks are actually enhanced by less synchronicity. In contrast, convergence communication tasks involve the process of reaching mutual agreement about the meaning of information, and these are enhanced by synchronicity. MST further contends that different media capabilities enable more or less synchronicity. Media that have

Conveyance communication tasks Communication tasks that involve disseminating information

Convergence communication tasks Communication tasks that involve reaching mutual agreement

higher transmission velocity (i.e., messages are received and processed close to when they are sent) and more symbol variety (i.e., more cues) are considered more synchronous. Those that allow for parallel communications (e.g., a report that has both a table of statistical data and a graph depicting them visually), rehearsal (e.g., a text message that can be erased and rewritten before sending), and reprocessing (e.g., an e-mail that can be re-read) are less synchronous.

To better understand MST, note that you are likely reading this chapter prior to a class during which you will discuss its contents. Many classes are set up this way: students first read the material individually, and then come together to discuss it in class. This structure is no accident, and the claims of MST explain why it often works well. The conveyance task of disseminating course content is facilitated by the asynchronous communication of written material. In readings, you can find parallel explanations, examples, and graphics that together compose the body of information. You can also reprocess (i.e., reread) sections to better comprehend them. You might even write a short essay reflecting on the content—an opportunity to rehearse the material. These asynchronous capabilities help you develop an individual appreciation for the information. However, with your reading completed, you now face the convergence task of reaching mutual understanding with others about the material. In class, with synchronous FTF communication, you can check your interpretation of the reading against the instructor and other students, and very quickly determine similarities and differences. This would be much harder and less successful if conducted with an asynchronous media such as e-mail.

When communication tasks are complex, they can have elements of both conveyance and convergence, and these tasks may be need to be handled with a mix of asynchronous and synchronous communication. A recent study (Brinker, Gastil, & Richards, 2015) examined how a nonprofit organization that ran a variety of civic engagement programs online tried to inform citizens about a complex political issue. Some of the organization's programs were asynchronous; for example, they created webpages where voters could read factual information about a political issue. Other programs were synchronous; for example, they hosted moderated real-time video chats where voters could discuss their personal values and experiences related to political issues. The researchers invited people to participate in these programs, and then asked them factual questions about the issues and asked for their opinion about politics. They found that low-synchronicity text and video programs produced more factual learning than interactive webcasts and group video chats. However, high-synchronicity programs were more effective in producing faith in civic collaboration and civil political discourse. The researchers concluded that civic engagement programs are most effective when they combine low-synchronicity individual learning interventions followed by high-synchronicity deliberation in groups.

Overall, CET and MST have begun to take the place of MRT in explaining how people choose media to fit the communication tasks they need to perform. At present, there are research findings that support these theories, but also findings that challenge their accuracy and utility (Walther, 2011). Thus, it remains

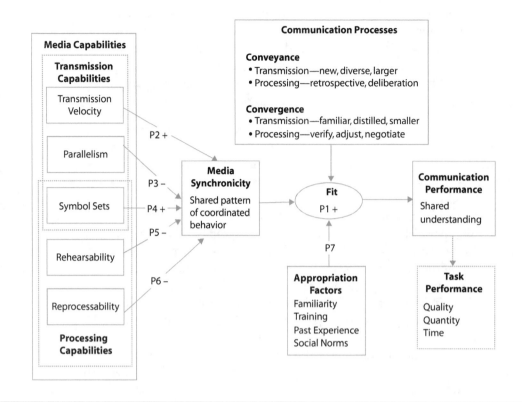

From MIS Quarterly, Volume 32 (3), September 2008 by Alan R. Denis, Robert M. Fuller, and Joseph S. Valacich. Copyright © 2008 by the Regents of the University of Minnesota. Reprinted by permission.

FIGURE 13.1 MEDIA SYNCHRONICITY THEORY.

to be seen whether these theories will be modified into successful replacements for MRT, or replaced with alternative theories. We now turn from these theories that focus on selecting the most appropriate media for particular communication tasks to theories that examine how people adapt to the characteristics of the media they use.

THEORIES OF ADAPTATION TO CMC

The final group of theories in this chapter emphasize human capacity to adapt to and even flourish within the constraints of computer-mediated interaction. Like cues-filtered-out theories, these adaptation theories recognize that computer-mediated interaction often lacks some of the nonverbal information that is exchanged in FTF; this is especially true for highly text-based forms of CMC such as e-mail or texting. Indeed, when the first of these theories (social information processing theory) was first proposed in the early 1990s, the CMC technologies available to most people were largely text-based (e.g., e-mail), lacking most of the capacity to integrate visual and aural information that we currently enjoy. However, unlike cues-filtered-out theories, the theories discussed in this section do not assume that the absence of certain cues dooms CMC to produce lower quality interactions and relationships. These theories also differ from channel selection theories because they emphasize adaptation to communication technologies rather than making choices between them.

SOCIAL INFORMATION PROCESSING THEORY

Developed by Joseph (Joe) Walther, social information processing theory (Walther, 1992) is an influential early theory of CMC that was developed as a direct challenge to the cues-filtered-out theories described earlier in this chapter. Social information processing theory (SIPT) explains "how, with time, CMC users are able to accrue impressions of and relations with others online, and these relations achieve the level of development that is expected through offline communication" (Walter, 2011, p. 458). In other words, SIPT is a theory that emphasizes the human capacity to tailor mediated communication, and especially language use, in ways that overcome limitations imposed by the technology.

Social information processing theory
A theory that explains how people adapt communication, especially language use, to develop impressions and create relationships in computer-mediated environments

SIPT makes two principal claims. First, the theory contends that people have an innate need to form impressions of other people, and correspondingly, that people will adapt their communication to develop and manage those impressions regardless of the medium being used. More specifically, when they are unable to use or interpret nonverbal cues, people interacting online will use language content and style to convey relational information such as liking (also called affinity or affiliation; see also Relational Framing Theory, Chapter 7). For example, people can disclose more or less personal information, be more agreeable or disagreeable, and converse brusquely or politely—all in the language they select. Emoticons can also be part of this process, but Walther notes that they are not the central focus of the theory or regarded as having the same level of importance as what is said with words, and how it is said (Walther, 2011).

In a foundational study testing the first principal claim of SIPT, Walther and colleagues (Walther, Loh, & Granka, 2005) had previously unacquainted college student participants interact with each other either via a computer chat program or FTF. In each dyad, one participant acted as a research confederate and was instructed to convey affinity (liking or friendliness) or disaffinity (disliking or unfriendliness) for the other person. To model normal interaction as closely as possible, the instruction emphasized that confederates should do this without "making it obvious." When the interactions were over, the naïve participants (i.e., those who were not confederates) were asked to rate how much their interaction partners (i.e., the confederates) liked them. The researchers also analyzed the text of the chat sessions and the video of the FTF sessions, classifying the types of nonverbal behavior that occurred in the FTF sessions, and the types of verbal behavior that occurred in both. The findings in this study clearly display the capacity for adaptation to CMC. Naïve participants correctly recognized when confederates were assigned to be friendly and unfriendly, rating the friendly confederates as conveying higher affinity.

This finding did not differ for FTF and CMC participants—despite their inability to use nonverbal behavior to convey affinity or disaffinity, confederates in the CMC condition were equally capable of making naïve participants feel liked or disliked. Analyses of the text and video showed how this occurred. In the FTF conditions, confederates principally made use of the nonverbal cues to convey affinity or disaffinity. Compared to unfriendly confederates, friendly confederates did many things differently to create a sense of liking, including higher quantities of smiling, orienting their bodies directly toward the naïve confederates, and gazing at them. There were only two verbal differences in the FTF interactions: Friendly confederates disclosed more personal information and delivered fewer insults than unfriendly confederates. In the CMC conditions, confederates utilized more verbal behavior to convey affinity or disaffinity. Compared to unfriendly confederates, the friendly confederates disclosed more personal information, offered encouragement, expressed joy, and spoke in longer turns; they also utilized more explicit statements of positive affection toward the naïve confederates and used more smiling emoticons.

The second principal claim of SIPT is that, compared to FTF, developing impressions and relationships via CMC requires more time; this claim has received research support in multiple studies that varied how long people were allowed to interact via CMC (Walther, Anderson, & Park, 1994). Nonverbal behavior conveys a great deal of information very quickly; without this information, CMC users need more time to exchange verbal messages and to develop impressions of each other from these exchanges. Additional time may also be necessary simply because most people type more slowly than they talk and because CMC is often used more asynchronously. However, this claim about requiring more time should still be understood as emphasizing adaptation, not limitation. SIPT contends that, given sufficient time and quantity of exchanges between people, personal and relational information builds up and eventually renders CMC equivalent to FTF communication for developing and maintaining relationships.

Walther has argued that SIPT has a broad scope and is applicable to a host of CMC settings that include, among others, virtual work groups (Walther & Bunz, 2005), chat rooms (Henderson & Gilding, 2004), and online dating (Gibbs, Ellison, & Heino, 2006). However, for today's student, SIPT's focus on text-based CMC and the capacity to develop impressions and relationships may seem outdated, possibly irrelevant. After all, images and links can now be embedded in e-mails and texts, and services like eHarmony.com and Match.com serve as testaments to the capacity for developing intimate relationships via CMC. As previously noted, keeping up with the development of communication technologies is a serious challenge for CMC theorists. Walther himself appears to have recently focused more attention on developing the hyperpersonal model and warranting theories (see below). Nonetheless, as Walther argues, deciding whether a theory should be retired requires that we "assess how the topography of new technologies' features meet or violate the assumptions of a theory" (2011, p. 471). Thus, the future viability of SIPT will depend on whether people continue to rely on largely text-based CMCs, and whether the theory can be "stretched" to explain how users respond to non-textual information that accompanies the text. At this point, despite the availability of phone calls and web conferencing (Skype, Google Hangout, etc.), people do continue to make substantial use of text-based CMC (e.g., phone-based texting, e-mail, and messaging functions within social media sites like Facebook). Further, there is accumulating evidence that adding visual information in principally text-based environments has only limited influence. One study compared people communicating FTF, a text-only instant messaging system, and a hybrid system that combined instant messaging with the ability to see (but not hear) the partner on screen. Across getting-to-know-you conversations conducted in these ways, there were no significant differences in interpersonal attraction, though the inclusion of visual cues increased the frequency of disclosure and personal questions (Antheunis, Valkenburg, & Peter, 2007). Future editions of this textbook will have to document how the future of SIPT unfolds.

EFFICIENCY FRAMEWORK

Although research testing social information processing theory shows that people are well-able to adapt to CMC, it remains true that people tend to report lower satisfaction with communication technologies in which more nonverbal cues are filtered out versus those that incorporate more nonverbal cues or FTF encounters. Further, users' low ratings of satisfaction about CMC do not necessarily inhibit task accomplishment (Walther, 2011). The efficiency framework, developed by Kristine Nowak, James Watt, and Joseph Walther, attempts to explain why some CMC technologies are perceived as unsatisfactory but are associated with high productivity and outcome quality (Nowak, Watt, & Walther, 2009; Walther, 2011). Specifically, Nowak and her colleagues argued that we must carefully distinguish between users' subjective ratings of satisfaction and the objective instrumental utility of a media.

Efficiency framework
A theory that explains why some CMC technologies are perceived as unsatisfactory but are associated with high productivity and outcome quality

The efficiency framework makes two assumptions about CMC and human behavior (Nowak et al., 2009). First, it assumes that CMC is generally effortful. Before interaction, users of CMC need to get familiar with the functions and constraints of a media form. For example, users of a videoconferencing system need to learn about how to call multiple people simultaneously and what video formats the system supports. During interaction, CMC users have to deal with a reduced amount of information transmitted, and accommodate interaction when the technology fails. Although CMC may be as good as face-to-face communication in task achievement, it takes more time and effort (Walther, 2011). Second, the efficiency framework assumes that humans are cognitive and behavioral misers, who have a natural preference for completing a task with the least amount of effort (Nowak et al., 2009).

Built on these assumptions, the efficiency framework posits that CMC users will have low satisfaction and preference for media that require a lot of effort to communicate. But this does not mean that people who are not satisfied about the media will have less success in communication than those who are satisfied.

Instead, the outcome quality (e.g., productivity) is determined by users' expenditure of effort rather than their preference for or satisfaction about a medium (Nowak et al., 2009). The more effort users put into using a particular medium, the better they can adapt and overcome the constraints imposed by the mediated technologies. Consequently, the increase in effort leads to better outcome quality.

Empirical research testing the efficiency framework is limited (Walther, 2011). In one experiment (Nowak et al., 2009), college students were assigned to form small groups to collaborate over a 5-week period on a class project. They were randomly assigned to use one of many forms of communication: face-to-face meetings, video conferencing, text-based real-time chats, asynchronous text messaging, and an asynchronous video-audio system where users can record messages and share with each other. The task required students to prepare a mock presentation to Congress about how to balance Internet privacy and national security. The presentation was videotaped and evaluated by independent coders. Participants filled in a survey assessing their media satisfaction and other variables of interest. The results showed that the communication systems with more cues were judged as more satisfactory, possibly because the high-cue systems make interaction less effortful. Yet, the coders judged that the asynchronous video-audio system best facilitated the quality of presentations, consistent with the idea that expenditure of effort produces outcome success (Nowak et al., 2009). Although the efficiency framework needs more empirical testing, the insight that "media that are the easiest to use may not, in fact, offer the greatest instrument benefit" has implications for both CMC research and practice (Walther, 2011, p. 469).

HYPERPERSONAL MODEL

Building and expanding from the foundation provided by social information processing theory, Joseph Walther developed the hyperpersonal model of CMC, designed to explain how CMC may not just produce impressions and relationships that are equivalent to those developed in person, but that are actually **hyperpersonal**, or superior in their desirability and intimacy (Walther, 2011). If you've had a relationship online that was in some way better than an FTF relationship, this theory helps to explain why and how that can occur. This model makes four broad claims, each tied to a major component of the communication process: (1) receiver, (2) sender, (3) channel, and (4) feedback.

First, the hyperpersonal model contends that, in the absence of nonverbal cues available in FTF interactions, message receivers tend to "fill in the blanks" or construct an impression of the message sender that goes beyond what they can actually verify. These impressions often draw on whatever is actually known about senders' group memberships (see SIDE theory, above), but may also pull in receivers' stereotypes and past experiences (Walther, 2011). When the initial impression is favorable, filling in the blanks typically takes the form of idealization, in which receivers imagine senders as better than they actually or probably are. For example, if you meet someone in a chat room focused on an activity that you enjoy, and learn that the person comes from your much-loved hometown or campus, the hyperpersonal model suggests you are likely to develop a more positive conception of that person than is warranted by these few things you have learned.

Second, the hyperpersonal model argues that text-based CMC encourages and supports selective self-presentation, or presenting a desired version of oneself. As Walther explains, "It need not be apparent to others what one's physical characteristics are (unless one discloses them verbally), nor do individuals generally transmit unconscious undesirable interaction behaviors such as interruptions, mismanaged eye contact, or nonverbal disfluencies of the kind that detract from desired impressions face-to-face. Instead, CMC senders may construct messages that portray themselves in preferential ways, emphasizing desirable characteristics and communicating in a manner that invites preferential reactions" (2011, p. 461). This ability to emphasize the best aspects of oneself and deemphasize or conceal others has obvious value for creating positive relationships online, though it may become problematic if the relationship moves offline and the selective self-presentation comes to be viewed as deceptive (Toma, Hancock, & Ellison, 2008). CMC users may also choose to portray themselves in ways that invite negative reactions. In one study (Walther, Van Der Heide, Tong, Carr, & Atkin, 2010), researchers paired strangers via CMC to discuss what they believed was the best hamburger restaurant in the area. One of the partners in each dyad was transformed into a confederate through instructions to make the other person like or dislike him or her (similar to the study described for social information processing theory, above). The "friendly" confederates were more agreeable than the "unfriendly" confederates, whereas the "unfriendly" confederates expressed more disagreement and negative opinions. The unfriendly confederates were also more likely to look up the partner's favorite hamburger—and to use that information to say negative things about it.

Third, the hyperpersonal model claims that characteristics of CMC, especially asynchrony, contribute to senders' ability to engage in selective self-presentation. When communication technology does not require or create expectations that communicators respond to each other immediately, people are able to put more time and effort into enhancing their messages, which may include editing, deleting, and rewriting. If you have found yourself repeatedly reworking a text, or rehearsing what you will say in a voicemail, you have experienced this phenomenon. In one study testing this claim from the hyperpersonal model (Walther, 2007), college students were led to believe that they were interacting asynchronously with different people online. These people were described in ways that increased or decreased their social desirability (i.e., attractiveness as interaction partners). Participants' messages were recorded as they wrote them. The more desirable the other person, the more they edited their messages (deletions, backspaces, and insertions).

Fourth, according to the hyperpersonal model, idealization, selective self-presentation, and channel effects (i.e., asynchrony), all work together in a feedback system that heightens the impact of each component. In other words,

Selective self-presentation
Presenting a desired version of oneself

because asynchronous CMC permits selective self-presentation, it promotes idealization, which in turn encourages more selective self-presentation. This loop increases the likelihood of a hyperpersonal relationship developing online. Although this component of the model has received less research attention than the other three components, there is evidence of behavioral confirmation, which is when one interaction partner's impression of the other partner motivates behavior that in turn encourages the other to behave in ways that align with the impression. In one recent study (Tong & Walther, 2015), the experimenters paired strangers to interact in a chat room. Before the interaction, one group of participants was led to believe that their conversational partners were in a bad mood, whereas the other group was led to believe that their conversational partners were in a good mood. The partners were actually not in any specific mood state. Participants who thought their partners were in a bad mood responded by exerting more effort to be sociable than those who thought their partners were in a good mood, and their (supposedly-bad-mood) partners responded with greater sociability themselves. This sociability in turn led the participants to believe that their partners had more pleasant personalities compared to partners in the good mood condition, when in fact it was their own conversational behavior that created the difference. Over time, behavioral confirmation can substantively change how people view themselves and communicate with others.

Behavioral confirmation
When one interaction partner's impression of the other partner motivates behavior that in turn encourages the other to behave in ways that align with the impression

SUMMARY

The theories in this chapter display communication scholars' considerable interest in understanding computer-mediated communication, a phenomenon that is made more difficult to theorize about because the media continue to change. Cues-filtered-out theories, including social presence theory, the lack of social context hypothesis, and the SIDE model, focus on the limitations of CMC as compared to FTF communication. Channel selection theories, including media richness theory, channel selection theory, and media synchronicity theory, focus on the selection of media to minimize limitations and maximize communication outcomes. A third set of theories, including social information processing theory, the efficiency framework, and the hyperpersonal model, are called theories of adaptation to CMC because they emphasize human capacity to work around and even benefit from the limitations of CMC.

KEY TERMS

Bandwidth

Behavioral confirmation

Channel expansion theory

Convergence communication tasks

Conveyance communication tasks

Deindividuation

Depersonalization

Efficiency framework

Equivocal

Hyperpersonal

Hypertextuality

Interactivity

Lack of social context cues hypothesis

Media richness

Media richness theory

Media synchronicity theory

Multimedia

Salience of social identity

Selective self-presentation

Social context cues

Social identity model of deindividuation effects

Social information processing theory

Social presence

Social presence theory

Synchronicity

Visual anonymity

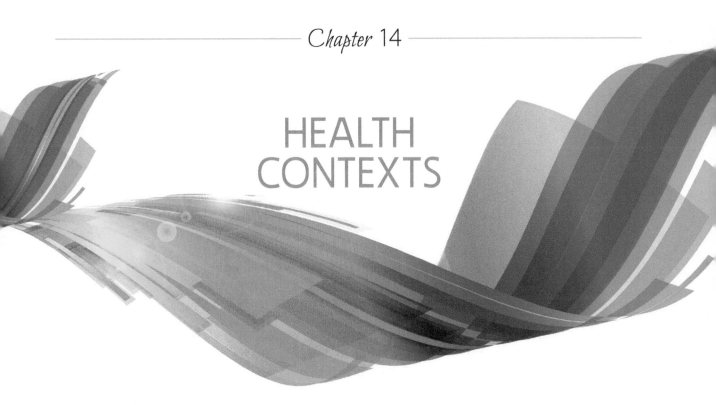

Chapter 14

HEALTH CONTEXTS

Over the last several decades, the field of communication studies has experienced incredible growth in both number of researchers and legitimization as an invaluable discipline that is becoming increasingly problem-focused. Perhaps one of the most influential factors for this growth can be traced to the proliferation of health communication theory and research. In the first edition of *Contemporary Communication Research*, we relegated the health communication context to a chapter titled *Tributary Contexts*. Today, the sheer mass of published data and theory building within health communication simply demands its own chapter. Further, as health care has become a focal point of national debate, whether it is the Affordable Care Act or changes to Medicare and Medicaid to reflect the quality of the patient experience in calculating reimbursement rates, the focus on communication and interpersonal relationships has never been greater. Theresa Thompson (2006) conducted a meta-analysis of articles published in *Health Communication* between the years of 1989 and 2003. Results indicated that 20.7 percent focused on patient-physician interaction, 13.4 percent focused on health campaigns, 11.8 percent on risky health behavior, 8.4 percent on aging, 7 percent on language or the creation of shared meaning, and 5.9 percent on issues related to the media.

The U.S. Department of Health and Human Services' Agency for Health Care Research and Quality (AHRQ) (2007) reported that communication errors accounted for more than 42,000 deaths annually. Further, Leonard Graham, and Bonacum (2004) reported that 70 percent of sentinel events (i.e., events causing serious injury or death to the patient) were directly related to communication and relational issues among members of the medical team (Polack &

Avtgis, 2011). These data are startling, especially when considering the fact that they are communication based, not medically based. It is data such as these that make the undeniable and compelling case for the development of quality health communication theory and research.

When discussing any concept, we need to have a clear conceptual definition. Similar to most any communication construct, definitions will differ depending on the particular scholar. A few examples include Linda Lederman (2009) defining health communication as "the study of the impact of communication on health and health care delivery, with attention to the role that communication plays in the definition of health and wellness, illness and disease, as well as in developing strategies for addressing ways to deal with those issues" (p. 236); Donohew and Ray (1990) define health communication as "the dissemination and interpretation of health-related messages" (p. 4); Ratzan, Stearns, Payne, Amato, Libergott, and Madoff (1994) define health communication as "...the art and technique of informing, influencing, and motivating individual, institutional, and public audiences about important health issues. Its scope includes disease prevention, health promotion, health-care policy, business, as well as enhancement of the quality of life and health of individuals within the community" (p. 362). These definitions are but a few of the many definitions available within the field of communication studies.

Kreps, Bonaguro, and Query (1998) attribute the explosion of interest in health communication to the fact that health communication, unlike many other communication contexts, went outside of the academy and into the "real world" to help solve everyday health issues. The Kreps et al. call for having research be socially relevant is still advocated today (see, for example, Thompson, Dorsey, Miller, & Parrot, 2003). At one point, there were two primary journals within which health communication scholars published their research. In 1989, *Health Communication* was the first journal within the field of communication studies dedicated to publishing high quality health communication research. This was followed by the 1996 creation of the *Journal of Health Communication*. These journals are not only prospering today, but there are literally dozens of interdisciplinary journals dedicated to publishing health communication theory and research.

Health communication theorists and researchers often focus their efforts on identifying, examining, and offering insights into how to improve health care and to promote taking responsibility for one's health. Communication has been associated with numerous health-related factors, including physical and psychological well-being, patient satisfaction, patient confidence in the doctor, malpractice rates, and patient-provider nonverbal communication to name but a few (Arntson & Droge, 1988; Street & Buller, 1988). Further, research has spanned well beyond the practice of health care to include the development of AIDS prevention (Brown, 1991), organ donation (Morgan & Miller, 2002), and bullying campaigns (Roberto & Eden, 2014).

Before presenting theories of health communication it is important to consider the different ways that people define health. Traditionally, people consumed health care from a sickness perspective in that people would seek out health care when they were ill. Further, when the health care practitioner gave a recommendation, the patient would follow those directions to the letter and not question any of the practitioner's orders. This is known as the paternalistic model. In contemporary health care, especially since the Vietnam War when people began to question authority, health care consumers are much more likely to educate themselves before the encounter with the health care provider and engage in a collaboration of joint input resulting in a mutually agreeable treatment protocol. This is known as the mutuality model (Polack & Avtgis, 2011).

FUNCTIONS OF COMMUNICATION IN THE HEALTH CONTEXT

Costello (1977) identified four functions of communication regarding patient/provider communication. These functions include elements of interpersonal and persuasive communication (see Figure 14.1).

- Diagnosis — the data-gathering, data-interpretation, and problem-solving skills used by the health care provider.
- Cooperation — communication concerning the nature of one's illness and the implication of measures prescribed for care.

Paternalistic model A patient following a health care practitioner's recommendation to the letter, not questioning any of the practitioner's orders

Mutuality model Health care consumer engaging in a collaboration of joint input with the health care provider resulting in a mutually agreeable treatment protocol

Diagnosis A function of health communication that involves data gathering, data interpretation, and problem-solving skills used by the health-care provider

Cooperation A function of health communication that involves communication concerning the nature of one's illness and the implication of measures prescribed for care

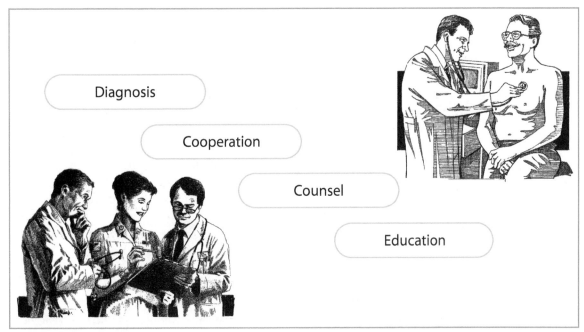

Diagnosis

Cooperation

Counsel

Education

© Kendall Hunt Publishing Company

FIGURE 14.1 FOUR FUNCTIONS OF HEALTH COMMUNICATION.

- Counsel — involves the role of the provider as "therapist." DeVito (2002) included therapeutic communication as one of the major purposes of interpersonal communication. The health care provider engaged in the therapeutic function deals with the client's "symbolic" symptoms.

- Education — health education is the process of disseminating information to individuals to attempt to reduce health risks and to increase the effectiveness of health care. Health education proceeds through channels ranging from informal patient/provider interaction to more formal mass-mediated campaigns designed to achieve clear and planned objectives. The Act Against AIDS campaign is one such example.

COMMUNICATION CONTEXTS WITHIN HEALTH COMMUNICATION

Researchers have attempted to provide some structure for studying health communication. Some believe it is helpful to categorize and define the study of health communication according to communication contexts (Ratzan, Payne, & Bishop, 1996). Much of the research in health communication has examined the interpersonal communication relationship between patient and health care provider. Other heavily research contexts within health communication include mass and mediated communication, which "focuses on effective message dissemination for health promotion, disease prevention, and health-related messages transmitted through mediated channels, including health marketing and policy-making" (Ratzen et al., 1996, p. 28).

For most people, the term "health communication" refers to the interpersonal context. In fact, in recent years, communication training has been part of many medical education curricula (see, for example, Polack, Avtgis, Rossi, & Shaffer, 2010). For example, the Accreditation Council for Graduate Medical Education (ACGME), the accrediting body for post-MD education programs, has made communication one of the six core competencies that all physicians are required to demonstrate. However, communication between patient and provider often assumes that both parties are competent communicators, which is far from reality. When a patient presents to a provider, the episode requires the patient to communicate their symptoms to the provider as accurately as possible. Similarly, the provider must be able to communicate instructions accurately and competently on how to relieve, eliminate, or manage health care problems. Ineffective communication is costly and concerted efforts are being put forth to increase health literacy at many levels. Such costs are not just financial, and misdiagnosis and incorrect treatment are also outcomes related to communication. Even if the instructions are delivered clearly, if the interaction between the health care provider and the patient is abrupt, hurried, and impersonal, the patient may not be satisfied, and compliance with provider recommendations may not result. At a minimum, effective interpersonal communication between patients and providers is a necessary prerequisite for the development of an open and trusting relationship, which is a critical factor within health communication contexts. Once an open and trusting relationship is established, diagnosis and treatment are likely to be much more accurate and effective. Further, quality relationships between patient and provider result in fewer malpractice suits.

While much of the theory-building research efforts have been developed focusing on interpersonal communication, several specific aspects of interpersonal interaction are especially important in the health communication context.

RELATIONAL CONTROL/COMPLIANCE

Many people feel that health care providers dominate most interactions. Providers can engage in control tactics before they even see clients by making them wait for an appointment and treatment. Health care providers control the interaction and conversation when they engage in one-way communication: asking questions but not encouraging others to do the same; interrupting; changing topics abruptly; or ignoring patients completely (Cline & Cardosi, 1983).

The model of relational interaction includes the message exchange patterns of control, trust, and intimacy. The control dimension refers to the process by which individuals establish the defining and directing actions of the relationship. Relational control is measured by redundancy, dominance, and power. Redundancy refers to the amount of change in the dyad's negotiations over rights. Dominance describes how much one individual commands the interaction. Power is the potential to influence or restrict another person's behaviors. Given the status differences that are inherent in the health context, the relational control approach is particularly useful.

Redundancy Refers to the amount of change in interactant's negotiations over rights

Dominance Degree to which one partner is said to dominate a dyad's interaction

Power The potential to influence or restrict another person's behaviors

Although the model was conceptualized and developed as a way to examine marital dyads, O'Hair (1989) applied the relational control component of the model to the study of the patient/provider relationship. He argued that the model is especially appropriate for researching patient/provider communication in general and control in particular. Patients are no longer passive participants in the health care relationship (i.e., paternalistic model). Patients regularly challenge the authority and control of the provider. The relational control model allows us to observe and examine the control strategies attempted by patients. Patients dissatisfied with the control exercised by the provider generally engage in fewer compliance behaviors. Thus, the relational control patterns of both the patient and the provider have direct influence on treatment outcomes.

To examine the issue of relational control in patient/provider communication, O'Hair (1989) recorded actual interactions and looked for indications of redundancy, dominance, and power. His findings indicated that patients attempted control almost as often as the provider. O'Hair calls this *competitive symmetry*. The following conversation illustrates this:

> **Doctor:** "I would continue on the antibiotics until your throat clears."
> **Client:** "They haven't helped. I would prefer a new medication."

Complementarity emerged as the second most frequently used control sequence. Messages are complementary if one speaker attempts control of the exchange, while the other yields, or if one speaker yields control while the other assumes control. O'Hair (1989) found that clients were twice as willing to yield control of the interaction after the physician sought control. For example:

> **Doctor:** "If you are going to travel long distances, be sure to stop periodically to empty your bladder."
>
> **Client:** "I'll schedule stops to make sure I do that."

The results of this application of interpersonal theory in the health care context show the benefits of extending an existing theory of communication. O'Hair (1989) suggested that relational control analyses could be used to examine incidences of patient noncompliance. For example, relational control analyses could help us determine which clients are willing to challenge the authority and competence of physicians; two factors that may predict noncompliance with physician recommendations.

Compliance is a critical dimension in the patient/provider relationship. Within health care, compliance can be defined as the degree to which the client engages in the provider's suggested lifestyle changes, treatment procedure, or other health related behaviors (e.g., adhering to a particular pharmaceutical regimen). Providers engage in many messages with their patients in an effort to guide them on a road to wellness. Kreps (1988) argued that from a relational perspective the responsibility for "getting well" is a joint function of both the patient and the provider. Compliance is influenced by strategic messages used by both parties.

Research into compliance in the health context has taken two distinct directions consisting of determining what kinds of compliance gaining strategies providers use effectively and the relationship between the use of specific strategies and outcomes such as client satisfaction with health care quality and individual health status. Michael and Judee Burgoon (1990) explored the use of both verbal and nonverbal physician compliance gaining strategies and concluded that physicians tend to use nonthreatening verbal strategies when attempting to convince their clients to follow suggested treatment regimens. Physicians emphasize their expertise as an incentive to comply. For example, "If you comply with my recommendations to lose weight and exercise, your blood pressure should go down." When there is resistance from the patient, the physician adopts more aggressive compliance gaining strategies such as "If you do not follow my instructions, you may very well have another and more severe heart attack!" Physicians rarely use positive reinforcing compliance gaining strategies with their patients (e.g., "If you lose weight, you will feel better about yourself.").

Providers employ a range of nonverbal communication behaviors which can serve to enhance or deter patient compliance. As discussed in Chapter 6, nonverbal immediacy is the use of behaviors that create liking and a psychological closeness (e.g., eye contact, little physical distance between patient and provider, smiling, etc.) whereas nonimmediate behaviors include excessive distance between patient and provider, frowning, lack of eye contact, etc.). In fact, J. Burgoon, Pfau, Parrott, Birk, Coker, and M. Burgoon (1987) found that patient compliance was greatly enhanced when physicians exhibited greater similarity to the patient, communicated greater receptivity, composure, immediacy/affection, and were moderately formal. Further, patient satisfaction was also found to be related to the use of an affiliative nonverbal style and less dominant behaviors by the physician (Street & Buller, 1987).

There is a plethora of applied research indicating the importance of compliance at both the interpersonal and public health campaign levels. Some these include using strategies to get patients with border-line personality disorders to comply with general health care suggestions (Sansone, Bohinc, & Wiederman, 2015); as a means of persuading minority, low income, and underinsured patients to participate in colon cancer screening (Hunleth, Steinmetz, McQueen, & James, 2016); to increase hand hygiene behavior in the clinical context (King, Vlaev, Everett-Thomas, Fitzpatrick, Darzi, & Birnbach, 2016); and as a means to optimize treatment adherence for low health literacy patients living with HIV (Pellowski, Kalichman, & Grebler, 2016).

COMMUNICATION TRAITS AND HEALTH BEHAVIOR

As with most other communication contexts, health communication has also utilized certain communication traits to explain and predict both patient and provider behavior. Such research continues, as the attempt to account for predispositions toward communication in the health context has proved fruitful in improving the quality of health care delivery.

Locus of Control. The construct of locus of control was originally applied to health communication by Brenders (1989). He argued that perceptions of personal control have been linked to such health-related factors as life stress, coping with illness, and the success of preventative practices. Individuals with internal locus of control expectancies perceive that outcomes in their lives are due to their own purposive behavior and that they are in control of their destiny. Individuals with external locus of control expectancies perceive that outcomes in their lives are controlled by outside forces such as luck, chance, and fate (Lefcourt, 1982). The major assumption of this work is that "persons are likely to evaluate information and advice from within the context of their perceived control orientation" (Brenders, 1989, p. 119). People with internal control expectancies are more assertive, proactive, and autonomous in interpersonal situations. After reviewing the array of research on locus of control in the health communication context, Brenders (1989) concluded: (a) Internals are more receptive to health care information and advice. (b) Internals may respond poorly to treatment unless provided with specific information about procedures and a rationale. (c) Choose congruent control messages, for example, providing an internal control oriented patient with information that is relayed in a way that is consistent with specific recommendations for the patient to control their own destiny regarding the specific health concern. (d) The interactions between control beliefs, communication, and health care are likely to yield promising theory building and practical results in health communication.

Locus of control
A personality trait that concerns how people interpret outcomes in their life

Internal locus of control
A perception that the person has direct control over their lives and behaviors

External locus of control
A perception that the person perceives that their lives and behavior are controlled by others

Brenders' conclusions have been evidenced in more recent research. Avtgis and Polack (2007) found that patients with an internal health locus of control also reported greater quality of health information exchange with their provider and higher levels of perceived physician communication competence than patients reporting an external locus of control. Further, Avtgis, Brann, and Staggers (2006) reported that patients who report high internal control expectancies, low chance control expectancies (e.g., belief in chance or fate controlling outcomes), and low powerful other control expectancies (e.g., people who believe that practitioners or religious figures control outcomes) reported high levels of provider information giving. However, when separated between scheduled health care visits and emergency room visits, patients who report high chance control expectancies reported engaging in information-verifying (e.g., clarifying messages for accuracy) when in an emergency visit situation yet report little information giving (i.e., patient providing information to the provider) in the scheduled visit condition. Avtgis et al. (2006) concluded "the medical situation influences the relationship between information exchange and socio-emotional support. The influence of the medical situation is so great that it confounds the simple linear notion that the relationship between information exchange and locus of control is static in all medical exchange situations" (p. 236).

Communicator Style. Recall that communicator style (Chapter 4) may be viewed as an overall impression of a number of different styles: contentious, open, dramatic, dominant, precise, relaxed, friendly, attentive, and animated with the overall impression comprising the communicator image. For example, a person can create an affirming communicator style (e.g., relaxed, friendly, and attentive styles) or a non-affirming style (e.g., contentious and dominant styles) when interacting with others.

Communicator style has been used to study how patients' perceptions of their health care provider's style link to patient satisfaction. Buller and Buller (1987) have identified communicator styles such as affiliation (i.e., friendly, open, attentive, and relaxed styles) and control (i.e., dominant and contentious styles), finding that the more a physician used an affiliative communicator style and the less a physician used the control style the more satisfied the patient was with the experience. Cardello, Ray, and Pettey (1995) reported that physicians who were perceived as being more attentive and animated and less dominant and contentious were perceived as more empathetic. In a study of physician-executives, Garko (1994) reported that, when trying to influence their superiors, physician-executives use different styles based on the communicator style of their superior. More specifically, when the superior was perceived as having an attractive communicator style the physician-executive reported using the attentive, dramatic, friendly, open, and relaxed style when exerting upward influence. Superiors who were perceived as having an unattractive communication style resulted in the physician-executive using animated, contentious, dominant, and precise style when trying to influence their superior. Physician communicator style was also found to influence nurses' well-being. More specifically, V. Wheeless, L. Wheeless, and Riffle (1989) reported that physician responsiveness was positively related to nurses' compliance decision style, as opposed to an avoidance decision style, and negatively related to decision quickness. Finally, in a study looking at predictors of empathy in health science students, the friendly and relaxed communicator styles were significant predictors of the students' level of empathy (Brown, Boyle, Williams, A. Molloy, Palermo, McKenna, & L. Molloy, 2011). Overall, the communicator style construct does influence relational tactics and outcomes within health care.

Verbal Aggressiveness. Verbal aggressiveness within the health context is extremely prevalent. According to Steadman, Mulvey, Monohan, Robbins, Applebaum, and Grisso (1998), 90 percent of all staff nurses experience at least one episode of abusive anger, condescension, or being globally rejected by a physician every 60 to 90 days. Further, 48 percent of nurses have been verbally and/or physically assaulted within the last year (Lanza, Zeiss, & Reardan, 2005). What contributes to this verbally aggressive culture? Nurses reported avoidance in reporting verbally aggressive incidence with 44 percent considering verbal aggression to be part of the job (Lanza et al., 2005). Structurally, there are verbal trigger events that lead to the onset of patient verbal aggressiveness. Wigley (2009) defines verbal trigger events as factors that, when present, result in an onset of verbal and potentially physical aggression. Utilizing this framework, Avtgis and Madlock (2008) identified the following verbal trigger events/ situations specific to health care; patient exhaustion and stress, frustration with the managed care industry, patient distrust in the provider and health care in general, and the culture of patient-oriented consumerism with regard to health care. Each of these trigger situations suggests that the uncertainty-laden environment that exists within the health context has a great influence on health communication behavior on behalf of both the patient and the provider.

HEALTH BELIEFS MODEL

Developed in the early 1950's, the health belief model (HBM) is considered one of the first systematic, theory-based research efforts in health communication and one of the most accepted models of behavioral change specific to health and safety issues. The first research effort on the HBM attempted to identify factors that underlie decisions to get a chest x-ray for the early detection of tuberculosis. The health belief model permits researchers to explain and predict complaint behavior and thereby allow people to control their behavior. One of the originators of the theory stated: "The early researchers concerned with the health belief model would work cooperatively, build on each other's work, develop a theory that would include a heavy component of motivation and the perceptional world of the behaving individual…toward developing a theory not only useful in explaining a particular program problem, but also adaptable to other problems" (Rosenstock, 1974, p. 329).

The HBM is composed of five components that may influence a person to take some type of action (e.g., to lessen the chances of getting a disease or suffering a health-related malady). These components are *perceived susceptibility, perceived seriousness or severity, perceived benefits, perceived barriers to taking action,* and *cues to action.*

Perceived susceptibility refers to the perceived subjective risks of contracting a disease or health-related condition (Rosenstock, 1974). Some people (low susceptibles) believe it is very unlikely that they would contract a particular disease or health-related condition. Other people (high susceptibles) perceive that it is very likely or inevitable that they will experience a disease or health condition. In between high and low susceptibles are the moderate susceptibles who operate on statistical probabilities when assessing their perception of susceptibility (e.g., "my mother and grandmother had Alzheimer's disease, therefore it is quite probable that I, too, will likely develop this condition").

Perceived seriousness or severity refers to an evaluation of the types of impact that potential health and safety conditions would have on our lives, emotional states, and the lives of families. Such assessments of severity include physical, emotional, and even financial assessments. This may include asking questions such as, "How much pain, suffering, and discomfort would I experience if I experience this condition?" "How will I cope with the financial costs due to loss of work or costly medical bills?" and "What emotional effects will the condition have on the rest of my family?"

Perceived benefits of taking action involve the assessment of the possible benefits of performing the recommended behaviors to lessen the chances of being affected by the health or safety threat. If the susceptibility of getting the condition is perceived to be high, the individual assesses the benefits of taking some type of action to prevent the disease. In essence, the individual performs a cost-benefit analysis. Decisions are often influenced by norms and group pressure, as well as recommendations by health professionals and physicians (Rosenstock, 1974). If the perceived benefits of taking action outweigh the perceived barriers, the likelihood of adopting the recommended preventative actions increases.

Perceived barriers to taking action refers to the assessment as to whether the suggested recommendations or preventative action will be expensive, painful, upsetting, time consuming, or inconvenient. If the individual perceives a high probability of encountering these conditions, then he or she may not adopt the recommended behaviors that could lead to better health and safety outcomes. If the perceived barriers of taking action outweigh the perceived benefits, the likelihood of adopting the recommended preventative actions decreases. Consider the option for the treatment of an opioid addiction. The patient in this case will have to weigh options of in-patient versus out-patient treatment, the types of psychological counseling options (individual versus group), pharmaceutical interventions (whether or not to use medications and if so, which ones [e.g., naltrexone, methadone, buprenorphine]), as well as the cost associated with each of these choices.

Cues to action are persuasive devices intended to motivate people to adopt or incorporate behaviors that could lead to a desired goal, such as better health or an increase in safety. The assumption is that, in addition to the individual's beliefs, certain health-related actions might need to be prompted or triggered. These cues to action are "the specific stimuli necessary to trigger appropriate health behavior (Mattson, 1999, p. 243). Cues to action within the health context can be internal or external in nature. Internal cues are more intrapersonal. That is, they are messages one sends to oneself about a health-related concern. For example, a person who chronically drives while legally drunk may have a close call in terms of an accident with another vehicle. Upon reflecting on this potentially life-altering experience, the person decides that they will no longer drive after drinking. External cues to action are communicated by someone or something outside of the person. For example, a conversation with a physician, friends, parents, media messages, postcards from practitioners, etc. all can serve to trigger changes in behaviors such as smoking cessation, breast cancer screening, and sexually transmitted infection testing, to name just a few (Chew, Palmer, & Kim, 1998; Rosenstock, 1974; Witte, Stokols, Ituarte, & Schneider, 1993).

The HBM has been one of the most utilized frameworks in health communication research. For example, researchers have used it in a study designed to promote the use of bicycle safety helmets. The goal of the study was to investigate how the HBM's perceived threat factor and cues to action influenced bicycle safety helmet practices (Witte et al., 1993). In interviews with parents, researchers asked, "How often do you worry about your child being involved in a bicycle accident?" and "Do you believe that most head injuries resulting from bicycle accidents are (serious/not serious)?" to measure perceived susceptibility and perceived severity. In addition, the researchers used several external cues to action, including a community event that demonstrated bicycle safety, public service announcements on the radio about bicycle safety, direct mail brochures designed to increase perceptions of susceptibility and severity of head injury when not wearing a helmet, phone messages that presented similar information, and bicycle helmet coupons redeemable for $10 off the price of a helmet distributed through the mail.

The results of the study generally supported the HBM. Those individuals receiving the external cues to action (e.g., the community event, mass media announcements, the telephone message) perceived bicycling injuries to be more serious and more likely to occur to their children than those not receiving the cues to action (Witte et al., 1993). Parents who perceived greater threat of bicycle injury had more favorable attitudes toward using bicycle helmets, were more likely to buy helmets for their children, and were more likely to insist that their children wear the bicycle helmet. In addition, the more cues to action received, the greater the perception of threat.

The HBM has also been used to guide research efforts designed to develop interpersonal communication strategies to prevent drug abuse by health care professionals and the elderly. The problems of impaired health care professionals are quite significant, with the incidence of health care professionals suffering from addiction to drugs and alcohol greatly exceeding that of the general population (Beisecker, 1991). The elderly are considered another at-risk group particularly susceptible to abuses of prescription and nonprescription medications. Beisecker (1991) recommended using the HBM to develop appropriate prevention strategies for both health care professionals and the elderly because the model focuses on two major needs of those groups, "education regarding the seriousness of substance abuse and a feeling of vulnerability and susceptibility to addiction" (p. 247). More specifically, it is recommended that the HBM cues to action be in the form of interpersonal contact cues for at-risk health care professionals, and that health care counselors provide the interpersonal contact cues for the elderly. The impact of another important HBM cue to action, a television program, was tested to determine its influence on healthy eating practices. A one-hour television program, *Eat Smart*, was used in a naturalistic setting to determine its impact on healthy eating habits (Chew et al., 1998). The results of the study suggested that those individuals who watched the program perceived increased health benefits and reduced health barriers to healthy eating habits. Further, participants who viewed the program became more concerned about food fitness, had more confidence in the recommendations about healthy eating, and reduced their consumption of unhealthy foods after exposure to the program.

Marifran Mattson (1999) focused on interpersonal communication itself as a critical cue to action. The study explored the influence of a counseling session during HIV testing. It was thought that this interpersonal interaction would be especially useful in influencing individuals to change risky sexual behaviors and to comply with the recommendations for engaging in safer sex practices. Participants received an interpersonal counseling session designed to increase their awareness of the severity and their susceptibility to HIV/AIDS. Mattson measured several HBM factors, including risk appraisal (perceived severity of HIV/AIDS and perceived susceptibility to the disease), perceived benefits and barriers to taking action (employing safer sex practices such as using condoms), and perceived self-efficacy (perceptions of their ability to perform the safer sex recommendations). The results supported the HBM. Participant perceptions of their susceptibility to HIV/AIDS after participation in the interpersonal counseling session were moderately related to their decisions to comply with the safer sex recommendations (primarily using condoms). In addition, after the counseling session, participants also perceived that the benefits of engaging in safer sex practices outweighed the barriers to engaging in safer sex practices. This research suggests that we move toward "reconceptualizing the HBM in favor of centralizing the role of communication cues to action" (p. 258). Thus, it is recommended that the cues to action, originally located on the periphery of the HBM, be moved to a more central position in the model given its major influence on behavior change.

UNCERTAINTY MANAGEMENT

Uncertainty management theory Explains how people react to health-related uncertainty

Uncertainty management theory (UMT) was developed by Dale Brashers (2001a) as a reaction to the simplistic way that the term uncertainty has been conceptualized in communication theory. He believed that uncertainty is a multifaceted concept that can be more valuable and serve many more functions if it is not treated as an aversive state that needs to be reduced (see uncertainty reduction theory in Chapter 8). Instead, Brashers believes that although UMT was developed to predict people's experience with uncertainty (i.e., post-positivist perspective), he readily acknowledges that the experience of uncertainty is also a situation-based phenomenon (Brashers, Goldsmith, & Hsieh, 2002).

UMT was originally conceptualized to explain how people react to health-related uncertainty (Brashers, 2001b; Brashers, Hsieh, Neidig, & Reynolds, 2006). According to Afifi and Matsunaga (2008), the three features of UMT consist of: (a) the meaning and the experience of uncertainty, (b) the role of an individual's response to uncertainty, and (c) the psychological and communicative strategies used to manage uncertainty. Unlike other theories that conceptualize uncertainty, a key term with UMT is "management of uncertainty" as opposed to "reduction of uncertainty." In fact, Brashers (2001a) argued that the equation of more "information = less uncertainty" is false. He argued that information and uncertainty are not unidimensional constructs, but that both are separate constructs. The key question is, "How much information is enough?" The concept of "enough" varies from person to person. Therefore, Brashers (2001a, 2001b) believed that when people feel insecure about the amount of knowledge they possess or the amount of knowledge available, uncertainty is present. Simply put, "abandon the assumption that uncertainty will produce anxiety" (Brashers, 2001a, p. 477). A person, when experiencing uncertainty, can experience a plethora of other emotions. For example, consider a student who is on the border between receiving a course grade of C– or D+. After the final exam the student's lack of effort in contacting the instructor about the course grade (i.e., little information about the final grade) may in fact serve as a comforting feeling, and the uncertainty may give the student "hope" of a better grade. This can also be seen in a person who sends out a resume for a position, then after one or two weeks does not follow up with a phone call to the employer to determine if they are still being considered for the position.

Uncertainty is ever present in health-related issues. In a study investigating the effects of illness on uncertainty, Brashers (2001b) investigated how HIV patients experience and manage uncertainty. Today, due to modern medicine and the reduced stigma associated with the disease, the diagnosis of being HIV positive is not thought of as the death sentence that it once was in the 1980s and 1990s. In terms of UMT, patients may actively seek out medical practitioners who provide them with uncertainty in an effort to give patients a sense of hope and a chance of some other outcome (e.g., controlling disease progression or cure). This provides an alternative to the certainty that the disease will eventually progress. Thus, uncertainty, in this case, can provide a sense of control and optimism (see Seligman, 1990). It has been revealed in a variety of medical studies that hope can prolong life and slow down the progression of the disease (Frank & Frank, 1991).

Another key component of UMT is that our reaction to uncertainty directly affects the influence of uncertainty on our psychological well-being. For instance, if a person interprets uncertainty in a negative way (i.e., negative emotional response) uncertainty is seen as a dangerous state that should be avoided whenever possible. On the other hand, when uncertainty is perceived as a positive experience (i.e., positive emotional response) uncertainty becomes

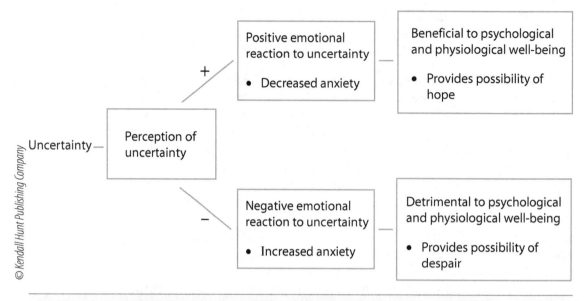

FIGURE 14.2 A MODEL OF UNCERTAINTY MANAGEMENT THEORY (UMT).

beneficial to our physiological and psychological well-being. Figure 14.2 illustrates this process.

Research on information seeking has provided scholars with an abundance of findings that primarily focus on the premise that the more information we seek, the more control it provides us. This process has been described from a skill development perspective as a way to gain control over a particular situation (Cegala & Lenzmeir-Broz, 2003) as well as a personality characteristic that predisposes people to seek information (Lefcourt, 1981). However, UMT holds that our perceptions of uncertainty (positive versus negative) directly affect the strategies and types of communication that we engage in and expose ourselves to. The following experiment will illustrate this point. Ask ten people you know, if they had a choice, would they want to know the types of diseases that they will develop in the future? Chances are that some people will respond "yes." In this case, uncertainty is perceived as a negative state that needs to be reduced to be effectively maintained. By "maintained," we mean that every person has a level of uncertainty that they feel comfortable managing. Some people can only effectively manage uncertainty if it is totally reduced, whereas others can effectively manage some levels of uncertainty. Still others feel comfortable in managing high levels of uncertainty. For these people, uncertainty is seen as a positive state that needs to be maintained, as it generates less anxiety to the person than knowing about the specific disease they might develop.

In the health care context, people do not simply either seek information or not, and Brashers (2001a) provided three additional ways in which people can interpret information regarding illness. First, some people who live with chronic disease or chronic states of uncertainty adapt to the state of chronic uncertainty (e.g., it is something that I have to deal with, so I must get used to it). Second, social networks consisting of family and friends as well as social role models, such as people acting in prosocial ways, may serve to aid in the management of high uncertainty. For example, a person with a spinal cord injury can rely on family and friends but may also rely on other people who have suffered a spinal cord injury. This experience is reflected by the late actor Christopher Reeve, who dedicated his life to helping people with spinal cord injuries, as well as by Michael J. Fox, who helps people cope with Parkinson's disease, and the late Princess Diana, who worked for land mine extraction throughout the world. Third, we engage in uncertainty management at a metalevel. That is, we manage our uncertainty in other areas. This is not to suggest that there is only so much management that we have to spread around (i.e., zero-sum game approach). Rather, our psychological efforts, in a proactive way, naturally determine where our uncertainty management efforts are needed (i.e., vital for effective management) and which are discretionary (i.e., desired but not vital). Second, through time and experience, people develop the flexibility to discern what information is trustworthy and relevant and what information is not in the management of uncertainty.

As noted earlier, research using UMT has been conducted primarily within the health context (see, for example, Brashers et al., 2006). UMT is in its early stages and, as such, has great potential for further testing and theoretical extension to other contexts. For example, within the family context, how does UMT explain issues in at-risk marriages? Sibling relationships? Stepfamilies? The theory has been questioned as to whether UMT can be rooted in both post-positivistic and interpretive paradigms (Afifi & Matsunaga, 2008). However, as discussed in Chapter 2 (see Craig, 1999), the constitutive metamodel of communication theory suggests that the blending of theoretical perspectives is something that is necessary for future communication theory-building efforts.

DIFFUSION OF INNOVATION

Diffusion of innovation theory (DIT) was forwarded by Everett Rogers (1983). DIT is concerned with how innovations, primarily new technology, are adopted and implemented by people. This theory is especially well-suited for the field of health communication because it provides a comprehensive theoretical framework through which to explain and predict the effectiveness of any given health campaign and the adoption of health technologies. In fact, dozens of studies have utilized DIT to explain a variety of health-related campaigns (see, for example, Kreps, 2009).

There are four main elements of DIT: (1) the innovation, (2) the channel through which the innovation is communicated, (3) over a particular time period, and (4) including members of a social system (Rogers, 1983). Now let's look more in depth at each of these elements.

Innovation. Innovations are believed to contain five attributes: relative advantage (i.e., the degree to which the new innovation is superior to existing options), compatibility (i.e., the degree of ease to which the new innovation is integrated within existing products or processes), complexity (i.e., the degree

Innovation Innovations contain five attributes: relative advantage, compatibility, complexity, reliability, and observability

to which the new innovation is understandable and usable), reliability (i.e., the degree to which the new innovation can consistently perform over time), and observability (i.e., the degree to which the new innovation performs as promised with measurable outcomes).

Communication channel. According to Rogers (1983), communication channel reflects the means through which messages about the innovation travel from one person to another. According to DIT theory, mass communication channels are believed to be most effective in bringing awareness and knowledge about a new innovation with interpersonal channels being more influential in forming, changing, or reinforcing attitudes toward the innovation. It is believed that most people evaluate new innovations through discussion with peers or respected others, not based on empirical data or scientific evidence.

Time. The element of time involved in the new innovation adoption process involves adoption decisiveness, timeliness of the decision (e.g., some people adopt new innovations sooner than others), and the rate of adoption or the time it takes to make its way through any given social system (Rogers, 1983). This time based decision making process involves the following steps: knowledge (i.e., becoming aware that the new innovation exists), persuasion (i.e., attitudes toward the new innovation), decision (i.e., whether or not the new innovation will be acquired), implementation (i.e., degree to which the new innovation is easily integrated into existing processes or procedures), and confirmation (i.e., evidence that the new innovation is as effective as anticipated).

Social system. The social system element is "a set of interrelated units that are engaged in joint problem-solving to accomplish a goal" (Rogers, 1983, p. 120). The composition of the system can either accelerate or hinder the diffusion of the new innovation. Similar to the two-step flow theory discussed in Chapter 12, there are particular individuals who serve as opinion leaders or those people who can influence others to either accept or reject the new innovation.

In terms of DIT and health communication, there are applications to public health campaigns and new technology. For example, the integration of electronic health records and personal health records has significantly changed the patient-provider dynamic. Research indicates that this new type of record keeping can serve to undermine the quality of the relationship between the patient and the provider (Avtgis, Polack, & Liberman, in press; Avtgis, Polack, Staggers, & Wiecorek, 2011). For example, generating the electronic health records requires the provider to enter information into the computer during the patient's presentation of their symptoms. This creates changes in verbal and nonverbal behavior (e.g., the provider faces the computer screen and is focused on inputting data as opposed to facing the patient and being entirely attentive to the needs of the patient). In terms of public health, DIT has successfully been applied to engaging students in school-wellness initiatives (Harringer, Lu, McKyer, E., Lisako, Pruitt, & Goodson, 2014) and to reducing the research-practice gap in autism intervention. That is, making sure that cutting-edge research on autism is quickly integrated into practitioners' treatment approaches (Dingfelder & Mandell, 2011).

TRANSTHEORETICAL MODEL

The transtheoretical model (TTM) was developed utilizing the stages of change framework regarding health-related issues (DiClemente, Prochaska, Fairhurst, Velicer, Rossi, & Velasquez, 1991; Prochaska, 2013; Prochaska & Velicer, 1997; Prochaska, Wright, & Velicer, 2008). These five stages consist of: the pre-contemplation stage (i.e., people who are not intending to change behavior in the next six months), the contemplation stage (i.e., people who are intending to change their behavior within the next six months), the preparation stage (i.e., people who intend to change their behavior within the next 30 days), the action stage (i.e., people who have actually made changes to the behavior), and the maintenance stage (i.e., people who continue engaging in the altered behavior). According to DiClemente et al. (1991), these stages have relationships with other measures of TTM such as processes of change, decisional balance, and self-efficacy (Fava, Velicer, & Abrams, 1995).

Processes of change reflect actual strategies that people engage in and contain both experiential and behavioral dimensions. Experiential processes consist of "consciousness raising, dramatic relief, environmental reevaluation, self-reevaluation, and social liberation" (Prochaska et al., 2008, p. 563). Behavioral processes consist of "stimulus control, counter conditioning, reinforcement management, self-liberation, and helping relationships" (Prochaska et al. p. 563). Decisional balance refers to the pros and cons reflecting cognitive and motivational factors in the decision making process (i.e., instrumental benefits to self, instrumental benefits to others, approval from self, approval from others, instrumental costs to self, instrumental costs to others, disapproval from self, and disapproval from others) (Janis & Mann, 1977). More specifically, people perceive more cons than pros to behavioral change before they engage in the behavioral change. On the other hand, people who have engaged in actual behavior change processes switch that perception to perceiving more pros than cons to such change. Similar patterns across stages were observed regarding self-efficacy. That is, self-efficacy increases as people move through actual behavioral change (Janis & Mann, 1977).

The transtheoretical model has been successfully utilized in many interventions for at-risk behaviors that include a variety of addictive behaviors (DiClemente & Prochaska, 1998), alcohol abstinence (Carbonari & DiClemente, 2000), smoking cessation (Fava, Velicer, & Abrahms, 1995; Ham & Lee, 2007; Velicer, Prochaska, Fava, Norman, & Redding, 1998), weight management (Johnson, Paiva, Cummins, Johnson, Dyment, Wright, Prochaska, Prochaska, & Sherman, 2008), exercise (Marcus & Simkin, 1994), organ donation (Morgan & Miller, 2002), and HIV prevention (Prochaska, Redding, Harlow, Rossi, & Veliver, 1994). However, similar to most theories, the transtheoretical model is not without its detractors. More specifically, the TTM has been criticized for its lack of empirical evidence (West, 2005) and lack of predictive validity (Sutton, 2001).

Transtheoretical model
Consists of five stages including the pre-contemplation stage, the contemplation stage, the preparation stage, the action stage, and the maintenance stage

SUMMARY

The health communication context continues to be one of the fastest growing areas of research in the field of communication studies. This chapter discusses the various ways in which health communication has been conceptualized. Whether it be interpersonal, organization, or mass and mediated approaches (to name but a few), the vast landscape of health within society and globally continues to intrigue researchers and practitioners alike. We covered the functions that communication serves within the patient/provider dyad and discussed the various influences on that relationship. Whether it concerns issues of relational control, mutual influence, communication traits, power status, or nonverbal behavior, there are myriad factors that have to be accounted for in efforts to improve health care and the patient/provider relationship.

Several models were presented regarding perceptions of health-related risks and ways to create effective health-related campaigns to inform and persuade publics to engage in wellness behavior. Some of these approaches include the health belief model, uncertainty management, and diffusion of innovation, all of which try to explain, describe, predict, and control health-related behavior. Regardless of the approach or theory we choose to focus on, researchers will continue theory-building efforts with the goal of improving communication and quality of life regarding health-related outcomes.

KEY TERMS

Communication channel	Innovation	Social system
Cooperation	Internal locus of control	Time
Counsel	Locus of control	Transtheorhetical model
Diagnosis	Mutuality model	Uncertainty management theory
Dominance	Paternalistic model	
Education	Power	
External locus of control	Redundancy	

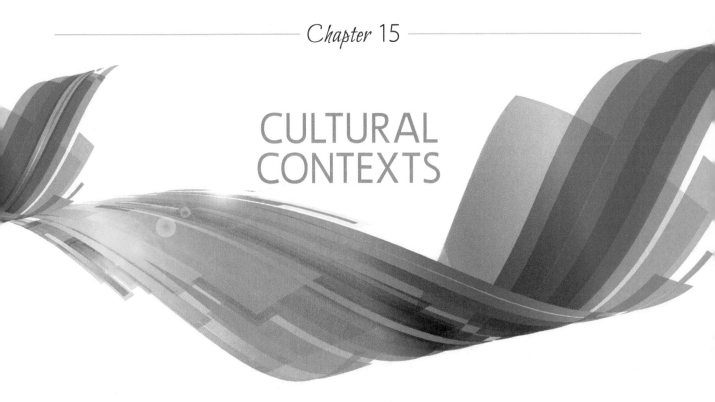

Chapter 15

CULTURAL CONTEXTS

Culture can be defined as "a learned system of meanings that fosters a particular sense of shared identity and community among its group members. It is a complex frame of reference that consists of patterns of traditions, beliefs, values, norms, symbols, and meanings that are shared by varying degrees by interacting" (Ting-Toomey, 2005, pp. 71–72). The study of cultural influence on how people relate is perhaps one of the most important areas of study for communication theorists. Partly due to technological advancements and economic pursuits, the world has become much more pluralistic in nature. It is the responsibility of any civilized society to investigate what makes cultures differ and to explain such differences in ways that promote mutual understanding from which relationships can be maintained and fostered. In many ways, the intercultural theorist serves as an ambassador because the theories that are developed help people from different cultures work through issues that, in earlier times, may have resulted in conflict or distrust. The theories presented in this chapter represent some of the most developed and comprehensive intercultural theories in the field of communication studies and have been applied for understanding many cultures throughout the world.

HOFSTEDE'S DIMENSIONS OF NATIONAL CULTURE

At the outset, it is important to understand that Hofstede's dimensions of national culture (DNC) is not a communication theory, per se: it is a theory

Dimensions of national culture A theory of how national cultures differ from each other

351

of how national cultures differ, and provides a language for describing and explaining why people from different countries sometimes find each other so difficult to understand and work with. As such, this theory has an extraordinarily powerful influence on how social scientists from multiple disciplines, including communication, understand and study culture, promoting the development of more predictive theories, such as face negotiation theory in communication (reviewed later in this chapter). Indeed, the introduction of the DNC in Hofstede's initial (1980) book, *Culture's Consequences*, has been described as shaping the central themes, structure, and controversies of comparative cross-cultural studies (Peterson, 2003). Accordingly, the DNC is presented here as an essential thoery for understanding communication in diverse cultural contexts.

In the late 1970s, Hofstede conducted surveys with more than 116,000 IBM employees from 72 countries, assessing values, beliefs, norms, and self-descriptions (Hofstede, 1980). From quantitative analysis of this data, he argued that many national differences could be explained with four major dimensions of national culture (Hofstede, Hofstede, & Minkov, 2010; Minkov & Hofstede, 2011). These dimensions were individualism-collectivism, power distance, uncertainty avoidance, and masculinity-femininity. Individualism-collectivism describes a distinction between cultures with a "loose-knit" social structure in which individuals are expected to look out only for themselves and their immediate families (individualistic) and cultures in which individuals are tightly connected to extended family or other in-groups with an expectation of mutual care and loyalty (collectivistic). National cultures especially high in individualism include the United States, Australia, Great Britain, Canada, and Hungary, whereas cultures especially high in collectivism (or low in individualism) include Colombia, Venezuela, Panama, Ecuador, and Guatemala. Power distance is a dimension representing how much the less powerful members of a society expect and accept that power is unequally distributed. In high power distance cultures, people accept hierarchy and disparity. In low power distance cultures, people want differences in power to be justified when necessary, and equalized when they are not. National cultures high in power distance include Malaysia, Slovakia, Guatemala, Panama, and the Philippines, whereas those low in power distance include Ireland, New Zealand, Denmark, Israel, and Austria. The United States exhibits an intermediate level of power distance. Uncertainty avoidance is a dimension representing how comfortable cultures are with uncertainty and ambiguity. Countries high in uncertainty avoidance are uncomfortable with the unpredictability of life, and try to control it with rigid codes of belief and behavior. Countries low in uncertainty avoidance are more accepting of unpredictability, and more relaxed about what people believe and how they behave. Cultures high in uncertainty avoidance include those of Greece, Portugal, Guatemala, Uruguay, and Russia, whereas cultures low in uncertainty avoidance include Hong Kong, Sweden, Denmark, Jamaica, and Singapore. United States culture is intermediate in uncertainty avoidance. Masculinity-femininity describes a dimension between "tough" and "tender" cultures. Masculine cultures value assertiveness, competition, success, heroism, and material rewards. Feminine cultures value modesty, cooperation and

Individualism-collectivism
A dimension of national culture distinguishing between cultures with a "loose-knit" social structure in which individuals are expected to look out only for themselves and their immediate families (individualistic) and cultures in which individuals are tightly connected to extended family or other in-groups with an expectation of mutual care and loyalty (collectivistic)

Power distance
A dimension of national culture that represents how much the less powerful members of a society expect and accept that power is unequally distributed

Uncertainty avoidance
A dimension of national culture that represents how comfortable cultures are with uncertainty and ambiguity

Masculinity-femininity
A dimension of national culture that represents the extent to which a culture is "tough" (i.e., masculine) versus "tender" (feminine)

consensus, caring, and quality of life. Cultures high in masculinity include those of Slovakia, Japan, Hungary, Austria, and Venezuela, whereas cultures high in femininity include Denmark, the Netherlands, Latvia, Norway, and Sweden. The United States has an intermediate score on this dimension, combining elements of both masculine and feminine cultures.

Between the initial book in 1980, and a revised edition in 2001, more than 800 studies tested the validity of Hofstede's dimensions in various ways. These studies included several massive-scale, multi-national research efforts similar to Hofstede's original work (Chinese Culture Connection, 1987; House, Hanges, Javidan, Dorfman, & Gupta, 2004). Research continued unabated between 2001 and a third edition of Hofstede's book in 2010, which included a study with data from 90 countries (Minkov, 2009). Collectively, this huge body of research has supported the addition of two other dimensions: long-term orientation and indulgence-restraint (Hofstede, Hofstede, & Minkov, 2010). **Long-term orientation** describes variation in the way cultures regard the past and present versus the future. Societies low in long-term orientation hang on to norms and traditions based in history and are suspicious of change, whereas societies high in long-term orientation look toward the future, emphasizing modern education and judicious use of resources. Cultures high in long-term orientation include South Korea, Taiwan, Japan, China, and the Ukraine, whereas cultures low in long-term orientation include Nigeria, Trinidad, Egypt, Ghana, and Puerto Rico. The United States is intermediate on long-term orientation, but closer to low long-term orientation countries than to high long-term orientation countries. **Indulgence-restraint** describes how societies vary in their response to the natural human desire to enjoy life and have fun. Cultures high in indulgence allow relatively unrestrained gratification of these desires, whereas cultures high in restraint attempt to suppress these desires and regulate them through social norms and sanctions. Cultures high in indulgence include Venezuela, Mexico, Puerto Rico, and El Salvador, whereas cultures high in restraint include Albania, Ukraine, Latvia, Egypt, and Pakistan. The United States is intermediate on indulgence-restraint, but closer to high indulgence countries than high restraint countries.

Starting in the first edition of his book, Hofstede described the dimensions in ways that incorporated communication behavior, or pointed to their implications for communication. For example, power distance was recognized from the outset as a dimension that influences how superiors and subordinates (e.g., employees and their supervisors) communicate with each other. In low power distance cultures, supervisors are more likely to solicit and receive employee ideas, recommendations, criticism, and other feedback, whereas in high power distance cultures communication between supervisors and employees flows largely downward from the more powerful supervisor to the less powerful employee (Hofstede, 1980; Hofstede et al., 2010). However, there has also been considerable research with a specific focus on testing the influence of various dimensions on multiple aspects of communication. Some of this research is captured by a recent meta-analysis (Merkin, Taras, & Steel, 2014) in which the authors synthesized the results of 60 empirical studies examining

Long-term orientation
A dimension of national culture that distinguishes between cultures that hold on to norms and traditions based in history and are suspicious of change (short-term orientation) versus cultures that look toward the future (long-term orientation), emphasizing modern education and judicious use of resources

Indulgence-restraint
A dimension of national culture that describes variation in cultural response to the human desire to enjoy life and have fun

relationships between the four original dimensions and patterns of communication behavior. To be included in the meta-analysis, the relationships had to have been examined in multiple studies. The results showed that: "(1) individualism is positively related to direct communication and self-promotion, and negatively related to sensitivity and face-saving concerns and indirect communication and the propensity to use deception; (2) high power distance is positively related to sensitivity and face-saving concerns and indirect communication and negatively related to a propensity to interrupt; (3) masculinity is positively related to a self-promoting communication style and direct communication and negatively related to sensitivity and face-saving concerns; and (4) uncertainty avoidance is positively related to both sensitivity and face-saving concerns" (Merkin, Taras, & Steel, 2014, p. 1). The impact of the long-term orientation and indulgence-restraint dimensions on communication were not examined because there were fewer studies examining these relationships, but they will likely receive more attention over time.

FACE NEGOTIATION THEORY

Face negotiation theory
A theory that explains how culture influences our behavior during conflict

Face negotiation theory (FNT) was developed by Stella Ting-Toomey (1988) to explain how culture influences our behavior during conflict. The theory helps to explain why it can be difficult for people from different cultures to understand and respond appropriately to each other's behavior when dealing with conflict issues, but in the process also sheds useful insight on the shared human concern for respect and consideration from others. The theory contends that national culture (individualism and collectivism) influences how people view themselves and others (self-construal and face concerns), and that these in turn predict how they typically handle conflict interactions (conflict styles). This set of relationships as explained by the theory is depicted in Figure 15.1 and described below.

CULTURE

The primary cultural distinction made by FNT is between individualistic cultures and collectivistic cultures, as described in Hofstede's dimensions of national culture (see above). People from individualistic cultures tend to emphasize the importance of the individual's interests over the group's interests and focus on their own feelings as opposed to the collective feelings of the group. People from collectivistic cultures tend to emphasize the importance of the group and group goals over the individual and individual goals. FNT contends that these dimensions have specific implications for conflict behavior, because of their impact on how people think about themselves and others.

SELF-CONSTRUAL

As previously noted, Hofstede's dimensions of national culture are intended to describe cultures, not individuals. Indeed, within an individualistic culture, there can be wide variation in the tendency to think and behave in ways that privilege the individual over the group, so that some people in an individualistic culture are more collectivistic in the way they personally think, feel, and act. Similarly, within a collectivistic culture, there are people whose personal orientation aligns better with an individualistic culture. However, it is also difficult to explain why culture affects communication behavior at the personal level without assuming that culture influences how people think, feel, and act. In FNT, the explanatory link is provided by self-construal, or way of seeing oneself relative to others (Markus & Kitayama, 1991, 1998). An independent self-construal involves viewing oneself as unique, with an individual repertoire of cognitions, emotions, and motivations that are separate from those of other people. An interdependent self-construal involves viewing oneself as intertwined in relationships with other people, sharing their cognitions, emotions, and motivations. These two types of self-construals are not mutually exclusive. For example, a person could have a biconstrual orientation (i.e., high on both independent and interdependent self-construals), independent orientation (i.e., high on independent and low on interdependent self-construals), interdependent orientation (i.e., person low on independent and high on interdependent self-construals), ambivalent orientation (i.e., person low on independent and interdependent self-construals), or other combination (involving moderate levels of one or both self-construals). For FNT, the most important observation is that people tend to have more independent and less interdependent self-construals in individualistic cultures (such as the United States), whereas people from collectivist cultures (such as Japan) tend to have more interdependent and less independent self-construals (Oetzel & Ting-Toomey, 2003). For that reason, FNT links cultural-level individualism and collectivism with personal-level (or construal-level) independence and interdependence.

FACE CONCERNS

Self-construals are in turn predicted to influence face concerns. In FNT, face is defined as "the claimed sense of favorable social self-worth and/or projected other-worth in a public situation" (Oetzel, Garcia, & Ting-Toomey, 2008). In other words, it is an image of ourselves or others as worthwhile for which we seek confirmation during interaction (Goffman, 1959; Brown and Levinson, 1987; see Politeness Theory in Ch. 5). Facework refers to the "specific verbal and nonverbal behaviors that we engage in to maintain or restore face loss and to uphold and honor face gain" (Ting-Toomey, 2005, p. 73). Facework allows us to avoid or try to repair face threats, which include any potential or actual damage to face that may occur during interaction. For example, if you believe yourself to be intelligent, you will engage in verbal and nonverbal behaviors that reflect this belief about yourself. If someone "talks down" to you, this constitutes a face threat. If someone else jumps in to observe that you have a lot of knowledge and expertise, this is a type of facework. Face loss occurs when people treat us in ways that are inconsistent with, or produce damage to, the self-image we are trying to project, and facework is not utilized or is unsuccessful in restoring face. Face gain occurs when people treat us in ways that enhance our existing self-image. As you can probably conclude, culture plays a central role in the formation of identities as well as the behaviors we enact to protect any threats to our face.

Self-construal A way of seeing oneself relative to others

Independent self-construal Viewing oneself as unique, with an individual repertoire of cognitions, emotions, and motivations that are separate from those of other people

Interdependent self-construal Viewing oneself as intertwined in relationships with other people, sharing their cognitions, emotions, and motivations

Biconstrual orientation An orientation that is based on high independent and high interdependent self-construal

Independent orientation An orientation that is based on high independent and low interdependent self-construal

Interdependent orientation An orientation that is based on high interdependent and low independent self-construal

Ambivalent orientation An orientation that is based on low independent and low interdependent self-construal

Face The claimed sense of favorable social self-worth and/or projected other-worth in a public situation

Facework Specific verbal and nonverbal behaviors that we engage in to maintain or restore face loss and to uphold and honor face

Face threat Potential or actual damage to face

Face loss Occurs when we are treated by others in ways that threaten our face, or when our own behavior produces face threat

Face gain Occurs when we are treated by others in ways that enhance our face, or when our own behavior produces face enhancement

Self-face concern The degree to which we are concerned with our own face needs during a conflict episode

Other-face concern The degree to which we are concerned with the face of the other party in a conflict episode

Mutual-face concern The degree to which we are simultaneously concerned for both our own face and that of others

Dominating style A conflict style that involves achieving personal goals without regard to the interests of the other party

Avoiding style A conflict style that involves avoiding discussion of the conflict issue, and may take the form of avoiding the opposing party or conflict situation

Obliging style A conflict style that prioritizes concern for the other party's position and interests above and beyond personal interests and goals

Compromising style A conflict style that involves conceding some personal interests and goals while attaining others in the effort to reach an equitable settlement

Consistent with other theories of face, identity, image, and interaction, FNT assumes that concern for face, and efforts to protect and enhance face, are universal. But consistent with its emphasis on cultural differences, FNT makes a distinction between self-face concern, or being concerned with our own face needs during conflict and other-face concern, or concern for the face of others in the conflict situation, especially "opposing" others. In addition, there can be mutual-face concern, when we are simultaneously concerned for both our own face and that of others.

FNT connects concern for self-face with independent self-construal, and concern for other-face and mutual-face with interdependent self-construal. To the extent that people view themselves as unique and separate from others, being more concerned with their own social self-worth is a natural consequence. Similarly, to the extent that people view themselves as intertwined with others through relationships, being more concerned with the social self-worth of others is the natural outcome. In this way, FNT connects culture, which influences self-construal, to face concern.

CONFLICT STYLES

The final piece of FNT is behavior during conflict. Several scholars have made similar distinctions between conflict styles, or general approaches that people take to interaction with others during conflict (see, for example, Blake & Mouton, 1964; Putnam & Wilson, 1982). Drawing on Rahim's (1983) conceptualization and measurement of conflict style, early presentations of FNT identified five different styles of conflict. The first is the dominating style (also known as the competitive style), which involves an effort to achieve personal goals without regard to the interests of the other party. The avoiding style involves eluding discussion of the conflict with the other party. This may even take the form of avoiding the person or situation producing the conflict. The obliging style (also known as the accommodating style) prioritizes concern for the other party's position above and beyond our own interests and goals. The compromising style is a "win some-lose some" style that involves conceding some personal interests and goals while attaining others in an effort to reach an equitable settlement. The final conflict style is the integrating style (also known as the collaborating style), which involves seeking a resolution that addresses individual interests of all parties involved. In essence, this is a "win-win" style.

FNT contends that these conflict styles represent different ways of managing self-face and other-face or mutual-face concerns. A dominating style exhibits high concern for self-face, and low concern for other-face and mutual-face. In contrast, the obliging style exhibits high concern for other-face and mutual-face, and low concern for self-face, and the avoiding style exhibits low concern for either aspect of face. The compromising style represents moderate concern for self-face and moderate concern for other-face and mutual-face, whereas the integrating style represents high concern for all aspects of face. Consequently, FNT asserts that higher self-face concern predicts greater use of conflict styles that represent this type of concern (e.g., dominating style), whereas higher other- or mutual-face concern predicts greater use of conflict styles that represent this type of concern (e.g., obliging style).

Integrating style
A conflict style that involves seeking a resolution that addresses individual interests of all parties involved

Although the five styles are conceptually different, more recent presentations of FNT often focus on dominating, integrating, and avoiding (Oetzel, et al., 2001; Oetzel & Ting-Toomey, 2003). These styles have distinct face implications and align with three dimensions of behavior observed within conflict interactions (as opposed to self-reported styles). Indeed, the compromising style is different from integrating only in the degree of concern for self-face and other-face, and avoiding and obliging behaviors can be difficult to distinguish. The resulting relationships predicted by the theory are shown in Figure 15.1. The theory emphasizes the paths connecting culture to self-construal, then to face concerns, and then to conflict style. In particular, cultural individualism predicts independent self-construal, which in turn predicts concern for self-face during conflict, which in turn predicts use of the dominating style, whereas cultural collectivism predicts interdependent self-construal, other-face concern during conflict, and use of the integrating and avoiding styles. However, the theory also allows for cultural individualism and collectivism to directly affect face concerns and conflict styles, aside from their influence on self-construal. The idea here is that regardless of how you see yourself (self-construal), you will be aware of what is normal in your culture. So, you may pay attention to the face of others and use the integrating or avoiding style partly because that is what you are expected to do (and partly because you see yourself as interdependent).

Ting-Toomey and her colleagues have tested FNT in various ways and built considerable support for the theory over time. One well-regarded study (Oetzel & Ting-Toomey, 2003) tested the model shown in Figure 15.1 with

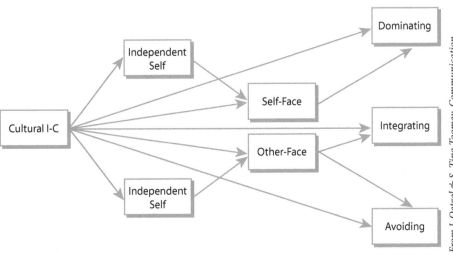

From J. Oetzel & S. Ting-Toomey, Communication Research, 30(6), 599–624. Copyright © 2003 by Sage Publications. Reprinted by permission of Sage Publications.

FIGURE 15.1 MODEL OF FACE NEGOTIATION.

participants from four cultures. Participants were college students from China, Japan, Germany, and the United States; the Asian countries represented collectivistic cultures, whereas Germany and the United States represented individualistic cultures. Participants completed standard self-report measures of self-construal, face concerns during conflict, and adherence to the dominating, avoiding, and integrating conflict styles. Statistical analysis of this data was largely supportive of the depicted model. One exception was the link between cultural collectivism and interdependent self-construal. In this particular study, participants from China and Japan did not view themselves as more interdependent than participants from the United States and Germany. The theorists suggested that this theoretically inconsistent finding resulted from the college student sample. Across nationalities, college students are at a point in their lives where they often seek to differentiate themselves from their families, and thus students from collectivistic cultures may report less interdependence than they would at earlier or later phases of their lives. Another study (Oetzel, Garcia, & Ting-Toomey, 2008) explored specific conflict behaviors associated with self-, other-, and mutual-face concern for individuals in these same four cultures. Across the cultures, participants in this study were largely consistent in identifying other-face concern as being associated with certain strategies, such as remaining calm, apologizing, having a private discussion, giving in, and pretending to be positive, but also expressing negative feelings. Self-face concern was positively associated with the strategy of defending oneself, whereas mutual face was associated negatively with aggression. An important implication of this study is that people are able to recognize efforts to address other-face concerns, even if their cultural group or self-construal does not predispose them to use those strategies. Very recent work has begun to examine the role of emotion in connecting self-construal, face concern, and conflict styles. Across cultures, the experience of anger during conflict is associated positively with independent self-construal, self-face concern, and the competing style, whereas the experience of compassion is associated positively with interdependent self-construal, other-face concern, and the integrating, compromising, and obliging styles (Zhang, Ting-Toomey, & Oetzel, 2014). Given the evidence supporting FNT and the utility of FNT for explaining how cultural influences affect our conflict behavior, this theory will continue to provide communication students and researchers a valuable tool for understanding conflict.

ANXIETY/UNCERTAINTY MANAGEMENT THEORY

Anxiety/uncertainty management theory (AUM) Is a theory that addresses the experience of interacting with unfamiliar others

Uncertainty In anxiety/uncertainty management theory, describes not knowing what will happen

Anxiety In anxiety/uncertainty management theory, describes a feeling that accompanies uncertainty

Anxiety/uncertainty management theory (AUM) is a theory that addresses the experience of interacting with unfamiliar others. This kind of situation typically involves both uncertainty, or not knowing what will happen, and anxiety, which is the emotional accompaniment to uncertainty. William Gudykunst (1985) began the construction of AUM based on uncertainty reduction theory (Berger & Calabrese, 1975; see Chapter 8), and it was originally designed to model the process of intergroup communication. Subsequently, he extended the theory to explain how people adapt to other cultures (see Gudykunst & Hammer, 1988), and that has been its principal focus since then.

Similar to some of the other theories presented in this text, AUM makes explicit metatheoretical assumptions. Some of these assumptions include (a) the basic underlying processes of communication are the same across cultures but culture provides rules for how the content of communication should be interpreted; (b) data that is considered useful for testing theory includes both communicators' perceptions or interpretations and their objective behaviors (what can be directly observed by others); and (c) communication is influenced by cultural and group membership as well as structural, situational, and environmental factors of which we may not be consciously aware.

AUM theory focuses on communication with people we do not know and who are themselves unfamiliar with us. The theory calls such people strangers, which represents both the idea of nearness in that the person is physically close, yet also has the concept of being remote in that they may have different values and utilize these values when making decisions about communicating. AUM contends that interaction with strangers is characterized by anxiety and uncertainty as previously described. For example, imagine yourself sitting in an airplane seat next to someone from another culture. Although the person is sitting next to you (i.e., physically close), their value system influencing communication behavior is different from yours and thus may cause you to become anxious and uncertain. Uncertainty can be defined as a cognitive phenomenon that affects how we think about strangers. Uncertainty is ubiquitous throughout all aspects of life and believed to be a "fundamental condition of human life" (Marris, 1996, p. 1). Further, uncertainty is a function of our own expectations about a situation and how that situation should be ordered or interpreted. We tend to have more accurate predictions about the behavior of people with whom we are familiar, or who inhabit the same social and cultural groups as we do, so we experience less uncertainty with them. On the other hand, we experience more uncertainty when communicating with people who belong to out-groups, or groups of people that we do not belong to or have membership with.

People react differently to uncertainty, and this reaction is heavily influenced by culture and ethnicity. Therefore, each person has a degree of certainty that, when experienced, allows them to remain comfortable when interacting with other people. For example, consider how your closest friends react to an upcoming house party; one friend probably has to know all the details about the party such as exactly where the house is located, what time you will arrive, who will be there, when you will be leaving, what you will be wearing, and who is driving. Another friend may only need to know when you are going to pick them up and is not too concerned about the details of who, what, where, or when. These two friends demonstrate how each person has a different level of uncertainty with which they are comfortable. "The highest amount of uncertainty we can have and think we can predict strangers' behavior sufficiently to feel comfortable interacting with them" is known as our maximum threshold for uncertainty (Gudykunst, 2005, p. 286). At the other end of the continuum, our

Strangers Concept in AUM theory representing people whom we do not know and who are themselves in an unfamiliar environment

Out-groups In anxiety/uncertainty management theory, describes groups of people that we do not belong to or have membership with

Maximum threshold for uncertainty A maximum level of uncertainty that, when not exceeded, allows people to remain comfortable when interacting with other people

Minimum threshold for uncertainty The minimal level of uncertainty that, when not exceeded, allows people to remain comfortable when interacting with other people

General level of uncertainty acceptance A level of uncertainty that exists between a person's maximum and minimum thresholds for uncertainty

Maximum threshold for anxiety A maximum level of anxiety that, when not exceeded, allows people to remain comfortable when interacting with other people

Minimum threshold for anxiety The minimum level of anxiety that, when not exceeded, allows people to remain comfortable when interacting with other people

General level of anxiety acceptance A level of anxiety that exists between a person's maximum and minimum thresholds for anxiety

Effective communication The degree to which the other person assigns or attaches a similar meaning to the meanings that were intended by the sender

Misinterpretation Occurs when communicators attach different meanings to the same communication behavior

Mindfulness A process of awareness where we become aware of our own frame of reference as well as the frame of reference of the receiver

minimum threshold for uncertainty is the "lowest amount of uncertainty we can have and not feel bored or overconfident about our predictions of strangers' behavior" (p. 286). If uncertainty levels exceed our maximum or minimum threshold levels, then we lose our ability to communicate effectively. However, if we remain within our maximum and minimum thresholds for uncertainty, we are within our general level of uncertainty acceptance, and thus, we have our greatest predictability about another person's behavior.

Anxiety, similar to uncertainty, is believed to be experienced when we encounter new intercultural situations. According to AUM, anxiety is the "affective equivalent of uncertainty" (Gudykunst, 2005, p. 287). In other words, uncertainty is more reflective of our cognitions, whereas anxiety reflects our emotional reaction to experiencing uncertainty. This can take the form of feeling uneasy, tense, worried, or apprehensive about communicative outcomes. The maximum threshold for anxiety is the highest amount of anxiety we can have and still feel comfortable interacting with strangers. If we exceed this maximum threshold, people tend to display communication avoidance behavior. Our lowest amount of anxiety that we can have and still feel comfortable interacting with strangers is our minimum threshold for anxiety. Should we fall below our minimum threshold for anxiety, we generally become lazy or complacent about communicating with other people. If our level of anxiety falls within our general level of anxiety acceptance, we can use this anxiety to our advantage as a motivating factor that "keeps us on our toes" and can result in a very competent interaction.

AUM theory is intended to make predictions about effective communication, or the degree to which a receiver assigns or attaches a similar meaning to communication as the meaning that was intended by the sender. When communication is ineffective, meanings are not shared, or are misinterpreted. Some misinterpretations can be readily identified, but many are never recognized. Misinterpretation is assumed to be a symptom of not being mindful of the messages we are creating and sending, as well as not ensuring that those messages are received in the ways in which we intended. The term "not being mindful when communicating" reflects a tendency for people, both the sender and receiver, to interpret messages based on their own frame of reference, not the frame of reference of the other person. The way to reduce these misinterpretations is to become aware of our own frame of reference as well as the frame of reference of the receiver(s). This process of awareness is known as mindfulness. Whereas mindlessness reflects an automatic process involving attention, intention, and control (Bargh, 1989), mindfulness assumes that there is a "(1) creation of new categories; (2) openness to new information; and (3) awareness of more than one perspective" (Langer, 1989, p. 62). Mindlessness assumes that people share our interpretive schema, whereas mindfulness assumes that different people interpret information differently than we do, and we need to account for these differences when communicating.

The central claim of this theory asserts that effective intercultural communication occurs when we experience levels of uncertainty and anxiety that fall between our minimum and maximum thresholds for uncertainty and anxiety,

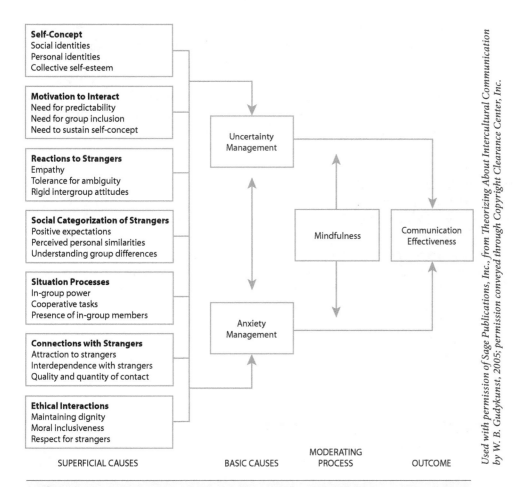

Self-Concept		Uncertainty Management		Communication Effectiveness

Self-Concept
Social identities
Personal identities
Collective self-esteem

Motivation to Interact
Need for predictability
Need for group inclusion
Need to sustain self-concept

Reactions to Strangers
Empathy
Tolerance for ambiguity
Rigid intergroup attitudes

Social Categorization of Strangers
Positive expectations
Perceived personal similarities
Understanding group differences

Situation Processes
In-group power
Cooperative tasks
Presence of in-group members

Connections with Strangers
Attraction to strangers
Interdependence with strangers
Quality and quantity of contact

Ethical Interactions
Maintaining dignity
Moral inclusiveness
Respect for strangers

Uncertainty Management

Mindfulness

Communication Effectiveness

Anxiety Management

SUPERFICIAL CAUSES   BASIC CAUSES   MODERATING PROCESS   OUTCOME

Used with permission of Sage Publications, Inc., from Theorizing About Intercultural Communication by W. B. Gudykunst, 2005; permission conveyed through Copyright Clearance Center, Inc.

FIGURE 15.2 ANXIETY/UNCERTAINTY MANAGEMENT THEORY.

and communicate mindfully in response to the uncertainty and anxiety we do experience. The theory, formally stated, posits 47 different axioms which deal more specifically with these ideas, resulting in a very complex conceptualization of intercultural communication. Figure 15.2 presents an overview of the theory and illustrates the factors involved in effective intercultural communication. It also reveals the difficulties of avoiding communication breakdowns when talking with people from other cultures.

The complexity of AUM has, to some extent, discouraged its testing and application. It is particularly challenging to identify when people are experiencing an acceptable or unacceptable level of uncertainty and anxiety, and thus, to test this theoretical claim. However, communication scholars continue to find value in AUM's identification of uncertainty and anxiety as potent influences on how effectively strangers from different cultures communicate with each other. One study (Nueliep, 2012) examined how intercultural communication apprehension (ICA) affected the extent to which participants in a cross-cultural conversation reduced their uncertainty about each other and were satisfied with the conversation. ICA can be understood as combining the uncertainty and anxiety elements identified by AUM. Participants were college students from the United States and a range of other countries (Belarus, Brazil, China, France, Japan, Korea, and Poland). None of them knew each other in advance of the study, and they were paired at random. Participants individually completed measures of ICA and ethnocentrism, which is the tendency to regard one's own cultural group as the center of everything and rate other groups in reference to it. Then, pairs were placed together in a room and instructed to become acquainted. After 10 minutes, the pairs were separated to complete the measures of uncertainty reduction and conversational satisfaction. The more ICA and ethnocentrism participants reported prior to interaction, the less they reported reducing uncertainty about each other during interaction, or being satisfied with the conversation. Presumably, participants who reported the higher levels of ICA were above their maximum thresholds for uncertainty and anxiety. However, the study did not assess that directly, nor did it try to identify participants who were below their minimum thresholds, and should have (according to AUM) also reduced less uncertainty and been less satisfied. Studies like this one suggest that AUM is on track with its focus on uncertainty and anxiety, but fall short of determining whether the more specific claims of the theory are true. The future of AUM as a theory will depend in large measure on direct tests of its claims, and modification of the theory as needed to fit the research evidence.

Ethnocentrism The tendency to regard one's own cultural group as the center of everything and rate other groups in reference to it

CROSS-CULTURAL ADAPTATION THEORY

Cross-cultural adaptation theory An intercultural theory that explains the process of how people adjust to a new environment

Enculturation Learning to interact and relate in ways that are considered normal for our home cultures

Young Kim (1988) developed cross-cultural adaptation theory to explain the process of how people adjust to a new environment. In this theory, environment refers to any cultural experience that is different from that person's home experience (i.e., the culture within which the person was raised). Growing up in our home cultures, each of us experiences enculturation, that is, "we learn to speak, listen, read, interpret, and understand verbal and nonverbal messages in such a fashion that the messages will be recognized and responded to by the individuals with whom we interact" (Kim, 2005, p. 382). Once enculturation has occurred, navigating the patterns of interaction and interpretation developed by other cultures requires adaptation, often substantial adaptation.

Previous attempts to explain the intersection of person and culture focused on how the new culture influences the person and that person's behavior. In other words, this process was traditionally viewed as linear in nature, with the culture exerting influence on the person who was considered passive in the process. Cross-cultural adaptation theory (CCAT) seeks to account for both the influence of the new culture as well as the influence of the person's previous cultural experience. For example, consider the culture of the university you are presently attending. This university has a culture that students, to one degree or another, identify with. If we were only to consider how the university influences the student and the student's adaptation without accounting for the student's prior culture (e.g., educational experiences before they came to college or other college experiences) and ways of doing things (i.e., cultural practices), this would be an incomplete explanation of the adaptation process.

CCAT is organized under a set of principles that frame the theory to reflect both universal assumptions about human behavior as well as culture-specific influences. First, adaptation is understood as a natural, universal phenomenon experienced by all human beings when adapting to a new environment. Kim describes it as "a basic human tendency that accompanies the internal struggle of individuals to regain control over their life changes in the face of environmental challenges" (Kim, 2005, p. 378). Second, adaptation is an evolutionary process. A person is believed to experience this process whenever attempting to make sense of a new environment. The adaptation process takes the form of changes occurring within the person based on influences from both the environment and the individual, as well as the interplay between the two. For example, consider meeting a dating partner's parents for the first time. Once we encounter the parents, our adaptation to the "new experience" changes our behavior, and our behavioral change alters the way we think about ourselves. Third, adaptation is a communication-based phenomenon. Given that adaptation is based on information from the new environment, the vehicle through which information travels is that of verbal and nonverbal communication. As such, adaptation is truly a communication process. This information is transmitted as long as the person and the environment continue to interact. Once a person is no longer interacting with the new environment, new information ceases to be exchanged. In our dating example, as long as we are in the new environment of our dating partner's parents, we will be constantly receiving and sending verbal and nonverbal messages that will affect the adaptation process. Fourth, CCAT does not address whether people adapt, as it is assumed that all people adapt to one degree or another. Rather, the theory seeks to address the *how* and *why* of adaptation.

One of the unique features of CCAT is that it utilizes both deductive and inductive theory-building approaches. Recall from Chapter 2 that deductive theory building consists of moving from general observations to more specific observations, whereas inductive theory building involves moving from specific observations to more general observations. This is achieved through the assumptions that all people experience the adaptation process (deductive approach), yet we must also account for a person's "lived story" to fully explain intercultural adaptation (inductive approach). That is, this theory accounts for general human tendencies while also accounting for the specific experiences of the person.

CROSS-CULTURAL ADAPTATION

The term *cross-cultural adaptation* is an umbrella term that consists of several smaller processes that a person experiences when encountering a new environment. The entire CCAT process includes several interconnected subprocesses, including acculturation, assimilation, adjustment, and integration.

The process of acculturation is the acquisition of beliefs and practices from a new culture or environment, or more succinctly, the activity of learning a new cultural system (Shibutani & Kwan, 1965). Acculturation is typically accompanied by some degree of deculturation, or unlearning some old cultural elements. For example, take a person who is born and raised in on the East Coast of the United States (e.g., New York or Boston). Given the practices of the home culture, this person comes to learn ways of behaving from that urban environment that may include being confrontational, direct, and to the point when communicating; use a great deal of sarcasm in humor production; and being opinionated, aggressive, and sometimes overtly disagreeable. This person learned these behaviors as a result of the enculturation process from his/her home culture. If this person should relocate to Iowa and have a desire to become an accepted member in the Midwest culture, he/she may have to learn new or different ways of behaving in that new culture (i.e., acculturation), which may consist of being less confrontational, less direct, use more subtlety when making a point, and reducing the level of sarcasm in humor production so as not to seem so "abrasive" or "aggressive." To learn these new ways of behaving, the person must simultaneously unlearn their old ways of behaving. Thus, to one degree or another, our East Coast person will take on Midwestern cultural characteristics and, thus, become "more Midwestern" and "less East Coast."

The overall outcome of cross-cultural adaptation is assimilation, or the degree to which a person accepts the influence of the new culture. It can also be described as intercultural transformation (see Figure 15.3). Assimilation includes both adjustment, or internal coping with encountering the new culture, and integration, or actively participating in the new culture. In research on CCAT, assimilation is often assessed with three more specific outcomes. One of these is functional fitness, or ability to function successfully in the new culture. A second is psychological health, or feelings of efficacy and fulfillment. A third is intercultural identity, or an orientation toward self and others that is not rigidly defined in terms of either the home culture or the new, host culture. Continuing our earlier example, as the East Coast person assimilates to Midwestern culture, this would be evident in his or her ability to interact with and form relationships with Midwesterners, feeling both competent and contented in his or her life in the Midwest, and no longer thinking of him or herself as solely Eastern (or Midwestern). It is important that we not consider cross-cultural adaptation as something that is either achieved or not achieved. Instead, consider adaptation as a degree to which some people experience, or are willing to experience, a cross-cultural adaptation that is more reflective of the new culture than others experience. Assimilation, in this case, should not be considered an attainable end result of cross-cultural adaptation as much as an ideal toward which people move via the cross-cultural adaptation process. Some people may realize assimilation during a lifetime of adapting, but more often than not, assimilation is a product of generations of cultural adaptation (Kim, 2001). CCAT describes the process of becoming assimilated as having a stress-adaptation-growth dynamic. New experiences in an unfamiliar culture are stressful and require adaptation, which produces internal growth, which in turn allows the individual to deal with more new experiences.

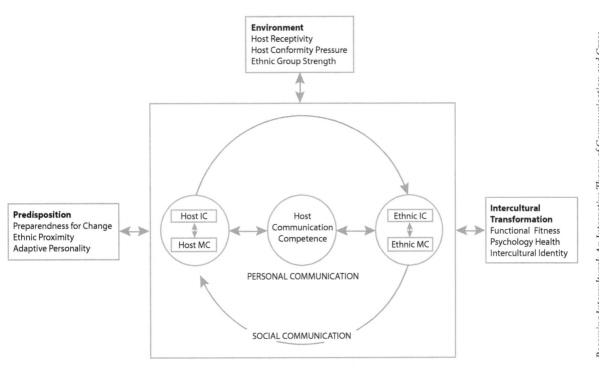

FIGURE 15.3 RELATIONSHIP AMONG CROSS-CULTURAL ADAPTATION CONCEPTS.

FACTORS INFLUENCING ADAPTATION

CCAT describes a set of factors that influence the rate at which people adapt to a new culture. These factors, depicted in Figure 15.3, include host communication competence, environmental factors, and predisposition factors (Kim, 2012). Host communication competence factors involve the outsider's ability to decode and encode information in ways that are consistent with normal communication practices in the new or "host" culture. In other words, these factors are about the individual's capacity to learn and perform as expected in the unfamiliar culture. Host communication competence includes cognitive competence (knowledge of host language, culture, history, social institutions, and rules for conduct), affective competence (emotional and motivational capacity to deal with the challenges of living in the new environment, including positivity, flexibility, and appreciation for the host way of life), and operational competence (ability to perform the correct verbal and nonverbal behaviors during interactions with members of the host culture). Thus, according to CCAT, people become acculturated more quickly to the extent that they learn the language, culture, etc., remain positive and flexible, and work at acting in culturally appropriate ways. CCAT also contends that host communication competence "is directly and reciprocally linked to participation in the social communication processes of the host society through interpersonal and mass communication channels" (p. 236). As a stranger in a culture, the more you engage in communication with members of the host culture, or observe their communication, the

Stress-adaptation-growth dynamic In CCAT, a process in which new experiences in an unfamiliar culture produce stress, requiring adaptation, producing internal growth, and allowing the individual to deal with subsequent new experiences

Host communication competence Factors that involve the outsider's ability to decode and encode information in ways that are consistent with normal communication practices in the new or "host" culture

Cognitive competence An aspect of host communication competence, involving knowledge of host language, culture, history, social institutions, and rules for conduct

more likely you are to develop host communication competence (e.g., language, appreciation, etc.), and in turn, as you develop host communication compe-tence, it becomes easier to interact with members of the host culture.

In addition to host communication competence factors, CCAT describes environmental factors that affect the ability to adapt and acculturate. Environmental factors are characteristics of the host culture and the relation-ship between host and home cultures. They include host receptivity, host con-formity pressure, and ethnic group strength. Host receptivity is the degree to which a culture welcomes and accepts strangers and offers them support. Host conformity pressure is the extent to which the host environment exerts influ-ence on strangers to act in accordance with the norms of the host culture, as opposed to being allowed to continue with habitual behaviors from their home cultures. Finally, ethnic group strength refers to the "relative status or stand-ing of a particular ethnic group in the context of the surrounding host society" (Kim, 2012, p. 237). Imagine two "study abroad" experiences. In one, you are mostly cut off from your home culture (your ethnic group strength is low), people in the host country are warm and friendly (host receptivity is high), and they expect you to participate in your host culture's way of life (host con-formity pressure is high). Under these circumstances, CCAT suggests that you will acculturate rapidly. In a contrasting experience, you might be traveling with a large but tight-knit group from your own country, with plenty of access to the comforts of home (your ethnic group strength is high), people in your host country do not seem welcoming of strangers (host receptivity is low), and you are allowed to behave much as you normally would, even when natives of the host culture do things differently. In this study abroad experience, CCAT indicates you would probably acculturate very little.

Finally, CCAT identifies predisposition factors, or qualities that people bring with them to their encounters with a host culture. The first of these is preparedness, or level of readiness to adapt, including what has been learned about the host language and culture, whether the encounter is expected to be temporary, or long-term, and whether the encounter is voluntary (e.g., study abroad) or involuntary (being relocated by your multi-national company, or worse, fleeing a war in your home country). As CCAT argues, being more pre-pared promotes greater adaptation. The second predisposition factor is ethnic proximity (or ethnic distance), which describes the extent to which a stranger is initially able to blend in with the host culture. This factor depends critically on physical appearance (do you look a lot like the host natives, or are your skin color, facial features, and height different?) but also on cultural values (see Hofstede's dimensions, above) and religious beliefs. Higher ethnic proximity (i.e., greater "blending in") also promotes greater adaptation. The third predis-position factor is personality. Are you open to, or resistant to, new information and experiences? Are you resilient and patient, or likely to crumble under pres-sure, and unable to let experiences evolve? Are you optimistic or pessimistic? CCAT says starting out with a more open, resilient, and optimistic personality helps strangers adapt more quickly to new cultures.

Elements of CCAT have been tested with diverse groups of strangers encountering similarly diverse cultures. For example, studies have focused on refugees (Kim, 1989), university students in study abroad programs (Pitts, 2009), and expatriates (Kim & Kim, 2004). A recent study focused on computer-mediated and non-mediated interpersonal communication as used by people who were born in various other countries but who had come to live in the United States near the University of Oklahoma, largely for education or employment (Kim & McKay-Semmler, 2013). The 51 participants in this study completed extensive interviews and surveys, probing their relationships and how they communicated with "native-born Americans" and "co-ethnics"; their self-reported functional fitness, or ability to function successfully in the American culture; and their psychological well-being, or feeling comfortable, satisfied, and happy with living in the United States. The findings showed that the non-natives interacted more frequently with native-born Americans than with co-ethnics, and that communication with co-ethnics who were outside the country was largely mediated by e-mail and the Internet. Importantly, non-natives' functional fitness and psychological well-being were affected by communication with natives. As the authors state, "non-natives who are more actively engaged in interpersonal communication with native-born Americans through dyadic relationships or through organizational memberships are likely to be more successful in pursuing their goals and psychologically better adjusted with respect to life in the United States" (Kim & McKay-Simmler, 2013, p. 109). Communication with co-ethnics did not have the same kind of influence, either positive or negative. This study helps to underscore CCAT's contention that interpersonal interaction with natives is critical for adaptation and acculturation.

Cross-cultural adaptation theory provides a holistic approach to explaining cultural adaptation because it takes both cultural and individual influences into consideration. As such, this theory is of great utility for researchers interested in understanding the dynamic process of acculturation, and anyone who wants more insight into their own experiences in host cultures.

Preparedness In cross-cultural adaptation theory, level of readiness to adapt, including what has been learned about the host language and culture, whether the encounter is expected to be temporary, or long-term, and whether the encounter is voluntary (e.g., study abroad) or involuntary

Ethnic proximity In cross-cultural adaptation theory, the extent to which a stranger is initially able to blend in with the host culture

SUMMARY

The theories in this chapter represent contemporary and influential efforts to understand how culture influences communication and its outcomes. Hofstede's dimensions of national culture framework provides a set of empirically validated constructs that help to explain why people from different countries exhibit different behaviors and expectations. Face negotiation theory explains cultural differences in conflict style as a function of individualism-collectivism, self-construal, and face concerns. Anxiety/uncertainty management theory addresses the experience of interacting with unfamiliar others, explaining the success of those interactions as a function of anxiety and uncertainty. Cross-cultural adaptation theory describes the complex process of adjusting to a new cultural environment. Each of these theories contributes to a better understanding of cultural differences, and how communication can more effectively bridge those differences.

KEY TERMS

Acculturation

Affective competence

Ambivalent orientation

Anxiety

Anxiety/uncertainty management theory

Assimilation

Avoiding style

Biconstrual orientation

Cognitive competence

Compromising style

Cross-cultural adaptation theory

Deculturation

Dimensions of national culture

Dominating style

Effective communication

Enculturation

Environmental factors

Ethnic group strength

Ethnic proximity

Ethnocentrism

Face

Face gain

Face loss

Face negotiation theory

Face threat

Facework

Functional fitness

General level of anxiety acceptance

General level of uncertainty acceptance

Host communication competence

Host conformity pressure

Host receptivity

Independent orientation

Independent self-construal

Individualism-collectivism

Indulgence-restraint

Integrating style

Intercultural identity

Interdependent orientation

Interdependent self-construal

Long-term orientation

Masculinity-femininity

Maximum threshold for anxiety

Maximum threshold for uncertainty

Mindfulness

Minimum threshold for anxiety

Minimum threshold for uncertainty

Misinterpretation

Mutual-face concern

Obliging style

Operational competence

Other-face concern

Out-groups

Power distance

Preparedness

Psychological health

Self-construal

Self-face concern

Strangers

Stress-adaptation-growth dynamic

Uncertainty

Uncertainty avoidance

REFERENCES

Adorno, T. W., Frenkel-Brunswik, E., Levinson. D. J., & Sanford. R. N. (1950). *The authoritarian personality.* New York: Harper & Row.

Afifi, W. A., & Matsunaga, M. (2008). Uncertainty management theories: Three approaches to a multifarious process. In L. A. Baxter & D. O. Braithwaite (Eds.), *Engaging theories in interpersonal communication: Multiple perspectives* (pp. 117–132). Thousand Oaks, CA: Sage.

Agency for Health Care Research and Quality, 2007. Retrieved on April 7, 2010 from www.ahrq.gov

Ajzen, I. (1985). From intentions to actions: A theory of planned behavior. In J. Kuhn & J. Beckman (Eds.). *Action-control: From cognitions to behavior* (pp. 11–39). Heidelberg: Springer.

Ajzen, I. (1988). *Attitudes, personality, and behavior.* Chicago, IL: The Dorsey Press.

Ajzen, I. (1991). The theory of planned behavior. *Organizational Behavior and Human Decision Processes, 50,* 179–211.

Ajzen, I. (2001). *Constructing a TpB questionnaire: Conceptual and methodological considerations.* Retrieved May 17, 2002 from http://www.unix.oit.umass.edu/~ajzen/tpb

Ajzen, I., & Fishbein, M. (1980). *Understanding attitudes and predicting social behavior.* Englewood Cliffs, NJ: Prentice-Hall.

Alberti, R. E., & Emmons, M. L. (1974). *Your perfect right: A guide to assertive behavior* (2nd ed.). San Luis Obispo, CA: Impact.

Althaus, S. L., & Tewksbury, D. (2002). Agenda setting and the "new" news: Patterns of issue importance among readers of the paper and online versions of the New York Times. *Communication Research, 29,* 180–207.

Andersen, J. F. (1979). The relationship between teacher immediacy and teaching effectiveness. In B. Ruben (Ed.), *Communication yearbook 3* (pp. 543–559). New Brunswick. NJ: Transactions Books.

Andersen, K., & Clevenger, T., Jr. (1963). A summary of experimental research in ethos. *Speech Monographs, 30*, 59–78.

Andersen, P. A. (1985). Nonverbal immediacy in interpersonal communication. In A. W. Siegman & S. Feldman (Eds.), *Multichannel integrations of nonverbal behavior* (pp. 1–36). Hillsdale, NJ: Lawrence Erlbaum.

Andersen, P. A. (1987). The it debate: A critical examination of the individual differences paradigm in interpersonal communication. In E. Dervin & M. J. Voigt (Eds.), *Progress in communication sciences* (Vol. 7, pp. 47–52). Norwood. NJ: Ablex.

Andersen, P. A. (1991). When one cannot not communicate: A challenge to Motley's traditional communication postulates. *Communication Studies, 42*, 309–325.

Andersen, P. A. (1998). The cognitive valence theory of intimate communication. In M. T. Palmer & G. A. Barnett (Eds.), *Progress in communication sciences, Vol. 14: Mutual influence in interpersonal communication theory and research in cognitive affect and behavior* (pp. 39–72). Norwood, NJ: Ablex.

Andersen, P. A. (1999). *Nonverbal communication: Forms and functions.* Mountain View, CA: Mayfield Publishing Co.

Anderson, C. M., & Martin, M. M. (November, 1995a). *Communication between mothers and their adult children: The path from motives to self-disclosure and satisfaction.* Paper presented at the annual meeting of the Speech Communication Association. San Antonio, TX.

Anderson, C. M., & Martin, M. M. (1995b). Communication motives of assertive and responsive communicators. *Communication Research Reports, 12*, 186–191.

Anderson, C. M., & Martin, M. M. (1995c). The effects of communication motives. interaction involvement, and loneliness on satisfaction. *Small Group Research, 26*, 118–137.

Anderson, C. M., & Martin, M. M. (1995d). Why employees speak to co-workers and bosses: Motives, gender, and organizational satisfaction. *The Journal of Business Communication, 32*, 249–265.

Anderson, C. R., & Schneier, C. E. (1978). Locus of control, leader behavior, and leader performance among management students. *Academy of Management Journal, 21*, 690–698.

Anderson, L. (1994). A new look at an old construct: Cross-cultural adaptation. *International Journal of Intercultural Relations, 18*, 293–328.

Antheunis, M. L., Valkenburg, P. M., & Peter, J. (2007). Computer-mediated communication and interpersonal attraction: An experimental test of two explanatory hypotheses. *Cyberpsychology & behavior, 10*(6), 831–836.

Argyris, C. (1965). *Organization and innovation.* Scarborough, Ontario, Canada: Irwin.

Argyris, C. (1985). *Strategy, change, and defensive routines.* London, England: Pitman.

Argyris, C. (1993). *Knowledge and action: A guide to overcoming barriers to change.* Hoboken, NJ: Jossey-Bass.

Argyris, C., & Schon, D. (1978). *Organizational learning: A theory of action perspective.* Boston: Addison-Wesley.

Arntson, P. (1985). Future research in health communication. *Journal of Applied Communication Research, 13,* 118–130.

Arntson, P., & Droge, D. (1988). Addressing the value dimension of health communication: A social science perspective. *Journal of Applied Communication Research. 16,* 1–15. doi: 10.1080/00909888809365267

Aronson, E., & Mills. J. (1959). The effect of severity of initiation on liking for a group. *Journal of Abnormal and Social Psychology, 59,* 177–181.

Auter, P. J. (1992). TV that talks back: An experimental validation of a parasocial interaction scale. *Journal of Broadcasting and Electronic Media. 36,* 173–181.

Avtgis, T. A. (2002). Adult-child conflict control expectancies: Effects on taking conflict personally toward parents. *Communication Research Reports, 19,* 226–236.

Avtgis, T. A., Brann, M., & Staggers, S. (2006). Information exchange and health control expectancies as influenced by a patient's medical interview situation. *Communication Research Reports, 23,* 231–237. doi: 10.1080/08824090600962284

Avtgis, T. A., & Madlock, P. E. (2008). Implications of the verbally patient: Creating a constructive environment in destructive situations. In E. P. Polack, V. P. Richmond, & J. C. McCroskey (Eds.), *Applied communication for health professions* (pp. 169–183). Dubuque, IA: Kendall Hunt.

Avtgis, T. A., & Myers, S. A. (1996, November). *Perceived control and communicative adaptability: How outlook on life influences ability to change.* Paper presented at the annual meeting of the Speech Communication Association, San Diego, CA.

Avtgis, T. A., & Polack, E. P. (2007). Predicting physician communication competence by patient perceived information exchange and health locus of control. *Human Communication, 10,* 136–144.

Avtgis, T. A., Polack, E. P., & Liberman, C. J. (in press). The impact of communication technology on healthcare organizations and patient-provider interactions. In K. B. Wright & L. Webb (Eds.), *Computer mediated communication in personal relationships* (2nd ed.). Cresskill, NJ: Hampton Press.

Avtgis, T. A., Polack, E. P., Staggers, S. M., & Wiecorek, S. M. (2011). Healthcare provider – recipient interactions: Is "on-line" interaction the next best thing to being there? In K. B. Wright & L. Webb (Eds.), *Computer mediated communication in personal relationships* (pp. 266–284). Cresskill, NJ: Hampton Press.

Avtgis, T. A., & Rancer, A. S. (2003). Personalization of conflict across cultures: A comparison among the United States, New Zealand, and Australia. *Journal of Intercultural Communication Research, 33,* 109–118.

Avtgis, T. A., & Rancer, A. S. (2007). The theory of independent-mindedness: An organizational theory for individualistic cultures. In M. Hinner (Ed.), *The role of communication in business transactions and relationships: Freiberger beitrage zur interkulturellen und wirtschaftskommunikation: A forum for general and intercultural business communication* (pp. 183–201). Frankfurt, Germany: Peter Lang.

Avtgis, T. A., & Rancer, A. S. (2010). *Arguments, aggression, and conflict: New directions in theory and research.* New York: Routledge.

Avtgis, T. A., West, D. V., & Anderson, T. L. (1998). Relationship stages: An inductive analysis identifying cognitive, affective, and behavioral dimensions of Knapp's relational stages model. *Communication Research Reports, 15,* 280–287.

Babrow, A. S., Black, D. R., & Tiffany, S. T. (1990). Beliefs, attitudes, intentions, and a smoking-cessation program: A planned behavior analysis of communication campaign development. *Health Communication, 2,* 145–163.

Ball-Rokeach, S. (1973). From pervasive ambiguity to definition of the situation. *Sociometry, 36,* 378–389.

Ball-Rokeach, S. J., & DeFleur, M. L. (1976). A dependency model of mass-media effects. *Communication Research, 3,* 3–21.

Ball-Rokeach, S. J., Power. G. J., Guthrie. K. K., & Waring, H. R. (1990). Value-framing abortion in the United States: An application of media system dependency theory. *International Journal of Public Opinion Research, 2,* 249–273.

Baran, S. J., & Davis, D. K. (1995). *Mass communication theory.* Belmont. CA: Wadsworth Publishing Company.

Barbato, C. A., Graham, E. E., & Perse, E. M. (2003). Communicating in the family: An examination of the relationship of family communication climate and interpersonal communication motives. *Journal of Family Communication, 3*(3), 123–148.

Barbato, C. A., & Perse, E. M. (1992). Interpersonal communication motives and the life position of elders. *Communication Research, 19,* 516–531.

Barbato, C. A., Perse, E. M., & Graham, E. E. (1995, Nov.). Interpersonal communication motives and family communication patterns: Interfacing mediated and interpersonal communication. Paper presented at the annual meeting of the Speech Communication Association, San Antonio. TX.

Barge, J. K., Downs, C. W., & Johnson, K. M. (1989). An analysis of effective and ineffective leader conversation. *Management Communication Quarterly, 2,* 357–386.

Bargh, J. (1989). Conditional automaticity. In J. Uleman & J. Bargh (Eds.), *Unintended thought* (pp. 3–51). New York: Guilford.

Barnlund, D. (1962). Toward a meaning centered philosophy of communication. *Journal of Communication, 2,* 197–211.

Barnlund, D., & Haiman. F. (1960). *The dynamics of discussion.* Boston: Houghton Mifflin.

Baseheart, J. R. (1971). Message opinionation and approval-dependence as determinants of receiver attitude change and recall. *Speech Monographs, 38,* 302–310.

Basen-Engquist, K., & Parcel, G. S. (1992). Attitudes, norms, and self-efficacy: A model of adolescents' HIV-related sexual risk behavior. *Health Education Quarterly, 19,* 263–277.

Bass, B. M., & Stogdill, R. M. (1990). *Bass & Stogdill's handbook of leadership: Theory, research, and managerial applications* (3rd ed.). New York: Free Press.

Bate, B. & Bowker, J. (1997). *Communication and the sexes* (2nd ed.). Prospect Heights, IL: Waveland Press.

Bateson, G. (1972). *Steps to an ecology of the mind.* New York: Ballantine Books.

Baukus, R. A. (1996). *Perception of mediated social conflict: Media dependency and involvement.* Unpublished manuscript, the Pennsylvania State University.

Bavelas, J. B. (1990). Behaving and communicating: A reply to Motley. *Western Journal of Speech Communication, 54,* 593–602.

Bavelas, J. B., & Segal, L. (1982). Family systems theory: Background and implications. *Journal of Communication, 32,* 99–107.

Beatty, M. J., & McCroskey, J. C. (1997). It's in our nature: Verbal aggressiveness as temperamental expression. *Communication Quarterly, 45,* 446–460.

Beatty, M. J., & McCroskey, J. C. (1998). Interpersonal communication as temperamental expression: A communibiological paradigm. In J. C. McCroskey, J. A. Daly, M. M. Martin, & M. J Beatty (Eds.). *Communication and personality: Trait perspectives* (pp. 41–67). Cresskill, NJ: Hampton Press.

Beatty, M. J., Marshall, L. A., & Rudd, J. E. (2001). A twin study of communicative adaptability: Heritability of individual differences. *Quarterly Journal of Speech, 87,* 366–377.

Beatty, M. J., McCroskey, J. C., & Floyd, K. (2009). *Biological dimensions of communication: Perspectives, methods, and research.* New York: Hampton Press.

Beatty, M. J., McCroskey. J. C., & Heisel, A. D. (1998). Communication apprehension as temperamental expression: A communibiological paradigm. *Communication Monographs, 65,* 197–219.

Beatty, M. J., & Pence, M. E. (2010). Verbal aggressiveness as an extension of selected biological influences. In T. A. Avtgis & A. S. Rancer (Ed.), *Arguments, aggression and conflict: New directions in theory and research* (pp. 3–25). New York: Routledge.

Beatty, M. J., Valencic, K. M., Rudd, J. E., & Dobos, J. A. (1999). A "darkside" of communication avoidance: Indirect interpersonal aggressiveness. *Communication Research Reports, 16,* 103–109.

Beck, K. H., & Davis, C. M. (1978). Effects of fear-arousing communications and topic importance on attitude change. *Journal of Social Psychology, 104,* 81–95.

Beebe, S. A., & Masterson, J. T. (2003). *Communicating in small groups: Principles and practices* (7th ed.). Boston: Allyn & Bacon.

Beisecker, A. E. (1991). Interpersonal communication strategies to prevent drug abuse by health professionals and the elderly: Contribution of the health belief mode. *Health Communication, 3,* 241–250. doi: 10.1207/s15327027hc0304_6

Bellefontaine, A., & Florea, J. (1983, March). *The effect of unemployment on family communication: A systems examination.* Paper presented to the DePauw University Communication Honors Conference, Greencastle. Indiana.

Bell, R. A., & Daly, J. A. (1984). The affinity-seeking function of communication. *Communication Monographs, 51*, 91–115.

Benne, K. D., & Sheats, P. (1948). Functional roles of group members. *Journal of Social Issues, 4*, 41–49.

Berger, C. R. (1979). Beyond initial interaction: Uncertainty, understanding, and the development of interpersonal relationships. In H. Giles & R. N. St. Clair (Eds.), *Language and social psychology* (pp. 122–144). Oxford: Basil Blackwell.

Berger, C. R. (1986). Uncertain outcome values in predicted relationships: Uncertainty reduction theory then and now. *Human Communication Research, 13*(1), 34–38. doi: 10.1111/j.1468-2958.1986.tb00093.x

Berger, C. R. (1991). Communication theories and other curios. *Communication Monographs, 58*, 101–113.

Berger, C. R. (1997). *Planning strategic interaction*. Mahwah, N.J.: Lawrence Erlbaum Associates.

Berger, C. R. (2007). Plans, planning, and communication effectiveness. In B. B. Whaley, & W. Samter, (Eds.), *Explaining communication: Contemporary theories and exemplars* (pp.149–162). Mahwah, N.J.: Lawrence Erlbaum Associates.

Berger, C. R. (2011). From explanation to application. *Journal of Applied Communication Research, 39*(2), 214–222.

Berger, C. R. (2015). Planning theory of communication: Goal attainment through communicative action. In D. O. Braithwaite & P. Schrodt (Eds.), *Emerging theories in interpersonal communication: Multiple perspectives* (2nd ed., pp. 89–102). Thousand Oaks, CA: Sage.

Berger, C. R., & Bell, R. A. (1988). Plans and the initiation of social relationships. *Human Communication Research, 15*(2), 217–235.

Berger, C. R., & Calabrese, R. J. (1975). Some explorations in initial interaction and beyond: Toward a developmental theory of interpersonal communication. *Human Communication Research, 1*, 99–112.

Berger, C. R., & Chaffee, S.H. (Eds.). (1987). *Handbook of communication science*. Newbury Park, CA: Sage.

Berkowitz, L. (1962). *Aggression: A social psychological analysis*. New York: McGraw-Hill.

Berlo, D. K. (1960). *The process of communication*. New York: Holt. Rinehart & Winston.

Berlo, D. K. (1977). Communication as process: Review and commentary. In B. D. Ruben (Ed.), *Communication yearbook 1* (pp. 11–27). New Brunswick, NJ: Transaction Books.

Berscheid, E. (1966). Opinion change and communicator-communicatee similarity and dissimilarity. *Journal of Personality and Social Psychology, 4*, 670–680.

Berscheid, E., & Walster, E. H. (1978). *Interpersonal attraction* (2nd ed.). Reading, MA: Addison-Wesley.

Bertalanffy, L. von (1968). *General systems theory.* New York: Braziller.

Blake, R. R., & Mouton, J. S. (1964). *The managerial grid.* Houston, TX: Gulf Publishing.

Blake, R. R., & Mouton, J. S. (1978). *The new managerial grid.* Houston, TX: Gulf Publishing.

Blake, R. R., & Mouton, J. S. (1982). A comparative analysis of situationalism and 9.9 management by principle. *Organizational Dynamics, 24*, 20–43.

Blumler, J. G. (1979). The role of theory in uses and gratifications studies. *Communication Research, 6*, 9–36.

Bochner, A. (1976). Conceptual frontiers in the study of communication in families: An introduction to the literature. *Human Communication Research, 2*, 381–397.

Bochner, A. R. & Eisenberg, E. M. (1987). Family process: System perspectives. In C. R. Berger & S. H. Chaffee (Eds.). *Handbook of communication science* (pp. 540–563). Newbury Park, CA: Sage.

Bond, C. F., & DePaulo, B. M. (2006). Accuracy of deception judgments. *Personality and Social Psychology Review, 10*(3), 214–234.

Bormann, E. G. (1972). Fantasy and rhetorical vision: The rhetorical criticism of social reality. *Quarterly Journal of Speech, 58*, 396–407.

Bormann, E. G. (1980). *Communication theory.* New York: Holt, Rinehart & Winston.

Bormann, E. G., Kroll, B., Watters, K.. & McFarland, D. (1984). Rhetorical visions of committed voters: Fantasy theme analysis of a large sample survey. *Critical Studies in Mass Communication, 1*, 287–310.

Boster, F. J., & Levine, T. (1988). Individual differences and compliance-gaining message selection: The effects of verbal aggressiveness, argumentativeness, dogmatism and negativism. *Communication Research Reports, 5*, 114–119.

Boster, F. J., Levine, T., & Kazoleas, D. (1989, November). *The impact of argumentativeness and verbal aggressiveness on strategic diversity and persistence in compliance-gaining.* Paper presented at the meeting of the Speech Communication Association. San Francisco.

Boster, F. J., & Mongeau, P. (1984). Fear-arousing persuasive messages. In R. N. Bostrom (Ed.), *Communication Yearbook 8* (pp. 330–375). Beverly Hills: Sage.

Bostrom, R. N. (1980). Altered physiological states: The central nervous system and persuasive communications. In M. Roloff & G. R. Miller (Eds.), *Persuasion: New directions in theory and research* (pp. 3–8). Beverly Hills, CA: Sage.

Bostrom, R. N. (1983). *Persuasion.* Englewood Cliffs. NJ: Prentice-Hall.

Bostrom, R. N., Baseheart, J., & Rossiter, C. (1973). The effects of three types of profane language in persuasive messages. *Journal of Communication, 23,* 461–475.

Bowers, J. W. (1963). Language intensity, social introversion, and attitude change. *Speech Monographs, 30,* 345–352.

Bowers, J. W., & Osborn, M. (1966). Attitudinal effects of selected types of concluding metaphors in persuasive speeches. *Speech Monographs, 33,* 147–155.

Bradac, J. J. (1988). Language variables: Conceptual and methodological problems of instantiation. In C. R. Tardy (Ed.), A *handbook for the study of human communication: Methods and instruments for observing, measuring, and assessing communication processes* (pp. 301–322). Norwood. NJ: Abler.

Bradac, J. J., Bowers, J. W., & Courtright, J. A. (1979). Three language variables in communication research: Intensity, immediacy, and diversity. *Human Communication Research. 5,* 257–269.

Bradford, L., & Petronio, S. (1998). Strategic embarrassment: The culprit of emotion. In P. A. Andersen, & L. K. Guerrero (Eds.), *Handbook of communication and emotion: Research, theory, applications, and contexts* (pp. 99–121). San Diego, CA: Academic Press.

Brannigan, A., & Zwerman, W. (2001). The real "Hawthorne effect." *Society, 38,* 55–61.

Brashers, D. E. (2001a). Communication and uncertainty management. *Journal of Communication, 51,* 477–497. doi: 10.1111/j.1460-2466.2001.tb02892.x

Brashers, D. E. (2001b). HIV and uncertainty: Managing treatment decision making. *Focus: A guide to AIDS research, 16,* 5–6.

Brashers, D. E., Goldsmith, D. J., & Hsieh, E. (2002). Information seeking and avoiding in health contexts. *Human Communication Research, 28,* 258–271. doi: 10.1111/j.1468-2958.2002.tb0887.x

Brashers, D. E., Hsieh, E., Neidig, J. L., & Reynolds, N. R. (2006). Managing uncertainty about illness: Health care providers as credible authorities. In B. LePoire & R. M. Dailey (Eds.), *Applied interpersonal communication matters: Family, health, and community relations* (pp. 219–240). New York: Peter Lang.

Brehm, J. W. (1966). *A theory of psychological reactance*. New York, NY: Academic Press.

Brehm, J. W., & Brehm, S. S. (1981). *Psychological reactance: A theory of freedom and control*. San Diego, CA: Academic Press.

Brenders, D. A. (1987). Fallacies in the coordinated management of meaning: A philosophy of language critique of the hierarchical organization of coherent conversation and related theory. *Quarterly Journal of Speech, 73*, 329–348.

Brenders, D. A. (1989). Perceived control and the interpersonal dimension of health care. *Health Communication, 1*, 117–135. doi: 10.1207/s15327027hc0102_3

Brinker, D. L., Gastil, J., & Richards, R. C. (2015). Inspiring and Informing Citizens Online: A Media Richness Analysis of Varied Civic Education Modalities. *Journal of Computer-Mediated Communication, 20*(5), 504–519.

Brooks, R. D. (1970). The generalizability of early reversals of attitudes toward communication sources. *Speech Monographs, 37*, 152–155.

Brooks, W. D. (1970). Perspectives on communication research. In P. H. Emmert & W. D. Brooks (Eds.), *Methods of research in communication*. Boston: Houghton Mifflin.

Brown, P., & Levinson, S. (1978). Universals in language usage: Politeness phenomena. In E. Goody (Ed.), *Questions and politeness: Strategies in social interaction* (pp. 256–289). New York, NY: Cambridge University Press.

Brown, P., & Levinson, S. C. (1987). *Politeness: Some universals in language usage*. Cambridge, U.K.: Cambridge University Press.

Brown, R. W., & Lenneberg, E. H. (1954). A study in language and cognition. *Journal of Abnormal and Social Psychology, 49*, 454–462.

Brown, T., Boyle, M., Williams, B., Molloy, A., Palermo, C., McKenna, L., & Molloy, L. (2011). Predictors of empathy in health science students. *Journal of Allied Health, 40*, 143–149. doi: 10.1037/t01093-000

Brown, W. J. (1991). An AIDS prevention campaign. *American Behavioral Scientist, 34*, 666–678.

Brown, W. J. (1991). An AIDS prevention campaign: Effects on attitudes, beliefs, and communication behavior. *American Behavioral Scientist, 34,* 666–678.

Buller, D. B., & Aune. R. K. (1988). The effects of vocalics and nonverbal sensitivity on compliance: A speech accommodation theory explanation. *Human Communication Research, 14,* 301–332.

Buller, D. B., & Burgoon, J. K. (1986). The effects of vocalics and nonverbal sensitivity on compliance: A replication and extension. *Human Communication Research, 13,* 126–144.

Buller, D. B., & Burgoon, J. K. (1996). Interpersonal deception theory. *Communication Theory, 6,* 203–242.

Buller, D. B., Burgoon, J. K., White, C., & Ebesu, A. S. (1994). Interpersonal deception: VII: Behavioral profiles in falsification, equivocation, and concealment. *Journal of Language and Social Psychology, 13,* 366–396.

Buller, D. B., Strzyzewski, K. D., & Hunsaker, F. G. (1991). Interpersonal deception: II. The inferiority of conversational participants as deception detectors. *Communication Monographs, 58,* 40.

Buller, M. K., & Buller, D. B. (1987). Physicians' communication style and patient satisfaction. *Journal of Health and Social Behavior, 28,* 375–388.

Burgoon, J., & Burgoon, M. (2001). Expectancy theories. In W. P. Robinson & H. Giles (Eds.), *The new handbook of language and social psychology* (2nd ed., pp. 79–102). Sussex, UK: Wiley.

Burgoon, J. K. (1978). A communication model of personal space violations: Explication and an initial test. *Human Communication Research, 4,* 129–142.

Burgoon, J. K. (1983). Nonverbal violations of expectations. In J. M. Wiemann & R. P. Harrison (Eds.), *Nonverbal interaction* (pp. 77–111). Beverly Hills. CA: Sage.

Burgoon, J. K. (1985). Nonverbal signals. In M. L. Knapp & G. R. Miller (Eds.), *Handbook of interpersonal communication* (pp. 344–390). Beverly Hills: Sage.

Burgoon, J. K., & Buller, D. B. (2004). Interpersonal deception theory. In J. S. Seiter & R. H. Gass (Eds.), *Perspectives on persuasion, social influence, and compliance gaining* (pp. 239–264). Boston: Allyn & Bacon.

Burgoon, J. K., & Buller, D. B. (2008). Interpersonal deception theory: Purposive and interdependent behavior during deception. In L. A. Baxter & D. O. Braithwaite (Eds.), *Engaging theories in interpersonal communication: Multiple perspectives* (pp. 227–239). Thousand Oaks, CA: Sage.

Burgoon, J. K., & Buller, D. B. (2015). Interpersonal deception theory: Purposive and interdependent behavior during deceptive interpersonal interactions. In D. O. Braithwaite & P. Schrodt (Eds.), *Engaging theories in interpersonal communication: Multiple perspectives* (pp. 349–362). Thousand Oaks, CA: Sage.

Burgoon, J. K., Buller, D. B., & Floyd, K. (2002). Does participation affect deception success? A test of the interactivity effect. *Human Communication Research, 27*, 503–534.

Burgoon, J. K., Buller, D. B., Guerrero, L. K., Afifi, W., & Feldman, C. (1996). Interpersonal deception: XII: Information management dimensions underlying deceptive and truthful messages. *Communication Monographs, 63*, 50–69.

Burgoon, J. K., Coker, D. A., & Coker, R. A. (1986). Communicative effects of gaze behavior: A test of two contrasting explanations. *Human Communication Research, 12*, 495–524.

Burgoon, J. K., & Ebesu Hubbard, A. S. (2005). Cross-cultural and intercultural applications of expectancy violations theory and interaction adaptation theory. In W. B. Gudykunst (Ed.), *Theorizing about intercultural communication* (pp. 149–171). Thousand Oaks, CA: Sage.

Burgoon, J. K., & Hale, J. L. (1988). Nonverbal expectancy violations: Model elaboration and application to immediacy behaviors. *Communication Monographs, 55*, 58–79.

Burgoon, J. K., & Jones. S. B. (1976). Toward a theory of personal space expectations and their violations. *Human Communication Research, 2*, 131–146.

Burgoon, J. K., LaPoire, B. A., & Rosenthal, R. (1995). Effects of preinteraction expectancies and target communication on perceiver reciprocity and compensation in dyadic interaction. *Journal of Experimental Social Psychology, 31*, 287–321.

Burgoon, J. K., Pfau, M., Parrott, R., Birk, T., Coker, R., & Burgoon, M. (1987). Relational communication, satisfaction, compliance-gaining strategies, and compliance communication between physicians and patients. *Communication Monographs, 54*, 307–324. doi: 10.1080/03637758709390235

Burgoon, J. K., & Walther, J. B. (1990). Nonverbal expectancies and the evaluative consequences of violations. *Human Communication Research, 17*, 232–265.

Burgoon, M. (1989). Messages and persuasive effects. In J. Bradac (Ed.), *Message effects in communication science* (pp. 129–164). Newbury Park, CA: Sage.

Burgoon, M. (1990). Language and social influence. In H. Giles & P. Robinson (Eds.), *Handbook of language and social psychology* (pp. 51–72). London, UK: Wiley.

Burgoon, M. (1995). Language expectancy theory: Elaboration, explication, and extension. In C. R. Berger & M. Burgoon (Eds.), *Communication and social influence process* (pp. 29–52). East Lansing, MI: Michigan State University Press.

Burgoon, M., & Bettinghaus, E. P. (1980). Persuasive message strategies. In M. E. Roloff & G. R. Miller (Eds.), *Persuasion: New directions in theory and research* (pp. 141–169). Beverly Hills: Sage.

Burgoon, M., Cohen, M., Miller, M. D., & Montgomery, C. L. (1978). An empirical test of a model of resistance to persuasion. *Human Communication Research, 5*, 27–39.

Burgoon, M., Denning, V. P., & Roberts, L. (2002). Language expectancy theory. In J. P. Dillard & M. Pfau (Eds.), *The persuasion handbook* (pp. 117–136). Thousand Oaks, CA: Sage.

Burgoon, M. H., & Burgoon, J. K. (1990). Compliance-gaining and health care. In J. P. Dillard (Ed.), *Seeking compliance* (pp. 161–188). Scottsdale, AZ: Gorsuch Scarisbrick.

Burgoon, M., Jones, S. B., & Stewart, D. (1975). Toward a message centered theory of persuasion: Three empirical investigations of language intensity. *Human Communication Research, 1*, 240–256.

Burke, K. (1950). *A rhetoric of motives*. New York: Prentice-Hall.

Burke, K. (1966). *Language and symbolic action*. Berkeley, CA: University of California Press.

Burleson, B. R. (1984). Role-taking and communication skills in childhood: Why they aren't related and what can be done about it. *Western Journal of Speech Communication, 48*, 155–170.

Burleson, B. R. (1992). Taking communication seriously. *Communication Monographs, 59*, 79–86.

Burleson, B. R. (2003). Emotional support skills. In J. O. Greene & B. R. Burleson (Eds.), *Handbook of communication and social interaction skills* (pp. 551–594). Mahwah, NJ: Erlbaum.

Burleson, B. R. (2007). Constructivism: A general theory of communication skill. In B. B. Whaley & W. Samter (Eds.), *Explaining communication: Contemporary theories and exemplars* (pp. 105–128). Mahwah, NJ: Erlbaum.

Burleson, B. R. (2010). The nature of interpersonal communication: A message-centered approach. In C. R. Berger, M. E. Roloff, & D. Roskos-Ewoldsen (Eds.), *The handbook of communication science* (2nd ed., pp. 145–163). Thousand Oaks, CA: Sage.

Burleson, B. R., & Caplan, S. E. (1998). Cognitive complexity. In J. C. McCroskey, J. A. Daly, M. M. Martin, & M. J. Beatty (Eds.), *Communication and personality: Trait perspectives* (pp. 233–286). Cresskill, NJ: Hampton Press.

Burrell, N. A., & Fitzpatrick, M. A. (1990). The psychological reality of marital conflict. In D. D. Cahn (Ed.), *Intimates in conflict: A communication perspective* (pp. 167–185). Hillsdale, NJ: Lawrence Erlbaum.

Byrne, D. (1971). *The attraction paradigm.* New York: Academic Press.

Byrne, D., Griffitt, W., & Stefaniak. D. (1967). Attraction and similarity of personality characteristics. *Journal of Personality and Social Psychology, 5,* 82–90.

Cacioppo, J. T., Petty, R. E., Feinstein, J. A., & Jarvis, W. B. G. (1996). Dispositional differences in cognitive motivation: The life and times of individuals varying in need for cognition. *Psychological Bulletin, 119,* 197–253.

Cahn, D. D. (1981, May). *A critique of Bertalanffy's general systems theory as a "new paradigm" for the study of human communication.* Paper presented to the International Communication Association, Minneapolis, Minnesota. Cambridge University Press.

Campbell, D. T. (1957). Factors relevant to the validity of experiments in social settings. *Psychological Bulletin, 54,* 297–312.

Campbell, D. T., & Stanley, J. C. (1963). Experimental and quasi-experimental designs for research on teaching. In N. L. Gage (Ed.), *Handbook of research on teaching* (pp. 171–246). Chicago: Rand McNally.

Canary, D. J., & Stafford, L. (1992). Relational maintenance strategies and equity in marriage. *Communication Monographs, 59*(3), 243–267.

Canary, D. J., & Stafford, L. (1994). Maintaining relationships through strategic and routine interaction. In D. J. Canary & L. Stafford (Eds.), *Maintaining relationships through strategic and routine interaction* (pp. 3–22). San Diego, CA: Academic Press.

Cappella, J. N. (1984). The relevance of the microstructure of interaction to relationship change. *Journal of Social and Personal Relationships, 1,* 239–264.

Carbonari, J. P., & DiClemente, C. C. (2000). Using transtheoretical model profiles to differentiate levels of alcohol abstinence success. *Journal of Consulting and Clinical Psychology, 68,* 810. doi: 10.1037/0022-D06x.68.5.810

Cardello, L. L. Ray, E. B., & Pettey, G. R. (1995). The relationship of perceived physician communicator style to patient satisfaction. *Communication Reports, 8,* 27–37. doi: 10.1080/08934219509367604

Carlson, J. R., & Zmud, R. W. (1999). Channel expansion theory and the experiential nature of media richness perceptions. *Academy of management journal, 42*(2), 153–170.

Carmichael, C., & Cronkhite, G. (1965). Frustration and language intensity. *Speech Monographs. 32,* 107–111.

Cathcart, R., & Gumpert, G. (1983). Mediated interpersonal communication: Toward a new typology. *Quarterly Journal of Speech, 69,* 267–277.

Cattell, R. B. (Ed.). (1966). *Handbook of multivariate experimental psychology.* Chicago: Rand McNally.

Caughlin, J. (2002). The demand/withdraw patterns of communication as a predictor of marital satisfaction over time. *Human Communication Research, 28,* 49–86.

Caughlin, J., & Afifi, T. (2004). When is topic avoidance unsatisfying? Examining moderators of the association between avoidance and dissatisfaction. *Human Communication Research, 30,* 479–513.

Caughlin, J. P. (2010). A multiple goals theory of personal relationships: Conceptual integration and program overview. *Journal of Social and Personal Relationships, 27*(6), 824–848.

Caughlin, J. P., Koerner, A. F., Schrodt, P., & Fitzpatrick, M. A. (2011). Interpersonal communication in family relationships. In M. L. Knapp & J. A. Daly (Eds.), *The SAGE Handbook of Interpersonal Communication* (pp. 679–714). Thousand Oaks, CA: SAGE.

Cegala, D. J. (1984). Affective and cognitive manifestations of interaction involvement during unstructured and competitive interactions. *Communication Monographs, 51,* 320–335.

Cegala, D. J., & Lenzmeier-Broz, S. (2003). Provider and patient communication skills training. In A. M. Dorsey, T. L. Thompson, K. I. Miller, & R. Parrot (Eds.), *Handbook of health communication* (pp. 95–120). Mahwah, NJ: Erlbaum.

Cegala, D. J., Savage, G. T., Brunner, C. C., & Conrad, A. B. (1982). An elaboration of the meaning of interaction involvement: Towards the development of a theoretical concept. *Communication Monographs, 49,* 229–245.

Chaffee, S. H., & Rogers, E.M. (Eds.). (1997). *The beginnings of communication study in America: A personal memoir by Wilbur Schramm.* Thousand Oaks, CA: Sage.

Chase, S. (1956). Forward. In J. B. Carroll (Ed.), *Benjamin Lee Whorf: Language, thought and reality* (pp. v–x). Cambridge, MA: The M.I.T. Press.

Cheek, J. M., & Buss, A. H. (1981). Shyness and sociability. *Journal of Personality and Social Psychology, 41,* 330–339.

Chesebro, J. L., & Martin, M. M. (2003). The relationship between conversational sensitivity, cognitive flexibility, verbal aggressiveness, and indirect interpersonal aggressiveness. *Communication Research Reports, 20,* 143–150.

Chew, F., Palmer, S., & Kim. S. (1998). Testing the influence of the health belief model and a television program on nutrition behavior. *Health Communication, 10,* 227–245. doi: 10.1207/s15327027hc/003_3

Child, J. T., Haridakis, P. M., & Petronio, S. (2012). Blogging privacy rule orientations, privacy management, and content deletion practices: The variability of online privacy management activity at different stages of social media use. *Computers in Human Behavior, 28*(5), 1859–1872.

Child, J. T., Petronio, S., Agyeman-Budu, E. A., & Westermann, D. A. (2011). Blog scrubbing: Exploring triggers that change privacy rules. *Computers in Human Behavior, 27*(5), 2017–2027.

Chinese Culture Connection (1987). Chinese values and the search for culture-free dimensions of culture. *International Journal of Psychology, 18,* 143–164.

Cialdini, R. B. (1987). Compliance principles of compliance professionals: Psychologists of necessity. In M. P. Zanna, J. M. Olson, & C. P. Herman (Eds.), *Social influence: The Ontario symposium* (Vol. 5). Hillsdale, NJ: Erlbaum.

Cialdini, R. B. (1988). *Influence: Science and practice* (2nd ed.). New York: Harper Collins.

Cialdini, R. B., & Ascani, K. (1976). Test of a concession procedure for inducing verbal behavior and further compliance with a request to give blood. *Journal of Applied Psychology, 61,* 295–300.

Clark, R. A., & Delia, J. G. (1976). The development of functional persuasive skills in childhood and early adolescence. *Child Development, 47,* 1008–1014.

Clark, R. A., & Delia, J. G. (1977). Cognitive complexity, social perspective-taking, and functional persuasive skills in second- to ninth-grade children. *Human Communication Research, 3,* 128–134.

Cline, R. J., & Cardosi, J. B. (1983). Interpersonal communication skills for physicians: A rationale for training. *Journal of Communication Therapy, 2,* 137–156.

Cobb, S., & Rifkin, J. (1991). Practice and paradox: Deconstructing neutrality in mediation. *Law and Social Inquiry, 35,* 35–62.

Cody, M. J., & McLaughlin, M. L. (1980). Perceptions of compliance-gaining situations: A dimensional analysis. *Communication Monographs, 47,* 132–148.

Cohen, B. (1963). *The press and foreign policy.* Princeton: Princeton University Press.

Colbert, K. R. (1993). The effects of debate participation on argumentativeness and verbal aggression. *Communication Education, 42,* 206–214.

Cole, J. G. (2000). A temperament perspective of nonverbal immediacy. *Communication Research Reports, 17,* 90–94.

Conger, J. A., Kanungo, R. N., & Associates. (1988). *Charismatic leadership: The elusive factor in organizational effectiveness.* San Francisco: Jossey-Bass.

Conlee, C. J., Olvera. J., & Vagim, N. N. (1993). The relationships among physician nonverbal immediacy and measures of patient satisfaction with physical care. *Communication Reports, 6,* 23–33.

Conley, T. M. (1990). *Rhetoric in the European tradition.* New York: Longman.

Cooley, C. H. (1902). *Human nature and the social order.* New York: Scribners.

Costello, D. E. (1977). Health communication theory and research: An overview. In B. Ruben (Ed.). *Communication Yearbook 1* (pp. 557–567). New Brunswick, NJ: Transaction Books.

Courtright, J. A. (1978). A laboratory investigation of groupthink. *Communication Monographs, 45,* 229–246.

Cragan, J. F., & Wright, D. W. (1999). *Communication in small groups* (5th ed.). Belmont, CA: Wadsworth.

Craig, R. T. (1993). Why are there so many communication theories? *Journal of Communication, 43*, 26–33.

Craig, R. T. (1999). Communication as a field. *Communication Theory, 9*, 119–161. doi: 10.1111/j.1468-2885.1999.tb00355.y

Craig, R. T. (2006). Communication as practice. In G. J. Shepherd, J. St. John, & T. Striphas (Eds.), *Communication as...Perspectives on theory* (pp. 38–47). Thousand Oaks, CA: Sage.

Craig, R. T. (2007). Pragmatism in the field of communication theory. *Communication Theory, 17*, 125–145.

Craig, R. T., & Muller, H. L. (2007). *Theorizing communication: Readings across traditions.* Los Angeles, CA: Sage.

Crockett, W. H. (1965). Cognitive complexity and impression formation. In B. A. Maher (Ed.), *Progress in experimental personality research* (Vol. 2, pp. 47–90). New York: Academic Press.

Cronen, V. E., Pearce, W. B., & Tomm, K. (1985). A dialectical view of personal change. In K. Gergen & K. Davis (Eds.), *The social construction of the person* (pp. 203–224). New York: Springer-Verlag.

Cronkhite, G. (1969). *Persuasion: Speech and behavioral change.* Indianapolis: Bobbs-Merrill.

Cronkhite, G. (1976). *Communication and awareness.* Menlo Park, CA: Cummings.

Cronkhite, G. (1986). On the focus, scope, and coherence of the study of human symbolic activity. *Quarterly Journal of Speech, 72*, 231–246.

Cronkhite, G., & Liska, J. R. (1980). The judgment of communicant acceptability. In M. E. Roloff & G. R. Miller (Eds.), *Persuasion: New directions in theory and research* (pp. 101–139). Beverly Hills: Sage.

Culnan, M. J., & Markus, M. L. (1987). Information technologies. In F. M. Jablin, L. L. Putnam, K. H. Roberts, & L. W. Porter (Eds.), *Handbook of organizational communication: An interdisciplinary perspective* (pp. 420–443). Newbury Park, CA: Sage.

Dainton, M., Stafford, L., & Canary, D. J. (1994). Maintenance strategies and physical affection as predictors of love, liking, and satisfaction in marriage. *Communication Reports, 7*(2), 88–98.

Dainton, M., & Zelley, E. D. (2015). *Applying communication theory for professional life, 3rd Ed.* Thousand Oaks, CA: Sage.

Daly, J. A. & McCroskey, J. C. (1984). *Avoiding communication.* Beverly Hills: Sage Publications.

Daly, J. A., Vangelisti, A., & Daughton, S. (1987). The nature and structure of conversational sensitivity. *Human Communication Research, 14,* 167–202.

Dansereau, F., Cashman, J., & Graen, G. B. (1973). Instrumentality theory and equity theory as complementary approaches in predicting the relationship of leaders and turnover among managers. *Organizational Behavior & Human Performance, 10,* 184–200.

Dansereau, F., Graen, G. B., & Haga, W. J. (1975). A vertical dyad linkage approach to leadership within formal organizations: A longitudinal investigation of the role making process. *Organizational Behavior & Human Performance, 13,* 46–78.

Davis, C. S., Powell, H., & Lachlan, K. A. (2013). *Straight talk about communication research methods.* Dubuque, IA: Kendall Hunt.

DeFleur, M. L., & Ball-Rokeach, S. (1982). *Theories of mass communication* (4th ed.). New York: Longman.

Delia, J. G. (1976). A constructivistic analysis of the concept of credibility. *Quarterly Journal of Speech, 62,* 361–375.

Delia, J. G. (1987). Communication research: A history. In C. R. Berger & S. H. Chaffee (Eds.), *Handbook of communication science* (pp. 20–98). Newbury Park, CA: Sage.

Delia, J. G., & Clark, R. A. (1977). Cognitive complexity, social perception, and the development of listener-adapted communication in six-, eight-, ten-, and twelve-year-old boys. *Communication Monographs, 44,* 326–345.

Delia, J. G., Crockett, W. H.. Press, A. N., & O'Keefe, D. J. (1975). The dependency of interpersonal evaluations on context relevant beliefs about the other. *Communication Monographs, 42,* 10–19.

Delia, J. G., O'Keefe, B. J., & O'Keefe, D. J. (1982). The constructivist approach to communication. In F. E. X. Dance (Ed.), *Human communication theory* (pp. 147–191). New York: Harper & Row.

Dennis, A. R., and Valacich, J. S. 1999. "Rethinking Media Richness: Towards a Theory of Media Synchronicity," in Proceedings of the 32nd Hawaii International Conference on System Sciences, Los Alamitos, CA: IEEE Computer Society Press, Volume 1.

Denton, R. E., Jr., & Woodward, G. C. (1998). *Political communication in America* (3rd ed.). New York: Praeger.

DePaulo, B. M., Kashy, D. A., Kirkendol, S. E., Wyer, M. M., & Epstein, J. A. (1996). Lying in everyday life. *Journal of Personality and Social Psychology, 70*(5), 979–995.

DeVito, J. A. (2001). *The interpersonal communication book* (9th ed.). Boston: Allyn & Bacon.

DeVito, J. A. (2002). *Human communication: The basic course* (9th ed.). Boston: Allyn & Bacon.

DiClemente, C. C., & Prochaska, J. O. (1998). Toward a comprehensive, transtheoretical model of change. Stages of change and addictive behaviors. In W. R. Miller & N. Heather (Eds.), *Treating addictive behaviors: Applied clinical psychology* (pp. 3–24). New York: Plenum Press. doi: 10.1007/978-1-4899-1934-2.1

DiClemente, C. C., Prochaska, J. O., Fairhurst, S., Velicer, W. F., Rossi, J. S., & Velasquez, M. (1991). The process of smoking cessation. *Journal of Consulting and Clinical Psychology, 59,* 295–304. doi: 10.1037/0022-D06x.59.2.295

Dillard, J. P. (1990). A goal-driven model of interpersonal influence. In J. P. Dillard (Ed.), *Seeking compliance: The production of interpersonal influence messages* (pp. 41–56). Scottsdale, AZ: Gorsuch-Scarisbrick.

Dillard, J. P. (1997). Explicating the goal construct: Tools for theorists. In J. O. Greene (Ed.*), Message production: Advances in communication theory* (pp. 47–69). Mahwah, N. J.: Lawrence Erlbaum Associates.

Dillard, J. P. (2008). Goals-Plans-Action theory of message production: Making influence messages. In L. A. Baxter & D. O. Braithwaite (Eds.), *Engaging theories in interpersonal communication* (pp. 65–76). Thousand Oaks, CA: Sage.

Dillard, J. P. (2015). Goals-plans-action theory of message production: Making influence messages. In D. Braithwaite & P. Schrodt (Eds.), *Engaging theories in interpersonal communication: Multiple perspectives* (pp. 63–74). Thousand Oaks, CA: Sage.

Dillard, J. P., Anderson, J. W., & Knobloch, L. K. (2002). Interpersonal influence. In M. L. Knapp & J. A. Daly (Eds.), *Handbook of interpersonal communication* (3rd ed., pp. 423–474). Thousand Oaks, CA: Sage.

Dillard, J. P. (Ed.) (1990). *Seeking compliance: The production of interpersonal influence* messages. Scottsdale, AZ: Gorsuch Scarisbrick.

Dillard, J. P., Segrin, C., & Harden, J. M. (1989). Primary and secondary goals in the production of interpersonal influence messages. *Communications Monographs, 56*(1), 19–38.

Dillard, J. P., Solomon, D. H., & Samp, J. A. (1996). Framing social reality: The relevance of relational judgments. *Communication Research, 23*(6), 703–723.

Dingfelder, H. E., & Mandell, D. S. (2011). Bridging the research-to-practice gap in autism intervention: An application of diffusion of innovation theory. *Journal of Autism & Developmental Disorders, 41,* 597–609. doi: 10.1007/s10803-010

Donohew, L., Palmgreen, P., & Rayburn, J. D. (1987). Social and psychological origins of media use: A lifestyle analysis. *Journal of Broadcasting and Electronic Media, 31,* 255–278.

Donohew, L., & Ray, E. B. (1990). Introduction: Systems perspectives on health communication. In E. B. Ray & L. Donohew (Eds.), *Communication and health* (pp. 3–8). Hillsdale, NJ: Lawrence Erlbaum.

Donsbach, W., Tsfati, Y., & Salmon, C. T. (2014). The legacy of spiral of silence theory. In W. Donsbach, C. T. Salmon, & Y. Tsfati, (Eds.), *The spiral of silence: New perspectives on communication and public opinion* (pp. 1–18). New York, NY: Routledge/Taylor & Francis.

Drew, P., & Chilton, K. (2000). Calling just to keep in touch: Regular and habitualized telephone calls as an environment for small talk. In J. Coupland (Ed.), *Small talk* (pp. 137–162). Harlow, UK: Pearson Education Limited.

Drew, P., & Heritage, J. (1992). Analyzing talk at work: An introduction. In P. Drew & J. Heritage (Eds.), *Talk at work* (pp. 3–65). Cambridge, MA: Cambridge University Press.

Duck, S., & Barnes, M. K. (1992). Disagreeing about agreement: Reconciling differences about similarity. *Communication Monographs, 59,* 199–208.

Duck, S. W. (1985). Social and personal relationships. In M. L. Knapp & G. R. Miller (Eds.), *Handbook of interpersonal communication* (pp. 655–686). Beverly Hills: Sage.

Duran, R. L. (1983). Communicative adaptability: A measure of social communicative competence. *Communication Quarterly, 31,* 253–258.

Duran, R. L. (1992). Communicative adaptability: A review of conceptualization and measurement. *Communication Quarterly, 40,* 253–268.

Duran, R. L., & Kelly, L. (1985). An investigation into the cognitive domain of communicating competence. *Communication Research Reports, 2,* 112–119.

Duran, R. L., Kelly, L., & Rotaru, T. (2011). Mobile phones in romantic relationships and the dialectic of autonomy versus connection. *Communication Quarterly, 59*(1), 19–36.

Duran, R. L., & Zakahi, W. R. (1984). Competence or style: What's in a name. *Communication Research Reports, 1,* 42–47.

Duran, R. L., & Zakahi, W. R. (1988). The influence of communicative competence upon roommate satisfaction. *Western Journal of Speech Communication, 52,* 135–146.

D'Urso, S. C., & Rains, S. A. (2008). Examining the scope of channel expansion: A test of channel expansion theory with new and traditional communication media. *Management Communication Quarterly.*

Eadie, W. F. (1990, November). Being applied: Communication research comes of age. *Journal of Applied Communication Research,* Special Issue, 1–6.

Edwards, A. L. (1972). *Experimental design in psychological research* (4th ed.). New York: Holt, Rinehart, and Winston.

Edwards, J. L. (1998). The very model of a modern major (media) candidate: Colin Powell and the theory of reasoned action. Communication *Quarterly, 46,* 163–176.

Ehninger, D. (1968). On systems of rhetoric. *Philosophy and Rhetoric, 1,* 131–144.

Eiser, J. R. (1980). Prolegomena to a more applied social psychology. In R. Gilmour & S. W. Duck (Eds.), *The development of social psychology* (pp. 271–292). New York: Academic Press.

Ekman, P. (1985). *Telling lies.* New York: Norton.

Ellis, D. G. (1992). *From language to communication.* Hillsdale, NJ: Lawrence Erlbaum.

Erdogan, B., Liden, R. C., & Kraimer, M. L. (2006). Justice and leader-member exchange: The moderating role of organizational culture. *Academy of Management Journal, 49,* 395–406.

Ewing, D. (1982). *"Do it my way or you're fired": Employee rights and the changing role of management perspectives.* New York: John Wiley & Sons.

Fallows, D. (2004). *Many Americans use the Internet for everyday activities, but traditional offline habits still dominate.* Retrieved August 12, 2008, from http://www.pewinternet.org/pdfs/PIP_Internet_and_Daily_Life.pdf

Fast, J. (1970). *Body language.* New York: Pocket Books.

Fava, J. L., Velicer, W. F., & Abrahms, D. B. (1995). *Two methods of assessing stages of change for smoking cessation.* Paper presented at the Ninth World Conference on Tobacco and Health, Paris, France.

Fava, J. L., Velicer, W. F., & Prochaska, J. O. (1985). Applying the transtheoretical model to a representative sample of smokers. *Addictive Behaviors, 20,* 189–203. doi: 10.1016/0306-4603(94)00062-x

Fayol, H. (1949). *General and industrial management.* New York: Pitman.

Feezel, J. D. (1974). A qualified certainty: Verbal probability in argument. *Speech Monographs, 41,* 348–356.

Festinger, L. (1957). *A theory of cognitive dissonance.* Stanford: Stanford University Press.

Fiedler, F. E. (1972). How do you make leaders more effective? *American Behavioral Scientist, 24,* 630–631.

Fishbein, M., & Ajzen, I. (1975). *Belief, attitude, intention and behavior: An introduction to theory and research.* Reading, MA: Addison-Wesley.

Fisher, B. A. (1970). Decision emergence: Phases in group decision making. *Speech Monographs, 37,* 53–66.

Fisher, J. Y. (1974). A Burkean analysis of the rhetorical dimensions of a multiple murder and suicide. *Quarterly Journal of Speech, 60,* 175–189.

Fitzpatrick, M. A. (1977). A typological approach to communication in relationships. In B. Ruben (Ed.), *Communication Yearbook 1* (pp. 263–275). New Brunswick, NJ: Transaction Books.

Fitzpatrick, M. A. (1983). Predicting couples' communication from couples' self reports. In R. N. Bostrom & B. H. Westley (Eds.), *Communication Yearbook 7* (pp. 49–82). Beverly Hills: Sage.

Fitzpatrick, M. A. (1984). A typological approach in marital interaction: Recent theory and research. In L. Berkowitz (Ed.). *Advances in experimental social psychology* (Vol. 18, pp. 1–47). Orlando: Academic Press.

Fitzpatrick, M. A. (1988). *Between husbands and wives: Communication in marriage.* Newbury Park, CA: Sage.

Fitzpatrick, M. A., & Ritchie, L. D. (1994). Communication schemata within the family: Multiple perspectives on family interaction. *Human Communication Research, 20,* 275–301.

Fitzpatrick, M. A., & Wamboldt, F. S. (1990). Where is all said and done? Toward an integration of intrapersonal and interpersonal models of marital and family communication. *Communication Research, 17,* 421–430.

Flew, T. (2002). *Newmedia.* Melbourne, Australia: Oxford University Press.

Florence, B. T. (1975). An empirical test of the relationship of evidence to belief systems and attitude change. *Human Communication Research, 1,* 145–158.

Floyd, K. (2011). Endocrinology in communication research. *Communication Research Reports, 28,* 369–372.

Floyd, K., & Burgoon, J. K. (1999). Reacting to nonverbal expressions of liking: A test of interaction adaptation theory. *Communication Monographs, 66,* 219–239.

Floyd, K., Ramirez, A., Jr., & Burgoon, J. K. (1999). Expectancy violations theory. In L. K. Guerrero, J. A. DeVito, & M. L. Hecht (Eds.), *The Nonverbal Communication Reader* (2nd ed., pp. 437–444). Prospect Heights. IL: Waveland Press.

Floyd, K., & Voloudakis, M. (1999). Affectionate behavior in adult platonic friendships: Interpreting and evaluating expectancy violations. *Human Communication Research, 25,* 341–369.

Foss, S., Foss, K., & Trapp, R. (1991). *Contemporary perspectives on rhetoric* (2nd Ed.). Prospect Heights, IL: Waveland Press.

Fox, J., Warber, K. M., & Makstaller, D. C. (2013). The role of Facebook in romantic relationship development. An exploration of Knapp's relational stage model. *Journal of Social and Personal Relationships, 30*(6), 771–794.

Franke, R. H., & Kaul, J. D. (1978). The Hawthorne experiments: First statistical interpretation. *American Sociological Review, 43,* 623–639.

Frank, J. D., & Frank, J. B. (1991). *Persuasion and healing: A comparative study of psychotherapy.* Baltimore: The Johns Hopkins University Press.

Frey, L. R. & Botan, C. H. (1988). The status of instruction in introductory undergraduate communication research methods. *Communication Education, 37,* 249–256.

Friedman, M. (1970, September 13). The social responsibility of business is to increase its profits. *The New York Times Magazine.*

Frisby, B. N., & Martin, M. M. (2010). Interpersonal motives and supportive communication. *Communication Research Reports, 27*(4), 320–329.

Fromm, E. (1947). *Man for himself.* New York, NY: Rinehart & Winston.

Galvin, K. M., & Brommel, B. J. (2000). *Family communication* (5th ed.). Boston: Allyn & Bacon.

Gangestad, S. W., & Snyder, M. (2000). Self-monitoring: Appraisal and reappraisal. *Psychological Bulletin, 126,* 530–555.

Garko, M. (1994). Communicator styles of powerful physician-executives in upward-influence situations. *Health Communication, 6,* 159–172. doi: 10.1207/s15327027hc0602_5

Gass, R. H., & Seiter, J. S. (2014). *Persuasion: Social influence and compliance gaining, 5th Ed.* Boston, MA: Pearson.

Gastil, J. (1995). An appraisal and revision of the constructivist research program. In B. R. Burleson (Ed.), *Communication yearbook 18* (pp. 83–104). Thousand Oaks, CA: Sage.

Gerbner, G., & Gross, L. (1976a). Living with television: The violence profile. *Journal of Communication, 26,* 172–199.

Gerbner, G., & Gross, L. (1976b). The scary world of TV's heavy viewer. *Psychology Today,* pp. 41–45, 89.

Gerbner, G., Gross, L., Morgan, M., & Signorielli, N. (1980). The "mainstreaming" of America: Violence profile no. 11. *Journal of Communication, 30,* 10–29.

Gerbner, G., Gross, L., Morgan, M., & Signorielli, N. (1986). Living with television: The dynamics of the cultivation process. In J. Bryant & D. Zillmann (Eds.). *Perspectives on media effects* (pp. 17–40). Hillsdale, NJ: Lawrence Erlbaum.

Gergen, K. J. (1980). Toward intellectual audacity in social psychology. In R. Gilmour & S. W. Duck (Eds.). *The development of social psychology* (pp. 239–270). New York: Academic Press.

Gibbs, J. L., Ellison, N. B., & Heino, R. D. (2006). Self-presentation in online personals: The role of anticipated future interaction, self-disclosure, and perceived success in Internet dating. *Communication Research, 33,* 1–26.

Gibbs, J. L., Ellison, N. B., & Lai, C.-H. (2011). First comes love, then comes Google: An investigation of uncertainty reduction strategies and self-disclosure in online dating. *Communication Research, 38*(1), 70–100.

Giffin, K., & Patton, B. R. (1971). *Fundamentals of interpersonal communication.* New York: Harper & Row.

Giles, H., Mulac, A., Bradac, J. J., & Johnson, P. (1987). Speech accommodation theory: The first decade and beyond. In M. McLaughlin (Ed.), *Communication Yearbook 10* (pp. 13–48). Newbury Park, CA: Sage.

Giles, H., & Wiemann, J. M. (1987). Language, social comparison, and power. In C. R. Berger & S. H. Chaffee (Eds.), *The handbook of communication science* (pp. 350–384). Newbury Park. CA: Sage.

Glynn, C. J., Hayes, A. F., & Shanahan, J. (1997). Perceived support for one's opinions and willingness to speak out: A meta-analysis of survey studies on the "spiral of silence." *Public* Opinion *Quarterly, 61,* 452–463.

Glynn, C. J., & Huge, M. E. (2014). Speaking in spirals: An updated meta-analysis of the spiral of silence. In W. Donsbach, C. T. Salmon & Y. Tsfati, (Eds.), *The spiral of silence: New perspectives on communication and public opinion* (pp. 65–72). New York, NY: Routledge/Taylor & Francis.

Glynn, C. J., & McLeod, J. M. (1985). Implications of the spiral of silence theory for communication and public opinion research. In K. R. Sanders, L. L. Kaid, & D. Nimmo (Eds.), *Political communication yearbook 1984* (pp. 43–65). Carbondale, IL: Southern Illinois University Press.

Goffman, E. (1959). *The presentation of self in everyday life*. Garden City, NY: Anchor/Doubleday.

Goffman, E. (1959). *The presentation of self in everyday life*. New York: Doubleday & Co.

Goffman, E. (1967). *Interaction ritual: Essays on face-face behavior*. Garden City, NY: Anchor Books.

Golden, J. L., Berquist, G. F., & Coleman, W. E. (1978). *The rhetoric of Western thought* (2nd Ed.). Dubuque, IA: Kendall/Hunt Publishing Co.

Goldsmith, D. J. (2007). Brown and Levinson's politeness theory. In B. B. Whaley, & W. Samter, (Eds.), *Explaining communication: Contemporary theories and exemplars* (pp. 219–236). Mahwah, NJ: Lawrence Erlbaum.

Goldsmith, D. J. (2008). Politeness theory: How we use language to save face. In L. Baxter, & D. O. Braithwaite, (Eds.), *Engaging theories in interpersonal communication* (pp. 255–267). Thousand Oaks, CA: Sage.

Goldsmith, D. J. (2009). Politeness theory. In S. W. Littlejohn, & K. Foss, (Eds.). *Encyclopedia of communication theory* (pp. 754–756). Los Angeles, CA: Sage.

Gonzenbach, W. J., King, C., & Jablonski. P. (1999). Homosexuals and the military: An analysis of the spiral of silence. *The Howard Journal of Communications, 10,* 281–296.

Goodboy, A. K., Martin, M. M., & Bolkan, S. (2009). The development and validation of the Student Communication Satisfaction Scale. *Communication Education, 58,* 372–396.

Gorden, W. I., Infante, D. A., & Braun, A. A. (1986). Communicator style: Is the metaphor appropriate? *Communication Research Reports, 3,* 13–19.

Gouran, D. S., & Hirokawa, R. Y. (1986). Counteractive functions of communication in effective group decision making. In R. Y. Hirokawa & M. S. Poole (Eds.), *Communication and group decision making* (pp. 81–90). Beverly Hills: Sage.

Graham, E. E., Barbato, C. A., & Perse, E. M. (1993). The interpersonal communication motives model. *Communication Quarterly, 41,* 172–186.

Grant, A. E., Guthrie. K. K., & Ball-Rokeach, S. J. (1991). Television shopping: A media system dependency perspective. *Communication Research, 18,* 773–798.

Grice, P. (1989). *Studies in the way of words*. Cambridge, MA: Harvard University Press.

Griffin, E. (2006). *A first look at communication theory* (6th ed.). Boston: McGraw-Hill.

Gruner, C. R. (1965). An experimental study of satire as persuasion. *Speech Monographs, 32,* 149–154.

Gruner, C. R. (1970). The effect of humor in dull and interesting informative speeches. *Central States Speech Journal, 21,* 160–166.

Gubrium, J. F., & Holstein, H. A. (2008). The constructionist mosaic. In J. A. Holstein & J. F. Gubrium (Eds.), *Handbook of constructionist research* (pp. 3–10). New York: Guilford.

Gudykunst, W. (1985). A model of uncertainty reduction in intercultural encounters. *Journal of Language and Social Psychology, 4,* 79–98.

Gudykunst, W. (2005). An anxiety/uncertainty management (AUM) theory of effective communication: Making the mesh of the net finer. In W. Gudykunst (Ed.), *Theorizing about intercultural communication* (pp. 281–322). Thousand Oaks, CA: Sage.

Gudykunst, W. B., & Nishida. T. (1984). Individual and cultural influence on uncertainty reduction. *Communication Monographs, 51,* 23–36.

Gudykunst, W., & Hammer, M. R. (1988). Strangers and hosts. In Y. Y. Kim & W. B. Gudykunst (Eds.), *Cross-cultural adaptation* (pp. 106–139). Newbury Park, CA: Sage.

Gulley, H., & Berlo, D. (1956). Effects of intercellular and intracellular speech structure on attitude change and learning. *Speech Monographs, 23,* 288–297.

Gumpert, G., & Cathcart, R. (Eds.). (1986). *Inter/Media: Interpersonal communication in a media world* (3rd ed.). New York: Oxford University Press.

Gunawardena, C. N. (1995). Social presence theory and implications for interaction and collaborative learning in computer conferences. *International Journal of Educational Telecommunications, 1,* 147–166.

Haas, S. M., & Stafford, L. (2005). Maintenance behaviors in same-sex and marital relationships: A matched sample comparison. *The Journal of Family Communication, 5*(1), 43–60.

Hackman, M. Z., & Johnson, C. E. (2000). *Leadership: A communication perspective*. Prospect Heights, IL: Waveland Press.

Haig, B. (2005). An abductive theory of scientific method. *Psychological Methods, 10,* 371–388.

Hall, J., Park, N., Song, H., & Cody, M. (2010). Strategic misrepresentation in online dating. *Journal of Social and Personal Relationships, 27,* 117–135.

Hamilton, M. A., Hunter, J. E., & Burgoon, M. (1990). An empirical test of an axiomatic model of the relationship between language intensity and persuasion. *Journal of Language and Social Psychology, 9,* 235–255.

Ham, O. K., & Lee, Y. J. (2007). Use of the transtheoretical model to predict stages of smoking cessation in Korean adolescents. *Journal of School Health, 77,* 319–326. doi: 10.1111/j.1746-1561.2007.00213.x

Hample, D. (1977). Testing a model of value argument and evidence. *Communication Monographs, 44,* 106–120.

Hample, D. (1979). Predicting belief and belief change using a cognitive theory of argument and evidence. *Communication Monographs, 46,* 142–146.

Hample, D. (1981, May). *Models of arguments using multiple bits of evidence.* Paper presented at the annual meeting of the International Communication Association, Minneapolis. MN.

Hample, D. (1999). The life space of personalized conflicts. In M. E. Roloff (Ed.), *Communication yearbook 22* (pp. 171–207). Thousand Oaks, CA: Sage.

Hample, D., & Dallinger, J. M. (1995). A Lewinian perspective on taking conflict personally. *Communication Quarterly, 43,* 297–319.

Harringer, D., Lu, W., McKyer, E. Lisako, J., Pruitt, B. E., & Goodson, P. (2014). Assessment of school wellness policies implementation by benchmarking against diffusion of innovation. *Journal of School Health, 84,* 275–283. doi: 10.1111/josh.12145

Hart, R. P., Carlson, R. E., & Eadie, W. F. (1980). Attitudes toward communication and the assessment of rhetorical sensitivity. *Communication Monographs, 47,* 1–22.

Hatfield, E., & Rapson, R. L. (1992). Similarity and attraction in close relationships. *Communication Monographs, 59,* 209–212.

Hawes, L.C. (1975). *Pragmatics of analoguing: Theory and model construction in communication.* Menlo Park, CA: Addison-Wesley Publishing Co.

Hawking, S. (1996). *The illustrated a brief history of time* (Updated and expanded ed.). New York: Bantam Books.

Hawkins, R. P., & Pingree, S. (1982). Television's influence on social reality. In D. Pearl, L. Bouthilet, & J. Lazar (Eds.), *Television and behavior: Ten years of scientific progress and implications for the eighties: Vol. 2. Technical reviews* (pp. 224–247). Washington. DC: U.S. Government Printing Office.

Heider, F. (1958). *Psychology of interpersonal relations.* New York: Wiley.

Heims, S. J. (1991). *The cybernetic group.* Cambridge, MA: MIT Press.

Heisel, A. D. (2010). Verbal aggression and prefrontal cortex asymmetry. In T. A. Avtgis, & A. S. Rancer (Eds.), *Arguments, aggression, and conflict: New directions in theory and research* (pp. 26–43). New York: Routledge.

Hempel, C. G. (1965). *Aspects of scientific explanation and other essays in the philosophy of science.* New York: The Free Press.

Henderson, S., & Gilding, M. (2004). "I've never clicked this much with anyone in my life": Trust and hyperpersonal communication in online friendships. *New Media & Society, 6,* 487–506.

Henningsen, M. L. M., Valde, K. S., Russell, G. A., & Russell, G. R. (2011). Student–faculty interactions about disappointing grades: Application of the goals–plans–actions model and the theory of planned behavior. *Communication Education, 60*(2), 174–190.

Henson, D. F., Dybvig-Pawelko, K. C., & Canary, D. J. (2004). The effects of loneliness on relational maintenance behaviors: An attributional perspective. *Communication Research Reports, 21*(4), 411–419.

Heritage, J. (1984). *Garfinkel and ethnomethodology.* Oxford, UK: Polity Press.

Hersey, P. (1984). *The situational leader.* Escondido, CA: Center for Leadership Studies.

Hersey, P., & Blanchard, K. H. (1977). *Management of organizational behavior: Utilizing human resources* (3rd ed.). Englewood Cliffs, NJ: Prentice Hall.

Herzberg, F. (1968). One more time: How do you motivate employees? *Harvard Business Review, 46,* 53–62.

Herzberg, F. (1982). *Managerial choice: To be efficient and to be human.* Provo, UT: Olympus.

Hiers, J. M., & Heckel, R. V. (1977). Seating choice, leadership, and locus of control. *Journal of Social Psychology, 103,* 313–314.

Hinkle, L. L. (1999). Nonverbal immediacy communication behaviors and liking in marital relationships. *Communication Research Reports, 16,* 81–90.

Hirokawa, R. Y. (1985). Discussion procedures and decision-making performance: A test of a functional perspective. *Human Communication Research, 12,* 203–224.

Hirokawa, R. Y. (1988). Group communication and decision-making performance: A continued test of the functional perspective. *Human Communication Research, 14,* 487–515.

Hirokawa, R. Y., & Pace, R. (1983). A descriptive investigation of the possible communication-based reasons for effective and ineffective group decision making. *Communication Monographs, 50,* 363–379.

Hirokawa, R. Y., & Scheerhorn, D. R. (1986). Communication in faulty group decision making. In R. Y. Hirokawa & M. S. Poole (Eds.), *Communication and group decision making* (pp. 63–80). Beverly Hills: Sage.

Hirschburg, P. L., Dillman, D. A., & Ball-Rokeach, S. J. (1986). Media system dependency theory: Responses to the eruption of Mount St. Helens. In S. Ball-Rokeach & M. G. Cantor (Eds.), *Media, audience, and social structure* (pp. 117–128). Newbury Park, CA: Sage Publications.

Hirsch, P. (1980). The "scary world" of the nonviewer and other anomalies. *Communication Research, 7,* 403–456.

Hofstede, G. (1980). *Culture's consequences: International differences in work-related values.* Beverly Hills, CA: Sage.

Hofstede, G. (2001). *Culture's consequences* (2nd ed.). Thousand Oaks, CA: Sage.

Hofstede, G., Hofstede, G. J., & Minkov, M. (2010). *Cultures and organizations: Software of the mind* (3rd ed.). New York, NY: McGraw-Hill.

Hoover, K. R. (1992). *The elements of social scientific thinking* (5th ed.). New York: St. Martin's Press.

Hopper, R.. Koch, S., & Mandelbaum. J. (1986). Conversation analysis methods. In D. G. Ellis & W. A. Donohue (Eds.). *Contemporary issues in language and discourse processes* (pp. 169–186). Hillsdale, NJ: Lawrence Erlbaum.

Horner, W. B. (Ed.). (1990). *The present state of scholarship in historical and contemporary rhetoric* (Rev. ed.). Columbia and London: University of Missouri Press.

Horton, D., & Wohl, R. R. (1956). Mass communication and parasocial interaction: Observations on intimacy at a distance. *Psychiatry, 19,* 215–229.

House, R. J., Hanges, P. J., Javidan, M., Dorfman, P. W., & Gupta, V. (2004). *Culture, leadership, and organizations: The GLOBE study of 62 societies.* Thousand Oaks, CA: Sage.

Hovland, C. (1948). Social communication. *Proceedings of the American Philosophical Society, 92,* 371–375.

Hovland, C. I. (Ed.) (1957). *The order of presentation in persuasion.* New Haven: Yale University Press.

Hovland, C. I., & Janis, I. L. (Eds.) (1959). *Personality and persuasibility.* New Haven: Yale University Press.

Hovland, C. I., Janis, I. L., & Kelley, H. H. (1953). *Communication and persuasion.* New Haven: Yale University Press.

Hughes, M. (1980). The fruits of cultivation analysis: A reexamination of some effects of television watching. *Public Opinion Quarterly, 44,* 287–302.

Hullman, G. A. (2007). Communicative adaptability scale: Evaluating its use as an "other-report" measure. *Communication Reports, 20,* 51–74.

Hu, M. (2015). The influence of a scandal on parasocial relationship, parasocial interaction, and parasocial breakup. *Psychology of Popular Media Culture, http://dx.doi.org/10.1037/ppm0000068.*

Hunleth, J. M., Steinmetz, E. K., McQueen, A., James, A. S. (2016). Beyond adherence: Health care disparities and the struggle to get screened for colon cancer. *Qualitative Health Research, 26,* 17–31. doi: 10.1177/1049732315593549

Hunter, J. & Boster, F. (1987). A model of compliance-gaining message selection. *Communication Monographs, 54,* 63–84.

Infante, D. A. (1973). Forewarnings in persuasion: Effects of opinionated language and forewarner and speaker authoritativeness. *Western Speech, 37,* 185–195.

Infante, D. A. (1975a). Differential functions of desirable and undesirable consequences in predicting attitude and attitude change toward proposals. *Speech Monographs, 42,* 115–134.

Infante, D. A. (1975b). The effects of opinionated language on communicator image and in conferring resistance to persuasion. *Western Journal of Speech Communication, 39,* 112–119.

Infante, D. A. (1975c). Richness of fantasy and beliefs about attempts to refute a proposal as determinants of attitude. *Speech Monographs, 42,* 75–79.

Infante, D. A. (1976). Persuasion as a function of the receiver's prior success or failure as a message source. *Communication Quarterly, 24,* 21–26.

Infante, D. A. (1978). Similarity between advocate and receiver: The role of instrumentality. *Central States Speech Journal, 24,* 187–193.

Infante, D. A. (1980). Verbal plans: A conceptualization and investigation. *Communication Quarterly, 28,* 3–10.

Infante, D. A. (1987a). Aggressiveness. In J. C. McCroskey & J. A. Daly (Eds.), *Personality and interpersonal communication* (pp. 157–192). Newbury Park, CA: Sage Publications.

Infante, D. A. (1987b, July). *Argumentativeness in superior-subordinate communication: An essential condition for organizational productivity.* Paper presented at the American Forensics Summer Conference of the Speech Communication Association, Alta, UT.

Infante, D. A. (1987). Enhancing the prediction of response to a communication situation from communication traits. *Communication Quarterly, 35,* 305–316.

Infante, D. A. (1987, May). *An independent-mindedness model of organizational productivity: The role of communication education.* Paper presented at the annual meeting of the Eastern Communication Association, Syracuse, NY.

Infante, D. A. (1988). *Arguing constructively.* Prospect Heights, IL: Waveland Press.

Infante, D. A. (1995). Teaching students to understand and control verbal aggression. *Communication Education, 44,* 51–63.

Infante, D. A., Anderson, C. M., Martin, M. M., Herington. A. D., & Kim, J. (1993). Subordinates' satisfaction and perceptions of verbal aggressiveness and style. *Management Communication Quarterly, 6,* 307–326.

Infante, D. A., Chandler, T. A., & Rudd, J. E. (1989). Test of an argumentative skill deficiency model of interspousal violence. *Communication Monographs, 56,* 163–177.

Infante, D. A., & Gorden, W. I. (1981). Similarities and differences in the communicator styles of superiors and subordinates: Relations to subordinate satisfaction. *Communication Quarterly, 30,* 67–71.

Infante, D. A., & Gorden, W. I. (1985). Superiors' argumentativeness and verbal aggressiveness as predictors of subordinates' satisfaction. *Human Communication Research, 12,* 117–125.

Infante, D. A., & Gorden, W. I. (1987). Superior and subordinate communication profiles: Implications for independent-mindedness and upward effectiveness. *Central States Speech Journal, 38,* 73–80.

Infante, D. A., & Gorden, W. I. (1989). Argumentativeness and affirming communicator style as predictors of satisfaction/dissatisfaction with subordinates. *Communication Quarterly, 37,* 81–90.

Infante, D. A., & Gorden, W. I. (1991). How employees see the boss: Test of an argumentative and affirming model of supervisors' communicative behavior. *Western Journal of Speech Communication, 55,* 294–304.

Infante, D. A., & Grimmett, R. A. (1971). Attitudinal effects of utilizing a critical method of analysis. *Central States Speech Journal, 22,* 213–217.

Infante, D. A., Parker, K. R., Clarke, C. H., Wilson, L., & Nathu, I. A. (1983). A comparison of factor and functional approaches to source credibility. *Communication Quarterly, 31,* 43–48.

Infante, D. A., & Rancer, A. S. (1982). A conceptualization and measure of argumentativeness. *Journal of Personality Assessment, 46,* 72–80.

Infante, D. A., & Rancer, A. S. (1996). Argumentativeness and verbal aggressiveness: A review of recent theory and research. In B. R. Burleson (Ed.), *Communication Yearbook 19* (pp. 319–351). Thousand Oaks, CA: Sage Publications.

Infante, D. A., Sabourin, T. C., Rudd. J. E., & Shannon, E. A. (1990). Verbal aggression in violent and nonviolent marital disputes, *Communication Quarterly, 38,* 361–371.

Infante, D. A., Trebing, J. D., Shepherd, P. E., & Seeds, D. E. (1984). The relationship of argumentativeness to verbal aggression. *Southern Speech Communication Journal, 50,* 67–77.

Infante, D. A., & Wigley, C. J. III. (1986). Verbal aggressiveness: An interpersonal model and measure. *Communication Monographs, 53,* 61–69.

Iyengar, S., & Kinder, D. R. (1985). Psychological accounts of agenda-setting. In S. Kraus & R. M. Perloff (Eds.), *Mass media and political thought* (pp. 117–140). Beverly Hills: Sage.

Jablin, F. M. (2001). Organizational entry, assimilation, and disengagement/exit. In F. M. Jablin, L. L. Putnam (Eds.), *The new handbook of organizational communication: Advances in theory, research, and methods* (pp. 732–818). Newbury Park, CA: Sage.

Jablin, F. M., & Putnam, L. L. (Eds.). (2001). *The new handbook of organizational communication: Advances in theory, research, and methods.* Newbury Park, CA: Sage.

Jacobs, S. (1980). Recent advances in discourse analysis. *Quarterly Journal of Speech, 66,* 450–472.

Jacobs, S. (1988). Evidence and inference in conversation analysis. In J. A. Anderson (Ed.), *Communication Yearbook 11* (pp. 433–443). Newbury Park, CA: Sage.

Janis, I. L. (1972, 1982). *Groupthink: Psychological studies of policy decisions and fiascoes* (2nd ed.). Boston: Houghton Mifflin.

Janis, I. L., & Feshbach, S. (1953). Effects of fear-arousing communications. *Journal of Abnormal and Social Psychology, 48,* 78–92.

Janis, I. L., & Mann, L. (1977). *Decision making.* London: Cassel & Collier Macmillan.

Jefferson, G. (2004). Glossary of transcript symbols with an introduction. In G. H. Lerner (Ed.), *Conversation analysis: Studies from the first generation* (pp. 225–256). Amsterdam: John Benjamins.

Jeffres, L. W., Neuendorf, K. A., & Atkin, D. (1999). Spirals of silence: Expressing opinions when the climate of opinion is unambiguous. *Political Communication, 16,* 115–131.

Johannesen, R. L. (1996). *Ethics in human communication* (4th ed.). Prospect Heights, IL: Waveland Press.

Johnson, A. (1990). Trends in political communication: A selective review of research in the 1980's. In D. L. Swanson & D. Nimmo (Eds.), *New directions in political communication* (pp. 329–362). Newbury Park, CA: Sage.

Johnson, D. W., & Johnson, R. T. (1979). Conflict in the classroom: Controversy and learning. *Review of Educational Research, 49,* 51–70.

Johnson, S. S., Paiva, A. L., Cummins, C. O., Johnson, J. L., Dyment, S. J., Wright, J. A., Prochaska, J. O., Prochaska, J. M., & Sherman, K. (2008). Transtheoretical model-based multiple behavior intervention for weight management: Effectiveness on a population basis. *Preventative Medicine, 46,* 238–246. doi: 10.1016/j.ypmed.2007.09.010

Johnston, J., & Ettema, J. S. (1986). Using television to best advantage: Research for prosocial television. In J. Bryant & D. Zillmann (Eds.), *Perspectives on media effects* (pp. 143–164). Hillsdale, NJ: Lawrence Erlbaum.

Jones, S. M., & Wirtz, J. (2006). How *does* the comforting process work?: An empirical test of an appraisal-based model of comforting. *Human Communication Research, 32,* 217–243. doi: 10.1111/j.1468-2958.2006.00274.x

Jordan, J. M., & Roloff, M. E. (1997). Planning skills and negotiator goal accomplishment. *Communication Research, 24,* 31–63.

Kanter, R. M. (1977). *Men and women of the corporation.* New York: Basic Books.

Kaplan, A. (1964). *The conduct of inquiry: Methodology for behavioral science.* San Francisco, CA: Chandler Publishing Company.

Kassing, J. W., & Avtgis, T. A. (1999). Examining the relationship between organizational dissent and aggressive communication. *Management Communication Quarterly, 13,* 100–115.

Kato, T. (2001). The end of lifetime employment in Japan?: Evidence from the national surveys and field research. *Journal of the Japanese and International Economies, 15,* 489–514.

Katz, E., & Lazarsfeld, P. F. (1955). *Personal influence: The part played by people in the flow of mass communication.* New York: Free Press.

Keltner, J. W. (1970). *Interpersonal speech-communication: Elements and structures.* Belmont. CA: Wadsworth.

Kennedy, G. (1963). *The art of persuasion in Greece.* Princeton, NJ: Princeton University Press.

Kerlinger, F. N. (1986). *Foundations of behavioral research.* New York: Holt, Rinehart, and Wilson.

Kiesler, C. A., & Kiesler, S. B. (1969). *Conformity.* Reading, MA: Addison-Wesley.

Kiesler, C., Collins. B., & Miller, N. (1969). *Attitude change: A critical analysis of theoretical approaches.* New York: John Wiley.

Kiesler, S., & Sproull, L. (1992). Group decision making and communication technology. *Organizational Behavior and Human Decision Processes, 52,* 96–123.

Kilduff, M., & Day, D. (1994). Do chameleons get ahead? The effects of self-monitoring on managerial careers. *Academy of Management Journal, 37,* 1047–1060.

Kim, Y. Y. (1988). *Communication and cross-cultural adaptation: An integrative theory.* Clevendon, UK: Multilingual Matters.

Kim, Y.Y. (1989) 'Personal, social, and economic adaptation: the case of 1975–79 arrivals in Illinois', in D. Haines (ed.) Refugees as Immigrants: Survey Research on Cambodians, Laotians, and Vietnamese in America, Totowa, NJ: Rowman and Littlefield, pp. 86–104.

Kim, Y. Y. (2001). *Becoming intercultural: An integrative theory of communication and cross-cultural adaptation.* Thousand Oaks, CA: Sage.

Kim, Y. Y. (2005). Adapting to a new culture: An integrative communication theory. In W. B. Gudykunst (Ed.), *Theorizing about intercultural communication* (pp. 375–400). Thousand Oaks, CA: Sage.

Kim, Y.Y. and Kim, Y.S. (2004) The role of the host environment in cross-cultural adaptation: a comparative analysis of Korean expatriates in the United States and their American counterparts in South Korea, Asian Communication Research, 1(1): 5–25

Kim, Y. Y., & McKay-Semmler, K. (2013). Social engagement and cross-cultural adaptation: An examination of direct-and mediated interpersonal communication activities of educated non-natives in the United States. *International Journal of Intercultural Relations, 37*(1), 99–112.

King, D., Vlaev, I., Everett-Thomas, R., Fitzpatrick, M., Darzi, A., & Birnbach, D. J. (2016). 'Priming' hand hygiene compliance in clinical environments. *Health Psychology, 35,* 96–101. doi: 10.1037/hea0000239

Kiousis, S., Mitrook, M., Wu, X., & Seltzer, T. (2006). First- and second-level agenda-building and agenda-setting effects: Exploring the linkages among candidate news releases, media coverage, and public opinion during the 2002 Florida gubernatorial election. *Journal of Public Relations Research, 18,* 265–285.

Kitcher, P. (1982). *Abusing science: The case against creationism.* Cambridge, MA: MIT Press.

Knapp, M. L. (1978). *Social intercourse: From greeting to goodbye.* Needham Heights, MA: Allyn & Bacon.

Knapp, M. L. (1984). Forward. In M. L. McLaughlin. *Conversation: How talk is organized.* Beverly Hills: Sage.

Knapp, M. L., & Comadena, M. E. (1979). Telling it like it isn't: A review of theory and research on deceptive communications. *Human Communication Research, 5,* 270–285.

Knapp, M. L., Hart, R. P., Friedrich, G. W., & Shulman, G. M. (1973). The rhetoric of goodbye: Verbal and nonverbal correlates of human leave-taking. *Speech Monographs, 40,* 182–198.

Knapp, M. L., & Vangelisti, A. L. (2005). *Interpersonal communication and human relationships.* Boston: Allyn & Bacon.

Knobloch, L. (2015). The relational turbulence model: Communicating during times of transition. In D. O. Braithwaite & P. Schrodt (Eds.), *Engaging theories in supportive communication* (pp. 377–388). Thousand Oaks, CA: Sage.

Knopper, S. (2013, June 12). Myspace Relaunches, But Does It Have a Chance? RollingStone. Retrieved February 27, 2016, from http://www.rollingstone.com/music/news/myspace-relaunches-but-does-it-have-a-chance-20130612

Knower, F. R. (1935). Experimental studies of attitude change I: A study of effect of oral argument on changes of attitude. *Journal of Abnormal and Social Psychology, 6,* 315–347.

Koenig, F., & Lesson, G. (1985). Viewers' relationship to television personalities. *Psychological Reports, 57,* 263–266.

Koermer, C., Goldstein, M., & Fortson, D. (1993). How supervisors communicatively convey immediacy to subordinates: An exploratory qualitative investigation. *Communication Quarterly, 41,* 269–281.

Koerner, A. F., & Fitzpatrick, M. A. (2002). Toward a theory of family communication. *Communication Theory, 12*(1), 70–91

Koerner, A. F., & Schrodt, P. (2014). An introduction to the special issue on family communication patterns theory. *Journal of Family Communication, 14*(1), 1–15.

Kotter, J. P. (1988). *The leadership factor.* New York: Free Press.

Kowalewski, J. (2014). It's not just a laughing matter: How entertainment news programs influence the transfer of the media's agenda to the public's agenda similiarly to traditional hard news. In T. J. Johnson (Ed.), *Agenda-setting in a 2.0 world* (pp. 134–155). New York, N.J.: Routledge/ Taylor & Francis.

Kreps, G. (1979). *Human communication and Weik's model of organizing: A field experimental test and revaluation* (Vol. 40): Dissertation Abstracts International.

Kreps, G. L. (1988). The pervasive role of information in health care: Implications for health communication policy. In J. Anderson (Ed.). *Communication Yearbook 11* (pp. 238–276). Newbury Park, CA: Sage.

Kreps, G. L. (2009). Health communication theories. In S. Littlejohn (Ed.), *Encyclopedia of communication theory* (pp. 465–469). Thousand Oaks, CA: Sage. doi: 10.4135/978141295938.n172

Kreps, G. L., & Atkin, C. (1991). Introduction: Current issues in health communication research. *American Behavioral Scientist, 34,* 648–651.

Kreps, G. L., Bonaguro, E., & Query, J. L. (1998). The history and development of the field of health communication. In L. Jackson & B. Duffy (Eds.), *Health communication research* (pp. 1–15). Westport, CT: Greenwood Press.

Kreps, G. L., Frey. L. R., & O'Hair. D. (1991). Applied communication research: Scholarship that can make a difference. *Journal of Applied Communication Research, 19,* 71–87.

Kreps, G. L., & Thornton, B. C. (1992). *Health communication: Theory and practice.* (2nd ed.) Prospect Heights, IL: Waveland Press.

Krupat, E. (1986, November). A delicate imbalance. *Psychology Today,* 22–26.

Kuhn, T. S. (1970). *The structure of scientific revolutions* (2nd ed.). Chicago, IL: University of Chicago Press.

LaBelle, S., Odenweller, K. G., & Myers, S. A. (2015). Applying instructor communication behaviors and learning outcomes to the pediatrician-parent context. *Southern Communication Journal, 80,* 55–73.

Lakoff, R. (1975). *Language and woman's place.* New York: Harper & Row.

Lane, S. (2002). *National magazine letters to the editor post-Columbine: Did a spiral of silence occur among those who hold pro-gun opinions?* Unpublished master's thesis, University of Akron, Akron. OH.

Langer, E. (1989). *Mindfulness.* Reading, MA: Addison-Wesley.

Lannutti, P. J., Laliker, M., & Hale, J. L. (2001). Violations of expectations and socio-sexual communication in student/professor interactions. *Communication Education, 50,* 69–82.

Lanza, M. L., Zeiss, R., & Rierdan, J. (2005, November). *Violence assessment, medication, and prevention.* Paper presented at the annual meeting of the American Nurses Conference, Washington, DC.

Lasagna, L. (1964). *Hippocratic Oath-Modern Version.* Retrieved March 14, 2008, from http://www.pbs.org/wgbh/nova/doctors/oath_010315.html

Lasswell, H. D. (1927). *Propaganda technique in world wars.* New York: Knopf.

Lasswell, H. D. (1948). The structure and function of communication in society. In L. Bryson (Ed.), *The communication of ideas (pp. 37–51).* New York: Harper.

Lazarsfeld, P. F., Berelson, B. R., & Gaudet, H. (1944). *The people's choice: How the voter makes up his mind in a presidential campaign.* New York: Columbia University Press.

Lazarsfeld, P. F. & Stanton, F. N. (1944). *Radio research 1942–1943.* New York: Duel, Sloan, and Pearce.

Lea, M., O'Shea, T., & Spears, R. (1992). "Flaming" in computer-mediated communication. In M. Lea (Ed.), *Contexts of computer-mediated-communication* (pp. 89–112). New York: Harvester Wheatsheaf.

Ledbetter, A. M. (2009). Family communication patterns and relational maintenance behavior: Direct and mediated associations with friendship closeness. *Human Communication Research, 35*(1), 130–147.

Ledbetter, A. M., & Kuznekoff, J. H. (2012). More than a game friendship relational maintenance and attitudes toward Xbox LIVE communication. *Communication Research, 39*(2), 269–290.

Lederman, L. C. (2009). Health communication: The first twenty-five years. In J. W. Chesebro (Ed.), *From 20th century beginnings to 21st century advances: Developing and evolving from a century of transformation: Studies in honor of the 100th anniversary of the eastern communication association* (pp. 236–254). Los Angeles, CA: Roxbury.

Lefcourt, H. M. (1981). *Research with the locus of control construct: Vol. 1: Assessment methods.* New York: Academic Press.

Lefcourt, H. M. (1982). *Locus of control: Current trends in theory and research*. Mahwah, NJ: Erlbaum.

Lefkowitz, M., Blake, R. R., & Mouton, J. S. (1955). Status factors in pedestrian violation of traffic signals. *Journal of Abnormal and Social Psychology, 51*, 704–706.

Leonard, M., Graham, S., & Bonacum, D. (2004). The human factor: The critical importance of effective teamwork in communication and-providing safe care. *Quality and Safety in Healthcare, 13*, 185–190. doi: 10.1136/qshc.2004.D10033

LePoire, B. A.. & Burgoon, J. K. (1994). Two contrasting explanations of involvement violations: Expectancy violations theory versus discrepancy arousal theory. *Human Communication Research, 20*, 560–591.

Levine, T. R. (2011). Quantitative social science methods of inquiry. In M. L. Knapp, & J. A. Daly, (Eds.), *The Sage handbook of interpersonal communication* (pp. 25–57). Thousand Oaks, CA, Sage.

Levine, T. R. (2014). Truth-Default Theory (TDT): A theory of human deception and deception detection. *Journal of Language and Social Psychology, 33*(4), 378–392.

Levine, T. R., Serota, K. B., Shulman, H., Clare, D. D., Park, H. S., Shaw, A. S., … Lee, J. H. (2011). Sender demeanor: Individual differences in sender believability have a powerful impact on deception detection judgments. *Human Communication Research, 37*(3), 377–403.

Levy, M. R. (1979). Watching TV news as parasocial interaction. *Journal of Broadcasting, 23*, 69–80.

Levy, M. R., & Windahl, S. (1984). Audience activity and gratifications: A conceptual clarification and exploration. *Communication Research, 11*, 51–78.

Likert, R. (1932). A technique for the measurement of attitudes. *Archives of Psychology, 22*, 1–55.

Likert, R. (1932). A technique for the measurement of attitudes. *Archives of Psychology* (No. 140).

Likert, R. (1961). *New patterns of management*. New York: McGraw-Hill.

Likert, R. (1967). *The human organization: Its management and value*. New York: McGraw-Hill.

Lin, C. A., & Salwen, M. B. (1997). Predicting the spiral of silence on a controversial public issue. *The Howard Journal of Communications, 8*, 129–141.

Lippman, W. (1922). *Public opinion*. New York: Macmillan.

Lipton, P. (2004). *Inference to the best explanation, 2nd Ed.* London, UK, Routledge.

Loevinger, L. (1979). The ambiguous mirror: The reflective-projective theory of broadcasting and mass communication. In G. Gumpert & R. Cathcart (Eds.), *Inter/Media: Interpersonal communication in a media world* (pp. 234–260). New York: Oxford University Press.

Loftus, E. F. (1979). *Eyewitness testimony.* Cambridge: Harvard University Press.

Loftus, E. F. (1980). *Memory.* Reading. MA: Addison-Wesley.

Loges, W. E., & Ball-Rokeach, S. J. (1993). Dependency relations and newspaper readership. *Journalism Quarterly, 70,* 602–614.

Lord, R. G., Phillips, J. S., & Rush, M. C. (1980). Effects of sex and personality on perceptions of emergent leadership, influence, and social power. *Journal of Applied Psychology, 65,* 176–182.

Lori, M., & More. W. W. (1980). Four dimensions of assertiveness. *Multivariate Behavioral Research, 2,* 127–135.

Lowenthal, P. R. (2009). Social presence. In P. Rogers, G. Berg, J. Boettcher, C. Howard, L. Justice, & K. Schenk (Eds.), *Encyclopedia of distance education and online learning* (2nd ed., pp. 932–936). Hershey, PA: IGI Global.

Lowery-Hart, R., & Pacheco, G. (2011). Understanding the first-generation student experience in higher education through a relational dialectic perspective. *New Directions for Teaching and Learning, 2011*(127), 55–68.

Lowery, S., & DeFleur, M. L. (1995). *Milestones in mass communication research: Media effects* (3rd ed.). New York: Longman.

Lull, J. (1982). A rules approach to the study of television and society. *Human Communication Research, 9,* 3–16.

MacGeorge, E. L. (2001). Support providers' interaction goals: The influence of attributions and emotions. *Communication Monographs, 68,* 72–97.

MacGeorge, E. L., Feng, B., & Burleson, B. R. (2011). Supportive communication. In M. L. Knapp & J. A. Daly (Eds.), *The Sage handbook of interpersonal communication* (4th ed., pp. 317–354). Thousand Oaks, CA: Sage.

MacKay, A. L. (1977). *The harvest of a quiet eye: A selection of scientific quotations.* London: Institute of Physics.

Madlock, P. E., Martin, M. M., Bogdan, L., & Ervin, M. (2007). The impact of communication traits on leader-member exchange. *Human Communication, 10,* 50–64.

Magnusson, D., & Endler, N. S. (1977). Interactional psychology: Present status and future prospects. In D. Magnusson & N. S. Endler (Eds.), *Personality at the crossroads: Current issues in interactional psychology* (pp. 3–35). Hillsdale, NJ: Erlbaum.

Mandelbaum, J. (2008). Conversational analysis theory. In L. A. Baxter & D. O. Braithwaite (Eds.), *Engaging theories in interpersonal communication: Multiple perspectives* (pp. 175–188). Thousand Oaks, CA: Sage.

Mander, J. (2015). GWI Social Q4 2014: The Latest Social Networking Trends. *GWI Social Q4 2014: The Latest Social Networking Trends.*

Marcoux, B. C., & Shope, J. T. (1997). Application of the theory of planned behavior to adolescent use and misuse of alcohol. *Health Education Research, 12,* 323–331.

Marcus, B. H., & Simkin, L. R. (1994). The transtheoretical model: Applications to exercise behavior. *Medicine & Science in Sports & Exercise, 26,* 1400–1404. doi: 10.1249100005768-199411000-00016

Markus, H. R., & Kitayama, S. (1991). Culture and self: Implication for cognition, emotion, and motivation. *Psychological Review, 98,* 224–253.

Markus, H. R., & Kitayama, S. (1998). The cultural psychology of personality. *Journal of Cross-Cultural Psychology, 29,* 63–87.

Marris, P. (1996). *The politics of uncertainty.* New York, NY: Routledge.

Martin, M. M., & Anderson, C. M. (1995). The father-young adult-relationship: Interpersonal motives, self-disclosure, and satisfaction. *Communication Quarterly. 43,* 119–130.

Martin, M. M., & Anderson, C. M. (2001). The relationship between cognitive flexibility and affinity-seeking strategies. *Advances in Psychological Research, 4,* 69–76.

Martin, M. M., & Anderson, C. M., & Sirimangkala, P. (1997, April). *The relationship between use of organizational conflict strategies with socio-communicative style and aggressive communication traits.* Paper presented at the annual meeting of the Eastern Communication Association, Baltimore, MD.

Martin, M. M., Anderson, C. M., & Thweatt, K. S. (1998). Individuals' perceptions of their communication behaviors: A validity study of the relationship between the Cognitive Flexibility Scale and the Communication Flexibility Scale with aggressive communication traits. *Journal of Social Behavior and Personality, 13,* 531–540.

Martin, M. M., & Rubin, R. B. (1995). A new measure of cognitive flexibility. *Psychological Reports, 76,* 623–626.

Marwell, G. & Schmitt, D. (1967). Dimensions of compliance-gaining behavior: An empirical analysis. *Sociometry, 30,* 350–364.

Maslow, A. H. (1943). A theory of human motivation. *Psychological Review, 50*, 370–396.

Mattson, M. (1999). Toward a reconceptualization of communication cues to action in the health belief model: H1V test counseling. *Communication Monographs, 66*, 240–265. doi: 10.1080/03637759909376476

Mayo, E. (1933). *The human problems of an industrial civilization*. New York: Macmillan.

May, S. (2006). Ethical perspectives and practices. In S. May (Ed.), *Case studies in organizational communication: Ethical perspectives and practices*. Thousand Oaks, CA: Sage.

McClelland, D. C. (1962). Business drive and national achievement. *Harvard Business Review, 40*, 99–112.

McClelland, D. C. (1975). *Power: The inner experience*. New York: Irvington.

McCombs, M. (2002, January). *The agenda-setting role of the mass media in the shaping of public opinion*. Paper presented at the Mass Media Economics Conference. London: UK, Infoamerica.org.

McCombs, M. E., & Shaw, D. L. (1972). The agenda-setting function of mass media. *Public Opinion Quarterly, 36*, 176–187.

McCornack, S. A. (1992). Information manipulation theory. *Communication Monographs, 59*, 1–16.

McCornack, S. A. (2008). Information manipulation theory. In L. Baxter, & D. O. Braithwaite (Eds.), *Engaging theories in interpersonal communication* (pp. 215–226). Thousand Oaks, CA, Sage.

McCornack, S. A., Morrison, K., Paik, J. E., Wisner, A. M., & Zhu, X. (2014). Information manipulation theory 2: A propositional theory of deceptive discourse production. *Journal of Language and Social Psychology, 33*(4), 348–377.

McCroskey, J. C. (1968). *An introduction to rhetorical communication*. Englewood Cliffs, NJ: Prentice-Hall.

McCroskey, J. C. (1969). A summary of experimental research on the effects of evidence in persuasive communication. *Quarterly Journal of Speech, 55*, 169–176.

McCroskey, J. C. (1970). Measures of communication-bound anxiety. *Speech Monographs, 37*, 269–277.

McCroskey, J. C. (1977). Oral communication apprehension: A summary of recent theory and research. *Human Communication Research, 4*, 75–96.

McCroskey, J. C. (2006). Tolerance for disagreement. In A. S. Rancer & T. A. Avtgis, *Argumentative and aggressive communication: Theory, research, and application* (pp. 244–245). Thousand Oaks, CA: Sage.

McCroskey, J. C., Larson, C., & Knapp, M. L. (1971). *An introduction to interpersonal communication.* Englewood Cliffs, NJ: Prentice-Hall.

McCroskey, J. C., Richmond, V. P., & Daly, J. A. (1975). The development of a measure of perceived homophily in interpersonal communication. *Human Communication Research, 1,* 323–332.

McCroskey, J. C., Sallinen, A., Fayer, J. M., Richmond, V. P., & Barraclough, R. A. (1996). Nonverbal immediacy and cognitive learning: A cross-cultural investigation. *Communication Education, 45,* 200–211.

McCroskey, J. C., & Wheeless, L. R. (1976). *An introduction to human communication.* Boston: Allyn & Bacon.

McCroskey, J. C., & Wright, D. W. (1971). A comparison of the effects of punishment-oriented and reward-oriented messages in persuasive communication. *Journal of Communication, 21,* 83–93.

McDonald, D. G., Glynn, C. J., Kim, S., & Ostman, R. E. (2001). The spiral of silence in the 1948 Presidential election. *Communication Research, 28,* 139–155.

McGlone, M. S., & Giles, H. (2011). Language and interpersonal communication. In M. L. Knapp, & J. A. Daly (Eds.), *The Sage Handbook of interpersonal communication, 4th Ed.* (pp. 201–237). Los Angeles, CA: Sage.

McGregor, D. (1960). *The human side of enterprise.* New York: McGraw-Hill.

McGregor, D. (1966). *Leadership and motivation.* Cambridge, MA: MIT Press.

McGuire, W. J. (1964). Inducing resistance to persuasion: Some contemporary approaches. In L. Berkowitz (Ed.). *Advances in experimental social psychology* (Vol. 1, pp. 191–229). New York: Academic Press.

McGuire, W. J. (1969). The nature of attitudes and attitude change. In G. Lindzey & E. Aronson (Eds.), *Handbook of social psychology* (Vol. 3, pp. 136–314). Reading, MA: Addison-Wesley.

McGuire, W. J. (1996). The Yale communication and attitude-change program in the 1950s. In E. E. Dennis & E. Wartella (Eds.), *American communication research: The remembered history* (pp. 39–60). Mahwah, NJ: Erlbaum.

McLaren, R. M., Dillard, J. P., Tusing, K. J., & Solomon, D. H. (2014). Relational framing theory: Utterance form and relational context as antecedents of frame salience. *Communication Quarterly, 62*(5), 518–535.

McLaren, R. M., & Solomon, D. H. (2015). Relational framing theory: Drawing inferences about relationships from interpersonal interactions. In D. Braithwaite & P. Schrodt (Eds.), *Engaging theories in interpersonal communication: Multiple perspectives* (pp. 115–127). Thousand Oaks, CA: Sage.

McLaughlin, M. L. (1984). *Conversation: How talk is organized.* Beverly Hills: Sage.

McLaughlin, M. L., & Cody, M. J. (1982). Awkward silences: Behavioral antecedents and consequences of conversational lapse. *Human Communication Research, 8,* 299–316.

McLaughlin, M. L., Cody, M. J., & O'Hair, H. D. (1983). The management of failure events: Some contextual determinants of accounting behavior. *Human Communication Research, 9,* 208–224.

McLaughlin, M. L., Cody, M. J., & Robey, C. S. (1980). Situational influences on the selection of strategies to resist compliance-gaining attempts. *Human Communication Research, 7,* 14–36.

McLaughlin, M. L., Louden, A. D., Cashion. J. L., Altendorf, D. M., Baaske, K. T., & Smith, S. W. (1985). Conversational planning and self-serving utterances: The manipulation of topical and functional structures in dyadic interaction. *Journal of Language and Social Psychology, 4,* 233–251.

McQuail, D. (1984). With the benefit of hindsight: Reflections on uses and gratifications research. *Critical Studies in Mass Communication, 1,* 177–193.

Mehrabian, A. (1971). *Silent messages.* Belmont, CA: Wadsworth Publishing Co.

Mehrabian, A. (1981). *Silent messages: Implicit communication of emotions and attitudes* (2nd ed.). Belmont, CA: Wadsworth.

Mehrley, R. S., & McCroskey, J. C. (1970). Opinionated statements and attitude intensity as predictors of attitude change and source credibility. *Speech Monographs, 37,* 47–52.

Merkin, R., Taras, V., & Steel, P. (2014). State of the art themes in cross-cultural communication research: a systematic and meta-analytic review. *International Journal of Intercultural Relations, 38,* 1–23.

Meyer, J. R. (2004). Effect of verbal aggressiveness on the perceived importance of secondary goals in messages. *Communication Studies, 55*(1), 168–184.

Millar, F. E., & Rogers, L. E (1976). A relational approach to interpersonal communication. In G. R. Miller (Ed.), *Explorations in interpersonal communication* (pp. 87–103). Beverly Hills: Sage.

Millar, F. E., & Rogers, L. E. (1987). Relational dimensions of interpersonal dynamics. In M. E. Roloff & G. R. Miller (Eds.), *Interpersonal processes: New directions in communication research* (pp. 117–139). Newbury Park, CA: Sage.

Miller, G. R. (1963). Studies on the use of fear appeals: A summary and analysis. *Central States Speech Journal, 14,* 117–125.

Miller, G. R. (1966). On defining communication: Another stab. *Journal of Communication, 16,* 88–98.

Miller, G. R. (1978). The current status of theory and research in interpersonal communication. *Human Communication Research, 4,* 164–178.

Miller, G. R., & Baseheart, J. (1969). Source trustworthiness, opinionated statements, and response to persuasive communication. *Speech Monographs, 36, 1–7.*

Miller, G. R., & Berger, C. R. (1978). On keeping the faith in matters scientific. *Western Journal of Speech Communication, 42,* 44–57.

Miller, G. R., Boster, F., Roloff, M., & Siebold, D. (1977). Compliance-gaining message strategies: A typology and some findings concerning effects of situational differences. *Communication Monographs, 44,* 37–51.

Miller, G. R., Burgoon, M., & Burgoon, J. K. (1984). The function of human communication in changing attitudes and gaining compliance. In C. C. Arnold & J. W. Bowers (Eds.), *Handbook of rhetorical and communication theory* (pp. 400–474). Boston: Allyn & Bacon.

Miller, G. R., de Turk, M. A., & Kalbfleisch, P. J. (1983). Self-monitoring. rehearsal, and deceptive communication. *Human Communication Research, 10,* 97–117.

Miller, G. R., & Lobe, J. (1967). Opinionated language, open- and closed-mindedness and responses to persuasive communications. *Journal of Communication, 17,* 333–341.

Miller, G. R., & McReynolds, M. (1973). Male chauvinism and source competence. *Speech Monographs, 40,* 154–155.

Miller, M. D., & Burgoon, M. (1979). The relationship between violations of expectations and the induction of resistance to persuasion. *Human Communication Research, 5,* 301–313.

Miller, V. D., & Jablin, F. M. (1991). Information-seeking during organizational entry: Influences, tactics, and a model of the process. *Academy of Management Review, 16,* 92–120.

Miller Waite, C., & Roloff, M. E. (2014). When hurt continues: Taking conflict personally leads to rumination, residual hurt, and negative emotions toward someone who hurt us. *Communication Quarterly, 62,* 193–213.

Minkov, M. (2009). Predictors of differences in subjective well-being across 97 nations. *Cross-Cultural Research, 43*(2), 152–179.

Minkov, M., & Hofstede, G. (2011). The evolution of Hofstede's doctrine. *Cross Cultural Management: An International Journal, 18*(1), 10–20.

Mischel, W. (1968). *Personality and assessment.* New York: John Wiley & Sons.

Mitchell, T. R. (1984). *Motivation and performance.* Chicago: Science Research Associates.

Moine, D. J. (1982, August). To trust perchance to buy. *Psychology Today, 16,* 50–54.

Mongeau, P. A. (1989). Individual differences as moderators of persuasive message processing and attitude-behavior relations. *Communication Research Reports, 6,* 1–6.

Mongeau, P. A., & Carey, C. M. (1996). Who's wooing whom II?: An experimental investigation of date-initiation and expectancy violation. *Western Journal of Communication, 60,* 195–213.

Mongeau, P. A., Hale, J. L., Johnson, K. L., & Hillis, J. D. (1993). Who's wooing whom?: An investigation of female initiated dating. In P. J. Kalbfleisch (Ed.), *Interpersonal Communication: Evolving Interpersonal Relationships* (pp. 51–68). Hillsdale, NJ: Lawrence Erlbaum.

Mongeau, P. A., & Johnson, K. L. (1995). Predicting cross-sex first date sexual expectations and involvement: Contextual and individuals factors. *Personal Relationships, 2,* 301–312.

Monge, P. R. (1973). Theory construction in the study of communication: The systems paradigm. *Journal of Communication, 23,* 5–16.

Montgomery, B. M., & Norton, R. W. (1981). Sex differences and similarities in communicator style. *Communication Monographs, 48,* 121–132.

Moor, P. J., Heuvelman, A., & Verleur, R. (2010). Flaming on youtube. *Computers in Human Behavior, 26*(6), 1536–1546.

Morgan, S. E., & Miller, J. K. (2002). Beyond the organ donor card: The effect of knowledge, attitudes, and values on willingness to communicate about organ donation to family members. *Health Communication, 14,* 122–134. New York: Springer. doi: 10.1207/S15327027HC1401_6

Morrison, E. W. (1993a). Longitudinal study of the effects of information-seeking on newcomer socialization. *Journal of Applied Psychology, 78,* 173–183.

Morrison, E. W. (1993b). Newcomer information-seeking: Exploring types, modes, sources, and outcomes. *Academy of Management Journal, 36,* 557–589.

Morrison, J. (1997). *Enacting involvement: Some conversational practices for being in relationships.* Unpublished doctoral dissertation, Temple University, Philadephia, PA.

Motivating adult smokers to kick the habit: Fear alone may not be enough. *Communication Currents 4,* 2014, Washington, D.C.: National Communication Association.

Motley, M. T. (1990a). On whether one can(not) not communicate: An examination via traditional communication postulates. *Western Journal of Speech Communication, 54,* 1–20.

Motley, M. T. (1990b). Communication as interaction: A reply to Beach and Bavelas. *Western Journal of Speech Communication, 54,* 613–623.

Motley, M. T. (1991). How one may not communicate: A reply to Andersen. *Communication Studies, 42,* 326–339.

Mulac, A., Bradac, J. J., & Gibbons, P. (2001). Empirical support for the gender-as-culture hypothesis: An intercultural analysis of male/female language differences. *Human Communication Research, 27,* 121–152.

Murphy, J. J. (1974). *Rhetoric in the Middle Ages: A history of rhetorical theory from Saint Augustine to the Renaissance.* Berkeley and Los Angeles: University of California Press.

Murphy, J. J. (Ed.). (1992). *A synoptic history of classical rhetoric.* New York: Random House.

Myers, S. A., Zhong, M., & Mitchell, W. (1995). The use of interpersonal communication motives in conflict resolution among romantic partners. *Ohio Speech Journal, 33,* 1–20.

Nelson, G. (1988, November). *Oliver North's testimony before the U.S. Congress' Select Committee on secret military assistance to Iran and Nicaraguan opposition: A fantasy theme analysis.* Paper presented at the meeting of the Speech Communication Association. New Orleans, LA.

Nemeth, C. J. (1986). Differential contributions of majority and minority influence. *Psychological Review, 93,* 23–32.

Neuliep, J. W. (2012). The relationship among intercultural communication apprehension, ethnocentrism, uncertainty reduction, and communication satisfaction during initial intercultural interaction: An extension of anxiety and uncertainty management (AUM) theory. *Journal of Intercultural Communication Research, 41*(1), 1–16.

Nicotera, A. M. (1995). The constructivist theory of Delia, Clark, and associates. In D. P. Cushman & B. Kovacic (Eds.), *Watershed research traditions in human communication theory* (pp. 45–66). Albany: State University of New York Press.

Nimmo, D., & Combs, J. E. (1982). Fantasies and melodramas in television network news: The case of Three Mile Island. *Western Journal of Speech Communication, 46,* 45–55.

Nimmo, D., & Combs, J. E. (1983). *Mediated political realities.* New York: Longman.

Nimmo, D. D., & Sanders, K. R. (1981). Introduction: The emergence of political communication as a field. In D. D. Nimmo & K. R. Sanders (Eds.), *Handbook of political communication* (pp. 11–36). Beverly Hills: Sage.

Nisbett, R. E., & Norenzayan, A. (2002). Culture and cognition. In D. L. Medin (Ed.), *Stevens' handbook of experimental psychology* (3rd ed., Vol. 2, pp. 561–597). New York: John Wiley & Sons.

Noelle-Neumann, E. (1984). *The spiral of silence: Public opinion—Our social skin.* Chicago, IL: University of Chicago Press.

Nofsinger, R. E. (1976). Answering questions indirectly. *Human Communication Research, 2,* 171–181.

Nofsinger, R. E. (1991). *Everyday conversation.* Newbury Park, CA: Sage.

Noll, A. M. (2007). *The evolution of media.* Lanham, MD: Rowman & Littlefield.

Norton, R. W. (1978). Foundation of a communication style construct. *Human Communication Research, 4,* 99–112.

Norton, R. W. (1983). *Communicator style.* Beverly Hills, CA: Sage.

Oetzel, J., Garcia, A. J., & Ting-Toomey, S. (2008). An analysis of the relationships among face concerns and facework behaviors in perceived conflict situations: A four-culture investigation. *International Journal of Conflict Management, 19*(4), 382–403.

Oetzel, J. G., & Ting-Toomey, S. (2003). Face concerns in interpersonal conflict a cross-cultural empirical test of the face negotiation theory. *Communication Research, 30*(6), 599–624.

Oetzel, J., Ting-Toomey, S., Masumoto, T., Yokochi, Y., Pan, X., Takai, J., & Wilcox, R. (2001). Face and facework in conflict: A cross-cultural comparison of China, Germany, Japan, and the United States. *Communication Monographs, 68*(3), 235–258.

O'Hair, D. (1989). Dimensions of relational communication and control during physician-patient interactions. *Health Communication, 1,* 97–115. doi: 10.1207/s/5327027/hc0102_2

O'Keefe, B. J., & Delia, J. G. (1979). Construct comprehensiveness and cognitive complexity as predictors of the number and strategic adaptation of arguments and appeals in a persuasive message. *Communication Monographs, 46,* 231–240.

O'Keefe, D. J. (1990). *Persuasion: Theory and research.* Newbury Park, CA: Sage. Park, H. S. (1998). The theory of reasoned action and self construal in predicting intention of studying among Korean college students. *Communication Research Reports* 15, 267–279.

Osgood, C. E., Suci, G. J., & Tannenbaum, P. H. (1957). *The measurement of meaning.* Urbana: University of Illinois Press.

Ostroff, C., & Kozlowski, S. (1992). Organizational socialization as a learning process: The role of information acquisition. *Personnel Psychology, 45,* 849–874.

Ouchi, W. G. (1981). *Theory Z: How American business can meet the Japanese challenge.* Reading, MA: Addison-Wesley.

Palomares, N. A. (2008). Toward a theory of goal detection in social interaction effects of contextual ambiguity and tactical functionality on goal inferences and inference certainty. *Communication Research, 35*(1), 109–148.

Park, H. S., Levine, T., McCornack, S., Morrison, K., & Ferrara, M. (2002). How people really detect lies. *Communication Monographs, 69*(2), 144–157.

Parks, M. R. (1994). Communication competence and interpersonal control. In M. L. Knapp & G. R. Miller (Eds.), *Handbook of interpersonal communication* (pp. 589–620). Beverly Hills, CA: Sage.

Parks, M. R., & Adelman, M. B. (1983). Communication networks and the development of romantic relationships: An expansion of uncertainty reduction theory. *Human Communication Research, 10,* 55–79.

Pearce, W. B. (2005). The coordinated management of meaning (CMM). In W. Gudykunst (Ed.), *Theorizing about intercultural communication* (pp. 35–54). Thousand Oaks, CA: Sage.

Pearce, W. B., & Cronen, V. E. (1980). *Communication, action, and meaning.* New York: Praeger.

Pearce, W. B., & Cushman, D. P. (1977). *Research about communication rules: A critique and appraisal.* Paper presented at the annual meeting of the Speech Communication Association, Washington, D. C.

Pearce, W. B., & Wiseman, R. L. (1983). Rules theories: Varieties, limitations, and potentials. In W. B. Gudykunst (Ed.), *Intercultural communication theory* (pp. 79–88). Beverly Hills, CA: Sage.

Pearson, J. C. (1995). *Gender and communication* (3rd ed.). New York: McGraw-Hill.

Pellowski, J. A., Kalichman, S. C., & Grebler, T. (2016). Optimal treatment adherence counseling outcomes for people living with HIV and limited health literacy. *Behavioral Medicine, 42,* 39–47. doi: 10.1080/08964289. 2014.963006

Perrin, A (December 8, 2015). One-fifth of Americans report going online 'almost constantly'. *Pew Research Center.* Retrieved from http://pewrsr. ch/1NIurjL.

Perrin, A., & Duggan, M. (2015). Americans' internet access: 2000–2015. *Pew Research Center, 26.*

Perse, E. M. (2001). *Media effects and society.* Mahwah, NJ: L. Erlbaum.

Perse, E. M., & Rubin, R. B. (1989). Attribution in social and parasocial relationships. *Communication Research, 16,* 59–77.

Peters, J. D. (1989). John Locke, the individual, and the origin of communication. *Quarterly Journal of Speech, 75,* 387–399.

Peterson, M. F. (2003). [Review of the book *Culture's Consequences: Comparing values, behaviors, institutions, and organizations across nations (2nd ed.),* by G. Hofstede]. *Administrative Science Quarterly, 48*(1), 127–131.

Peters, T., & Waterman, R. (1982). *In search of excellence.* New York: Harper & Row.

Petronio, S. (2002). *Boundaries of privacy: Dialectics of disclosure.* Albany: SUNY Press.

Petronio, S. (2013). Brief status report on communication privacy management theory. *Journal of Family Communication, 13*(1), 6–14.

Petronio, S., & Braithwaite, D. O. (1993). The contributions and challenges of family communication to the field of communication. *Journal of Applied Communication Research, 21,* 103–110.

Petronio, S., & Durham, W. T. (2008). Communication privacy management theory: Significance for interpersonal communication. In L. A. Baxter & D. O. Braithwaite (Eds.), *Engaging theories in interpersonal communication: Multiple perspectives* (pp. 309–322). Thousand Oaks, CA: Sage.

Petronio, S., Jones, S. S., & Morr, M. (2003). Family privacy dilemmas: A communication privacy management perspective. In L. Frey (Ed.), *Bona fide groups* (pp. 23–56). Mahwah, NJ: Erlbaum.

Pettegrew, L. S., & Logan, R. (1987). The health care context. In C. R. Berger & S. H. Chaffee (Eds.), *Handbook of communication science* (pp. 675–710). Newbury Park, CA: Sage.

Petty, R. E., & Cacioppo, J. T. (1986). *Communication and persuasion: Central and peripheral routes to attitude change.* New York: Springer-Verlag.

Philipsen, G. (1995). The coordinated management of meaning theory of Pearce, Cronen, and Associates. In D. P. Cushman & B. Kovacic (Eds.), *Watershed research traditions in human communication theory* (pp. 13–43). Albany: State University of New York Press.

Pitts, M. (2009) Identity and the role of expectations, stress, and talk in short-term student sojourner adjustment: an application of the integrative theory of communication and cross-cultural adaptation. International Journal of Intercultural Relations, 33(6): 450–62.

Pitts, M. J., Fowler, C., Fisher, C. L., & Smith, S. A. (2014). Politeness strategies in imagined conversation openers about eldercare. *Journal of Language and Social Psychology, 33,* 29–48.

Plax, T. G., Kearney, P., McCroskey, J. C., & Richmond, V. P. (1986). Power in the classroom VI: Verbal control strategies, nonverbal immediacy, and affective learning. *Communication Education, 35,* 43–55.

Polack, E. P., & Avtgis, T. A. (2011). *Medical communication: Defining the discipline.* Dubuque, IA: Kendall Hunt.

Polack, E. P., Avtgis, T. A., Rossi, D., & Shaffer, L. (2010). A team approach in communication instruction: A qualitative approach. *Journal of Surgical Education, 67,* 125–128. doi: 10.1016/jsurg.2010.02.004

Polya, G. (1945). *How to solve it: A new aspect of mathematical method.* Princeton, NJ: Princeton University Press.

Poole, M. S. (1981). Decision development in small groups I: A comparison of two models. *Communication Monographs, 48,* 1–24.

Poole, M. S. (1983a). Decision development in small groups II: A study of multiple sequences in decision making. *Communication Monographs, 50,* 206–232.

Poole, M. S. (1983b). Decision development in small groups, III: A multiple sequence of models of group decision development. *Communication Monographs, 50,* 321–341.

Poole, M. S., & Roth, J. (1989). Decision development in small groups IV: A typology of group decision paths. *Human Communication Research, 15,* 323–356.

Popper, K. (1963). *Conjectures and refutations.* London, UK: Routledge.

Popper, K. (1996). *The myth of framework: In defense of science and rationality.* New York: Routledge.

Postmes, T. (2010). Social identity model of deindividuation effects. In J. M. Levine & M. A. Hogg (Eds.), *Encyclopedia of group processes & intergroup relations* (pp. 794–797). Thousand Oaks, CA: Sage.

Potter, W. J. (1986). Perceived reality and the cultivation hypothesis. *Journal of Broadcasting and Electronic Media, 30,* 159–174.

Pritchard, M. (1991). *On becoming responsible.* Lawrence, KS: University of Kansas Press.

Prochaska, J. O. (2013). Transtheoretical model of behavior change. *Encyclopedia of behavioral medicine.* (pp. 1997–2000). New York: Springer.

Prochaska, J. O., & Redding, C. A., Harlow, L. L., Rossi, J. S., & Velicer, W. F. (1994). The transtheoretical model of change and HIV prevention: A review. *Health Education & Behavior, 21,* 471–486. doi: 10.1177/109019815402100410

Prochaska, J. O., & Velicer, W. F. (1997). The transtheoretical model of health behavior change. *American Journal of Health Promotion, 12,* 38–48. doi: 10.4278/0890-1171-12_1.38

Prochaska, J. O., Wright, J. A., & Velicer (2008). Evaluating theories of health behavior change: A hierarchy of criteria applied to the transtheoretical model. *Applied Psychology: An International Review, 57,* 561–588. doi: 10.1111/j.464-0597.2008.00345.x

Pugh, D. S., & Hickson, D. J. (1997). *Writers on organizations* (5th ed.). Thousand Oaks, CA: Sage.

Purcell, W. M. (1992). Are there so few communication theories? *Communication Monographs, 59,* 94–97.

Putnam, L., & Wilson, C. E. (1982). Communicative strategies in organizational conflicts: Reliability and validity of a measurement scale. In M. Burgoon (Ed.), *Communication yearbook 6* (pp. 629–652). Beverly Hills, CA: Sage.

Quick, B. L., Scott, A. M., & Ledbetter, A. (2011). A close examination of trait reactance and issue involvement as moderators of psychological reactance theory. *Journal of Health Communication, 16,* 660–679.

Quick, B. L., Shen, L., & Dillard, J. P. (2013). Reactance theory and persuasion. In J. P. Dillard, & L. Shen (Eds.), *The Sage handbook of persuasion, 2nd Ed* (pp. 167–183). Thousand Oaks, CA: Sage.

Quick, B. L., & Stephenson, M. T. (2007). The reactance restoration scale (RSS): A measure of direct and indirect restoration. *Communication Research Reports, 24,* 131–138.

Rahim, M. A. (1983). A measure of styles of handling interpersonal conflict. *Academy of Management Journal, 26*(2), 368–376.

Ramirez, A. (2008). An examination of the tripartite approach to commitment: An actor-partner interdependence model analysis of the effect of relational maintenance behavior. *Journal of Social and Personal Relationships, 25*(6), 943–965.

Ramirez Jr., A., Sunnafrank, M., & Goei, R. (2010). Predicted outcome value theory in ongoing relationships. *Communication Monographs, 77*(1), 27–50.

Rancer, A. S., & Avtgis, T. A. (2014). *Argumentative and aggressive communication: Theory, research, and application.* New York: Peter Lang Publishers.

Rancer, A. S., & Avtgis, T. A. (2006). *Argumentative and aggressive communication: Theory, research, and application.* Thousand Oaks, CA: Sage.

Rancer, A. S., & Avtgis, T. A. (2009). Communication theory and research: Bridging the chasms of controversy. In J. W. Chesebro (Ed.), *A century of transformation: Studies in honor of the 100th anniversary of the Eastern Communication Association.* New York: Oxford University Press.

Ratzan, S. C. (1994). Education for the health professional. *American Behavioral Scientist. 38,* 361–380.

Ratzan, S. C., Payne, J. G., & Bishop, C. (1996). The status and scope of health communication. *Journal of Health Communication, 1,* 25–41. doi: 10.1080/108107396128211

Ratzan, S. C., Stearns, N. S., Payne, J. G., Amato, P. P., Libergott, J., & Madoff, M. A. (1994). Education for the health professional. *American Behavioral Scientist. 38,* 361–380. doi: 10.1177/0002764294038002015

Ray, E. B., & Miller, K. I. (1990). Communication in health-care organizations. In E. B. Ray & L. Donohew (Eds.), *Communication and health* (pp. 92–107). Hillsdale, NJ: Lawrence Erlbaum.

Raymond, G., & Heritage, J. (2006). Physicians' opening questions and patients' satisfaction. *Patient Education and Counseling, 60,* 279–285.

Redding, C. W. (1972). *Communication within the organization.* New York: Industrial Communication Counsel.

Reicher, S., Spears, R., & Postmes, T. (1995). A social identity model of deindividuation phenomena. In W. Stroebe & M. Hewstone (Eds.), *European review of social psychology* (Vol. 6, pp. 161–198). Chichester, England: Wiley.

Richmond, V. P., & McCroskey, J. C. (1979). Management communicator style, tolerance for disagreement, and innovativeness as predictors of employee satisfaction: A comparision of single-factor, two-factor, and multiple factor approaches. In D. Nimmo (Ed.), *Communication yearbook 3* (Vol. 3, pp. 359–373). New Brunswick, NJ: Transaction Books.

Richmond, V. P., & McCroskey, J. C. (1985). *Communication: Apprehension, avoidance, and effectiveness.* Scottsdale, AZ: Gorsuch Scarisbrick. Publishers.

Richmond, V. P., & McCroskey, J. C. (2000a). The impact of supervisor and subordinate immediacy on relational and organizational outcomes. *Communication Monographs, 67,* 85–95.

Richmond, V. P., & McCroskey, J. C. (2000b). *Nonverbal behavior in interpersonal relations* (4th ed.). Needham Heights, MA: Allyn & Bacon.

Richmond, V. P., McCroskey, J. C., & McCroskey, L. L. (2005). *Organizational communication: Making work, work.* Boston: Pearson.

Richmond, V. P., Smith, R. S., Jr., Heisel, A. D., & McCroskey, J. C. (2001). Nonverbal immediacy in the physician/patient relationship. *Communication Research Reports, 18,* 211–216.

Ritchie, L. D. (1991). Family communication patterns: An epistemic analysis and conceptual reinterpretation. *Communication Research, 18*(4), 548–565.

Ritchie, L. D., & Fitzpatrick, M. A. (1990). Family communication patterns measuring intrapersonal perceptions of interpersonal relationships. *Communication Research, 17*(4), 523–544.

Roberson, D., Davies, I., & Davidoff, J. (2000). Color categories are not universal: Replications and new evidence from a stone-age culture. *Journal of Experimental Psychology: General, 129,* 369–398.

Roberto, A. J., & Eden, J. (2014). Prevalence and predictors of cyberbullying perpetration by high school seniors. *Communication Quarterly, 62,* 97–114. doi: 10.1080/01463373.860906

Roberto, A. J., Meyer. G., & Boster, F. J. (2001). Predicting adolescents' decisions about fighting: A test of the theory of planned behavior. *Communication Research Reports, 18,* 315–323.

Rocca, K. A., Martin, M. M., & Dunleavy, K. N. (2010). Siblings' motives for talking to each other. *The Journal of psychology, 144*(2), 205–219.

Roethlisberger, F. J., & Dickson, W. J. (1949). *Management and the worker.* Cambridge, MA: Harvard University Press.

Rogers, E. M. (1983). *Communication technology: The new media in society.* New York: The Free Press.

Rogers, E. M. (1994). *A history of communication study.* New York: The Free Press.

Rogers, E. M. (1995). *Diffusion of innovations* (4th ed.). New York: Free Press.

Rogers, E. M., & Bhowmik. D. K. (1970). Homophily-heterophily: Relational concepts for communication research. *Public Opinion Quarterly, 34,* 523–538.

Rokeach, M. (1960). *The open and closed mind.* New York: Basic Books.

Roloff, M. E. (1980). Self-awareness and the persuasion process: Do we really know what we're doing? In M. E. Roloff & G. R. Miller (Eds.), *Persuasion: New directions in theory and research* (pp. 29–66). Beverly Hills: Sage.

Rosenstock, I. M. (1974). Historical origins of the health belief model. *Health Education Monographs, 2,* 354–385. doi: 10.1177/109019817400200403

Rosenthal, R., Hall, J. A., DiMatteo, M. R., Rogers, P. L., & Archer, D. (1979). *Sensitivity to nonverbal communication.* Baltimore, MD: Johns Hopkins University Press.

Rotter, J. B. (1966). Generalized expectancies for internal versus external control of reinforcement. *Psychological Monographs, 80* (Whole No. 609).

Ruben, B. D. (1983). A system-theoretic approach to intercultural communication. In W. B. Gudykunst (Ed.), *Intercultural communication theory: Current perspectives* (pp. 131–145). Beverly Hills, CA: Sage.

Rubin, A. M. (1979). Television use by children and adolescents. *Human Communication Research, 5,* 109–120.

Rubin, A. M. (1983). Television uses and gratifications: The interactions of viewing patterns and motivations. *Journal of Broadcasting, 27,* 37–51.

Rubin, A. M. (1984). Ritualized and instrumental television viewing. *Journal of Communication, 34,* 67–77.

Rubin, A. M. (1985). Uses and gratifications: Quasi-functional analysis. In J. R. Dominick & J. E. Fletcher (Eds.), *Broadcasting research methods* (pp. 202–220). Boston, MA: Allyn and Bacon.

Rubin, A. M., Perse, E. M., & Powell, R. A. (1985). Loneliness, parasocial interaction, and local television news viewing. *Human Communication Research, 12,* 155–180.

Rubin, A. M., & Rubin, R. B. (1985). Interface of personal and mediated communication: A research agenda. *Critical Studies in Mass Communication, 2,* 36–53.

Rubin, A. M., & Windahl, S. (1986). The uses and dependency model of mass communication. *Critical Studies in Mass Communication, 3,* 184–199.

Rubin, R. B. (1982). Assessing speaking and listening competence at the college level: The Communication Competency Assessment Instrument. *Communication Education, 31,* 19–32.

Rubin, R. B. (1985). The validity of the Communication Competency Assessment Instrument. *Communication Monographs, 52,* 173–185.

Rubin, R. B., Fernandez-Collado, C., & Hernandez-Sampieri, R. (1992). A cross-cultural examination of interpersonal communication motives in Mexico and the United States. *International Journal of Intercultural Relations, 16,* 145–157.

Rubin, R. B., & Martin, M. M. (1994). The interpersonal communication competence scale. *Communication Research Reports, 11,* 33–44.

Rubin, R. B., & McHugh, M. P. (1987). Development of parasocial interaction relationships. *Journal of Broadcasting and Electronic Media, 31,* 279–292.

Rubin, R. B., Perse, E. M., & Barbato, C. A. (1988). Conceptualization and measurement of interpersonal communication motives. *Human Communication Research, 14.* 602–628.

Rubin, R. B., & Rubin, A. M. (1992). Antecedents of interpersonal communication motivation. *Communication Quarterly, 40,* 305–317.

Ruechelle, R. C. (1958). An experimental study of audience recognition of emotional and intellectual appeals in persuasion. *Speech Monographs, 25,* 49–58.

Sacks, H. (1992). Lectures on conversations: Volumes 1–2. In G. Jefferson (Ed.). Cambridge, MA: Blackwell.

Salmon, C. T., & Glynn, C. J. (1996). Spiral of silence: Communication and public opinion as social control. In M. B. Salwen & D. W. Stacks (Eds.), *An integrated approach to communication theory and research* (pp. 165–180). Mahwah. NJ: L. Erlbaum.

Salmon, C. T., & Moh, C. Y. (1992). The spiral of silence: Linking individual and society through communication. In J. D. Kennamer (Ed.), *Public opinion, the press, and public policy* (pp. 145–161). Westport, CT: Praeger.

Samp, J. A., & Solomon, D. H. (1999). Communicative responses to problematic events in close relationships II: The influence of five facets of goals on message features. *Communication Research, 26*(2), 193–239.

Sanders, J. A., Gass, R. H., Wiseman, R. L., & Bruschke, J. (1992). Ethnic comparison and measurement of argumentativeness, verbal aggressiveness, and need for cognition. *Communication Reports, 5*, 50–56.

Sanders, J. A., Wiseman, R. L., & Gass, R. H. (1994) Does teaching argumentation facilitate critical thinking? *Communication Reports, 7*, 27–35.

Sansone, R. A., Bohinc, R., & Wiederman, M. W. (2015). Borderline personality symptomatology and compliance with general health care among internal medicine outpatients. *International Journal of Psychiatry in Clinical Practice, 19*, 132–136. doi: 10.3109/13651501.2014.988269

Sapir, E. (1958, 1964). In D. G. Mandelbaum (Ed.), *Selected writings of Edward Sapir in language, culture and personality.* Berkeley: University of California.

Satir, V. (1972). *Peoplemaking.* Palo Alto, CA: Science and Behavior Books.

Scandura, T. A., Graen, G. B., & Novak, M. A. (1986). When managers decide not to decide automatically: An investigation of leader-member exchange and decision influence. *Journal of Applied Psychology, 71*, 579–584.

Schegloff, E. A., Jefferson, G., & Sacks, H. (1977). The preference for self-correction in the organization of repair in conversation. *Language, 53*, 361–382.

Scheidel, T. M. (1963). Sex and persuasibility. *Speech Monographs, 30*, 353–358.

Schein, E. H. (1989). *Organizational culture and leadership.* San Francisco: Jossey-Bass.

Schein, E. H. (1992). *Organizational culture and leadership* (2nd ed.). San Francisco: Jossey-Bass.

Scheufele, D. A., & Moy, P. (2000). Twenty-five years of the spiral of silence: A conceptual review and empirical outlook. *International Journal of Public Opinion Research, 12*, 3–28.

Scheufele, D. A., Shanahan, J., & Lee, E. (2001). Real talk: Manipulating the dependent variable in spiral of silence research. *Communication Research, 28*, 304–324.

Schifter, D. E., & Ajzen, I. (1985). Intention, perceived control, and weight loss: An application of the theory of planned behavior. *Journal of Personality and Social Psychology, 49,* 843–851.

Schneider, B. (2000). The psychological life of organizations. In N. M. Ashkanasy & M. F. Peterson (Eds.), *Handbook of organizational culture and climate* (pp. 18–21). Thousand Oaks, CA: Sage.

Schoening, G. T., & Anderson, J. A. (1995). Social action media studies: Foundational arguments and common premises. *Communication Theory, 5,* 93–116.

Schramm, W. (Ed.). (1954). *The process and effects of mass communication.* Urbana: University of Illinois Press.

Schramm, W., Lyle, J.. & Parker. E. (1961). *Television in the lives of our children.* Palo Alto, CA: Stanford University Press.

Schrodt, P., & Carr, K. (2012). Trait verbal aggressiveness as a function of family communication patterns. *Communication Research Reports, 29*(1), 54–63.

Schrodt, P., & Wheeless, L. R. (2001). Aggressive communication and informational reception apprehension: The influence of listening anxiety and intellectual inflexibility on trait argumentativeness and trait verbal aggressiveness. *Communication Quarterly, 49,* 53–69.

Schrodt, P., Wheeless, L. R., & Ptacek, K. M. (2000). Informational reception apprehension, educational motivation, and achievement. *Communication Quarterly, 48,* 60–73.

Schrodt, P., Witt, P. L., & Messersmith, A. S. (2008). A meta-analytical review of family communication patterns and their associations with information processing, behavioral, and psychosocial outcomes. *Communication Monographs, 75*(3), 248–269.

Schutz, W. C. (1958). *FIRO: A three-dimensional theory of interpersonal behavior.* Oxford, UK: Rinehart.

Scott, M., & Hurt, T. (1978). Social influence as a function of communication and message type. *Southern Speech Communication Journal, 43,* 146–161.

Searle, J. R. (1969). *Speech acts: An essay in the philosophy of language.* Cambridge: Cambridge University Press.

Seligman, M. E. P. (1990). *Learned optimism: How to change your mind and your life.* New York: Pocket Books.

Seligman, M. E. P. (1992). *Helplessness: On development, depression, and death.* New York: Freeman.

Sereno, K., & Bodaken, E. (1972). Ego-involvement and attitude change: Toward a reconceptualization of persuasive effect. *Speech Monographs, 39,* 151–158.

Serota, K. B., & Levine, T. R. (2014). A few prolific liars: Variation in the prevalence of lying. *Journal of Language and Social Psychology, 34*(2), 138–157.

Severin, W. J., & Tankard, J. W. (2001). *Communication theories: Origins, methods and uses in the mass media* (5th ed.). Boston: Allyn & Bacon.

Sharf, B. F. (1993). Reading the vital signs: Research in health care communication. *Communication Monographs, 60,* 35–41.

Shaw, D. L., & McCombs, M. E. (1977). The emergence of American-political issues: The agenda-setting function of the press. St. Paul, MN: West Publishing Co.

Shaw, M. E., & Costanzo, P. R. (1970). *Theories of social psychology.* New York: McGraw-Hill.

Sheer, V. C., & Cline, R. J. (1995). Testing a model of perceived information adequacy and uncertainty reduction in physician-patient interactions. *Journal of Applied Communication Research, 23,* 44–59.

Shen, L., & Dillard, J. P. (2005). Psychometric properties of the Hong Psychological Reactance Scale. *Journal of Personality Assessment, 85,* 74–81.

Sherif, C. W., Sherif, M., & Nebergall, R. W. (1965). *Attitude and attitude-change: The social judgment-involvement approach.* Philadelphia: Saunders.

Shibutani, T., & Kwan, K.M. (1965). *Ethnic stratification: A comparative approach.* New York: Macmillan.

Shields, D. C. (1981). A dramatistic approach to applied communication research: Theory, methods, and applications. In J. F. Cragan & D. C. Shields (Eds.), *Applied communication research: A dramatistic approach* (pp. 5–13). Prospect Heights, IL: Waveland Press.

Shimanoff, S. B. (1980). *Communication rules.* Beverly Hills, CA: Sage.

Short, J., Williams, E., & Christie, B. (1976). *The social psychology of telecommunications.* London: Wiley

Siegel, J., Dubrovsky, V., Kiesler, S., & Mcguire, T. W. (1986). Group processes in computer-mediated communication. *Organizational Behavior and Human Decision Processes, 37,* 157–187.

Smith, B. L., Lasswell, H. D., & Casey, R. D. (1946). *Propaganda, communication, and public opinion.* Princeton, NJ: Princeton University Press.

Smith, M. J. (1982). *Persuasion and human action*. Belmont, CA: Wadsworth.

Snyder, M. (1974). Self-monitoring of expressive behavior. *Journal of Personality and Social Psychology, 30*, 526–537.

Snyder, M. (1979). Self-monitoring processes. In L. Berkowitz (Ed.). *Advances in experimental social psychology* (Vol. 12, pp. 85–128). New York: Academic Press.

Snyder, M. (1980). The many me's of the self-monitor. *Psychology Today*, 33–40.

Snyder, M. (1987). *Public appearances, private realities: The psychology of self-monitoring*. New York, NY: W. H. Freeman and Company.

Solomon, D. H. (2006). A relational framing perspective on perceptions of social-sexual communication at work. In R. Dailey & B. LePoire (Eds.), *Applied research in interpersonal communication: Family communication, health communication, and communicating across social boundaries* (pp. 271–298). New York: Peter Lang.

Solomon, D. H., & Knobloch, L. K. (2001). Relationship uncertainty, partner interference, and intimacy within dating relationships. *Journal of Social and Personal Relationships, 18*(6), 804–820.

Solomon, D. H., & Knobloch, L. K. (2004). A model of relational turbulence: The role of intimacy, relational uncertainty, and interference from partners in appraisals of irritations. *Journal of Social and Personal Relationships, 21*(6), 795–816.

Solomon, D. H., & Vangelisti, A. L. (2014). Relationship development. In C. R. Berger (Ed.), *Interpersonal Communication* (pp. 347–370). Berlin, Germany: De Gruyter.

Solomon, D. H., Weber, K. M., & Steuber, K. R. (2010). Turbulence in relational transitions. In S. Smith & S. Wilson (Eds.), *New directions in interpersonal communication research* (pp. 115–134). Thousand Oaks, CA: Sage.

Spears, R., & Lea, M. (1992). Social influence and the influence of the 'social' in computer-mediated communication. In M. Lea (Ed.), *Contexts of computer-mediated communication* (pp. 30–65). Hemel Hempstead, England: Harvester Wheatsheaf.

Spears, R., & Postmes, T. (2015). Group identity, social influence and collective action online: Extensions and applications of the SIDE model. In S. Sundar (Ed.), *The handbook of psychology of communication technology*. Oxford, UK: Blackwell.

Spillman, B. (1979). The impact of value and self-esteem messages in persuasion. *Central States Speech Journal, 30*, 67–74.

Spitzberg, B. H., & Cupach, W. R. (1984). *Interpersonal communication competence.* Beverly Hills: Sage Publications.

Sproull, L., & Kiesler, S. (1986). Reducing social context cues: Electronic mail in organizational communication. *Management Science, 32,* 1492–1512.

Stachel, J. (1989). *The collected papers of Albert Einstein, Vol. 2. The Swiss years: Writings 1900–1909.* Princeton, NJ: Princeton University Press.

Stafford, L. (2011). Measuring relationship maintenance behaviors: Critique and development of the revised relationship maintenance behavior scale. *Journal of Social and Personal Relationships, 28*(2), 278–303.

Staub, E. (1989). *The roots of evil.* New York: Cambridge University Press.

Steadman, H., Mulvey, E., Monohan, J., Robbins, P., Applebaum, P., & Grisso, T. (1998). Violence by people discharged from active psychiatric in-patient facilities and by others in the same neighborhoods. *Archives of General Psychiatry, 55,* 393–401. doi: 10.1001/archpsyc.55.5.393

Stefanone, M. A., & Jang, C. Y. (2007). Writing for friends and family:- The interpersonal nature of blogs. *Journal of Computer-Mediated Communication, 13,* 123–140.

Steinfatt, T. M. (1977). *Human communication: An interpersonal introduction.* Indianapolis, IlN: Bobbs-Merrill.

Steinfatt, T. M. (1987). Personality and communication: Classical approaches. In J. C. McCroskev & J. A. Daly (Eds.). *Personality and interpersonal communication* (pp. 42–126). Newbury Park. CA: Sage Publications.

Stephen, T. (1990, June). *Research on the New Frontier: A review of the communication literature on marriage and the family.* Paper presented at the meeting of the International Communication Association. Dublin, Ireland.

Stevens, S. S. (1950). A definition of communication. *Journal of the Acoustical Society of America, 22,* 689–690.

Stewart, C. J., Smith, C. A., & Denton, R. E., Jr. (1994). *Persuasion and social movements* (3rd Ed.). Prospect Heights, IL: Waveland Press.

Stewart, L. P., Stewart, A. D., Cooper, P. J., & Friedley, S. A. (1996). *Communication and gender* (3rd ed.). Scottsdale. AZ: Gorsuch Scarisbrick.

Stewart, R. A., & Roach, K. D. (1998). Argumentativeness and the theory of reasoned action. *Communication Quarterly, 46,* 177–193.

Stiff, J. B. (1986). Cognitive processing of persuasive message cues: A meta-analytic review of the effects of supporting information on attitudes. *Communication Monographs, 53,* 75–89.

Stogdill, R. M. (1948). Personal factors associated with leadership: A survey of the literature. *Journal of Psychology, 25*, 35–71.

Stogdill, R. M. (1974). *Handbook of leadership: A survey of theory and research*. New York: Free Press.

Stogdill, R. M., & Bass, B. M. (1981). *Stogdill's handbook of leadership: A survey of theory and research*. New York: Free Press.

Stotland, E., & Patchen, M. (1961). Identification and change in prejudice and authoritarianism. *Journal of Abnormal and Social Psychology, 62*, 250–256.

Straus, M. (1974). Leveling, civility, and violence in the family. *Journal of Marriage and the Family, 36*, 13–30.

Street, R. L., Jr., & Buller, D. B. (1987). Nonverbal response patterns in physician-patient interactions: A functional analysis. *Journal of Nonverbal Behavior, 11*, 234–253. doi: 10.1007/BF00987255

Street, R. L., Jr., & Buller, D. B. (1988). Patients' characteristics affecting physician-patient nonverbal communication. *Human Communication Research, 15*, 60–90. doi: 10.1111/j.1468-2958.1988.tb00171.x

Street, R. L., Jr., & Giles, H. (1982). Speech accommodation theory: A social cognitive approach to language and speech behavior. In M. Roloff & C. R. Berger (Eds.), *Social cognition and communication* (pp. 193–226). Beverly Hills: Sage.

Suedfeld, P., Bochner, S., & Matas, C. (1971). Petitioner's attire and petition signing by peace demonstrators. *Journal of Applied Social Psychology, 1*, 278–283.

Sunnafrank, M. (1983). Attitude similarity and interpersonal attraction in communication processes: In pursuit of an ephemeral influence. *Communication Monographs, 50*, 273–284.

Sunnafrank, M. (1985). Attitude similarity and interpersonal attraction during early communicative relationships: A research note on the generalizability of findings to opposite-sex relationships. *Western Journal of Speech Communication, 49*, 73–80.

Sunnafrank, M. (1986). Predicted outcome value during initial interactions: A reformulation of uncertainty reduction theory. *Human Communication Research, 13*(1), 3–33.

Sunnafrank, M. (1990). Predicted outcome value and uncertainty reduction theories: A test of competing perspectives. *Human Communication Research, 17*(1), 76–103.

Sunnafrank, M. (1992). On debunking the attitude similarity myth. *Communications Monographs, 59*(2), 164–179.

Sunnafrank, M. J., & Miller, G. R. (1981). The role of initial conversations in determining attraction to similar and dissimilar strangers. *Human Communication Research, 8,* 16–25.

Sunnafrank, M., & Ramirez, A. (2004). At first sight: Persistent relational effects of get-acquainted conversations. *Journal of Social and Personal Relationships, 21*(3), 361–379.

Sussman, L. (1973). Ancients and moderns on fear and fear appeals: A comparative analysis. *Central States Speech Journal, 24,* 206–211.

Sutton, S. (2001). Back to the drawing board? A review of applications of the transtheoretical model to substance abuse. *Addiction, 96,* 175–186. doi: 10.1046/j.1360-0443.2001.96117513.x

Swanson, D. L. (1981). A constructivist approach. In D. D. Nimmo & K. R. Sanders (Eds.), *Handbook of political communication* (pp. 169–191). Beverly Hills: Sage.

Sweetser, K. D., Golan, G. J., & Wanta, W. (2008). Intermedia agenda-setting in television, advertising, and blogs during the 2004 election. *Mass Communication and Society, 11,* 197–216.

Sypher, H. E., Davenport-Sypher, B., & Haas, J. W. (1988). Getting emotional: The role of affect in interpersonal communication. *American Behavioral Scientist, 31,* 372–383.

Taylor, F. W. (1911). *The principle of scientific management.* New York: Harper and Brothers.

Teven, J. J., McCroskey, J. C., & Richmond, V. P. (1998). Measurement of tolerance for disagreement. *Communication Research Reports, 15,* 209–217.

Theiss, J. A., & Knobloch, L. K. (2013). A relational turbulence model of military service members' relational communication during reintegration. *Journal of Communication, 63*(6), 1109–1129.

Thistlethwaite, D. L., Kamenetsky. J., & Schmidt, H. (1956). Refutation and attitude change. *Speech Monographs, 23,* 14–25.

Thompson, T. L. (1986). *Communication for health professionals.* New York: Harper & Row.

Thompson, T. L. (1990). Patient health care: Issues in interpersonal communication. In E. B. Ray & L. Donohew (Eds.), *Communication and health* (pp. 27–50). Hillsdale, NJ: Lawrence Erlbaum.

Thompson, T. L. (2006). Seventy-five (count 'em – 75!) issues in health communication: An analysis of emerging themes. *Health Communication, 20,* 117–122. doi: 10.1207/s15327027hc2002_2

Thompson, T. L., Dorsey, A. M., Miller, K. I., & Parrott, R. (Eds.). (2003). *Handbook of health communication.* Mahwah, NJ: Erlbaum.

Thweatt, K. S., & McCroskey, J. C. (1998). The impact of teacher immediacy and misbehaviors on teacher credibility. *Communication Education, 47,* 348–357.

Tichy, N., & Devanna, M. A. (1986). *The transformational leader.* New York: Wiley & Sons.

Ting-Toomey, S. (1988). Intercultural conflicts: A face negotiation theory. In Y. Kim & W. Gudykunst (Eds.), *Theories in intercultural communication* (pp. 213–235). Newbury Park, CA: Sage.

Ting-Toomey, S. (2005). The matrix of face: An updated face-negotiation theory. In W. Gudykunst (Ed.), *Theorizing about intercultural communication* (pp. 71–92). Thousand Oaks, CA: Sage.

Ting-Toomey, S., & Kurogi, A. (1998). Facework competence in intercultural conflict: An updated face-negotiation theory. *International Journal of Intercultural Relations, 22,* 187–225.

Tjosvold, D. (1984). Effects of leader warmth and directiveness on subordinate performance on a subsequent task. *Journal of Applied Psychology, 69,* 222–232.

Toller, P. W., & McBride, M. C. (2013). Enacting privacy rules and protecting disclosure recipients: Parents' communication with children following the death of a family member. *Journal of Family Communication, 13*(1), 32–45.

Toma, C. L., Hancock, J. T., & Ellison, N. B. (2008). Separating fact from fiction: An examination of deceptive self-presentation in online dating profiles. *Personality and Social Psychology Bulletin, 34*(8), 1023–1036.

Tominaga, J., Gudykunst, W. B., & Ota, H. (2003, May). *Perceptions of effective communication in the United States and Japan.* Paper presented at the annual meeting of the International Communication Association, San Diego, CA.

Tompkins, P. K., Fisher, J. Y., Infante, D. A., & Tompkins, E. L. (1975). Kenneth Burke and the inherent characteristics of formal organizations: A field study. *Communication Monographs, 42,* 135–142.

Tong, S. T., & Walther, J. B. (2015). The confirmation and disconfirmation of expectancies in computer-mediated Communication. *Communication Research, 42*(2), 186–212. doi: 10.1177/0093650212466257

Tran, H. (2014). Online agenda setting: A new frontier for theory development. In T. J. Johnson (Ed.), *Agenda-setting in a 2.0 world* (pp. 205–229). New York, NY: Routledge/Taylor & Francis.

Triandis, H. C. (1995). *Individualism and collectivism.* Boulder, CO: Westview.

Trost, J. (1990). Do we mean the same by the concept of family? *Communication Research, 17*(4), 431–443.

Tubbs, S. (1968). Explicit versus implicit audience conclusions and audience commitment. *Speech Monographs, 35,* 14–19.

Turner, J. R. (1993). Interpersonal and psychological predictors of parasocial interaction with different television performers. *Communication Quarterly, 41,* 443–453.

Vangelisti, A. L. (1993). Communication in the family: The influence of time, relational prototypes, and irrationality. *Communication Monographs, 60,* 42–54.

Vangelisti, A. L. (2011). Interpersonal processes in romantic relationships. In M. L. Knapp & J. A. Daly (Eds.), *The SAGE Handbook of Interpersonal Communication* (pp. 597–632). Thousand Oaks, CA: SAGE.

Van Swol, L. M. (2014). Questioning the assumptions of deception research. *Journal of Language and Social Psychology, 33*(4), 411–416.

Velicer, W. F., Prochaska, J. O., Fava, J. L., Norman, G. J., & Redding, C. A. (1998). Smoking cessation and stress management. Application of the transtheoretical model of behavior change. *Homeostasis in Health and Disease: International Journal Devoted to Integrative Brain Functions and Homeostatic Systems,* 216–233.

Waldron, V. R. (1997). Toward a theory of interactive conversational planning. In J. O. Green (Ed.), *Message production: Advances in communication theory.* (pp. 195–220). Mahwah, N.J.:, Lawrence Erlbaum Associates.

Walther, J. B. (1992). Interpersonal effects in computer-mediated interaction a relational perspective. *Communication Research, 19,* 52–90.

Walther, J. B. (1993). Impression development in computer-mediated interaction. *Western Journal of Communication, 57,* 381–398.

Walther, J. B. (1996). Computer-mediated communication: Impersonal, interpersonal, and hyperpersonal interaction. *Communication Research, 19,* 50–88.

Walther, J. B. (2007). Selective self-presentation in computer-mediated communication: Hyperpersonal dimensions of technology, language, and cognition. Computers in Human Behavior, 23, 2538–2557.

Walther, J. B. (2008). Social information processing theory: Impressions and relationship development online. In L. A. Baxter & D. O. Braithwaite (Eds.), *Engaging theories in interpersonal communication: Multiple perspectives* (pp. 391–404). Thousand Oaks, CA: Sage.

Walther, J. B. (2011). Theories of computer-mediated communication and interpersonal relations. In M. L. Knapp & J. A. Daly (Eds.), *The handbook of interpersonal communication* (4 ed.). Thousand Oaks, CA: Sage.

Walther, J. B. (2011). Theories of computer-mediated communication and interpersonal relations. In M. L. Knapp & J. A. Daly (Eds.), *The Sage Handbook of Interpersonal Communication* (pp. 443–479). Thousand Oaks, CA: Sage.

Walther, J. B., Anderson, J. F., & Park, D. (1994). Interpersonal effects in computer-mediated interaction: A meta-analysis of social and anti-social communication. Communication Research, 21, 460–487.

Walther, J. B., & Bunz, U. (2005). The rules of virtual groups: Trust, liking, and performance in computer-mediated communication. *Journal of Communication, 55*, 828–846.

Walther, J. B., & Carr, C. T. (2010). Internet interaction and intergroup dynamics: Problems and solutions in computer-mediated communication. In H. Giles, S. Reid, & J. Harwood (Eds.), *The dynamics of intergroup communication* (pp. 209–220). New York, NY: Peter Lang.

Walther, J. B., Loh, T., & Granka, L. (2005). Let me count the ways the interchange of verbal and nonverbal cues in computer-mediated and face-to-face affinity. *Journal of Language and Social Psychology, 24*(1), 36–65.

Walther, J. B., & Parks, M. R. (2002). Cues filtered out, cues filtered in: Computer-mediated communication and relationships. In M. L. Knapp & J. A. Daly (Eds.), *Handbook of interpersonal communication* (3rd ed., pp. 529–563). Thousand Oaks, CA: Sage.

Watzlawick, P., Beavin, J. H., & Jackson, D. D. (1967). *Pragmatics of human communication: A study of interaction patterns, pathologies, and paradoxes.* New York: Norton.

Weaver, D. (1987). Media agenda-setting and elections: Assumptions and implications. In D. L. Paletz (Ed.), *Political communication research* (pp. 176–193). Norwood, NJ: Ablex.

Weaver, D. H., Graber, D. A., McCombs, M. E.. & Eyal, C. H. (1981). *Media agenda setting in a presidential election: Issues, images, and interest.* New York: Praeger.

Weber, M. (1947). *The theory of social and economic organization* (A. M. Henderson & T. Parsons, Trans.). New York: Oxford.

Weick, K. E. (1979). *The social psychology of organizing* (2nd ed.). Reading, MA: Addison-Wesley.

Weick, K. E. (1995). *Sensemaking in organizations.* Thousand Oaks, CA: Sage.

Weiner, N. (1948). *Cybernetics*. New York: John Wiley.

Welch, S. A., & Rubin, R. B. (2002). Development of relationship stage model. *Communication Quarterly, 50*, 24–40.

Wellmon, T. A. (1988). Conceptualizing organizational communication competence: A rules-based perspective. *Management Communication Quarterly, 1*, 515–534.

West, R. (2005). Time for a change: Putting the transtheoretical (stages of change) model to test. *Addiction, 100*, 1036–1039. doi: 10.1111/j.1360-0443.2005.01139.x

Wheeless, L. R. (1975). An investigation of receiver apprehension and social context dimensions of communication apprehension. *The Speech Teacher, 24*, 261–265.

Wheeless, L. R., Eddleman-Spears, L., Magness, L. D., & Preiss, R. W. (2005). Informational reception apprehension and information from technology aversion: Development and test of a new construct. *Communication Quarterly, 53*, 143–158.

Wheeless, L. R., Preiss, R. W., & Gayle, B. M. (1997). Receiver apprehension, informational receptivity, and cognitive processing. In J. C. McCroskey, J. A. Daly, J. Ayres, T. Hopf, & D. M. Ayres (Eds.), *Avoiding communication: Shyness, reticence, and apprehension* (2nd ed., pp. 151–187). Cresskill, NJ: Hampton Press.

Wheeless, L. R., & Schrodt, P. (2001). An examination of cognitive foundations of informational reception apprehension: Political identification, religious affiliation, and family. *Communication Research Reports, 18*, 1–10.

Wheeless, V. E. (1984). A test of the theory of speech accommodation using language and gender orientation. *Women's Studies in Communication, 7*, 13–22.

Wheeless, V. E., Wheeless, L. R., & Riffle, S. (1989). The role of situation, physician communicator style, and hospital rules climate on nurses' decision styles and communication satisfaction. *Health Communication, 1*, 189–206. 10.1207/s15327027hc0104_1

White, C. H. (2008). Expectancy violations theory and interaction adaptation theory: From expectations to adaptation. In L. A. Baxter & D. O. Braithwaite (Eds.), *Engaging theories in interpersonal communication: Multiple perspectives* (pp. 189–202). Thousand Oaks, CA: Sage Publications.

White, C. H., & Burgoon, J. K. (2001). Adaptation and communicative design: Patterns of interaction in truthful and deceptive conversations. *Human Communication Research, 17*, 3–27.

White, R. K. & Lippett, R. (1968). Leader behavior and member reaction in three social climates. In D. Cartwright & A. Zander (Eds.), *Group dynamics: Research and theory* (3rd ed., pp. 318–335). New York: Harper and Row.

Whorf, B. L. (1956). In J. Carroll (Ed.). *Language, thought and reality: Selected writings of Benjamin Lee Whorf.* Cambridge, NIA: Technology Press, MIT.

Wiemann, J. M. (1977). Explication and test of a model of communication competence. *Human Communication Research, 3,* 195–213.

Wigley, C. J. (2006). Verbal triggering events. In A. S. Rancer & T. A. Avtgis, *Argumentative and aggressive communication: Theory, research, and application* (pp. 243–244). Thousand Oaks, CA: Sage.

Wigley, C. J. (2009, November). *Verbal trigger events (VTEs) and the measurement of reactive verbal aggression (RVA).* Paper presented at the annual meeting of the National Communication Association, Chicago, IL.

Wilkie, W. H. (1934). An experimental comparison of the speech, the radio, and the printed page as propaganda devices. *Archives of Psychology, 25,* No. 169.

Wilson, S. R., & Feng, H. (2007). Interaction goals and message production: Conceptual and methodological developments. In D. R. Roskos-Ewoldsen, & J. L. Monahan (Eds.), *Communication and social cognition: Theories and methods* (pp. 71–95). Mahwah, N.J.: Lawrence Erlbaum Associates.

Windahl, S. (1981). Uses and gratifications at the crossroads. In G. C. Wilhoit & H. deBock (Eds.), *Mass Communication Review Yearbook* (Vol. 2, pp. 174–185). Beverly Hills: Sage.

Witte, K. (1992). Putting the fear back into fear appeals: Reconciling the literature. *Communication Monographs, 59,* 329–349.

Witte, K. (1994). Fear control and danger control: A test of the extended parallel process model (EPPM). *Communication Monographs, 61,* 113–132.

Witte, K., & Allen, M. (2000). A meta-analysis of fear appeals: Implications for effective public health campaigns. *Health Education & Behavior, 27,* 591–615.

Witte, K., Cameron, K. A., McKeon, J., & Berkowitz, J. (1996). Predicting risk behaviors: Development and validation of a diagnostic scale. *Journal of Health Communication, 1,* 317–341.

Witte, K., Stokols, D., Ituarte, P., & Schneider, M. (1993). Testing the health belief model in a field study to promote bicycle safety helmets. *Communication Research, 20,* 564–586. doi:10.1177/005365093020004004

Witte, P. L., Wheeless, L. R., & Allen, M. (2004). A meta-analytical review of the relationship between teacher immediacy and student learning. *Communication Monographs, 71*, 184–207.

Wong, N. C. H., & Capella, J. N. (2009). Antismoking threat and efficacy appeals: Effects on smoking cessation intentions for smokers with low and high readiness to quit. *Journal of Applied Communication Research, 37*, 1–20.

Wright, C. N., Holloway, A., & Roloff, M. E. (2007). The dark side of self-monitoring: How high self-monitors view their romantic relationships. *Communication Reports, 20*, 101–114.

Wright, C. R. (1960). Functional analysis and mass communication. *Public Opinion Quarterly, 24*, 606–620.

Yerby, J., Buerkel-Rothfuss, N., & Bochner, A. R. (1990). *Understanding family communication.* Scottsdale, AZ: Gorsuch Scarisbrick.

Zaccaro, S. J., Foti, R. J., & Kenny, D. A. (1991). Self-monitoring and trait based variance in leadership: An investigation of leader flexibility across multiple group situations. *Journal of Applied Psychology, 76*, 308–315.

Zaidel, S. F., & Mehrabian, A. (1969). The ability to communicate and infer positive and negative attitudes facially and vocally. *Journal of Experimental Research in Personality, 3*, 233–241.

Zakahi, W. R. (1985). The relationship of assertiveness to communicative competence and communication satisfaction: A dyadic assessment. *Communication Research Reports, 2*, 36–40.

Zhang, Q., Ting-Toomey, S., & Oetzel, J. G. (2014). Linking emotion to the conflict face-negotiation theory: A US–China investigation of the mediating effects of anger, compassion, and guilt in interpersonal conflict. *Human Communication Research, 40*(3), 373–395.

Zillmann, D. (1972). Rhetorical elicitation of agreement in persuasion. *Journal of Abnormal and Social Psychology, 21*, 159–165.

Zuckerman, M., DePaulo, B. M., & Rosenthal, R. (1981). Verbal and non-verbal communication of deception. In L. Berkowitz (Ed.), *Advances in experimental social psychology* (pp. 1–59). New York: Academic Press.

GLOSSARY

Acculturation The degree to which a person acquires the beliefs and practices of the new culture or environment

Acquired needs theory Theory of motivation that holds that people are motivated to behave in order to acquire things that the culture at large deems important

Active strategy An uncertainty reduction strategy that requires effort to discover information, but there is still no direct contact between the two parties

Affective competence An aspect of host communication competence, involving emotional and motivational capacity to deal with the challenges of living in the new environment, including positivity, flexibility, and appreciation for the host way of life

Affiliation-disaffiliation In relational framing theory, a cognitive frame that focuses attention on regard, liking, or admiration

Agenda setting A theory that holds that intense media attention increases the importance of certain topics, issues, and individuals

Ambivalent orientation An orientation that is based on low independent and low interdependent self-construal

Amount A dimension of disclosiveness that pertains to the frequency of disclosure relative to other people

Anxiety In anxiety/uncertainty management theory, describes a feeling that accompanies uncertainty

Anxiety/uncertainty management theory (AUM) Is a theory that addresses the experience of interacting with unfamiliar others

Apathetic feelings Experienced by a moderately argumentative person who is low on both approach and avoidance

Appropriate disclosure A dimension of communicative adaptability that reflects the degree to which a person reveals personal information in the appropriate amount as dictated by any given situation

Argumentative skill deficiency Cause of verbal aggression due to an inability to argue skillfully; attack and defend needs are not satisfied

Argumentativeness A person's tendency to present and defend positions on controversial issues while attempting to refute the positions others take

Articulation A dimension of communicative adaptability that reflects the degree to which a person is proficient or skilled in the expression of ideas

Assimilation The degree to which a person accepts the influence of the new culture or environment; it involves both internal adjustment and active participation; also called intercultural transformation

Assurances A type of relationship maintenance behavior that involves messages about the desire to continue the relationship

Attitude How favorably we evaluate something

Attitude similarity The degree to which people's attitudes are consistent with each other

Authority heuristic A compliance-gaining strategy that assumes that people should be more willing to follow the suggestions of an individual who is a legitimate authority

Avoiding stage A stage in the relationship interaction stages model that reflects the physical or communication avoidance of a relational partner

Avoiding style A conflict style that involves avoiding discussion of the conflict issue, and may take the form of avoiding the opposing party or conflict situation

Axiology The discovery of worlds beyond the obvious and how these worlds contribute to the overall quality of human experience

Axiom A proposition that is not proven or demonstrated, but simply considered true in nature

Bandwidth The capacity of a medium to transmit nonverbal communication cues

Behavioral confirmation When one interaction partner's impression of the other partner motivates behavior that in turn encourages the other to behave in ways that align with the impression

Behavioral intention A person's intention of performing a given behavior is the best predictor of whether or not the person will actually perform the behavior

Behavioral observation Involves observing behavior, classifying it according to a framework, and determining the reliability of the classification

Belief A perception of how two or more things are related

Biconstrual orientation An orientation that is based on high independent and high interdependent self-construal

Bonding stage A stage in the relationship interaction stages model that reflects a strong emotional and psychological link between relational partners

Bureaucratic management A management perspective that advocates a tight structure with many levels in the hierarchy as well as control over employees

Central route The favorable thinking about the message content causes a favorable attitude to form toward the object of the message

Change agents Professionals who encourage opinion leaders to adopt or reject an innovation

Channel expansion theory A theory that defines media richness as a perception of the user and argues that it is influenced by channel, topic, organizational context, and communication partners

Channel The means by which the message is conveyed from source to receiver

Circumscribing stage A stage in the relationship interaction stages model that reflects relational partners focusing communication on everyday matters in order to avoid conflict

Classical management perspective A management perspective that seeks to maximize productivity and has little concern for the worker

Co-orientation Two or more people attending to the same social or physical "object"

Co-owners People with whom an original owner shares private information

Coercion Source applies force or pressure as a substitute for the motivation provided by attitudes

Cognitive competence An aspect of host communication competence, involving knowledge of host language, culture, history, social institutions, and rules for conduct

Cognitive complexity The extent to which a person's construct system is differentiated, abstract, and well-organized

Cognitive dissonance theory Assumes that two beliefs are related either in a state of consonance or dissonance

Cognitive valence theory A perceived increase in immediacy behaviors from one person in a relationship activates expectations

Cohesiveness The feeling of "oneness" in a group, being "close-knit," bound to one another, and united as members of a team

Commitment and consistency heuristic A compliance-gaining strategy that assumes that when people take a stand on an issue, there is internal pressure to be consistent with what they committed to

Commitment and intimacy A characteristic of families; typically, families experience a stronger sense of inseparability and interconnection than in other relationships

Communication accommodation theory A language theory of how we have our language converge or diverge with the language of others

Communication apprehension A broadly based anxiety related to oral communication

Communication channel Reflects the means through which messages about the innovation travel from one person to another

Communication plan A set of behaviors that the person believes will accomplish a purpose

Communication privacy management theory A theory that explains how people reveal private information as well as how people conceal private information

Communication trait An abstraction constructed to account for enduring consistencies and differences in message-sending and message-receiving behaviors among individuals

Communicative adaptability A trait that is the ability to perceive socio-interpersonal relationships and adapt interaction goals and interpersonal behaviors appropriately

Communicator image An overall impression of a communicator that is composed of at least ten traits

Communicator style The way a person verbally and paraverbally interacts to signal how literal meaning should be taken, interpreted, filtered, or understood

Compliance Social influence attempts designed to influence another person to behave in a particular manner

Compromising style A conflict style that involves conceding some personal interests and goals while attaining others in the effort to reach an equitable settlement

Conflict Part of the tolerance for disagreement communication trait that reflects competition, suspicion, distrust, dislike, hostility, and self-perpetuation

Conflicted feelings Experienced by a moderate argumentative person who is high in both approach and avoidance

Conformity orientation The extent to which family communication emphasizes homogeneity of beliefs, values, and attitudes

Confounding variables A type of extraneous variable and serve to complicate relationships between the variables

Connection-autonomy From relational dialectics theory, an internal dialectic between the desire to link your activities with those of your relational partner and the desire to act independently

Connotative meaning Subjective associations, personal, or emotional attachments people associate with symbols

Consensual families Families high in conformity orientation and high in conversation orientation

Constitutive definitions Define a concept by using other concepts

Constructivism Cognitive theory of communication that explains how people use personal constructs (bi-polar opposites) to produce and interpret messages

Content analysis Method of measurement for studying the content of messages, which utilizes a category system and check the reliability of categorizing message units

Context A particular type of communication situation

Contextual view Behavior is consistent within contexts but varies across contexts

Continuous variables When there are meaningful degrees of a variable between the highest and lowest values

Control The ability to alter elements in the present to achieve a specified outcome given certain situational factors in the future

Controllability People's belief that they have control over the behavior, that the performance of the behavior is or is not up to them

Convergence A dimension of communication accommodation theory that is a strategy where individuals alter their speech to adapt to each other

Convergence communication tasks Communication tasks that involve reaching mutual agreement

Conversation orientation The degree to which families encourage unrestrained interaction about a wide range of topics

Conveyance communication tasks Communication tasks that involve disseminating information

Cooperation A function of health communication that involves communication concerning the nature of one's illness and the implication of measures prescribed for care

Coordinated linkage rules A rule coordinated between original and co-owners of private information, controlling who else is allowed to know the information

Coordinated ownership rules A rule coordinated between original and co-owners of private information, controlling whether co-owners are allowed to share the information independent of the original owner

Coordinated permeability rules A rule coordinated between original and co-owners of private information, controlling how much information is shared

Correlation A dimension of the functional theory of mass communication that concerns how the mass media select, interpret, and criticize the information they present to the public

Costs Anything that we see as a punishment or detriment from a relationship

Counsel A function of health communication that involves the role of the provider as "therapist"

Critical tradition Goal is to expose hidden elements that distort communication and to advocate efforts to resist the use of power by these elements

Cross-cultural adaptation theory An intercultural theory that explains the process of how people adjust to a new environment

Cultivation theory of mass communication This theory asserts that television influences our view of reality

Cultural transmission A dimension of the functional theory of mass communication that concerns the media's ability to communicate norms, rules, and values of a society

Cybernetic tradition Treats communication theory building as information processing and concerns analyzing communication problems in a system

Deculturation The degree to which a person unlearns the beliefs and practices of a culture or environment

Defense of rights and interests A willingness to confront others to protect rights and interests

Deindividuation Temporary loss of one's own uniqueness or individuality

Denotative meaning The objective, descriptive, or agreed-upon meaning of a word. A dictionary definition

Dependent variables Presumed effect in cause-effect relationship with independent variables

Depersonalization The inability to tell that other people are uniquely different from one another

Depth A dimension of disclosiveness that refers to how superficial or intimate the information is

Description Focuses the attention of scholars on particular parts of an event or phenomenon

Development of self-concept A characteristic of families; our self-concepts are strongly influenced by interactions with family members

Diagnosis A function of health communication that involves data gathering, data interpretation, and problem-solving skills used by the health-care provider

Dialectic of expression In relational dialectics theory, a tension around how much should be disclosed or kept private

Dialectic of integration In relational dialectics theory, a tension around being involved versus being separate

Dichotomous variables Variable with two discrete values

Differential salience hypothesis In relational framing theory, the claim that only one cognitive frame will be in use at any given time

Differentiation stage A stage in the relationship interaction stages model that reflects highlighting how different you are from your relational partner

Diffusion theory The study of how new ideas spread among groups of people

Dimensions of national culture A theory of how national cultures differ from each other

Direct personalization A dimension of taking conflict personally reflecting the hurt a person experiences during a conflict episode

Directiveness A dimension of assertiveness that involves leadership: taking charge in group situations and seeking positions where one can influence others

Disagreement Part of the tolerance for disagreement communication trait that reflects the difference of opinion on issues

Disclosiveness Personality trait that reflects a person's predilection to disclose to other people in general

Disdain Cause of verbal aggression that involves the desire to communicate dislike for a person through verbally aggressive messages

Disengaged homemaker A lifestyle type indicating primarily female, middle-aged, lower in education and income, and use the media for companionship and to pass time

Divergence A dimension of communication accommodation theory that reflects accentuating vocal and linguistic differences to underscore social differences between speakers

Dogmatism The individual's willingness to consider other belief systems

Dominance Degree to which one partner is said to dominate a dyad's interaction

Dominance-submissiveness In relational framing theory, a cognitive frame that focuses attention on status, power, and control

Dominating style A conflict style that involves achieving personal goals without regard to the interests of the other party

Door in the face technique A compliance-gaining strategy that utilizes a large request followed by a smaller request. People are more likely to agree to the smaller request after rejecting the larger request

Education A function of health communication that assumes health education is the process of disseminating information to individuals in order to attempt to reduce health risks and to increase the effectiveness of health care

Effective communication The degree to which the other person assigns or attaches a similar meaning to the meanings that were intended by the sender

Effective management theory A theory that assumes management action should be composed of planning for the future, organizing, commanding, coordinating, and controlling

Efficiency framework A theory that explains why some CMC technologies are perceived as unsatisfactory but are associated with high productivity and outcome quality

Ego-involvement Characterized by a wide latitude of rejection and narrow latitudes of acceptance and noncommitment

Elaboration likelihood model A model of persuasion that assumes persuasion results primarily from characteristics of the persuasive message or from characteristics of the situation

Emotional leakage A term used to describe when a person's feelings "leak out" through one or more nonverbal channels

Empirical Information gathered by observation

Enculturation A type of cultural adaptation reflecting when we learn to speak, listen, read, interpret, and understand verbal and nonverbal messages in such a fashion that the messages will be recognized and responded to by the individuals with whom we communicate; learning to interact and relate in ways that are considered normal for our home cultures

Entertainment A dimension of the functional theory of mass communication that reflects how mass communication helps fill our leisure time by presenting messages filled with comedy, tragedy, play, and performance

Entry phase Dimension of uncertainty reduction theory that reflects the initial phase of relationships where physical appearance, sex, age, socioeconomic status, and other biographic and demographic information is most important

Environmental factors In cross-cultural adaptation theory, characteristics of the host culture and the relationship between host and home cultures

Epistemology How we come to know knowledge as well as how the theorist investigates the theory

Equivocal Open to multiple interpretations

Ethnic group strength The relative status or standing of a particular ethnic group in the context of the surrounding host society; an environmental factor in cross-cultural adaptation theory

Ethnic proximity In cross-cultural adaptation theory, the extent to which a stranger is initially able to blend in with the host culture

Ethnocentrism The tendency to regard one's own cultural group as the center of everything and rate other groups in reference to it

Exchange approaches to leadership A leadership approach that assumes the quality of the relationship is believed to be the determining factor for effective leadership

Exit phase Dimension of uncertainty reduction theory that assumes that during this phase, the communicators decide on future interaction plans

Experimental operational definition Outlines the procedures followed in manipulating a variable

Experimenting stage A stage in the relationship interaction stages model that reflects relational partners focusing on finding similarities between them

Explanation Understanding how a phenomenon or event occurs

Extension Process in which a theory grows by adding knowledge and new concepts

External dialectics In relational dialectics theory, a set of opposing forces or tensions that result from the embedding of the dyadic relationship in a larger social network

External locus of control A perception that the person perceives that their lives and behavior are controlled by others

External validity Concerned with the generalizability of a study; major threats are pretesting, experimental arrangements, sampling, and multiple treatment effects

Extraneous variables Variables that are uncontrolled or not part of the intended research but may have an impact on your study

Eye behavior Nonverbal behavior that communicates attitude, interest, dominance, or submission

Face The claimed sense of favorable social self-worth and/or projected other-worth in a public situation

Face gain Occurs when we are treated by others in ways that enhance our face, or when our own behavior produces face enhancement

Face loss Occurs when we are treated by others in ways that threaten our face, or when our own behavior produces face threat

Face negotiation theory A theory that explains how culture influences our behavior during conflict

Face threat Potential or actual damage to face

Facework Specific verbal and nonverbal behaviors that we engage in to maintain or restore face loss and to uphold and honor face

Factor model of credibility Aspects of credibility are a source's expertise, character, and goodwill

Falsification To find a theory to be false

Family communication patterns theory A theory that differentiates types of families based on their routine ways of communicating with each other, and connects such patterns with outcomes for family members, especially children

Feedback Allows a source to have a means of assessing how a message is being decoded

Forewarnings Messages that warn the audience by mentioning the type of arguments an opposing speaker will present

Functional fitness In CCAT, the ability to function successfully in a new culture; an indicator of assimilation

Functional model of credibility Credibility is determined by the extent to which a source fulfills the receiver's needs

Gatekeepers People who control the flow of information to a given group of people

General intensifier hypothesis In relational framing theory, the claim that perceptions of involvement polarize judgments within the other two frames (dominance-submissiveness, affiliation-disaffiliation)

General level of anxiety acceptance A level of anxiety that exists between a person's maximum and minimum thresholds for anxiety

General level of uncertainty acceptance A level of uncertainty that exists between a person's maximum and minimum thresholds for uncertainty

Goals Future states of affairs that an individual is committed to achieving or maintaining

Goals-plans-action theory A theory that explains message production as resulting from goals and the plans made to achieve them

Heuristic value A theory's ability to solve problems or provide solutions that are the closest to the "best solution"

Hierarchy principle The tendency, when faced with plan failure, to change concrete rather than abstract elements of the plan

Honesty A dimension of disclosiveness that involves the sincerity of disclosure

Host communication competence Factors that involve the outsider's ability to decode and encode information in ways that are consistent with normal communication practices in the new or "host" culture

Host conformity pressure The extent to which the host environment exerts influence on strangers to act in accordance with the norms of the host culture, as opposed to being allowed to continue with habitual behaviors from their home cultures; an environmental factor in cross-cultural adaptation theory

Host receptivity The degree to which a culture welcomes and accepts strangers and offers them support; an environmental factor in cross-cultural adaptation theory

Human relations perspective A management approach that advocates that management should satisfy the interpersonal and emotional needs of workers

Human resource management perspective A management approach that assumes employees are a valuable asset who should be developed for the benefit of both the organization as well as the worker

Hypertextuality A quality of CMC, referencing the extent to which it includes interlinking of information

Hypothesis Tentative statement about the relationships between concepts of a theory; a statement of prediction about the relationships between variables

Immediacy behaviors Messages that signal feelings of warmth, closeness, and involvement with another person

Incentive In uncertainty reduction theory, the motive to reduce uncertainty about people who control rewards or who can satisfy our needs

Inclusion-seclusion From relational dialectics theory, an external dialectic between the desire to spend time as a dyad with family and friends versus the desire to spend time with the relational partner apart from everyone else

Independence A dimension of assertiveness that involves maintaining personal convictions even when in the minority and receiving pressure from the majority to conform

Independent orientation An orientation that is based on high independent and low interdependent self-construal

Independent self-construal Viewing oneself as unique, with an individual repertoire of cognitions, emotions, and motivations that are separate from those of other people

Independent variables Variables that cause and/or predict dependent variables

Individualism-collectivism A dimension of national culture distinguishing between cultures with a "loose-knit" social structure in which individuals are expected to look out only for themselves and their immediate families (individualistic) and cultures in which individuals are tightly connected to extended family or other in-groups with an expectation of mutual care and loyalty (collectivistic)

Indulgence-restraint A dimension of national culture that describes variation in cultural response to the human desire to enjoy life and have fun

Information systems theory An information processing theory that seeks to explain how information and sense-making is a perceptual process that varies from person to person

Informational reception apprehension A pattern of anxiety and antipathy that filters informational reception, perception, and processing, and/or adjustment (psychologically, verbally, physically) associated with complexity, abstractness, and flexibility

Initiation stage A stage of the relationship interaction stages model that reflects the first interactions of relational partners

Innovation Innovations contain five attributes: relative advantage, compatibility, complexity, reliability, and observability

Inoculation theory Approach to preventing persuasion based on the biological analogy of preventing disease

Instrumental use Using television viewing primarily for information acquisition

Integrating stage A stage in the relationship interaction stages model that reflects when relational partners begin to talk about the future together and share a sense of being committed

Integrating style A conflict style that involves seeking a resolution that addresses individual interests of all parties involved

Intellectual inflexibility The degree to which people are unwilling to consider different points of view

Intensifying stage A stage in the relationship interaction stages model that reflects relational partners seeking to find similarities in terms of morals and values

Intent A dimension of self-disclosure that involves the degree of awareness that one is revealing information about oneself

Intention Process in which a theory grows by developing a deeper understanding of the original concepts and variables

Intentional Knowingly influencing the receiver of the message

Interaction adaptation theory A theory of how we alter our behavior in response to the behavior of another person

Interactionist position Assumes that behavior in a particular situation is a joint product of a person's traits and of variables in the situation

Interactive strategy An uncertainty reduction strategy that consists of obtaining information directly through asking questions (interrogation) and offering personal information about yourself

Interactivity A quality of CMC, referencing the extent to which message sender and receiver are interchangeable roles and exert influence on each other

Intercultural identity In CCAT, an orientation toward self and others that is not rigidly defined in terms of either the home culture or the new culture; an indicator of assimilation

Interdependent orientation An orientation that is based on high interdependent and low independent self-construal

Interdependent self-construal Viewing oneself as intertwined in relationships with other people, sharing their cognitions, emotions, and motivations

Internal dialectics In relational dialectics theory, a set of opposing forces or tensions that are internal to the dyadic relationship

Internal locus of control A perception that the person has direct control over their lives and behaviors

Internal validity Check to determine whether something other than the independent variables such as history, maturation, measurement, or selection, could be responsible for results

Interval level of measurement Contains the properties of nominal and ordinal levels of measurement plus the intervals between data points that are equal, or approximately equal

Involvement In relational framing theory, the degree to which interacting parties are coordinated, engaged, and immediate with each other

Involvement with social networks A type of relationship maintenance behavior that involves interacting with friends and relatives

Irritability A dimension of hostility that is reflected in a quick temper in response to the slightest provocation, being generally moody and grouchy, showing little patience, being exasperated when there is a delay or something goes wrong, and being rude and inconsiderate of others' feelings

Lack of social context cues hypothesis A theory that explains how reduced social context cues affect communication behavior

Laissez-faire families Families low in conformity orientation and low in conversation orientation

Language expectancy theory A message-based theory of persuasion that focuses on how cultural expectation of language use affects both the change and reinforcement of attitudes and beliefs

Language intensity Quality of speaker's language about objects or concepts that indicates a difference in attitude from neutral

Latitude of acceptance Consists of all statements the person finds acceptable. This can include the favorite position or the anchor

Latitude of noncommitment Consists of all of the positions a person neither accepts nor rejects

Latitude of rejection Consists of all of the positions on an issue the person rejects

Like/dislike valence A dimension of taking conflict personally that reflects the degree to which people enjoy engaging in conflict

Likelihood of future interaction In uncertainty reduction theory, the motive to reduce uncertainty about people whom we anticipate meeting again

Likert scales Rating scales that utilize a five or seven point agree-disagree format to rate value statements about an object

Liking heuristic A compliance-gaining strategy that assumes that we comply with requests because we like the person

Listening apprehension The fear associated with either anticipated or real listening situations

Locus of control A personality trait that concerns how people interpret outcomes in their life

Long-term orientation A dimension of national culture that distinguishes between cultures that hold on to norms and traditions based in history and are suspicious of change (short-term orientation) versus cultures that look toward the future (long-term orientation), emphasizing modern education and judicious use of resources

Longevity of influence A characteristic of families; the influence of one's family endures for a lifetime

Machiavellianism An orientation in which people believe that manipulating others is a basic strategy of social influence

Magic bullet theory A theory of mass communication that suggests media influences people directly and uniformly

Mainstreaming The power of television to present relatively uniform images acceptable to a majority of viewers

Managerial grid theory A theory that contains two continua resulting in five managerial profiles ranging in concern for task and concern for relationship

Masculinity-femininity A dimension of national culture that represents the extent to which a culture is "tough" (i.e., masculine) versus "tender" (feminine)

Maximum threshold for anxiety A maximum level of anxiety that, when not exceeded, allows people to remain comfortable when interacting with other people

Maximum threshold for uncertainty A maximum level of uncertainty that, when not exceeded, allows people to remain comfortable when interacting with other people

Media dependency theory A theory of mass communication that assumes that the more dependent an individual is on the media for having his or her needs filled, the more important the media will be to the person

Media richness Features of a medium that give it the capacity to resolve equivocality and uncertainty

Media richness theory A theory that characterizes communication media as "richer" or "leaner" to summarize how well they facilitate mutual understanding, and contends that selecting the right channel for particular tasks is key to maximizing the efficacy of these communications

Media synchronicity theory A theory that divides communication into two kinds of tasks: conveying information and converging on meaning. The theory claims that information is better conveyed asynchronously, while shared meaning is more effectively reached synchronously

Mediating variables Variables that come in between two variables and explain the relationship between them

Message The stimulus that the source transmits to the receiver

Mindfulness A process of awareness where we become aware of our own frame of reference as well as the frame of reference of the receiver

Minimum threshold for anxiety The minimum level of anxiety that, when not exceeded, allows people to remain comfortable when interacting with other people

Minimum threshold for uncertainty The minimal level of uncertainty that, when not exceeded, allows people to remain comfortable when interacting with other people

Misinterpretation Occurs when communicators attach different meanings to the same communication behavior

Mobilization A dimension of the functional theory of mass communication that reflects the ability of the media to promote national interests

Model I approach Management approach that assumes unilateral goals, self-reliance, failure to disclose negative opinions, and reliance on objectivity and logic

Model II approach Management approach that assumes pro-action, consultative decision making, solution implementation, and the ability to adapt should the solution need adjustment

Moderating variables Variables that moderate, or change, the influence of variable A on variable B

Motive An internal state of readiness to act to achieve a goal

Multimedia A quality of CMC, referencing the extent to which it includes not only text, but visual images and sound, including the range of human nonverbal behavior

Multiple-act A behavioral prediction in research based on a set of relevant behaviors ideally observed more than once over a period of time

Mutual-face concern The degree to which we are simultaneously concerned for both our own face and that of others

Mutuality model Health care consumer engaging in a collaboration of joint input with the health care provider resulting in a mutually agreeable treatment protocol

Need for cognition A stable individual difference in people's tendency to engage in and enjoy effortful cognitive activity

Need for orientation Part of the agenda-setting theory of mass communication concerning the relevance of information to an individual and the degree of uncertainty

Need for social approval A person's need for approval from others influences how they react to persuasive messages that imply approval-disapproval

Negative relational effects A dimension of taking conflict personally that reflects the extent to which people feel that conflict communication can have negative outcomes for both social and task relationships

Negativism A dimension of hostility that is expressed by refusing to cooperate, expressing unwarranted pessimism about the outcome of something when other people are very hopeful, and voicing antagonism concerning authority, rules, and social conventions

Noble self A person who believes in expressing exactly what they think or feel. Noble selves do not value flexibility in adapting to different audiences

Noise Any stimulus that inhibits the receiver's accurate reception of a given message

Nominal level of measurement Level of measurement that results in assigning an object of judgment into a category

Nonsummativity and interdependence A characteristic of families; families are more complex than their set of members, and each member influences all others

Nonverbal expectancy violations theory Theory that explains a wide range of communication outcomes associated with violations of expectations about nonverbal communication behavior

Nonverbal response matching Matching another's nonverbal behavior in order to create perceived similarity, which leads to trust

Nonvoluntary A characteristic of many family relationships; we do not choose to be born to a specific family

Null hypothesis Statement that relations observed in a study were due to chance

Obliging style A conflict style that prioritizes concern for the other party's position and interests above and beyond personal interests and goals

Occam's razor Term used to represent the precision of theoretical explanation; stresses simplicity

Ontology What it is the theorist is examining and what is considered the exact nature of reality and the most basic measuring units of reality

Openness-closedness From relational dialectics theory, an internal dialectic between the desire to share intimate ideas and feelings with one's relational partner and the desire to maintain individual privacy

Operational competence An aspect of host communication competence, involving the ability to perform the correct verbal and nonverbal behaviors during interactions with members of the host culture

Operational definitions Define something in terms of the operations or procedures that were followed to experience the object of definition

Opinion leader A component of the two-step flow theory that reflects a person who pays close attention to the mass media then exerts their influence on others concerning the messages received from the media

Opinionated acceptance Language that expresses a favorable attitude toward people who agree with the speaker

Opinionated language Highly intense language that indicates a speaker's attitude toward topics and attitude toward others

Opinionated rejection Language that expresses an unfavorable attitude toward people who disagree with the speaker

Ordinal level of measurement Level of measurement where objects are rank ordered according to some standard

Other-face concern The degree to which we are concerned with the face of the other party in a conflict episode

Out-groups In anxiety/uncertainty management theory, describes groups of people that we do not belong to or have membership with

Outgoing activist A lifestyle type primarily consisting of female, younger, well educated, with a high need for stimulation, good income, and less likely to marry

Parasocial interaction A relationship that exists between television viewers and remote media communicators

Parsimony Reducing a theory to its simplest form possible

Partner interference Influence of a relational partner that disrupts life routines

Passive strategy An uncertainty reduction strategy that involves watching someone without being observed

Paternalistic model A patient following a health care practitioner's recommendation to the letter, not questioning any of the practitioner's orders

Perceived behavioral control The degree to which a person believes that they control any given behavior

Perceived control The degree to which people believe that they have control over a situation or behavior

Perceived similarity The degree to which we believe another's attitudes are similar to ours

Perception A process through which individuals interpret sensory information

Peripheral route When there is little or no elaboration of a message, situational cues persuade people instead of the message

Persecution feelings A dimension of taking conflict personally that reflects the perception that other people are just seeking to pick a fight with you and purposely seek to engage in conflict

Personal constructs The elements (i.e., bi-polar opposites) which individuals use to interpret, anticipate, evaluate, and make sense of the world

Personal phase A dimension of uncertainty reduction theory that reflects communicating attitudes, beliefs, values, and more personal data

Personal space Zones of space that surround us: intimate, casual-personal, socioconsultative, public

Persuasibility Personality trait indicating willingness to be persuaded

Phenomenological tradition Views communication as dialogue or experience to otherness

Pimary goals Principal reasons for interaction, determining subsequent plans and actions

Plan complexity The specificity of a plan, including its level of detail and number of contingencies

Planning Processes involved in developing plans

Planning theory A theory that describes message effectiveness as a consequence of plan characteristics, especially plan complexity

Plans Cognitive representations of actions to be taken to achieve goals

Pluralistic families Families low in conformity orientation and high in conversation orientation

Positive relational effects A dimension of taking conflict personally that reflects the extent to which people feel conflict communication can be positive for both social and task relationships

Positiveness A dimension of disclosiveness that measures the extent to which the information revealed about the self is positive or negative

Positivity A type of relationship maintenance behavior that involves being optimistic and cheerful with the relationship partner

Postulate A proposition that is not proven or demonstrated, but simply considered true in nature

Power The potential to influence or restrict another person's behaviors

Power distance A dimension of national culture that represents how much the less powerful members of a society expect and accept that power is unequally distributed

Predicted outcome value A prediction about whether a relationship is likely to be rewarding (positive) or costly (negative)

Predicted outcome value theory Theory that explains behavior in initial interactions and subsequent relationship development as a consequence of predicted rewards and costs of the relationship

Prediction The concept of knowing what events will occur in the future

Preparedness In cross-cultural adaptation theory, level of readiness to adapt, including what has been learned about the host language and culture, whether the encounter is expected to be temporary, or long-term, and whether the encounter is voluntary (e.g., study abroad) or involuntary

Principle of privacy control People's belief in the right to control what others know about them, and to make decisions about the disclosure of their private information to others

Principle of privacy ownership The belief people have that their private information belongs to them

Principle of privacy turbulence The tendency for privacy violations to arise when owners and co-owners do not sufficiently coordinate privacy boundaries

Principle of reinforcement The idea that we like and are attracted to those people who reward us

Privacy boundary A distinction between someone who has private information and someone who does not have that same information

Privacy rules Personal guidelines that specify when and how to disclose private information; influenced by culture, gender, motivation, context, and risk-benefit ratio

Protective families Families high in conformity orientation and low in conversation orientation

Proxemics How people use space to coammunicate

Psychological health In CCAT, feelings of efficacy and fulfillment; an indicator of assimilation to a new culture

Public-private dialectic The ongoing tension, or opposition, between revealing and concealing private information

Questions of fact Concern whether something is or isn't, occurred or didn't occur, will or will not occur

Questions of policy Concern whether something should or shouldn't be done

Questions of value Concern whether something is good or bad or favorable or unfavorable

Ratio level of measurement Level of measurement that contains properties of nominal, ordinal, and interval levels of measurement plus an absolute zero point

Reactive In the relational turbulence model, refers to excessive emotional and cognitive response to a partner's behavior

Reading anxiety Refers to the degree of anxiety a person experiences when reading information

Receiver Decodes and interprets the message sent

Receiver apprehension Fear of misinterpreting, inadequately processing, and/or not being able to adjust psychologically to messages sent by others

Reciprocity heuristic A compliance-gaining strategy that assumes that when someone gives you something, you should give them something in return

Redundancy Refers to the amount of change in interactant's negotiations over rights

Reflective-projective theory of mass communication A theory that asserts that the mass media act like a mirror for society

Relational dialectics A set of opposing forces or tensions that individuals experience as a consequence of being in a dyadic relationship

Relational dialectics theory A theory that describes opposing forces or tensions (relational dialectics) that affect relationships

Relational framing theory A theory that explains cognitive structures through which we interpret communication behavior and its effects

Relational turbulence model A model that explains why relationships experience periods in which they are experienced as unstable

Relational uncertainty The degree of confidence individuals have in their perceptions of involvement in a relationship

Relationship interaction stages model A model that describes change in communication as relationships change over time

Relationship maintenance model A model of actions and activities that sustain desired relational definitions

Relationship talk A type of relationship maintenance behavior that involves discussing the nature of the relationship and what is desired for it

Reliability The ability to be consistent or obtain a high degree of agreement between items in a scale or between/among raters, among others

Replicable A study similar to an earlier study which determines if the results of the original study are similar when repeated

Research hypothesis The prediction of the results of an experiment

Research question Question guiding investigation; usually used when a hypothesis is not warranted

Resentment A dimension of hostility that involves expressing jealousy and hatred, brooding about real or imagined mistreatment so that feelings of anger develop, and indicating that others do not really deserve success

Resonance Argues that media's influences on perceptions are intensified when media depict "real life"

Restrained activist A lifestyle type primarily male and female who are older, highly educated, opinion leaders likely to marry, and have high incomes

Revelation-concealment From relational dialectics theory, an external dialectic between the desire to share information from the relationship to the social network and the desire to keep information private, within the relationship

Rewards Anything that we see as a benefit from a relationship

Rhetorical reflector People who have the tendency to conceive their "selves" not as fixed entities, but as social "characters" who take on whatever role is necessary for the particular situation

Rhetorical sensitive A person who believes there is no single self but a complex network of selves. The rhetorical sensitive person is in between the noble self and the rhetorical reflector

Rhetorical tradition Conceptualizes communication as the art of discourse

Ritual A third type of sign that is a combination of being naturally produced and being arbitrary or created

Ritualized use Using television viewing primarily as a diversion

Salience of a social identity The extent to which feelings of belonging to a social group are present and important

Sampling A method of studying part of a population in order to draw conclusions about the entire population

Scarcity heuristic A compliance-gaining strategy that assumes that people want to try to secure those opportunities that are scarce

Scientific management theory A management perspective that assumes any worker can be productive if given a scientifically efficient task

Secondary goals Concerns that arise when pursuing a primary goal

Selective exposure Exposing oneself only to agreeable messages; avoiding situations, such as public speeches by a political opponent, requiring us to listen to those with whom we disagree

Selective self-presentation Presenting a desired version of oneself

Self-construal A way of seeing oneself relative to others

Self-disclosure A type of relationship maintenance behavior that involves sharing thoughts and feelings that are not specifically about the relationship

Self-efficacy The degree of ease or difficulty in performing the behavior or likelihood that a person can actually perform a behavior

Self-esteem How favorably the individual evaluates himself or herself is related to persuasion

Self-face concern The degree to which we are concerned with our own face needs during a conflict episode

Self-monitoring of expressive behavior A trait that involves monitoring one's nonverbal behavior and adapting it to situations in order to achieve communication goals

Semantic differential scales Rating scales that utilize a seven-point continuum bound by bipolar terms in order to locate an object in semantic space

Semiotic tradition Conceptualizes communication as intersubjective mediation by signs

Sharing tasks A type of relationship maintenance behavior that involves performing responsibilities, such as household chores

Sign Something that stands for or represents another thing

Situational leadership approach Assumes that there is no such thing as a born leader as much as people acting as leaders depending on the specific situation

Situationist Approach to understanding communication that emphasizes the impact of situational variables

Small-group communication Communication in gatherings that vary in size from three to about fifteen persons

Smaller bandwidth A term from language expectancy theory that reflects when people have a smaller variety of persuasive linguistic strategies that will be seen as appropriate or within an expected range

Social assertiveness A dimension of assertiveness that reflects an individual being able to start conversations with strangers, feeling comfortable around a wide variety of people, and generally being able to initiate desired relationships

Social composure A dimension of communicative adaptability that reflects the degree to which a person is calm, cool, and collected in social situations

Social confirmation A dimension of communicative adaptability that reflects the degree to which a person can affirm or maintain the other person's face or self-image while interacting

Social context cues Cues that define the nature of social situations and the relationships between communicators

Social experience A dimension of communicative adaptability that reflects the degree to which a person actually experiences, or is willing to experience, novel situations

Social identity model of deindividuation effects A theory that explains how people develop perceptions of others and regulate their own behavior based on identification with social groups to which they belong

Social information processing theory A theory that explains how people adapt communication, especially language use, to develop impressions and create relationships in computer-mediated environments

Social learning Cause of verbal aggression brought about by direct reinforcement of verbally aggressive behavior or by modeling the behavior after an esteemed person

Social presence The degree to which a communicator is aware of the presence of his or her interactional partner

Social presence theory A theory that explains the effects of a communication medium on the way people communicate

Social proof heuristic A compliance-gaining strategy that assumes that we determine what is correct by finding out what other people think is correct

Social scientific method Using the concept of systematic thought and the application of scientific principles

Social system A set of interrelated units that are engaged in joint problem-solving to accomplish a goal

Sociocultural tradition Addresses problems of diversity and relativity as well as cultural change

Sociopsychological tradition Assumes that communication is a process of social interaction

Source Designates the originator of a message

Spiral of silence theory A theory about how minority viewpoints disappear from public awareness. People remain silent because of the fear of being different and isolated. The media play a major role in informing people about what is normative

Stagnation stage A stage in the relationship interaction stages model that reflects the boredom experienced in a relationship

Stakeholder theory A theory that assumes the sole responsibility of an organization is to those people who own the instruments of production

State behavior Behavior that varies from one situation to another within the same context

Statistical hypothesis A statement of the research made in mathematical terms

Statistical significance Reflects whether the results are due to chance

Strangers Concept in AUM theory representing people whom we do not know and who are themselves in an unfamiliar environment

Stress-adaptation-growth dynamic In CCAT, a process in which new experiences in an unfamiliar culture produce stress, requiring adaptation, producing internal growth, and allowing the individual to deal with subsequent new experiences

Stress reaction A dimension of taking conflict personally that reflects the level of physiological response one has when in a conflict episode

Subjective norm The pressure a person feels to conform to the will of others to perform or not perform a behavior

Surveillance A dimension of the functional theory of mass communication that is the information and news providing function of mass communication

Suspicion A dimension of hostility that is reflective of expressing an unjustified distrust of people, expecting that others do not have goodwill, believing that others are planning to harm you, and treating people as if their characters are flawed

Symbol A second type of sign created to stand for something else

Symptom One type of sign that bears a natural relation to an object

Synchronicity A quality of CMC, referencing the immediacy of response between interacting parties

Taking conflict personally A communication trait that reflects the degree to which we have a negative emotional reaction to participating in a conflict

Terminating stage A stage in the relationship interaction stages model that reflects the ending of a relationship

Testable Quality of a good theory; capable of being disproved or falsified

Theoretical significance The empirical findings either support or do not support the theory

Theory A set of related statements designed to describe, explain, and/or predict reality

Theory of independent mindedness A communication based organizational theory that advocates cultural congruity between the organization and the larger culture within which it operates

Theory of interpersonal communication motives A theory that identifies the motives people have for interpersonal communication

Theory of linguistic relativity Assumes that all higher level of thought depends on language and the structure of the language we use influences the way we understand our environment

Theory of reasoned action A theory of persuasion that is based on attitudes, belief strength, and the evaluation of the meaning of the belief

Time The element of time involved in the new innovation adoption process involves adoption decisiveness, timeliness of the decision, and the rate of adoption or the time it takes to make its way through any given social system

Tolerance for disagreement A communication trait that reflects the amount of disagreement a person can tolerate before he or she perceives the existence of a conflict in a relationship

Trait approach to leadership Assumes that leaders have traits that distinguish them from followers

Trait behavior Behavior is assumed to be consistent across contexts and specific situations within particular contexts

Trait position Approach to communication that maintains there are broad predispositions that account for behavior

Transactional process Communication involves people sending each other messages that reflect the motivations of the participants

Transference Cause of verbal aggression that involves using verbal aggression against people who remind one of unresolved sources of conflict and pain

Transition In the relational turbulence model, refers to a life event or circumstance that tends to provoke relationship change

Transtheoretical model Consists of five stages including the pre-contemplation stage, the contemplation stage, the preparation stage, the action stage, and the maintenance stage

Truth default The presumption of honesty that usually underlies interaction

Truth default theory A theory of credibility assessment and deception detection in interpersonal communication based on the idea that people typically presume others to be honest (truth default)

Two-step flow Theory that asserts information from media is processed first by opinion leaders who then pass it along via interpersonal channels

Uncertainty In anxiety/uncertainty management theory, describes not knowing what will happen

Uncertainty avoidance A dimension of national culture that represents how comfortable cultures are with uncertainty and ambiguity

Uncertainty management theory Explains how people react to health-related uncertainty

Understanding A type of relationship maintenance behavior that encompasses understanding, cooperation, and patience with the relationship partner

Unitary sequence model Model of group decision making that identifies stages that groups go through as they move toward a decision

Unpredictable behavior In uncertainty reduction theory, the motive to reduce uncertainty about people whose behavior deviates from our expectations

Uses and gratifications theory A theory of mass communication that attempts to explain the uses and functions of the media for individuals, groups, and society in general

Validity The degree to which we are measuring what we are intending to measure

Variable Term referring to a theoretical concept emphasizing its variation and measurability

Verbal aggressiveness Attacking the self-concepts of people instead of, or in addition to, their positions on issues

Visual anonymity Occurs when CMC users exchange messages without seeing people to whom they are communicating

Voluntary relationships Relationships we choose for ourselves

Wide bandwidth A term from language expectancy theory that reflects when people have a greater variety of persuasive linguistic strategies that will be seen as appropriate or within an expected range

Wit A dimension of communicative adaptability that reflects the degree to which a person utilizes humor in appropriate situations to diffuse escalating aggressive communication exchanges

Working class climber A lifestyle type primarily consisting of males, lower in education and income, middle-aged, and married

X, Y management theory A theory of management that contains bi-polar assumptions about employee behavior

SUBJECT INDEX

A

Abductive reasoning, 25
Abductive theory building, 25–26
Accommodation. *See* Communication accommodation theory (CAT)
Accreditation Council for Graduate Medical Education (ACGME), 336
Acculturation, 364
Accuracy, 56
ACGME. *See* Accreditation Council for Graduate Medical Education
Acquaintances, 293
Acquaintanceships, 293
Acquired needs theory, 273–274 *See also* Worker motivational theories
Acquiring information, communication and, 17–18
Active strategies, uncertainty reduction, 210
Activity track, 247, 248
  in multiple sequence model, 247, 248
  relational activity track, 247
  task activity track, 247
  topical activity track, 247–248
  See also Breakpoints
Adaptation traits
  appropriate disclosure, 80
  articulation, 80
  communicative adaptability, 79–81
  compensates, 135
  noble selves, 81
  reciprocates, 134–135
  rhetorical reflector, 81–82
  rhetorical sensitivity, 82
  social composure, 80
  social confirmation, 80

  social experience, 80
  wit, 80
  See also Trait approaches
Advertising theory, 34–35
Advocacy for ideas, 3
Affective competence, 365–366
Affect management goals, 196
Affiliation-disaffiliation frame, 203, 204
Agency for Health Care Research and Quality (AHRQ), 333
Agenda-setting theory, 290–292
  need for orientation, 291
  See also Mass communication; Mass media; Political communication
Aggression traits
  argumentativeness, 85–87
  hostility, 87–88
  taking conflict personally, 90–92
  tolerance for disagreement, 92–93
  verbal aggressiveness, 88–90
  See also Trait approaches
AHRQ. *See* Agency for Health Care Research and Quality
AIDS prevention, 334
Alternate forms reliability, 50
Ambivalent orientation, 355
American Psychological Association (APA), 294
Amount, self-disclosure, 79
Anchoring approach, 179
Anderson, Carl, 267
Androgynous leadership style, 268
Anger. *See* Aggression traits; Argumentation; Hostility; Taking conflict personally (TCP); Verbal aggressiveness
Animated communication style, 265
Animated communicator style, 78

P

W

X

NAME INDEX

Z